Strategic Corporate Finance

I dedicate this book in loving memory of my mother

Gina Davies (1923–2007)

Strategic Corporate Finance

Tony Davies, Tony Boczko, and Jean Chen

McGraw-Hill
Higher Education

London   Boston   Burr Ridge, IL   Dubuque, IA   Madison, WI   New York   San Francisco
St. Louis   Bangkok   Bogotá   Caracas   Kuala Lumpur   Lisbon   Madrid   Mexico City
Milan   Montreal   New Delhi   Santiago   Seoul   Singapore   Sydney   Taipei   Toronto

Strategic Corporate Finance
Tony Davies, Tony Boczko and Jean Chen

ISBN-13 978-0-07-710941-7
ISBN-10 0-07-710941-4

McGraw-Hill
Higher Education

Published by McGraw-Hill Education
Shoppenhangers Road
Maidenhead
Berkshire
SL6 2QL
Telephone: 44 (0) 1628 502 500
Fax: 44 (0) 1628 770 224
Website: www.mcgraw-hill.co.uk

British Library Cataloguing in Publication Data
A catalogue record for this book is available from the British Library

Library of Congress Cataloguing in Publication Data
The Library of Congress data for this book has been applied for from the Library of Congress

Acquisitions Editor: Mark Kavanagh
Head of Development: Caroline Prodger
Marketing Manager: Vanessa Boddington
Head of Production: Beverley Shields

Text Design by Hard Lines
Cover design by SCW
Printed and bound in Italy by Rotolito Lombarda

ISBN-13 978-0-07-710941-7
ISBN-10 0-07-710941-4

Brief table of contents

Detailed table of contents

Press extracts

Illustrations

Preface

Coverage of financial issues by the press and media increases almost daily in both volume and complexity. It includes topics such as stock market performance, investment and growth, mergers and acquisitions, venture capitalists and private equity, derivatives, debt, interest rates, foreign currency exchange rates, and corporate financial fraud. Each of these topics is in some way concerned with the risks faced by government organisations, and individuals, financial institutions, banks, manufacturing and service companies, and their shareholders and lenders, and the corresponding cash returns that they expect to receive in reward for acceptance of such risks.

Corporate finance is concerned with all these financial issues, which impact on us all in one way or another and are forever changing in their composition and focus. The discipline of corporate finance is about:

- the way in which financial resources are acquired
- how these resources are most effectively used
- the control of these activities.

The topicality and critical importance of these topics therefore makes their study exciting and very relevant to a better understanding of the performance of countries' economies, and businesses, and the decisions and problems they face.

This new textbook is called *Strategic Corporate Finance* because it includes not only the theory and key areas of corporate finance and the range of techniques that may be used and applied in practice, but also the appropriate financial strategies that may be adopted in order to optimise the use of the scarce resource of money (or cash flow).

One of the main objectives in writing this book was to produce a clear and user-friendly text, which embraces both the core principles and practice of corporate finance and also financial strategy. This book uses a comprehensive set of learning features, illustrative worked examples, and assessment material to support and reinforce your study. It is aimed primarily at students who are undertaking a degree or diploma in accounting, finance, economics, or business management, which includes a course in corporate finance or financial strategy, or both. It is also aimed at students undertaking postgraduate finance and business masters degrees, MBA students, and students pursuing professional accounting and finance courses.

Content and structure

The content and structure of the text have been carefully researched to follow closely the typical requirements of most introductory corporate finance and financial strategy courses at both the undergraduate and postgraduate level. This text assumes no prior knowledge of the subject: we start at square one and take you step by step through the concepts and application of techniques, with clear explanations and numerous examples.

The text comprises 18 chapters, and is structured into two parts: corporate finance, and financial strategy.

Corporate finance is broadly concerned with the effective acquisition and use of financial resources in creating corporate value, and its translation into shareholder value. It includes a wide range of strategic financial management techniques and decision-making relating to capital investment; capital structure; working capital; the management of financial risk; financial planning; international operations and investment. It also covers accountability of company directors and their relationships with shareholders and other stakeholders.

Financial strategy decisions in general relate to the levels of:

- investment in the assets of the business, and the choice of types of asset
- most appropriate methods of funding – debt or equity
- profit retention
- profit distribution
- gearing, or capital structure of the business and
- management of financial risk

with the aim of maximisation of shareholder wealth.

Financial strategy is concerned with the creation of corporate value, but also how this is then reflected in increased shareholder wealth through creation of shareholder value consistent with levels of perceived risk and the returns required by investors.

Each of these areas and their component chapters are outlined in the introductory section to each part of the text.

A further key objective in writing this text was to provide a flexible study resource. There is a linkage between each of the chapters, which follow a structure that has been designed to facilitate effective learning of the subject in a progressive way. However, each chapter may also be used on a stand-alone basis; equally, chapters may be excluded from study if they relate to subjects that are not essential for a specific course. Therefore, the text is intended to be suitable for modules of either one or two semesters' duration.

Each chapter aims to help students understand the broader context and relevance of corporate finance and financial strategy in the business environment, and how they may assist in improving both corporate value and shareholder value. To put each topic in context we have provided numerous examples and commentary on company activity within each chapter, including at least one cutting from the press and financial media; companies featured include BSkyB, Samsung, Enron, Matalan, Umbro, and Marks & Spencer. In addition, the book includes extracts and analysis of the actual Report and Accounts 2007 of Johnson Matthey, a major UK plc.

Using this book

To support your study and reinforce the topics covered, we have included a comprehensive range of learning features and assessment material in each chapter, including:

- learning objectives
- introduction
- highlighted key terms
- fully-worked examples
- integrated progress checks
- key points summary

- glossary of key terms
- questions
- discussion points
- exercises

Within each chapter we have also included numerous diagrams and charts that illustrate and reinforce important concepts and ideas. The Guided Tour that follows overleaf summarises the purpose of these learning features and the chapter-end assessment material. To gain maximum benefit from this text and to help you succeed in your study and exams, you are encouraged to familiarise yourself with these elements now, before you start the first chapter.

It is easy, but mistaken, to read on cruise control, highlighting the odd sentence and gliding through the worked examples, progress checks, and chapter-end questions and exercises. Active learning needs to be interactive: if you haven't followed a topic or an example, go back and work through it again; try to think of other examples to which particular topics may be applied. The only way to check you have a comprehensive understanding of things is to attempt all the integrated progress checks and worked examples, and the chapter-end assessment material, and then to compare with the text and answers provided. Fully-worked solutions are given immediately after each example, and solutions to around 45% of the chapter-end exercises (those with their numbers in colour) are provided in Appendix 2. Additional self-assessment material is available in the student centre of the book's accompanying website (see page xxiii).

Case studies

Throughout the book there are six case studies that may be tackled either individually or as a team. The case studies are a little more weighty than the chapter-end exercises and integrate many of the topics covered in the book. Each case study therefore gives you an opportunity to apply the knowledge and techniques gained, and to develop these together with the analytical skills, judgement, and strategic approach required to deal with real-life business problems. Additional cases are provided on the accompanying website.

We hope this textbook will enhance your interest, understanding and skills. Above all, relax, learn, and enjoy!

Guided Tour

Learning objectives

Listed at the start of each chapter, these bullet points identify the core learning outcomes you should have acquired after completing each chapter. This is followed by an introduction to the coverage and purpose of each chapter, and how it links to the previous chapter.

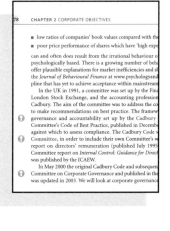

Key terms

These are highlighted the first time they are introduced, alerting you to the core concepts and techniques in each chapter. A full explanation is contained in the glossary of key terms section at the end of each chapter.

Progress checks

Each topic within each chapter includes one or more of these short questions that enable you to check and apply your understanding of the preceding key topics before you progress to the next one in the chapter.

Packed with examples

The numerous worked examples in each chapter provide an application of the learning points and techniques included within each topic. By following and working though the step-by-step solutions, you have an opportunity to check your knowledge at frequent intervals.

Press extracts

Included in every chapter, these topical extracts feature real company examples from the press, including commentary that highlights the practical application of accounting and finance in the business environment.

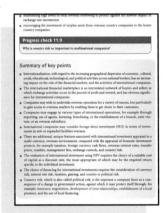

Summary of key points

Following the final section in each chapter there is a comprehensive summary of the key points in terms of the learning outcomes listed at the start of each chapter. These allow you to check that you understand all the main points covered before moving onto the next chapter.

Glossary of key terms

At the end of each chapter, a glossary of key terms in alphabetical order provides full definitions of all the main terms that have been introduced throughout each chapter. The numbers of the pages on which key term definitions appear are colour-highlighted in the index.

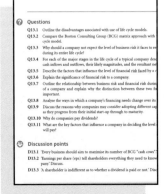

Questions

These are short narrative type questions that encourage you to review and check your understanding of all the key topics. There are typically 7 to 10 of these questions at the end of every chapter.

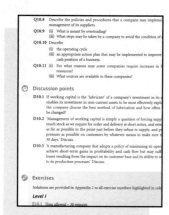

Discussion points

This section typically includes 2 to 4 thought-provoking ideas and questions that encourage you to critically apply your understanding and further develop some of the topics introduced in each chapter, either individually or in team discussion.

Exercises

These comprehensive examination-style questions are graded by their level of difficulty, and also indicate the time typically required to complete them. They are designed to assess your knowledge and application of the principles and techniques covered in each chapter. There are typically 7 to 9 exercises at the end of each chapter. Full solutions to the colour-highlighted exercise numbers are provided in Appendix 2 to allow you to self-assess your progress.

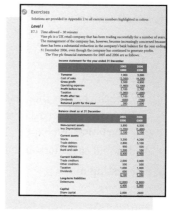

Technology to enhance learning and teaching

Visit www.mcgraw-hill.co.uk/textbooks/davies today

Online Learning Centre (OLC)

After completing each chapter, log on to the supporting Online Learning Centre website. Take advantage of the study tools offered to reinforce the material you have read in the text, and to develop your knowledge in a fun and effective way.

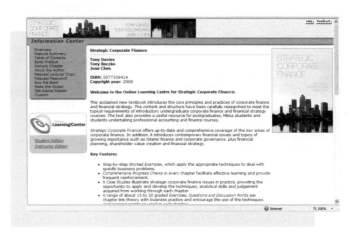

Resources for students include:

- Additional chapter-based exercises
- Solutions to all additional chapter-based exercises
- Additional case studies
- Self-testing multiple-choice questions (by chapter) with automatic grading
- Revision notes (by chapter)
- Glossary of key terms
- The press room
- Annotated weblinks

Resources for lecturers include:

- Solutions to all chapter-end exercises
- Additional chapter-based exercises
- Solutions to all additional chapter-based exercises
- Additional case studies
- Debriefings to all case studies
- PowerPoint lecture slides
- Illustrations
- PageOut

Custom Publishing Solutions: Let us help make our content your solution

At McGraw-Hill Education our aim is to help the lecturer find the most suitable content for their needs and the most appropriate way to deliver the content their students Our **custom publishing solutions** offer the ideal combination of content delivered in the way which suits lecturer and students the best.

The idea behind our custom publishing programme is that via a database of over two million pages called Primis, www.primisonline.com, the lecturer can select just the material they wish to deliver to their students:

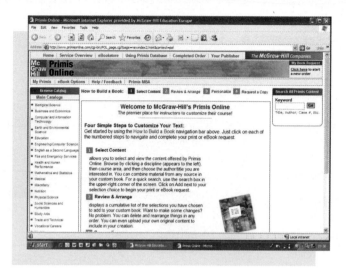

Lecturers can select chapters from:

- textbooks
- professional books
- case books – Harvard Articles, Insead, Ivey, Darden, Thunderbird and BusinessWeek
- Taking Sides – debate materials

Across the following imprints:

- McGraw-Hill Education
- Open University Press
- Harvard Business School Press
- US and European material

There is also the option to include material authored by lecturers in the custom product – this does not necessarily have to be in English.

We will take care of everything from start to finish in the process of developing and delivering a custom product to ensure that lecturers and students receive exactly the material needed in the most suitable way.

With a **Custom Publishing Solution**, students enjoy the best selection of material deemed to be the most suitable for learning everything they need for their courses – something of real value to support their learning. Teachers are able to use exactly the material they want, in the way they want, to support their teaching on the course.

Please contact your local McGraw-Hill representative with any questions or alternatively contact Warren Eels **e:** warren_eels@mcgraw-hill.com.

Make the grade!

30% off any Study Skills book!

Our Study Skills books are packed with practical advice and tips that are easy to put into practice and will really improve the way you study. Topics include:

- Techniques to help you pass exams
- Advice to improve your essay writing
- Help in putting together the perfect seminar presentation
- Tips on how to balance studying and your personal life

www.openup.co.uk/studyskills
Visit our website to read helpful hints about essays, exams, dissertations and much more.

Special offer! As a valued customer, buy online and receive 30% off any of our Study Skills books by entering the promo code **getahead**

Acknowledgements

Our thanks go to the following reviewers for their comments at various stages in the text's development:

John McLaren, Southampton Solent University
Graham Sara, Warwick Business School
Shishir Malde, Nottingham Trent University
Graham Diggle, Oxford Brookes University
John Stittle, University of Essex
Jill Solomon, Cardiff Business School
Bob Stradling, Durham Business School
Parminder Johal, University of Derby
John Wyld, Staffordshire University

Authors' acknowledgements

Thank you to all the university lecturers who were involved in the initial market research, and to those who provided useful review comments and technical checks of the draft chapters during the development phase of this project.

Thank you to CIMA (the Chartered Institute of Management Accountants) for their permission to include extracts from their Management Accounting Official Terminology 2005 edition.

Thank you to Johnson Matthey plc for permission to use extracts of their Report and Accounts 2007 as an excellent example of the information provided to shareholders by a major UK plc, and to *Accountancy Age*, the *Daily Telegraph*, *The Times*, the *Guardian*, *Management Today*, and *The Manufacturer* for their permission to use extracts from their publications.

Thank you to the HSBC for their invaluable comments with regard to the section on Islamic banking and Islamic finance.

Thank you to Mark Kavanagh and Bev Shields of McGraw-Hill for their support and encouragement in the writing of this book and the development of the website.

Every effort has been made to trace and acknowledge ownership of copyright and to clear permission for material reproduced in this book. The publishers will be pleased to make suitable arrangements to clear permission with any copyright holders whom it has not been possible to contact.

Corporate finance

Part contents

Introduction to Part I

Part I of this book is about corporate finance, which is concerned with the effective use of financial resources in creating corporate value. It looks at the financial environment in which businesses operate, their financial aims and objectives, and includes a wide range of strategic financial management techniques related to financial decision-making. These include, for example, capital investment, capital structure, working capital, the management of financial risk, financial planning, and international operations and investment. It also considers the ways in which compliance with various corporate governance guidelines broadly support the achievement of business objectives in determining the responsibilities and accountability of company directors and their relationships with shareholders and other stakeholders.

In Chapter 1, Fig. 1.1 provides the framework of strategic corporate finance on which this book is based. The topics included in each of the shaded areas in Fig. 1.1 are covered in Chapters 1 to 12, except for financial strategy, which is covered in Chapters 13 to 18 in Part II of this book.

Part I is concerned primarily with the creation of corporate value and its translation into shareholder value. Part II of this book is about the use of appropriate financial strategies, as distinct from business strategies. This looks at what companies may do to ensure not only the creation of corporate value, but also that the performance of the business is reflected in the maximisation of shareholder value. Companies may do all the right things in terms of creating value from investments in value-creating projects. However, if this performance is not translated into and reflected in optimal shareholder value through dividend growth and an increasing share price then the primary objective of the business – maximisation of shareholder wealth – is not being achieved.

The providers of the capital for a business, its shareholders and lenders, require appropriate returns on their investments from dividends, interest, and share price increases, commensurate with the levels of risk they are prepared to accept associated with the type of businesses and industrial sectors in which they invest. The directors or managers of a company have the responsibility for pursuit of the objective of shareholder wealth maximisation. Faced with different types and levels of risk at each stage in a company's development, directors' responsibilities include therefore not only ensuring that value is added to the business, that is corporate value, through making 'real' investments in projects that return the highest possible positive net present values of cash flows, but also ensuring that appropriate financial strategies are adopted that reflect this in the value created for shareholders, that is shareholder wealth.

These 'real' investment types of decision and their financing are dealt with in Part I. Part II looks at how companies are exposed to varying levels of financial risk at each of the different stages in their development, and in response to these how they may apply the techniques dealt with in Part I. Part II also considers how the creation of corporate value by companies at each stage of their development may then be reflected in increased shareholder value though the use of appropriate financial strategies and exploitation of market imperfections. We will explore how different financial strategies may apply at different stages in the development of a company.

Shareholder value is provided in two ways, from increases in the price of shares and the payment of dividends on those shares. In Part II we look at the ways in which strategic financial decisions may be made relating to the levels of:

- investment in the assets of the business, and the types of assets
- most appropriate methods of funding – debt or equity
- profit retention
- profit distribution
- gearing, or capital structure of the business,

with the aim of maximisation of shareholder wealth through creation of shareholder value consistent with levels of perceived risk and returns required by investors and lenders.

To provide a framework for Part II in which to consider these decisions we will use a simplified, theoretical 'business life cycle' model, the BLC, which describes the stages through which businesses may typically progress from their initial start-up through to their ultimate decline and possible demise. The financial parameters particular to each stage of this simplified business life cycle will be identified and appropriate financial strategies will be discussed that may be used to exploit the specific circumstances in order to create shareholder value.

Chapter 1 looks at the financial environment in which businesses operate and their financial aims and objectives. This chapter provides the framework of strategic corporate finance on which this book is based.

Chapter 2 considers the objectives of businesses. Businesses raise money from shareholders and lenders to invest in assets, which are used to increase the wealth of the business and its owners. The underlying fundamental economic objective of a company is to maximise shareholder wealth.

In Chapter 3 we provide an introduction to corporate governance, a topic that is becoming increasingly important, as the responsibilities of directors continue to increase. We look at the ways in which compliance with the various corporate governance guidelines broadly support the achievement of the aims and objectives of companies in determining the responsibilities and accountability of company directors and their relationships with shareholders and other stakeholders. The burden lies with management to run businesses in strict compliance with statutory, regulatory, and accounting requirements, so it is crucial that directors are aware of the rules and codes of practice that are in place to regulate the behaviour of directors of limited companies.

Chapter 4 considers how businesses make decisions about potential investments that may be made, in order to ensure that the wealth of the business will be increased. This is an important area of decision-making that usually involves a great deal of money and relatively long-term commitments. It therefore requires appropriate techniques to ensure that the financial objectives of the company are in line with the interests of the shareholders.

Chapter 5 examines the relationship between risk and return and how diversification may be used to mitigate and reduce risk. It considers the impact of diversification and looks at the portfolio theory developed by Markowitz.

Chapter 6 considers the way in which a company's average cost of capital may be determined from the costs of its various types of capital financing. The average cost of a company's capital is an important factor in determining the value of a business. In theory the minimisation of the combined cost of equity, debt, and retained earnings used by a company to finance its business should increase its value. The average cost of a company's capital may also be used as the discount rate with which to evaluate proposed investments in new capital projects. Chapter 6 considers whether an optimal capital structure is of fundamental importance to its average cost of capital and looks at the various approaches taken to determine this.

Chapter 7 deals primarily with long-term, external sources of business finance for investment in businesses. This relates to the various types of funding available to a business, including the raising of funds from the owners of the business (the shareholders) and from lenders external to the business. Chapter 7 closes with an introduction to the fast-growing area of Islamic banking and Islamic finance.

Chapter 8 is headed *Financial analysis*. The three main financial statements provide information about business performance. Much more may be gleaned about the performance of the business through further analysis of the financial statements, using financial ratios and other techniques, for example trend analysis, industrial and inter-company analysis. Chapter 8 looks at the analysis and interpretation of the published accounts of a business. It uses the Report and Accounts for the year ended 31 March 2007 of Johnson Matthey plc to illustrate the type of financial and non-financial information provided by a major UK public company. The chapter closes with a look at some of the measures that approximate to cash flow, for example earnings before interest, tax, depreciation, and amortisation (EBITDA), and economic value added (EVA), that may be used to evaluate company performance.

Chapter 9 deals with the way in which businesses, as part of their strategic management process, translate their long-term objectives into financial plans. This chapter includes consideration of the role of forecasting, financial modelling, and planning for growth.

In Chapter 10 we look at one of the sources of finance internal to a business, its working capital, and the impact that its effective management has on cash flow, profitability, and return on capital. Working capital comprises the short-term assets of the business, stocks (or inventory), trade debtors, and cash and claims on the business, trade creditors. This chapter deals with how these important items may be more effectively managed.

We are now living in a global economy in which businesses trade internationally and also may exist in a number of countries. In Chapter 11 the implications of internationalisation are discussed with regard to companies' involvement in overseas operations, directly and indirectly, and considers the appraisal and financing of international investments.

Chapter 12 looks at financial risk faced by businesses resulting from the variation in interest rates, and currency exchange rates, from one period to another. We consider the different ways in which these risks may be approached by companies, and the techniques that may be used to manage such risks. Finally, the use of derivatives is discussed together with examples of their use by companies (and their misuse, which we have seen over the past ten years or so).

Chapter 1

The financial environment

Chapter contents

LEARNING OBJECTIVES

Completion of this chapter will enable you to:

- ☑ Outline the framework of corporate finance and its link with financial strategy.
- ☑ Illustrate the different types of business entity: sole traders, partnerships, private limited companies, public limited companies.
- ☑ Explain the role of the finance function within a business organisational structure.

▶   ☑ Explain the nature and purpose of financial statements.

     ☑ Consider the issues of accountability and financial reporting.

     ☑ Describe what is meant by accounting and corporate finance.

     ☑ Outline how the corporate finance function is managed to meet business objectives.

     ☑ Explain the underlying principles of corporate finance.

Introduction

This chapter explains why finance is such a key element of business life. For aspiring finance directors, finance managers, and accountants, and those of you who may not continue to study finance and accounting, the underlying principles of finance are important topics. A broad appreciation will be useful not only in dealing with the subsequent text, but also in the context of the day-to-day management of a business.

The chapter begins by explaining how the discipline of corporate finance was established and developed. It provides the framework on which each of the subsequent chapters is based. It also explains the links between corporate finance and strategy, and how the financial models and techniques covered in the first part of the book are used in the adoption of appropriate financial strategies by companies at different stages in their development.

The owners or shareholders of the range of business entities may be assumed to have the primary objective of maximisation of their wealth. Directors of the business manage the resources of the business to meet shareholders' objectives. Directors and managers are responsible for running businesses, and their accountability to shareholders is maintained through their regular reporting on the activities of the business.

The finance function plays a crucially important part in all organisations. Its responsibilities include both accounting and corporate finance, the latter relating to the management and control of the financial resources at its disposal. The effective management of corporate finance is essential in ensuring that the business meets its prime objective of maximisation of shareholder wealth. This chapter closes by introducing the fundamental concepts and principles of corporate finance.

A large number of financial terms are used throughout this book, the definitions of which may be found in the glossaries of key terms at the end of each chapter.

Corporate finance and financial strategy

The business environment comprises companies that have just started up or are in various stages of their development. Each has its own reason for being in business and each has its own financing requirements. In the early part of the 20th century when new industries and technologies were emerging there was a growing requirement for new financing, particularly from external sources. This requirement saw increasing interest in various types of securities, particularly equity shares, and also led to the establishment of finance as a discipline separate from economics, in which it had its origins.

The growth in equity shareholdings increased (and continued to increase up to the present day) but confidence was drastically dented during the economic depression and as a result of the financial scandals of the 1930s. As bankruptcy became a real possibility more attention began to be focused on companies' liquidity and financial structure, and there was a need for increased disclosure of financial information and its analysis. The 1940s saw an increase in financial analysis of cash flow, planning, and methods of control. In the 1950s capital budgeting emerged together with the financial management of assets, and an awareness of how financial decision-making impacted on the value of businesses. This all led to the establishment of the discipline of corporate finance in the early 1960s supported by the publication of a number of academic papers on topics such as the capital markets, and share prices, which had previously been considered only in the areas of economics and statistics.

Corporate finance continues to be developed from its beginnings at the start of the 20th century, as do the techniques used in the management of corporate finance, and with an increasing emphasis on international aspects of trade, investment and financing. This book covers all the main areas of corporate finance and its management (financial management).

Let's consider each of the elements of the chart in Fig. 1.1, which provides the framework on which this book is based. It is not strictly a flow chart but contains the topics, roles, and techniques covered in this book (and the relationships between them), which are represented by the elements of the chart that are shaded.

Corporate objectives (see Chapter 2) are formulated by a business, in alignment with its underlying mission and company policy, and may include for example profit maximisation, or market share maximisation. Its mission is the company's general sense of purpose or underlying belief. Its policy is a long-lasting, usually unquantified, statement of guidance about the way in which the company seeks to behave in relation to its stakeholders. A company normally has social and environmental responsibilities, responsibilities to its employees, and responsibilities to all its other stakeholders. However, this should not be inconsistent with its primary responsibility to its shareholders. We are assuming that the aim of a business is to add value for its shareholders with the primary objective of maximising shareholder wealth. Shareholder wealth comprises the dividends paid to shareholders on the shares they hold, and the gains achieved from the increase in the market price of their shares.

The directors of a business are appointed by the shareholders to manage the business on their behalf. The directors are responsible for developing appropriate strategies that determine *what* the company is going to do to achieve its objectives, with the primary aim of maximising shareholder wealth. A strategy is a course of action that includes a specification of resources required to achieve a specific objective; it is *what* the company needs to do long term to achieve its objectives, but it does not include *how* to achieve them.

A company's strategy includes its business strategy, which establishes the type of business, its location, its products and services, its markets, its use of resources, and its growth objectives. These areas are assessed with regard to the risks associated with them for which appropriate risk management techniques may be put in place. The company's business strategy is quantified for the long term (typically three years, five years, or ten years) through its financial planning function (see Chapter 9). The short term is quantified in the company's six-monthly or yearly budgets.

A company's strategy also includes financial strategy. This book links corporate finance and financial management with financial strategy. Chapters 1 to 12 discuss the various aspects, models, and hypotheses relating to the discipline of corporate finance, and the techniques and methods used in the financial management of a business. Chapters 13 to 18 deal with the various stages in the development of a business from its initial start-up, each chapter considering the most appropriate financial strategies that may be adopted by companies, with regard to their current stage of development. 'Most appropriate financial strategies' means those financial

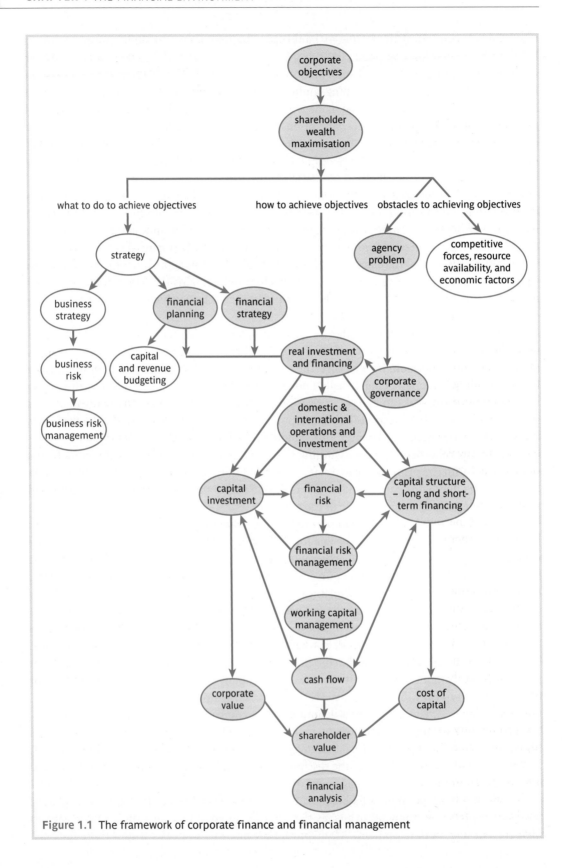

Figure 1.1 The framework of corporate finance and financial management

strategies that result in the optimisation of the value of the business, with the aim of maximising shareholder wealth. An example of such a strategy is a company that may buy insurance to cover the risks relating to the achievement of its commercial objectives. The cost of the insurance premiums means that the short-term profits of the company are reduced, but the long-term value of the business to the shareholders will be increased because of the removal of uncertainty about the company's future earnings.

At the heart of corporate finance is *how* the company will achieve its objectives, and specifically its financial objective of maximisation of shareholder wealth. The first part of this relates to the allocation and use of financial resources for real capital investment (see Chapter 4) in, for example, new product development, land and buildings, and plant and equipment (as distinct from the popular meaning of investment in securities, stocks, and shares). The second part relates to the financing of such investments, which may be internal to the company from the retained earnings of the business or from improvements in its management of working capital (see Chapter 10) or from external financing. External financing broadly comprises loans and equity share capital provided to companies by investors and which may be acquired and traded in capital markets like, for example, the London Stock Exchange (see Chapter 7).

Capital investments may be made by companies in their own domestic countries, but companies are also now becoming increasingly involved in international operations and investment (see Chapter 11), and international financing (see Chapter 7). Domestic and international investment, and domestic and international financing all face various types of risk (see Chapter 5), including financial risk, the management of which is discussed in Chapter 12.

If good decisions are made by a company's managers and directors, which result in value-adding investments then corporate value will be increased and reflected in increased cash flow. It is crucially important to appreciate that it is cash flow (in real terms) and not profits, which reflects the true value of a business. If good decisions are made with regard to financing then the capital structure of the company will result in the cost of capital of the company being at a level that will also enhance its corporate value (see Chapter 6). However, an increase in corporate value may not necessarily result in an increase in shareholder value. That will depend partly on how much of the cash flow that has been generated is used to pay out dividends (or retained for future investment), and partly in the increase (or not) in the share price. The share price will depend on the market's perception of the financial health of the business, and the demand for and level of trading in the company's shares. The analysis of the financial performance and the financial position of a business is considered in Chapter 8.

In theory, the creation of value through adoption of appropriate strategies, and making the right decisions, looks simple and straightforward. In practice, there are of course many obstacles in the way to prevent a company from achieving its objectives. There are competitive forces in most markets from existing companies, from new entrants to the market, and from substitute and alternative products and services. There may be pressures on revenues, costs, and profitability from powerful customers or groups of customers who may demand lower selling prices, or higher levels of quality or service for the same price. There may be pressures on costs and profitability from suppliers or groups of suppliers who may increase prices or control the supply of materials, components, or services. There may be constraints in terms of market demand, availability of materials and people, knowledge, technology, legislation, taxation, import tariffs, social and environmental responsibilities, and media and political pressure.

In addition to the predominantly external obstacles to achieving corporate objectives outlined above, there may also be a major internal obstacle, which is called the agency problem (see Chapter 2). As we have said, the shareholders appoint the directors to manage the company on their behalf. The primary role of the directors is to make decisions and manage the business consistent with the objective of maximisation of shareholder wealth. The agency problem is concerned mainly with situations in which there is a lack of goal congruence between the directors and shareholders of a company, and the decisions of the directors are not aligned with the requirements of the shareholders. The most serious examples of this have been seen in the numerous cases of fraud and corporate excesses over the past 20 years, which have been extensively reported in the financial press. In the UK, the USA, and many other countries throughout the world the concern about financial reporting and accountability and the effect of such financial scandals resulted in the development of various codes of corporate governance (see Chapter 3). Corporate governance is broadly the system by which companies are directed and controlled, and how directors report on the activities and progress of companies to their shareholders.

In the section above we have been talking about businesses and companies in general with regard to corporate finance and financial strategy. Many of the financial techniques covered in this book relate primarily, although not exclusively, to medium-sized and large limited companies. However, it is useful to consider all the various types of business entity that exist and exactly what we mean by a **private limited company (Ltd)** and a **public limited company (plc)**, which is all discussed in the next section.

Types of business entity

Business entities are involved either in manufacturing (for example, food and automotive components) or in providing services (for example, retailing, hospitals, or television broadcasting). Such entities include profit-making and not-for-profit organisations, and charities. The main types of entity and the environments in which they operate are represented in Fig. 1.2. The four main types of profit-making organisations are explained in the sections that follow.

The variety of business entities can be seen to range from quangos (quasi-autonomous non-government organisations) to partnerships to limited companies.

Sole traders

A sole trader entity is applicable for most types of small business. It is owned and financed by one individual, who receives all the profit made by the business, even though more than one person may work in the business.

The individual sole trader has complete flexibility regarding:

- the type of (legal) activities in which the business may be engaged
- when to start up or cease the business
- the way in which business is conducted.

The individual sole trader also has responsibility for:

- financing the business
- risk-taking
- decision-making
- employing staff
- any debts or loans that the business may have (the responsibility for which is unlimited, and cases of financial difficulty may result in personal property being used to repay debts).

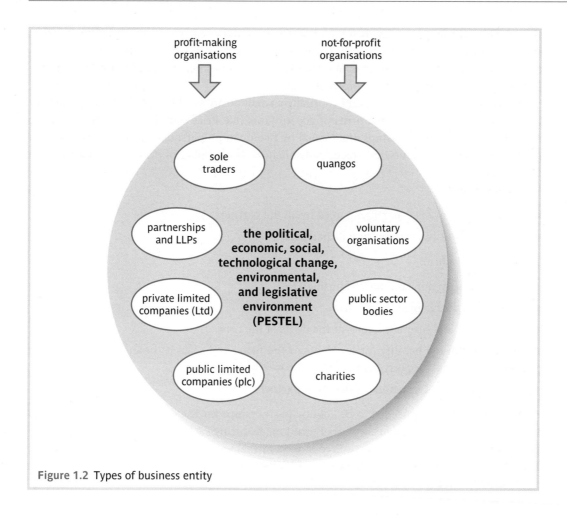

Figure 1.2 Types of business entity

A sole trader business is simple and cheap to set up. There are no legal or administrative set-up costs as the business does not have to be registered since it is not a legal entity separate from its owner. As we shall see, this is unlike the legal position of owners, or shareholders, of limited companies who are recognised as separate legal entities from the businesses they own.

Accounting records are needed to be kept by sole traders for the day-to-day management of the business and to provide an account of profit made during each tax year. Unlike limited companies, sole traders are not required to file a formal report and accounts each year with the **Registrar of Companies**. However, sole traders must prepare accounts on an annual basis to provide the appropriate financial information for inclusion in their annual tax return for submission to HMRC (Her Majesty's Revenue and Customs).

Sole traders normally remain quite small businesses, which may be seen as a disadvantage. The breadth of business skills is likely to be lacking since there are no co-owners with which to share the management and development of the business.

Partnerships

Partnerships are similar to sole traders except that the ownership of the business is in the hands of two or more persons. The main differences are in respect of how much money each of the partners puts into the business, who is responsible for what, and how the profits are to be shared. These factors are normally set out in formal partnership agreements, and if the partnership agreement is not specific then the provisions of the Partnership Act 1890 apply. There is usually a written partnership agreement (but this is not absolutely necessary) and so there are initial legal costs of setting up the business.

A partnership is called a firm and is usually a small business, although there are some very large partnerships, for example firms of accountants like PriceWaterhouseCoopers, and the retailer John Lewis. Partnerships are formed by two or more persons and, apart from certain professions like accountants, architects, and solicitors, the number of persons in a partnership is limited to 20.

A partnership:

- can carry out any legal activities agreed by all the partners
- is not a legal entity separate from its partners.

The partners in a firm:

- can all be involved in running the business
- all share the profits made by the firm
- are all jointly and severally liable for the debts of the firm
- all have unlimited liability for the debts of the firm (and cases of financial difficulty may result in personal property being used to repay debts)
- are each liable for the actions of the other partners.

Accounting records are needed to be kept by partnerships for the day-to-day management of the business and to provide an account of profit made during each tax year. Unlike limited companies, partnership firms are not required to file a formal report and accounts each year with the Registrar of Companies, but partners must submit annual returns for tax purposes to HMRC.

A new type of legal entity was established in 2001, the limited liability partnership (LLP). This is a variation on the traditional partnership, and has a separate legal identity from the partners, which therefore protects them from personal bankruptcy.

One of the main benefits of a partnership is that derived from its broader base of business skills than that of a sole trader. A partnership is also able to share risk-taking, decision-making, and the general management of the firm.

Limited companies

A limited company is a legal entity separate from the owners of the business, which may enter into contracts, own property, and take or receive legal action. The owners limit their obligations to the amount of finance they have put into the company by way of the share of the company they have paid for. Normally, the maximum that may be claimed from shareholders is no more than they have paid for their shares, regardless of what happens to the company. Equally, there is no certainty that shareholders may recover their original investment if they wish to dispose of their shares or if the business is wound up, for whatever reason.

A company with unlimited liability does not give the owners, or members, of the company the protection of limited liability. If the business were to fail, the members would be liable, without limitation, for all the debts of the business.

A further class of company is a company limited by guarantee, which is normally incorporated for non-profit-making functions. The company has no share capital and has members rather than shareholders. The members of the company guarantee to contribute a predetermined sum to the liabilities of the company, which becomes due in the event of the company being wound up.

The legal requirements relating to the registration and operation of limited companies is contained within the Companies Act 1985 as amended by the Companies Act 1989. Limited companies are required to be registered with the Registrar of Companies as either a private limited company (Ltd) or a public limited company (plc).

Private limited companies (Ltd)

Private limited companies are designated as Ltd. There are legal formalities involved in setting up a Ltd company which result in costs for the company. These formalities include the drafting of the company's Memorandum and Articles of Association (M and A) that describe what the company is and what it is allowed to do, registering the company and its director(s) with the Registrar of Companies, and registering the name of the company.

The shareholders provide the financing of the business in the form of share capital, of which there is no minimum requirement, and are therefore the owners of the business. The shareholders must appoint at least one director of the company, who may also be the company secretary, who carries out the day-to-day management of the business. A Ltd company may only carry out the activities included in its M and A.

Ltd companies must regularly produce annual accounts for their shareholders and file a copy with the Registrar of Companies, and therefore the general public may have access to this information. A Ltd company's accounts must be audited by a suitably qualified accountant, unless it is exempt from this requirement, currently (with effect from 30 March 2004) by having annual sales of less than £5.6m and a balance sheet total of less than £2.8m. The exemption is not compulsory and having no audit may be a disadvantage: banks, financial institutions, customers, and suppliers may rely on information from Companies House to assess creditworthiness and they are usually reassured by an independent audit. Ltd companies must also provide copies of their annual accounts to HMRC and also generally provide a separate computation of their profit on which corporation tax is payable. The accounting profit of a Ltd company is adjusted for:

- various expenses that may not be allowable in computing taxable profit
- tax allowances that may be deducted in computing taxable profit.

Limited companies tend to be family businesses and smaller businesses with the ownership split among a few shareholders, although there have been many examples of very large private limited companies. The shares of Ltd companies may be bought and sold but they may not be offered for sale to the general public. Since ownership is usually with family and friends there is rarely a ready market for the shares and so their sale usually requires a valuation of the business.

Progress check 1.1

Which features of a limited company are similar to those of a sole trader?

Public limited companies (plc)

Public limited companies are designated as plc. A plc usually starts its life as a Ltd company and then becomes a public limited company by applying for registration as a plc and a listing of its shares on the Stock Exchange or the **Alternative Investment Market (AIM)**, and making a public offer for sale of shares in the company. Plcs must have a minimum issued share capital of (currently) £50,000. The offer for sale, dealt with by a financial institution and the company's legal representatives, is very costly. The formalities also include the redrafting of the company's M and A, reflecting its status as a plc, registering the company and its director(s) with the Registrar of Companies, and registering the name of the plc.

The shareholders must appoint at least two directors of the company, who carry out the day-to-day management of the business, and a suitably qualified company secretary to ensure the plc's compliance with company law. A plc may only carry out the activities included in its M and A.

Plcs must regularly produce annual accounts, a copy of which they must send to all their shareholders. They must also file a copy with the Registrar of Companies, and therefore the general public may have access to this information. The larger plcs usually provide printed glossy annual reports and accounts which they distribute to their shareholders and other interested parties. A plc's accounts must be audited by a suitably qualified accountant, unless it is exempt from this requirement by (currently) having annual sales of less than £5.6m and a balance sheet total of less than £2.8m. The same drawback applies to having no audit as applies with a Ltd company. Plcs must also provide copies of their annual accounts to HMRC and also generally provide a separate computation of their profit on which corporation tax is payable. The accounting profit of a plc is adjusted for:

- various expenses that may not be allowable in computing taxable profit
- tax allowances that may be deducted in computing taxable profit.

The shareholders provide the financing of the plc in the form of share capital and are therefore the owners of the business. The ownership of a plc can therefore be seen to be spread amongst many shareholders (individuals and institutions like insurance companies and pension funds), and the shares may be freely traded and bought and sold by the general public.

Progress check 1.2

What are the different types of business entity? Can you think of some examples of each?

Worked Example 1.1

Ike Andoowit is in the process of planning the setting up of a new residential training centre. Ike has discussed with a number of his friends the question of registering the business as a limited company, or being a sole trader. Most of Ike's friends have highlighted the advantages of limiting his liability to the original share capital that he would need to put into the company to finance the business. Ike feels a bit uneasy about the whole question and decides to obtain the advice of a professional accountant to find out:

(i)   the main disadvantages of setting up a limited company as opposed to a sole trader

(ii)   if Ike's friends are correct about the advantage of limiting one's liability

(iii)   what other advantages there are to registering the business as a limited company.

The accountant may answer Ike's questions as follows:

Setting up as a sole trader is a lot simpler and easier than setting up a limited company. A limited company is bound by the provisions of the Companies Act 1985 as amended by the Companies Act 1989, and, for example, is required to have an independent annual audit. A limited company is required to be much more open about its affairs.

The financial structure of a limited company is more complicated than that of a sole trader. There are also additional costs involved in the setting up, and in the administrative functions of a limited company.

Running a business as a limited company requires registration of the business with the Registrar of Companies.

As Ike's friends have pointed out, the financial obligations of a shareholder in a limited company are generally restricted to the amount he/she has paid for his/her shares. In addition, the number of shareholders is potentially unlimited, which widens the scope for raising additional capital.

It should also be noted that:

- a limited company is restricted in its choice of business name

- if its annual sales exceed £1m, a limited company is required to hold an annual general meeting (AGM)

- any additional finance provided for a company by a bank is likely to require a personal guarantee from one or more shareholders.

Progress check 1.3

There are some differences between those businesses that have been established as sole traders and those established as partnerships, and there are also differences between private limited companies and public limited companies. What are these differences, and what are the similarities?

Throughout this book, when we talk about companies we are generally referring to limited companies, as distinct from sole traders and partnerships (or firms – although this term is frequently wrongly used to refer to companies). As we have discussed, limited liability companies have an identity separate from their owners, the shareholders, and the liability of shareholders is limited to the amount of money they have invested in the company, that is their shares in the company.

Ownership of a business is separated from its stewardship, or management, by the shareholders' assignment to a board of directors the responsibility for running the company. The directors of the company are accountable to the shareholders, and both parties must play their part in making that accountability effective.

Business organisational structures

The board of directors of a limited company includes a managing director (or CEO – chief executive officer), and a number of functional executive directors and may include one or more professionally qualified accountants, one of which may be the finance director. The directors of the company necessarily delegate to middle managers and junior managers the responsibility for the day-to-day management of the business. It is certainly likely that this body of managers, who report to the board of directors, will include a further one or more qualified accountants responsible for managing the finance function.

The traditional structure of the finance function in a medium to large sized company (see Fig. 1.3) splits responsibilities broadly between accounting and finance, both being the responsibility of the finance director (or CFO – chief financial officer). Accounting is managed by the financial controller (or chief accountant), and cash and corporate finance may be managed by a corporate treasurer (or financial manager), and they both report to the finance director. Historically, the IT function (information technology or data processing) has also been the responsibility of the finance director in the majority of companies. This is because the accounting function was the first major user of computers for payroll and then accounting ledgers, financial reporting, budgeting, financial information, etc. In most large companies the IT function, including communications generally, has become a separate responsibility under an IT

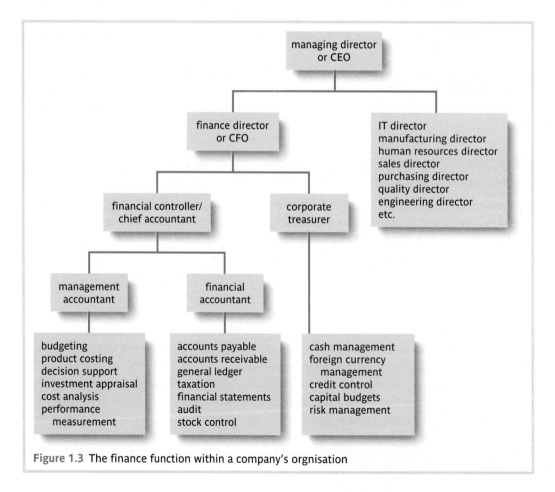

Figure 1.3 The finance function within a company's orgnisation

director. In the same way, the responsibility for the payroll function has moved away from the finance function to being the responsibility of the HR (human resources) director.

Accounting

The original, basic purposes of accounting were to classify and record monetary transactions and present the financial results of the activities of an entity, in other words the scorecard that shows how the business is doing. As the business and economic environment has become more complex the accounting profession has evolved, and accounting techniques have been developed for use in a much broader business context. To look at the current nature of accounting and the broad purposes of accounting systems we need to consider the three questions these days generally answered by accounting information:

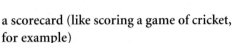

- how are we doing, and are we doing well or badly?   **a scorecard (like scoring a game of cricket, for example)**
- which problems should be looked at?   **attention-directing**
- which is the best alternative for doing a job?   **problem solving**

Although accountants and the accounting profession have retained their fundamental roles they have grown into various branches of the profession, which have developed their own specialisms and responsibilities.

The accounting system is a part of the information system within an organisation. Accounting also exists as a service function, which ensures that the financial information that is presented meets the needs of the users of financial information. To achieve this, accountants must not only ensure that information is accurate, reliable and timely, but also that it is relevant for the purpose for which it is being provided, consistent for comparability, and easily understood (see Fig. 1.4).

In order to be useful to the users of financial information, the accounting data from which it is prepared, together with its analysis and presentation, must be:

- accurate – free from error of content or principle
- reliable – representing the information that users believe it represents
- timely – available in time to support decision-making
- relevant – applicable to the purpose required, for example a decision regarding a future event or to support an explanation of what has already happened
- consistent – the same methods and standards of measurement of data and presentation of information to allow like-for-like comparison
- clear – capable of being understood by those for whom the information has been prepared.

Progress check 1.4

What are the main purposes of accounting?

The provision of a great deal of financial information is mandatory; it is needed to comply with, for example, the requirements of Acts of Parliament and HMRC. However, there is a cost of

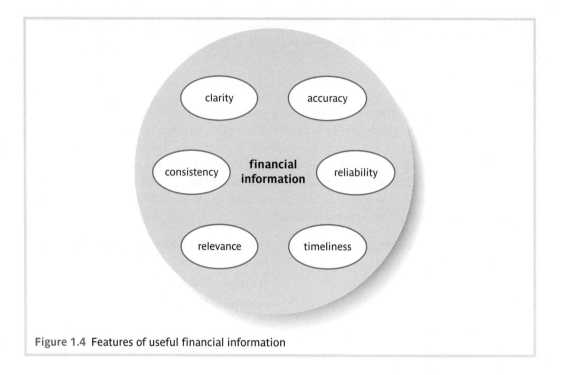

Figure 1.4 Features of useful financial information

providing information that has all the features that have been described, which therefore renders it potentially useful information. The benefits from producing information, in addition to mandatory information, should therefore be considered and compared with the cost of producing that information to decide on which information is 'really' required.

Accountants may be employed by accounting firms, which provide a range of accounting-related services to individuals, companies, public services, and other organisations. Alternatively, accountants may be employed within companies, public services, and other organisations. Accounting firms may specialise in **audit**, corporate taxation, personal taxation, VAT (value added tax), or consultancy (see the right hand column of Fig. 1.5). Accountants within companies, public service organisations etc., may be employed in the main functions of **financial accounting**, **management accounting**, and **treasury management** (see the left hand column of Fig. 1.5), and also in general management. Accounting skills may also be required in the area of **financial management** (or the management of corporate finance), which may also include treasury management. Within companies this may include responsibility for investments, and the management of cash and interest and foreign currency risk. External to companies this may include advice relating to mergers and acquisitions, and Stock Exchange **flotations**, or initial public offerings (IPOs).

Progress check 1.5

Does all accounting data provide useful financial information?

Financial accounting is primarily concerned with the first question answered by accounting information, the scorecard function. Taking a car-driving analogy, financial accounting makes

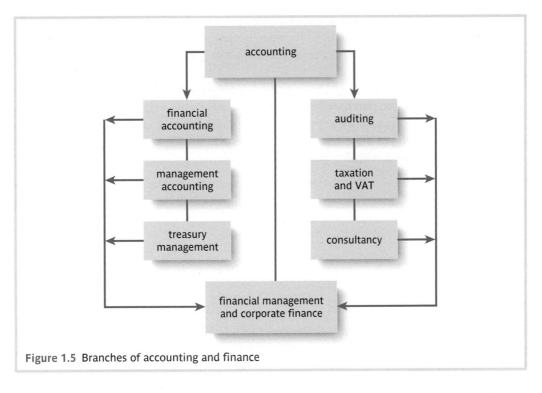

Figure 1.5 Branches of accounting and finance

greater use of the rear-view mirror than the windscreen; financial accounting is primarily concerned with historical information.

Financial accounting is the function responsible in general for the reporting of financial information to the owners of a business, and specifically for preparation of the periodic external reporting of financial information, statutorily required, for shareholders. It also provides similar information as required for Government and other interested third parties, such as potential investors, employees, lenders, suppliers, customers, and financial analysts. Financial accounting is concerned with the three key **financial statements**: the balance sheet; **income statement** (or profit and loss account); **cash flow statement**. It assists in ensuring that financial statements are included in published reports and accounts in a way that provides ease of analysis and interpretation of company performance.

The role of financial accounting is therefore concerned with maintaining the scorecard for the entity. Financial accounting is concerned with the classification and recording of the monetary transactions of an entity in accordance with established **accounting concepts**, principles, **accounting standards** and legal requirements and their presentation, by means of income statements, balance sheets, and cash flow statements, during and at the end of an **accounting period**.

Within most companies, the financial accounting role usually involves much more than the preparation of the three main financial statements. A great deal of analysis is required to support such statements and to prepare information both for internal management and in preparation for the annual audit by the company's external **auditors**. This includes sales analyses, bank reconciliations, and analyses of various types of expenditure.

A typical finance department in a medium to large sized company has the following additional functions within the financial accounting role: control of **accounts payable** to suppliers (the purchase ledger); control of **accounts receivable** from customers (the sales ledger). The financial accounting role also includes the responsibility for the control of fixed assets, stock control, and traditionally included responsibility for payroll, whether processed internally or by an external agency. However, a number of companies elect to transfer the responsibility for payroll to the personnel, or human resources department, bringing with it the possibility of loss of internal control.

The breadth of functions involved in financial accounting can require the processing of high volumes of data relating to purchase invoices, supplier payments, sales invoices, receipts from customers, other cash transactions, petty cash, employee expense claims, and payroll data. Control and monitoring of these functions therefore additionally requires a large number of reports generated by the accounting systems, for example:

- analysis of accounts receivable (debtors): those who owe money to the company – by age of debt
- analysis of accounts payable (creditors): those to whom the company owes money – by age of invoice
- sales analyses
- cheque and electronic payments
- records of fixed assets
- invoice lists.

Past performance is never a totally reliable basis for predicting the future. However, the vast amount of data required for the preparation of financial statements, and maintenance of the further subsidiary accounting functions, provides an indispensable source of data for use in another branch of accounting, namely management accounting. Management accounting is primarily concerned with the provision of information to managers within the organisation for product costing, planning and control, and decision-making, and is to a lesser extent involved in providing information for external reporting.

The functions of management accounting are wide and varied. Whereas financial accounting is primarily concerned with past performance, management accounting makes use of historical data, but focuses almost entirely on the present and the future. Management accounting is involved with the scorecard role of accounting, but in addition is particularly concerned with the other two areas of accounting, namely problem solving and attention directing. These include cost analysis, decision-making, sales pricing, forecasting, and budgeting.

Progress check 1.6

What roles are included within the accounting function?

Financial management

The discipline of corporate finance has its roots in economics, although it also uses many of the techniques used in accounting. Financial management (or the management of corporate finance) is broadly defined as the management of all the processes associated with the efficient acquisition and deployment of both short- and long-term financial resources. The financial management role assists an organisation's operations management to reach its financial objectives. This includes, for example, evaluation of investment opportunities, responsibility for treasury management, which is concerned with the management and control of cash, relationships with banks and other financial institutions, the management of interest rate and foreign currency exchange rate risk, and credit control. The cashier function includes responsibility for cash payments, cash receipts, managers' expenses, petty cash, etc.

The management of an organisation generally involves the three overlapping and inter-linking roles of strategic management, risk management, and operations management. Financial management supports these roles to enable management to achieve the financial objectives of the shareholders. The corporate finance function assists in the way that financial results are reported to the users of financial information, for example shareholders, lenders, and employees.

The responsibility of the finance function for managing corporate finance includes the set-ting up and running of reporting and control systems, raising and managing funds, investment, the management of relationships with financial institutions, and the use of information and analysis to advise management regarding planning, policy, and capital investment. The over-riding requirement of the corporate finance function is to ensure that the financial objectives of the company are in line with the interests of the shareholders, the prime objective being to maximise shareholder wealth.

The finance function therefore includes both accounting and corporate finance, which inevitably overlap in some areas. Financial management includes the management and control of corporate funds, in line with company policy. This includes the management of banking rela-tionships, borrowings, and investment. Treasury management may also include the use of the various financial instruments, which may be used to hedge the risk to the business of changes in interest rates and foreign currency exchange rates, and advising on how company strategy may be developed to benefit from changes in the economic environment and the market in which the business operates.

Progress check 1.7

In what way does corporate finance and the financial management function use account-ing information?

Worked Example 1.2

A friend of yours is thinking about pursuing a career in accounting and would like some views on the major differences between accounting and the management of corporate finance (financial management).

The following notes provide a summary that identifies the key differences.

Accounting: The financial accounting function deals with the recording of past and current transactions, usually with the aid of computerised accounting systems. Of the various reports prepared, the key reports for external users include the income statement, balance sheet, and the cash flow statement. In a plc, such reports must be prepared at least every six months, and must comply with current legal and reporting requirements.

The management accounting function works alongside the financial accounting function, using a number of the day-to-day financial accounting reports from the accounting system. Management accounting is concerned largely with looking at current issues and problems and the future in terms of decision-making and forecasting, for example the consideration of 'what if' scenarios during the course of preparation of forecasts and budgets. Management accounting outputs are mainly for internal users, with much confidential reporting, for example to the direc-tors of the company.

▶

> **Financial management:** The financial management function includes responsibility for corporate finance and the treasury function. Corporate finance includes the management and control of corporate funds, within parameters specified by the board of directors. The role includes the management of company borrowings, investment of surplus funds, the management of both interest rate and exchange rate risk, and giving advice on economic and market changes and the exploitation of opportunities. This function is not necessarily staffed by accountants. Plcs report on the treasury activities of the company in their periodic reporting and financial review.

The press extract below, which appeared in the *Daily Telegraph*, relates to the sale by Corus in February 2004 to St Modwen Properties of some of its surplus property, the former Llanwern steelworks site in Wales. They also revealed plans to invest more than £200m in the site over the next 10 years. The project would create 7,000 jobs and lead to a total end value of £750m, and they hoped to be on site towards the end of 2005. The acquisition of the Llanwern site was the fifth major land deal St Modwen completed with Corus, which retained a further 1,500 acres at Llanwern, including the operational steelworks. This illustrates some of the important applications of financial management, which include:

- planning activities, particularly with regard to restructuring of the business
- negotiations with bankers
- evaluation of investments in new steelworks.

Financial management in action

'Corus puts land up for sale to raise funds for rescue package',
by Edward Simkins and Mary Fagan

Corus, the troubled steel producer, is quietly marketing around 7,000 acres of surplus property in a bid to raise funds and streamline its business as it prepares for a radical restructuring of its UK operations.

Corus, formed though a merger of British Steel and Hoogovens of the Netherlands in 1999, requires around £250m to pay for redundancies and investments in its plan to turn around its ailing UK business.

Corus is unable to put a value on its surplus property because of the expensive cleaning up which some sites may require. Corus is legally liable to carry out the remediation work which can sometimes cost more than the value of the site.

Since the merger, Corus has cut around 10,000 jobs in the UK and is planning to cut a further 1,100 as it closes more unprofitable plants. The number of redundancies could rise by another 2,000 if its Teesside steel plant cannot be brought into profit.

However, the company intends to invest in modernising two or three steelworks in the UK in order to boost its output.

Earlier this month Corus announced that it had secured a new £800m debt facility, but the £250m needed for the UK restructuring is likely to come from either a rights issue or from fresh loans.

It is also planning to dispose of most of its US business after years of poor performance.

Philippe Varin, the new Corus chief executive who was appointed three months ago from the French aluminium producer Pechiney, has said the money is required 'the sooner the better'.

Despite selling several smaller portfolios earlier this year – including one to Threadneedle, the fund manager, for £48m in July – realising the value of its property portfolio is likely to be a slow process.

The company won planning permission in April to redevelop the 1,125 acre site of the former Ravenscraig steelworks in Scotland more than 11 years after the last steel was poured there.

© *Daily Telegraph*, 24 August 2003

Progress check 1.8

What are the main differences between accounting and corporate finance?

Financial statements

Limited companies produce financial statements for each accounting period to provide information about how the company has been doing. There are three main financial statements – balance sheet, income statement (or profit and loss account), and cash flow statement. Companies are obliged to provide financial statements at each year end to provide information for their shareholders, HMRC, and the Registrar of Companies.

Balance sheet

The balance sheet summarises the financial position of the business; it is a financial snapshot at a moment in time. It may be compared to looking at a DVD. In 'play' mode the DVD is showing what is happening as time goes by, second by second. If you press 'pause' the DVD stops on a picture. The picture does not tell you what has happened over the period of time up to the pause (or what is going to happen after the pause). The balance sheet is the financial position of the company at the 'pause' position. It is the consequence of everything that has happened up to that time. It does not explain how the company got to that position, it just shows the results of financial impacts of events and decisions up to the balance sheet date. The year end may be 31 December, but other dates may be chosen. A company's year end date is (normally) the same date each year.

The balance sheet comprises a number of categories, within the three main elements (see Fig. 1.6), which are labelled **assets**, **liabilities** and **shareholders' equity** (usually referred to as just equity). The balance sheet is always in balance so that:

$$\text{total assets (TA)} = \text{equity (E)} + \text{total liabilities (TL)}$$

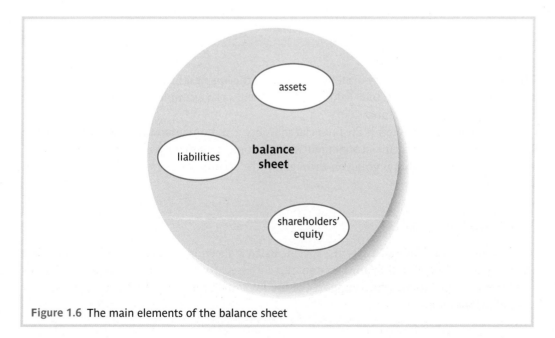

Figure 1.6 The main elements of the balance sheet

Flatco plc
Balance sheet as at 31 December 2007

Figures in £000

Non-current assets			
Intangible			416
Tangible			1,884
Financial			248
			2,548
Current assets			
Stocks		311	
Debtors		573	
Prepayments		589	
Cash		327	
			1,800
Current liabilities (less than one year)			
Financial debt		50	
Creditors		553	
Accruals		202	
		805	
Net current assets			995
(working capital)			
Total assets			
less current liabilities			3,543
less			
Non-current liabilities (over one year)			
Financial debt		173	
Creditors		154	327
less			
Provisions			222
Net assets			2,994
Capital and reserves			
Share capital			1,200
Share premium account			200
Retained earnings			1,594
			2,994

Figure 1.7 An example of a balance sheet

The balance sheet is a summary of all the accounts of the business in which the total assets equal the shareholders' equity plus total liabilities. Fig. 1.7 shows an example of a typical balance sheet for Flatco plc as at 31 December 2007.

Whereas the balance sheet is the financial snapshot at a moment in time – the 'pause' on the DVD – the two other financial statements, the income statement and cash flow statement, are the equivalent of what is going on throughout the accounting period – the 'play' mode on the DVD.

Valuation of assets

The question of valuation of assets at a specific balance sheet date arises in respect of choosing the most accurate methods relating to non-current assets (or fixed assets), stocks and debtors (and similarly creditors), which support the fundamental requirement to give a true and fair view of the business.

Companies must be very careful to ensure that their assets are valued in a way that realistically reflects their ability to generate future cash flows. This applies to both current assets such as stocks, and non-current assets such as land and buildings. The balance sheets of companies rarely reflect either the current market values of non-current assets, or their future earnings potential, since they are based on historical costs. During 2004, Marks & Spencer plc was facing a takeover bid from entrepreneur Philip Green. The directors of Marks & Spencer plc prepared to fight off the takeover bid on the basis that the offer price was a long way short of the true value of its assets. As a measure to protect it against takeover, Marks & Spencer then revalued its portfolio of freehold property, which the directors felt was worth £2bn more than stated in its balance sheet. Directors of companies must take care in recommending such valuation increases because they may reflect the impact of property price inflation, which may not be sustained, and ignore the future earning potential of the assets.

Differences between the methods chosen to value various assets (and liabilities) at the end of accounting periods may have a significant impact on the results reported in the income statement for those periods. Examples of this may be seen in:

- non-current assets and depreciation
- stocks valuations and cost of sales
- valuations of accounts payable and accounts receivable denominated in foreign currencies
- valuations of accounts receivable and provisions for doubtful debts.

The rules applicable to the valuation of balance sheet items are laid down in the Companies Act 1985, as amended by the Companies Act 1989. These rules allow companies to prepare their financial statements under the historical cost convention (the gross value of the asset being the purchase price or production cost), or alternative conventions of historical cost modified to include certain assets at a revalued amount or current cost.

Under alternative conventions, the gross value of the asset is either the market value at the most recent valuation date or its current cost: tangible non-current assets should be valued at market value or at current cost; non-current asset investments (for example, in subsidiary companies) are valued at market value or at any value considered appropriate by the directors; current asset investments (for example, in marketable non-associated companies) are valued at current cost; stocks are valued at current cost. If a reduction in value of any non-current assets is expected to be permanent then provision for this must be made. The same applies to investments even if the reduction is not expected to be permanent.

Non-current assets with finite lives are subject to depreciation charges. Current assets must be written down to the amount for which they could be disposed of (their **net realisable value**), if that value is lower than cost or an alternative valuation. It should be noted that provisions for reductions in value no longer considered necessary must be written back to the profit and loss account.

The valuation of assets is therefore an extremely subjective area. There is an element of choice between alternative valuation methods that may be adopted by businesses. As a consequence of that, different levels of profit may be reported by the same company through the use of alternative asset valuation methods. Profit is therefore an extremely subjective measure and because of this difficulties may arise in trying to provide consistent comparisons of the financial performance and financial position of companies even within the same industrial sectors.

If changes in accounting policies have been introduced, further inconsistencies arise in trying to provide a realistic comparison of just one company's performance between one accounting period and another. The Companies Acts 1985/1989, accounting concepts, and the accounting standards (SSAPs and FRSs) lay down certain rules for the valuation of balance sheet items.

Income statement (or profit and loss account)

The profit and loss account and income statement are two terms that really mean the same thing. Profit (or loss) may be considered in two ways, which both give the same result. The profit and loss account shows the change in the book value of the wealth of the business over a period. The book value of the wealth of the business is the amount it is worth to the owners, the shareholders. The accumulation of the total change in wealth since the business began, up to a particular point in time, is reflected within the equity section of the balance sheet under the heading retained profits. Using the DVD analogy, the profit and loss account measures the change in the balance sheet from one 'pause' to another. An increase in equity is a profit and a decrease in equity is a loss.

However, for measurement purposes, the income statement is considered with regard to the trading performance of the business (see Fig. 1.8). The profit and loss account calculates whether or not the company has made a profit or loss on its operations during the period, through producing and selling its goods or services. The result, the net earnings or **net profit** (or loss), is derived from deducting expenses incurred from revenues earned throughout the period between two 'pauses'.

The net profit or loss is reflected in the balance sheet of the business under the heading retained profits, which is part of 'shareholders' equity'. Figure 1.9 shows an example of a typical income statement for Flatco plc for the year ended 31 December 2007.

There are three main points to consider regarding the income statement and why it differs from a cash flow statement. First, revenues (or sales or income) and expenses (or costs

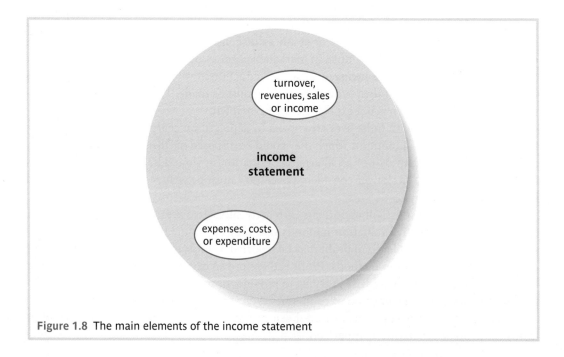

Figure 1.8 The main elements of the income statement

Flatco plc
Income statement for the year ended 31 December 2007

	£000
Turnover	3,500
Cost of sales	(2,500)
Gross profit	1,000
Distribution costs	(300)
Administrative expenses	(250)
	450
Other operating income	100
Operating profit	550
Income from other investments	100
Profit before interest and tax	650
Net interest	(60)
Profit before tax	590
Tax on profit on ordinary activities	(50)
Net profit (profit on ordinary activities after tax, or earnings, or net income)	540
Dividends	(70)
Retained profit for the financial year	470

Figure 1.9 An example of an income statement

or expenditure) are not necessarily received or paid in cash when the transactions occur, and stocks are not always used as soon as they are purchased. Sales are normally accounted for when goods or services are delivered and accepted by the customer. Cash will rarely be received immediately from the customer, except in businesses like high-street retailers and supermarkets; it is normally received weeks or months later.

Second, the income statement does not take into account all the events that impact on the financial position of the company. For example, cash paid for an investment in assets, and cash received from an issue of new shares in the company, or a loan to the company, will reduce or increase cash but they are neither revenue nor expenses.

Third, non-cash flow items, for example depreciation and provisions for doubtful debts, reduce the profit, or increase the loss, of the company but do not represent outflows of cash.

Therefore it can be seen that net profit is not the same as cash flow. A company may get into financial difficulties if it suffers a severe cash shortage even though it may have positive net earnings (or profit).

Cash flow statement

Between them, the balance sheet and income statement show a company's financial position at the beginning and at the end of an accounting period, and its financial performance in the profit or loss that has been achieved during that period.

The balance sheet and income statement do not show or directly analyse some of the key changes that have taken place in the company's financial position, for example:

■ how much capital expenditure (for example, on equipment, machinery, and buildings) has the company made, and how did it fund the expenditure?

- what was the extent of new borrowing and how much debt was repaid?

- how much did the company need to fund new working capital (which includes, for example, an increase in debtors and stock requirements as a result of increased business activity)?

- how much of the company's funding was met by funds generated from its trading activities, and how much by new external funding (for example, from banks and other lenders, or new shareholders)?

Figure 1.10 shows the main elements of a cash flow statement and Fig. 1.11 is an example of a typical cash flow statement for Flatco plc for the year ended 31 December 2007.

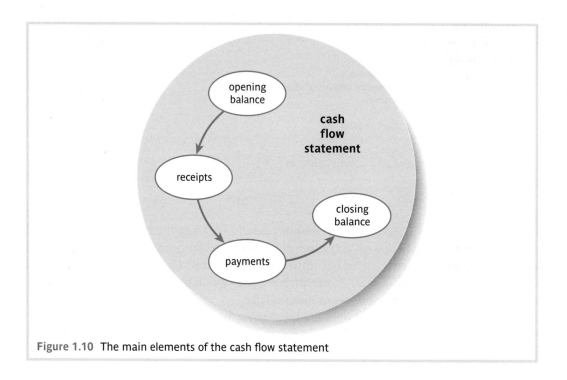

Figure 1.10 The main elements of the cash flow statement

Cash flow statement	
	£000
Net cash inflow from operating activities	936
Returns on investments and servicing of finance (note 1)	40
Taxation	(44)
Capital expenditure (note 1)	(299)
	633
Equity dividends paid	(67)
	566
Management of liquid resources (note 1)	–
Financing (note 1)	373
Increase in cash	939

Figure 1.11 An example of a cash flow statement

The income statement and the cash flow statement are the two 'DVDs' which are running in parallel between the two 'pauses' – the balance sheets at the start and the finish of an accounting period. However, the cash flow statement goes further in answering the questions like those shown above. The aim of the cash flow statement is to summarise the cash inflows and outflows and calculate the net change in the cash position for the company throughout the period between two 'pauses'.

Worked Example 1.3

James Brown, a graduate trainee in the finance department of a large engineering group, pursued his accounting studies with enthusiasm. Although James was more interested in business planning and getting involved with new development projects, his job and his studies required him to become totally familiar with, and to be able to prepare, the financial statements of a company. James was explaining the subject of financial statements and what they involved to a friend of his, Jack, another graduate trainee in human resources. James explained the subject of financial statements to Jack, bearing in mind that he is very much a non-financial person.

Limited companies are required to produce three main financial statements for each accounting period with information about company performance for:

■ shareholders
■ the Inland Revenue
■ banks
■ City analysts
■ investing institutions
■ the public in general.

The three key financial statements are the:

(i) balance sheet
(ii) income statement
(iii) cash flow statement.

(i) **Balance sheet:** a financial snapshot at a moment in time, or the financial position of the company comparable with pressing the 'pause' button on a DVD. The DVD in 'play' mode shows what is happening as time goes on second by second, but when you press 'pause' the DVD stops on a picture; the picture does not tell you what has happened over the period of time up to the pause (or what is going to happen after the pause). The balance sheet is the consequence of everything that has happened up to the balance sheet date. It does not explain how the company got to that position.

(ii) **Income statement:** this is the DVD in 'play' mode. It is used to calculate whether or not the company has made a gain or deficit on its operations during the period, its financial performance, through producing and selling its goods or services. Net earnings or net profit is calculated from revenues derived throughout the period between two 'pauses', minus costs incurred in deriving those revenues.

(iii) **Cash flow statement:** this is the DVD again in 'play' mode, but net earnings is not the same as cash flow, since cash is not necessarily received and paid when revenues and costs occur. Sales are accounted for when goods or services are delivered and accepted by the

> ▶ customer but cash may not be received until some time later. The income statement does not reflect non-trading events like an issue of shares or a loan that will increase cash but are not revenues or costs. The cash flow statement summarises cash inflows and cash outflows and calculates the net change in the cash position for the company throughout the period between two 'pauses'.

The information provided by plcs in particular is frequently used by City analysts, investing institutions, and the public in general. After each year end plcs prepare their **annual report and accounts** for their shareholders. Copies of the annual report and accounts are filed with the Registrar of Companies and copies are available to other interested parties such as financial institutions, major suppliers, and other investors. In addition to the income statement and cash flow statement for the year and the balance sheet as at the year end date, the annual report and accounts includes notes to the accounts, **accounting policies**, and much more financial and non-financial information such as company policies, financial indicators, corporate governance compliance, directors' remuneration, employee numbers, business analysis, and segmental analysis. The annual report also includes the chief executive's review of the business, a report of the auditors of the company, and the chairman's statement.

The auditors' report states compliance or otherwise with accounting standards and that the accounts are free from material misstatement, and that they give a true and fair view prepared on the assumption that the company is a going concern. The chairman's statement offers an opportunity for the chairman of the company to report in unquantified and unaudited terms on the performance of the company during the past financial period and on likely future developments. However, the auditors would object if there was anything in the chairman's statement that was inconsistent with the audited accounts.

In theory, the balance sheet of a private limited company or a plc should tell us all about the company's financial structure and liquidity – the extent to which its assets and liabilities are held in cash or in a near cash form (for example, bank accounts and deposits). It should also tell us about the assets held by the company, the proportion of current assets, and the extent to which they may be used to meet current obligations. However, an element of caution should be noted in analysing balance sheet information. The balance sheet is a historical document. It may have looked entirely different six months or a year ago, or even one week ago. There is not always consistency between the information included in one company's balance sheet with that of another company. Two companies even within the same industry are usually very difficult to compare. Added to that, different analysts very often use alternative calculations for financial ratios or use them in different ways. In addition to the wide choice of valuation methods, the information in a typical published balance sheet does not tell us anything about the quality of the assets, their real value in money terms or their value to the business.

The audit report provided by external auditors in a company's annual report and accounts normally states that they represent a true and fair view of the business. For a number of reasons, which we will discuss in Chapter 3, companies' reports and accounts may not in fact represent a true and fair view and may hide fraudulent activities or may have been subjected to some **creative accounting**, such as **off balance sheet financing** and **window dressing**. Off balance sheet financing relates to the funding of operations in such a way that the relevant assets and liabilities are not disclosed in the balance sheet of the company concerned. Window dressing is a practice in which changes in short-term funding have the effect of disguising or improving the reported liquidity (cash and near cash) position of the reporting organisation. The auditors of WorldCom and Enron stated that their reports and accounts provided a true and fair view of those businesses. The reality was somewhat different, as we can see from Worked Examples 1.4 and 1.5.

Worked Example 1.4

WorldCom was one of the world's largest telecommunications companies with 20 million consumer customers, thousands of corporate clients and 80,000 employees. During 2001/2002 WorldCom improperly recorded US$3.8bn as capital expenditure instead of revenue expenditure, which distorted its reported cash flow and profit. In reality, WorldCom should have reported a loss instead of the US$1.4bn net income in 2002. WorldCom's accounting irregularities were thought to have begun in 2000. Instead of accounting for expenses when they were incurred, WorldCom hid the expenses by pushing them into the future, giving the appearance of spending less and therefore making more profit. This apparent profitability obviously pleased Wall Street analysts and investors, which was reflected in increases in the WorldCom share price up until the accounting irregularities were discovered. WorldCom filed for bankruptcy, and many of the directors and employees subsequently received custodial sentences for fraud.

Worked Example 1.5

The story of Enron, which was guilty of using off balance sheet financing, is complex. Enron began life as a natural gas company started up by Kenneth Lay. He saw an opportunity to profit from the deregulation of the natural gas industry, for which the core business was established. In its early days Enron did the right things for the right reasons and gained substantial credibility on Wall Street. In its latter years successful operations were replaced with the illusion of successful operations.

The business started to use its substantial credibility to sustain operations through loans to acquire companies on a global basis. In the course of acquiring companies the enterprise recruited a team of financial market experts whose original function was to manage operational risks that the company faced. This team became involved in market speculation and either by luck or perhaps by deception apparently made a lot of money. The directors of the enterprise that became Enron thought that the profits being made were dependable. They therefore kept the team of experts, who were then called market traders, as an integral part of the company.

However, the company also tried to disguise the nature of the operations of the team. After some initial successes the traders began to have some financial failures and Enron was no longer really making a profit. The market traders were really only people who were gambling or speculating for very high stakes, and became no longer a source of profits for the business but a source of huge losses. The company covered up its losses in a number of ways relating to a manipulation of the rules relating to the accounting for securities. Any funding shortfalls that the company had were covered by borrowing money in such a way that it did not have to be disclosed in the company's balance sheet.

The company grew enormously from both domestic and international ventures and at the same time so did cases of management spending of corporate funds on unnecessary luxury items. In the years prior to its bankruptcy Enron executives paid for such luxuries out of company borrowing because it had no real profits, which was therefore at the expense of lenders to the company.

Enron eventually became bankrupt, but it also had a large amount of assets that were sold off to partly meet its even greater liabilities. In 2004, Enron's two key executives, Kenneth Lay and Jeff Skilling, were tried for fraud and convicted in 2006. Kenneth Lay, before his imprisonment, died at the age of 64.

Progress check 1.9

What are the three main financial statements reported by a business? How are business transactions ultimately reflected in financial statements?

Users of financial information

Financial information is important to a wide range of groups both internal and external to the organisation. Such information is required, for example, by individuals outside the organisation to make decisions about whether or not to invest in one company or another, or by potential suppliers who wish to assess the reliability and financial strength of the organisation. It is also required by managers within the organisation as an aid to decision-making. The main users of financial information are shown in Fig. 1.12, which are discussed in Worked Example 1.6.

Worked Example 1.6

Kevin Green, a trainee accountant, has recently joined the finance department of a newly formed public limited company. Kevin has been asked to work with the company's auditors who have been commissioned to prepare some alternative formats for the company's annual report.

As part of his preparation for this, Kevin's manager has asked him to prepare a draft report about who is likely to use the information contained in the annual report, and how they might use such information.

Kevin's preparatory notes for his report included the following:

- **Competitors** as part of their industry competitive analysis studies to look at market share, and financial strength.

- **Customers** to determine the ability to provide a regular, reliable supply of goods and services, and to assess customer dependence.

- **Employees** to assess the potential for providing continued employment and assess levels of remuneration.

- **General public** to assess general employment opportunities, social, political and environmental issues, and to consider potential for investment.

- **Government** for VAT and corporate taxation, Government statistics, grants and financial assistance, monopolies and mergers.

- **Investment analysts** to assess investment potential for individuals and institutions with regard to past and future performance, strength of management, and risk versus reward.

- **Lenders** to assess the capacity and the ability of the company to service debt and repay capital.

- **Managers/directors** to aid decision-making, to a certain extent, but such relevant information should already have been available internally.

- **Shareholders/investors** as a tool of accountability to maintain a check on how effectively the directors/managers are running the business, and to assess the financial strength and future developments.

- **Suppliers** to assess long-term viability and whether the company is able to meet its obligations and pay suppliers on an ongoing basis.

Figure 1.12 Users of financial and accounting information

Progress check 1.10

How many users of financial information can you think of and in what ways do you think they may use this information?

Accountability and financial reporting

The directors of a company are appointed by the shareholders to manage the business on their behalf. The accountability of the directors is maintained by reporting on the financial performance and the financial position of the company to shareholders on both a yearly and an interim basis. The reporting made in the form of the financial statements includes the balance sheet, income statement, and cash flow statement.

There are guidelines, or standards, which have been developed by the accounting profession to ensure truth, fairness, and consistency in the preparation and presentation of financial information.

A number of bodies have been established to draft accounting policy, set accounting standards, and to monitor compliance with standards and the provisions of the Companies Act. The Financial Reporting Council (FRC), whose chairman is appointed by the Department of Trade and Industry (DTI) and the Bank of England, develops accounting standards policy and gives guidance on issues of public concern. In the UK the Accounting Standards Board (ASB), which is composed of members of the accountancy profession, and on which the Government has an observer status, has responsibility for development, issue, and withdrawal of accounting standards.

The accounting standards are called **Financial Reporting Standards (FRSs)**. Up to 1990 the accounting standards were known as **Statements of Standard Accounting Practice (SSAPs)**, and were issued by the Accounting Standards Committee (ASC), the forerunner of the ASB. Although some SSAPs have now been withdrawn there are, in addition to the new FRSs, a large number of SSAPs that are still in force.

The ASB is supported by the Urgent Issues Task Force (UITF). Its main role is to assist the ASB in areas where an accounting standard or Companies Act provision exists, but where unsatisfactory or conflicting interpretations have developed or seem likely to develop. The UITF also deals with issues that need to be resolved more quickly than through the issuing of an accounting standard. A recent example of this was the Y2K problem, which involved ensuring that computerised accounting transactions were not corrupted when we moved from the year 1999 to the year 2000.

The Financial Reporting Review Panel (FRRP) reviews comments and complaints from users of financial information. It enquires into the annual accounts of companies where it appears that the requirements of the Companies Act, including the requirement that annual accounts shall show a true and fair view, might have been breached. The Stock Exchange rules covering financial disclosure of publicly quoted companies require such companies to comply with accounting standards, and reasons for non-compliance must be disclosed.

Pressure groups, organisations, and individuals may also have influence on the provisions of the Companies Act and FRSs (and SSAPs). These may include some Government departments (for example, HM Revenue & Customs, Office of Fair Trading) in addition to the DTI and employer organisations such as the Confederation of British Industry (CBI), and professional bodies like the Law Society, Institute of Directors, and Chartered Management Institute.

There are therefore many diverse influences on the form and content of company accounts. In addition to legislation, standards are continually being refined, updated and replaced, and further enhanced by various codes of best practice. As a response to this the UK Generally Accepted Accounting Practices (UK GAAP), first published in 1989, includes all practices that are considered to be permissible or legitimate, either through support by statute, accounting standard or official pronouncement, or through consistency with the needs of users and of meeting the fundamental requirement to present a true and fair view, or even simply through authoritative support in the accounting literature. UK GAAP is therefore a dynamic concept, which changes in response to changing circumstances.

Within the scope of current legislation, best practice, and accounting standards, each company needs to develop its own specific accounting policies. Accounting policies are the specific accounting bases selected and consistently followed by an entity as being, in the opinion of the management, appropriate to its circumstances and best suited to present fairly its results and financial position. Examples are the various alternative methods of valuing stocks of materials, or charging the cost of a machine over its useful life, that is, its depreciation.

The accounting framework therefore includes a large number of concepts, standards, and regulation, and there are a number of strong arguments in favour of such regulation:

■ It is very important that the credibility of financial statement reporting is maintained so that actual and potential investors are protected as far as possible against inappropriate accounting practices.

- Generally, being able to distinguish between the good and not so good companies also provides some stability in the financial markets.
- The auditors of companies must have some rules on which to base their **true and fair view** of financial position and financial performance, which they give to the shareholders and other users of the financial statements.

External auditors are appointed by, and report independently to, the shareholders. They are professionally qualified accountants who are required to provide objective verification to shareholders and other users that the financial statements have been prepared properly and in accordance with legislative and regulatory requirements; that they present the information truthfully and fairly; and that they conform to the best accounting practice in their treatment of the various measurements and valuations. The audit is defined by the **Auditing Practices Board (APB)** as 'an independent examination of, and expression of an opinion on, the financial statements of the enterprise'.

The financial reporting of the company includes preparation of the financial statements, notes and reports, which are audited and given an opinion on by the external auditors. A regulatory framework exists to see fair play, the responsibility for which is held jointly by the Government and the private sector, including the accountancy profession and the Stock Exchange.

The Government exercises influence through bodies such as the Department of Trade and Industry (DTI) and through Parliament by the enactment of legislation, for example the Companies Act. Such legal regulation began with the Joint Stock Companies Act 1844. Subsequent statutes exerted greater influence on company reporting: the Companies Acts 1948, 1967, and 1981. The provisions included in these Acts were consolidated into the Companies Act 1985, which was then amended in 1989. The Companies Act 1985, as amended in 1989, contains the overall current legal framework.

The **International Accounting Standards Committee (IASC)** set up in 1973, which is supported by each of the major professional accounting bodies, fosters the harmonisation of accounting standards internationally. To this end each UK Financial Reporting Standard (FRS) includes a section explaining its relationship to any relevant international accounting standard.

There are wide variations in the accounting practices that have been developed in different countries. These reflect the purposes for which financial information is required by the different users of that information, in each of those countries. There is a different focus on the type of information and the relative importance of each of the users of financial information in each country. This is because each country may differ in terms of:

- who finances the businesses – individual equity shareholders, institutional equity shareholders, debenture holders, banks, etc.
- tax systems, either aligned with or separate from accounting rules
- the level of government control and regulation
- the degree of transparency of information.

The increase in international trade and globalisation has led to a need for convergence, or harmonisation, of accounting rules and practices. The IASC was created in order to develop international accounting standards, but these have been slow in appearing because of the difficulties in bringing together differences in accounting procedures. Until 2000 these standards were called **International Accounting Standards (IASs)**. The successor to the IASC, the

International Accounting Standards Board (IASB) was set up in April 2001 to make financial statements more comparable on a worldwide basis. The IASB publishes its standards in a series of pronouncements called **International Financial Reporting Standards (IFRSs)**. It has also adopted the body of standards issued by the IASC, which continue to be designated IASs. However, the IFRSs have not been provided as a substitute for the IASs.

The UK ASB contributes to the development of IFRS as a part of the IASB team and is committed to achieve convergence of UK GAAP towards IFRS. In the UK, all listed companies have now adopted IFRS; only non-listed companies and small businesses are exempted. IFRSs originated primarily from the Anglo-American GAAPs and are, therefore, similar to UK GAAP in all major aspects. However, there are still some small discrepancies between IFRSs and UK GAAP. The accounting firm KPMG has provided a detailed comparison between IFRSs and UK GAAP in *Implementing IAS: IAS compared with US GAAP and UK GAAP*, published in 2003.

The chairman of the IASB, Sir David Tweedie, has said that 'the aim of the globalisation of accounting standards is to simplify accounting practices and to make it easier for investors to compare the financial statements of companies worldwide'. He also said that 'this will break down barriers to investment and trade and ultimately reduce the cost of capital and stimulate growth' (*Business Week*, 7 June 2004).

On 1 January 2005 there was convergence in the mandatory application of the IFRSs by listed companies within each of the European Union Member States. However, it is interesting to note, for example, the differences in company reporting requirements that continue to exist, for instance, between the German commercial code (the German *Handelsgesetzbuch (HGB)*, the French accounting plan (the French *Plan Comptable*), and UK financial reporting standards in areas such as:

- valuation of assets
- recognition of income
- accounting for provisions and reserves.

There are differences in approach towards company financial reporting requirements for a number of reasons. For example, differences between the USA and the UK exist primarily because of the alternative approaches adopted by accounting and financial reporting standard setters in the USA and the UK. The 'rules based' approach used in the USA predominantly seeks to codify practices and specify particular techniques, while the 'principles based' approach used in the UK seeks to provide organisations with choices from a range of practices and techniques.

Despite significant progress towards a standardised international approach, there continue to be very many differences between UK GAAP and IFRSs, for example in the areas of:

- accounting for pension costs for defined benefit schemes
- accounting for deferred tax
- accounting for derivatives
- accounting for investments at fair values
- hedge accounting
- preference shares and convertible bonds
- merger accounting
- goodwill amortisation

- the treatment of negative goodwill
- accounting for investment properties, especially the treatment of revaluations
- accounting for proposed dividends
- accounting for finance leases – for example, operating leases under UK GAAP may be finance leases under IFRS.

It may be argued that the increasing amount of accounting regulation itself stifles responses to changes in economic and business environments, and discourages the development of improved financial reporting. As the various conceptual frameworks continue to be developed it is apparent that there is wide disagreement about what constitutes accounting best practice. The resistance to acceptance of IASs may be for political reasons, the rules perhaps reflecting the requirements of specific interest groups or countries.

Despite increasing accounting regulation there have been an increasing number of well-publicised financial scandals in the USA in particular, where the accounting systems are very much 'rule-based', as well as in the UK, Italy, and Japan. However, these scandals have usually been the result of fraudulent activity. This leads to another question as to why the auditors of such companies did not detect or prevent such fraud. The answer is that, despite the widespread perception of the general public to the contrary, auditors are not appointed to detect or prevent fraud. Rather, they are appointed by the shareholders to give their opinion as to whether the financial statements show a true and fair view and comply with statutory, regulatory, and accounting and financial reporting standards requirements.

Progress check 1.11

In what ways may the reliability of financial reporting be ensured?

Worked Example 1.7

You are thinking of changing jobs (within marketing) and moving from a local, well-established retailer that has been in business for over 20 years. You have been asked to attend an interview at a new plc that started up around two years ago. The plc is a retailer via the Internet. Your family has suggested that you investigate the company thoroughly before your interview, paying particular attention to its financial resources. There is a chance the plc may not be a going concern if its business plan does not succeed.

You will certainly want to include the following questions at your interview.

(i) Are any published accounts available for review?

(ii) What is the share capital of the company (for example, is it £10,000 or £1,000,000)?

(iii) Is the company profitable?

(iv) Does the company have loan commitments?

(v) Is the company working within its bank overdraft facilities?

(vi) Are any press analyses of the company available?

(vii) What is the current customer base?

The answers may suggest whether the company can continue trading for the foreseeable future.

Managing corporate finance

The finance function, or more specifically the finance director of a business, has the responsibility for managing the financial resources of the business to meet the objectives of the business. The finance director's corporate finance responsibilities involve:

- raising and controlling the provision of funds for the business
- deciding on the deployment of these funds – the assets, new projects, and operational expenditure required to increase the wealth of the business
- controlling the resources of the business to ensure that they are being managed effectively
- managing financial risks such as exposures relating to movements in interest rates and foreign currency exchange rates.

The finance director is also responsible for the accounting function of the business, but it is a separate and different discipline to corporate finance. The management of corporate finance, or financial management, draws on the techniques of both financial accounting and management accounting, relating to decision-making and financial reporting. However, corporate finance is concerned with the future and relates to the management of the financial resources of the business in order to optimise the returns to investors in the business. In this context the finance directors must decide on:

- what level of assets should the company have?
- how should investment projects be chosen and how should they be funded?
- in what proportions should the company's funding be regarding shareholders' equity and borrowings?
- what proportions of profit after tax should be paid out in dividends or retained for future investment?

Accounting may assist in these decisions, for example capital investment appraisal (management accounting) and the impact on financial statement reporting (financial accounting). Therefore, the two disciplines of corporate finance and accounting are both the responsibility of the finance director, and although they are separate disciplines the former is very much supported by the latter.

Progress check 1.12

What are the key responsibilities of the finance director with regard to the financial management of a business?

Underlying principles of corporate finance

We have seen that corporate finance is about obtaining and managing the financial resources of a business in order to achieve the objectives of the business. The primary objective of the business is the maximisation of shareholder wealth, and there are a number of principles that underpin the decision-making of financial managers in pursuit of this objective.

Shareholder wealth maximisation

The maximisation of shareholder wealth is the prime objective of the majority of companies. The reason why investors put funds into a business is to receive returns that are better than the returns that they may receive from alternative investments. It is the responsibility of the directors of the company to make the optimum use of these funds to ensure that shareholder returns are maximised. But, how do they do this and what is shareholder wealth?

Shareholder wealth is derived by shareholders from two sources:

- dividends paid on their equity, or ordinary, shares
- capital appreciation from the increase in the price of their ordinary shares.

As illustrated in Worked Example 1.8, dividends do not have to be paid by a company. Dividends are paid out of the profits of the company available for distribution after interest and corporation tax has been paid, and assuming that the company has sufficient cash for their payment. The increase in share price depends generally on the demand for the company's shares and the volume of dealing activity in those shares.

Worked Example 1.8

In early 2004 the satellite broadcaster BSkyB restored paying a dividend after a gap of more than five years. BSkyB had suspended its dividend for several years while it rolled out its digital TV service. The announcement of an interim payout of 2.75p per share was announced as the UK pay-TV giant unveiled an 84% jump in half-year operating profits to £283m (US$529.5m).

A company's shares may be in demand because prospective share buyers believe that there are good prospects of future share price increases and/or increased dividend payments. The reason for such optimism may be that the company has demonstrated its success in investing in value-creating projects ('real' investment) and its ongoing intention of making even greater value-adding investments. The success of such investments in cash terms will provide the future cash flow for the payment of dividends and sustained future investment in new projects.

Cash flow

It is the 'success' of investments in new projects that provides the key to future growth in both dividends and the company's share price (see Chapter 4). In this context, by success we mean returns in cash terms over and above the cost of the funds used for those investments and above the average returns in that particular market. It is cash flow from investments and not profit that is important here. Profit is an accounting term, which is subjective and open to many interpretations. Cash is a fact and its measurement is completely objective – you either have it or you don't. Real funds can be seen in cash but not in accounting profit. Interest charges become payable as soon as money is made available, for example, from a lender to a borrower, not when an agreement is made or when a contract is signed. Therefore, in corporate finance it is cash flow which is important rather than profit.

Worked Example 1.9

Cox Ltd is a local electrical retailer with retail outlets throughout the north of England. The company is currently considering opening a new temporary retail outlet, and is considering three alternative development options. As the company's financial adviser, you have been asked to evaluate the financial aspects of each of the options and advise which option the company should select, from a purely cash flow perspective (ignoring the time value of money, which is discussed in the next section).

The following financial information has been made available:

Year	Option 1 £000	Option 2 £000	Option 3 £000
		Investment	
0	12,000	12,000	12,000
		Cash receipts	
1	9,500	3,000	6,000
2	8,500	4,500	6,000
3	3,500	8,000	6,000
4	2,500	8,500	6,000

In cash flow terms all three options provide the same net cash flow, but the timings of the cash flow receipts differ significantly. Given that the future is invariably uncertain, it is likely that from a purely cash flow perspective, the rational choice would be to maximise the cash flows derived earlier rather than later, in which case the selection would be Option 1.

Time value of money

It is not only the cash flows themselves from investments that are important in terms of their size but also when they are received – the timing of cash flows, and their certainty of being received at all – the risk relating to cash flows. This has not been considered at all in Worked Example 1.9.

A receipt of £100 today has greater value than receipt of £100 in one year's time. Its value changes over time primarily because:

- the money could have been alternatively invested to receive interest
- purchasing power will have been lost over a year due to inflation.

The percentage rate by which the value of money may be eroded over one year is called the discount rate, and the amount by which the value of money is eroded over one year is calculated by dividing it by what is called the discount factor [1/(1 + discount rate %)]. The value of money continues to be reduced by application of the discount factor (or using the appropriate discount factor if the discount rate has changed); its value therefore normally becomes less and less. Using this method, a discount factor may be applied to future cash flows to calculate the today values of future cash flows. This technique is called discounted cash flow (DCF). It is the today values of cash flows, their present values, which are the relevant cash flows with regard to investments. We will return to DCF in more detail in Chapter 4.

Risk

Increases in shareholder wealth comprise dividends and capital gains from share price increases, which together are termed returns to investors. Interest paid on loans to companies is called the return to debt holders, or lenders. The returns from 'real' investments in new assets and projects are the present values of the cash flows derived from the profits from such investments. Whichever return we are considering, we are talking specifically about future expected cash flows from investments. There is a close correlation between the returns and the level of risk relating to these investments.

An actual return on an investment will never be exactly what was expected – it will be either higher or lower, better or worse. Risk relates to the possibility that an actual return will be different from an expected return. The more risky an investment, the greater is the possibility that the return will be different from that expected. The higher the risk of an investment, the higher will be the expected return; the lower the risk of an investment, the lower will be the expected return. Throughout this book we will return to risk many times in:

■ Chapter 4 when we look at capital investment decisions
■ Chapter 5 when we look at the cost of capital – the funds used for investments
■ Chapter 6 when we look at the type of funds used by companies – equity or loans
■ Chapter 9 when we look at financial planning
■ Chapter 11 when we look at international operations and investment
■ Chapter 12 when we look at financial risk management
■ Part II when we look at financial strategy.

Progress check 1.13

What is meant by shareholder wealth maximisation?

Summary of key points

■ The four main types of profit-making businesses in the UK are sole traders, partnerships, limited companies (Ltd), and public limited companies (plc).
■ The finance function has an important position within an organisation, and includes responsibility for accounting and corporate finance.
■ Accountability of directors is maintained by reporting on the financial performance and the financial position of the company to shareholders on both a yearly and a half-yearly basis, and the audit function.
■ Financial statements are produced by companies for each accounting period to provide information about how the business has been doing.
■ The three main financial statements that appear within a business's annual report and accounts, together with the chairman's statement, directors' report, and auditors' report, are the balance sheet, income statement, and cash flow statement.

▶

▶
- Corporate finance and accounting are both the responsibility of the finance director, and although they are separate disciplines corporate finance is very much supported by the accounting function.
- The effective management of corporate finance impacts greatly on how well the company is able to achieve its prime objective of maximisation of shareholder wealth.
- The underlying principles of corporate finance include cash flow (rather than profit), the time value of money, and the risk and uncertainty relating to future cash flows.

🔑 Glossary of key terms

accounting The classification and recording of monetary transactions, the presentation and interpretation of the results of those transactions in order to assess performance over a period and the financial position at a given date, and the monetary projection of future activities arising from alternative planned courses of action.

accounting concepts The principles underpinning the preparation of accounting information. Fundamental accounting concepts are the broad basic assumptions which underlie the periodic financial accounts of business enterprises.

accounting period The time period covered by the accounting statements of an entity.

accounting policies The specific accounting bases selected and consistently followed by an entity as being, in the opinion of the management, appropriate to its circumstances and best suited to present fairly its results and financial position (FRS 18 and Companies Act).

accounting standard Authoritative statement of how particular types of transaction and other events should be reflected in financial statements. Compliance with accounting standards will normally be necessary for financial statements to give a true and fair view (ASB).

Accounting Standards Board (ASB) A UK standard-setting body set up in 1990 to develop, issue and withdraw accounting standards. Its aims are to 'establish and improve standards of financial accounting and reporting, for the benefit of users, preparers and auditors of financial information'.

accounts payable Also called trade creditors, is the money owed to suppliers for goods and services.

accounts receivable Also called trade debtors, is the money owed to entities by customers.

Alternative Investment Market (AIM) A securities market designed primarily for small companies, regulated by the Stock Exchange but with less demanding rules than apply to the Stock Exchange official list of companies.

annual report and accounts A set of statements which may comprise a management report (in the case of companies, a directors' report), an auditors' report, and the financial statements of the entity.

asset A right or other access to future economic benefits controlled by an entity as a result of past transactions or events (FRS 5).

audit A systematic examination of the activities and status of an entity, based primarily on investigation and analysis of its systems, controls, and records. A statutory annual audit of a company is defined by the APB as an independent examination of, and expression of an opinion on, the financial statements of the enterprise.

Auditing Practices Board (APB) A body formed in 1991 by an agreement between the six members of the Consultative Committee of Accountancy Bodies, to be responsible for developing and issuing professional standards for auditors in the United Kingdom and the Republic of Ireland.

auditor A professionally qualified accountant who is appointed by, and reports independently to, the shareholders, providing an objective verification to shareholders and other users that the financial statements have been prepared properly and in accordance with legislative and regulatory requirements; that they present the information truthfully and fairly, and that they conform to the best accounting practice in their treatment of the various measurements and valuations.

balance sheet A statement of the financial position of an entity at a given date disclosing the assets, liabilities, and accumulated funds such as shareholders' contributions and reserves, prepared to give a true and fair view of the financial state of the entity at that date.

cash flow statement A statement that summarises the inflows and outflows of cash for a period, classified under the following standard headings (FRS 1):

- operating activities
- returns on investment and servicing of finance
- taxation
- investing activities
- liquid funds
- equity dividends
- financing.

creative accounting A form of accounting which, while complying with all regulations, nevertheless gives a biased (generally favourable) impression of a company's performance.

financial accounting Financial accounting is the function responsible for the periodic external reporting, statutorily required, for shareholders. It also provides such similar information as required for Government and other interested third parties, such as potential investors, employees, lenders, suppliers, customers, and financial analysts.

financial management (or management of corporate finance) The management of all the processes associated with the efficient acquisition and deployment of both short- and long-term financial resources. Within an organisation financial management assists operations management to reach their financial objectives.

▶

▶ **Financial Reporting Council (FRC)** The UK body responsible for:

(i) guiding the standard setting body (ASB) on work programmes and issues of public concern

(ii) seeing that work on accounting standards is properly financed

(iii) acting as a proactive public influence for securing good accounting practice.

Financial Reporting Standards (FRSs) The accounting standards of practice published by the Accounting Standards Board since 1 August 1990, and which are gradually replacing the Standard Statements of Accounting Practice (SSAPs), which were published by the Accounting Standards Committee up to 1 August 1990.

financial statements Summaries of accounts, whether to internal or external parties, to provide information for interested parties. The three key financial statements are: income statement; balance sheet; cash flow statement. Other financial statements are: report of the auditors; statement of recognised gains and losses; reconciliation of movements in shareholders' funds.

flotation A flotation, or initial public offering (IPO), is the obtaining of a listing by a company on a stock exchange, through the offering of its shares to the general public, financial institutions, or private sector businesses.

income statement (or profit and loss account) Measures whether or not the company has made a profit or loss on its operations during the period, through producing and selling its goods or services.

internal control As defined in the Cadbury Report, it is the whole system of controls, financial or otherwise, established in order to provide reasonable assurance of:

(i) effective and efficient operation

(ii) internal financial control

(iii) compliance with laws and regulations.

International Accounting Standard (IAS) The international financial reporting standards issued by the IASC, which are very similar to the SSAPs and FRSs, which are used in the UK.

International Accounting Standards Board (IASB) The IASB is the body that is responsible for setting and publishing International Financial Reporting Standards (IFRSs). It was formed on 1 April 2001 and succeeded the International Accounting Standards Committee (IASC) which had been formed in 1973. The parent body of the IASB is the International Accounting Standards Committee Foundation, which was incorporated in the USA in March 2001, and was also responsible for issuing International Accounting Standards (IASs).

International Accounting Standards Committee (IASC) A committee supported by many national accounting bodies worldwide, whose objects are:

(i) to facilitate and publish in the public interest, accounting standards to be observed in the presentation of financial statements, and to promote their worldwide acceptance and observance

(ii) to work generally for the improvement of harmonisation of regulations, accounting standards, and procedures relating to the presentation of financial statements (IASC).

International Financial Reporting Standard (IFRS) The international financial reporting standards issued by the IASB, which incorporate the IASs, issued by the IASC.

liability An entity's obligation to transfer economic benefits as a result of past transactions or events (FRS 5).

management accounting The application of the principles of accounting and financial management to create, protect, preserve and increase value so as to deliver that value to the stakeholders of profit and not-for-profit enterprises, both public and private. Management accounting is an integral part of management, requiring the identification, generation, presentation, interpretation and use of information relevant to:

- formulating business strategy
- planning and controlling activities
- decision-making
- efficient resource usage
- performance improvement and value enhancement
- safeguarding tangible and intangible assets
- corporate governance and internal control.

net profit (or profit after tax) Profit before tax (PBT) less corporation tax.

net realisable value The amount for which an asset could be disposed, less any direct selling costs (SSAP 9).

off balance sheet financing The funding of operations in such a way that the relevant assets and liabilities are not disclosed in the balance sheet of the company concerned.

private limited company (Ltd) A Ltd company is one in which the liability of members for the company's debts is limited to the amount paid and, if any, unpaid on the shares taken up by them.

public limited company (plc) A plc is a company limited by shares or by guarantee, with a share capital, whose memorandum states that it is public and that it has complied with the registration procedures for such a company. A public company is distinguished from a private company in the following ways: a minimum issued share capital of £50,000; public limited company, or plc, at the end of the name; public company clause in the memorandum; freedom to offer securities to the public.

qualified accountant A member of the accountancy profession, and in the UK a member of one of the six professional accountancy bodies: CIMA; ICAEW; ICAS; ICAI; ACCA; CIPFA.

Registrar of Companies Government official agency that is responsible for initial registration of new companies and for collecting and arranging public access to the annual reports of all limited companies.

▶ **shareholders' equity** The total investment of the shareholders in the company – the total wealth. Equity comprises capital, share premiums, and retained earnings.

Statements of Standard Accounting Practice (SSAPs) The accounting standards of practice published by the Accounting Standards Committee up to 1 August 1990.

treasury management The corporate handling of all financial matters, the generation of external and internal funds for business, the management of currencies and cash flows, and the complex strategies, policies, and procedures of corporate finance.

true and fair view The requirement for financial statements prepared in compliance with the Companies Act to 'give a true and fair view' overrides any other requirements. Although not precisely defined in the Companies Act, this is generally accepted to mean that accounts show a true and fair view if they are unlikely to mislead a user of financial information by giving a false impression of the company.

window dressing A creative accounting practice in which changes in short-term funding have the effect of disguising or improving the reported liquidity position of the reporting organisation.

❓ Questions

Q1.1 What are the different types of business entity and what are the fundamental differences between them?

Q1.2 (i) Why is financial information produced?
(ii) Who is it produced for and what do they use it for?

Q1.3 Outline the responsibilities of the finance director of a large public limited company (plc).

Q1.4 Which are the three key financial statements that are used to provide information to shareholders and others about the company's financial position and financial performance, and what are their limitations?

Q1.5 (i) What information does a balance sheet provide?
(ii) What information does an income statement (or profit and loss account) provide?
(iii) What information does a cash flow statement provide?

Q1.6 How do financial statements ensure that accountability for the reporting of timely and accurate information to shareholders is maintained?

Q1.7 (i) What is corporate finance?
(ii) How does corporate finance relate to accounting and perhaps other disciplines?

Q1.8 Describe the main corporate finance responsibilities of the finance director of a large public limited company (plc).

Q1.9 Explain the key principles that underpin the discipline of corporate finance.

Discussion points

D1.1 The managing director of a large public limited company stated: 'I've built up my business over the past 15 years from a one-man band to a large plc. As we grew we seemed to spend more and more money on accountants, financial managers, and auditors. During the next few months we are restructuring to go back to being a private limited company. This will be much simpler and we can save a fortune on finance departments and auditing costs.' Discuss.

　　(Hint: You may wish to research Richard Branson and, for example, Virgin Air, on the Internet to provide some background for this discussion.)

D1.2 'So long that, as a company, we continue to report profits each year then the shareholders will have no reason to complain.' Discuss.

Exercises

Solutions are provided in Appendix 2 to all exercise numbers highlighted in colour.

Level I

E1.1 *Time allowed – 30 minutes*

At a recent meeting of the local branch of the Women's Institute they had a discussion about what sort of organisation they were. The discussion broadened into a general debate about all types of organisation, and someone brought up the term 'business entity'. Although there were many opinions, there was little sound knowledge about what business entities are. Jane Cross said that her husband was an accountant and she was sure he would not mind spending an hour one evening to enlighten them on the subject. Chris Cross fished out his textbooks to refresh his knowledge of the subject and came up with a schedule of all the different business entities he could think of together with the detail of their defining features and key points of difference and similarity.

Prepare the sort of schedule that Chris might have drafted for his talk and identify the category that the Women's Institute might fall into.

E1.2 *Time allowed – 30 minutes*

Mary Andrews was a finance manager but is now semi-retired. She has been asked by her local comprehensive school careers officer to give a talk entitled: 'What is corporate finance and what is financial management?'

Prepare a list of bullet points that covers everything necessary for Mary to give a comprehensive and easy-to-understand presentation to a group of sixth-formers at the school.

E1.3 *Time allowed – 30 minutes*

It is sometimes said that the only user of financial information is the accountant.

Outline the range of other users of financial information.

Level II

E1.4 *Time allowed – 30 minutes*

Financial statements are produced each year by businesses, using prescribed formats.

▶

▶ **Should major plcs be allowed to reflect their individuality in their own financial statements?**

E1.5 *Time allowed – 45 minutes*

Professionals in the UK, for example, doctors, solicitors, accountants, etc., normally work within partnerships. Many tradesmen, such as plumbers, car mechanics, carpenters, etc., operate as sole traders. Software engineers seem to work for corporations and limited companies.

Consider the size of operation, range of products, financing, the marketplace, and the geographical area served, to discuss why companies like Microsoft and Yahoo should operate as plcs.

E1.6 *Time allowed – 60 minutes*

Bill Walsh has just been appointed Finance Director of a medium-sized engineering company, Nutsan Ltd, which has a high level of exports and is very sensitive to economic changes throughout the UK and the rest of the world. One of the tasks on Bill's action list is a review of the accounting and finance function.

What are the senior financial roles that Bill would expect to be in place and what are the important functions for which they should be responsible?

E1.7 *Time allowed – 60 minutes*

The Millennium Dome was opened to the general public in the UK for the year 2000 and was planned to close at the end of 2000 for the site to be used for some other purpose. There were problems financing the construction and the general day-to-day operations. There were many crises reported in the press during 2000. A proposed takeover of the site fell through in September 2000, with various reasons given by the potential acquirer.

You are required to research into the Dome using the BBC, the *Financial Times* **and the other serious newspapers, and the Internet, and summarise the financial aspects of the project that you gather. You should focus on the attitudes expressed by the general public, select committees of MPs, Government ministers, the Opposition, the Dome's management, and consider examples of bias, non-timeliness, and lack of transparency.**

Chapter 2

Corporate objectives

Chapter contents

LEARNING OBJECTIVES

Completion of this chapter will enable you to:

☑ Outline the strategic management process with regard to mission, corporate objectives, corporate appraisal, and strategic choice.

☑ Explain why the maximisation of shareholder wealth is the primary corporate objective.

▶ ☑ Consider the secondary, or surrogate objectives of a company.

☑ Appreciate the importance of how companies may adopt appropriate financial strategies to create shareholder value.

☑ Explain the efficient market hypothesis and its place in corporate financial theory.

☑ Describe the concept of shareholder value.

☑ Outline the key strategic financial decisions faced by companies.

☑ Explain agency theory and what is meant by the agency problem.

☑ Describe the range of alternative incentive schemes that may be used to overcome the agency problem.

Introduction

This chapter begins by looking generally at the strategic management process. It puts the corporate objectives of the company into context and how they are linked to shareholder value and financial strategy. We will consider the range of corporate objectives of a business, and in particular the primary objective of maximisation of shareholder wealth. Other objectives, which are considered secondary to the main objective, are often described as substitute or surrogate objectives. These may exist in support of the primary objective, or because of the diverse interests of the other stakeholders in a business apart from the shareholders, for example employees, the general public, suppliers, and customers. This chapter deals with what is meant by shareholder value and its relationship with corporate value, and the key financial decisions faced by businesses in their endeavours to achieve their primary objective. An introduction to the subject of financial strategy will indicate how the appropriate financial strategy may be used to increase value. The chapter closes with a look at why the objective of maximisation of shareholder wealth may not always be aligned with the goals of the managers of a business because of the agency problem. The ways in which the agency problem may be dealt with is expanded on in Chapter 3 where we discuss corporate governance.

Strategic management

The origins of strategy are in military campaigns and manoeuvring. Strategy is fundamentally long term. It is concerned with the long-term 'whats' of the company rather than the 'hows', for example what it wants to do, what it wants the organisation to be, and where it wants the organisation to go, including the specification of resources required to achieve specific objectives. Strategy is not the 'how' to achieve those things. Tactics are the short-term plans for achieving the objectives of the organisation. They are the shorter-term 'hows'.

The **strategic management** process includes making decisions on:

■ the objectives of the organisation

■ changes in these objectives

■ the resources used to attain these objectives

■ the policies that are to govern the acquisition, use, and disposition of these resources.

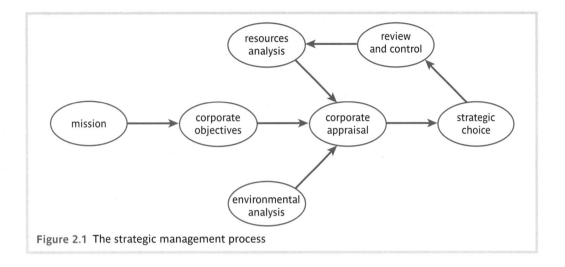

Figure 2.1 The strategic management process

Strategic management includes strategic planning, which it is incorrect to assume is just an extension of budgeting, but there is a close relationship between these processes. A strategic plan (see Chapter 9) looks at the long term, which is more than a year and typically five or ten years. A budget is a short-term quantified statement, for a defined period of time, which may include planned investments, revenues, expenses, assets, liabilities, and cash flows. A budget provides a focus for the organisation, aids the co-ordination of activities, and facilitates control.

The way in which a typical strategic management process may be carried out in an organisation is illustrated in the flow chart in Fig. 2.1. The flow chart shows particularly how analysis is used to develop strategies and actions.

It is fundamental for every company to have a **mission** developed from a vision of what it would like to be achieved. The mission statement may be a summary of goals and policies, which does not have to be in writing, but is generally a sense of purpose or underlying belief of the company. A mission includes four elements, defined in the Ashridge Mission Model developed by Andrew Campbell in 1992: purpose; company values; strategies; and standards and behaviour. In addition it should answer the strategic question 'what do we do?' by defining the scope of the business in terms of markets and products. The most important thing about a company's mission is that it should be understood and believed in by every employee in the business.

Strategic decisions cannot generally be collated by a company into some sort of total decision matrix to arrive at an optimum overall strategy. Life is never as simple as this because there are too many variables, which are changing constantly, and also limitations with regard to knowledge and processes. In practice, strategy tends to emerge and develop in an incremental way in order to maintain a strategic fit between corporate goals and resources and changing market opportunities.

An organisation's policy is the framework expressing the limits within which actions should occur. Whereas policy is a long-lasting, usually unquantified, statement of guidance about the way in which an organisation seeks to behave in relation to its stakeholders, corporate **objectives** are the visionary statements set out by the company before it starts its detailed planning.

Corporate objectives

A company is owned by its shareholders who have invested money in the business in order to increase the value of, and maximise the return from, their investment. The primary objective of

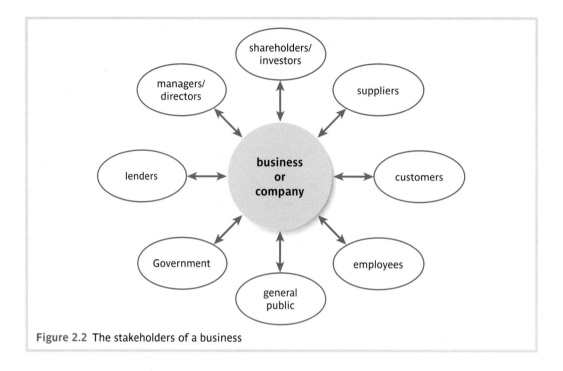

Figure 2.2 The stakeholders of a business

a business is therefore assumed to be the maximisation of shareholder wealth. A company is managed by its directors on behalf of its shareholders. Directors are appointed by shareholders and are charged with the primary aim of achievement of the shareholder wealth maximisation objective. An increase in shareholder wealth is derived from cash received by shareholders from the receipt of dividends and from capital gains from increases in the market price of their shares.

The shareholders are not the only stakeholders in a business; there are many others, which are shown in Fig. 2.2. Their aims and objectives do not necessarily coincide with the objectives of the shareholders.

Surrogate objectives

Although we are assuming throughout this book that the primary objective of a company is the maximisation of shareholder wealth, there are many other objectives including business objectives, operational objectives, and individual objectives that should be formalised and in writing. Other aims and objectives of the business, which must be secondary to the primary objective, are called surrogate, or alternative objectives (see Fig. 2.3), and may include:

- profit maximisation
- market share maximisation
- earnings per share growth
- social responsibility
- sales maximisation
- survival
- dividend growth,

and may include non-financial objectives such as customer satisfaction and delivery reliability.

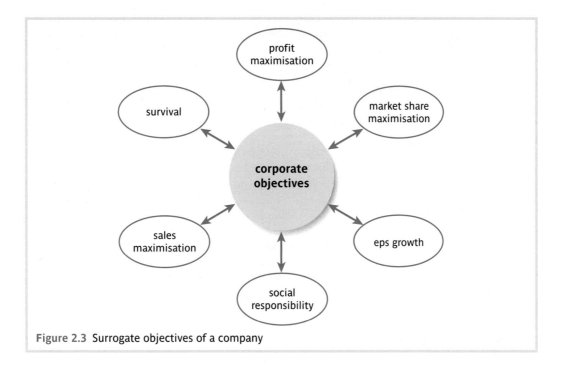

Figure 2.3 Surrogate objectives of a company

There are a number of problems associated with these **surrogate objectives**:

- the choice of timescale applicable to profit maximisation may be long or short term
- the measurement of profit is very subjective
- a profit-maximising strategy is not without risk
- with a sales maximisation strategy there is sometimes a danger of overtrading, in which there is a lack of adequate working capital to support such increases in levels of business
- survival, whilst an important objective, cannot be a long-term objective of a business
- a business cannot exist merely to meet its social responsibility, for example to please its employees, the local community, etc.
- surrogate or secondary objectives may actually be contrary to or may undermine the primary objective of shareholder wealth maximisation.

Progress check 2.1

Why is maximisation of shareholder wealth a company's primary objective?

The relationships between the objectives of a company should ensure that there is no conflict. Their importance should also be assigned by ranking priorities. Objectives are set in order to support the planning process and to assign responsibility to individuals. They should aim to integrate each area of the company so that they are all moving in the same direction in alignment with the company's mission and shareholders' requirements. Objectives are also used to motivate employees and to enable performance evaluation of individuals, departments, business units, and companies.

> ## Worked Example 2.1
>
> During a discussion at a recent board meeting the finance director of Moon plc explained that traditional financial theory suggests that companies should pursue a primary objective of long-term shareholder wealth maximisation. He went on to explain that most companies also pursue one or more surrogate corporate objectives, and that Moon plc should pursue an objective of short-term share price maximisation.
>
> How can the adoption of such a surrogate corporate objective be justified?
>
> Maximisation of shareholder wealth may be considered in terms of maximisation of shareholder returns. Shareholder returns are derived from two sources – a regular flow of dividends and capital growth from an increase in share price. A shareholder will invariably demand a required rate of return, which is the present value of anticipated future flows of dividends, discounted at the shareholder's required rate of return. This is often used to determine the fundamental value of a share. While this fundamental value may not necessarily be the market value of the shares it often represents a close approximation, and as a consequence is often used as a substitute for measuring shareholder wealth. This is a possible justification for Moon's adoption of its surrogate corporate objective of short-term share price maximisation.

The attitudes of the company's stakeholders should be considered by the company in terms of assessment of their expectations and reactions and the repercussions of decisions taken. This can only be a broad assessment since in practice it is obviously difficult to determine the attitudes of all stakeholders. Corporate and cultural power should be considered, which include the shared beliefs, values, and attitudes that serve to define objectives. These must be prioritised and may include objectives within the current scope and the current culture, or they may involve moves in new directions that possibly require culture changes. Consideration of corporate culture in setting objectives should involve influence consultation, which means identification of the people in the organisation that can make things happen and therefore help in ensuring that objectives are met. Objectives also need to be structured in such a way as to facilitate their implementation and achievement. The time limits and prioritisation for completion of these objectives and the measures of their performance should also be specified.

Corporate appraisal

Having established its objectives, a company's strategic management process continues to consider many ideas and options and 'what-ifs'. The purpose of this is to try and provide the best 'fit' between the company and its environment, to enable it to focus on its most important objectives, and to assist in determining how the company may achieve its objectives. The first part of the process involves a corporate appraisal, which includes a review of the business in terms of external factors (**environmental analysis**) and internal factors (**resources analysis**, or position audit) to assess the possibility of attaining objectives, and considers the basis of the company's competitive advantage (Porter's generic strategy).

An environmental analysis of the company includes consideration of, for example:

- the nature of the company's environment, whether it is complex or simple, and whether the company is slow or dynamic in reacting to what is going on in the environment
- analysis of PESTEL (political, economic, social, technological change, environmental, and legislative) factors

- external elements of a SWOT (strengths, weaknesses, opportunities, threats) analysis – the part of the SWOT analysis (see an example in Chapter 8) that looks at major external threats to the company and how these may be avoided, turned round, or exploited along with all other opportunities
- structural analysis of the competitive environment (Porter), which looks at the competitive reactions of current and potential competitors in the industry and how they may compete, and considers:
  - analysis of the market characteristics of supply and demand
  - forecasting (see Chapter 9) and the use of databases and a range of information sources.

The position audit or resources analysis of the company considers things like, for example:

- availability and control of the 5Ms – the resources of people (men), materials, plant and equipment (machines), cash flow (money), and markets
- the company's industrial sectors and its products
- internal elements of a SWOT analysis (see an example in Chapter 8) that look at the major internal weaknesses of the company and how these may be eliminated and how the company may capitalise on its strengths
- portfolio analysis of the company – product life cycle (plc) and the Boston Consulting Group (BCG) matrix (see Chapter 13)
- gap analysis, which looks at gaps that may exist between the company and the best in the industry and considers areas such as levels of productivity, quality, distribution, and service efficiency
- skills and flexibility analysis – the human resources analysis of the strengths, knowledge and experience of all employees and their ability to work in teams
- financial analysis (see Chapter 8)
- comparative analysis of historical performance and industry norms, using benchmarking and the company's own records
- the learning curve with regard to new employees, new products and processes.

Porter's generic strategy describes the way in which a business may derive a competitive advantage through either cost leadership, or differentiation of its products and services from its competitors on the basis of, for example, technology, quality, service, or branding. Having chosen cost leadership or differentiation, the company may then focus on either broad markets or narrow markets of specific products and customers.

Strategic choice

The next steps in the company's strategic management process consider strategic choice, which uses the information provided from the corporate appraisal to evaluate the suitability, feasibility, and acceptability of the development of alternative strategies through:

- screening options, using ranking, decision trees, scenario analysis and simulation
- financial analysis using, for example, cost/benefit analysis, break-even analysis, return on capital employed (see Chapter 8), payback, and DCF (see Chapter 4)
- risk analysis (see Chapter 12)

and strategic method, which deals with the ways in which a company may develop and grow.

Corporate development and growth may be either through internal organic development or through acquisitions, mergers, or joint ventures. Organic growth is achieved from investment by the company in value-adding projects (see Chapter 4), and the development of new products and services, processes, and markets.

Strategic method may use techniques such as the Ansoff growth vector analysis, which considers gaps in the market and the products and markets in which the business wishes to compete. The company may adopt a strategy of doing nothing, withdrawing from a market, penetrating and developing a market, consolidating the company's position, or diversifying. The Ansoff diversification model considers the various methods of diversification, which may be related (horizontal, or vertical backward and forward) or unrelated to the company's current areas of business through conglomerate growth involving acquisitions (see Chapter 16).

Implementation of strategy requires consideration of the planning and allocation of resources, development of an appropriate organisational structure and the people and systems within the corporate environment. It also requires consideration of how strategies will be managed as they are rolled out and systems put in place for their review and control. The outcomes of review and control systems are usually fed back into a company's systems of resources analysis in order that refinements or changes may be made to strategy as necessary.

Worked Example 2.2

We are required to identify a policy, a strategy, and tactics for Mediatrix plc, which is a designer and manufacturer of hi-tech consumer products, and which wants to develop a specific multimedia product that is number one in the market place.

The policy for Mediatrix may be to aim for a product that is technically superior to the competition.

The strategy for Mediatrix may involve planning to spend 15% of its sales turnover on research and development.

A tactic for Mediatrix may be to set up a cross-functional new product development team.

A further level below the tactical level is operational control. In the case of Mediatrix this may involve the monitoring of feedback from the cross-functional team.

Progress check 2.2

What is strategy?

Financial strategy

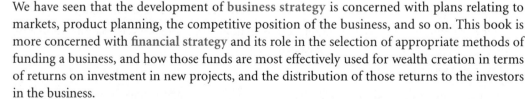

We have seen that the development of business strategy is concerned with plans relating to markets, product planning, the competitive position of the business, and so on. This book is more concerned with financial strategy and its role in the selection of appropriate methods of funding a business, and how those funds are most effectively used for wealth creation in terms of returns on investment in new projects, and the distribution of those returns to the investors in the business.

Individual shareholders and others, for example pension funds and other financial institutions, invest in companies to achieve investor, or shareholder value. Here we are talking about the popular meaning of investment – the purchase of shares in a company. **Shareholder value** (or investor value) may be reflected in the expected returns of the capital markets mirrored in the value placed on the company's securities by the markets. This may be the market value of the shares of the business, or it may be a value of the business derived by a range of other methods (which we will discuss in Chapter 16 when we look at mergers and acquisitions).

Companies invest in a range of projects with an aim of spreading risk and creating corporate value in order to try and provide value for the shareholders. Here we are talking about 'real' investments by companies in strategies and projects to provide growth and make them better businesses. The expected future returns are valued at a discount rate appropriate to the business. **Corporate value** is defined as the value today of the expected future returns from current business strategies and future investment projects, valued at an appropriate discount rate (see Chapter 4). Sometimes companies may invest in a combination of projects to spread the risk, but the result may not be a reduction in overall risk. Very often overall risk may be increased, without any corresponding increase in value and although eps (earnings per share) may be increased, shareholder value may actually be destroyed. Examples of this may be seen in conglomerates who have acquired a business in which they have no real expertise, or if too high a price has been paid for the acquisition of a company, or if the method of financing an acquisition is not cost-effective.

The BSkyB press extract below illustrates how inappropriate financial strategies resulted in the destruction of shareholder value, albeit over a fairly short period. Investors and analysts were very critical of BSkyB's capital investment policy and its dividend and share buyback strategies (see Chapter 7), the impact of which will have been reflected in the fall in its share price. Analysis of the share price over a relatively longer period may provide even more convincing support for the argument that shareholder value may be destroyed through use of an inappropriate financial strategy.

How an inappropriate financial strategy can destroy shareholder value

The Sky is not falling in – in the exclusive interview below, James Murdoch tries to persuade Guy Dennis that the 20 per cent fall in BSkyB's share price is a blip.

James Murdoch has just suffered the debut from hell. Last week the chief executive of British Sky Broadcasting unveiled annual results for the first time after taking up the post nine months ago, and set out his strategy.

The immediate result was a drop in the share price of nearly 20 per cent; more than £2bn of shareholder value was destroyed in a day. And the longer Murdoch yabbered in front of analysts and journalists, the further the shares fell – as the City worried that Sky's future profitability may not be as fabulous as it believed.

And yet when we interview James Rupert Murdoch, to use his full name, he is chipper – until we ask a question that seriously riles him. Has he seen the anonymous quote in a newspaper suggesting that his job is to get Sky's share price down so that his father, Rupert Murdoch – the media mogul whose News Corp owns 35.5 per cent of Sky and who is also Sky's chairman – can buy the company on the cheap.

'That', spits Murdoch Junior, 'is ridiculous. I'm not even going to dignify that by replying'. Through his wire-rimmed, thick-lensed glasses, he stares at the table.

When James Murdoch took the helm at Sky in November it was one of the business controversies of the year. Why, asked many

▶

shareholders, was the chairman's son getting the job? And what about the conflict of interest when the chief executive is the son of the biggest shareholder? Such questions will always dog him but, unsurprisingly, he wants to draw a line under them.

'Look, I just do my job, okay', he says in a gentle, New England cadence, reflecting his upbringing in the US. 'I get paid for one thing, and that's to build this company into the most valuable company it can be for all our shareholders, and that's really all I focus on'.

Speaking to the *Telegraph* in the only face-to-face interview he gives after the results, Murdoch, 31, accentuates the positive in the company's results. And dressed casually in a white open-necked shirt, black blazer and grey chinos, he offers a view for the first time of where the company is going and where he thinks all of us who watch television are going.

For an hour, he dances through the trends and numbers in detailed answers that manifest a palpable excitement for the game. Even so, it must have felt awful to see the share price plummet.

'We were disappointed by it', he says. 'I mean we're in the business of trying to make money for shareholders and we think we've got a good plan to deliver value to shareholders over time, and it's certainly disappointing when your shareholders lose a bunch of money'.

What must have made it all the more galling is that Sky delivered stunning profit growth. Even annual net income, the most stringent measure that looks at profits after tax and every cost in the business, rose 75 per cent to £322m.

'This business has never been in better financial shape', Murdoch says, pointedly.

The difficulty for Sky is that its share price is built not on profits today, but on the hope of even greater profits in the future, and the key to these is the growing number of people installing satellite television in their homes and what they are prepared to pay for the service. Unfortunately for Murdoch, and for Sky, this growth rate has been slowing.

Within the 21 pages of results was news that in the last quarter of the company's financial year – the three months to the end of June – the number of Sky subscribers grew by 81,000. This is 40 per cent down on the 134,000 for the same period last year, and 62 per cent down on the 214,000 for the year before that.

'I know it's been slowing for some period of time', Murdoch says. 'Its something that the business is very focused on reversing. It's not something that you reverse overnight'.

But apart from the actual decline in subscription growth, there was also a problem of investors' excessive expectations in advance of the results – as the scale of the share-price fall made clear. To put it bluntly, shouldn't the company have done more to ensure that shareholders had anticipated the lower growth rate?

'First of all, we were in a quiet period before the results, so it's not a mistake, it's that we don't disclose those numbers in advance of going out with our whole thing [the full annual results]', Murdoch says. 'The problem, I think, was there were a couple of people [analysts] who raised their estimates'.

Another contributor to the share price rout is thought to have been the unwinding of 'long' positions by hedge funds. They may have picked up stock the previous week when Goldman Sachs, the investment bank, placed 30m shares for Scottish Widows – which seems to have timed its disposal to perfection.

But declining sales growth was not the only statistic that rattled investors. Some also question the need for an increase in capital spending of £450m over the next four years, in addition to the £100m BSkyB already spends annually. At a time when investors are crying out for bigger dividends and share buybacks today, Murdoch is promising jam tomorrow. Why?

'The most important thing is building the infrastructure for a business that is going to be of a scale much higher than it is today', he says. 'It does require people, it does require more robust infrastructure'. At the moment, he says, Sky does not even own all the buildings at its West London headquarters – a legacy perhaps of its rapid growth over the last 10 years.

His main mission is to grow the number of homes with a Sky box from 7.4m to 10m, a rise of 35 per cent, by 2010. And only when you think about it in terms of growth per quarter does the magnitude of the challenge become apparent. Sky needs to add subscribers at an average rate of 104,166 a quarter – which is almost 30 per cent more than the 81,000 of new subscribers last quarter.

How is he going to do that? In the past, Murdoch says, the company emphasised its more expensive television packages, leading people to see Sky as the preserve of those with significant disposable income rather than a standard household utility.

'It's the right time to go out and knock some of those misperceptions on the head, and to start really focusing on what are, in many cases, really, emotional barriers to purchase, and we don't think they should exist', he says.

'We think our midrange packages between £13.50 and £33 [a month], including the family pack at £19.50, are mass-market propositions; we think there is room for meaningful price points below £20'.

Many potential customers, however, are moving from standard, five-channel analogue television, to digital terrestrial TV in the form of Freeview. It promises an extra 21 channels plus digital radio stations free of charge once customers have paid about £60 for a set-top box. More than 3.5m households now use Freeview – just under half the number that have Sky.

Freeview could, then, be seen as a threat, as people who want more television channels could switch to it instead of Sky. Interestingly, however, Sky is one of the partners in the consortium that promotes Freeview, along with the BBC, and Crown Castle, the transmitter company.

Murdoch insists the notion that Freeview's growth poses a threat to Sky is wrong and rests on the assumption that people make a choice between five-channel television in their homes, and multi-channel, rather than a choice between free television and pay-TV. 'We don't think it affects the long-term migration from free-to-air to pay', he says. 'We're seeing customers who bought Freeview coming to Sky'.

Murdoch also has other plans to win customers, and raise profits. These include an offer to be launched in October where customers will get a range of satellite channels free once they've bought a Sky dish. And there will be a push to raise the take-up of Sky+, the service that incorporates a digital video recorder, to 25 per cent of domestic subscribers from the current 5.3 per cent.

But it is not all about future returns. This year, shareholders are receiving a full-year dividend for the first time since 1998. And there is a plan for Sky to buy back up to 5 per cent of its shares, which requires shareholder approval later this year.

Some investors have noted that a buyback could leave his father's News Corp with an even greater percentage of the stock, unless it decides to participate and sell shares back to Sky. Is it likely to do this?

'It's not for me to say', he says. 'Seriously, it's not for me to say. I don't know'. There's not even a hint of a grin.

© *Daily Telegraph*, 8 August 2004

Another example of destruction of shareholder value was seen in the Eurotunnel project. Since the world's biggest privately funded project (at that time) began in 1987, by 2004 Eurotunnel's share price had dropped by 90% to under 20p. By 2005 it had fallen even further to around 17p but recovered a little to around 25p during 2006.

Eurotunnel incurred huge losses and debts counted in billions of £ sterling, which it could not afford to service or repay. At the outset Eurotunnel had been extremely over-optimistic in its forecasts. It actually attracted around 35% of the original prediction of 16 million passengers per year, and only around 25% of its initial forecast of an annual 7 million tonnes of freight business. The initial costs of the project were greatly exceeded, with the cost of building the tunnel at £10bn instead of an estimated £6bn. That problem was further exacerbated by their high loan interest rates in the early 1990s of between 11% and 17%, which subsequently fell to between 5% and 7%. Eurotunnel was also hit by an economic downturn, which resulted in a fall in numbers of people travelling, and increased price competition from the cross-Channel ferries, and discount airlines such as easyJet and Ryanair. Eurotunnel's fate was blamed by some on the fact that when Margaret Thatcher, and former French premier François Mitterrand, gave the final go-ahead for the tunnel in 1987, Mrs Thatcher insisted that the project should be completely privately funded, and with no subsequent government help.

In a perfectly competitive market it may be argued that the return from a portfolio, or spread, of investments exactly matches the return demanded by shareholders and other investors and so no (additional) value is created. Financial strategy is to do with decisions related to the financing of the business or individual projects, using debt or equity. The appraisal of the individual 'real' investment project opportunities available to a business, which is discussed in Chapter 4, is used to determine if they are viable and will add value to the business. Financial strategy is also to do with decisions about capital structure, and how much profit should be paid in interest or dividends and how much should be retained for investment in new projects. It is also to do with decisions about the choice of which type of loan may be most appropriate, the management of financial risk, the use of derivatives, and mergers and acquisitions.

Imagine the following hypothetical scenario:

- all information about companies and their markets is fully known by all investors
- all companies' capital is homogenous and debt is the same as equity in terms of its risk and cost
- dividends are not paid
- all investment projects have the same risk and returns
- there is no corporation tax
- companies' share prices reflect the book values of their net assets.

Clearly in the above scenario financial strategy has little significance. In such a perfectly competitive market all investors would receive the same returns and no value would be created, and investors would have no financial reason to invest in one company rather than another. It is because each of the above hypothetical situations do not apply in practice, and because companies and investors do not have access to, or do not know all relevant information, that opportunities arise which enable financial strategies to be adopted that provide value over and above market expectations.

In reality, capital is not homogeneous in terms of its characteristics, risks and returns, and different costs. In addition, different returns may exist for the same type of loan, for example, in different sectors of the same market or in alternative markets. A company has a choice as to whether or not it pays a dividend to its shareholders. The appropriate financial strategy will be one that selects the required type of capital at the lowest cost, and adopts a corresponding dividend policy that both result in an optimisation of corporate value and shareholder value.

Actual investment projects vary considerably with regard to their risks and returns. Their actual returns will also differ from their expected returns because of variations in original investment costs, the timings and values of future cash flows, and variations in the cost of capital. Financial strategy with regard to 'real' investment relates to the use of appropriate capital investment evaluation methods, use of relevant discount rates, and the assessment and management of risk that result in an optimisation of corporate value.

Corporation tax is normally payable by companies in the UK. The levels of tax incurred by a company will depend on the financial measures taken by the company to avoid and mitigate its corporation tax payable, with the aim of optimisation of corporate value.

If a company makes all the 'right' decisions, which result in the optimisation of its level of corporate value, this may not necessarily be reflected in the maximisation of shareholder wealth in terms of dividends and the market price of its shares. To achieve this a company must therefore also adopt the 'right' financial strategies relating to, for example, levels of gearing and dividend policy. It must also pursue other strategies that have an impact on the share price, which may include:

- creation of competitive advantages and barriers to market entry, through for example, effective marketing, establishment of strong brand names, and economies of scale

- employment of a strong management team with the credibility that inspires confidence among investors, City analysts, and potential investors

- development of efficient communication channels and public relations that emphasise company achievements and awareness of future plans

- actions that reduce risk to the level commensurate with returns required by the shareholders, for example insurance, and the hedging of interest rate and foreign currency exchange rate risk (see Chapter 12).

Progress check 2.3

What is meant by corporate value and how is it different from shareholder value?

Financial strategy is therefore broadly concerned with corporate value and shareholder value, and the courses of action required to achieve the specific objective of creating shareholder value above the returns expected for that specific type of company in that particular market. The use of appropriate financial strategies by a company will depend on its stage of development and also the behaviour of the financial markets in which it operates. Companies may benefit from the adoption of financial strategies that exploit imperfections and inefficiencies in the markets relating to each of the factors we have discussed, which we will explore in more detail throughout this book. The following section looks broadly at what is meant by market efficiency and inefficiency with regard to the capital or financial markets.

Efficient market hypothesis

The efficient market hypothesis states that the stock market responds immediately to all available information. An individual investor cannot therefore, in the long run, expect greater than average returns from a diversified portfolio of shares. Efficient market hypothesis research evidence suggests that accounting tricks and manipulations employed by companies do not increase company value, because the market is able to see through them. However, we may question whether in practice any market can respond immediately to all available information. As we have seen over the past few years, many creative techniques have been used to disguise presumably widely understood accounting transactions, for example WorldCom and Enron (see Chapter 1).

There are three types of market efficiency:

- pricing efficiency, which refers to the notion or understanding that prices rapidly reflect all available information in an unbiased way

- operational efficiency, which refers to the level of costs of carrying out transactions in capital markets in the most cost-effective way

- allocational efficiency, which refers to the extent to which capital is allocated to the most profitable enterprise, and should be a product of pricing efficiency.

There are three forms of market efficiency, which are subsets of pricing efficiency:

- weak form efficiency, which is seen in a market in which security prices instantaneously reflect all information on past price and volume changes in the market

- semi-strong form efficiency, which is seen in a market in which security prices reflect all publicly available information

- strong form efficiency, which is seen in a market in which security prices reflect instantaneously all information available to investors, whether publicly available or not.

In terms of financial markets the term efficiency generally refers to pricing efficiency. In the financial markets, like other markets in general, the price of a financial asset or a currency will be an equilibrium price between rational, well-informed, profit-seeking buyers and sellers. All information available in the public domain will be discounted into the price of a financial asset or currency.

A perfect market has the following characteristics:

- information is freely available to everyone in the market

- there is a large number of buyers and sellers who may freely enter and leave the market

- there is no taxation

- there are no transaction costs

- there is perfect competition and no single buyer or seller dominates the market

- everyone in the market will be aware of any creative accounting and window dressing of the financial information contained in companies' reports and accounts

- financial assets are infinitely divisible

- bankruptcies may occur but are without any cost.

Perfect markets imply efficient markets. However, efficient markets are not required to be perfect markets. Market efficiency promotes:

- investor trust in the market and thus encourages capital investment

- allocational efficiency,

and improves market information and therefore the choice of investments.

Substantial research has been carried out with regard to each form of efficiency to test how efficient security markets, equity markets, and currency markets really are, for example:

- weak form efficiency – Beechley M, Gruen D, Vickery J (2000) 'The efficient market hypothesis: a survey' *Research Paper Reserve Bank of Australia*; Fama EF (1965) 'The behaviour of stock market prices' *Journal of Business*, January, 34–106; Roberts HV (1959) 'Stock market patterns and financial analysis: methodological suggestions' *Journal of Finance*, March, 1–10

- semi-strong form efficiency – Ball R, Brown P (1968) 'An empirical evaluation of accounting income numbers' *Journal of Accounting Research*, Autumn, 159–178; Fama EF, Fisher L, Jensen MC, Roll R (1969) 'The adjustment of stock prices to new information' *International Economic Review*, 10(1) February, 1–21

- strong form efficiency – Jensen MC (1968) 'The performance of mutual funds in the period 1945–1964' *Journal of Finance*, May, 389–416.

In general, these tests are categorised as:

- weak form efficiency tests
- semi-strong form efficiency tests
- strong form efficiency tests,

and they have sought to evaluate the relative efficiency of such markets.

Weak form efficiency tests have sought to test the theory that prices follow patterns that can be used to predict future prices. This means that all prices fully reflect information contained in past price movements. Such studies have found no discernible pattern that can be used to predict future prices, but have indicated that prices follow a random walk, which means that:

- prices have no memory
- yesterday's prices cannot predict tomorrow's prices

and therefore

- only new information causes price changes.

The random walk theory suggests that share price movements are independent of each other and that today's share price cannot be used to predict tomorrow's share price. Therefore, the movement of a share price follows no predictable pattern, but moves in a random fashion with no discernible trend. This notion of random variability in the pricing of shares originates from the work of Kendall, M (1953, 'The analysis of economic time-series prices' *Journal of the Royal Statistical Society*, 96, 11–25) in which he examined security and commodity price movements over a period of time. He was looking for regular price cycles, but was unable to identify any. Essentially, Kendall's theory states that the random walk occurs because, at any point in time, a share price will reflect all information available about the share and the company, and will only change as new information becomes available. However, because the next piece of information to arrive will be independent of the last piece of information to arrive, share prices react and move in an unpredictable fashion.

Semi-strong form efficiency tests have sought to test the theory that security prices fully reflect all information in the public domain. This means that all prices fully reflect all relevant publicly available information. These studies have also not produced any conclusive evidence that exceptional returns can be earned from information widely available in the public domain.

Strong form efficiency tests have sought to test the theory that security prices reflect all information, including insider information. This means that all prices fully reflect all relevant information including information that is privately held. Such studies have shown that insiders can make exceptional returns over and above those available from information in the public domain, usually only for a short period.

The implications of the efficiency tests described above may be summarised by saying that in efficient markets there is no bargain today, there is no memory of yesterday, and there is no knowledge of tomorrow. From this it may be concluded that markets generally follow a weak form efficiency, which means that pricing is generally regarded as inefficient.

Progress check 2.4

What is the efficient market hypothesis?

Worked Example 2.3 illustrates the efficient market hypothesis and how information may impact on a company's share price.

Worked Example 2.3

Predator plc has issued share capital of 24,000,000 shares, and Target plc has issued share capital of 8,000,000 shares. The following details relate to the time period days 1 to 10.

Day 1   The market value per share is Target plc £4 and Predator plc £6.

Day 3   The directors of Predator plc decide at a private and confidential meeting to make a cash bid for Target plc at a price of £6 per share with settlement on day 16. The takeover will result in large operating savings with a present value of £21m.

Day 7   Predator plc publicly announces an unconditional offer to purchase all the shares in Target plc at a price of £6 per share. Details of the large operating savings are not announced and are not public knowledge.

Day 10   Predator plc makes a public announcement of the operating savings which will be realised from the takeover, and the share price increases to £6.21.

We will assume semi-strong efficiency of the market, and consider the values of Predator plc and Target plc on days 1, 3, 7, and 10.

Days 1 and 3
Market value of Predator £24m × £6 = £144m
Market value of Target 8m × £4 = £32m

Day 7
Cost to Predator of offer for Target = [(8m × £6) – (8m × £4)] = £16m
Market value of Predator = 24m × £6 = £144m less £16m price offered for Target = £128m
Share price of Predator = £128m/24m = £5.33 per share

Day 10
Market value of Predator = 24m × £6.21 = £149m
If the market has the semi-strong form of efficiency then in theory the prices on day 1, 3, 7, and 10 should be as follows:

	Target £	Predator £
Days 1 and 3	4.00	6.00
Day 7	6.00	5.33
Day 10	6.00	6.21

The decision made on day 3 will have no impact on the share prices of Predator or Target, unless there has been a leak of information.

On day 7, following the announcement of the cash offer by Predator plc of £6 per share for Target plc the market price of Target's shares should increase from £4 to the bid price of £6. The value of Predator is likely to be reduced from £144m to £128m (£144m – £16m) or £5.33 per share. The share price was likely to fall because there did not appear to be any benefits from the acquisition.

On day 10, following the announcement of the benefit of operating savings with a present value of £21m (three days after the initial offer announcement), the share price of Predator plc increases to £6.21 per share and therefore its market value increases to £149m (24m × £6.21).

In reality, the share prices may not react in this way because there are many other factors that impact on share price movements.

Worked Example 2.4

A colleague of yours has recently attended a series of finance seminars run by a local university. During one of the seminars your colleague recollects the speaker suggesting that 'an efficient market is good for all profit-orientated organisations', and has asked you to explain why that is the case.

There are a number of points that could be considered, the main points being that an efficient market:

- promotes investor confidence
- reduces risk and uncertainty
- increases degrees of predictability
- reduces market costs
- reduces the need for excessive regulation
- reduces need for proactive monitoring
- reduces costs of regulation.

In the financial markets the complicating role of governments and their central banks to influence the market operations of other institutional organisations and international companies as they constantly battle for the right to maximise potential financial reward is of major importance. While imperfections may exist within the market, such imperfections may not necessarily exist due to problems in the supply and demand of information. They may be the direct consequence of political protectionism rather than a product of the economic supply and demand.

The concept of the efficient market is the basis of many of the ideas of traditional corporate financial theory and its implications are, for example:

- that the market will have already discounted any manipulation of accounting information in share prices
- it is not possible to obtain any information that will result in better than average returns
- share prices reflect only investors' required returns for perceived levels of risk
- shares are never under-priced
- that it is not possible to achieve better than average stock market returns.

Although the UK stock market and other capital markets apparently respond relatively efficiently to new information as soon as it becomes available, the assumptions of efficient markets may be open to debate. The efficient market hypothesis is a theoretical, analytical framework. In a perfectly efficient market investors would receive their required returns dependent on the level of risk they are prepared to take, and no shareholder value would be created. In the real world markets are not perfectly efficient. Shareholder value may be created by companies using appropriate financial strategies to exploit the different perceptions of the market, which are called market imperfections. These imperfections include, for example, the information asymmetry that exists with regard to each of the stakeholders in companies. For example, managers, directors, lenders, and shareholders each have different levels and aspects of information about companies and their assets. There may also be significant periods of time between when important information is revealed or acquired by each of the different stakeholders.

Shareholder value

Value is a function of the relationship between perceived risk and the return required by shareholders and other key stakeholders. The higher the risk that is associated with a particular security, the higher is the required rate of return (see Fig. 2.4). For the borrower, short-term debt (such as an overdraft) is riskier than long-term debt. There are a number of reasons for this:

- an overdraft is repayable on demand
- a short-term debt or overdraft may not be renewed, or if it is re-negotiated then the terms may be less favourable
- interest rates are more volatile in the short term, particularly for overdrafts which have variable interest rates.

The difference between the interest rate paid on Government securities, which is effectively risk-free, and the interest rate that a company pays on loans is called the risk premium. Shareholders' equity is even riskier than shorter-term corporate debt (for example, a loan made to a company). Therefore, the earnings of the company need to be at a level such that the shareholders get a return in line with their level of risk. This should be the return on Government securities plus a risk premium, which is even higher than the risk premium payable on the corporate debt.

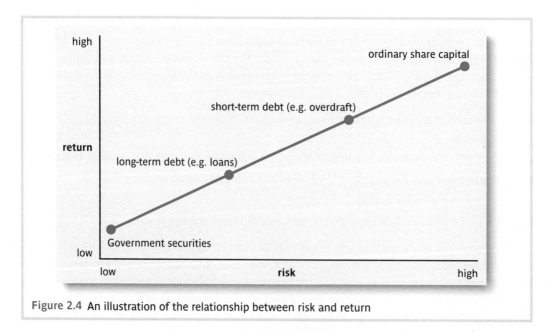

Figure 2.4 An illustration of the relationship between risk and return

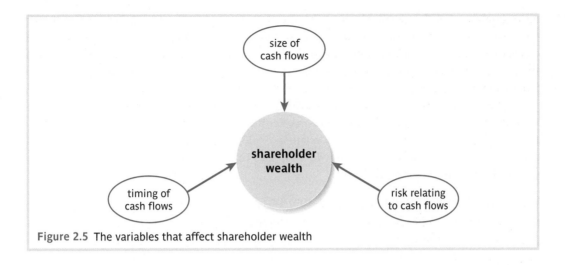

Figure 2.5 The variables that affect shareholder wealth

An increase in shareholders' wealth is derived from cash received by shareholders through dividends and capital gains from the increased market price of shares held. There are three variables that directly affect shareholders' wealth (see Fig. 2.5):

- the size of the company's cash flows – cash flows are considered rather than profit, which is subjective and involves problems in its measurement
- the time value of cash flows – £100 cash received today is generally worth more than £100 cash received in one year's time
- the risk associated with cash flows – risk impacts on the rate of return earned on the investment in the business, and therefore the cost of capital that affects today's value of cash received in the future.

Providing value means being better than the market, by providing better than expectation. This can be compared to a perfect market, in which all investors would in theory receive their risk-adjusted required rates of return. A perfect market rarely exists because:

- information and knowledge may not always be freely and equally shared by all the players in the market
- entry and exit into and out of markets is generally not without cost
- all players may not act rationally, and they may have different expectations
- markets are usually dominated by a small number of players because of their buying power, possession of scarce resources, unique knowledge, technologies, or skills
- taxes and costs of transacting act as barriers to selling and buying.

Many financial theorists currently believe that the use of financial strategies and techniques by companies does not create and increase value, on the basis that today's financial markets are efficient and can easily and quickly identify and allow for the above factors. In theory this may be the case, but in practice financial managers actually do employ financial strategies that result in providing value over and above market expectation.

It is argued by some that markets are efficient but more volatile due to technological advances. It is true that markets are perhaps becoming more efficient as information becomes more freely and widely available, and the speed and cost of transactions are reduced (for example, through the use of electronic transactions and the Internet). However, the future cannot be forecast with certainty and so the market value of a business may rarely reflect the present value of its expected future cash flows. Also, investors' returns are related to the perceived risks of their investments, but this relationship may not be the same for all investors.

It may therefore be argued that markets are still not totally efficient. Therefore, shareholder value may be increased by exploitation of market imperfections, even though such imperfections may only be temporary. This may relate to exploitation of business competitive advantages, and the use of appropriate financial strategies that result in an increase in shareholder wealth. This includes, for example:

- cost reduction and profit improvement measures
- an optimal mix of products, services, and businesses
- investment in only those projects that provide increased cash flows in real terms
- minimisation of the company's after-tax cost of capital
- establishment of an optimal financial structure for the business
- appropriate use of debt financing
- the use of appropriate financial instruments, including derivatives
- appropriate dividend policy.

Progress check 2.5

Describe the variables that directly affect maximisation of shareholder wealth.

Shareholder value may be measured using two approaches, either book value (using accounting-based measures) or market value (using measures based on share price), and include the following performance indicators:

 ■ **residual income (RI)**
 ■ **shareholder value added (SVA)**
 ■ **economic value added (EVA™)**
■ shareholder return

which are considered in the four sections that follow.

Residual income (RI)

Residual income (RI) may be calculated by deducting a notional interest charge for capital invested from profit before tax, and is therefore a measure of performance and an absolute measure of value added.

If profit after tax = PAT
Capital invested = I
Interest on capital invested = i

$$RI = PAT - (i \times I)$$

Worked Example 2.5

Let's consider two divisions within a company that have an opportunity to invest in projects that both have an initial cost of £10m. The notional cost of capital for the company is 15% per annum. The expected operating profits from each investment are shown below:

	Company A	Company B
Expected profit before tax	£2.0m	£1.3m
Cost of capital charge (15%)	£1.5m	£1.5m
Residual income (loss)	+£0.5m	−£0.2m

Shareholder value added (SVA)

Alfred Rappaport (Rappaport A (1998) London: free Press *Creating Shareholder Value*) considered that there were seven drivers of shareholder value. The first five drivers:

- sales growth
- operating profit margin
- the cash tax rate
- incremental capital expenditure investment
- investment in working capital

are used to determine forecast 'free cash flows' relating to the sixth driver

- a time period of competitive advantage, the planning horizon

and using the seventh driver

- the cost of capital

to discount the cash flows to present day values to provide an enterprise value (SVA).

   Shareholder value added is best illustrated in an example. Worked Example 2.6 shows how SVA may be calculated in practice.

Worked Example 2.6

Flag plc is a UK company whose shareholders require an annual return of 8%. The calculation of Flag plc's free cash flow for the current year highlights Rappaport's first five drivers of shareholder value:

		£m
sales growth	Turnover	5.0
	Operating costs	(3.0)
operating profit margin	Operating profit	2.0
cash tax rate	Tax	(0.5)
	Profit after tax	1.5
	Depreciation	0.4
		1.9
capital investment	Capital expenditure	(0.6)
investment in working capital	Additional working capital	(0.3)
	Free cash flow	1.0

▶

▶ In addition, Flag plc has estimated its free cash flow for the next five years as: £1.5m, £1.8m, £2.2m, £2.4m, and £2.8m. Flag plc's planning horizon is six years and its estimated net asset value at the end of the planning horizon is £2.9m.

The value in perpetuity of the estimated net assets at the end of year 6 is:

$$£2.9m/8\% = £36.25m$$

We can use the 'in perpetuity' value of Flag plc's net assets plus the free cash flows for years 1 to 6 to calculate the company's shareholder value added (SVA).

Year	Free cash flow £m	Discount factor at 8%	Present value £m
1	1.0	0.93	0.93
2	1.5	0.86	1.29
3	1.8	0.79	1.42
4	2.2	0.74	1.63
5	2.4	0.68	1.63
6	2.8	0.63	1.76
6	36.25	0.63	22.84
		SVA	31.50

The enterprise value of Flag plc, its shareholder value added (SVA) is therefore £31.5m.

Economic value added (EVA™)

A variation on RI is economic value added (EVA™), which aims to provide a measure that is highly correlated with shareholder wealth as well as divisional performance. EVA is calculated by deducting a financial charge from profit after tax for the use of the company's net assets. The net assets number reported in the accounts is usually adjusted (in a variety of different ways) to reflect as realistic a valuation as possible of the company's net assets. The basis for the financial charge is usually the weighted average cost of the capital used by the company (see Chapter 6).

If profit after tax = PAT
Weighted average cost of capital = WACC
Net assets = adjusted book value of net capital = NA

$$EVA = PAT - (WACC \times NA)$$

Shareholder return

Residual income and EVA are both measures of the surplus of profit after allowing in some way for a cost of capital. However, they are really more measures of performance than measures of value, but they can show value created in a single period. SVA is a measure that relates to the life of a business or a project, but cannot be used to consider value added during a single period. These are all essentially 'internal' measures made by a company.

Total shareholder return (TSR) is a measure of how value is created for shareholders, and it is a measure that can be made external to the business. The total returns received by a share-holder in a period include the increase in their share price plus the dividends they have received. However, as a measure of value it also has disadvantages. Although there may be a correlation between dividends and how well the company is performing, the share price may be depressed because of, for example, rumours that the CEO may be resigning, even though the company may actually be performing very well. Equally, a company's share price may be artificially high because of, for example, possible takeover interest, or the patenting of a new 'miracle' drug, even though the company may actually be performing poorly.

If the share price at the beginning of the year = S1
Share price at the end of the year = S2
Dividends paid during the year = v

$$TSR = S2 - S1 + v$$

Progress check 2.6

In what ways may shareholder value be measured?

Strategic financial decisions

We have looked at a few measures of shareholder value. RI, SVA, and EVA are measures that are based on factors 'within' the business, such as sales, profit, capital employed, and the cost of capital. Shareholder return is a measure that is based on factors 'external' to the business: the dividend payouts and gains from share price increases. It has many shortcomings as a measure, primarily because to a large extent it is outside the control of the company. A company's share price may rise or fall for reasons completely unrelated to its economic performance, being more closely related to market expectations. Despite its shortcomings, shareholder return is perhaps the most useful measure of shareholder value because dividends and gains from increases in share price are what shareholders actually receive, and which they may monitor on a continuous basis. Let's look at the underlying decisions that a company, or rather its directors, are required to make to achieve value.

A business uses its assets, through 'real' investment, to generate profits. Profits may be used for dividends paid to shareholders. Or, profits may be retained to finance future growth, which is an alternative to increasing debt or equity. The profit available for dividends is dependent on how much is left after interest has been deducted from pre-tax profit. Actual dividends are then an appropriation of post-tax profit. A company's level of interest payments is dependent on the level of its debt. High debt means paying high levels of interest, and so less profit is available for dividends and for further investment.

The decisions relating to the types and levels of investment, levels of debt, levels of retained earnings, and levels of dividends are all concerned with financial strategy. The directors of a company, therefore, broadly have four key decisions to make concerning financial strategy, which are all very closely linked:

- how large should the company's asset base be? – the capital budgeting or investment decisions relating to the level of 'real' investment to be made by the business
- what proportions of the company's financing should be debt or equity? – its capital structure, or gearing; if a company has a target ratio of debt to equity, then in theory an increase in its equity means that it can take on more debt
- should the company issue new equity or new debt? – for expansion of the company's funding
- how much profit should be paid out in dividends, and how much retained? – dividend policy.

Progress check 2.7

Outline the strategic financial decisions faced by companies.

In Part II of this book we will look at a number of ways in which the use of appropriate financial strategies at the relevant stages in the development of a business may be used to derive shareholder value.

The agency problem

We have talked about shareholder wealth maximisation as the primary objective of a business. But can we assume that the managers and directors of the business are making decisions and taking actions that are consistent with the objective of maximising shareholder wealth? Certainly managers and directors should make decisions consistent with the objective of shareholder wealth maximisation, because that is what they are appointed to do by the shareholders. In practice, this may not actually happen, because their goals may be different and they may be seeking to enhance their status, secure their positions, or maximise their own wealth rather than that of the shareholders.

The **agency problem** occurs when directors and managers are not acting in the best interests of shareholders. Directors and managers of a company run the business day to day and have access to internal management accounting information and financial reports, but shareholders only see the external annual and six-monthly reports. Annual and interim reporting may also, of course, be subject to manipulation by management.

The agency problem of directors not acting in the best interests of shareholders may be seen in, for example:

- a high retention of profits and cash by directors to provide a cushion for easier day-to-day management of operations, rather than for investment in new projects

- an unwillingness by directors to invest in risky projects in line with shareholders' required returns, because of fear of failure and possibly losing their jobs, particularly if they are close to retirement age and wish to protect their pension benefits

- receipt of high salaries, benefits, and perks by directors and chief executives, regardless of how well, or not, the business has performed

- participation by directors and managers in profit or eps-related bonus and incentive schemes, which encourage short-term profit maximisation rather than creation of shareholder value.

Why should the agency problem exist? Well, it is management who are in the position, and who have the opportunity, to pursue the maximisation of their own wealth without detection by the owners of the business. Additionally, both financial analysts and managers and directors of companies have an obsession with eps as a measure of financial performance. This is despite the fact that profit is a totally subjective measure and that it is future cash flows and not short-term profit from which the real value of a business is determined.

A growth in eps does not necessarily translate into a sustained increase in shareholder value. Conglomerates may have acquired businesses to effectively 'buy' additional eps by increasing earnings without having to make corresponding increases in share capital. An example of this is the performance of Tomkins plc during the 1990s, when it was still a conglomerate. The company had grown enormously through acquisitions and Tomkins plc's eps increased consistently each year from around 12 pence in 1991 to around 28 pence in 2000, an average increase of 9.8% per annum. However, its share price averaged around £2.50 during the same period, although it briefly reached a high of £3.75 in early 1998, and then gradually fell again to around £1.50 by the beginning of 2000.

The agency problem manifests itself through a conflict of interest. There may be different views about risks and returns, for example. The shareholders may be interested in the long term, whereas the rewards paid to managers, for example, may be based on short-term performance. To address the agency problem between agents and principals – managers and shareholders – a number of initiatives may be implemented to encourage the achievement of goal congruence:

- audit of results
- reporting of manager performance
- work shadowing of managers and directors
- the use of external analysts.

Progress check 2.8

What are the conflicts that may arise between the managers and the shareholders of a business?

In addition to the agency problem relating to the directors and shareholders of a company, there may be a conflict between debt holders and shareholders, who may exploit their relationship with debt holders. The agency problem here is that shareholders may prefer the use of debt for investments by the company in new high-risk projects. Shareholders then subsequently benefit from the rewards gained from the success of such investments, but it is the debt holders who bear the risk. Debt holders may protect their interests by having security over specific assets or the assets in general of the company. They may also include restrictive covenants in their loan agreements with the company, for example with regard to decision-making, and levels of gearing.

There has been an increasing influence of institutional investors in the UK, which to some degree has helped in dealing with the agency problem. Institutional shareholders like banks, pension funds, and fund management companies have been getting tougher with companies who do not comply with the appropriate standards of behaviour, and in particular with the appropriate **corporate governance** requirements (see Chapter 3).

In the mid-1990s one of the UK's largest life assurers, Standard Life, provided an example of financial institutions' 'get tough' policy on lax corporate governance. Standard Life expressed its concern about protecting its customers by focusing on directors' contracts and their remuneration, and the importance of non-executive directors. Standard Life also registered their opposition to shareholder returns (dividends plus share price increases) as a measure of management performance because they said that they had little to do with management success.

Corporate governance has become a hot topic throughout the 1990s to date, because of the increasing numbers of corporate financial scandals that have been revealed through the media:

- 1990 Polly Peck
- 1991 Robert Maxwell companies
- 1991 BCCI
- 1995 Barings Bank (Nick Leeson)
- 2001 Enron
- 2001 Marconi
- 2002 WorldCom
- 2004 Parmalat.

Corporate governance is concerned with the relationship between company management, its directors, and its owners, the shareholders. It is the structure and the mechanisms by which the owners of the business 'govern' the management or the directors of the business. Its importance has been highlighted as a result of the increasing concern about the conduct of companies, following the spate of financial scandals, but also by concerns about senior executive remuneration. Such conduct has promoted a new area of study concerned with the psychology of financial decision-making and understanding the rationality or otherwise, of economic agents such as managers and directors of companies, shareholders, and providers of loan finance. This area of research is commonly referred to as behavioural finance.

Behavioural finance suggests that:

- unpredicted share price movements
- inexplicably high dividend yields
- low ratios of companies' book values compared with their market capitalisation
- poor price performance of shares which have 'high expectation'

can and often does result from the irrational behaviour of economic agents, and is essentially psychologically based. There is a growing number of behavioural finance-related models that offer plausible explanations for market inefficiencies and share price volatility (see, for example, the *Journal of Behavioural Finance* at www.psychologyandmarkets.org). However, it is a discipline that has yet to achieve acceptance within mainstream financial management.

In the UK in 1991, a committee was set up by the Financial Reporting Council (FRC), the London Stock Exchange, and the accounting profession, which was chaired by Sir Adrian Cadbury. The aim of the committee was to address the concerns about company conduct and to make recommendations on best practice. The framework for establishing good corporate governance and accountability set up by the Cadbury Committee was formulated as the Committee's Code of Best Practice, published in December 1992. This provided a benchmark against which to assess compliance. The Cadbury Code was updated in 1998 by the Hampel Committee, in order to include their own Committee's work, and the Greenbury Committee report on directors' remuneration (published July 1995). In September 1999 the Turnbull Committee report on *Internal Control: Guidance for Directors on the Combined Code of Practice* was published by the ICAEW.

In May 2000 the original Cadbury Code and subsequent reports were all consolidated by the Committee on Corporate Governance and published in the Combined Code of Practice, which was updated in 2003. We will look at corporate governance in more detail in Chapter 3.

Worked Example 2.7

The directors of a company are discussing which strategies they may adopt to try and minimise the impact of agency-related problems.

Their discussion may include the following:

The agency problem emerges when managers make decisions that are inconsistent with the objective of shareholder wealth maximisation. There are a number of alternative approaches a company can adopt to minimise the possible impact of such a problem, and whilst these would differ from company to company, in general such approaches would range between:

■ the encouragement of goal congruence between shareholders and managers through the monitoring of managerial behaviour and the assessment of management decision outcomes

and

■ the enforcement of goal congruence between shareholders and managers through the incorporation of formalised obligations and conditions of employment into management contracts.

Any such approach would invariably be associated with some form of remuneration package to include an incentive scheme to reward managers, such as performance related pay, or executive share options.

Progress check 2.9

Outline how the agency problem may occur between the shareholders, directors, and lenders of a business.

We have seen that agency problems may exist not only between directors and shareholders but also between any of the stakeholders of the business: its employees; managers; shareholders; lenders; suppliers; customers. However, it is the agency problems arising between directors and shareholders with which we are primarily concerned in the current chapter, and in the next section we will look at how incentive schemes may be used to try and address such problems.

Incentive schemes

A big part of the corporate governance framework is concerned with directors' remuneration. Many different types of pay schemes have been developed to try and overcome the managers and shareholders agency problem. For example, performance related pay schemes may use performance measures like profit, and return on capital employed (ROCE) to compare against pre-agreed targets for the calculation of additional remuneration. As we have already seen, there are problems with these measures relating to their accuracy and the fact that they are open to manipulation. Perhaps even more importantly, these measures are not necessarily indicators of shareholder wealth.

Executive share option schemes have become increasingly popular because of the problems associated with performance related pay schemes. Managers become potential shareholders and so they should have the same aims. Therefore the achievement of goal congruence is seen as a big benefit of such schemes. There are many examples of company directors participating in some extremely lucrative share option schemes. For example, in 1985 the co-founder of Apple Computers, Steve Jobs, was forced to resign when company performance took a downturn. He left owning 7m Apple shares worth US$120m and went on to form Pixar, which went public in 1995, and in which his 80% stake was worth US$1.1bn. In 1997 Apple rehired Jobs as CEO and in 2000 the board of directors of Apple granted Jobs share options worth US$200m (plus US$90m for the purchase and maintenance of a Gulfstream V jet). In May 2006 Disney paid US$8.06bn for Pixar, which resulted in Steve Jobs becoming the Disney Corporation's largest shareholder.

However, executive share option schemes do have disadvantages. There are many external impacts on share price, which are outside the influence or the control of managers. Therefore, there is not a completely direct link between managers' performance and their rewards. There may be disagreement and discontent arising out of the decision as to which managers are chosen to participate in executive share option schemes. This may therefore be de-motivational and have a negative impact on the achievement of goal congruence.

Regardless of the disadvantages, executive share option schemes (rather like the company car used to be) are regarded as a 'must have' benefit. But are they a 'one-sided bet' for the managers? If the shares go down in price then the managers receive no penalty. However, share options do tend to be longer term and so there may be no reward if the managers leave the company.

There has also been an increase in the popularity of eps growth-based management incentives. Here, there are still potential problems concerned with accuracy and manipulation of the numbers, and as we saw in the Tomkins example an increase in eps does not necessarily result in an increase in shareholder value.

Progress check 2.10

How may directors' bonus incentive schemes be used to deal with the agency problem?

Summary of key points

- A company's strategic management process begins by defining its mission, its underlying belief, and continues with the establishment of corporate objectives, corporate appraisal analyses, and then development of its strategies and plans.
- The maximisation of shareholder wealth is the primary financial objective of companies.
- There may be a number of secondary or surrogate objectives of a company, for example profit maximisation, sales maximisation, and survival.
- It is important that companies adopt appropriate financial strategies in pursuit of the objective of maximisation of shareholder wealth.
- The efficient market hypothesis is an important corporate finance theory, but in practice capital markets are generally regarded as inefficient.
- Shareholder wealth is derived from dividends and capital gains from the increase in share price.

- The key strategic financial decisions faced by companies are concerned with levels of 'real' investment and gearing, and dividend policy.
- Agency theory considers why the goals and aims of the various stakeholders of a company are not always aligned, particularly with regard to a company's managers and its shareholders.
- Incentive schemes may be used by companies to overcome the agency problem with regard to their directors and shareholders.

🔑 Glossary of key terms

agency problem Agency theory is a hypothesis that attempts to explain elements of organisational behaviour through an understanding of the relationships between principals (such as shareholders) and agents (such as company managers). The agency problem manifests itself in a conflict that may exist between the actions undertaken by agents in furtherance of their own self-interest, and those required to promote the interests of the principals. Within the hierarchy of companies, the same lack of goal congruence may occur when divisional managers promote their own self-interest over those of other divisions and of the company generally.

behavioural finance An area of study concerned with the psychology of financial decision-making and understanding the rationality or otherwise, of economic agents such as managers and directors of companies, shareholders, and providers of loan finance.

business strategy Strategy is the 'what' we want the organisation to be, what we want to do, and where we want the organisation to go, rather than the 'how' to achieve those things. Business strategy is concerned with these 'whats' in terms of plans relating to markets, product planning, the competitive position of the business.

Cadbury Committee Report of the Cadbury Committee (December 1992) on the Financial Aspects of Corporate Governance, set up to consider issues in relation to financial reporting and accountability, and to make recommendations on good practice, relating to:

- responsibilities of executive and non-executive directors
- establishment of company audit committees
- responsibility of auditors
- links between shareholders, directors, and auditors
- any other relevant matters.

The report established a Code of Best Practice, now succeeded by the Combined Code of Practice.

Combined Code of Practice The successor to the Cadbury Code, established by the Hampel Committee. The code consists of a set of principles of corporate governance and detailed code provisions embracing the work of the Cadbury, Greenbury, and Hampel Committees. Section 1 of the code contains the principles and provisions applicable to UK

▶

▶ listed companies, while section 2 contains the principles and provisions applicable to institutional shareholders in their relationships with companies.

corporate governance The system by which companies are directed and controlled. Boards of directors are responsible for the governance of their companies. The shareholders' role in governance is to appoint the directors and the auditors and to satisfy themselves that an appropriate governance structure is in place.

corporate value The present value of the returns expected from the range of 'real' investments made and business strategies pursued by a company.

economic value added (EVA™) Profit after tax adjusted for distortions in operating performance (such as goodwill, extraordinary losses, and operating leases) less a charge for the amount of capital employed to create that profit (calculated from the adjusted book value of net assets multiplied by the company's weighted average cost of capital).

efficient market hypothesis A hypothesis that the stock market responds immediately to all available information, with the effect that an individual investor cannot, in the long run, expect to obtain greater than average returns from a diversified portfolio of shares. There are three forms:

- weak form, which is a market in which security prices instantaneously reflect all information on past price and volume changes in the market

- semi-strong form, which is a market in which security prices reflect all publicly available information

- strong form, which is a market in which security prices reflect instantaneously all information available to investors, whether publicly available or not.

environmental analysis A part of corporate appraisal, which includes a review of the business in terms of its external factors.

financial strategy Financial strategy is concerned with investor value, and the courses of action required to achieve the specific objective of creating shareholder value above the returns expected for the specific type of investment and market. Financial strategy is to do with decisions related to the financing of the business, investments in individual projects, the use of debt or equity, and decisions about how much profit should be paid in dividends and how much should be retained for investment in new projects.

Hampel Committee The 1998 report of the Hampel Committee on Corporate Governance was set up to conduct a review of the Cadbury Code and its implications, and considered:

- a review of the role of directors

- matters arising from the Greenbury Study Group on directors' remuneration

- the role of shareholders and auditors

- other relevant matters.

The Hampel Committee was responsible for publication of the corporate governance Combined Code of Practice.

mission A summary of goals and policies, which does not have to be in writing, but is generally a sense of purpose or underlying belief of the organisation.

objectives Objectives are the visionary statements set out by the company before it starts its detailed planning, its primary financial objective being the maximisation of shareholder wealth.

residual income (RI) Profit before tax less an imputed interest charge for invested capital, which may be used to assess the performance of a division or a branch of a business.

resources analysis A part of corporate appraisal, which includes a review of the business in terms of its internal factors.

shareholder value (or investor value) The required returns from a company expected by the market, reflected in the value of its securities.

shareholder value added (SVA) A measure of shareholder value derived from cash forecasts over the specific time period of a company's competitive advantage using its sales growth, operating profit, tax rate, and investments in capital expenditure and working capital, discounted to present day values using the company's cost of capital.

strategic choice Strategic choice uses the information provided from the corporate appraisal (resources analysis and environmental analysis) to evaluate the suitability, feasibility, and acceptability of the development of alternative strategies through screening options, financial analysis, risk analysis, and strategic method, which deals with the ways in which a company may develop and grow.

strategic management The strategic management process, which includes strategic planning, is involved with making decisions on the objectives of the organisation, changes in these objectives, the resources used to attain these objectives, the policies that are to govern the acquisition, and the use and disposition of resources.

surrogate objectives The primary objective of a company is the maximisation of shareholder wealth but there are many other objectives in support of, but considered secondary to, the main objective that are described as substitute or surrogate objectives. These may include profit maximisation, share price maximisation, market share maximisation, earnings per share growth, sales maximisation, survival, dividend growth, social responsibility, non-financial objectives (like customer satisfaction and delivery reliability).

❓ Questions

Q2.1 Outline the primary objective of a company, the maximisation of shareholder wealth, and how it may be achieved.

Q2.2 What are some of the surrogate objectives that a business may have and what is their relevance?

Q2.3 Outline the efficient market hypothesis with regard to corporate financial theory.

Q2.4 Explain the ways in which shareholder value may be measured.

Q2.5 What is financial strategy, and how does it differ from business strategy?

Q2.6 In what ways may strategic financial decisions impact on shareholder value?

Q2.7 Outline the agency problem and the ways in which it may manifest itself.

Q2.8 How may incentive schemes help deal with the agency problem?

 Discussion points

D2.1 The CEO of a diversified multinational company said: 'So long as I continue to report an increase in eps for the business each year then I am doing my job and the shareholders should be pleased.' Discuss.

D2.2 Can the goal of maximisation of the value of the company conflict with other goals, such as avoiding unethical or illegal behaviour? Do the goals of, for example, customer and employee safety, the environment, and the general good of society fit within this framework, or are they essentially ignored?

D2.3 Company ownership varies around the world. Historically, individuals have owned the majority of shares in public companies in the United States. In Germany and Japan, however, banks, other large financial institutions, and other companies own most of the shares in public companies. Discuss whether agency problems are likely to be more or less severe in Germany and Japan than in the United States and why.

D2.4 In recent years, large financial institutions such as mutual funds and pension funds have increasingly become the owners of shares in the United States, and these institutions are becoming more active in corporate affairs. Discuss what the implications of this trend may be with regard to agency problems.

D2.5 Discuss the increasing popularity of share option schemes as an important element of executive remuneration.

D2.6 Why do you think there may have been such a proliferation of financial scandals in the USA, UK, and Europe during the 1990s and early 2000s?

Exercises

Solutions are provided in Appendix 2 to all exercise numbers highlighted in colour.

Level I

E2.1 *Time allowed – 15 minutes*

Identify the components of shareholder wealth and explain how the strategic financial decisions made by a company impact on each of them.

E2.2 *Time allowed – 15 minutes*

Explain what is meant by shareholder value and consider the value-creating alternatives. Outline three ways of measuring shareholder value.

E2.3 *Time allowed – 30 minutes*

Explain how alternative methods may be used to measure shareholder value and give your view as to which may be the most appropriate measure.

Level II

E2.4 *Time allowed – 30 minutes*

At a recent board meeting the managing director of Angel plc announced that the company directors had been awarded substantial cash bonuses, and share options despite the company incurring substantial losses during the last financial year. Explain why the above represents an agency problem within a company between the directors and the shareholders, and the ways in which it may be resolved.

E2.5 *Time allowed – 30 minutes*

In 2006 Chancer Ltd announced that to finance the development of a new head office in the centre of London, the company would need to borrow £30m secured against the company's existing assets. As a result the company's gearing ratio would rise from 20% to 85%. Outline the agency problem that may exist with regard to managers, shareholders, and debt holders of the company, and suggest ways in which this agency problem may be reduced.

E2.6 *Time allowed – 30 minutes*

Research evidence suggests a large amount of support for the efficient market hypothesis. Examine the reasons why the movements in the share prices of companies may not be consistent with this theory.

E2.7 *Time allowed – 30 minutes*

At a recent press briefing at the London Stock Exchange, a senior manager was quoted as saying 'an efficient market is a good market, which is good for the market, good for business, and good for profit'. Discuss what the senior manager meant and whether the statement is correct.

E2.8 *Time allowed – 30 minutes*

Crosby plc has a stock market valuation of £25m, and Nash plc has a stock market valuation of £18m (the market valuation equals number of shares in issue multiplied by the share price).

Both companies have similar profit profiles, as follows:

	Crosby plc £m	Nash plc £m
2000	1.3	1.8
2001	1.7	1.2
2002	1.2	2.3
2003	1.5	1.5
2004	2.3	1.8
2005	2.0	1.4

Explain the reasons why shareholders may regard Crosby plc as being worth £7m more than Nash, despite their having had the same total profits over the past six years.

E2.9 *Time allowed – 30 minutes*

In the context of the efficient markets hypothesis, distinguish between pricing efficiency, allocational efficiency, and operational efficiency.

E2.10 *Time allowed – 30 minutes*

Briefly explain the implications of the efficient markets hypothesis for the financial managers of a medium-sized company that is seeking a public listing.

E2.11 *Time allowed – 30 minutes*

Explain the range of remuneration incentive schemes and how they may be used to encourage managers of companies to make decisions that are consistent with the objective of maximisation of shareholder wealth.

Corporate governance

Chapter contents

LEARNING OBJECTIVES

Completion of this chapter will enable you to:

- ☑ Describe how the framework for establishing good corporate governance and accountability has been established in a UK Combined Code of Practice, developed from the work of the Cadbury, Greenbury, Hampel, and Turnbull Committees.

- ☑ Outline the corporate governance codes that have been developed in other countries, for example throughout Europe, China, and the Middle East, and including the USA's Sarbanes-Oxley Act 2002.

- ☑ Appreciate the importance of corporate social responsibility (CSR) reporting by companies.

- ☑ Outline the various approaches to dealing with the agency problem, including corporate governance frameworks but also with consideration to the ethical dimension.

- ☑ Explain the statutory requirement for the audit of limited companies, the election by shareholders of suitably qualified, independent auditors, and the role of the auditors.

- ☑ Outline directors' specific responsibility to shareholders, and responsibilities to society in general, for the management and conduct of companies.

- ☑ Recognise the fiduciary duties that directors have to the company, and their duty of care to all stakeholders and to the community at large, particularly with regard to the Companies Act 1985/1989, Health and Safety at Work Act 1974, and Financial Services Act 1986.

- ☑ Explain the implications for companies and their directors that may arise from the UK Corporate Manslaughter & Corporate Homicide Act 2006.

- ☑ Appreciate the importance of directors' duties regarding insolvency, the Insolvency Act 1986, and the Enterprise Act 2002.

- ☑ Consider the implications for directors of wrongful trading, and recognise the difference between this and the offence of fraudulent trading, and the possibility of criminal penalties.

- ☑ Outline the implication for directors of the Company Directors Disqualification Act 1986, and the Enterprise Act 2002.

- ☑ Explain the actions that directors of companies should take to ensure compliance with their obligations and responsibilities, and to protect themselves against possible non-compliance.

Introduction

The reports and accounts of public limited companies now increasingly include large sections that report on their systems of corporate governance. Corporate governance relates to the policies, procedures, and rules governing the relationships between the shareholders and the directors of a company. This chapter looks at how these have been developed in the UK, the USA, and many other countries in response to worldwide concerns about the ways companies are run following a spate of financial scandals over the past 20 years or so. Corporate governance codes offer guidance as to how the relationship between the various stakeholders of the business should be managed, and particularly the relationship between directors and shareholders.

In Chapter 1 we discussed the way in which the limited company exists in perpetuity as a legal entity, separate from the lives of those individuals who both own and manage it. The limited company has many rights, responsibilities, and liabilities in the same way as individual people. As a separate legal entity the company is responsible for its own liabilities. These are not the obligations of the shareholders who have paid for their shares, being the limit of their obligations to the company. The management and regulation of a company as a separate legal entity lies with the directors and the auditors. The directors are within, and part of, the company, and the auditors are external to, and not part of, the company. This chapter examines the roles and responsibilities of directors and auditors. It will also consider the obligations of directors, particularly with regard to the UK corporate governance Combined Code of Practice, and the many Acts that are now in place to regulate the behaviour of directors of limited companies. The chapter closes with a look at some of the steps that directors may take to protect themselves against possible non-compliance.

Corporate governance code of practice

Concerns about financial reporting and accountability, and the impact on the business community (see Fig. 3.1), grew during the 1980s following increasing numbers of company failures and financial scandals.

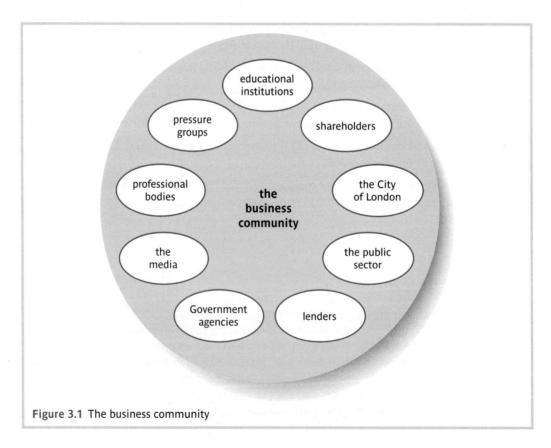

Figure 3.1 The business community

During the 1980s and 1990s there was huge concern within the business community following the financial scandals surrounding, for example, BCCI, Polly Peck, and Robert Maxwell's companies. These concerns continued to increase as we saw even larger scandals in the USA involving the companies Enron and WorldCom, and particularly the involvement of the consulting arms of firms like Arthur Andersen. These concerns were seen in a lack of confidence in financial reporting, and in shareholders and others being unable to rely on auditors to provide the necessary safeguards for their reliance on company annual reports.

The main factors underlying the lack of confidence in financial reporting were:

- loose accounting standards, which allowed considerable latitude (an example has been the treatment of extraordinary items and exceptional items in financial reporting)
- lack of a clear framework to ensure directors were able to continuously review business controls
- competitive pressure within companies and on auditors, making it difficult for auditors to maintain independence from demanding boards and bullying chairmen
- lack of apparent accountability regarding directors' remuneration and compensation for loss of office.

To address the concerns about financial reporting and make recommendations on good practice the Cadbury Committee, chaired by Sir Adrian Cadbury, was set up in May 1991 by the Financial Reporting Council, the London Stock Exchange, and the accounting profession.

The Cadbury Committee defined corporate governance (see Fig. 3.2) as:

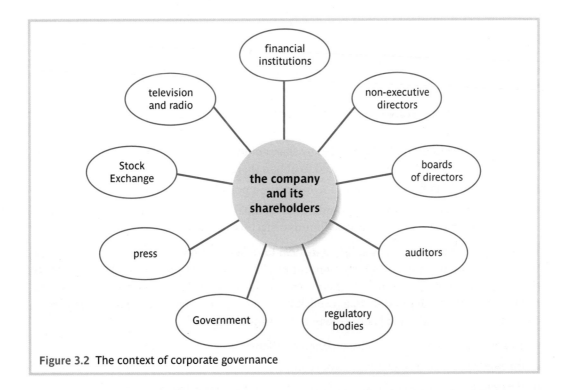

Figure 3.2 The context of corporate governance

> the system by which companies are directed and controlled. Boards of directors are responsible for the governance of their companies. The shareholders' role in governance is to appoint the directors and the auditors and to satisfy themselves that an appropriate governance structure is in place. The responsibilities of the board include setting the company's strategic aims, providing the leadership to put them into effect, supervising the management of the business and reporting to shareholders on their stewardship. The board's actions are subject to laws, regulations and the shareholders in general meeting.

The financial aspects within the framework described by Cadbury are the ways in which the company's board sets financial policy and oversees its implementation, the use of financial controls, and how the board reports on activities and progress of the company to shareholders.

The framework for establishing good corporate governance and accountability set up by the Cadbury Committee was formulated as the Committee's Code of Best Practice, published in December 1992. The main proposals and recommendations of the code were as follows:

- executive directors' service contracts should not exceed three years
- non-executive directors should be appointed to companies' boards of directors for specified terms
- the majority of non-executive directors should be independent of management and free from any business or other relationship
- executive remuneration should be subject to the recommendations of a Remuneration Committee made up entirely or mainly of non-executive directors
- an Audit Committee, comprising at least three non-executives, should be established.

The Cadbury Committee's Code of Best Practice provided a benchmark against which to assess compliance.

The Greenbury Committee's findings on directors' remuneration were published in the Greenbury Report in July 1995. It incorporated a Code of Best Practice on Director's Remuneration, which dealt with four main issues:

- the role of a Remuneration Committee in setting the remuneration packages for the CEO and other directors
- the required level of disclosure needed by shareholders regarding details of directors' remuneration, and whether there is the need to obtain shareholder approval
- specific guidelines for determining a remuneration policy for directors
- service contracts and provisions binding the company to pay compensation to a director, particularly in the event of dismissal for unsatisfactory performance.

The Hampel Committee was established in 1996 to review and revise the earlier recommendations of the Cadbury and Greenbury Committees. The Cadbury Code was updated in 1998 by the Hampel Committee, to include their own Committee's work. The report emphasised the need for good governance rather than explicit rules in order to reduce the regulatory burden on companies. In particular, the Hampel Report recommended:

- greater shareholder involvement in company affairs
- the need for a sound system of internal control
- the need for executives to be accountable for all aspects of risk management.

In September 1999 the Turnbull Committee report on *Internal Control: Guidance for Directors on the Combined Code*, known as the Turnbull Report, was issued by the ICAEW. The aim of the report was to provide guidance to ensure that all companies trading on the London Stock Exchange (LSE) have in place an adequate system of internal control in order to facilitate the management of business risk. The report was based on the adoption of a risk-based approach in establishing a sound system of internal control. It required companies to develop ongoing processes and procedures for:

- identifying, evaluating, and managing the significant business risks
- reviewing the effectiveness of the system of internal control
- ensuring adequate procedures exist for the management and disclosure of internal control problems and issues.

The Turnbull Report provided that in assessing internal controls, consideration should be given to:

- the nature and extent of the risks facing the organisation
- the extent and categories of risk which are regarded as acceptable
- the likelihood of the risks concerned materialising
- the company's ability to reduce the incidence and impact on the organisation of risks that do materialise.

The Turnbull Report also suggested that internal controls should be:

- embedded in the operation of the organisation and form part of its culture
- capable of responding quickly to evolving risks,

and procedures should be included for reporting any significant control failings immediately to appropriate levels of management.

In May 2000 the original Cadbury Code and subsequent reports were all consolidated by the Committee on Corporate Governance and published in the Combined Code of Practice.

The underlying principles of the Code are:

- openness
- integrity
- accountability.

Openness

Openness from companies is constrained within the limits of their competitive position but is the basis for the confidence that needs to exist between a business and all those who have a stake in its success. Openness in disclosure of information adds to the effectiveness of the market economy. It forces boards to take action and allows shareholders and others to be able to look more closely and thoroughly into companies.

Integrity

Integrity means straightforward dealing and completeness. Financial reporting should be honest and present a balanced view of the state of the company's affairs. The integrity of the company's reports will depend on the integrity of the people responsible for preparing and presenting them.

The annual reports and financial statements of the majority of UK plcs now include a number of sections under the heading *Corporate Governance*. These sections of the annual reports are required to comply with provisions set out in the Combined Code of Practice (principles of good governance and code of best practice), embracing the principles of the Cadbury, Greenbury, Hampel, and Turnbull Committees, appended to the Listing Rules of the LSE.

The corporate governance section of a company's annual report and accounts may contain details under the following headings:

- directors' biographies
- board responsibilities
- board composition and functions
- board committees:
    - audit committee
    - nomination committee
    - remuneration committee
    - IT committee
    - capital expenditure committee
    - **non-executive directors'** committee
- directors' remuneration
- relations with shareholders
- internal financial control
- incentive compensation
- directors' pensions
- corporate strategy.

This may not be a complete list but it gives a broad indication of the areas of compliance under the Combined Code of Practice. The annual reports and accounts of most UK plcs include corporate governance reports that are generally in compliance.

Accountability

Accountability of boards of directors to their shareholders requires the commitment from both to make the accountability effective. Boards of directors must play their part by ensuring the quality of information that is provided to shareholders. Shareholders must exercise their responsibilities as owners of the business. The major investing institutions (for example, pension funds and insurance companies) are usually in regular contact with the directors of UK plcs to discuss past, current, and future performance.

Companies listed on the Stock Exchange are requested to comply with the Code, but other companies may also benefit from compliance. It is not compulsory for any company, but rather a target of best practice to aim for. The revised Code continued to include the 'comply or explain' approach that was introduced by Cadbury. This means that companies listed on the Stock Exchange are required to include in their annual report and accounts a statement to confirm that they have complied with the Code's provisions throughout the accounting period, or to provide an explanation if that is not the case.

Subsequent to 2000, further reviews of various aspects of corporate governance were set up. The *Audit Committees Combined Code guidance* was published in January 2003, by a group led by Sir Robert Smith. The *Review of the role and effectiveness of non-executive directors* by Derek Higgs was also published in January 2003.

The above reviews were undertaken during a period in which investor confidence had been badly shaken, both by lapses in corporate governance and by the high-profile failure of some corporate strategies, the latter two being very much in response to these events. The reviews were reflected in a revision to the 1998 Combined Code of Practice, which was published by the Financial Reporting Council (FRC) in July 2003 – the Revised Code on Corporate Governance.

The Higgs Report examined the role, independence, and recruitment of non-executive directors, and outlined a series of tests of independence such as length of service (10 years), associations with executive management, financial interests, and significant shareholdings. With regard to recruitment, Higgs recommended stronger provisions governing nomination committees, and called for all listed companies to establish a nomination committee, chaired by an independent non-executive director (not the chairman) and comprising a majority of independent non-executive directors.

Other important recommendations of the Higgs Report included:

- the board of directors should review its own performance, the performance of its committees and individual directors at least once a year
- the company secretary should be accountable to the board of directors through the chairman on all governance matters
- the terms of reference of the remuneration committee should be published.

In October 2005, following a review of the Turnbull Report, the FRC published updated guidance notes. The guidance notes apply to all listed companies for financial years beginning on or after 1 January 2006.

Hermes Pensions Management Ltd is a company that embraces the UK Combined Code on Corporate Governance. Hermes is an independent fund manager, with over 20 years experience of managing money for its initial sponsors, British Telecom and the Post Office. In 1995 it became wholly owned by the BT Pension Scheme. The summary of Hermes corporate governance codes shown below includes their endorsement of the UK Combined Code on Corporate Governance (2003). We can see that Hermes corporate governance principles go even further in covering a number of additional corporate governance issues that they regard as important:

- Endorsement of Combined Code on Corporate Governance
  We welcome the publication of the Combined Code on Corporate Governance in 2003 and endorse its principles, provisions and suggestions as well as the Guidance on Internal Control and the Guidance on Audit Committees. We regard the Combined Code as the UK's official corporate governance guidelines and encourage companies either to comply with the Combined Code or to explain their reasons for non-compliance. Hermes will make staff available to play its part in the dialogue, which the 'comply or explain' principle demands of all parties, and we will enter into discussions with companies where we do not feel that their public explanations for any non-compliance are satisfactory. The Combined Code does not cover all corporate governance issues we regard as important. We would therefore make the following additional points.

- Remuneration
  We endorse the Combined Code's principles, provisions and good practice suggestions on remuneration. We also encourage companies to refer to the Principles and Guidelines on

Executive Remuneration issued by the Association of British Insurers, including the joint statement by the Association of British Insurers and the National Association of Pension Funds entitled Best Practice on Executive Contracts and Severance, and the Guidance on Remuneration Policy issued by the Performance Pay Group.

- Social, Ethical and Environmental Responsibility
  Hermes believes that the effective management of the risks associated with social, ethical and environmental matters can lead to long-term financial benefits for the companies concerned. We support the Disclosure Guidelines on Socially Responsible Investment issued by the Association of British Insurers and encourage companies to take these, as well as the Guidance on Internal Control (the Turnbull Guidance) attached to the Combined Code, into account in their management and reporting of risks in this area. We will engage with companies which, in our view, are not managing these risks effectively or which we feel could improve the quality of their disclosure, to encourage positive change.

It is not only the UK that has introduced codes of corporate governance. On a worldwide basis many countries are continuing to develop their own approaches to this issue. The Hermes summary of its corporate governance principles also makes similar comments with regard to their endorsement of the corporate governance principles adopted in Japan, the USA, and in a number of other European countries:

- France – Principles for the Corporate Governance of Listed Companies (2003), which consolidates the reports of the Association Française des Enterprises Privées and the Mouvement des Enterprises de France
- Italy – Italian Corporate Governance Code (2006)
- Germany – German Corporate Governance Code (2005)
- Japan – Tokyo Stock Exchange Principles of Corporate Governance for Listed Companies (2004)
- USA – California Public Employees' Retirement System governance principles.

Further information about Hermes' corporate governance codes may be found at www. hermes.co.uk/publications/publications_corporate_governance.htm.

The USA's response to concerns about major corporate financial scandals, including Enron, Tyco International, and WorldCom (now MCI), resulted in the passing of a United States federal law on 30 July 2002, called the Sarbanes-Oxley Act. This Act is also known as the Public Company Accounting Reform and Investor Protection Act of 2002, and is generally referred to as SOX or SARBOX. It was named after its sponsors, Senator Paul Sarbanes and Representative Michael G Oxley.

The Sarbanes-Oxley Act established new wide-ranging standards for all US public companies covering issues such as auditor independence, corporate governance, corporate responsibilities, and financial disclosure. The main provisions of the Sarbanes-Oxley Act include:

- the creation of the Public Company Accounting Oversight Board
- a requirement for public companies to evaluate and disclose the effectiveness of their internal controls as they relate to financial reporting
- the certification of financial reports by chief executive officers and chief financial officers
- a requirement for auditor independence
- a requirement that companies listed on stock exchanges must possess fully independent audit committees to oversee the relationship between the company and its auditor
- a prohibition on most personal loans to any executive officer or director

- a requirement for accelerated reporting of insider trading
- enhanced criminal and civil penalties for violations of US securities law
- the imposition of significantly longer maximum jail sentences and larger fines for corporate executives who knowingly and wilfully mis-state financial statements.

For non-compliance with SOX requirements, penalties range from fines of up to US$5m and/or imprisonment for up to 20 years. The Sarbanes-Oxley Act 2002 covers similar areas to those within UK corporate governance requirements. In addition, the SOX requirements increasingly have a wide-ranging impact on corporate governance and issues associated with managerial control and accountability on a worldwide basis.

The development of corporate governance systems in specific countries is related very much to each country's particular business environment and the diverse range of problems they face. The importance of corporate governance has gathered pace in the GCC (Gulf Cooperation Council) countries (Bahrain, Kuwait, Oman, Qatar, Saudi Arabia, and United Arab Emirates) over the past few years. In October 2006 the outcome of the first corporate governance survey of GCC countries by the Institute of International Finance (IIF) and Hawkamah, the Institute of Corporate Governance was reported. It found that in general, corporate governance in GCC countries lagged significantly behind international corporate governance best practices among emerging markets.

The IIF and Hawkamah survey report was part of a coordinated strategy towards the harmonisation of corporate governance standards in the GCC and their alignment with international best practices. However, the survey also found a great degree of variation between corporate governance frameworks in the six countries. Oman was the only country in the GCC that had a code of corporate governance and had the strongest corporate governance framework complying with about 70% of IIF guidelines. This was followed by Kuwait and Saudi Arabia with about 50% compliance, and Bahrain and UAE with 40% compliance with IIF guidelines. The greatest room for improvement was found in Qatar where corporate governance requirements complied with only 35% of IIF guidelines. Improvements were expected as the authorities were taking steps to improve governance practices in listed companies. The study identified three key factors that were driving the introduction of improved governance practices in the GCC:

- policy makers' reaction to the volatility in the prices of securities
- the importance of IPOs (initial public offerings) in the growth of GCC equity markets
- foreign direct investment (FDI).

The study also observed that efforts were being made to strengthen corporate governance in the region.

A different set of problems faced the development of corporate governance in China, which has also gathered momentum over the past few years. The state policy of maintaining a full or controlling ownership interest in enterprises in several business sectors creates a dilemma. The state wants enterprises to be run efficiently, but not necessarily with the objective of maximisation of shareholder wealth. The state may have alternative objectives, for example in areas of employment levels and control of sensitive industries. This means that objectives cannot easily be measured, which therefore creates monitoring difficulties. Continuing state involvement results in a conflict of interest between the state as controlling shareholder and other shareholders. In this way the state uses its control for purposes other than shareholder wealth maximisation, and therefore exploits the other minority shareholders who have no other way to benefit from their investment.

Progress check 3.1

What is corporate governance and how is it implemented?

Let's take a look at the Johnson Matthey section on corporate governance, included in pages 38 to 49 of their Report and Accounts 2007, and reproduced on pages 93 to 104 of this book. This section includes the corporate governance report itself, and the audit committee report, nomination committee report, management development and remuneration committee report, the responsibility of directors report, and independent auditors report.

The company states that:

> " The group was in compliance with the provisions of the Code throughout the year except that the board has taken the view that it is not necessarily practical, efficient or desired by shareholders for the Senior Independent Director to attend meetings with major shareholders in order to learn their issues and concerns unless such discussions are requested by shareholders. "

Johnson Matthey then expand on the ways in which shareholders' views are communicated in the section headed 'Relations with Shareholders'. Communication with shareholders includes the company's interim and year-end reports and the AGM (annual general meeting). It also includes presentations to major shareholders, analysts and the media, and the use of the company's website. Contact with major shareholders is the responsibility of the chief executive and group finance director. Canvassing of shareholders' views also takes place, as well as meetings between the chairman and major shareholders as required with regard to corporate governance and company strategy.

A number of the headings, which are part of the overall corporate governance reporting, are not included within Johnson Matthey plc's main corporate governance report but are shown elsewhere in the report and accounts. For example, the composition and functions of the board, and directors' and senior managers' biographies are shown on pages 34 and 35 of the Report and Accounts 2007, and are not reproduced in this book.

Worked Example 3.1

A number of basic problems may be encountered by shareholders with small shareholdings as they enter a new relationship with the company they effectively part own.

Most major plcs are owned by shareholders with both large and small shareholdings, the analysis of which can be found in their annual reports and accounts.

Usually within a very short time of acquiring their shares, most new small shareholders realise they have neither influence nor power.

As plcs have become multi-activity and multinational, so the directors have become more distanced from the shareholders. (Compare this with, for example, locally based building societies.)

During the move towards growth and expanded activities by companies, considerable disquiet regarding accountability developed in the business community and the Committee on the Financial Aspects of Corporate Governance (Cadbury Committee) was appointed, which produced its report in December 1992.

There has also been unease regarding directors' remuneration, bonus schemes, option schemes and contracts. The various committees on corporate governance, subsequent to Cadbury, have reviewed each of these areas.

CORPORATE GOVERNANCE

Statement of Compliance with the Combined Code

The company has applied all of the principles set out in section 1 of the Combined Code on Corporate Governance (the Code) relating to the structure and composition of the board, the remuneration of the directors, relations with shareholders and procedures for financial reporting, internal control and audit. This statement describes how the principles of the Code have been applied. The group was in compliance with the provisions of the Code throughout the year except that the board has taken the view that it is not necessarily practical, efficient or desired by shareholders for the Senior Independent Director to attend meetings with major shareholders in order to learn their issues and concerns unless such discussions are requested by shareholders. The methods by which major shareholders' views are communicated to the board as a whole are discussed under 'Relations with Shareholders' on page 39.

Directors and the Board

The board is responsible to the company's shareholders for the group's system of corporate governance, its strategic objectives and the stewardship of the company's resources and is ultimately responsible for social, environmental and ethical matters. The board held seven meetings in the year and in addition met separately to review the group's long term strategy. The board delegates specific responsibilities to board committees, as described below. The board reviews the key activities of the business and receives papers and presentations to enable it to do so effectively. The Company Secretary is responsible to the board, and is available to individual directors, in respect of board procedures.

Mr N A P Carson is the Chief Executive. The board currently comprises the Chairman, the Chief Executive, four other executive directors and five independent non-executive directors. Sir John Banham became Chairman on 1st April 2006 following the retirement of Mr H M P Miles. Sir John Banham's other commitments are disclosed on page 34. The roles of Chairman and Chief Executive are separate. The Chairman leads the board, ensuring that each director, particularly the non-executive directors, is able to make an effective contribution. He monitors, with assistance from the Company Secretary, the information distributed to the board to ensure that it is sufficient, accurate, timely and clear. The Chief Executive maintains day-to-day management responsibility for the company's operations, implementing group strategies and policies agreed by the board.

Mr C D Mackay is the Senior Independent Director. The role of non-executive directors is to enhance independence and objectivity of the board's deliberations and decisions. All non-executive directors are independent of management and free from any business or other relationship which could materially interfere with the exercise of their independent judgment. The executive directors have specific responsibilities, which are detailed on pages 34 and 35, and have direct responsibility for all operations and activities.

All directors submit themselves for re-election at least once every three years. The board composition allows for changes to be made with minimum disruption.

During the year the board undertook a formal evaluation of its performance and the performance of its committees and the individual directors. A questionnaire, prepared by the Chairman with the assistance of the Company Secretary, was completed by all directors other than the Chairman. The questionnaire focused on the operation of the board, its committees and individual directors' contributions. A summary of the responses was prepared by the Company Secretary and discussed at a board meeting. In addition, led by the Senior Independent Director, the non-executive directors met without the Chairman present to consider evaluation of the Chairman's performance.

Committees of the Board

The **Chief Executive's Committee** is responsible for the recommendation to the board of strategic and operating plans and on decisions reserved to the board where appropriate. It is also responsible for the executive management of the group's business. The Committee is chaired by the Chief Executive and meets monthly. It comprises the executive directors and three senior executives of the company.

The **Audit Committee** is a sub-committee of the board whose purpose is to assist the board in the effective discharge of its responsibilities for financial reporting and corporate control. The Committee meets quarterly and is chaired by Mr A M Thomson. It comprises all the independent non-executive directors with the group Chairman, the Chief Executive, the Group Finance Director and the external and internal auditors attending by invitation. A report from the Committee on its activities is given on page 41.

The **Nomination Committee** is a sub-committee of the board responsible for advising the board and making recommendations on the appointment of new directors. The Committee is chaired by Sir John Banham and also comprises all the independent non-executive directors. A report from the Committee on its activities is given on page 40.

The **Management Development and Remuneration Committee (MDRC)** is a sub-committee of the board, which determines on behalf of the board the remuneration of the executive directors. The Committee is chaired by Mr C D Mackay and comprises all the independent non-executive directors of the company together with the group Chairman who was appointed to the Committee during the year. The Chief Executive and the Director of Human Resources attend by invitation except when their own performance and remuneration are discussed. Further details are set out in the Remuneration Report on pages 42 to 48.

CORPORATE GOVERNANCE

Committees of the Board (continued)

Attendance at the board and board committee meetings in 2006/07 was as follows:

Director	Full Board Eligible to attend	Full Board Attended	MDRC Eligible to attend	MDRC Attended	Nomination Committee Eligible to attend	Nomination Committee Attended	Audit Committee Eligible to attend	Audit Committee Attended
Sir John Banham	7	7	2	4[1]	3	3	–	4[1]
N A P Carson	7	7	–	4[1]	–	3[1]	–	4[1]
M B Dearden	7	7	4	4	3	3	4	4
P N Hawker	7	7	–	–	–	–	–	–
C D Mackay	7	7	4	4	3	3	4	4
D W Morgan	7	7	–	–	–	–	–	–
L C Pentz	7	7	–	–	–	–	–	–
J N Sheldrick	7	7	–	–	–	–	–	4[1]
I C Strachan	7	6	4	4	3	3	4	3
A M Thomson	7	7	4	4	3	3	4	4
R J W Walvis	7	7	4	4	3	3	4	4

[1] Includes meetings attended by invitation for all or part of meeting.

Directors' Remuneration

The Remuneration Report on pages 42 to 48 includes details of remuneration policies and of the remuneration of the directors.

Relations with Shareholders

The board considers effective communication with shareholders, whether institutional investors, private or employee shareholders, to be extremely important.

The company reports formally to shareholders twice a year, when its half year and full year results are announced and an interim report and a full report are issued to shareholders. These reports are posted on Johnson Matthey's website (www.matthey.com). At the same time, executive directors give presentations on the results to institutional investors, analysts and the media in London and other international centres. Copies of major presentations are also posted on the company's website.

The company's annual general meeting (AGM) takes place in London and formal notification is sent to shareholders with the Annual Report at least 20 working days in advance of the meeting. The directors are available for questions, formally during the AGM and informally afterwards. Details of the 2007 AGM are set out in the notice of the meeting enclosed with this Annual Report.

Contact with major shareholders is principally maintained by the Chief Executive and the Group Finance Director, who ensure that their views are communicated to the board as a whole. The Chairman also discusses governance and other matters directly with major shareholders. The board believes that appropriate steps have been taken during the year to ensure that the members of the board, and in particular the non-executive directors, develop an understanding of the issues and concerns of major shareholders about the company. The board is provided with brokers' reports and feedback from shareholder meetings on a six-monthly basis. The canvassing of major shareholders' views for the board in a detailed investor survey is usually conducted every two years by external consultants. The board has taken the view that these methods, taken together, are a practical and efficient way both for the Chairman to keep in touch with major shareholder opinion on governance and strategy and for the Senior Independent Director to learn the views of major shareholders and to develop a balanced understanding of their issues and concerns. The Senior Independent Director is available to attend meetings with major shareholders if requested.

Accountability, Audit and Control

The statement of the Responsibility of Directors for the preparation of the Annual Report and the accounts is set out on page 48.

In its reporting to shareholders, the board aims to present a balanced and understandable assessment of the group's financial position and prospects.

The group's organisational structure is focused on its three divisions. These are all separately managed but report to the board through a board director. The executive management team receives monthly summaries of financial results from each division through a standardised reporting process.

The group has in place a comprehensive annual budgeting process including forecasts for the next two years. Variances from budget are closely monitored.

The board has overall responsibility for the group's systems of internal control and for reviewing their effectiveness. The internal control systems are designed to meet the group's needs and address the risks to which it is exposed. Such systems can provide reasonable but not absolute assurance against material misstatement or loss.

There is a continuous process for identifying, evaluating and managing the significant risks faced by the company, which has been in place during the year under review and up to the date of approval of the Annual Report and Accounts. The board regularly reviews this process.

The assessment of group and strategic risks is reviewed by the board and updated on an annual basis. At the business level, the processes to identify and manage the key risks are an integral part of the control environment. Key risks and internal controls are the subject of regular reporting to the Chief Executive's Committee.

The Group Control Manual, which is distributed to all group operations, clearly sets out the composition, responsibilities and authority limits of the various board and executive committees and also specifies what may be decided without central approval. It is supplemented by other specialist policy and procedures manuals issued by the group, divisions and individual business units or departments. The high intrinsic value of many of the metals with which the group is associated necessitates stringent physical controls over precious metals held at the group's sites.

CORPORATE GOVERNANCE

Accountability, Audit and Control (continued)

The internal audit function is responsible for monitoring the group's systems of internal financial controls and the control of the integrity of the financial information reported to the board. The Audit Committee approves the plans for internal audit reviews and receives the reports produced by the internal audit function on a regular basis. Actions are agreed with management in response to the internal audit reports produced.

In addition, significant business units provide assurance on the maintenance of financial and non-financial controls and compliance with group policies. These assessments are summarised by the internal audit function and a report is made annually to the Audit Committee.

The directors confirm that the system of internal control for the year ended 31st March 2007 and the period up to 5th June 2007 has been established in accordance with the Turnbull Guidance included with the Code and that they have reviewed the effectiveness of the system of internal control.

Corporate Social Responsibility

Measures to ensure responsible business conduct and the identification and assessment of risks associated with social, ethical and environmental matters are managed in conjunction with all other business risks and reviewed at regular meetings of the board and the Chief Executive's Committee.

A review of the group's policies and targets for corporate social responsibility (CSR) is set out on pages 25 to 33. A full version of the CSR report is available on the company's website.

The identification, assessment and management of environment, health and safety (EHS) risks are the responsibility of the CSR Compliance Committee, which is a sub-committee of the Chief Executive's Committee, comprising the division directors, the Director of EHS, the Company Secretary and other appropriate professional staff. Performance is monitored using monthly statistics and detailed site audit reports. EHS performance is reviewed on a regular basis by the Chief Executive's Committee and an annual review is undertaken by the board.

Risks from employment and people issues are identified and assessed by the Chief Executive's Committee and reported to the board.

Employment contracts, handbooks and policies specify acceptable business practices and the group's position on ethical issues. The Group Control Manual and security manuals provide further operational guidelines to reinforce these.

The Audit Committee reviews risks associated with corporate social responsibility on an annual basis and monitors performance through the annual control self-assessment process conducted by the internal audit function.

NOMINATION COMMITTEE REPORT

Role of the Nomination Committee

The Nomination Committee is a sub-committee of the board whose purpose is to advise the board on the appointment and, if necessary, dismissal of executive and non-executive directors. The full terms of reference of the Nomination Committee are provided on the company's website at www.matthey.com.

Composition of the Nomination Committee

The Nomination Committee comprises all the independent non-executive directors together with the group Chairman. The quorum necessary for the transaction of business is two, each of whom must be an independent non-executive director. Biographical details of the independent directors and the group Chairman are set out on pages 34 and 35. Their remuneration is set out on page 44.

The group Chairman acts as the Chairman of the Committee, although the group Chairman may not chair the Committee when it is dealing with the matter of succession to the Chairmanship of the company. A non-executive director may not chair the Committee when it is dealing with a matter relating to that non-executive director.

Only members of the Committee have the right to attend Committee meetings. However, other individuals, such as the Chief Executive, the Director of Human Resources and external advisers, may be invited to attend for all or part of any meeting as and when appropriate.

The Company Secretary is secretary to the Committee.

The Committee has the authority to seek any information that it requires from any officer or employee of the company or its subsidiaries. In connection with its duties, the Committee is

authorised by the board to take such independent advice (including legal or other professional advice, at the company's expense) as it considers necessary, including requests for information from or commissioning investigations by external advisers.

Main Activities of the Nomination Committee

During the financial year ended 31st March 2007, the Nomination Committee conducted a process to identify additional non-executive directors for the company with the assistance of external search consultants. Open advertising was not used. The Nomination Committee met three times during the year in connection with the selection process. The Committee met on 20th November 2006 to review the selection process, on 23rd January 2007 at which it recommended the appointment of Mr M J Roney to the board, and on 27th March 2007 at which it recommended the appointment of Mrs D C Thompson to the board. As announced on 16th April 2007, Mr Roney joined the board as a non-executive director with effect from 1st June 2007. As announced on 30th May 2007, Mrs Thompson will join the board as a non-executive director with effect from 1st September 2007.

On behalf of the Committee:

Sir John Banham
Chairman of the Nomination Committee

AUDIT COMMITTEE REPORT

Role of the Audit Committee

The Audit Committee is a sub-committee of the board whose responsibilities include:

- Reviewing the interim and full year accounts and results announcements of the company and any other formal announcements relating to the company's financial performance and recommending them to the board for approval.

- Reviewing the group's systems for internal financial control and risk management.

- Monitoring and reviewing the effectiveness of the company's internal audit function and considering regular reports from internal audit on internal financial controls and risk management.

- Considering the appointment of the external auditors; overseeing the process for their selection; and making recommendations to the board in relation to their appointment to be put to shareholders for approval at a general meeting.

- Monitoring and reviewing the effectiveness and independence of the external auditors, agreeing the nature and scope of their audit, agreeing their remuneration, and considering their reports on the company's accounts, reports to shareholders and their evaluation of the systems of internal financial control and risk management.

The full terms of reference of the Audit Committee are provided on the company's website at www.matthey.com.

Composition of the Audit Committee

The Audit Committee comprises all the independent non-executive directors. Biographical details of the independent directors are set out on pages 34 and 35. Their remuneration is set out on page 44. The Chairman of the Audit Committee is Mr A M Thomson. The group Chairman, Chief Executive, Group Finance Director, Head of Internal Audit and external auditors (KPMG Audit Plc) attend Audit Committee meetings by invitation. The Committee also meets separately with the Head of Internal Audit and with the external auditors without management being present. The Company Secretary is secretary to the Audit Committee.

Main Activities of the Audit Committee

The Audit Committee met four times during the financial year ended 31st March 2007. At its meeting on 24th May 2006 the Committee reviewed the company's preliminary announcement of its results for the financial year ended 31st March 2006, and the draft report and accounts for that year. The Committee received reports from the external auditors on the conduct of their audit, their review of the accounts, including accounting policies and areas of judgment, and their comments on risk management and control matters. The Committee reviewed the group's Corporate Social Responsibility Report which is available on the company's website at www.matthey.com. The Committee also reviewed shareholder resolutions to be proposed at the forthcoming AGM.

The Audit Committee met on 24th July 2006 to receive reports on internal controls from both the internal and external auditors. The external auditors also presented their proposed fees and scope for the forthcoming year. The Committee also reviewed the performance of both the internal and external auditors.

At its meeting on 20th November 2006 the Audit Committee reviewed the company's interim results, the half year report and the external auditors' review.

At its meeting on 23rd January 2007 the Audit Committee reviewed management's and internal audit's reports on the effectiveness of the company's systems for internal financial control and risk management. The Committee reviewed the group's credit control procedures and risks, controls over precious metals, IT controls and corporate social responsibility reporting arrangements. Changes to the Group Control Manual were ratified.

Independence of External Auditors

Both the board and the external auditors have for many years had safeguards in place to avoid the possibility that the auditors' objectivity and independence could be compromised. Our policy in respect of services provided by the external auditors is as follows:

- Audit related services – the external auditors are invited to provide services which, in their position as auditors, they must or are best placed to undertake. This includes formalities relating to borrowings, shareholders' and other circulars, various other regulatory reports and work in respect of acquisitions and disposals.

- Tax consulting – in cases where they are best suited, we use the external auditors. All other significant tax consulting work is put out to tender.

- General consulting – in recognition of public concern over the effect of consulting services on auditors' independence, our policy is that the external auditors are not invited to tender for general consulting work.

The split between audit and non-audit fees for the year ended 31st March 2007 and information on the nature of non-audit fees appear in note 5 on the accounts.

Internal Audit

During the year the Audit Committee reviewed the performance of the internal audit function, the findings of the audits completed during the year and the department's resource requirements and also approved the internal audit plan for the year ending 31st March 2008.

Internal audit independently reviews the risks and control processes operated by management. It carries out independent audits in accordance with an internal audit plan which is agreed with the Audit Committee before the start of the financial year.

The plan provides a high degree of financial and geographical coverage and devotes significant effort to the review of the risk management framework surrounding the major business risks.

Internal audit reports include recommendations to improve internal controls together with agreed management action plans to resolve the issues raised. Internal audit follows up the implementation of recommendations and reports progress to senior management and the Audit Committee.

The Audit Committee receives reports from the Head of Internal Audit on the department's work and findings.

The effectiveness of the internal audit function is reviewed and discussed on an annual basis with the Head of Internal Audit.

On behalf of the Committee:

Alan Thomson
Chairman of the Audit Committee

REMUNERATION REPORT

Remuneration Report to Shareholders

Management Development and Remuneration Committee and its Terms of Reference

The Management Development and Remuneration Committee of the board comprises all the independent non-executive directors of the company as set out on pages 34 and 35 and the group Chairman, who was appointed to the Committee during the year. The Chairman of the Committee is Mr C D Mackay.

The Committee's terms of reference include determination on behalf of the board of fair remuneration for the executive directors and of the group Chairman (in which case the group Chairman does not participate), which recognises their individual contributions to the company's overall performance. In addition, the Committee assists the board in ensuring that the senior management of the group are recruited, developed and remunerated in an appropriate fashion. The Director of Human Resources, Mr I F Stephenson, acts as secretary to the Committee. The full terms of reference of the Committee are available on the company's website at www.matthey.com.

Non-executive directors' remuneration is determined by the board, within the limits prescribed by the company's Articles of Association. The remuneration consists of fees, which are set following advice taken from independent consultants and are reviewed at regular intervals.

Executive Remuneration Policy

The Committee believes strongly that remuneration policy should be closely aligned with shareholder interests. The Committee recognises that, in order to maximise shareholder value, it is necessary to have a competitive pay and benefits structure. The Committee also recognises that there is a highly competitive market for successful executives and that the provision of appropriate rewards for superior performance is vital to the continued growth of the business. To assist with this, the Committee appoints and receives advice from independent remuneration consultants on the pay and incentive arrangements prevailing in comparably sized industrial companies in each country in which Johnson Matthey has operations. During the year, such advice was received from the Hay Group, which also provided advice on job evaluation, and PricewaterhouseCoopers LLP. PricewaterhouseCoopers LLP also provided expatriate tax advice, tax audit work, completion of overseas tax returns, advice on set up of new overseas operations and some overseas payroll services. The Committee also receives recommendations from the Chief Executive on the remuneration of those reporting to him as well as advice from the Director of Human Resources. Total potential rewards are earned through the achievement of demanding performance targets based on measures that represent the best interests of shareholders.

The remuneration policy is reviewed by the Committee annually and a formal review is undertaken every three years. Remuneration consists of basic salary, annual bonus, a long term incentive plan, share options and other benefits. Salaries are based on median market rates with incentives providing the opportunity for upper quartile total remuneration, but only for achieving outstanding performance.

To ensure the interests of the executive directors remain aligned with those of the shareholders, they are encouraged to build up over time and hold a shareholding in the company equal to at least one times their basic salary.

During 2006/07 the Committee undertook a comprehensive review of the executive director and senior management remuneration arrangements within the group, which included advice from independent consultants PricewaterhouseCoopers LLP and consultation with the company's major institutional shareholders and representative organisations. As a result of this review, changes are proposed to remuneration relating to annual bonus, long term

incentive plan and share options. These proposals in respect of the long term incentive plan are submitted to shareholders for approval at this year's annual general meeting (AGM) and are explained in the circular containing the notice of the AGM. A copy of the circular may be viewed at www.matthey.com. The arrangements which have been in place to date are described below.

Executive directors' remuneration consists of the following:

- **Basic Salary** – which is in line with the median market salary for each director's responsibilities as determined by independent surveys. Basic salary is normally reviewed on 1st August each year and the Committee takes into account individual performance and promotion during the year. Where an internal promotion takes place, the median salary relative to the market would usually be reached over a period of a few years, which can give rise to higher than normal salary increases while this is being achieved.

- **Annual Bonus** – which is paid as a percentage of basic salary under the terms of the company's Executive Compensation Plan (which also applies to the group's 160 or so most senior executives). The executive directors' bonus award is based on consolidated profit before tax and one-off items (PBT) compared with the annual budget. The board of directors rigorously reviews the annual budget to ensure that the budgeted PBT is sufficiently stretching. An annual bonus payment of 30% of basic salary (prevailing at 31st March) is paid if the group meets the annual budget. This bonus may rise to 65% of basic salary if the group achieves PBT of 107.5% of budget. A maximum 100% of basic salary may be paid to the Chief Executive and the other executive directors if 115% of budgeted PBT is achieved. PBT must reach 95% of budget for a minimum bonus of 15% to be payable. The Committee has discretion to vary the awards made. The bonus awarded to executive directors for 2006/07 was 51.47% of salary at 31st March 2007 based on an achieved PBT of 104.6% of budget.

- **Long Term Incentive Plan (LTIP)** – which is designed to achieve above average performance and growth. It allows share allocations of up to a maximum of 125% of basic annual salary each year to directors and executives. The allocation in 2006 was 100% of basic annual salary for executive directors and 125% for the Chief Executive. The release of the share allocation is subject to the achievement of certain stretching performance targets measured over the three year period from the date of allocation.

Share allocations made prior to 2004 – Share allocations made prior to 2004 are subject to the achievement of performance targets which contain two components – relative total shareholder return (TSR) and absolute TSR.

The first component (50% of the allocation) compares the company's TSR over the three year performance period with that of a comparator group. The comparator group comprises those companies placed 51-150 in the FTSE Index. All of the shares are released if the company ranks in the 76th percentile or above. None of the shares are released if the company ranks in the 50th percentile or below. If the company ranks between these percentiles 35% to 100% of the shares are released on a straight line basis. In addition, the company's earnings per share (EPS) must be at least equal to the increase in UK RPI plus 2% per annum over the three year performance period before any release is made.

The second component (50% of the allocation) measures absolute TSR. All of the shares are released if the absolute TSR growth over the three year performance period is 45% or more. Pro rata allocations on a straight line basis of between 50% and 100% are released if absolute TSR growth is between 30% and 45%. Half of the allocated shares are released if TSR growth is 30%. No shares are released for TSR growth of less than 30%.

REMUNERATION REPORT

Share allocations made from 2004 onwards – Share allocations made in 2004 onwards are subject to a relative TSR performance target. This compares the company's TSR over a three year performance period commencing in the year of allocation with that of a comparator group which comprises those companies placed 51-150 in the FTSE Index. All of the allocated shares are released if the company ranks in the 76th percentile or above. None of the shares are released if the company ranks in the 50th percentile or below. If the company ranks between these percentiles 35% to 100% of the shares are released on a straight line basis. In addition, the company's EPS must be at least equal to the increase in UK RPI plus 2% per annum over the three year performance period before any release is made.

- **Share Options** – Since 2001 options have been granted under the Johnson Matthey 2001 Share Option Scheme (the 2001 Scheme). Options are granted at the market value of the company's shares at the time of grant and are subject to performance targets over a three year period. Options may be exercised upon satisfaction of the relevant performance targets. Approximately 800 employees are granted options under the 2001 Scheme each year.

Options granted prior to 2004 – Prior to 2004, options granted to the executive directors under the 2001 Scheme were up to a maximum of 100% of basic annual salary each year. Such options can only be exercised if the company's EPS has grown by at least UK RPI plus 4% per annum over any three consecutive years during the life of the option. These options are subject to annual retesting until they lapse on the tenth anniversary of grant.

There are also options outstanding under the Johnson Matthey 1995 UK and Overseas Executive Share Option Scheme. The last option grant under this scheme was made in 2000. All options were granted in annual tranches up to the maximum permitted of four times earnings and were subject to a performance target of EPS growth of UK RPI plus 2% over the three year performance period. Option grants were not made to executive directors in the years 1998, 1999 and 2000.

Options granted from 2004 onwards – Grants made from 2004 onwards are not eligible for retesting and are subject to a three year performance target of EPS growth of UK RPI plus 3% per annum. If the performance target is not met at the end of the three year performance period, the options will lapse. In addition, to reduce the cost calculated under the International Financial Reporting Standard IFRS 2 – 'Share-based Payment', gains are capped at 100% of the grant price.

The Committee has the discretion to award grants greater than 100% of basic annual salary. Grants above this threshold are, however, subject to increasingly stretching performance targets. Grants between 100% and 125% of basic annual salary are subject to EPS growth of UK RPI plus 4% per annum and grants between 125% and 150% of basic annual salary are subject to EPS growth of UK RPI plus 5% per annum. In 2006 the executive directors were granted options equal to 150% of basic annual salary.

- **Pensions** – All the executive directors are members of the Johnson Matthey Employees Pension Scheme in the UK. Messrs Carson and Hawker ceased to accrue pensionable service in the scheme on 31st March 2006. Mr L C Pentz, a US citizen, joined the scheme in January 2006. Prior to this he was a member of the Johnson Matthey Inc. Salaried Employees Pension Plan in the US. Under the UK scheme, members are entitled to a pension based on their pensionable service and final pensionable salary. The scheme also provides life assurance cover of four times annual salary. The normal scheme pension age for directors is 60. None of the non-executive directors are members of the scheme. Details of the individual arrangements for executive directors are given on pages 46 and 47.

- **Other Benefits** – Available to the executive directors are private medical insurance, a company car and membership of the group's employee share incentive plans which are open to all employees in the countries in which the group operates such schemes.

- **Service Contracts** – The executive directors are employed on contracts subject to one year's notice at any time. On early termination of their contracts the directors would normally be entitled to 12 months' salary and benefits.

Directors' Emoluments 2006/07

	Date of service agreement	Date of appointment	Base salary £'000	Payment in lieu of pension[1] £'000	Annual bonus £'000	Benefits £'000	Total excluding pension £'000	Total prior year excluding pension £'000
Executive								
N A P Carson	1.8.99	1.8.99	590	147	314	29	1,080	785
P N Hawker	1.8.03	1.8.03	287	72	152	21	532	387
D W Morgan	1.8.99	1.8.99	293	–	154	26	473	422
L C Pentz [2]	1.1.06	1.8.03	287	–	152	272	711	534
J N Sheldrick [3]	24.11.97	3.9.90	392	–	206	14	612	544
Total			1,849	219	978	362	3,408	2,672

REMUNERATION REPORT

Directors' Emoluments 2006/07 (continued)

	Date of letter of appointment	Date of appointment	Fees £'000	Total excluding pension £'000	Total prior year excluding pension[7] £'000
Non-Executive [4]					
Sir John Banham (Chairman)	10.12.05	1.1.06	250	250	31
M B Dearden	5.1.99	1.4.99	40	40	40
C D Mackay	5.1.99	27.1.99	45[5]	45	45
I C Strachan	10.12.01	23.1.02	40	40	40
A M Thomson	1.8.02	24.9.02	45[6]	45	45
R J W Walvis	1.8.02	24.9.02	40	40	40
Total			**460**	**460**	**241**

Notes

[1] Mr Carson and Dr Hawker ceased to accrue pensionable service in the UK pension scheme with effect from 31st March 2006. They received a cash payment in lieu of pension equal to 25% of basic salary. This is taxable under the PAYE system.

[2] Mr Pentz's emoluments from 1st January 2006 are based on UK salary and benefits. Prior to that Mr Pentz's emoluments were based on US basic salary adjusted for the cost of living differential in the UK including UK taxation. Associated with his localisation to UK salary and benefits and the purchase of a UK residence, Mr Pentz was provided with a package of transitional assistance including a housing allowance and relocation expenses commensurate with the company's relocation policy.

[3] Mr Sheldrick is a non-executive director of GKN plc. His fees for the year were £54,000. This amount is excluded from the table above and retained by him.

[4] Non-executive fees (other than for the Chairman) were reviewed on 1st April 2004 for the period to 31st March 2007, and on 1st May 2007 for the period from 1st April 2007. The new fees are £45,000 per annum, with the fee for chairmanship of committees remaining at £5,000.

[5] Includes £5,000 per annum for chairmanship of the Management Development and Remuneration Committee.

[6] Includes £5,000 per annum for chairmanship of the Audit Committee.

[7] Excludes the emoluments of Mr Miles who retired as Chairman on 31st March 2006. His emoluments were £220,000, bringing the total to £461,000.

Former Directors

During the year a payment of £8,000 was made to Mr Miles who retired as Chairman on 31st March 2006.

Directors' Interests

The interests of the directors as at 31st March 2007 in the shares of the company according to the register required to be kept by section 325(1) of the Companies Act 1985 were:

1. Ordinary Shares

	31st March 2007	31st March 2006
Sir John Banham	8,000	4,000
N A P Carson	61,310	50,919
M B Dearden	2,000	2,000
P N Hawker	15,327	7,966
C D Mackay	12,500	12,500
D W Morgan	40,582	36,257
L C Pentz	18,526	11,414
J N Sheldrick	74,517	63,321
I C Strachan	1,000	1,000
A M Thomson	2,213	2,165
R J W Walvis	1,000	1,000

All of the above interests were beneficial. The executive directors are also deemed to be interested in shares held by two employee share ownership trusts (see note 31 on page 88).

Directors' interests as at 31st May 2007 were unchanged from those listed above, other than that the Trustees of the Johnson Matthey Share Incentive Plan have purchased on behalf of Messrs Carson, Hawker, Morgan and Sheldrick a further 45 ordinary shares each and on behalf of Mr Pentz a further 48 ordinary shares.

REMUNERATION REPORT

Directors' Interests (continued)

2. Share Options

As at 31st March 2007, individual holdings under the company's executive share option schemes were as set out below. Options are not granted to non-executive directors.

	Date of grant	Ordinary shares under option	Exercise price (pence)	Date from which exercisable[1]	Expiry date	Total number of ordinary shares under option
N A P Carson	14.7.98	15,964	524.0	14.7.01	14.7.08	
	22.7.99	18,035	585.5	22.7.02	22.7.09	
	18.7.01	19,391	1,083.0	18.7.04	18.7.11	
	17.7.02	28,901	865.0	17.7.05	17.7.12	
	17.7.03	33,407	898.0	17.7.06	17.7.13	
	21.7.04	75,678	892.0	21.7.07	21.7.14	
	20.7.05	77,102	1,070.0	20.7.08	20.7.15	
	26.7.06	71,378	1,282.0	26.7.09	26.7.16	339,856 (2006 268,478)
P N Hawker	18.7.01	10,253	1,083.0	18.7.04	18.7.11	
	17.7.02	15,606	865.0	17.7.05	17.7.12	
	17.7.03	21,158	898.0	17.7.06	17.7.13	
	21.7.04	36,746	892.0	21.7.07	21.7.14	
	20.7.05	37,850	1,070.0	20.7.08	20.7.15	
	26.7.06	34,518	1,282.0	26.7.09	26.7.16	156,131 (2006 127,743)
D W Morgan	18.7.01	18,098	1,083.0	18.7.04	18.7.11	
	17.7.02	25,433	865.0	17.7.05	17.7.12	
	17.7.03	26,726	898.0	17.7.06	17.7.13	
	21.7.04	44,397	892.0	21.7.07	21.7.14	
	20.7.05	39,252	1,070.0	20.7.08	20.7.15	
	26.7.06	35,104	1,282.0	26.7.09	26.7.16	189,010 (2006 153,906)
L C Pentz	22.7.99	12,158	585.5	22.7.02	22.7.09	
	19.7.00	8,224	942.0	19.7.03	19.7.10	
	18.7.01	12,952	1,083.0	18.7.04	18.7.11	
	17.7.02	17,730	865.0	17.7.05	17.7.12	
	17.7.03	22,185	898.0	17.7.06	17.7.13	
	21.7.04	34,857	892.0	21.7.07	21.7.14	
	20.7.05	37,850	1,070.0	20.7.08	20.7.15	
	26.7.06	34,518	1,282.0	26.7.09	26.7.16	180,474 (2006 145,956)
J N Sheldrick	18.7.01	25,854	1,083.0	18.7.04	18.7.11	
	17.7.02	34,682	865.0	17.7.05	17.7.12	
	17.7.03	36,191	898.0	17.7.06	17.7.13	
	21.7.04	58,861	892.0	21.7.07	21.7.14	
	20.7.05	52,570	1,070.0	20.7.08	20.7.15	
	26.7.06	46,804	1,282.0	26.7.09	26.7.16	254,962 (2006 208,158)

[1] subject to meeting the relevant performance targets.

Between 1st April 2006 and 31st March 2007 the following options were exercised:

	Date of grant	Date of exercise	Options exercised	Exercise price (pence)	Market price on exercise (pence)
P N Hawker	19.7.00	6.2.07	6,130	942.0	1,583.0

Gains made on exercise of options by directors during the year totalled £39,293 (2006 £645,429).

The closing market price of the company's shares at 30th March 2007 was 1,576 pence and the range during 2006/07 was 1,237 pence to 1,639 pence.

REMUNERATION REPORT

Directors' Interests (continued)

3. LTIP Allocations

Number of allocated shares:

	As at 31st March 2006	Allocations during the year	Market price at date of allocation (pence)	Shares released during the year	Allocations lapsed during the year	As at 31st March 2007
N A P Carson	165,787	56,148	1,358.0	16,968	16,968	187,999
P N Hawker	73,003	21,723	1,358.0	10,747	10,746	73,233
D W Morgan	84,775	22,091	1,358.0	13,575	13,574	79,717
L C Pentz	72,783	21,723	1,358.0	11,269	11,268	71,969
J N Sheldrick	113,540	29,455	1,358.0	18,382	18,382	106,231

On 1st August 2006 the 2003 LTIP allocation was released to participants. The release of this allocation was subject to the achievement of performance targets which contained two components – relative TSR and absolute TSR. Further details of the performance targets can be found on page 42. The company's TSR performance relative to the comparator group was below the 50th percentile, which qualified for a nil release of half the allocated shares. The company achieved absolute TSR growth of 66.9% during the performance period. This qualified for a full release of the other half of the allocated shares and resulted in the following gains:

	Number of shares released	Share price when released (pence)	Gain £
N A P Carson	16,968	1,291.5	219,142
P N Hawker	10,747	1,291.5	138,798
D W Morgan	13,575	1,291.5	175,321
L C Pentz	11,269	1,291.5	145,539
J N Sheldrick	18,382	1,291.5	237,404

Pensions

Pensions and life assurance benefits for the executive directors are provided through the company's final salary occupational pension scheme for UK employees – the Johnson Matthey Employees Pension Scheme (JMEPS) – which is constituted under a separate Trust Deed. JMEPS is an exempt approved scheme under Chapter I of Part XIV of the Income & Corporation Taxes Act 1988. It is a registered scheme for the purposes of the Finance Act 2004.

On 6th April 2006 the Finance Act 2004 introduced changes to the taxation of benefits payable from registered UK pension schemes. Unless protected under transitional arrangements, retirement benefits that exceed a capital value – called the Life Time Allowance – will be subject to an additional tax charge. Any such tax charge arising out of membership of JMEPS will be paid by the trustees at the point of retirement and the member's benefits will be reduced accordingly. Executive directors whose retirement benefits are valued in excess of the Life Time Allowance may withdraw from service in JMEPS and receive instead a supplemental payment of 25% of basic salary each year, which is taxable. Messrs Carson and Hawker withdrew from JMEPS and ceased paying member contributions on 31st March 2006. No pensionable service in JMEPS has been accrued by either director since that date. The increase in accrued pension in the tables below is attributable to the increase in basic salary.

The Finance Act 2004 also enables authorised schemes to remove the restriction imposed by the 'earnings cap' under the Finance Act No. 2, 1989. As a result, the accrued pensions for Messrs Morgan and Sheldrick for service from 6th April 2006 are calculated by reference to normal JMEPS rules and actual basic salary. Accrued pensions in respect of service prior to that date remain restricted by reference to the 'earnings cap' (see note 6 below).

From 1st April 2007, member contributions paid by executive directors to JMEPS will increase from 4% to 5% of pensionable pay (i.e. basic salary). There will be further increases to 6% and 7% on 1st April 2008 and 1st April 2009 respectively.

Disclosure of directors' pension benefits has been made under the requirements of the United Kingdom Listing Authority Listing Rules and in accordance with the Directors' Remuneration Report Regulations 2002. The information below sets out the disclosures under the two sets of requirements.

a. United Kingdom Listing Authority Listing Rules

	Age at 31st March 2007	Years of pensionable service at 31st March 2007	Directors' contributions to JMEPS in the year[1] £'000	Increase in accrued pension during the year (net of inflation)[2] £'000 pa	Total accrued pension at 31st March 2007[3] £'000 pa	Total accrued pension at 31st March 2006 £'000 pa	Transfer value of increase (less directors' contributions)[4] £'000
N A P Carson[5]	49	25	–	19	287	259	226
P N Hawker[5]	53	20	–	7	138	127	101
D W Morgan[6]	49	18	12	6	47	40	55
L C Pentz[7]	51	22	11	3	46	42	90
J N Sheldrick[6]	57	16	16	8	55	46	112

REMUNERATION REPORT

Pensions (continued)

b. Directors' Remuneration Report Regulations 2002

	Directors' contributions to JMEPS in the year[1] £'000	Increase in accrued pension during the year £'000 pa	Total accrued pension at 31st March 2007[3] £'000 pa	Transfer value of accrued pension at 31st March 2007[4] £'000	Transfer value of accrued pension at 31st March 2006[4] £'000	Increase in transfer value (net of directors' contributions) £'000
N A P Carson[5]	–	28	287	3,431	2,887	544
P N Hawker[5]	–	11	138	1,954	1,707	247
D W Morgan[6]	12	7	47	539	426	101
L C Pentz[7]	11	4	46	411	311	89
J N Sheldrick[6]	16	9	55	907	735	156

Notes

[1] Members' contributions were paid at the general scheme rate of 4% of pensionable pay (i.e. basic salary). This general rate will increase to 5% on 1st April 2007, with further increases to 6% and 7% on 1st April 2008 and 1st April 2009 respectively.

[2] The increase in accrued pension during the year excludes any increase for inflation.

[3] The entitlement shown under 'Total accrued pension at 31st March 2007' is the pension which would be paid annually on retirement, based on pensionable service to 31st March 2007, although pensionable service for Messrs Carson and Hawker ceased on 31st March 2006. The pension would, however, be subject to an actuarial reduction of 0.3% per month for each month that retirement precedes age 60.

[4] The transfer values have been calculated on the basis of actuarial advice in accordance with Actuarial Guidance Note 11. No allowance has been made in the transfer values for any discretionary benefits that have been or may be awarded under JMEPS. The transfer values in the Directors' Remuneration Report Regulations 2002 have been calculated at the start and the end of the year and, therefore, also take account of market movements.

[5] Mr Carson and Dr Hawker ceased to accrue pensionable service in JMEPS with effect from 31st March 2006. A cash payment in lieu of pension equal to 25% of basic salary has been made. This is taxable under the PAYE system and is included in the emoluments table on page 43.

[6] The JMEPS' benefits and contributions for Messrs Morgan and Sheldrick in respect of pensionable service up to 5th April 2006 are restricted by reference to the 'earnings cap' imposed by the Finance Act No. 2, 1989. Between 1st April 2000 and 31st March 2006, contributions were paid to Funded Unapproved Retirement Benefit Schemes (FURBS) to provide retirement and death benefits in relation to basic salary in excess of the 'earnings cap'. FURBS were not exempt approved under Chapter I of Part XIV of the Income & Corporation Taxes Act 1988 and so payments were also made to meet the tax liabilities in respect of these contributions. No FURBS payments have been made after 31st March 2006. Benefits and contributions in respect of service from 6th April 2006 have been provided by JMEPS in accordance with the normal scheme rules.

[7] Mr Pentz is a US citizen but became a member of JMEPS on 1st January 2006. Prior to that he was a member of the Johnson Matthey Inc. Salaried Employees Pension Plan (a non-contributory defined benefit arrangement) and a US savings plan (401k). He also has benefits in a Senior Executive Retirement Plan. The pension values reported above are the aggregate for his separate membership of the UK and US pension schemes and the Senior Executive Retirement Plan. US entitlements have been converted to sterling by reference to exchange rates on 31st March 2006 and 31st March 2007. Mr Pentz's US pension was fixed on 31st December 2005. The sterling equivalent of it has fallen over the year as a result of exchange rate movements and this reduction is reflected in the 'Increase in accrued pension during the year'. The 'Transfer value of increase' is the full value of the increase in his UK pension.

REMUNERATION REPORT

Johnson Matthey Total Shareholder Return and FTSE 100 rebased to 100

The following graph charts total cumulative shareholder return of the company for the five year period from 31st March 2002 to 31st March 2007 against the FTSE 100 as the most appropriate comparator group, rebased to 100 at 1st April 2002. Johnson Matthey joined the FTSE 100 on 12th June 2002.

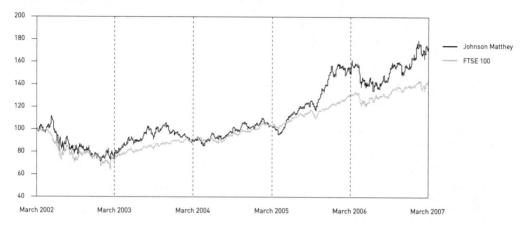

The Remuneration Report was approved by the Board of Directors on 5th June 2007 and signed on its behalf by:

Charles Mackay
Chairman of the Management Development and Remuneration Committee

RESPONSIBILITY OF DIRECTORS
for the preparation of the Annual Report and the accounts

The directors are responsible for preparing the Annual Report and the group and parent company accounts in accordance with applicable law and regulations.

Company law requires the directors to prepare group and parent company accounts for each financial year. Under that law they are required to prepare the group accounts in accordance with International Financial Reporting Standards (IFRS) as adopted by the European Union (EU) and applicable law and have elected to prepare the parent company accounts on the same basis.

The group and parent company accounts are required by law and IFRS as adopted by the EU to present fairly the financial position of the group and the parent company and the performance for that period; the Companies Act 1985 provides in relation to such accounts that references in the relevant part of that Act to accounts giving a true and fair view are references to their achieving a fair presentation.

In preparing each of the group and parent company accounts, the directors are required to:

- select suitable accounting policies and apply them consistently;
- make judgments and estimates that are reasonable and prudent;

- state whether they have been prepared in accordance with IFRS as adopted by the EU; and
- prepare the accounts on the going concern basis unless it is inappropriate to presume that the group and parent company will continue in business.

The directors are responsible for keeping proper accounting records which disclose with reasonable accuracy at any time the financial position of the parent company and enable them to ensure that its accounts comply with the Companies Act 1985. They have a general responsibility for taking such steps as are reasonably open to them to safeguard the assets of the group and to prevent and detect fraud and other irregularities.

Under applicable law and regulations the directors are also responsible for preparing a Directors' Report, Directors' Remuneration Report and Corporate Governance Statement that comply with that law and those regulations.

The directors are responsible for the maintenance and integrity of the corporate and financial information included on the company's website. Legislation in the UK governing the preparation and dissemination of accounts may differ from legislation in other jurisdictions.

INDEPENDENT AUDITORS' REPORT

to the members of Johnson Matthey Public Limited Company

We have audited the group and parent company accounts (the 'accounts') of Johnson Matthey Plc for the year ended 31st March 2007 which comprise the Consolidated Income Statement, the Consolidated and Parent Company Balance Sheets, the Consolidated and Parent Company Cash Flow Statements, the Consolidated and Parent Company Statements of Recognised Income and Expense and the related notes. These accounts have been prepared under the accounting policies set out therein. We have also audited the tabulated information and related footnotes set out in the directors' Remuneration Report on pages 42 to 48 disclosing the directors' emoluments and compensation, share options, long term incentive plan, pensions and other matters specified by Part 3 of Schedule 7A to the Companies Act 1985.

This report is made solely to the company's members, as a body, in accordance with section 235 of the Companies Act 1985. Our audit work has been undertaken so that we might state to the company's members those matters we are required to state to them in an auditor's report and for no other purpose. To the fullest extent permitted by law, we do not accept or assume responsibility to anyone other than the company and the company's members as a body, for our audit work, for this report, or for the opinions we have formed.

Respective Responsibilities of Directors and Auditors

The directors are responsible for preparing the Annual Report, the directors' Remuneration Report, the Corporate Governance statement and the accounts in accordance with applicable law and International Financial Reporting Standards (IFRS) as adopted by the EU as set out in the Responsibility of Directors statement on page 48.

Our responsibility is to audit the accounts and the part of the directors' Remuneration Report to be audited in accordance with relevant legal and regulatory requirements and International Standards on Auditing (UK and Ireland).

We report to you our opinion as to whether the accounts give a true and fair view and whether the accounts and the part of the directors' Remuneration Report to be audited have been properly prepared in accordance with the Companies Act 1985 and, as regards the group accounts, Article 4 of the IAS Regulation. We also report to you whether in our opinion the information given in the Directors' Report is consistent with the accounts. The information given in the Directors' Report includes that specific information presented in the Operating and Financial Review that is cross referenced from the Business Review section of the Directors' Report. In addition we report to you, if in our opinion, the company has not kept proper accounting records, if we have not received all the information and explanations we require for our audit, or if information specified by law regarding directors' remuneration and other transactions is not disclosed.

We review whether the Corporate Governance statement reflects the company's compliance with the nine provisions of the 2003 Combined Code specified for our review by the Listing Rules of the Financial Services Authority, and we report if it does not. We are not required to consider whether the board's statements on internal control cover all risks and controls, or form an opinion on the effectiveness of the group's corporate governance procedures or its risk and control procedures.

We read the other information contained in the Annual Report and consider whether it is consistent with the audited accounts. We consider the implications for our report if we become aware of any apparent misstatements or material inconsistencies with the accounts. Our responsibilities do not extend to any other information.

Basis of Audit Opinion

We conducted our audit in accordance with International Standards on Auditing (UK and Ireland) issued by the Auditing Practices Board. An audit includes examination, on a test basis, of evidence relevant to the amounts and disclosures in the accounts and the part of the directors' Remuneration Report to be audited. It also includes an assessment of the significant estimates and judgments made by the directors in the preparation of the accounts, and of whether the accounting policies are appropriate to the group's and company's circumstances, consistently applied and adequately disclosed.

We planned and performed our audit so as to obtain all the information and explanations which we considered necessary in order to provide us with sufficient evidence to give reasonable assurance that the accounts and the part of the directors' Remuneration Report to be audited are free from material misstatement, whether caused by fraud or other irregularity or error. In forming our opinion we also evaluated the overall adequacy of the presentation of information in the accounts and the part of the directors' Remuneration Report to be audited.

Opinion

In our opinion:

- the group accounts give a true and fair view, in accordance with IFRS as adopted by the EU, of the state of the group's affairs as at 31st March 2007 and of its profit for the year then ended;

- the parent company accounts give a true and fair view, in accordance with IFRS as adopted by the EU as applied in accordance with the provisions of the Companies Act 1985, of the state of the parent company's affairs as at 31st March 2007;

- the accounts and the part of the directors' Remuneration Report to be audited have been properly prepared in accordance with the Companies Act 1985 and, as regards the group accounts, Article 4 of the IAS Regulation; and

- the information given in the Directors' Report is consistent with the accounts.

KPMG Audit Plc
Chartered Accountants
Registered Auditor
London
5th June 2007

Johnson Matthey plc's corporate governance report, included on pages 38 to 40 of the Report and Accounts 2007, explains the roles and composition of each of the corporate governance committees:

- the chief executive's committee is responsible for recommending strategic and operating plans to the board of directors, and is chaired by the chief executive and comprises all the executive directors and three senior company executives
- the audit committee is a sub-committee of the board of directors and assists the board in meeting its responsibilities for financial reporting and corporate control, and is chaired by a non-executive director and comprises all non-executive directors plus the chairman, chief executive, and group finance director by invitation
- the nomination committee is a sub-committee of the board of directors responsible for advising the board and making recommendations on appointment of new directors, and is chaired by the chairman (contrary to the Higgs Report recommendation) and comprises all non-executive directors
- the management development and remuneration committee determines the remuneration of executive directors on behalf of the board of directors, and is chaired by a non-executive director and comprises all non-executive directors, and the chairman, chief executive, and human resources director attend by invitation except when their own performance and remuneration are being discussed.

The company does not appear to have an information technology (IT) committee or a capital expenditure committee, and so IT and capital expenditure are presumably the responsibility of the chief executive's committee.

Corporate social responsibility (CSR) reporting

Throughout the past 15 years or so companies have started to show greater interest in their position with regard to environmental and social issues. General corporate awareness has increased as to how the adoption of particular policies may have adverse social and environmental effects. Environmental issues naturally focus on our inability to sustain our use of non-renewable resources, the disappearance of the ozone layer, and deforestation, pollution, and waste treatment. Social issues may include problems associated with race, gender, disability, sexual orientation, and age, and the way that companies manage bullying, the incidence of accidents, employee welfare, training and development.

The increase in awareness of environmental and social issues has followed the concern that the focus of traditional reporting has been weighted too heavily towards the requirements of shareholders, with too little regard for the other stakeholders. This has led to an over-emphasis on the financial performance, particularly the profitability, of the business. The accountancy profession and other interested parties have given thought to the widening of the annual report and accounts to meet the requirements of all stakeholders, and not just the shareholders of the business.

In March 2000, the UK Government appointed a Minister for Corporate Social Responsibility. The Government's first report on corporate social responsibility (CSR) was published in March 2001, which has been followed by subsequent reports, all of which can be accessed from its website devoted to CSR, www.CSR.gov.uk. The Government sees CSR as the business contribution to sustainable development goals. They regard CSR as essentially about how business takes account of its economic, social, and environmental impacts in the way it operates – maximising the benefits and minimising the downsides. CSR is about companies moving beyond a base of legal compliance to integrating socially responsible behaviour into their core values, in recognition of the sound business benefits in doing so. In principle, CSR applies to small and medium enterprises (SMEs) as well as to large companies, who are now generally increasing their reporting on their CSR performance, which includes areas such as health and safety, the environment, equal opportunities, employee development, and ethical issues. Johnson Matthey's Report and Accounts 2007 includes a comprehensive report on its corporate social responsibility performance. The importance of CSR is emphasised by Johnson Matthey – it not only has its own separate section of the report and accounts on pages 25 to 33, but it is mentioned in the chairman's report, the chief executive's report (with regard to acid gas emissions, global warming potential, energy consumption, water consumption, and total waste), and is also referred to in the corporate governance section.

There is currently no consensus of 'best practice' in the area of social and environmental reporting. Nor is there a compulsory requirement for companies to include such statements in their annual reports and accounts. The Government's approach is to encourage the adoption and reporting of CSR through best practice guidance, including development of its Corporate Responsibility Index and, where appropriate, intelligent regulation and fiscal incentives. Most large companies have reacted positively to the need for such reporting, although the quality, style and content, and the motives for inclusion, may vary. Motives may range from a genuine wish to contribute to the goal of sustainable development to simple reassurance, or attempts to mould and change opinion, and political lobbying.

Companies that include CSR reporting in their annual reports and accounts are now endeavouring to go beyond a simple outline of their environmental and social policies. Many companies include reports expanding on these policies in qualitative terms, which explain the performance of the business in its compliance with national and international standards. Some companies have taken the next step to provide detailed quantitative reports of targets and performance and the financial impact of social and environmental issues.

CSR performance reporting is still in its infancy. The current UK Government is actively supporting the creation of a shift in the UK enterprise culture. It has emphasised how companies engaged in CSR are reporting benefits to their reputation and their bottom line. It seems likely that as the focus on standardisation of targets, indicators, and audit of social and environmental performance increases, then the pressure for wider reporting will increase, and be supported by a CSR performance reporting standard.

The audit and the role of auditors

The annual audit of the accounts is a statutory requirement for all limited companies, excluding smaller limited companies. The auditors of a limited company are appointed by, and are responsible to, the shareholders. Their primary responsibility is to make an objective report to shareholders and others as to whether, in their opinion, the financial statements show a true and fair view, and comply with statutory, regulatory, and accounting and financial reporting standard requirements. The auditors appointed by the shareholders are not employees of the company, but individual accountants or firms of accountants who are referred to as external auditors. Their roles and responsibilities are completely different to those of internal auditors.

Internal auditors are employees of the company. They are responsible and normally accountable to a non-executive director's audit committee within the company and independent of any functional activity or procedure within the company. The primary functions of an internal auditor are to:

- examine and evaluate how the company is managing its operational or strategic risks
- provide the company (audit committee or the board of directors) with information about whether risks have been identified, and how well such risks are being managed
- offer an independent opinion on the effectiveness and efficiency of internal controls (current operation protocols, policies, and procedures)
- review accounting information systems development to ensure that appropriate internal controls policies and procedures are maintained
- provide consultancy services and undertake special reviews at the request of management.

The role of an internal auditor includes:

- appraisal of the efficiency of operational activities of the company
- assessment of the effectiveness of internal administrative and accounting controls
- evaluation of conformance with managerial procedures and policies

and generally involves undertaking a wide range of audits, examinations, and reviews, including:

- systems based audits
- internal control evaluations
- risk appraisals
- governance reviews
- security audits, particularly of computer-based information systems.

An external auditor is independent of the company and is appointed or reappointed annually at the company's annual general meeting (AGM). The role and duties of an external auditor in the UK are regulated by provisions of UK corporate legislation. The external auditor's primary functions and duties are provided in the UK within the Companies Act 1985 (s 235 and s 237). Under these provisions, as part of a statutory annual audit, an external auditor is required to report to the company shareholders stating whether in their opinion:

- the company's financial statements provide a true and fair view of the company's state of affairs as at the end of the financial year, and its profit and loss accounting for the year
- that such financial statements have been properly prepared in accordance with the requirements of the Companies Act 1985 (as amended 1989).

Essentially, an external auditor is required to ensure that the company has maintained proper underlying accounting records, and the financial statements are in agreement with the underlying accounting records.

As noted earlier, an annual audit of the accounts is a statutory requirement for all limited companies, except for those currently having an annual turnover of less than £5.6m and a balance sheet total of less than £2.8m (refer to the Department of Trade and Industry website www.dti.com for changes to these limits). The shareholders of a limited company are responsible for appointing suitably qualified, independent persons, either individually or as a firm, to act as auditors. The external auditors are not part of the company but are responsible to the shareholders, with a main duty of objectively reporting to shareholders and others as to whether, in their opinion, the financial statements show a true and fair view, and comply with statutory, regulatory, and accounting requirements. Such an opinion is referred to as an unqualified opinion.

The report of the auditors is usually very short and additionally includes:

- reference to the directors' responsibility for preparation of the annual report and accounts
- reference to the responsibility as auditors being established by:
  - UK statute
  - the Auditing Practices Board (APB)
  - the Listing Rules of the Financial Services Authority
  - the accountancy profession's ethical guidance.

The auditors are required to explain the basis of the audit, and report if in their opinion:

- the directors' report is not consistent with the accounts
- the company has not kept proper accounting records
- they have not received all the information and explanations required for the audit
- information specified by law, or the Listing Rules regarding directors' remuneration and transactions with the company, is not disclosed
- company policies are appropriate and consistently applied and adequately disclosed
- all information and explanations considered necessary provide sufficient evidence to give reasonable assurance that the accounts are free from material misstatement
- the overall presentation of information in the accounts is adequate.

There may very occasionally be circumstances when the financial statements are affected by an inherent, and fundamental uncertainty. In such cases the auditors are obliged to draw attention to the fundamental uncertainty. If the fundamental uncertainty is adequately accounted for and disclosed in the financial statements then the opinion of the auditors may remain unqualified. If there is inadequate disclosure about the fundamental uncertainty then the auditors must give what is termed a qualified opinion. A qualified **audit report** is something that may destroy company credibility and create uncertainty, and is obviously something to be avoided.

In addition to their reporting on the financial statements of the company, auditors' reports now include a statement of the company's corporate governance compliance with the seven provisions of the Combined Code of Practice. This review is in accordance with guidelines issued by the APB. The auditors are not required to:

- consider whether the statements by the directors on internal control cover all risks and controls
- form an opinion on the effectiveness of the company's corporate governance procedures or its risk management and internal control procedures
- form an opinion on the ability of the company to continue in operational existence.

The audit and the perceived role of auditors has been the subject of much criticism over the years and there is a gap between what the audit provides and what people think it provides. The responsibility of the auditors does not, for example, include guarantees that:

- the financial statements are correct
- the company will not fail
- there has been no fraud.

This gap, 'the expectations gap', between public expectation and what the audit actually provides is understandable in the light of the numerous examples of company failures and financial scandals over the past 20 years. These led to a lack of confidence of the business community in financial reporting, and in shareholders being unable to rely on safeguards they assumed would be provided by their auditors.

The problem is that 'correctness' of financial statements is an unachievable result. We have seen from our consideration of both the balance sheet and income statement in Chapter 1 that there is a great deal of inconsistency in the area of asset valuation, and a high level of subjective judgement required in their preparation. Directors are required to prepare accounts, on which auditors are required to give an opinion that they give a true and fair view rather than that they are deemed 'correct'.

Companies and therefore their shareholders increasingly face a greater diversity and level of risk in a number of areas:

■ financial risk
■ commercial risk
■ operational risk,

and the increasing possibility of corporate failure is very real. Although the financial statements of companies are based on the going concern concept, the directors and auditors cannot realistically give any assurance that those businesses will not fail.

An area of risk that is of increasing concern to companies is fraud. This is perhaps due to:

■ the increasing pace of economic, social, political, and technological change
■ widespread use of computer systems
■ ease and speed of communications and transfer of funds
■ use of the Internet
■ increase in staff mobility
■ increasing dependence on specific knowledge (for example, Nick Leeson and Barings, and dot.com companies' IT experts).

Fraud is perhaps something on which auditors may arguably be expected to give an opinion. This is not something that is currently required from an external audit. It is something for which an **internal audit** department may be responsible for investigating. In the same way, external auditors could be requested to report on the adequacy or otherwise of systems of internal control.

Major corporate fraud is now increasingly associated with communications and IT systems. The use of internal (or external) audit for the:

■ detection of fraud
■ minimisation of fraud
■ elimination of fraud

therefore tends to be specialised and is something for which the costs and benefits must be carefully evaluated.

Progress check 3.2

What is an external audit and to whom are the auditors responsible, and for what?

The report of the independent auditors, KPMG, to the shareholders of Johnson Matthey plc, included on page 49 of the Report and Accounts 2007, is reproduced on page 104. Johnson Matthey plc can be seen to have complied with the standard audit reporting requirements relating to the company's financial statements and all other information disclosure. The audit report also includes a section on the responsibilities of the directors and auditors, and the basis of their audit opinion. The report includes confirmation that Johnson Matthey's corporate governance report reflects the company's compliance with the nine provisions of the 2003 FRC Combined Code, specified for their review by the Listing Rules of the Financial Services Authority. KPMG also state that they are not required to consider whether the board's statements on internal control cover all risks and controls, or form an opinion on the effectiveness of the group's corporate governance procedures or its risk and control procedures.

KPMG's audit report concludes with their opinion that:

- the group accounts give a 'true and fair view' of the state of the group's affairs in 2007
- the group accounts comply with the IFRS as adopted by the European Union, and with the provisions of the UK Companies Act 1985
- the accounts and the part of the directors' remuneration report which is audited have been prepared in accordance with the Companies Act 1985 and relevant IAS
- the directors' report is consistent with the accounts.

It may be interesting to compare the auditors' report for, say, 1997 with the same report for the year 2007, in which so many more areas are covered, and now highlight the current importance of corporate governance.

Worked Example 3.2

The audit is the objective review (or sometimes the detailed examination) of business systems and transactions. A business may employ internal and external auditors. The latter are considered the more independent, although both are paid by the business. External auditors are appointed by, and report to, the shareholders, whereas the internal auditors report to the company's audit committee.

(i) Why should the external auditors of a plc report direct to the shareholders and not to the chairman of the company?

(ii) Why should the internal auditors of a plc report to the audit committee and not to the finance director?

(iii) In what ways may the independence of a company's audit committee be demonstrated?

The answers to these questions are:

(i) The external auditors are appointed by and are responsible to the shareholders. The AGM is the formal meeting of directors, shareholders, and auditors. Conceivably, the chairman could shelve the report, with shareholders unaware of the contents. The law is quite strict on auditors' access to the shareholders.

(ii) The finance director is responsible for the system of recording transactions. The finance director could prevent vital information from the internal auditors being distributed to others in the organisation.

(iii) The audit committee may request the non-executive directors to review specific areas, for example, the output from the internal auditors. The audit committee meets many times during the year and it offers a degree of objectivity. The careers of its members do not depend on the continuance of their directorship.

The directors of a company may not be accountants and they very rarely have any hands-on involvement with the actual putting-together of a set of accounts for the company. However, directors of companies must make it their business to be fully conversant with the content of the accounts of their companies. Directors are responsible for ensuring that proper accounting records are maintained, and for ensuring reasonably accurate reporting of the financial position and financial performance of their company, and ensuring their compliance with the Companies Act 1985/1989. Johnson Matthey plc's Report and Accounts 2007 includes on page 48 a section headed Responsibility of Directors, which details the responsibilities of its directors in the preparation of its accounts.

We will consider the role of directors and their responsibilities in more detail, and with regard to the corporate governance Combined Code of Practice. We will also look at some of the circumstances in which directors of limited companies are particularly vulnerable, and how these may lead to disqualification of directors.

The fact that a corporate governance Code of Practice exists or even that the appropriate corporate governance committees have been established is not necessarily a guarantee of effective corporate governance. There have been many examples of companies that have had corporate governance committees in place relating to directors and their remuneration, relations with shareholders, accountability, and audit. Nevertheless, these companies have given cause for great concern from shareholders following much-publicised revelations about financial scandals and apparent loosely-adhered-to corporate governance practices.

Such examples have been by no means confined to the UK, as the press extract below illustrates. Dennis Kozlowski was the head of the conglomerate Tyco International from 1992 to 2002, which enjoyed phenomenal growth from the acquisition of hundreds of companies involved in widely diverse industries. Kozlowski once told a reporter: 'We don't believe in perks, not even executive parking spots.' In the USA, during an extremely long and complicated case against Kozlowski for fraud, it appears that he in fact received an inordinately large volume of perks himself, either legally or illegally.

Tyco – another huge fraud case in the USA?

'Time for Kozlowski to pick up the tab?', by Richard Sykes

Dennis Kozlowski fancied himself as Jack Welch and Warren Buffett genetically melded into the body of a beefy, regular guy from New Jersey.

As head of the conglomerate Tyco International from 1992 to 2002, he oversaw the dizzying takeover of hundreds of big and small companies at a cost of $60bn (£34bn), in businesses as diverse as surgical equipment, disposable nappies and security systems. What's more, Koz pitched himself as a legendary tight-fist, and became a Wall Street darling.

For a company with more than 200,000 employees scattered across 2,342 subsidiaries and generating $36bn in annual revenues, Tyco's head office in a bland two-storey wooden building in Exeter, New Hampshire, housed just 20 full-time employees.

'We don't believe in perks,' Kozlowski once told a visiting journalist. 'Not even executive parking spots.'

It turns out Koz may have been fudging it a smidge. In the indictment against Kozlowski and his chief financial officer, Mark Swartz, by the New York District Attorney Robert Morgenthau, Tyco's headquarters while under their command is charmingly referred to as TEXCE. That is short for 'Top Executive Criminal Enterprise'.

The DA's case against them argues that the perception of 'frugality' and the tiny number of people with their hands in the till helped make Tyco a 'personal piggy bank' for the duo. For the past six months Koz, 57, and Swartz, 43, have been on trial for allegedly pilfering a staggering $600m (£341m).

▶

▶ Prosecutors say they snagged $170m through unauthorised bonuses and abuses of a company loan programme and netted another $430m by pumping Tyco shares by misleading the stock market about Tyco's results and then dumping their holdings.

Compared with the 'Marthathon', the lengthy and complex Tyco proceedings haven't received heaps of attention. (There is one odd similarity, however: both Koz and Stewart – her maiden name is Koystra – hailed from working-class Polish families in New Jersey.)

But Koz may be ready for his close-up now that the trial is wrapped up: the jury could deliver its verdict as soon as this week.

In fact, Stewart's obstruction of justice doesn't even register compared with the epic scale of the charges against Kozlowski. It is the first real attempt by a criminal court to hold accountable corporate executives for the alleged fraudulent pumping of their stocks during the bull market.

Indeed, as 'nothing exceeds like excess' scandals go, Koz's ordeal offered something for everyone. Toys? Check. Koz has plenty, including three Harley-Davidson motorcycles, a classic sailing yacht and a private plane to whisk him between his grand homes in New York, New Hampshire, Nantucket and Florida.

Furnishings and antiques – including the now legendary $6,000 wastebasket and $15,000 umbrella stand – were charged to the company account.

Ladies? Check. The trial featured testimony from former Koz paramours and the disclosure of his divorce agreement with former wife Angie, who was entitled to $30m in cash plus two New York apartments and homes in Connecticut, New Hampshire and Florida – not to mention a new Mercedes every three years. These obligations were depicted by prosecutors as the potential motivation for a successful executive making millions a year to carry on looting his company for much more.

Parties? Check. There was of course the infamous 40th birthday party held for his wife Karen in Sardinia in 2001, half of its $2m cost – including a vodka-peeing ice sculpture and Jimmy Buffett performance – on the Tyco tab.

Interesting pals? Check. Probably the most fascinating tale to emerge during the testimony was Koz's closeness to Phua Young, an analyst hired to cover Tyco for Merrill Lynch after Koz complained to Merrill's CEO about his company's coverage in 1999.

In addition to being unfailingly bullish on Tyco stock – Young once described himself as being 'indirectly paid by Tyco' – the analyst also fell in love during those heady times with a woman he met in Singapore. Young then did what any person in that situation would do: he asked Tyco for assistance in hiring a private detective to investigate her, which Kozlowski agreed to do at a cost of some $20,000.

Fortunately, the woman checked out, and she and the analyst were married. Unfortunately, Young was fired by Merrill in 2002 for improper conduct and has been charged by securities regulators with publishing misleading research on Tyco.

'Greed is greed, and sometimes when you have a lot you want more,' Ann Donnelly, the assistant district attorney, said of Kozlowski and Swartz. 'They have an extravagant lifestyle and there is nothing wrong with that. But you have to pay for it. Don't these guys have credit cards? Don't they have chequebooks? Why does Tyco have to buy a house for every place they travel to?'

For their closing arguments last week, Donnelly and her colleagues displayed a large chart outlining for the jury the 32 counts against Koz and Swartz, just as they did when the case opened. The charges include grand larceny, conspiracy, falsifying business records and violating state business laws.

The grand larceny charge alone is punishable by up to 25 years in prison. (Earlier this month the judge did throw out a charge of 'enterprise corruption', a statute normally applied to mob figures.)

It all seems very sensational, but the reality is that the proceedings have been convoluted and tiring. Kozlowski's lawyer, Stephen Kaufman, argued to the jury that his client might be culpable in a civil court for misusing shareholder funds but he is no criminal.

And he played a bit of a post-Martha card when he urged the jury not to view his client's case as a chance to 'win one for the little guy'. He pointed out that 'we're not WorldCom, we're not Adelphia, we're not Enron'.

Indeed, those three companies, whose former CEOs are being prosecuted for fraud, are all now bankrupt. Tyco stock isn't the high flier it was in Koz's day, but it's still plugging along.

In his two hours of instruction to the jury, Judge Michael Obus told them that their purpose is a 'narrow one' and that they should not 'evaluate any other cases you might have heard about' or be 'judges of corporate governance'.

Indeed, the only question is whether Kozlowski, the man who 'doesn't believe in perks', was legally entitled to an obscenely super-sized helping of them.

© *Daily Telegraph*, 21 March 2004

The case against Mr Kozlowski and the former chief financial officer of Tyco, Mark Swartz, collapsed in a mistrial in April 2004 when a juror began receiving threats. However, a retrial was arranged and both Dennis Kozlowski and Mark Swartz were sentenced to 25 years in jail for stealing more than US$150m (£82m) from the company (see the press extract below).

Tyco – the conclusion

'Tyco two get up to 25 years jail', story from BBC News

Two former bosses of US manufacturer Tyco have been sentenced to up to 25 years in jail for stealing more than $150m (£82m) from the company.

Former Tyco chief executive Dennis Kozlowski and finance chief Mark Swartz were taken from the court in handcuffs.

They were also ordered to repay most of the money, which they spent on expensive jewellery, luxury apartments and giant $2m Mediterranean parties.

The pair, who denied the charges, were convicted in June at their retrial.

Their first trial collapsed in April 2004 after a juror received a threatening phone call and letter. Both were heard in New York.

Appeals planned

Judge Michael Obus sentenced the pair to between 8 1/3 years and 25 years.

The judge ordered them to pay $134m in restitution. In addition, Kozlowski was fined $70m and Swartz $35m.

Kozlowski, 58, and Swartz, 44, have said they will appeal against the verdicts.

During the trial, the court heard that the former bosses took the money through secret loans that were then simply forgotten, as well as unauthorised bonuses.

Examples of their lavish lifestyle quoted in court included a $2m toga party on a Mediterranean island for Kozlowski's wife's birthday and an $18m apartment in Manhattan.

Tyco employs 250,000 people in 2,000 locations around the world and sells electronic, healthcare, and plastics supplies.

© BBC MMVI, 19 September 2005

Directors' responsibilities

The board of directors of a limited company is appointed by, and is responsible to, the shareholders for the management of the company, maintained through their regular reporting on the activities of the business. Some directors may be senior managers employed within the business. Other directors may be non-executive directors who are not employed by the company. As we saw in Chapter 1 from the organisation chart in Fig. 1.3, in addition to a chairman, the board of directors comprises a chief executive (or managing director), and may include non-executive directors and executive directors responsible for each of the key areas of the business, for example:

- research and development
- sales and marketing
- human resources
- purchasing
- quality
- engineering

- manufacturing
- logistics
- information technology
- finance and accounting.

From Johnson Matthey's Report and Accounts 2007 we can see on page 34 that its board of directors comprises a chairman, chief executive, four executive directors, and five non-executive directors.

Even though each director may have specific functional responsibilities, they also have general responsibilities as agents of the shareholders to manage the business in accordance with the objectives of the shareholders. The responsibilities of directors, however, are wider than to just the shareholders. They are also responsible for acting correctly towards their employees, suppliers, customers, and the public at large.

Agency and the ethical dimension

In Chapter 2 we introduced agency theory and saw how directors and managers of a company may not always act in the best interests of the shareholders. The agency problem manifests itself in a number of ways, for example through improper behaviour by managers and directors, such as:

- fraudulent activity
- misuse of company assets
- empire building
- awarding themselves excessive salaries, benefits, and perks.

The agency problem may also manifest itself in poor decision-making by managers and directors resulting in:

- a lack of investment in high risk, value-adding projects investments – managers may prefer 'safer' options that do not put their jobs at risk
- investment in projects that generate negative NPVs (net present values) – managers may use inappropriate investment appraisal techniques
- a focus on earnings per share (eps) maximisation (which may be the basis of directors' incentive schemes), instead of shareholder wealth maximisation.

Jensen and Meckling (Jensen MC, Meckling WH (1976) 'Theory of the firm: managerial behaviour, agency costs, and ownership structure' *Journal of Financial Economics 3* October, 305–360) identified alternative approaches to try and ensure that managers' and directors' objectives are aligned with shareholders' objectives. Their first approach considers how managers' and directors' behaviour may be monitored by shareholders by obtaining reports on their performance, work shadowing, and independent audits and analysis. This approach may be costly compared with the benefits derived from the alignment of managers' behaviour. It may also be impossible to spread such costs between all shareholders, and so the burden may fall on a few major shareholders, but with any resultant benefits being received by all shareholders.

Jensen and Meckling's alternative approach to achievement of goal congruence is to try and induce managers and directors on a contractual basis. Service contracts for directors and senior managers may include incentives to motivate goal congruence such as performance related pay and share option schemes, as discussed in Chapter 2.

Both approaches therefore incur agency costs of monitoring or inducement. Regardless of whichever approach has been adopted by companies, there have been obvious failures, which is apparent from the number of corporate financial scandals that have occurred. It was not only the 1980s and early 1990s that saw corporate scandals and irregularities (for example, Polly Peck, and the Maxwell companies). At the end of 1999, accounting irregularities caused trading in engineering company TransTec shares to be suspended, with Arthur Andersen called in as administrative receiver. The case was fuelled by the revelation by former TransTec chief accountant Max Ayris that nearly £500,000 of a total of £1.3m in grants from the Department of Trade and Industry was obtained fraudulently. TransTec, founded by former Government minister Geoffrey Robinson, collapsed in December 1999, after the accounting irregularities were discovered, with debts of more than £70m. Following the collapse of the company the role of the auditors to the company, PricewaterhouseCoopers, was also examined by the Joint Disciplinary Scheme, the accountancy professions' senior watchdog.

Also during 1999, the trade finance group Versailles discovered that there had been some double counting of transactions, which prompted the Department of Trade and Industry to take a close interest in its affairs. Actual and apparent corporate misdemeanours continued, on an even larger scale, through the late 1990s and on into the 21st century, including the Barings debacle, Tyco (see the earlier press extracts), and perhaps most notably WorldCom and Enron which were described in Chapter 1.

As we have seen, in the wake of these financial scandals corporate governance guidelines have been developed on a worldwide basis essentially to try and deal with the agency problem relating to directors and shareholders. However, it may also be useful to consider the ethical dimension of agency rather than just the governance framework.

We made the assumption at the start of this book that maximisation of shareholder wealth is the primary objective of companies. Should we believe that in the real world the majority of company directors and managers act with integrity, and are they law-abiding, honest, and conscientious in their efforts to maximise shareholder wealth? Alternatively, should we believe that the majority of company directors are greedy individuals who act purely in their own self-interest rather than looking after the interests of the shareholders? It has been suggested that perhaps managers should not be required to act in the best interests of shareholders. There is a body of opinion that argues that managers and directors of companies should actually look after themselves rather than the interests of the shareholders.

However, there may not actually be a conflict between the value-adding objective and acting with integrity and honesty. At the outset, in order to create any wealth at all directors and managers must ensure that the business is run on a cost-effective basis and satisfies its customers by providing goods and services at the quality and price they require. To achieve this, managers and directors will generally observe the unwritten rules and codes of good business behaviour. They do this because such codes have stood the test of time and generally work in everyone's interest. Directors and managers of companies are also aware that the credibility and good name of their businesses are key assets, and therefore their honesty, integrity, and trustworthiness are paramount.

In the area of corporate finance the reputation of a business is particularly important because there is not always absolute certainty about the product being bought and sold. For example, there is a big difference between buying a security and buying a refrigerator with regard to information asymmetry. When you buy a refrigerator you probably know as much about the product as the seller, which is unlikely to be the case when you buy a security. The businesses of financial institutions and banks are built on establishing unblemished reputations for honesty, integrity, and square dealing. Anything that dents that reputation will be regarded as unacceptable and may cost them dearly.

Even if we assume that managers and directors of businesses generally act with honesty and integrity it is not always clear what is and what is not ethical behaviour. There are many grey areas and many not so grey areas of what may be considered unethical, for example:

- importing of clothing, footwear, and consumer goods from countries which exploit employment of children and other low cost labour
- supply of cosmetics and pharmaceuticals which have been developed using testing on animals
- manufacture and sale of tobacco products
- manufacture and sale of alcohol
- a company's employment of men and women with the same experience and qualifications at different salary levels
- the sale of car fuel at different prices in different areas of the country
- a bank's issue of an identical loan at one rate of interest to one company and another rate of interest to another company.

Whether or not companies rely on:

- performance monitoring of managers and directors, or
- contractual inducements, or
- unwritten codes of good business behaviour, or
- corporate governance systems

the 'good' management of a business is really dependent on individuals' personal values and ethical standards. Perhaps unethical people (for example the Tyco executives) will always find ways of getting round the system, whereas people of character will not.

Directors' obligations

The responsibilities of directors, in terms of the Combined Code of Practice, can be seen to be important and far-reaching. It has been said that being a director is easy, but being a responsible director is not. It is important for all directors to develop an understanding and awareness of their ever-increasing legal obligations and responsibilities to avoid the potential personal liabilities, and even disqualification, which are imposed if those obligations are ignored.

It can be seen that the aims of most of the codes of practice and legislation have been to promote better standards of management in companies. This has also meant penalising irresponsible directors, the effect of which has been to create an increasingly heavy burden on directors regardless of the size or nature of the business they manage. The Government is actively banning offending directors.

Directors' duties are mainly embodied in the:

- Companies Act 1985/1989
- Insolvency Act 1986 (as amended by the Enterprise Act 2002)
- Company Directors Disqualification Act 1986 (as amended by the Enterprise Act 2002)
- Enterprise Act 2002

- Health and Safety at Work Act 1974
- Financial Services Act 1986

and there is

- potential for legal action on **corporate manslaughter**.

In addition, it should be noted that further statutory provisions giving rise to vicarious liability of directors for corporate offences are included in Acts of Parliament, which currently number well over 200! Directors can be:

- forced to pay a company's losses
- fined
- prevented from running businesses
- imprisoned.

The Directors' Remuneration Report Regulations 2002 (Statutory Instrument 2002 No 1986) are now in force and require the directors of a company to prepare a remuneration report that is clear, transparent, and understandable to shareholders. Many smaller companies without continuous legal advice are unaware about how much the rules have tightened. It is usually not until there is wide publicity surrounding high-profile business problems that boards of directors are alerted to the demands and penalties to which they may be subjected if things go wrong.

Non-executive directors are legally expected to know as much as executive directors about what is going on in the company. Ignorance is not a defence. Directors must be aware of what is going on and have knowledge of the law relating to their duties and responsibilities. Fundamentally, directors must:

- use their common sense
- be careful in what they do
- look after shareholders
- look after creditors
- look after employees.

Progress check 3.3

What are the main responsibilities of directors with regard to the accounting and financial reporting of their companies?

Duty of care

It is the duty of a director to exercise his or her powers in the best interests of the company, which includes not acting for his or her personal benefit, nor improper use of company assets. In the year 2000, Greg Hutchings, the chairman of a major plc, Tomkins, was criticised for alleged excessive perks, unauthorised donations, and inclusion of members of his family and household staff on the company payroll, without proper disclosure. Investors' concern over corporate governance practices at the group had been triggered by a fall in the share price of over 50% in two years. The resignation of the chairman followed an initial investigation. The new chairman very quickly launched a full inquiry into executive perks within the group, overseen by him personally.

Duty of care means doing the job with the skill and care that somebody with the necessary knowledge and experience would exercise if they were acting on their own behalf. Delegation of directors' power must be 'properly and sensibly done'. If a director of a company does not choose the right people or supervise them properly, all the directors may be liable for the misdeeds and mistakes of the people they have appointed.

When a company fails and is found to be insolvent, the receiver appointed will leave no stone unturned to identify whether any money may be recovered in order to pay off creditors. This will include checking for any oversights by directors for items they should have spotted 'if they had exercised their proper level of skill'.

Progress check 3.4

What is a director's duty of care?

Fiduciary duty

Directors have a fiduciary duty to act in the best interests of the company. Courts will support directors who act honestly and in good faith. Acting in the best interests of the company includes not making personal profit at the company's expense, not letting personal interest interfere with the proper running of the business, or doing business which favours directors or their close associates. In the late 1990s and early 2000s there were several business failures within the dot.com sector, where directors did act in the best interests of the company although their business plans may not have been commercially successful (for example, www.breathe.com).

Progress check 3.5

What is a director's fiduciary duty?

Corporate manslaughter

There is an offence of corporate manslaughter, which a company may be guilty of if a failure by its management is the cause of a person's death, and their failure is because their conduct is well below what can be reasonably expected. Before 1999 there were only five prosecutions in the UK for corporate manslaughter, resulting in two convictions. The risk for companies and their directors is remote but very real, and should therefore be managed in terms of awareness, training, preventative measures, and liability insurance.

In earlier years companies were outside the criminal law. Witness the many thousands of Welsh coalminers who lost their lives or were severely disabled in the 19th and 20th centuries as a result of blatant disregard for personal safety and an unbridled pursuit of profit by mine owners. As one judge put it, 'a company had a soul to damn and no body to kick', meaning that because a company did not have an actual existence it could not be guilty of a crime because it could not have a guilty will. In 1965 a case established the validity of the indictment of a company for manslaughter. Since then over 19,000 people have been killed as a result of corporate activity, but no company stood trial for manslaughter, apart from P&O European Ferries (Dover) Ltd after the capsize and sinking of the *Herald of Free Enterprise* off Zeebrugge in 1987. The directors of P&O Ferries did stand trial, but were acquitted because the trial collapsed halfway through. To succeed in a case of corporate manslaughter against a company there is a need to prove gross negligence and to prove that at least one sufficiently senior official was guilty of that same gross negligence.

Although each year hundreds of people are killed at work or in commercially related activity, if companies have been prosecuted at all they have been charged under the Health and Safety at Work Act (1974) and other regulatory legislation. Many of the companies implicated in work fatalities and public transport disasters operate with diffuse management systems and much delegated power. Such systems that appear to have no 'controlling mind' make it difficult to meet the requirement of the law because of the difficulty in identifying the individual(s) who may possess the mental element for the crime.

A case that was successfully prosecuted involved a small company, OLL Ltd, which organised a canoe expedition at Lyme Bay in 1993, in which four teenage schoolchildren died. In 1994 the jury in the case found OLL Ltd guilty of manslaughter – a historic decision. Peter Kite, the managing director of the activity centre responsible for the canoeing disaster, was jailed for three years for manslaughter, and OLL Ltd was fined £60,000. OLL Ltd was the first company in the UK ever to be found guilty of manslaughter, in a decision that swept away 400 years of legal history.

The Lyme Bay case was atypical of corporate homicide incidents. The company was small, so it was relatively easy to discover the 'controlling mind'; the risks to which pupils were exposed were serious and obvious and, critically, they were not technical or esoteric in any way. Moreover, very unusually, the directors could not claim ignorance of the risks because of a damning letter they had received from former instructors telling them to improve safety at the centre.

Progress check 3.6

Why should companies be aware of the risk of corporate manslaughter?

Corporate manslaughter and the 'controlling mind'

'Rail chiefs on Hatfield manslaughter charges', by PA News and Angela Jameson

Six senior managers from Network Rail and Balfour Beatty were charged with manslaughter today in connection with the Hatfield train disaster. The two companies – Railtrack's successor and its maintenance firm – have also been charged with manslaughter and failure to discharge a duty under the Health and Safety at Work Act, the Crown Prosecution Service announced. Another six men received summonses for an offence under health and safety legislation, including Gerald Corbett, the former chief executive of Railtrack who is now the chairman of Woolworths.

British Transport Police confirmed that six men – four from Railtrack and two from Balfour – had been charged with gross

▶ negligence manslaughter and a health and safety offence. The maximum sentence for individuals is life in prison, while the companies face unlimited fines if found guilty. The prosecutions were revealed in *The Times* earlier this week. All are due to appear before Central Hertfordshire Magistrates' Court in St Albans on Monday morning.

Four people died in the October 17 2000 crash when a GNER express train derailed half a mile south of Hatfield station in Hertfordshire. Thirty police officers are understood to have been working on the case and to have interviewed about 100 people. The London to Leeds train derailed because of a broken rail, which both Railtrack and Balfour Beatty allegedly knew about.

The accident led to a network-wide inspection of tracks and speed restrictions on trains while work took place. Train punctuality has still not returned to pre-Hatfield levels and is not expected to for some years.

Solicitors representing the injured and families of the victims welcomed news of prosecutions, as did rail safety groups. Carol Bell, co-chairman of the Safe Trains Action Group, said: 'It is going to be really important for the families because it gives them a chance to put some kind of closure on it. If they decide to go to court it will be difficult but they will be glad that someone is taking responsibility for it'. Mrs Bell is a survivor of the 1997 Southall rail crash. But Balfour Beatty criticised the decision and defended its safety record.

In a statement, the company said: 'The charge of manslaughter against our maintenance business will be firmly defended as we see no plausible basis for it in law or on the evidence. The individuals charged will have the company's fullest support in their defence of the charges against them'. Network Rail also pledged to defend itself and its employees against the charges. 'As the company stated last week, we believe that our employees conduct their duties to the best of their abilities with the sole intention of delivering a safe, reliable and efficient railway network. It is now a matter for the courts and it would be inappropriate to comment further,' a statement said.

Andrew Faiers, a Crown Prosecutor, said that the decision to press charges was based on 'substantial evidence'. More than 1,500 witnesses gave evidence during the two-and-a-half year long probe. The police seized more than one million pages of documentary evidence.

The families of those who died at Hatfield have campaigned for a corporate manslaughter prosecution, as have relatives of victims of other rail accidents. It is difficult to obtain a conviction on such a charge, however. Great Western Trains was acquitted of the charge on a point of law when it was prosecuted for the 1997 Southall rail crash, but it was fined £1.5 million under health and safety legislation. Labour promised to update corporate manslaughter law in its 1997 manifesto and the Home Secretary has said that he intends to introduce a draft law in October to make it easier to prosecute companies, but that would not target individual directors. Under present corporate manslaughter law, a company can be convicted only if a person is identified as its 'controlling mind' and is found responsible for someone's death. If he or she is found not guilty, the company is cleared as well.

If a junior member of staff is responsible for safety, he or she is not regarded as a controlling mind and again the company escapes prosecution. In the Southall case, the CPS did not charge any individual with manslaughter, so the case against the company failed. Only small companies, where it is easy to establish the lines of responsibility, have been convicted of corporate manslaughter.

In 1994 Peter Kite, managing director of an activity centre responsible for a canoeing disaster that killed four children, was jailed for three years after his company became the first in the country to be convicted of manslaughter. It was fined £60,000. P&O European Ferries was prosecuted after the 1987 Zeebrugge disaster, but the case collapsed half-way through the trial.

© *The Times*, 9 July 2003

Great Western Trains was fined £1.5m over the Southall (1997) rail crash in which seven people were killed, following a Health and Safety Executive (HSE) prosecution. But no individual within the company was charged with manslaughter.

In 1999 the Paddington rail crash case resulted in 31 people being killed and over 400 injured. A case was again brought by the HSE. The company, Thames Trains, was fined £2m in

April 2004, but even though the HSE said its enquiries had revealed 'serious failing in management', there was no prosecution for corporate manslaughter.

In February 2004 in Tebay, Cumbria, one man from Cumbria and three men from Lancashire died after they were hit by a runaway railway wagon. The wagon was carrying 16 tonnes of steel rail tracks and it hit them when they were working on the west coast main line. Mark Connolly, the boss of MAC Machinery Services had deliberately disconnected the hydraulic brakes on two wagons because it was cheaper than repairing the wagons properly, and filled the cables with ball bearings instead of hydraulic fluid to give the impression that everything was OK. The crane operator, Roy Kennett used a large crane to lift lengths of steel on to the wagons. One wagon started to roll down the track because the brakes wouldn't hold it. The four men who died had no warning of its approach because of the noise of an on-site generator. The British Transport Police condemned Connolly for his greed and 'blatant and premeditated disregard for safety'. Kennett and Connolly were each found guilty on four counts of manslaughter and jailed for two years and nine years respectively. Mark Connolly was also found guilty on three counts, and Roy Kennett on one count, of breach of health and safety laws. Both men had denied the charges of manslaughter by criminal negligence but in March 2006 the jury returned a majority verdict of guilty.

A few years ago the legal profession considered that the promised review of the Law Commission's recommendation for an Involuntary Homicide Act 'could result in company directors being made personally responsible for safety and therefore potentially liable in cases of avoidable accidents'. The current Government promised to legislate on the issue of corporate manslaughter. In its consultation document in 2000 it considered a proposed offence of corporate killing, allowing easier prosecution of any employing organisation for a death that results from a serious management failure.

In May 2003 the Government said that it would issue a draft Bill on corporate manslaughter, and that it would target the companies themselves and not the criminal liability of individual directors, and would not set up a system of standards in parallel with existing health and safety standards. In November 2004 the Government included the issue of corporate manslaughter in the Queen's Speech, and placed it on their legislative agenda for 2005. The Bill went before Parliament in the latter part of 2006 and had 24 clauses and 2 schedules. It created a new offence in England, Wales, and Northern Ireland, called corporate manslaughter and, in Scotland, called corporate homicide. The Corporate Manslaughter & Corporate Homicide Act 2006 will apply to companies and other incorporated bodies, Government departments and similar bodies, and police forces.

Progress check 3.7

Why is it so difficult to bring a successful prosecution for corporate manslaughter?

Other responsibilities

Directors do not owe a direct duty to shareholders, but to the company itself. Directors have no contractual or fiduciary duty to outsiders and are generally not liable unless they have acted in breach of their authority. Directors must have regard to the interests of employees but this is enforceable against directors only by the company and not by the employees.

Insolvency

Insolvency, or when a company becomes insolvent, is when the company is unable to pay creditors' debts in full after realisation of all the assets of the business. The penalties imposed on directors of companies continuing to trade while insolvent may be disqualification and personal liability. Many directors have lost their houses (as well as their businesses) as a result of being successfully pursued by the receivers appointed to their insolvent companies.

The Insolvency Act 1986 (as amended by the Enterprise Act 2002) provides guidance on matters to be considered by liquidators and receivers in the reports, which they are required to prepare on the conduct of directors. These matters include:

- breaches of fiduciary and other duties to the company
- misapplication or retention of monies or other property of the company
- causing the company to enter into transactions which defrauded the creditors
- failure to keep proper accounting and statutory records
- failure to make annual returns to the Registrar of Companies and prepare and file annual accounts.

If a company is insolvent, the courts assess the directors' responsibility for:

- the cause of the company becoming insolvent
- the company's failure to supply goods or services which had been paid for
- the company entering into fraudulent transactions or giving preference to particular creditors
- failure of the company to adhere to the rules regarding creditors' meetings in a creditors' **voluntary winding-up**
- failure to provide a **statement of affairs** or to deliver up any proper books or information regarding the company.

Progress check 3.8

How does insolvency impact on directors and what are their responsibilities in this regard?

Wrongful trading

A major innovation of the Insolvency Act 1986 was to create the statutory tort (civil wrong) of **wrongful trading**. It occurs where a director knows or ought to have known before the commencement of winding up that there was no reasonable prospect of the company avoiding insolvency and he or she does not take every step to minimise loss to creditors. If the court is satisfied of this it may:

- order the director to contribute to the assets of the business

and

- disqualify him or her from further involvement in corporate management for a specified period.

A director will not be liable for wrongful trading if he or she can show that from the relevant time he or she 'took every step with a view to minimising the potential loss to the company's creditors as (assuming him or her to have known that there was no reasonable prospect that the company would avoid going into insolvent liquidation) he or she ought to have taken'. A company goes into insolvent liquidation, for this purpose, if it does so at a time when its assets are insufficient for the payment of its debts and other liabilities and the expenses of winding-up.

Both subjective tests and objective tests are made with regard to directors. A director who is responsible, for example, for manufacturing, quality, purchasing, or human resources, is likely to have less skill and knowledge regarding the financial affairs of the company than the **finance director**, unless otherwise fully briefed. Directors with financial or legal experience will certainly be expected to bear a greater responsibility than other directors because of their specialist knowledge.

Progress check 3.9

What is wrongful trading?

Fraudulent trading

Fraudulent trading is an offence committed by persons who are knowingly party to the continuance of a company trading in circumstances where creditors are defrauded, or for other fraudulent purposes. Generally, this means that the company incurs more debts at a time when it is known that those debts will not be met. Persons responsible for acting in this way are personally liable without limitation for the debts of the company. The offence also carries criminal penalties.

The offence of fraudulent trading may apply at any time, not just in or after a winding-up. If a company is wound up and fraudulent trading has taken place, an additional civil liability arises in respect of any person who was knowingly a party to it.

Progress check 3.10

What is fraudulent trading and how does it differ, if at all, from wrongful trading?

Disqualification of directors

Worked Example 3.3

A director of a Hampshire building and double-glazing contractor was disqualified for six years after his company collapsed owing creditors £364,000. Ronald Norris, director of the Aldershot-based Berg Group, which was wound up on 6 January 1999, was found guilty of trading while insolvent since 3 December 1997. Norris, from West Sussex, stood before Reading County Court on 8 January 1999. The other grounds for his disqualification were the transfer of a pension fund, of which Norris was a beneficiary, on a property owned by Berg, failing to ensure that VAT was collected as due, and failing to ensure that monies due to Berg from connected companies were collected.

There are some fundamental reasons why it is necessary for society to ban certain individuals from becoming directors of limited companies. The limited liability company is a very efficient means of conducting business, but if used by unscrupulous persons then innocent people can lose money, through no fault of their own. The limited liability company can offer a financial shield to protect employees and investors if things go wrong and the company ceases trading, and is unable to pay its creditors. UK law is now quite strict and will attack an obviously unscrupulous person taking advantage of the limited liability company and leaving various creditors out of pocket.

In recent times the UK Government has been banning an increasing number of persons from becoming directors, as well as publishing their names in the public domain (for example, on the Internet). Almost certainly the recently introduced regime is showing its teeth and punishing guilty directors in a most practical manner.

Disqualification means that a person cannot be, for a specified period of time, a director or manager of any company without the permission of the courts. Disqualification is governed under the Company Directors (Disqualification) Act 1986, and may result from breaches under:

- the Companies Act 1985/1989 – from cases of fraud or other breaches of duty by a director
- the Insolvency Act 1986 (as amended by the Enterprise Act 2002) – if the courts consider that the conduct of a director makes him or her unfit to be concerned in the future management of a company.

While there are serious implications for directors of companies under the Company Directors (Disqualification) Act 1986, it should be noted that the Act is not restricted to company directors. Over one half of the liabilities fall on 'any persons' as well as company directors. 'Any persons' in this context potentially includes any employee within the organisation.

The following offences, and their penalties, under the Act relate to any persons:

- being convicted of an indictable offence – disqualification from company directorships for up to 5 years, and possibly for up to 15 years
- fraud in a winding up – disqualification from company directorships for up to 15 years
- participation in fraudulent or wrongful trading – disqualification from company directorships for up to 15 years
- acting as a director while an undischarged bankrupt, and failure to make payments under a county court administration order – imprisonment for up to 2 years, or a fine, or both
- personal liability for a company's debts where the person acts while disqualified – civil personal liability.

The following offences, and their penalties, under the Act relate to directors (but in some instances include other managers or officers of the company):

- persistent breaches of company legislation – disqualification from company directorships for up to 5 years
- convictions for not less than three default orders in respect of a failure to comply with any provisions of companies' legislation requiring a return, account, or other document to be filed, delivered, sent, etc., to the Registrar of Companies (whether or not it is a failure of the company or the director) – disqualification from company directorships for up to 5 years
- finding of unfitness to run a company in the event of the company's insolvency – disqualification from company directorships for a period of between 2 years and 15 years

- if after investigation of a company the conduct of a director makes him unfit to manage a company – disqualification from company directorships for up to 15 years
- attribution of offences by the company to others if such persons consent, connive, or are negligent – imprisonment for up to 2 years, or a fine, or both, or possibly imprisonment for not more than 6 months, or a fine.

In some circumstances directors may be disqualified automatically. Automatic disqualification occurs in the case of an individual who revokes a county court administration order, and in the case of an undischarged bankrupt unless leave of the court is obtained. In all other situations the right to act as a director may be withdrawn only by an order of the court, unless a company through its Articles of Association provides for specific circumstances in which a director's appointment may be terminated. The City of London has seen a major toughening of the regime where persons have found themselves unemployable (for example, the fallout from the Barings Bank debacle in the mid-1990s).

Progress check 3.11

In what circumstances may a director be disqualified?

Summary of directors' obligations and responsibilities

In summary, the following may serve as useful checklists of the board of directors' and non-executive directors' obligations and responsibilities.

Board of directors

A board of directors:

- is collectively responsible for the success of the company
- is responsible for determining the company's aims and the policies and strategies, and the plans to achieve those aims; it is responsible for monitoring progress in the achievement of those aims both from a company perspective and also in terms of analysis and evaluation of their own performance as a board and as individual directors
- is responsible for appointing a chief executive officer with appropriate leadership qualities
- should undertake a formal and rigorous annual evaluation of its own performance and that of its committees and individual directors
- should assign a sufficient number of non-executive board members capable of exercising independent judgement to tasks where there is a potential for conflict of interest.

Non-executive directors

Non-executive directors:

- should act as a control or counterweight to executive directors to help to ensure that an individual person or group cannot unduly influence the board's decisions
- should make a contribution to the overall leadership and development of the company.

Executive directors

The following may serve as a useful checklist of executive directors' obligations and responsibilities:

- it is the duty of executive directors to act with care, look after the finances and act within their powers, and look after employees
- directors of companies are responsible for keeping proper books of account and presenting shareholders with accounts, and their failure to do so may ultimately result in their disqualification
- directors should understand the accounts and be able to interpret them
- the directors are responsible for filing accounts with the Registrar of Companies and must also notify changes to the board of directors and changes to the registered address
- directors are responsible for calling and holding annual general meetings, and ensuring minutes of all meetings are appropriately recorded
- directors are responsible for ensuring that the company complies with its memorandum and articles of association
- if a company continues to trade while technically insolvent and goes into receivership a director may be forced to contribute personally to repaying creditors
- a director trading fraudulently is liable to be called on for money
- any director who knew or ought to have known that insolvency was unavoidable without minimising loss to the creditors becomes liable
- directors can be disqualified for paying themselves too much
- inadequate attention paid to the financial affairs of the company can result in disqualification
- directors are required to prepare a remuneration report.

We have seen the onerous burden of responsibility placed on directors of limited companies in terms of compliance with guidelines and legislation. The obligations of directors continue to grow with the increase in Government regulation and legislation. During the past few years, very many new directives have been introduced, relating to such issues as employee working conditions, health and safety, and, for example, administration of a minimum wage policy.

How can directors make sure that they comply and cover themselves in the event of things going wrong?

Actions to ensure compliance

Directors of companies need to be aware of the dividing line between the commission of a criminal offence and the commission of technical offences of the Companies Act. Directors should take the necessary actions to ensure compliance with their obligations and responsibilities, and to protect themselves against possible non-compliance:

- directors may delegate their responsibilities within or outside the company and in such circumstances they must ensure that the work is being done by competent, able, and honest people
- directors of small companies in particular should get professional help to ensure compliance with statutory responsibilities

- directors must ensure that they are kept fully informed about the affairs of the company by having regular meetings and keeping minutes and recording material decisions
- directors should ensure they have service contracts that cover their duties, rights, obligations, and benefits
- directors must ensure that detailed, timely management accounts are prepared, and, if necessary, professional help sought to provide, for example, monthly reporting systems and assistance with interpretation of information produced and actions required.

It is essential that directors carefully watch for warning signs of any decline in the company's position, for example:

- falling sales or market share
- overdependence on one product, customer or supplier
- overtrading (see Chapter 10)
- pressure on bank borrowings
- increases in trade creditors
- requirements for cash paid in advance
- increasing stock levels
- poor financial controls.

The protection that directors may obtain is extremely limited. All directors should certainly take out individual professional liability insurance. But above all it is probably more important that all directors clearly understand their obligations and responsibilities, closely watch company performance, and take immediate, appropriate action, as necessary, to ensure compliance and minimise their exposure to the type of personal risks we have discussed above.

Progress check 3.12

What actions should directors take to ensure they meet their obligations, and to protect themselves should things go wrong?

Summary of key points

- The framework for establishing good corporate governance and accountability has been established in a revised UK Combined Code of Practice, developed from the work of the Cadbury, Greenbury, Hampel, and Turnbull Committees.
- Corporate governance codes are increasingly being developed in many other countries, for example throughout Europe, China, and the Middle East, and including the USA's Sarbanes-Oxley Act 2002.
- Corporate social responsibility (CSR) reporting by companies is becoming increasingly important and includes areas such as environmental and social issues, global warming, waste management, and the efficient use of resources such as water and energy.

▶
- There are various approaches to dealing with the agency problem, including monitoring performance and offering inducements to company managers and directors, and development of corporate governance systems, but consideration should also be given to the ethical dimension.
- There is a statutory requirement for the audit of the accounts of limited companies, except for smaller limited companies.
- The election of suitably qualified, independent auditors is the responsibility of the shareholders, to whom they are responsible.
- Directors of limited companies have a specific responsibility to shareholders, and general responsibilities to all stakeholders and the community, for the management and conduct of companies. (Note the continued activities of pressure groups such as Greenpeace and Friends of the Earth.)
- Directors of limited companies have a fiduciary duty to act in the best interests of the company, and a duty of care to all stakeholders and to the community at large, particularly with regard to the Companies Act 1985/1989, Health and Safety at Work Act 1974, Financial Services Act 1986, Insolvency Act 1986, and Enterprise Act 2002.
- The risk for companies and their directors from the UK Corporate Manslaughter & Corporate Homicide Act 2006 may be remote but very real, and should therefore be managed in terms of awareness, training, preventative measures, and liability insurance.
- The implications for directors for wrongful trading may be to contribute to the assets of the business, and disqualification from further involvement in corporate management for a specified period.
- The implications for directors for fraudulent trading may be to contribute to the assets of the business without limit, disqualification, and possible criminal and civil penalties.
- The implications of the Company Directors (Disqualification) Act 1986 (as amended by the Enterprise Act 2002) apply not only to company directors, and over 50% of the provisions relate to any persons.
- Directors of limited companies, in addition to taking out individual professional liability insurance, must ensure that they clearly understand their obligations and responsibilities.

🔑 Glossary of key terms

audit report An objective verification to shareholders and other users that the financial statements have been prepared properly and in accordance with legislative and regulatory requirements; that they present the information truthfully and fairly; and that they conform to the best accounting practice in their treatment of the various measurements and valuations.

corporate manslaughter An offence for which a company may be guilty if a failure by its management is the cause of a person's death, and their failure is because their conduct is well below what can be reasonably expected.

corporate social responsibility (CSR) CSR is the decision-making and implementation process that guides all company activities in the protection and promotion of international human rights, labour and environmental standards, and compliance with legal requirements within its operations and in its relations to the societies and communities where it operates. CSR involves a commitment to contribute to the economic, environmental, and social sustainability of communities through the ongoing engagement of stakeholders, the active participation of communities impacted by company activities, and the public reporting of company policies and performance in the economic, environmental and social arenas (www.bench-marks.org).

director A person elected under the company's articles of association to be responsible for the overall direction of the company's affairs. Directors usually act collectively as a board and carry out such functions as are specified in the articles of association or the Companies Acts, but they may also act individually in an executive capacity.

duty of care A duty of care means doing the job with the skill and care that somebody with the necessary knowledge and experience would exercise if they were acting on their own behalf, and if a director of a company does not choose the right people or supervise them properly, all the directors may be liable for the misdeeds and mistakes of the people they have appointed.

fiduciary duty A duty of directors to act in the best interests of the company, and with a duty of care to all stakeholders and to the community at large, particularly with regard to the Companies Act 1985/1989, Health and Safety at Work Act 1974, Financial Services Act 1986, Insolvency Act 1986, and Enterprise Act 2002.

finance director The finance director of an organisation is actively involved in broad strategic and policy-making activities involving financial considerations. The finance director provides the board of directors with advice on financing, capital expenditure, acquisitions, dividends, the implications of changes in the economic environment, and the financial aspects of legislation. The finance director is responsible for the planning and control functions, the financial systems, financial reporting, and the management of funds.

fraudulent trading An offence committed by persons who are knowingly party to the continuance of a company trading in circumstances where creditors are defrauded or for other fraudulent purposes. Generally, this means that the company incurs more debts at a time when it is known that those debts will not be met. Persons responsible for so acting are personally liable without limitation for the debts of the company. The offence also carries criminal penalties.

insolvency The inability of a company, partnership, or individual to pay creditors' debts in full after realisation of all the assets of the business.

internal audit An independent appraisal function established within an organisation to examine and evaluate its activities as a service to the organisation. The objective of internal auditing is to assist members of the organisation in the effective discharge of their responsibilities. To this end, internal auditing furnishes them with analyses, appraisals, recommendations, counsel, and information concerning the activities reviewed (Institute of Internal Auditors – UK).

▶

▶ **leave of the court** This is where the court will make a decision after hearing all the relevant information.

non-executive director A director who does not have an executive function to perform within the company's management. The usual involvement is to attend board meetings and chair and attend corporate governance committee meetings.

receiver A person appointed by secured creditors or by the court to take control of company property, usually following the failure of the company to pay principal sums or interest due to debenture holders whose debt is secured by fixed or floating charges over the assets of the company. The receiver takes control of the charged assets and may operate the company's business with a view to selling it as a going concern. In practice, receivership is usually closely followed by liquidation.

statement of affairs Details submitted to the receiver during the winding-up of a company identifying the assets and liabilities of the company. The details are prepared by the company directors, or other persons specified by the receiver, and must be submitted within 14 days of the winding-up order or the appointment of a provisional liquidator.

voluntary winding-up A voluntary winding-up of a company occurs where the company passes a resolution that it shall liquidate and the court is not involved in the process. A voluntary winding-up may be made by the members (the shareholders) of the company or by its creditors, if the company has failed to declare its solvency.

wrongful trading Wrongful trading occurs where a director knows or ought to have known before the commencement of winding-up that there was no reasonable prospect of the company avoiding insolvency and he or she does not take every step to minimise loss to creditors. If the court is satisfied of this it may (i) order the director to contribute to the assets of the business, and (ii) disqualify him or her from further involvement in corporate management for a specified period (Insolvency Act 1986).

❓ Questions

Q3.1 (i)   How was the corporate governance UK Combined Code of Practice developed?
      (ii) Why was it considered necessary?

Q3.2 Refer to the Johnson Matthey section on corporate governance in their annual Report and Accounts 2007 on pages 93 to 104 to illustrate the areas of compliance under the Combined Code of Practice.

Q3.3 (i)   Which areas of the business do auditors' opinions cover?
      (ii) What happens if there is any fundamental uncertainty as to compliance?

Q3.4 Explain the implications of the 'expectation gap' with regard to external auditors.

Q3.5 Explain the obligations of directors of limited companies in terms of their duty of care, their fiduciary duty, and the Corporate Manslaughter & Corporate Homicide Act 2006.

Q3.6 If the severity of the penalty is determined by the seriousness of the offence, describe the half dozen or so most serious offences under the Company Directors (Disqualification) Act 1986 (as amended by the Enterprise Act 2002), which relate to directors of limited companies.

Q3.7 Outline the general responsibilities of a director of a limited company with regard to the company, its shareholders, and other stakeholders.

Q3.8 What are the key actions that a director of a limited company may take to ensure compliance with his or her obligations and responsibilities?

Discussion points

D3.1 Discuss and illustrate with some examples to what extent the corporate governance UK Combined Code of Practice is effective in preventing the kind of corporate excesses we have seen in the recent past.

D3.2 'I pay my auditors a fortune in audit fees. I look upon this almost as another insurance premium to make sure that I'm protected against every kind of financial risk.' Discuss.

D3.3 'Everyone who embarks on a career in industry or commerce aspires to becoming a director of their organisation, because then all their troubles are over! Directors just make a few decisions, swan around in their company cars, and pick up a fat cheque at the end of each month for doing virtually nothing.' Discuss.

D3.4 In an age of increasingly sophisticated computer systems is the traditional role of the auditor coming to an end?

Exercises

Solutions are provided in Appendix 2 to all exercise numbers highlighted in colour.

Level I

E3.1   *Time allowed – 15 minutes*

What role does accounting information play in corporate governance?

E3.2   *Time allowed – 30 minutes*

Identify the major participants within the corporate financial environment and explain how they contribute to effective corporate governance.

E3.3   *Time allowed – 30 minutes*

Discuss why users of financial statements should have information on awards to directors of share options, allowing them to subscribe to shares at fixed prices in the future.

E3.4   *Time allowed – 30 minutes*

Outline the basic reasons why there should be openness regarding directors' benefits and 'perks'.

E3.5   *Time allowed – 30 minutes*

Can you think of any reasons why directors of UK plcs found that their contracts were no longer to be open-ended under the new regime of corporate governance?

E3.6   *Time allowed – 60 minutes*

William Mason is the managing director of Classical Gas plc, a recently formed manufacturing company in the chemical industry, and he has asked you as finance director to prepare a report that covers the topics, together with a brief explanation, to be included in a section on corporate governance in their forthcoming annual report and accounts.

▶ ## *Level II*

E3.7   *Time allowed – 60 minutes*

After the birth of her twins Vimla Shah decided to take a couple of years away from her career as a company lawyer. During one of her coffee mornings with Joan Turnbull, Joan confided in her that although she was delighted at her husband Ronnie's promotion to commercial director of his company, which was a large UK plc in the food industry, she had heard many horror stories about problems that company directors had encountered, seemingly through no fault of their own. She was worried about the implications of these obligations and responsibilities (whatever they were) that Ronnie had taken on. Vimla said she would write some notes about what being a director of a plc meant, and provide some guidelines as to the type of things that Ronnie should be aware of, and to include some ways in which Ronnie might protect himself, that may all offer some reassurance to Joan.

Prepare a draft of what you think Vimla's notes for Joan may have included.

E3.8   *Time allowed – 60 minutes*

Li Nan has recently been appointed managing director of Pingers plc, which is a company that supplies table tennis equipment to clubs and individuals throughout the UK and Europe. Li Nan is surprised at the high figure that appeared in last year's accounts under audit fees.

Li Nan is not completely familiar with UK business practices and has requested you to prepare a detailed report on what the audit fees cover, and to include the general responsibilities of directors in respect of the external audit.

E3.9   *Time allowed – 60 minutes*

Use the following information, extracted from Tomkins plc report and accounts as a basis for discussing the needs of users of financial information for information on directors' remuneration.

	Basic salary	Benefits in kind	Bonuses
G Hutchings, executive director	£975,000	£45,000	£443,000
G Gates (USA), non-executive director	nil, but has a US$ 250,000 consultancy agreement		
R Holland, non-executive director	£23,000	Nil	Nil

E3.10 *Time allowed – 60 minutes*

Explain what is meant by insolvency and outline the responsibilities of receivers appointed to insolvent companies.

Capital investment decisions

LEARNING OBJECTIVES

Completion of this chapter will enable you to:

- ☑ Explain what is meant by an investment.

- ☑ Outline the key principles underlying investment selection criteria.

- ☑ Calculate simple and compound interest, annuities, and perpetuities.

- ☑ Outline the strengths and weaknesses of the five investment appraisal criteria.

- ☑ Explain what is meant by discounted cash flow (DCF).

- ☑ Consider investment selection using the appraisal criteria of net present value (NPV) and internal rate of return (IRR).

- ☑ Explain the effects of inflation, working capital requirements, length and timing of projects, taxation, and risk and uncertainty on investment criteria calculations.

- ☑ Evaluate the impact of risk and uncertainty and the use of sensitivity analysis, scenario analysis, and simulation in decision-making.

- ☑ Use capital budgeting techniques, including the profitability index for single period capital rationing.

- ☑ Consider the ways in which capital projects may be controlled and reviewed.

- ☑ Appreciate the importance of the project post-completion audit.

Introduction

This chapter looks at the specific area of decision-making that relates to investment. Such decisions may relate to whether or not to invest in a project, or choices between investment in alternative projects which are competing for resources.

We will begin by looking at exactly what an investment is, and outlining the techniques used to decide on whether or not to invest, and how to choose between alternative investments.

We shall evaluate the advantages and disadvantages of the five main investment appraisal criteria used by companies and consider examples that demonstrate their use. The most important of these are the discounted cash flow methods of net present value (NPV), and internal rate of return (IRR). The technique of discounted cash flow (DCF) will be fully explained.

In addition to the initial costs of an investment and the returns expected from it, a number of other factors usually need to be taken into account in investment decision-making. These include, for example, inflation, the need for working capital, taxation, and the length and timing of the project. We will consider the possible impact of these factors and how the effects of risk and uncertainty on the appraisal of investments may be quantified using sensitivity analysis, scenario analysis, and simulation.

Capital budgeting is a process that assists managers to make optimal investment decisions with the aim of maximisation of shareholder wealth. Capital budgeting may be required where the level of funds available is rationed for one period or for successive future periods – single period and multiple period capital rationing. This chapter considers the use of the profitability index method for single period capital rationing.

> Appraisal of an investment is more than an accounting exercise. An investment decision is a crucially significant and important decision for a business. It is usually a highly politically charged area in the management of an organisation, which if mismanaged is capable of destroying shareholder value. Once an investment decision has been made the project may then be planned and implemented. This chapter closes with an introduction to the ways in which capital investment projects may be controlled and reviewed.

What is an investment?

For the accountant an investment appears within the assets section of the balance sheet under non-current assets. For the finance director an investment is any decision that implies expenditure today with the expectation that it will generate cash inflows tomorrow.

Investment decisions are extremely important because they are invariably concerned with the future survival, prosperity, and growth of the organisation. The organisation's primary objective of maximisation of shareholder wealth is a basic assumption that continues to hold true. Investments must be made not only to maintain shareholder wealth but more importantly to increase it. To meet the shareholder wealth maximisation objective it is crucial that those managing the organisation make optimal decisions that are based on the best information available and use of the most appropriate appraisal techniques.

At the corporate level, investment (in shares) relates to the amount that shareholders are willing to invest in the equity of a company in the expectation of future cash flows in the form of dividends and enhancement of share price. The level of future dividends and share price enhancement are in turn dependent on the extent to which the company is able to optimise returns on 'real' investment (investment in companies, plant, machinery, working capital) in new products, projects, new business, and so on. There is a great deal of pressure on chief executives to ensure that profitable 'real' investments are made to provide sustained dividend growth and increasing share prices.

Investment decisions faced by companies are therefore financially driven, and so if performance is deemed inadequate or unlikely to meet shareholder expectations, then the pressure becomes even greater to identify alternative, more profitable projects. Decisions are made by managers and not by the management accountant. Levels of authority within the management hierarchy are determined by company policy. Companies normally establish limits at each management level for each type of decision, and the level of expenditure allowed. The approval of one or more directors is normally required for all capital expenditure and for major projects.

Investment may appear in the balance sheet within non-current assets in line with the accountants' definition, for example land, buildings, plant, machinery, etc. It may also appear in the income statement in terms of public relations, staff training, or research and development. In some cases the amount of money gained as a result of making an investment is relatively easy to measure, such as cost savings, capacity increases, etc. In other cases, it may be impossible to measure the gains – company image, knowledge, and so on. The amount of spend may be easily forecast, for example the costs of computerisation of a process to reduce the production of non-quality products. In other projects, such as research and development, costs and benefits may be more uncertain.

Regardless, an investment decision is required before spending shareholders' and lenders' funds. The decision made needs to be one that shareholders and lenders would be happy with;

it is one that is expected to provide anticipated gains in real terms that greatly exceed the funds spent today, in other words a good return on the money invested. Otherwise the investment should not be made.

Investments in new projects selected by a company invariably have different levels of risks associated with them, some being more risky and some less risky than others. The use of a company's cost of capital to evaluate such an investment may over- or understate its net present value (NPV). This is because the company's cost of capital only represents an average discount rate appropriate for use with average or normal risk investments. Such a situation may be avoided by using a risk-adjusted discount rate to compensate for the additional risk and uncertainty that may exist regarding the timing and value of a project's cash flows.

In general, financial managers should use a discount rate higher than the company's cost of capital where an investment project is considered to be of a higher than average risk, and a discount rate lower than the company's cost of capital where a project is considered to be of a lower than average risk.

Determination of an appropriate risk-adjusted discount rate (RADR) for each investment project can be problematic. A common approach is to use investment project risk classes to assign a different discount rate to each class of risk. For example, a company may take a certainty approach to classifying investment projects by certainty or uncertainty of demand – a higher discount rate may be assigned to those projects of greater uncertainty. Such uncertainty may be estimated using historical data to calculate the coefficient of variation of various investment projects to determine their relative uncertainty, or an actual discount rate may be estimated using either:

- scenario analysis or sensitivity analysis to estimate an appropriate cost of capital, which we will consider later in this chapter

- the **capital asset pricing model (CAPM)**, to estimate a risk-adjusted cost of capital, which is covered in Chapter 6.

Progress check 4.1

Describe what is meant by investment.

Future values, present values, perpetuities, and annuities

Simple interest is interest that is calculated over successive periods based only on the principal amount of a loan. Compound interest is calculated over successive periods based on the principal loan plus interest, which has accrued to date.

Future values and present values

A future value (FV) is the amount to which a sum of money will grow over a number of successive periods after earning interest, which is compounded each period. If I is the initial loan, r is the annual interest rate, and t is the number of years, then

$$\text{FV} = \text{I} \times (1 + r)^t$$

Worked Example 4.1

We can calculate the future value of £1,000 if interest is compounded annually at a rate of 4% for ten years.

$$FV = £1,000 \times (1 + 0.04)^{10} = £1,480.24$$

Worked Example 4.2

An often-quoted example of compound interest and future value is the purchase of Manhattan Island. Peter Minuit of the Dutch West India Company legitimised the claim of Dutch settlers by buying this land from local Indians for 60 Dutch Guilders in the year 1626. This was equivalent to around US$24, and we can calculate the FV to see what US$24 is worth in 2007 if it is compounded at say 8% per annum.

$$FV = US\$24 \times (1 + 0.08)^{381} = US\$130.215 \text{ trillion}$$

Was it a good deal or not in 1626? Well possibly, although the value of Manhattan Island was perhaps considerably lower than US$130.215 trillion in 2007. However, 8% may be an unrealistic average interest rate to use over the 381 years.

A present value is the cash equivalent now of a sum receivable or payable at a future date. It is the value today of a future cash flow. The principle is effectively the same as using compound interest to calculate a future value, but in reverse. If PV is the present value and r is the interest rate for the period, then:

$$PV = \frac{FV \text{ after } t \text{ periods}}{(1 + r)^t}$$

Worked Example 4.3

Assume that you are buying a new car for £30,000, for which payment is due in two years' time, interest free. If you can earn 6% per annum on your money, how much money should you set aside today (the PV) in order to make the payment when due in two years?

$$PV = \frac{£30,000}{(1 + 0.06)^2} = £26,700$$

You need to set aside £26,700 now, which will earn 6% per annum compounded over two years to become £30,000 with which to pay for the car.

The present value of a future payment of £1, US$1, 1 Riyal, or any other currency is called a discount factor. The interest rate r, used to calculate a present value (PV) of future cash flows over a number of successive periods (t) is called a discount rate (which may also be referred to as the cost of capital). The discount factor (DF) of £1 or US$1 for t periods is:

$$DF = \frac{1}{(1+r)^t}$$

A discount factor can be used to calculate the present value of a cash flow occurring at any time in the future. A discount factor may also be used to calculate the present value (PV) of any number of future cash flows C1, C2, C3, etc. occurring in successive future periods:

$$PV = \frac{C1}{(1+r)^1} + \frac{C2}{(1+r)^2} + \frac{C3}{(1+r)^3} + \cdots$$

where C1, C2 etc. represent the cash flows in each future period, 1, 2, 3 and so on, and r is the discount rate, or interest rate.

Worked Example 4.4

Lovely Laptops Ltd has offered you alternative ways to pay for a new laptop computer. You may pay £2,000 cash immediately, or make three payments: £1,000 immediately, and £600 at the end of the next two years. If you are able to borrow money at 7% per annum, which is your cheapest option?

Immediate payment		£1,000.00
PV of £600 next year	$\dfrac{£600}{(1+0.07)^1} =$	£560.75
PV of £600 following year	$\dfrac{£600}{(1+0.07)^2} =$	£524.06
Total PV		= £2,084.81

The instalment plan total cost of £2,084.81 is more expensive than the £2,000 immediate purchase and so outright purchase appears to be the preferred option.

When decisions need to be made regarding investment in new capital projects some appraisal techniques use an extension of the method shown in Worked Example 4.4 to calculate the present value of future project cash flows. The principles underlying this method are cash flow (as opposed to profit), and the time value of money. The method is called **discounted cash flow (DCF)**, which is used to discount projected future net cash flows to ascertain their present values, using an appropriate discount rate, or cost of capital. This will be discussed in more detail later in this chapter when we look at net present value.

Perpetuities and annuities

A **perpetuity** is a periodic payment continuing for a limitless period – a stream of level cash payments that never ends. The present value (PV) of a perpetuity, where C is the annual cash payment and r the per annum interest rate is:

$$PV = \frac{C}{r}$$

Worked Example 4.5

Suppose that an individual wishes to set aside a sum of money (an endowment), which pays £150,000 per year forever. We can calculate how much money must be set aside today if the rate of interest is 5% per annum. In other words, we need to calculate the present value of £150,000 a year in perpetuity at 6% per annum.

$$PV = \frac{C}{r} = \frac{£150,000}{0.06} = £2,500,000$$

Alternatively, if it is decided that the first £150,000 payment should not be received until five years from today, we can calculate the different sum of money that needs to be set aside today.

$$PV = \frac{2,500,000}{(1 + 0.06)^5} = £1,868,145$$

An **annuity** comprises an equally spaced level stream of cash flows for a limited period of time. The present value (PV) of an annuity, where C is the annual cash payment, r is the per annum interest rate, and t is the number of years each cash payment is received is:

$$PV = C \times \left[\frac{1}{r} - \frac{1}{r(1+r)^t} \right]$$

where

$$\left[\frac{1}{r} - \frac{1}{r(1+r)^t} \right]$$

is described as the present value annuity factor (PVAF), which is the present value of £1 a year for each of t years, and therefore:

$$PV = C \times PVAF$$

Worked Example 4.6

Let's assume that you are planning to purchase a car, which requires payment by four annual installments of £6,000 per year. We can calculate the real total cost you will incur for purchase of the car, assuming a rate of interest of 6% (in other words the PV).

$$PV = C \times \left[\frac{1}{r} - \frac{1}{r(1+r)^t} \right]$$

$$PV = £6,000 \times \left[\frac{1}{0.06} - \frac{1}{0.06(1 + 0.06)^4} \right]$$

real total cost PV = £20,794.00

This is obviously considerably below the total of the actual cash payments for the four years which is £24,000 (4 × £6,000).

As we discussed earlier in this chapter, the relationship between present value and future value is:

$$PV = \frac{FV}{(1+r)^t}$$

and therefore

$$FV = PV \times (1+r)^t$$

We also saw that:

$$PV = C \times PVAF$$

Therefore, by combining each of the above two equations, we can see that the future value (FV) of equal annual payments over *t* periods is:

$$FV = (C \times PVAF) \times (1+r)^t$$

Worked Example 4.7

Let's assume that you plan to save £7,000 every year for 30 years and then retire, and the rate of interest is 5% per annum. We can calculate the future value (FV) of your retirement fund as follows:

$$FV = (C \times PVAF) \times (1+r)^t$$

or

$$FV = C \times \left[\frac{1}{r} - \frac{1}{r(1+r)^t}\right] \times (1+r)^t$$

$$FV = £7,000 \times \left[\frac{1}{0.05} - \frac{1}{0.05(1+0.05)^{30}}\right] \times (1+0.05)^{30}$$

value of fund at retirement FV = £465,072

Investment appraisal methods

The five main methods used in investment appraisal are shown in Fig. 4.1:

- the **accounting rate of return (ARR)** for appraising capital investment projects is based on profits and the costs of investment; it takes no account of cash flows or the time value of money
- the **payback** method for appraising capital investment projects is based on cash flows, but also ignores the time value of money
- **net present value (NPV)** is one of the two most widely used investment decision criteria that are based on cash flow and the time value of money
- **internal rate of return (IRR)** is the second of the two most widely used investment decision criteria that are based on cash flow and the time value of money
- the **discounted payback** appraisal method is also based on cash flow and the time value of money.

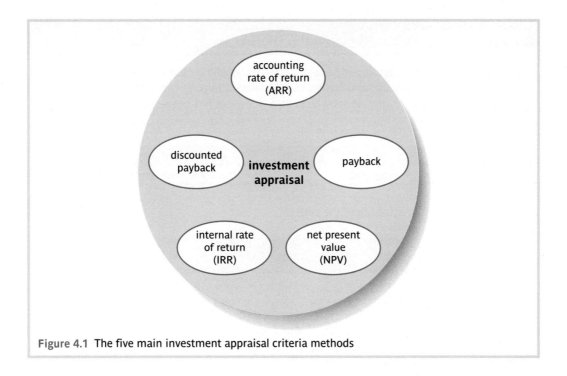

Figure 4.1 The five main investment appraisal criteria methods

We will look at examples of each of the five appraisal criteria and the advantages and disadvantages of using each of them.

Accounting rate of return (ARR)

ARR is a simple measure that may be used for investment appraisal. It is a form of return on capital employed, based on profits rather than cash flows, and ignores the time value of money.

ARR may be calculated using:

$$\frac{\text{average annual accounting profit over the life of the project}}{\text{initial investment}} \times 100\%$$

There are alternative ways of calculating ARR. For example, total profit may be used instead of average profit, or average investment may be used instead of initial investment. It should be noted that in such a case if, for example, a machine originally cost £800,000 and its final scrap value was £50,000 then the average investment is £850,000/2, or £425,000. This is because the investment at the start is valued at £800,000, and the investment at the end of the project is £50,000. The average value over the period of the project is then the addition of these two values divided by two.

It should also be noted that the method of calculation of ARR that is selected must be used consistently. However, ARR, although simple to use, is not recommended as a primary appraisal method. The method can provide an 'overview' of a new project but it lacks the sophistication of other methods. The impact of cash flows and time on the value of money really should be considered in investment appraisal, which we will discuss in a later section about key principles underlying investment selection criteria.

Worked Example 4.8

Alpha Engineering Ltd is a company that has recently implemented an investment appraisal system. Its investment authorisation policy usually allows it to go ahead with a capital project if the accounting rate of return is greater than 25%. A project has been submitted for appraisal with the following data:

	£000
Initial investment	100 (residual scrap value zero)

Per annum profit over the life of the project:

Year	Profit £000
1	25
2	35
3	35
4	25

The capital project may be evaluated using ARR.

$$\text{Average profit over the life of the project} = \frac{£25,000 + £35,000 + £35,000 + £25,000}{4}$$

$$= £30,000$$

$$\text{Accounting rate of return} = \frac{£30,000}{£100,000} \times 100\% = 30\%$$

which is greater than 25% and so acceptance of the project may be recommended.

Progress check 4.2

What is the accounting rate of return (ARR) and how is it calculated?

Payback

Payback is defined as the number of years it takes the cash inflows from a capital investment project to equal the cash outflows. An organisation may have a target payback period, above which projects are rejected. It is useful and sometimes used as an initial screening process in evaluating two mutually exclusive projects. The project that pays back in the shortest time may on the face of it be the one to accept.

Worked Example 4.9

Beta Engineering Ltd's investment authorisation policy requires all capital projects to pay back within three years, and views projects with shorter payback periods as even more desirable. Two mutually exclusive projects are currently being considered with the following data:

	Project 1 £000	Project 2 £000
Initial investment	200	200 (residual scrap value zero)

Per annum cash inflows over the life of each project:

Year	Project 1		Project 2	
	Yearly cash flow £000	Cumulative cash flow £000	Yearly cash flow £000	Cumulative cash flow £000
1	60	60	100	100
2	80	140	150	250
3	80	220	30	280
4	90	310	10	290

The projects may be evaluated by considering their payback periods.

■ Project 1 derives total cash inflows of £310,000 over the life of the project and pays back the initial £200,000 investment three quarters of the way into year three, when the cumulative cash inflows reach £200,000 [£60,000 + £80,000 + £60,000 (75% of £80,000)].

■ Project 2 derives total cash inflows of £290,000 over the life of the project and pays back the initial £200,000 investment two thirds of the way into year two, when the cumulative cash inflows reach £200,000 [£100,000 + £100,000 (67% of £150,000)].

■ Both projects meet Beta Engineering Ltd's three-year payback criteria.

■ Project 2 pays back within two years and so is the preferred project, using Beta's investment guidelines.

Worked Example 4.9 shows how payback may be used to compare projects. The total returns from a project should also be considered, in addition to the timing of the cash flows and their value in real terms. As with ARR, although from experience the use of payback appears to be widespread amongst companies, payback is not recommended as a primary appraisal method. This method can also provide an 'overview' but should not be the primary appraisal method used in larger companies or with regard to large projects because it ignores the time value of money.

Progress check 4.3

What is payback and how is it calculated?

Key principles underlying investment selection criteria: cash flow, the time value of money, and discounted cash flow (DCF)

The first two appraisal criteria we have considered are simple methods that have limitations in their usefulness in making optimal capital investment decisions. The three further appraisal criteria are NPV, IRR, and discounted payback. Whichever of these three methods is used, three basic principles apply: *cash is king, time value of money*, and *discounted cash flow (DCF)* (see pages 144 to 147).

We may assume that a specific sum of money can be held in reserve for some unforeseen future need, or used:

- to earn interest in a bank or building society account over the following year
- to buy some bottles of champagne (for example) at today's price
- to buy some bottles of champagne at the price in one year's time, which we may assume will be at a higher price because of inflation.

We may assume that the bank or building society interest earned for one year, or the amount by which the price of champagne goes up due to inflation over one year is, say, 5%. Then we can see that £100 would be worth £105 if left in the building society for one year, and £100 spent on champagne today would actually buy just over £95 worth of champagne in one year's time because of its price increase.

Cash is king

Real funds can be seen in cash but not in accounting profit.

Interest charges become payable as soon as money is made available, for example, from a lender to a borrower, not when an agreement is made or when a contract is signed.

Time value of money

A receipt of £100 today has greater value than a receipt of £100 in one year's time.

There are two reasons for this. First, the money could have been invested alternatively in, say, risk-free Government gilt-edged securities – in fact, the actual rate of interest that will have to be paid will be higher than the Government rate, to include a risk premium, because neither companies nor individuals are risk-free borrowers. Generally, the higher the risk of the investment, the higher the return the investor will expect from it. Second, purchasing power will have been lost over a year due to inflation.

The percentage rate by which the value of money may be eroded over one year is called the discount rate. The amount by which the value of, say, £100 is eroded over one year is calculated by multiplying it by what is called the discount factor:

$$£100 \times \frac{1}{(1 + \textbf{discount rate \%})}$$

So, for example, we could buy champagne in one year's time worth:

$$£100/(1 + 5\%) \text{ or } £100/1.05 = £95.24$$

If the £95.24 were left for another year, and assuming that prices continued to increase at 5% per annum, we could buy champagne after a further year worth:

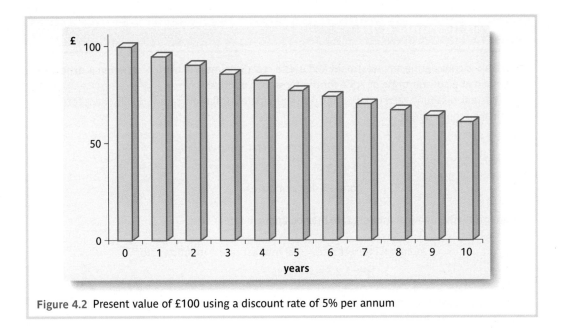

Figure 4.2 Present value of £100 using a discount rate of 5% per annum

$$\text{£}95.24/(1 + 5\%) \text{ or } \text{£}95.24/1.05 = \text{£}90.70$$

The yearly buying power continues to be reduced by application of the discount factor (or using the appropriate discount factor if the discount rate has changed). If the money is not used either to earn interest or to buy something, its value therefore normally becomes less and less. The discount factor for each year obviously depends on the discount rate. The successive year-by-year impact on £100 using an unchanging discount rate of 5% per annum may be illustrated using a simple graph showing its value from the start until the end of 10 years. The graph shown in Fig. 4.2 illustrates the concept of the time value of money.

In Fig. 4.2 we have used a discount rate of 5%. But exactly what type of discount rate is it? Actual interest rates, costs of capital, or rates of return, are often referred to as nominal rates, whereas nominal rates adjusted for inflation are referred to as real interest rates, costs of capital, or rates of return, and can be calculated as follows:

$$1 + \text{real interest rate} = \frac{1 + \text{nominal interest rate}}{1 + \text{inflation rate}}$$

or

$$1 + \text{nominal interest rate} = (1 + \text{real interest rate}) \times (1 + \text{inflation rate})$$

Alternatively, an approximate value may be calculated as follows:

$$\text{real interest rate} = \text{nominal interest rate} - \text{inflation rate}$$

How do we determine whether to use a real or nominal interest rate or discount rate? Discounting nominal cash flows using nominal discount rates actually gives the same result as discounting real inflation adjusted cash flows using real discount rates. Most financial analysts find it more convenient to use nominal rates and nominal cash flows.

Worked Example 4.10

Bruce plc is considering an investment and uses a real discount rate of 10%. Inflation is expected to remain at a constant rate of 2.5% for the foreseeable future.

The real discount rate is 10%, and the anticipated inflation rate is 2.5%, therefore the nominal discount rate is:

$$(1 + \text{real interest rate}) \times (1 + \text{inflation rate})$$
$$(1 + 10\%) \times (1 + 2.5\%) = 1.1275$$
$$\text{nominal discount rate} = 12.75\%$$

Alternatively the nominal interest rate may be approximated:

$$\text{nominal interest rate} = \text{real interest rate} + \text{inflation rate}$$
$$10\% + 2.5\% = 12.5\%$$

Both calculations give a nominal interest rate of between 12% and 13%.

Discounted cash flow (DCF)

Whichever of the three methods of appraisal is used, NPV, IRR, or discounted payback, a technique of discounting the projected cash flows of a project is used to ascertain its **present value**. Such methods are called discounted cash flow or DCF techniques. They require the use of a discount rate to carry out the appropriate calculation.

If we consider a simple company balance sheet:

$$\text{net assets} = \text{equity} + \text{financial debt}$$

we can see that an investment is an additional asset that may be financed by equity or debt or by both.

Shareholders and lenders each require a return on their investment that is high enough to pay for the risk they are taking in funding the company and its assets. The expected return on equity will be higher than the cost of debt because the shareholders take a higher risk than the lenders (see Chapter 6 which discusses the cost of various types of capital and their associated levels of risk). The average cost of these financial resources provided to the company is called the weighted average cost of capital (WACC). An important rule is that the return generated by a new investment undertaken by a company must be higher than the WACC, which reflects the discount rate – the rate of financing the investment. If, say, a company's WACC is 10%, an investment may be accepted if the expected rate of return is 15% or 16%. The importance of WACC and the significance of the debt and equity financial structure of a business will be examined in more detail in Chapter 6.

Other discount rates may be used, such as a borrowing interest rate or even the accounting rate of return. However, the company's cost of capital – the WACC – is usually a more suitable hurdle rate, the opportunity cost of funds, with which to evaluate new investments.

A hurdle rate may be defined as a rate of return that must be achieved by a proposed capital project if it is to be accepted. There are many alternative rates a company may use as a hurdle rate (see Arnold G, Hatzopoulos PD (2000) 'The theory practice gap in capital budgeting: evidence from the United Kingdom' *Journal of Business Finance and Accounting* 27(5) and 27(6) June/July, 603–626), for example:

- the cost of equity (using CAPM)
- interest payable on debt capital (where debt financing is used)
- dividend yield on shares plus an estimated capital growth in share price
- earnings yield on shares
- an arbitrarily chosen figure.

Companies use WACC (to which they may sometimes add a premium) as a hurdle rate to ensure that only those projects that offer a return in excess of WACC will be accepted. This therefore ensures that these projects will contribute to the overall funds of the company. However, methods of calculating WACC may differ greatly between companies.

Arnold and Hatzopoulos (2000) found that only 41% of small companies, 63% of medium sized companies, and 61% of large companies used WACC as a hurdle rate. Although specific reasons are difficult to establish in general, the main reason why many companies continue to use a hurdle rate other than a WACC-based hurdle rate appeared to be a lack of understanding of WACC. It is perhaps worth noting that Francis and Minchington (Francis G, Minchington C (2000) 'Value-based metrics as divisional performance measures' in Arnold G, Davis M (editors) *Value Based Management*, Wiley, London) found that in large divisional based companies approximately 24% of companies used a divisional cost of capital that only reflected the cost of debt rather than WACC, with 69% of such companies failing to use a risk adjusted rate for different divisions to reflect different levels of risk.

In the earlier section about future values and present values we saw how present values may be determined using interest rates. The same calculation may be applied using discount rates. If i represents the cost of capital (the discount rate), and n the number of periods (for example years), these can be used to derive a present value discount factor:

$$\text{discount factor} = \frac{1}{(1+i)^n}$$

where n may have a value from 0 to infinity.

(Note the similarity between this and the way we calculated the present values of £100 illustrated in Fig. 4.2).

If we consider a project where the initial investment in year 0 is I, and each subsequent year's net cash flows are C1, C2, C3, C4 and so on for n years up to Cn, and the cost of capital is i, then the

$$\text{present value of the cash flows} = -I + C1/(1+i) + C2/(1+i)^2 + \cdots + Cn/(1+i)^n$$

The present value of the cash flows using an appropriate cost of capital, or discount rate, is called the net present value or NPV.

Progress check 4.4

What do we mean by discounted cash flow (DCF) and what are the principles on which it is based?

Net present value (NPV)

NPV is today's value of the difference between cash inflows and outflows projected at future dates, attributable to capital investments or long-term projects. The value now of these net cash flows is obtained by using the discounted cash flow method with a specified discount rate.

Worked Example 4.11

An investment of £5,000 is made in year 0. For the purpose of NPV, year 0 is regarded as being today. The investment generates subsequent yearly cash flows of £1,000, £3,000, £3,000, and £2,000. The cost of capital is 10%.

We can evaluate the investment using an NPV approach.

$$NPV = -£5,000 + £1,000/1.1 + £3,000/1.1^2 + £3,000/1.1^3 + £2,000/1.1^4$$

$$NPV = -£5,000 + (£1,000 \times 0.91) + (£3,000 \times 0.83) + (£3,000 \times 0.75) + (£2,000 \times 0.68)$$

$$NPV = -£5,000 + £910 + £2,490 + £2,250 + £1,360$$

$NPV = +£2,010$ which is greater than 0, and being positive the investment should probably be made.

Such an analysis is more usefully presented in tabular form. The discount rates for each year: $1/1.1$, $1/1.1^2$, $1/1.1^3$, $1/1.1^4$, may be shown in the table as discount factor values which are calculated, or alternatively obtained from present value tables (see the extract below from the Present Value table in Appendix 1 at the end of this book).

Rate r % After n years	1	2	3	4	5	6	7	8	9	10	11	12
1	0.99	0.98	0.97	0.96	0.95	0.94	0.93	0.93	0.92	**0.91**	0.90	0.89
2	0.98	0.96	0.94	0.92	0.91	0.89	0.87	0.86	0.84	**0.83**	0.81	0.80
3	0.97	0.94	0.92	0.89	0.86	0.84	0.82	0.79	0.77	**0.75**	0.73	0.71
4	0.96	0.92	0.89	0.85	0.82	0.79	0.76	0.74	0.71	**0.68**	0.66	0.64
5	0.95	0.91	0.86	0.82	0.78	0.75	0.71	0.68	0.65	0.62	0.59	0.57

Tabular format of NPV analysis

Year	Cash outflows £	Cash inflows £	Net cash flow £	Discount factor at 10%	Present values £
0	−5,000		−5,000	1.00	−5,000
1		1,000	1,000	0.91	910
2		3,000	3,000	0.83	2,490
3		3,000	3,000	0.75	2,250
4		2,000	2,000	0.68	1,360
				NPV	+2,010

Progress check 4.5

What is net present value (NPV) and how is it calculated?

Internal rate of return (IRR)

The NPV of a capital investment project is calculated by:

■ discounting, using a rate of return, discount rate, or cost of capital, to obtain
■ the difference in present values between cash inflows and cash outflows.

   The internal rate of return (IRR) method calculates:

■ the rate of return, where
■ the difference between the present values of cash inflows and outflows, the NPV, is zero.

Through this calculation, the IRR provides the exact rate of return that the project is expected to achieve. An organisation would then undertake the project if the expected rate of return, the IRR, exceeds its target rate of return.

   IRR may be determined through interpolation, which assumes a linear relationship between the NPVs and the discount rates of a capital investment project derived using different discount rates. The NPV line is actually a curve, but the NPV/discount rate relationship approximates to a straight line because a curve actually comprises a very large number of small straight lines, each relating to a small range of values. Joining each of these together provides a curve over the complete range of values. We may therefore assume that we are considering a small range of values and therefore a liner relationship. Nevertheless, this is an approximation and therefore the resultant IRR calculation is also an approximation.

   If a project generates a positive NPV of £50,000 using a discount rate of 10% and a negative NPV of £5,000 using a discount rate of 20%, then the IRR (at which point NPV is zero) must be somewhere between 10% and 20%. The exact rate may be determined graphically or calculated algebraically, as illustrated in Fig. 4.3.

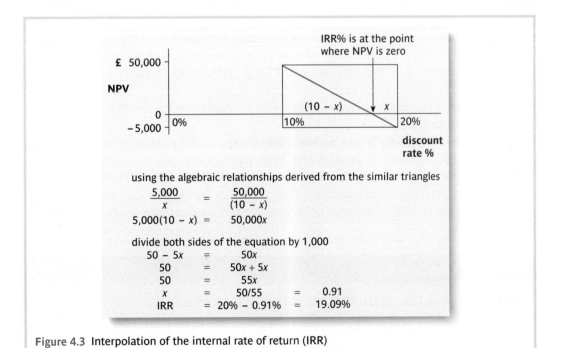

Figure 4.3 Interpolation of the internal rate of return (IRR)

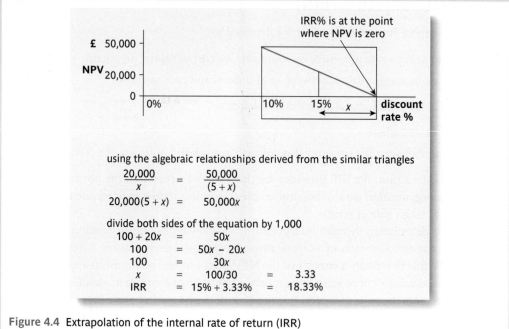

Figure 4.4 Extrapolation of the internal rate of return (IRR)

A similar approach may be adopted if both NPVs are positive. Consider a different project, which generates a positive NPV of £50,000 using a discount rate of 10% and a positive NPV of £20,000 using a discount rate of 15%, then the IRR (at which point NPV is zero) may be extrapolated as shown in Fig. 4.4.

As an alternative to the graphical approach, the calculation of IRR can be carried out manually using a trial and error process, which is a quite laborious task. This may be overcome since IRR can also be determined using the appropriate spreadsheet function in Excel, for example. However, there are a couple of further serious difficulties with the use of IRR.

Discount rates of return may change over the life of a project because of changes in the general level of interest rates. The IRR calculated for a project may therefore be greater than expected rates of return in some years and less in other years, which makes a decision on the project very difficult to make. Alternatively, the NPV approach may use different discount rates for each year of a project.

The cash flows of projects do not normally fall into the simple pattern of an outflow at the start of the project followed by positive cash flows during each successive year. Project cash flows may be positive at the start, or may vary between negative and positive throughout the life of a project. Such unconventional cash flow sequences throughout each period may lead to a project having no IRR or multiple IRRs. Multiple IRRs make it impossible to use IRR for decision-making.

Progress check 4.6

What is the internal rate of return (IRR) and how is it calculated?

Worked Example 4.12 illustrates the use of both NPV and IRR, using conventional cash flows.

Worked Example 4.12

Gamma plc is a diversified multinational group that wishes to acquire a computer system costing £600,000, which is expected to generate cash gains of £170,000 per year over five years. The computer system will have a residual value of zero after five years. The suggested cost of capital is 12%. For this example we may ignore taxation. Gamma has a target IRR of 15%. Gamma plc evaluates the computer system investment by considering its IRR.

Yearly cash gains   £170,000

Year	Cash outflows £000	Cash inflows £000	Net cash flow £000	Discount factor at 12%	Present values £000
0	−600		−600	1.00	−600.0
1		170	170	0.89	151.3
2		170	170	0.80	136.0
3		170	170	0.71	120.7
4		170	170	0.64	108.8
5		170	170	0.57	96.9
				NPV	+13.7

Alternatively, using the cumulative present values in the Present Value tables in Appendix 1, the present value of £1 at 12% over five years is £3.61, therefore:

$$NPV = -£600,000 + (£170,000 \times 3.61) = +£13,700$$

The project gives a positive NPV of £13,700 over five years. If Gamma plc used NPV to appraise capital projects then acceptance of this project may be recommended because NPV is positive.

The IRR is the rate of return that would give an NPV of zero. The interpolation technique shown in Fig. 4.3 may be used to derive the internal rate of return of the project.

If we assume a rate of return of 20%, the five-year cumulative discount rate is 2.99 (from the cumulative present value of £1 in the Present Value tables).

The new NPV would be:

$$-£600,000 + (£170,000 \times 2.99) = -£91,700$$

(Note that if Gamma plc used NPV to appraise capital projects then acceptance of this project would not be recommended at a cost of capital of 20% because it is negative.)

We have already calculated the positive NPV of £13,700 using a cost of capital of 12%. The IRR must be at some point between 20% and 12% (difference 8%). Using a similar calculation to that used in Fig. 4.3:

$$\frac{£91,700}{x} = \frac{£13,700}{(8-x)}$$

$$£91,700(8 - x) = £13,700x$$

$$(£91,700 \times 8) - £91,700x = £13,700x$$

$$£733,600 - £91,700x = £13,700x$$

$$£733,600 = £13,700x + £91,700x$$

▶

▶

$$£733,600 = £105,400x$$

$$x = \frac{£733,600}{£105,400}$$

$$x = 6.96$$

Therefore, interpolation gives us an IRR of 20% less 6.96%, which is 13.04%.

   If the Gamma group uses IRR to appraise capital projects then this project may be rejected as the target rate is 15%. Because of the NPV and discount rate linearity assumption discussed above, the 13.04% IRR is an approximation. A solution to Worked Example 4.12 using Excel is shown on the website that accompanies this book. From that solution we can see that NPV is £12,812, and IRR is more accurately calculated at 12.86%, compared with £13,700 and 13.04% calculated manually.

NPV or IRR?

We have looked at the two main capital appraisal methods, which use the DCF technique. Which method should an organisation adopt for the appraisal of capital investment projects? Which is the better method?

   IRR is relatively easy to understand, particularly for non-financial managers. It can be stated in terms that do not include financial jargon, for example 'a project will cost £1m and will return 20% per annum, which is better than the company's target of 15%'. Whereas, NPV is not quite so clear, for example 'a project will cost £1,000,000 and have an NPV of £250,000 using the company's weighted average cost of capital of 12%'. But there are major disadvantages with the use of IRR:

■ IRR is very difficult to use for decision-making where expected rates of return may change over the life of a project

■ if project cash flows do not follow the usual 'outflow at the start of the project followed by inflows over the life of the project' the result may be no IRR, or two or more IRRs, which can lead to uncertainties and difficulties in interpretation

■ IRR should not be used to decide between mutually exclusive projects because of its inability to allow for the relative size of investments.

IRR ignores the size of investment projects, because it is a percentage measure of a return on a project rather than an absolute cash return number. Two projects, one with a large initial investment and one with a small initial investment, may have the same IRR, but one project may return many times the cash flow returned by the other project. So, if the projects were judged solely on IRR they would seem to rank equally.

   We have already discussed the use of hurdle rates by companies to evaluate proposed investments. While their use by companies is widespread they may lead to sub-optimal decisions being made because otherwise good, value-adding projects may be rejected because they return just below the required hurdle rate.

   If mutually exclusive projects need to be compared then the following rules for acceptance generally apply:

■ is the IRR greater than the hurdle rate (usually the WACC)?

If so

■ the project with the highest NPV should be chosen assuming the NPV is greater than zero.

A company may be considering a number of projects in which it may invest. If there is a limited amount of funds available then **capital rationing** is required (see later in this chapter). This method requires ranking the competing projects in terms of NPV per each £ of investment in each project. Investment funds may then be allocated according to NPV rankings, given the assumption that the investments are infinitely divisible.

Progress check 4.7

What are the disadvantages in the use of internal rate of return (IRR) in the support of capital investment appraisal decisions?

Despite the apparent advantages of using NPV and the disadvantages with using IRR as an appraisal method, many companies appear to prefer IRR. As a consequence, IRR is sometimes used in a slightly different way in order to adjust IRR to bring it in line with the reinvestment assumption of the NPV approach. This is referred to as the modified internal rate of return (MIRR).

Modified internal rate of return (MIRR)

As with IRR, the modified internal rate of return (MIRR) is the rate of return that gives an NPV of zero. However, with MIRR it is the rate of return when the initial investment is compared with the terminal value of the project's net cash flows reinvested at the cost of capital. Therefore, it is necessary to calculate the terminal value of the investment by compounding, using the cost of capital, all cash flows through to the end of the project. The MIRR is then the return at which the terminal value equals the initial cost.

Worked Example 4.13

Dancer Ltd is considering a £35,000 investment in a manufacturing process improvement. The savings resulting from the investment are expected to result in cash flows of £17,000 in each of the first two years of the project and £13,000 in the third and fourth years. The company's cost of capital is 15% per annum. The IRR has been calculated at 23.9%, but the company wishes to determine the MIRR of the project.

Year	Cash flows £	Future value factor at 15%	Terminal value £
1	17,000	$(1.15)^3$	25,855
2	17,000	$(1.15)^2$	22,483
3	13,000	$(1.15)^1$	14,950
4	13,000	$(1.15)^0$	13,000
			76,288

▶

▶ We can now find the discount rate that gives the present value interest factor obtained by dividing the initial investment by the terminal value of the cash flows.

$$\text{present value discount factor} = \frac{£35,000}{£76,288} = 0.46$$

From the Present Value table in Appendix 1 at the end of this book, we can see that for a four-year project this value relates to a discount rate of approximately 21.5% per annum. The MIRR is therefore 21.5%, compared with the IRR of 23.9%.

Discounted payback

The discounted payback appraisal method requires a discount rate to be chosen to calculate the present values of cash inflows and then the payback is the number of years required to repay the original investment.

Worked Example 4.14

A new leisure facility project is being considered by Denton City Council. It will cost £600,000 and is expected to generate the following cash inflows over six years:

Year	£
1	40,000
2	100,000
3	200,000
4	350,000
5	400,000
6	50,000

The cost of capital is 10% per annum.
　　Denton City Council evaluates projects using discounted payback.

Year	Net cash flow £000	Cumulative net cash flow £000	Discount factor at 10%	Present values £000	Cumulative present values £000
0	−600	−600	1.00	−600.0	−600.0
1	40	−560	0.91	36.4	−563.6
2	100	−460	0.83	83.0	−480.6
3	200	−260	0.75	150.0	−330.6
4	350	90	0.68	238.0	−92.6
5	400	490	0.62	248.0	155.4
6	50	540	0.56	28.0	183.4
	540		NPV	+183.4	

Taking a simple payback approach we can see that the project starts to pay back at nearly three quarters of the way through year four. The discounted payback approach shows that with a cost of capital of 10% the project does not really start to pay back until just over a third of the way into year five. This example also highlights the large difference between the real total value of the project of £183,400 in discounted cash flow terms, and the arithmetic total of cash flows of £540,000.

Progress check 4.8

What is discounted payback and how is it calculated?

Advantages and disadvantages of the five investment appraisal methods

We have discussed the five capital investment methods and seen examples of their application. The table in Fig. 4.5 summarises each of the methods and the advantages and disadvantages of their practical use in investment appraisal.

Two reports over the past 15 years have identified the incidence of use of various investment appraisal methods in the UK:

- Drury C, Braund S, Osbourne P, Tayles M (1993) 'A survey of management accounting practices in UK companies' *Certified Research Report No 32*, ACCA

- Arnold GC, Hatzopoulos PD (2000) 'The theory-practice gap in capital budgeting: evidence from the United Kingdom' *Journal of Business Finance & Accounting*, 27 June 2000

In the 1993 survey, the payback method appears to have been the most popular appraisal method used within UK companies. The use of NPV and ARR (or ROCE) appeared to be equal second, sharing around the same level of popularity. IRR was the least used method. However, differences were seen between large and small companies. Larger companies tended to prefer DCF methods while smaller companies preferred payback, but most companies used more than one method.

The 2000 report indicated that a change in the practices of UK companies had occurred since 1993. There had been an increase in popularity in the use of DCF methods in both large and small companies, with NPV and IRR being the most popular methods. Larger companies continued to prefer DCF methods, with IRR being slightly more popular than NPV, both of which were more popular than payback. Smaller companies preferred payback, but were also increasingly using DCF methods. The majority of companies used more than one investment appraisal method. Some companies may say that they use multiple measures for investment appraisal. However, the reality may be that they use the simple techniques for small straightforward investment projects, and NPV and IRR on larger strategic projects.

It should be emphasised that the whole area of capital investment appraisal is one that requires a great deal of expertise and experience. In real-life decision-making situations these types of appraisal are generally carried out by the accountant or the finance director. These longer-term decisions are concerned primarily with the maximisation of shareholder wealth, but they also impact on issues relating to the financial health and future development of the business. Therefore, such decisions are normally based on qualitative as well as quantitative factors.

In practice, in addition to financial criteria, the use of non-financial measures is also of fundamental importance. These measures are becoming some of the key factors considered by businesses in their appraisal of new projects, with the financial evaluation being used to justify the decision. These non-financial indicators may include measures, for example, relating to:

- customer relationships
- employee welfare
- legal issues

	definition	advantages	disadvantages
accounting rate of return (ARR)	average accounting profit over the life of the project divided by the initial or average investment	quick and easy to calculate and simple to use	based on accounting profit rather than cash flows
		the concept of a % return is a familiar one	a relative measure and so no account is taken of the size of the project
		very similar to ROCE	ignores the timing of cash flows and the cost of capital
payback	the point where the cumulative value of a project's cash flows becomes positive	easily understood	ignores the timing of cash flows
		considers liquidity	ignores cash flows that occur after the payback point
		looks only at relevant cash flows	ignores the cost of capital, and therefore the time value of money
net present value (NPV)	the total present values of each of a project's cash flows, using a present value discount factor	uses relevant cash flows	its use requires an estimate of the cost of capital
		allows for the time value of money	
		absolute measure and therefore useful, for example, for comparison of the change in shareholder wealth	
		it is additive which means that if the cash flow is doubled then the NPV is doubled	
internal rate of return (IRR)	the discount rate at which the NPV of a project becomes zero	does not need an estimate of the cost of capital	it is a relative rate of return and so no account is taken of the size of the project
		because the result is stated as a % it is easily understood	its use may rank projects incorrectly
			as cash flows change signs −ve to +ve or *vice versa* throughout the project there may be more than one IRR
			it is difficult to use if changes in the cost of capital are forecast
discounted payback	the point where the cumulative value of a project's discounted cash flows becomes positive	easily understood	its use requires an estimate of the cost of capital
		considers liquidity	ignores cash flows that occur after the payback point
		looks only at relevant cash flows	
		allows for the time value of money	

Figure 4.5 Advantages and disadvantages of the five investment appraisal methods

- health and safety requirements
- the fit with general business strategy
- competition
- availability of scarce resources such as skills and specialised knowledge.

In addition, there are a number of other important quantitative factors, which are discussed in the next section, which should also be considered in new project appraisal. The impact of taxation, for example, is sometimes forgotten with regard to the allowances against tax on the purchase of capital items and tax payable on profits, and therefore cash flows, resulting from a capital project. The uncertainty surrounding future expectations and the sensitivity of the outcome of a project to changes affecting the various elements of an appraisal calculation, are factors that also require measured assessment.

Progress check 4.9

Which technique do you think is the most appropriate to use in capital investment appraisal, and why?

Other factors affecting investment decisions

A number of further factors may have an additional impact on investment criteria calculations:

- the effect of inflation on the cost of capital
- whether additional working capital is required for the project
- taxation
- the length of the project
- risk and uncertainty.

Inflation

We have already discussed earlier in this chapter the difference between actual (or nominal) interest rates or costs of capital, and real interest rates or costs of capital, which are nominal rates adjusted for inflation.

$$1 + \text{nominal interest rate} = (1 + \text{real interest rate}) \times (1 + \text{inflation rate})$$

If i is the real interest rate or cost of capital and the inflation rate is f, then the actual (or money or nominal) interest rate or cost of capital a may be denoted as follows:

$$(1 + a) = (1 + i) \times (1 + f)$$

Therefore

$$\text{actual cost of capital } a = (1 + i) \times (1 + f) - 1$$

Worked Example 4.15

What is a company's real cost of capital if its actual (money) cost of capital is 11% (a) and inflation is running at 2% (f)?

$$\text{real cost of capital} = \frac{(1+a)}{(1+f)} - 1$$

$$= \frac{(1+11\%)}{(1+2\%)} - 1$$

$$= 0.088 \text{ or } 8.8\%$$

This would normally then be rounded to say 9% and forecast cash flows that have been adjusted for inflation may then be discounted using this real cost of capital. Alternatively, if forecast cash flows have not been adjusted for inflation, then these money cash flows would be discounted using the company's actual cost of capital. The result is the same using either method.

Working capital

In addition to capital investments, any increases in working capital required for a project need to be shown as cash outflows as necessary in one or more years, offset by cash inflows to bring the total to zero by the end of the project, at which time it is assumed that all working capital will have been liquidated.

Worked Example 4.16

Delta Precision plc, a manufacturing company, has the opportunity to invest in a machine costing £110,000 that will generate net cash inflows from the investment of £30,000 for five years after which time the machine will be worth nothing. Cost of capital is 10%. We may ignore inflation and taxation in our evaluation of the project using NPV.

Year	Cash outflows £000	Cash inflows £000	Net cash flow £000	Discount factor at 10%	Present values £000
0	−110		−110	1.00	−110.0
1		30	30	0.91	27.3
2		30	30	0.83	24.9
3		30	30	0.75	22.5
4		30	30	0.68	20.4
5		30	30	0.62	18.6
				NPV	+3.7

The positive NPV of £3,700 would indicate acceptance of this investment.

Suppose that in addition to the above factors, for this project Delta required:

- £20,000 working capital in year 1
- £40,000 working capital in year 2, but then
- zero working capital in years 3, 4 and 5.

The revised cash flows would be:

Year	0 £000	1 £000	2 £000	3 £000	4 £000	5 £000	Total £000
Investment	–110						–110
Cash inflows		30	30	30	30	30	150
Working capital		–20		20			0
			–40	40			0
Total	–110	10	–10	90	30	30	40

We can see from the table above that the working capital requirement in year 1 results in a £20,000 reduction in cash for that year. We are told that there is no working capital requirement in years 3, 4 and 5, and so we can assume that the £20,000 cash outflow in year 1 is effectively 'repaid' with an inflow of £20,000 cash in year 3. Similarly, we can also see from the table that the working capital requirement in year 2 means a £40,000 reduction in cash for that year. Again, since we are told that there is no working capital requirement in years 3, 4 and 5, we can assume that the £40,000 cash outflow in year 2 is effectively 'repaid' with an inflow of £40,000 cash in year 3.

The total cash flow of the project is still the same at £40,000, which it was with no working capital requirements. With the inclusion of working capital requirements it is only the timings of the cash flows that are now different.

Year	Net cash flows £000	Discount factor at 10%	Present values £000
0	–110	1.00	–110.0
1	10	0.91	9.1
2	–10	0.83	–8.3
3	90	0.75	67.5
4	30	0.68	20.4
5	30	0.62	18.6
		NPV	–2.7

The need for, and the timing of, working capital results in a negative NPV of £2,700 which would now indicate rejection of this investment.

Taxation

In practice, tax must always be allowed for in any capital investment appraisal calculations. The following two examples provide an introduction to this topic.

Worked Example 4.17

Epsilon Ltd is a company that manufactures and distributes consumer products. It is currently considering the acquisition of a machine costing £2,700,000 to market a new product.

The machine will be worth nothing after 10 years but is expected to produce 10,000 units of a product per year during that period, with variable costs of £35 per unit.

▶ The product can be sold for £120 per unit.

Non-current costs directly attributed to this product will be £300,000 per year.

The company's cost of capital is 10%.

We may assume that all costs and revenues are paid and received during each year.

We may further assume that corporation tax is paid in the year that profit is made and calculated at 30% of profit, and that for tax purposes each year's depreciation is equal to capital allowances.

The acquisition of the machine can be evaluated using NPV.

	£000	
Sales revenue	1,200	[10,000 × £120]
Variable costs	(350)	[10,000 × £35]
Depreciation	(270)	[2,700,000 over 10-year life]
Non-current costs	(300)	
Taxable profit	280	
Corporation tax at 30%	(84)	[based on taxable profit plus depreciation less capital allowances]
Profit after tax	196	
Add back depreciation	270	[non-cash flow]
Yearly cash flow	466	

Using the cumulative Present Value tables (see Appendix 1) the present value of £1 at 10% over 10 years is 6.15, therefore:

$$NPV = -£2,700,000 + (£466,000 \times 6.15) = +£165,900$$

The NPV is positive and greater than 0 and the project is therefore acceptable.

Corporation tax is normally payable by a company in the year following the year in which profit is earned. If a project lasts for, say, four years then cash flow in respect of tax must also be shown in the fifth year. The length of the project is then effectively five years. Tax payable in respect of operating profit must be shown separately from cash flows in respect of capital allowances. The first investment year is normally shown as year 0 and the first tax allowance year is therefore year 1. Worked Example 4.18 uses a UK tax scenario to illustrate the importance of the timing of the tax cash flows in investments appraisal.

Worked Example 4.18

Zeta plc has the opportunity to invest in a machine costing £100,000 that will generate cash profits of £30,000 per year for the next four years after which the machine would be sold for £10,000. The company's after tax cost of capital is 8% per annum.

We may assume:

■ corporation tax at 30%

■ annual writing down allowances in each year are on the investment reducing balance at 25%

■ there will be a balancing charge or allowance on disposal of the machine.

We can consider whether or not the investment should be made, using an NPV approach.

Capital allowances:

Year	Opening balance £	Capital allowance at 25% £	Closing balance £
0	100,000	25,000	75,000
1	75,000	18,750	56,250
2	56,250	14,063	42,187
3	42,187	10,547	31,640
4	31,640	7,910	23,730
		Proceeds	(10,000)
	Total capital allowances 76,270	Balancing allowance	13,730

Note that the totals of the capital allowances and balancing allowance equal £90,000, the net cost of the machine £100,000 less £10,000.

Next, we can calculate the taxable profit, and the tax payable.

Year	0 £	1 £	2 £	3 £	4 £
Profit		30,000	30,000	30,000	30,000
Capital allowances	25,000	18,750	14,063	10,547	21,640
Taxable 'profit'	−25,000	11,250	15,937	19,453	8,360
Tax receivable/payable at 30%	7,500	−3,375	−4,781	−5,836	−2,508

The balancing allowance of £13,730 has been added to the 25% allowance £7,910 for year 4 to give a total of £21,640.

We can now calculate the net cash flows and the present values of the project and note how tax receivable and tax payable appear in the year following the year they relate to:

Year	Investment £	Profit £	Tax £	Net cash flow £	Discount factor at 8%	Present values £
0	−100,000			−100,000	1.00	−100,000
1		30,000	7,500	37,500	0.93	34,875
2		30,000	−3,375	26,625	0.86	22,897
3		30,000	−4,781	25,219	0.79	19,923
4	10,000	30,000	−5,836	34,164	0.74	25,281
5			−2,508	−2,508	0.68	−1,705
					NPV	+1,271

The positive NPV of £1,271 would indicate acceptance of this investment.

Progress check 4.10

Why and how should inflation and working capital be allowed for in making capital investment decisions?

Capital investment decisions take on a wider dimension for international corporations with the consideration of a further factor, the uncertainty associated with foreign currency exchange rate fluctuations. For UK-based companies this has had a particular significance over the past few years with the uncertainty surrounding the UK's adoption of the euro.

Back in 2001, Nissan's decision to build its new Micra car in Sunderland in the UK illustrated the importance of some of the additional factors that influence investment appraisal decisions. The strength of the £ sterling against the euro had damaged Sunderland's chances of winning the contract. But the level of Government support and the flexibility of the Sunderland workforce were factors that impacted favourably on the Nissan decision, in addition to their positive initial financial appraisal of the investment. As we can see from the press extract below, the fact that the UK had still not joined the euro was now threatening any future new investment in the plant.

The same press extract highlights an additional factor influencing investment decisions – the cost of labour. The labour cost differentials between the UK and, for example, the Far East and Eastern Europe have resulted increasingly in companies making new investments in countries like Poland, Czechoslovakia, and China. Despite the receipt from the UK Government of huge grants, interest-free loans, and fully subsidised staff training, Samsung decided to re-invest in plants in China and Slovakia.

The impact of high UK costs on investments by large foreign companies

'High labour cost drives Samsung out of Britain', by Edmund Conway

Electronics group Samsung yesterday announced it was shutting down its UK manufacturing operation, resulting in the loss of 425 jobs in the north-east.

The South Korean conglomerate said UK labour costs were too high, forcing it to move all of its factories to the Far East and Slovakia.

The Department for Trade and Industry said it would decide whether Samsung should pay back £10.5m of government aid granted it when the two Billingham factories were built for £450m in 1995.

Samsung UK's deputy managing director of manufacturing, John Slider, said the closure was 'the only practical way forward'.

He said: 'It's very sad news. This factory won the gold medal for productivity in the Samsung empire, which is no mean feat. The problem is the expense of the UK. We pay £4.50 to £5.50 an hour, which is not that much over here, but, when you compare that with 50p an hour in China, and £1 an hour in Slovakia, it's clear we can't compete.'

The microwave and flat-panel monitor plant's closure – timetabled for April – threatens another 1,000 jobs with suppliers in the area. It also follows Samsung's closure in 1999 of a nearby factory making fax machines.

Yesterday's move cast further doubt on the Government's policy of attempting to lure large foreign companies to build in the UK with grants and aid. When originally announced at the end of 1994, Michael Heseltine, then President of the Board of Trade, had called the Samsung deal 'a wonderful opportunity.'

The company was promised a total of £58m in grants, provided it created 3,000 jobs in the following five years, but, because employment only reached 1,500 at its peak, it received only £10.5m.

Samsung was also offered a £13m interest-free loan and £20m worth of training provided by a combination of local authorities and quangos. It said yesterday it used £1m of this to build a training centre, and did not take up the loan.

About £11m was also invested by local authorities and English Partnerships in improving the site itself and its transport facilities.

Unions and MPs rounded on Samsung last night, demanding that the grant be repaid in full. Frank Cook, Labour MP for Stockton North, said: 'They were allocated £58m and given every kind of consideration. They had every possible convenience provided for them. They claimed they have only drawn down

£10.5m as if they have done us some kind of a favour. Words fail me.'

A DTI spokesman said: 'Offers of this kind include claw-back provisions for the recovery of grant paid where projects run into difficulty or firms withdraw from an investment,' she said. 'The Government has given funding to local agencies to help those affected by today's announcement.'

Another local recipient of government aid, Nissan, has hinted that it might move production abroad. The Japanese car company was most recently awarded £3.26m to build its Micra cabriolet in Sunderland, but its president, Carlos Ghosn, last week threatened to pull the replacement for the Almera from the plant unless the UK joined the euro.

Many of those losing their jobs yesterday live in Prime Minister Tony Blair's Sedgefield constituency. Yesterday he said: 'This is part of the world economy in which we live. There will be occasions when companies close plants.'

© *Daily Telegraph*, 16 January 2004

Foreign currency exchange rate risk is not discussed in detail in this chapter but is an important topic that we will return to in Chapters 11 and 12.

Risk and uncertainty and decision-making – sensitivity analysis

The decision-making process includes a comparison of actual results following implementation of the decision with the expected outcome. Our own experience tells us that actual outcomes usually differ considerably from expected outcomes. In terms of capital investment, the greater the timescale of the project the more time there is for more things to go wrong; the larger the investment, the greater may be the impact.

As a final step in evaluation of the investment in a project it is prudent to carry out some sort of sensitivity analysis. Sensitivity analysis may be used to assess the risk associated with a capital investment project. A project having a positive NPV may on the face of it seem viable. It is useful to calculate how much the NPV may change should there be changes to the factors used in the appraisal exercise. These factors are shown in Fig. 4.6.

Sensitivity may be illustrated graphically:

- NPV is plotted on the y vertical axis
- the percentage change in the variable factors, used in the appraisal, is plotted on the x horizontal axis.

This process is then carried out for each variable, for example:

- sales
- cost savings
- investment
- scrap value

and the most sensitive variable is the one with the steepest gradient.

Sensitivity may also be evaluated through numerical analysis, which is illustrated in Worked Examples 4.19 to 4.23.

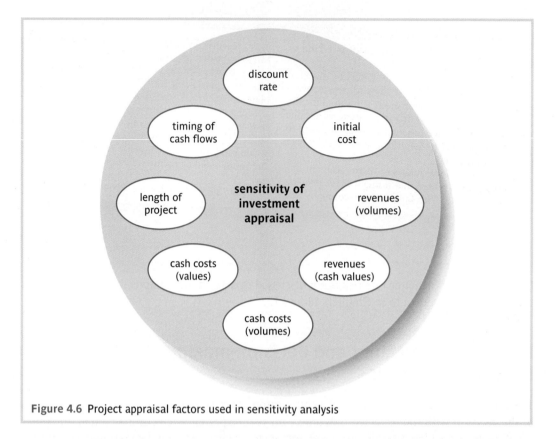

Figure 4.6 Project appraisal factors used in sensitivity analysis

Worked Example 4.19

Theta Ltd has the opportunity to invest in a project with an initial cost of £100,000 that will generate estimated net cash flows of £35,000 at the end of each year for five years. The company's cost of capital is 12% per annum. For simplicity we can ignore the effects of tax and inflation.

The sensitivity of the initial investment in the project can be evaluated using an NPV approach.

The cumulative Present Value tables show us that the annuity factor over five years at 12% per annum is 3.61 (see Appendix 1).

Therefore the NPV of the project is:

$$-£100,000 + (£35,000 \times 3.61)$$
$$= -£100,000 + £126,350$$
$$NPV = +£26,350$$

The positive NPV of £26,350 would indicate going ahead with the investment in this project.

We can consider the sensitivity analysis of the project to changes in the initial investment.

Initial investment
The NPV of the project is £26,350. If the initial investment rose by £26,350 to £126,350 (£100,000 + £26,350) the NPV would become zero and it would not be worth taking on the project. This represents an increase of 26.4% on the initial investment.

Worked Example 4.20

Using the data from Worked Example 4.19 we can evaluate the sensitivity of the project to changes in the annual cash flows from the project, using an NPV approach.

Annual cash flow
If we again consider what needs to happen to bring the NPV to zero then

$$\text{NPV} = 0 = -£100,000 + (a \times 3.61)$$

where a is the annual cash flow

$$a = £100,000/3.61$$
$$a = £27,700$$

which is a reduction of 20.9% from the original per annum cash flow of £35,000.

Worked Example 4.21

Using the data from Worked Example 4.19 we can evaluate the sensitivity of the project to changes in the cost of capital of the project for Theta Ltd, using an NPV approach.

Cost of capital
When the NPV is zero the internal rate of return (IRR) is equal to the cost of capital. If the cost of capital is greater than the IRR then the project should be rejected.

In this case, therefore, we first need to calculate the cumulative discount factor at which the NPV is zero.

$$\text{NPV} = 0 = -£100,000 + (£35,000 \times d)$$

Where d is the cumulative discount factor for five years

$$d = £100,000/£35,000$$
$$d = 2.857$$

The cumulative Present Value tables show us that the annuity factor over five years of 2.86 represents an interest rate of 22%.

The IRR is therefore approximately 22%, which is an 83.3% increase over the cost of capital of 12%.

Worked Example 4.22

Using the data from Worked Example 4.19 we can evaluate the sensitivity to changes in the length of the project for Theta Ltd, using an NPV approach.

Length of project
The original project was five years for which we calculated the NPV at £26,350. We may consider what would be the effect if the project ended after say four years or three years.

▶

▶   If the project was four years, the cumulative discount factor (from the tables) is 3.04 so the NPV of the project is:

$$-£100,000 + (£35,000 \times 3.04)$$
$$= -£100,000 + £106,400$$
$$NPV = +£6,400$$

The positive NPV of £6,400 still indicates going ahead with the investment in this project.

If the project was three years the cumulative discount factor (from the tables) is 2.40 so the NPV of the project is:

$$-£100,000 + (£35,000 \times 2.40)$$
$$= -£100,000 + £84,000$$
$$NPV = -£16,000$$

The negative NPV of £16,000 indicates not going ahead with the investment in this project if the length of the project drops below four years, which is the year in which NPV becomes negative. This is a change of 20% (that is a drop from five years to four years).

Worked Example 4.23

Each of the sensitivities that have been calculated in Worked Examples 4.19 to 4.22 may be summarised and we can draw some conclusions about the sensitivity of the project that are apparent from the summary.

The sensitivity analysis that we have carried out is more usefully summarised to show each of the factors we have considered, to show:

- the values used in the original appraisal
- the critical values of those factors
- the percentage change over the original values that they represent.

Factor	Original value	Critical value	% change
Initial investment	£100,000	£126,350	26.4
Annual cash flow	£35,000	£27,700	−20.9
Cost of capital	12%	22%	83.3
Length of project	5 years	4 years	−20.0

The following conclusions can be drawn from our sensitivity analysis:

- none of the factors used in the appraisal was critical, their critical values all being at least +/−20%
- cost of capital is the least critical factor at 83.3%, which is useful to know since the accuracy of the calculation of cost of capital may not always be totally reliable.

The same technique of sensitivity analysis may be used as an early warning system before a project begins to show a loss. It can be seen from the factors outlined in this section that a board of directors should request a sensitivity analysis on major projects. However, there are limitations to the use of sensitivity analysis. In the worked examples we have considered we have looked at the effect of changes to individual factors in isolation. In reality two or more factors may change simultaneously. The impact of such changes may be assessed using the more sophisticated technique of linear programming. A further limitation may be the absence of clear rules governing acceptance or rejection of the project and the need for the subjective judgement of management.

Simulation analysis

The risk associated with an investment project may also be considered by using a probability simulation. Worked Example 4.24 uses the weighting of cash flows of a project by the probabilities of their occurrence in order to calculate an expected NPV.

Worked Example 4.24

Kappa plc has the opportunity of engaging in a two-year project for a specific client. It would require an initial investment in a machine costing £200,000. The machine is capable of running three separate processes. The process used will depend on the level of demand from the client's final customers. Each process will therefore generate different yearly net cash flows, each with a different likelihood of occurrence. The company's cost of capital is 15% per annum.

The forecast probabilities and net cash flows for each year are:

Process	Probability of occurrence	Per annum cash flow
Process 1	0.5	£150,000
Process 2	0.1	£15,000
Process 3	0.4	£90,000
	1.0	

The total of the probabilities is 1.0, which indicates that one of the options is certain to occur.

Even though one process will definitely be used should Kappa take on the project?

We first need to use the probabilities to calculate the weighted average of the expected outcomes for each year.

Process	Cash flow £	Probability	Expected cash flow £
1	150,000	0.5	75,000
2	15,000	0.1	1,500
3	90,000	0.4	36,000
Expected per annum cash flows			112,500

To calculate the expected NPV of the project we need to discount the expected annual cash flows using the discount rate of 15% per annum.

▶

Year	Expected cash flow £	Discount factor at 15%	Expected present value £
1	112,500	0.87	97,875
2	112,500	0.76	85,500
Total	225,000		183,375
Initial investment (year 0)			200,000
Expected NPV			−16,625

The negative expected NPV of £16,625 indicates that Kappa plc should reject investment in this project.

Although the technique of expected net present value is a clear decision rule with a single numerical outcome there are caveats:

- this technique uses an average number which in the above example is not actually capable of occurrence

- use of an average number may cloud the issue if the underlying risk of outcomes worse than the average are ignored.

Consider, for example, the impact on Kappa if the expected per annum cash flow from Process 1 had been £300,000 and the expected NPV had been positive, but that the client then actually required the use of Process 2.

Progress check 4.11

Risk and uncertainty increasingly impact on investment decisions. What are these risk factors, and how may we evaluate their impact?

Scenario analysis

The examples of the sensitivity analysis techniques we have considered only deal with changing each variable or key factor one at a time. These techniques don't consider, for example, questions like 'what would be the outcome if the worst happens?' or 'what is the best outcome?' Uncertainty analysis (as distinct from risk analysis) is an unquantified approach that takes the view that just how much actual outcomes are worse or better than rational estimates can't be quantified. Uncertainty in terms of worst, best, and likely outcomes may be considered using the technique of scenario analysis. Risk analysis is a quantified approach about how future outcomes may vary expressed as probabilities. Risk analysis techniques include simulation analysis using probabilities, which is an extension of scenario analysis.

Monte Carlo simulation

The probability simulation we used in Worked Example 4.24 is a simple example that considers probabilities of only a very small number of outcomes. In real life situations there may be many variables subject to random variation. Also, the number of likely combinations of events may be massive, and therefore it may be very difficult to calculate a solution. The simulation of a large number of events may be carried out using what is called a Monte Carlo simulation, which employs a random device for what happens at a given point in a situation.

Because of the large amount of data, Monte Carlo simulation is necessarily a computerised technique. The computer uses random numbers to generate thousands of possible combinations of variables according to a pre-specified probability distribution. The Monte Carlo simulation applied to investment analysis provides an NPV outcome from each scenario and the NPVs of each scenario provide a probability distribution of outcomes. Companies may therefore use the Monte Carlo method, and other simulation techniques that use probabilities, to assess risk relating to future cash flows of investments. However, these techniques do not provide any help with regard to the selection of an appropriate discount rate.

Real options

It should be noted that the techniques of both sensitivity analysis and Monte Carlo simulation do not recognise the ability to change projects. The various options that may be considered in order to modify projects use what are called real options. A real option is particularly useful in investment appraisal if:

■ there is a great deal of uncertainty surrounding the project
■ the project requires a high level of flexibility
■ the NPV analysis provides a borderline result.

There are four main types of real options applicable to investment decisions:

■ expansion options, using, for example, decision trees to evaluate alternatives, which identify opportunities to invest and expand on the success of the original investment
■ abandonment options, which enable the company to shrink or get out of a project if cash flows are below expectations and therefore recover some of the costs of plant and equipment and any other project assets
■ timing options provide the options of waiting and learning before going ahead with investment in a project even if it has a positive NPV – a company may want to go ahead with an investment immediately to take advantage of market opportunities, or it may prefer to wait if there are market uncertainties
■ strategic production options, which give companies the flexibility to vary the inputs or outputs of the production process – this may relate to the use in a capital project of, for example, alternative sources of energy like gas or oil, dependent on price and availability.

Real options in practice may relate to advantages of projects that may be perceived as being intangible, but which may be fundamental to the investment decision.

Equivalent annual cost (EAC)

The calculation of a net present value (NPV) takes the cash flows of future periods and converts them into one sum which represents their value expressed in today's US$, £ sterling, Riyals, Dirhams, euros, or any other currency. It is possible to carry out this calculation in reverse by taking the total of today's original investment and converting it into a stream of equivalent future cash flows. These equivalent future cash flows are called equivalent annual costs (EACs). EAC is a particularly useful financial tool, which we have illustrated in Worked Example 4.25.

Worked Example 4.25

A water company in the Middle East required a significant capital investment in order to upgrade its desalination plants. This prompted the question 'How much would the price of water have to be increased following this investment?' It was estimated that an upgrade of a desalination plant would require the company to invest 5 billion Dirhams. The company's real (inflation-adjusted) cost of capital is 5% and the new equipment will last for 20 years. The desalination plant's total clean water production will be 4.5 million litres a year. For simplicity it may be assumed that the upgrade will not require any additional materials or changes to operating costs. The company needed to know how many Dirhams per litre it would have to charge to recover the investment cost. We will use EAC to answer that question and ignoring taxation, which is not payable in this Middle Eastern country.

To calculate how much additional income the desalination plant would need for each of the 20 years to cover the 5 billion Dirhams investment we need to calculate the 20 year annuity (see the earlier section about annuities) with a present value of 5 billion Dirhams.

$$\text{present value of an annuity} = \text{annuity payment} \times \text{annuity factor}$$

therefore

$$\text{annuity payment} = \frac{\text{present value of an annuity}}{\text{annuity factor}}$$

Using a cost of capital or 5% per annum the 20 year

$$\text{annuity factor} = \left[\frac{1}{r} - \frac{1}{r(1+r)^t} \right] = \left[\frac{1}{0.05} - \frac{1}{0.05 \times 1.05^{20}} \right] = 12.46$$

$$\text{annuity payment} = \frac{5,000,000 \text{ Dirhams}}{12.46} = 401,284 \text{ Dirhams per annum}$$

The amount per litre is

$$\frac{401,284 \text{ Dirhams}}{4,500,000 \text{ litres}} = 0.0892 \text{ Dirhams per litre}$$

Progress check 4.12

With regard to investment appraisal what is an equivalent annual cost (EAC)?

Capital budgeting

Investment appraisal techniques are just one part of the capital investment process. They may be used in one form or another as part of a company's capital budgeting process. Capital budgeting should be an incremental decision-making process involving many departments within a business, and not just the finance department, or the accountant, or financial analyst.

Capital budgeting is a process with a distinct number of stages. The capital investment procedures in companies must be designed to allow managers to make optimal investments with the aim of maximisation of shareholder wealth. The main aim of capital budgeting is to ensure that resources are made available to implement capital projects that are wealth-creating and are aligned with corporate goals. Good investment ideas should not be held back and poor investment ideas rejected or further refined. The steps in the capital budgeting process are:

- determination of the budget
- the search for and development of new investment projects
- evaluation of alternative investment projects
- obtaining approval for new projects
- monitoring and controlling projects.

Capital rationing – the profitability index (PI)

Companies normally consider many alternative projects in which they may invest. If the business has limited funds available for investment then capital rationing is required. Capital rationing is a restriction on an organisation's ability to invest capital funds and comprises two types: soft capital rationing and hard capital rationing:

- soft capital rationing is a restriction that is caused by an internal budget ceiling being imposed on capital expenditure by management, for example via departmental or company capital budgets
- hard capital rationing is caused by external limitations being applied to the organisation, for example when additional borrowed funds cannot be obtained.

A company may impose a restriction on the amount of funds available to individual divisional heads in order to direct investment funds into particular areas or activities of the company to maximise its returns. Such a restriction would be an example of soft capital rationing. However, where such a restriction exists because of external constraints such a restriction would be an example of hard capital rationing. Examples of this may be seen where a company may not be able to raise funds because of a lack of security or collateral, or where restrictions are imposed by existing lenders (for example to limit the level of the company's gearing).

If capital rationing exists, how should a company choose between alternative investment opportunities? One widely used technique is the profitability index, which is an attempt to identify the relationship between the costs and benefits of a proposed project through the use of a ratio. The profitability index ratio is:

$$PI = \frac{\text{present value of future cash flows}}{\text{initial investment}}$$

A ratio of 1 is the lowest acceptable measure of the index since any value lower than 1 would indicate that the project's present value of future cash flows is less than the initial investment required to generate the cash flows. Consequently, as the value of the profitability index increases, so does the financial attractiveness of a proposed project. Where there is no restriction on investment capital, all projects with a profitability ratio greater than 1 may be accepted.

It should be noted that the profitability index is only useful where single period capital rationing exists. This relates to situations where there is a limit on the availability of finance for positive NPV projects for one year only. Where multi-period capital rationing exists there is a limit on the availability of finance for positive NPV projects for more than one year, and therefore in that situation the profitability index cannot be used. In multi-period capital rationing where financial constraints are expected over a number of years the allocation of funds to investment projects may be calculated using the statistical approach of linear programming.

Appraisal of investments in single period capital rationing situations requires the evaluation of competing projects. This uses the profitability index technique, which is also sometimes referred to as DPI (dollar per investment). The PI method requires the ranking of competing projects in terms of their NPVs per each dollar of investment in each project. Of course the PI technique is not just restricted to the US$ and relates to the ranking of competing investments denominated in any currency. Competing investment funds may then be allocated according to the NPV rankings of each investment. Funds should then be allocated for investment in the project with the highest PI, and then funds allocated for investment in the next highest ranked PI and so on. In this way, the company continues to allocate funds for investment in the 'best' projects up to the total of the capital investment budget that has been set either through soft or hard capital rationing.

Worked Example 4.26

A company is considering two projects A and B, with the following estimates of investment cost, present values of future cash flows, and NPVs.

Project	Investment	Present values of future cash flows	NPV
	£	£	£
A	400,000	560,000	160,000
B	800,000	880,000	80,000

Both projects have an NPV greater than zero and may therefore be accepted. If the projects are mutually exclusive then the company will choose project B because it has a higher NPV than project A.

If the company has capital rationing with a constraint on the amount of funds available for investment then it should consider a PI approach.

$$\text{Project A} \quad \text{PI} = \frac{£560,000}{£400,000} = 1.4$$

$$\text{Project B} \quad \text{PI} = \frac{£880,000}{£800,000} = 1.1$$

Project A has a higher PI than project B, which means that it will return more NPV per £ invested than project B, a return of 40% compared with 10%. Therefore, if the company uses PI criteria then it will choose project A. Assume that there are a number of projects with the same investment and NPV as project A and the maximum available for investment is £800,000. The company could invest in two projects of type A which will produce a total NPV of $2 \times £160,000 = £320,000$, compared with an £80,000 NPV from project B.

The PI approach gives the right decision in a single-period capital rationing situation as we have seen in Worked Example 4.26, if the total amount of funds available can be used. If there is more than one period then the PI approach will not work. If capital rationing is expected to continue from the current period into future periods then the timing of future cash flows must be considered. For multiple-period capital rationing the NPV per amount available for investment (the limiting factor) must still be maximised but on the assumption that projects may be divisible, and then an optimal solution may be found using linear programming.

Control of capital investment projects

Once a project has been appraised and a sensitivity analysis carried out and the approval has been given at the relevant level in the organisation, project controls must be established and then post-project completion audits carried out. The project controls should cover the three main areas of:

- capital spend – note the number of subjective areas where things can go wrong
- project-timing – delays appear to be 'routine' in many major projects as evidenced almost daily in the financial press
- benefits – evidenced almost as frequently in the financial press, this is another area where things may not turn out as planned.

Capital spending limits are usually put in place by most organisations with levels of spend requiring authorisation at the appropriate managerial level. Capital expenditure proposals should be documented to show:

- project details, including costs, benefits and the life of the project
- appraisal calculations and comparisons with the organisation's targets
- assumptions
- names of the project manager and the project team
- name(s) and signature(s) of the manager(s) authorising the project
- the period(s) in which expenditure should take place.

Material delays in capital spend or in the progress of the project should prompt a re-submitted proposal together with the reasons for delay. A good project manager with the appropriate level of responsibility and authority should ensure that projects run to plan.

Benefits from projects are not easy to control because they are usually derived over many years. The importance of having a good project manager in place cannot be over-emphasised. The project manager should ensure that expected benefits actually materialise and are as large in value as anticipated. The project manager should also ensure that costs are kept in line with expectation.

Post-implementation audits should be carried out for all projects if possible. Although after the event corrective action cannot usually be taken, variances may be analysed to use the project as an information and learning tool:

- to appraise manager performance
- to identify strengths and weaknesses in the company's forecasting and estimating techniques
- to identify areas of improvement in the capital investment process
- to advertise the fact that both project and manager performance are being monitored.

Progress check 4.13

In what ways can we ensure that capital investment projects are adequately controlled?

Summary of key points

- An investment requires expenditure on something today that is expected to provide a benefit in the future.

- The decision to make an investment is extremely important because it implies the expectation that expenditure today will generate future cash gains in real terms that greatly exceed the funds spent today.

- '£1 received today is worth more than £1 received in a year's time' is an expression of what is meant by the 'time value of money'.

- The present value of a perpetuity may be calculated for a stream of level cash payments that continues indefinitely. The present value of an annuity may be calculated for an equally spaced level stream of cash flows for a limited period of time.

- The principles underlying the investment appraisal techniques that use the discounted cash flow (DCF) method are cash flow (as opposed to profit), and the time value of money.

- Five main criteria are used to appraise investments: accounting rate of return (ARR); payback; net present value (NPV); internal rate of return (IRR); and discounted payback – the last three being DCF techniques.

- The technique of discounted cash flow discounts the projected net cash flows of a capital project to ascertain its present value, using an appropriate discount rate, or cost of capital.

- Additional factors impacting on investment criteria calculations are: the effect of inflation on cash flows and the cost of capital; working capital requirements; length of project; taxation; risk and uncertainty.

- There may be a number of risks associated with each of the variables included in a capital investment appraisal decision: estimates of initial costs; uncertainty about the timing and values of future cash revenues and costs; the length of project; variations in the discount rate.

- Sensitivity analysis, scenario analysis, and simulation may be used to assess the risk and uncertainty associated with a capital investment project.

- To establish the appropriate levels of control, the appointment of a good project manager with the appropriate level of responsibility and authority, together with regular project reviews, are absolute essentials to ensure that projects run to plan.

- The techniques of capital investment appraisal require a great deal of expertise and experience, and specialised training is essential in order to use them in real life decision-making situations.

🔑 Glossary of key terms

accounting rate of return (ARR) Annual profit divided by investment. It is a form of return on capital employed. Unlike NPV and IRR, it is based on profits, not cash flows.

annuity A fixed periodic payment which continues either for a specified time, or until the occurrence of a specified event.

capital asset pricing model (CAPM) A theory which predicts that the expected risk premium for an individual share will be proportional to its beta, such that the expected risk premium on a share equals beta multiplied by the expected risk premium in the market. The risk premium is defined as the expected incremental return for making a risky investment rather than a safe one.

capital rationing This is a restriction on an organisation's ability to invest capital funds, caused by an internal budget ceiling being imposed on such expenditure by management (soft capital rationing), or by external limitations being applied to the organisation, for example when additional borrowed funds cannot be obtained (hard capital rationing).

discounted cash flow (DCF) The discounting of the projected net cash flows of a capital project to ascertain its present value, using a yield or internal rate of return (IRR), net present value (NPV) or discounted payback.

discounted payback The number of years required to repay an original investment using a specified discount rate.

equivalent annual cost (EAC) The yearly annuity payments (or the annual cash flows) sufficient to recover a capital investment, including the cost of capital for that investment, over the investment's economic life.

internal rate of return (IRR) The annual percentage return achieved by a project, at which the sum of the discounted cash inflows over the life of the project is equal to the sum of the discounted cash outflows, that is, when NPV equals zero.

investment Any application of funds which is intended to provide a return by way of interest, dividend, or capital appreciation.

net present value (NPV) The difference between the sums of the projected discounted cash inflows and outflows attributable to a capital investment or other long-term project.

payback The number of years it takes the cash inflows from a capital investment project to equal the cash outflows. An organisation may have a target payback period, above which projects are rejected.

perpetuity A periodic payment continuing for a limitless period.

present value The cash equivalent now of a sum receivable or payable at a future date.

sensitivity analysis A modelling and risk assessment technique in which changes are made to significant variables in order to determine the effect of these changes on the planned outcome. Particular attention is thereafter paid to variables identified as being of special significance.

Questions

Q4.1 (i) What is capital investment?

(ii) Why are capital investment decisions so important to companies?

Q4.2 Outline the five main investment appraisal criteria.

Q4.3 Describe the two key principles underlying DCF investment selection criteria.

Q4.4 What are the advantages in the use of NPV over IRR in investment appraisal?

Q4.5 What are the factors that impact on capital investment decisions?

Q4.6 (i) What is meant by risk with regard to investment?

(ii) How does sensitivity analysis help?

Q4.7 Describe how capital investment projects may be controlled and reviewed.

Discussion points

D4.1 'I know that cash and profit are not always the same thing but surely eventually they end up being equal. Therefore, surely we should look at the likely ultimate profit from a capital investment before deciding whether or not to invest?' Discuss.

D4.2 'This discounted cash flow business seems like just a bit more work for the accountants to me. Cash is cash whenever it's received or paid. I say let's keep capital investment appraisal simple.' Discuss.

D4.3 'If you don't take a risk you will not make any money.' Discuss.

Exercises

Solutions are provided in Appendix 2 to all exercise numbers highlighted in colour.

Level I

E4.1 *Time allowed – 30 minutes*

Global Sights & Sounds Ltd (GSS) sells multi-media equipment and software through its retail outlets. GSS is considering investing in some major refurbishment of one of its outlets, to enable it to provide improved customer service, until the lease expires at the end of four years. GSS is currently talking to two contractors, Smith Ltd and Jones Ltd. Whichever contractor is used, the improved customer service has been estimated to generate increased net cash inflows as follows:

Year	£
1	75,000
2	190,000
3	190,000
4	225,000

Smith:

The capital costs will be £125,000 at the start of the project, and £175,000 at the end of each of years 1 and 2.

► **Jones:**
The capital costs will be the same in total, but payment to the contractor can be delayed. Capital payments will be £50,000 at the start of the project, £75,000 at the end of each of years 1, 2 and 3, and the balance of capital cost at the end of year 4. In return for the delayed payments the contractor will receive a 20% share of the cash inflows generated from the improved services, payable at the end of each year. In the interim period, the unutilised capital will be invested in a short-term project in another department store, generating a cash inflow of £60,000 at the end of each of years 1, 2 and 3.

It may be assumed that all cash flows occur at the end of each year.

The effects of taxation and inflation may be ignored.

You are required to advise GSS Ltd on whether to select Smith or Jones, ignoring the time value of money, using the appraisal basis of:

(i) accounting rate of return (ARR), and

(ii) comment on the appraisal method you have used.

E4.2 *Time allowed – 30 minutes*

Using the information on Global Sights & Sounds Ltd from Exercise E4.1, you are required to advise GSS Ltd on whether to select Smith or Jones, ignoring the time value of money, using the appraisal basis of:

(i) payback, and

(ii) comment on the appraisal method you have used.

E4.3 *Time allowed – 60 minutes*

Rainbow plc's business is organised into divisions. For operating purposes, each division is regarded as an investment centre, with divisional managers enjoying substantial autonomy in their selection of investment projects. Divisional managers are rewarded via a remuneration package, which is linked to a return on investment (ROI) performance measure. The ROI calculation is based on the net book value of assets at the beginning of the year. Although there is a high degree of autonomy in investment selection, approval to go ahead has to be obtained from group management at the head office in order to release the finance.

Red Division is currently investigating three independent investment proposals. If they appear acceptable, it wishes to assign each a priority in the event that funds may not be available to cover all three. The WACC (weighted average cost of capital) for the company is the hurdle rate used for new investments and is estimated at 15% per annum.

The details of the three proposals are as follows:

	Project A £000	Project B £000	Project C £000
Initial cash outlay on non-current assets	60	60	60
Net cash inflow in year 1	21	25	10
Net cash inflow in year 2	21	20	20
Net cash inflow in year 3	21	20	30
Net cash inflow in year 4	21	15	40

Taxation and the residual values of the non-current assets may be ignored.

Depreciation is straight line over the asset life, which is four years in each case. ►

▶ You are required to:

(i) give an appraisal of the three investment proposals with regard to divisional performance, using ROI and RI

(ii) give an appraisal of the three investment proposals with regard to company performance, using a DCF approach

(iii) explain any divergence between the two points of view, expressed in (i) and (ii) above, and outline how the views of both the division and the company can be brought into line.

Level II

E4.4 *Time allowed – 30 minutes*

Using the information on Global Sights & Sounds Ltd from Exercise E4.1, you are required to:

(i) advise GSS Ltd on whether to select Smith or Jones, using the appraisal basis of net present value (NPV), using a cost of capital of 12% per annum to discount the cash flows to their present value

(ii) comment on the appraisal method you have used.

E4.5 *Time allowed – 30 minutes*

Using the information on Global Sights & Sounds Ltd from Exercise E4.1, you are required to:

(i) advise GSS Ltd on whether to select Smith or Jones, using the appraisal basis of discounted payback, using a cost of capital of 12% per annum to discount the cash flows to their present value

(ii) comment on the appraisal method you have used.

E4.6 *Time allowed – 45 minutes*

Using the information on Global Sights & Sounds Ltd from Exercise E4.1, you are required to:

(i) advise GSS Ltd on whether to select Smith or Jones, using the appraisal basis of internal rate of return (IRR)

(ii) comment on the appraisal method you have used.

E4.7 *Time allowed – 45 minutes*

In Exercise E4.1 we are told that a 20% share of the improved cash inflow has been agreed with Jones Ltd.

You are required to:

(i) calculate the percentage share at which GSS Ltd would be indifferent, on a financial basis, as to which of the contractors Smith or Jones should carry out the work

(ii) outline the other factors, in addition to your financial analyses in (i), that should be considered in making the choice between Smith and Jones.

E4.8 *Time allowed – 60 minutes*

Alive & Kicking Ltd (AAK) owns a disused warehouse in which a promoter runs regular small gigs.

There are currently no facilities to provide drinks. The owners of AAK intend to provide such facilities and can obtain funding to cover capital costs. This would have to be repaid over five years at an annual rate of 10%.

The capital costs are estimated at £120,000 for equipment that will have a life of five years and no residual value. To provide drinks, the running costs of staff, etc., will be £40,000 in the first year, increasing by £4,000 in each subsequent year. AAK proposes to charge £10,000 per annum for lighting, heating, and other property expenses, and wants a nominal £5,000 per annum to cover any unforeseen contingencies. Apart from this, AAK is not looking for any profit as such from the provision of these facilities, because it believes that there may be additional future benefits from increased use of the facility. It is proposed that costs will be recovered by setting drinks prices at double the direct costs.

It is not expected that the full sales level will be reached until year 3. The proportions of that level estimated to be reached in years 1 and 2 are 40% and 70% respectively.

You are required to:

(i)   calculate the sales that need to be achieved in each of the five years to meet the proposed targets

(ii) comment briefly on four aspects of the proposals that you consider merit further investigation.

You may ignore the possible effects of taxation and inflation.

E4.9   *Time allowed – 90 minutes*

Lew Rolls plc is an international group that manufactures and distributes bathroom fittings to major building supply retailers and DIY chains. The board of Rolls is currently considering four projects to work with four different customers to develop new bathroom ranges (toilet, bidet, bath, basin, and shower).

Rolls has a limit on funds for investment for the current year of £24m. The four projects represent levels of 'luxury' bathrooms. The product ranges are aimed at different markets. The lengths of time to bring to market, lives of product, and timings of cash flows are different for each product range.

The Super bathroom project will cost £3m and generate £5m net cash flows spread equally over five years.

The Superluxury bathroom project will cost £7m and generate £10m net cash flows spread equally over five years.

The Executive bathroom project will take a long time to start paying back. It will cost £12m and generate £21m net cash flows, zero for the first two years and then £7m for each of the next three years.

The Excelsior bathroom project will cost £15m and generate £10m net cash flows for two years.

For ease of calculation it may be assumed that all cash flows occur on the last day of each year.

Projects may be undertaken in part or in total in the current year, and next year there will be no restriction on investment. Lew Rolls plc's cost of capital is 10%.

You are required to:

(i)   calculate the NPV for each project

(ii)   calculate the approximate IRR for each project

(iii) advise on the acceptance of these projects on the basis of NPV or IRR or any other method of ranking the projects

▶   **(iv)** list the advantages of the appraisal method you have adopted for Lew Rolls plc

    (v) comment on what other factors should be used in the final evaluations before the recommendations are implemented.

E4.10 *Time allowed – 90 minutes*

A UK subsidiary of a large multinational is considering investment in four mutually exclusive projects. The managing director, Indira Patel, is anxious to choose a combination of projects that will maximise shareholder wealth.

At the current time the company can embark on projects up to a maximum total of £230m. The four projects require the following initial investments:

£20m in project Doh
£195m in project Ray
£35m in project Mee
£80m in project Fah

The projects are expected to generate the following net cash flows over the three years following each investment. No project will last longer than three years.

Project Year	Doh £m	Ray £m	Mee £m	Fah £m
1	15	45	15	20
2	30	75	25	25
3		180	60	100

The company's WACC is 12% per annum, which is used to evaluate investments in new projects. The impact of tax and inflation may be ignored.

Advise Indira with regard to the projects in which the company should invest on the basis of maximisation of shareholder wealth, given the limiting factor of the total funds currently available for investment.

Chapter 5

Risk, return, and portfolio theory

Chapter contents

LEARNING OBJECTIVES

Completion of this chapter will enable you to:

☑ Explain the relationship between risk and return.

☑ Outline investor attitudes to risk.

☑ Describe what is meant by business risk and financial risk.

☑ Consider the impact of risk on financing.

☑ Describe what is meant by systematic and unsystematic risk.

☑ Explain the role of diversification in the mitigation of unsystematic risk.

☑ Explain portfolio theory.

☑ Appreciate the significance of risk-free investments, investors' preferences, and the capital market line (CML).

Introduction

This chapter looks at the uncertainty and risk surrounding decisions made by both the shareholders and managers and directors of businesses and how these relate to the returns or paybacks achieved following such decisions.

The fundamental objective of a business is to maximise the wealth of the shareholders, or the owners of the business. The increase in the wealth of shareholders, or total shareholder return, is derived from dividends and increases in the market prices of their shares. The ability of a company to pay dividends is ultimately determined by its decision-making success with regard to its 'real' investment in value creating projects. The market price of a company's shares is determined by the demand for its shares, which in turn depends on the market perception of the business and its ability to generate future cash flows.

When an investor buys shares there is uncertainty with regard to the level of future dividends that may be received. There is also uncertainty with regard to how much the share price may increase, or decrease. The level of total shareholder returns is therefore uncertain and some shares are more uncertain or riskier than others. For example, the expected returns from an investment in the shares of a hi-tech company will generally be far riskier than the expected returns from an investment in the shares of a bank.

When the directors of a business make 'real' investments in new projects there is uncertainty not only with regard to each of the factors relating to a project like its investment cost, its cost of capital etc., but particularly with regard to the expected returns on the investments. The level of returns from 'real' investments is therefore uncertain, and some projects are more uncertain or riskier than others.

This chapter will consider the relationship between the risks and returns from both investments in shares and investments in 'real' projects. We will consider the way in which approaches to risk are different from one individual to another, and how risk may be mitigated or reduced by investing in a range or portfolio of shares or projects.

The chapter examines Markowitz's portfolio theory, which deals with the way in which investors are able to diversify risk by holding combinations of different securities. This chapter closes with a look at investors' preferences with regard to investments in risk-free and market risk securities and the proportions of both which may be shown on the capital market line (CML).

The relationship between risk and return

There is a fundamental relationship that exists between risk and return. We will consider this relationship, and also investor attitudes to risk, the different types of risk and their impact on the business, its cost of capital, and its strategies.

Decision-making relates to alternative outcomes that may occur as a result of whichever decision is taken. The likelihood of a particular outcome occurring is never certain. The return or payback resulting from a particular decision may be more or less than expected. The level of uncertainty relating to the expected outcome that may be quantified is the level of the risk of that outcome not occurring. Generally, the higher the level of risk the higher will be the expected return. The lower the level of risk, the lower will be the expected return. As we have seen in earlier chapters, the directors of businesses make decisions to invest in new projects only if they are expected to provide value added to the business in real terms.

Worked Example 5.1

Eryl Ltd is considering investing surplus cash in one of the following companies:

Company	Expected return %	Risk %
AB plc	10	12
CD plc	10	24
EF plc	20	24
GH plc	20	28

We are required to advise Eryl Ltd as to which investment should be selected.

If Eryl Ltd is a rational and risk-averse investor, then it would invest in AB plc (minimum investment risk). If Eryl Ltd is a rational but risk-taking investor, then it would invest in EF plc (maximum return).

Neither CD plc, nor GH plc should be selected since CD plc has the same return as AB plc but higher risk, and GH plc has the same return as EF plc but a higher risk.

Let's consider a company, which has a risk-return profile represented by the line YXZ in Fig. 5.1. This means that the company will maintain the same level of value wherever it may position itself along line YXZ in terms of combinations of risk and return.

If the company is assumed to be at point X in terms of its perceived risk and required return from current projects we can consider the impact of any strategic move by the company from point X, along the line YXZ, and to either above or below line YXZ.

Increasing value is not just about increasing return or reducing risk, but it is to do with the level of increased required return compared with the increased perception of risk. A move down the line XY reduces risk but proportionately reduces returns, and a move up the line XZ increases returns but proportionately increases risk. Either way, value is neither created nor destroyed.

Any strategic move (1) to below line YXZ will destroy existing value, because risk is disproportionately higher for any increased returns when compared against the current risk-return profile YXZ.

Any strategic move above line YXZ will create shareholder value. A move (2) above the line WXZ will increase returns for any given reduction in risk and by proportionately more than any

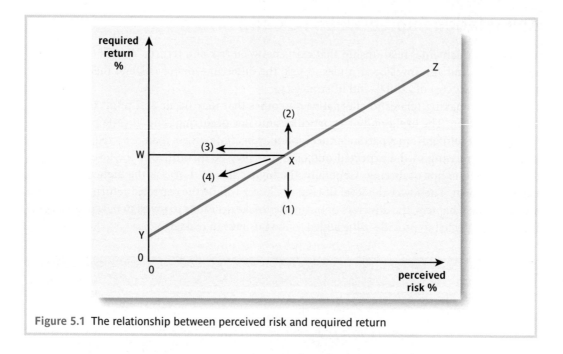

Figure 5.1 The relationship between perceived risk and required return

increase in risk. We can clearly see that a move (3) along the line XW will reduce risk, while at the same time maintaining the same level of return. However, a move (4) to within the triangle WXY will reduce risk but by proportionately less than any increase in required return, but it is still value adding. An example of this may be seen when a company decides to pay out large insurance premiums to cover specific risks faced by the company. This has the effect of reducing profit, but it also reduces risk and therefore protects the company's future cash flows and so increases the value of the business.

There is also a degree of risk involved whenever any investment is made in a company's securities. The total actual return on investment in ordinary shares (equity capital) may be better or worse than hoped for. Unless the investor settles for risk-free securities a certain element of risk is unavoidable.

Progress check 5.1

What is the relationship between risk and return?

However, investors in companies or in projects can diversify their investments in a suitably wide portfolio. Some investments may do better and some worse than expected. In this way, average returns should turn out much as expected. Risk that is possible to be diversified away in this way is referred to as unsystematic risk.

Some investments are by their very nature more risky than others. This is nothing to do with chance variations in actual compared with expected returns. It is inherent risk that cannot be diversified away. This type of risk is referred to as systematic risk or market risk, as distinct from unsystematic risk (risk that is unique to a specific company). The investor must therefore accept systematic risk, unless they invest entirely in risk-free investments. In return for accepting systematic risk an investor will expect to earn a return, which is higher than the return on risk-free investment.

The two broad components of systematic risk are business risk and financial risk. The amount of systematic risk depends, for example, on the industry or the type of project. If an investor has a completely balanced portfolio of shares they may incur exactly the same systematic risk as the average systematic risk of the stock market as a whole. The capital asset pricing model (CAPM), which we will discuss further in Chapter 6, is mainly concerned with how systematic risk is measured and how systematic risk affects required returns and share prices. It was first formulated for investments in shares on the stock exchange, but is now also used for company investments in capital projects.

Systematic risk is measured using what are known as beta (β) factors. A **beta factor** (β) is the measure of the volatility of a share in terms of market risk. The CAPM is a statement of the principles outlined above. An investor can use the beta factor in such a way that a high factor will automatically suggest a share is to be avoided because of its considerable high risk in the past.

Consider the possible impact in January 2001 on the beta factor of Iceland plc caused by the resignation from the board of the major shareholder, Malcolm Walker, together with the issue of a profits warning by the company. Given that Iceland was plunged into a £120m loss after an amazing £145m of exceptional items, it is very likely that Iceland's beta factor increased significantly because there would have been a great deal of volatility in the trading of its shares. Many senior managers were forced to leave the company in 2002, at which time the company was also renamed The Big Food Group. The Big Food Group's sales levels, profits, and share price continued to fluctuate with a downward trend over the subsequent few years during which time it is likely that the company's beta value remained fairly high. In 2005 The Big Food Group's shareholders accepted an offer for the business by a consortium led by Baugur, an investment group based coincidentally in Iceland! After 21 years on the stock market, Iceland (Big Food Group) became a private company once more, with shareholders receiving only a fraction of the value that the group had enjoyed at its peak. The business was subsequently split into its main component parts and Iceland placed under the management of Malcolm Walker and other senior executives who had been ejected in 2001.

Progress check 5.2

Describe what is meant by systematic risk and unsystematic risk.

Investor attitudes to risk

There is a potential conflict between the risk and return perceptions of managers and investors. They may generally display one of three attitudes to risk. These may be:

- risk-taking, in which case they have a preference for a high return in exchange for taking a high level of risk
- risk neutral, in which case they are indifferent to the level of risk faced
- risk-averse, in which case they have a preference for low-risk, low-return investments.

Attitudes to risk may also be considered with regard to their impact on an individual's level of utility. A risk-taker and a risk-averse person may both take on the same risk, but the risk-averse person would require a higher potential return than the risk taker before making an investment. For example, one person might be willing to bet on a horse in a race if odds of 2 to 1 were offered, while another person might only bet on the same horse in the same race if they could be offered better odds of say 4 to 1. The risk taker accepts a potentially lower return for the same level of risk as the risk-averse person who would expect a higher return. If the risk-averse person cannot obtain the return (or odds) that they require then they will not invest (or bet). This is also situationally specific in that on another occasion roles might be reversed as their perspectives of the risk involved might change.

Investors also display different attitudes to risk. While equity shareholders are generally risk takers, providers of debt capital are generally risk-averse. There may also be conflicts. For example, risk-loving venture capitalists may have aims that may clash with the aims of the risk-averse senior managers of a business. As a consequence, the company may not go ahead with high-risk investments necessary to provide the high returns expected by venture capitalists.

Progress check 5.3

What is meant by an individual's attitude to risk?

Business risk and financial risk

One part of systematic or market risk is business risk. Business risk is due to the variability of a company's operating profits or cash flows given the line of business in which the company is operating. These are risks to the company's operating results that are dependent on the industry in which the company is operating.

The wide range of factors relating to business risk is shown in Fig. 5.2, relating to each of the main elements of cost, price, demand, growth, business environment, and financial factors that impact on the level of a company's operating profits and cash flows.

COST
Number of suppliers
Suppliers' financial stability
Reliance on specific materials
Operating gearing
Committed costs

PRICE
Marketing mix
Economic conditions
Price competition
Substitute products
Complementary products

DEMAND
Marketing mix
Fashion and taste
Competition
Shorter product life cycle

GROWTH
New product development
Management skills
Production facilities
Location

BUSINESS ENVIRONMENT
PESTEL factors
Environmental issues
Industrial factors

FINANCIAL
Interest rate changes
Foreign currency exposure
Working capital requirements

Figure 5.2 Factors relating to business risk

DEBT	
Low financial risk for the investor and High financial risk for the company	Interest must be paid contractually according to the loan agreement The loan must be repaid contractually on the agreed date A loan is usually secured on company assets and assets may be repossessed
EQUITY	
High financial risk for the investor and Low financial risk for the company	It is the company's choice to pay dividends and dividends do not have to be paid Equity capital does not have to be repaid under normal circumstances Capital growth from expected share price increases may not happen

Figure 5.3 Levels of financial risk for the investor and the company

Progress check 5.4

What is business risk?

Financial risk comprises the other element of systematic risk and arises from fluctuations in interest rates causing reductions in a company's after-tax earnings and hence its ability to pay dividends. This risk can be measured by using a gearing ratio (the relationship between a company's debt and equity), since it is a risk inherent in the company's choice of financial structure. The financial risk is seen in the sensitivity of the company's cash flows to changes in the interest payments it has to make on its debt. Financial risk increases as gearing increases.

Figure 5.3 illustrates the ways in which financial risk impacts on the lenders (providers of debt), equity shareholders, and on the company. For example, it can be seen that while equity capital represents high financial risk for the investor, it represents low financial risk for the company.

Progress check 5.5

What is financial risk?

The impact of risk on financing

The premium required for business risk is an increase in the required rate of return due to uncertainty about the company's future prospects.

The premium for financial risk relates to the danger of high gearing (an increasing level of debt compared with equity capital). The higher the gearing, the greater the financial risk to ordinary shareholders, reflected in a higher risk premium and therefore higher cost of capital.

Business risk and financial risk are the two elements of non-diversifiable systematic risk, or market risk. Systematic risk may not be diversified away by investors through holding a portfolio of shares in different companies because it relates to macroeconomic factors such as interest rates, exchange rates, and taxation, which affect all companies.

Progress check 5.6

How is financial risk related to a company's financial gearing?

Systematic and unsystematic risk

The total risk in a security faced by investors may be separated into unsystematic risk and systematic risk. Systematic risk represents, for example, how investment returns are affected by business cycles, trade tariffs, and the possibilities of war, etc. It is inherent risk that cannot be diversified away. Systematic risk represents the relative effect on the returns of an individual security of changes in the market as a whole. Systematic risk may be measured using what are called β factors (see earlier in this chapter). β is a measure of the volatility of the return on a share relative to the market. The β factor for the market as a whole is 1. If a share were to rise in price at double the market rate then it would have a β factor of 2. Some investments are by their very nature more risky than others; this is nothing to do with chance variations in actual compared with expected returns.

It is generally assumed that on average systematic risk accounts for about 30% of the total risk attached to an individual share. Bruno Solnik (Solnik B (1995) 'Why not diversify internationally rather than domestically?' *Financial Analysts Journal*, January/February, reprinted from July/August 1974), suggested that for shares in the UK systematic risk is approximately 34% of the total risk of a share. Unsystematic risk is therefore generally assumed on average to account for about 70% of the total risk attached to an individual share.

Unsystematic risk is unique risk specific to a company. It is the risk of the company performing badly, or the risk of it going into liquidation. Unsystematic risk can therefore be diversified away by spreading money over a portfolio of investments. The proportion of total risk attached to an individual share relating to unsystematic risk is high at around 70%, but an investor may progressively reduce this type of risk by maintaining a diversified portfolio of projects or securities.

Worked Example 5.2

A colleague of yours has recently applied for the post of assistant finance officer of Flag plc, a medium-sized investment company. As part of the interview process she was asked to make a 15-minute presentation on risk, and in particular about the different types of risk an investment company like Flag plc may face.

We will consider the main points that she would have included in her presentation.

First, she may have given a broad definition of risk. Risk can be defined as '. . . the chance or possibility of loss or bad consequence', which arises from a past, present, or future hazard or group of hazards about which some uncertainty exists regarding possible effects or consequences. Whereas a hazard or group of hazards is a source of danger, risk is the likelihood of such a hazard or group of hazards causing actual adverse consequences or effects. In this context, uncertainty relates to the measure of variability in possible outcomes – the variability (qualitatively rather than quantitatively) of the possible impact and consequences or effects of such hazards. While such uncertainty can arise as a result of a whole host of complex and often interrelated reasons, in the corporate context in particular it more often than not arises as a result of a lack of knowledge or a lack of information and understanding.

Second, what are the types of risk? As with the never-ending variety that is symptomatic of modernity, there are many types of risk, many of which overlap in terms of definition and context, for example:

- social risk – the possibility that intervention (whether socio-cultural, political, or institutional) will create, fortify, or reinforce inequity and promote social conflict

- political risk – the possibility that changes in government policies will have an adverse and negative impact on the role and functioning of institutions and individuals

- economic risk – the risk that events (both national and international) will impact on a country's business environment and adversely affect the profit and other goals of particular companies and other business-related enterprises

- market risk – the risk of a decline in the price of a security due to general adverse market conditions, also called systematic risk

- financial risk – the possibility that a given investment or loan will fail to provide a return and may result in a loss of the original investment or loan

- business risk – the risk associated with the uncertainty of realising expected future returns of the business.

Diversification

As we have discussed, unsystematic risk (or non-market risk) is diversifiable. Businesses that have reached a mature stage of their development sometime use diversification as a strategy to mitigate unsystematic risk. However, it should be noted that diversification by its very nature also increases the risk of the unknown!

Companies may diversify their activities by buying businesses engaged in providing products and services in different business sectors to the ones in which they currently operate. They may also diversify by investing in new projects for new products and services in different markets and different geographical areas.

Individual investors may also diversify by effectively creating a portfolio of investments that include their own mixes of growing and maturing companies in a variety of market sectors in order to mitigate risk. During the early part of 2006 the UK stock market started to become a little volatile. In the press extract that follows the analysts suggest that appropriate diversification of investments is crucial to try and minimise risk of impacts from an uncertain future and boom-and-bust cycles.

Diversify or die?

'Keep your balance', by Paul Farrow

With the bulls and the bears at loggerheads over the direction of global markets, the adage about having a balanced portfolio has been brought into sharp focus.

Stock markets across the globe fell sharply last week, with the FTSE100 index shedding 254 points to close on Friday at 5,657.40. However, the jury is still firmly out on whether there is worse to come. 'The market is entering a period of uncertainty', says Ted Scott of F&C, the fund manager. 'The likelihood is of a mini bear market rather than just a correction.'

The directors of British companies have been selling twice as many shares as they have been buying, suggesting that they are not placing much faith in their companies' shares.

But many fund managers have been swift to dismiss fears of a sharp fall in markets.

'I am absolutely convinced this is not the start of a bear market. It is simply a healthy correction', says Richard Buxton of Schroders. Robin Geffen of Neptune Investment Management agrees. 'In a nutshell, this is a buying opportunity', he says.

No one can predict what will happen and the best way to avoid boom-and-bust cycles is to make objective investment decisions that ignore fashions.

Diversification and getting the balance right are vital. Fail to achieve that and it is easy either to purchase the wrong kind of investment or to create a portfolio that is vulnerable to shocks.

'Now would be an opportune time to review portfolios and ensure they are well placed to cope with more challenging market conditions', says Justin Modray of Best Invest. 'Investors have enjoyed three exceptionally favourable years and I fear some may have become over-excited, taking on more risk than is sensible.

'In our experience, too many investors realise they have poor asset allocation only when it is too late. Prevention is most definitely better than cure.'

It is important to have exposure to some assets that are not heavily correlated. Britain and the US, for instance, have a strong tendency to move together. This was evident a week ago when Wall Street tumbled on Friday and the London market followed suit when it opened on Monday morning.

However, commercial property has often performed contra-cyclically to equities, while Japan's stock market has little correlation to those in the West. In the three-year period that followed the market crash in 2000, corporate bonds and property were negatively correlated with the FTSE All-Share index – they performed well as London equities nose-dived.

That said, the eventual mix of assets in your portfolio will depend on your age, attitude to risk and objectives.

Risk is not just about potential capital losses – there is also the risk of inflation and of a reduction in income. Investors should take into account the amount of risk they wish to tolerate, both psychologically and in terms of their needs.

To give you some pointers we have talked to the top three balanced managed fund managers since 2002 (rated by Citywire, the financial analyst) to see how they are mixing their assets. We chose balanced managed funds because, by definition, they are able to invest in a range of assets from equities and bonds to property and cash and so are akin to individual investors' portfolios.

© *Daily Telegraph*, 24 May 2006

In diversified groups, or conglomerates, the signalling given by such groups to the financial markets via their dividend or gearing policy is not as clear as in a one product company. Conglomerates may, in theory, be evaluated using a minimum weighted average price/earnings ratio of the component businesses. The excess of the market value over this minimum, in theory, represents value created by the conglomerate. In reality, the share value of most conglomerates is below this minimum, which is why most such groups have increasingly been broken up in recent years. We will look further at diversification in Part II of this book when we discuss mergers and acquisitions in Chapters 16 and 17.

Progress check 5.7

What is meant by diversification?

Risk measurement

Risk is an important factor with regard to investor preferences as it is to the 'real' investment decisions taken by the directors of companies. It may be measured in a number of ways, for instance using probability distributions. For example, although the outcomes of a decision to buy a particular security may be uncertain, probabilities may be assigned to the various alternative outcomes. Estimates of probabilities are likely to be obtained from an analysis of previous experience or of similar scenarios. Probabilities are used to measure the likelihood that an event will occur, and a probability distribution lists all possible outcomes for an event and the probability that each will occur.

Worked Example 5.3

Imagine you are contemplating buying shares in company A or B, and you have been given the following estimates about whether the share prices are likely to move up or down.

Outcome	Share A probability	Share B probability
x	p	p
Share price will increase	0.90	0.60
Share price will fall	0.10	0.40
	1.00	1.00

The table above is a probability distribution that tells us that share A appears less risky than share B because it is less likely to fall in price and consequently more likely to increase in price. Probability distributions provide more meaningful information than stating the most likely outcome, for example that both shares are more likely to increase and less likely to fall in price.

Instead of presenting probability distributions for each alternative, summary measures of risk may be used, for example:

- expected value (EV)
- standard deviation (σ).

Expected value

The expected value is the weighted average of the possible outcomes of a decision, and it represents the long-run average outcome if the decision were to be repeated many times.

$$EV = \text{the sum of } (p \times x)$$

Worked Example 5.4

The expected price of a share is shown in the following table, and the probability has been estimated of it being one price or another.

probability p	£ estimated share price x
0.40	2.00
0.35	3.00
0.25	5.00

Expected value of the share price:

probability p	£ estimated share price x	EV $p \times x$
0.40	2.00	£0.80
0.35	3.00	£1.05
0.25	5.00	£1.25
		£3.10

The expected value of the share price is the average expected price, except as we can see £3.10 is not a specific share price that may actually be expected.

Expected values may give an indication with regard to a decision based on the limited amount of information available. There is a distinction between the two types of information, perfect information and imperfect information. Perfect information is information that predicts what will happen with certainty and when, which in practice does not exist. Imperfect information adds to what the investor, for example, already knows, but the information cannot be relied on with certainty, and the information may be wrong. Most information, in practice, for example forecast economic outlooks and expected share price movements, is imperfect. However, a decision-maker may obtain more information before making a decision about buying a particular share and the cost of that information should be quantified to be justified by potential benefits. There are no potential benefits unless the extra information might make the investor choose a different decision option. Let's look at an example of this.

Worked Example 5.5

An investment of £10,000 in the shares of each of three companies is expected to generate gains from share price increases over the next year, depending on the state of the stock market. Probabilities of each market state occurring have been estimated as   I: 0.5   II: 0.2   III: 0.3.

The following is an incremental payoff table that includes the likely gain from each share for each market state.

Share	Market state I £	II £	III £
A	750	200	50
B	450	800	550
C	350	600	900

Assuming that the share with the highest EV should be chosen, which share should be chosen? We need to calculate expected values of each share and each market state to determine this, by multiplying probabilities by likely gains.

Market state	Probability	Expected values		
		A £	B £	C £
I	0.50	375	225	175
II	0.20	40	160	120
III	0.30	15	165	270
EV of gains		430	550	565

The shares in company C should be purchased because that choice provides the highest EV, which is an average of £565.

Assume hypothetically that information about the likely state of the market could be purchased for £150 from a broker who has specialist knowledge. With perfect information about the future state of the market the choice of share will be the one giving the highest expected gain for the market state which the perfect information predicts will occur.

If State I is forecast, share A would be chosen, to gain £750.
If State II is forecast, share B would be chosen, to gain £800.
If State III is forecast, share C would be chosen, to gain £900.

EVs of gains given perfect information about the market

Market state	Share choice	Gain £	Probability	EV £000
I	A	750	0.50	375
II	B	800	0.20	160
III	C	900	0.30	270
EV of gain with perfect information				805

Choosing share C without information gives an EV £565
The value of the benefit from information is £805 − £565 = £240
Therefore, it would be worth buying the information from the broker for £150.

Standard deviation

A standard deviation measures the risk of the possible variations, the dispersion, around an expected value.

$$\text{Variance or } \sigma^2 = \text{the sum of } p(x - EV)^2$$

The standard deviation is the square root of the statistical variance:

$$\text{Standard deviation or } \sigma = \sqrt{\text{variance}}$$

Use of the standard deviation is appropriate for comparison if EVs are the same – the higher the standard deviation the higher the risk.

Worked Example 5.6

Shares in companies Q and R have the following estimated share prices (x), probabilities of occurring (p) , and expected values (EV) over the next month.

	Probability p	Estimated share price £	EV £
Company Q	0.30	2.00	0.60
	0.40	3.00	1.20
	0.30	4.00	1.20
			3.00
Company R	0.20	1.00	0.20
	0.20	2.00	0.40
	0.20	3.00	0.60
	0.20	4.00	0.80
	0.20	5.00	1.00
			3.00

Both companies have the same share price expected value. How should an investor choose which is the best share to buy? Since the expected value of the share price is the same for both companies the share chosen should be the one with the smallest risk, the one with the lowest standard deviation.

	Probability p	Share price – EV (x – EV)	Variance p(x – EV)²	σ = √variance
Company Q	0.30	−1.00	0.30	
	0.40	0.00	0.00	
	0.30	+1.00	0.30	
			0.60	σ = √0.6 = 0.775
Company R	0.20	−2.00	0.80	
	0.20	−1.00	0.20	
	0.20	0.00	0.00	
	0.20	+1.00	0.20	
	0.20	+2.00	0.80	
			2.00	σ = √2.0 = 1.414

A risk-averse investor would choose to invest in company Q. Its forecast share price has the smallest standard deviation and therefore the lowest risk.

Portfolio risks and returns

Investors may be companies, individuals, or institutions that make investments on behalf of private individuals. While short-term investments should certainly hold their original value and be capable of being converted into cash at short notice, funds are generally invested to make the highest return at an acceptable level of risk. If all funds are put into an investment in one type of project or one type of security then there is a risk that if the investment performs badly, there will be a total loss. A more prudent approach may be to spread investments over several types of project or security, so that losses on some may be offset by gains on others.

The use of portfolios of different investments may relate to 'real' investments in capital projects or investments in stocks and shares. The major factors relating to the choice of investments are, as we have already seen, cash flow and the time value of money, together with the return expected by the investor and the perceived risk associated with that investment.

If an investor has a portfolio of securities, then it will be expected that the portfolio itself will provide a certain return on investment. The expected return from the portfolio is the weighted average of the expected returns of the investments in the portfolio, weighted by the proportion of total funds invested in each. If W_S is the percentage of the portfolio that relates to an investment S that is expected to yield $s\%$ and W_T is the percentage of the portfolio that relates to an investment T that is expected to yield $t\%$, the portfolio's expected return is:

$$(W_S \times s) + (W_T \times t)$$

For example, if 60% of the portfolio relates to an investment that is expected to yield 8% and 40% to an investment that is expected to yield 10%, the portfolio's expected return is:

$$(60\% \times 8\%) + (40\% \times 10\%) = 8.8\%$$

The risk associated with either an investment or a portfolio of investments is that the actual return will not be the same as the expected return. The actual return may be higher or it may be lower than the expected return. It is rarely likely to equal the expected return. A prudent investor will want to avoid as much risk as possible so that actual returns may be as close as possible to expected returns. The risk associated with a single investment or in a portfolio of investments may be measured by the standard deviation of expected returns using estimated probabilities of actual returns.

Worked Example 5.7

A single investment has the following probabilities of earning alternative expected returns:

Return % x	Probability p	Expected value $p \times x$
10	0.30	3.00
15	0.40	6.00
20	0.20	4.00
25	0.20	5.00
		18.00

The expected return is 18% and may be denoted as EVx, and the standard deviation of the expected return can be calculated as follows:

Return x %	$x - EV_x$ %	p	$p(x - EV_x)^2$
10	−8.00	0.30	19.20
15	−3.00	0.40	3.60
20	2.00	0.20	8.80
25	7.00	0.20	9.80
		Variance	41.40

The standard deviation is the square root of the variance $\sqrt{41.4}$ which equals 6.43%, and so the expected return of the investment is 18% with a risk of 6.43%.

The risk of an investment might be high or low, depending on the nature of the investment. There is a positive correlation between risk and return so that in general low risk investments usually give low returns, and high-risk investments usually provide high returns.

Within a portfolio, the individual investments should not only be looked at in terms of their own risks and returns. In a portfolio the relationships between the return from one investment and the return from other investments are very important. The relationship between two investments can be one of three types:

- positive correlation – if one investment does well or badly it is likely that the other investment will perform likewise, so you would expect an investment in a company making umbrellas and in another which sells raincoats both to do badly in dry weather

- negative correlation – if one investment does well the other will do badly, and *vice versa*, so you would expect an investment in a company making umbrellas to do badly in dry weather and well in wet weather, and you would expect an investment in a company which sells ice cream to do well in dry weather and badly in wet weather – the weather will affect each company differently

- zero correlation, where the performance of one investment will be independent of how the other performs, so you would not expect there to be any relationship between the returns from an investment in a pharmaceutical company and an investment in a communications company.

This relationship between the returns from different investments is measured by the **correlation coefficient**. A correlation coefficient that approaches +1 indicates a high positive correlation, and a correlation coefficient that approaches −1 indicates a high negative correlation. Zero indicates no correlation at all. If alternative investments show a high negative correlation then overall risk may be reduced by combining them in a portfolio. Risk may also be reduced by combining in a portfolio of investments that have no correlation at all.

Worked Example 5.8

Shares in two companies S and T have the following expected returns:

Probability p	Company S return %	Company T return %
0.20	10	5
0.60	20	25
0.20	30	45

The expected return from each security is as follows:

Probability	Company S		Company T	
	Return s	EV$_s$	Return t	EV$_T$
p	%	%	%	%
0.20	10	2	5	1
0.60	20	12	25	15
0.20	30	6	45	9
	Expected return EV$_S$ =	20	Expected return EV$_T$ =	25

The variance of the expected return for each company is the sum of each $p(s - EV_S)^2$ and $p(t - EV_T)^2$

Probability	Company S			Company T		
	Return			Return		
p	s	$s - EV_S$	$p(s - EV_S)^2$	t	$t - EV_T$	$p(t - EV_T)^2$
0.20	10	(10)	20	5	(20)	80
0.60	20	0	0	25	0	0
0.20	30	10	20	45	20	80
	$EV_S = 20$		Variance = 40	$EV_T = 25$		Variance = 160

The standard deviation is the square root of the variances.

Company S risk $= \sqrt{40} = 6.32\%$

Company T risk $= \sqrt{160} = 12.65\%$

Company T therefore offers a higher return than company S, but at a greater risk.

Let's now assume that an investor acquires a portfolio P consisting of 50% shares in company S and 50% shares in company T.

The expected return from the portfolio (EV_P) will be $(0.5 \times 20\%) + (0.5 \times 25\%) = 22.5\%$. This is less than the expected return from company T alone, but more than that from company S. The combined portfolio should be less risky than an investment in company T alone (although in this example of just a two-investment portfolio, it will be more risky than an investment in company S alone except when returns are not at all correlated).

We can calculate the standard deviation of the expected return if there is:

- perfect positive correlation between the returns from each security, so that if S gives a return of 10%, then T will give a return of 5%; if S gives a return of 20%, then T will give a return of 25%; if S gives a return of 30%, then T will give a return of 45%

- perfect negative correlation between the returns from each security, so that if S gives a return of 10%, T will yield 45%; if S gives a return of 30%, T will yield 5%; if S gives a return of 20%, T will yield 25%

- no correlation between returns, for which the probability distribution of returns is as follows:

S %	T %		p
10	5	(0.2×0.2)	0.04
10	25	(0.2×0.6)	0.12
10	45	(0.2×0.2)	0.04
20	5	(0.6×0.2)	0.12
20	25	(0.6×0.6)	0.36
20	45	(0.6×0.2)	0.12
30	5	(0.2×0.2)	0.04
30	25	(0.2×0.6)	0.12
30	45	(0.2×0.2)	0.04
			1.00

Perfect positive correlation

Given an expected return EV_P of 22.5%, the standard deviation of the portfolio is as follows:

Probability	Return from 50% S	Return from 50% T	Combined portfolio return		
p	%	%	P %	(P − EVP)	p(P − EVP)²
0.20	5	2.50	7.50	(15)	45
0.60	10	12.50	22.50	0	0
0.20	15	22.50	37.50	15	45
				Variance =	90

The standard deviation or risk is $\sqrt{90} = 9.49\%$

Perfect negative correlation

Given an expected return EVP of 22.5%, the standard deviation of the portfolio is as follows:

Probability	Return from 50% S	Return from 50% T	Combined portfolio return		
p	%	%	P %	(P − EVP)	p(P − EVP)²
0.20	5	22.50	27.50	5	5
0.60	10	12.50	22.50	0	0
0.20	15	2.50	17.50	(5)	5
				Variance =	10

The standard deviation or risk is $\sqrt{10} = 3.16\%$

Zero correlation

Given an expected return EVP of 22.5%, the standard deviation of the portfolio is as follows:

Probability	Return from 50% S	Return from 50% T	Combined portfolio return		
p	%	%	P %	(P − EVP)	p(P − EVP)²
0.04	5	2.5	7.5	(15)	9
0.12	5	12.5	17.5	(5)	3
0.04	5	22.5	27.5	5	1
0.12	10	2.5	12.5	(10)	12
0.36	10	12.5	22.5	0	0
0.12	10	22.5	32.5	10	12
0.04	15	2.5	17.5	(5)	1
0.12	15	12.5	27.5	5	3
0.04	15	22.5	37.5	15	9
				Variance =	50

The standard deviation is $\sqrt{50} = 7.07\%$

Therefore, for the same expected return of 22.5% the risk expressed in the standard deviation is:

- highest at 9.49% when there is perfect positive correlation between the returns of the individual securities in the portfolio
- lowest at 3.16% when there is perfect negative correlation – the risk is then less than for either individual security taken on its own
- low at 7.07% when there is no correlation.

An alternative way of calculating the standard deviation of a portfolio of two investments is to use the formula:

$$\sigma_p = \sqrt{(\alpha_S^2 \times \sigma_S^2) + (\alpha_T^2 \times \sigma_T^2) + (2 \times \alpha_S \times \alpha_T \times r \times \sigma_S \times \sigma_T)}$$

where: σ_p is the standard deviation of a portfolio of the two investments, S and T
σ_S is the standard deviation of the returns from investment S
σ_T is the standard deviation of the returns from investment T
σ_S^2, σ_T^2 are the variances of returns from investment S and T (the squares of the standard deviations)
α_S is the weighting or proportion of investment S in the portfolio
α_T is the weighting or proportion of investment T in the portfolio
r is the correlation coefficient of returns from investment S and T, which is

$$\frac{\text{covariance of investments S and T}}{\sigma_S \times \sigma_T}$$

and the covariance is the sum of:

$$\text{probability} \times (\text{return}_S - EV_S) \times (\text{return}_T - EV_T)$$

Worked Example 5.9

We can use the data from Worked Example 5.8 for a portfolio of a 50% investment in company S and a 50% investment in company T to illustrate the alternative way of calculating the standard deviation of a portfolio of two investments.

When there is perfect positive correlation between the returns from S and T, $r = 1$.

$$\sigma_p^2 = (0.5^2 \times 40) + (0.5^2 \times 160) + (2 \times 0.5 \times 0.5 \times 1 \times \sqrt{40} \times \sqrt{160})$$
$$= 10 + 40 + (0.5 \times 6.325 \times 12.649)$$
$$= 90$$

The standard deviation or risk of the portfolio is $\sqrt{90} = 9.49\%$

Worked Example 5.10 is an illustration of how the correlation between two investments may be calculated.

Worked Example 5.10

PLT plc is considering investing in two companies CHT plc and HGT plc, for which the following information is available:

Probability P	CHT plc return RC	HGT plc return RH
0.25	24%	28%
0.50	12%	12%
0.25	0%	4%
Expected return e	12%	14%
Variance σ^2	72	76
Standard deviation σ	8.49	8.72

▶

▶ We are required to calculate the correlation coefficient of the above companies, and advise PLT plc what this means with regard to their decision to invest.

The relationship or correlation between the two investments can be calculated as follows:

The covariance of CHT and HGT = the sum of the probability × (return – expected return for investment CHT) × (return – expected return for investment HGT)

or

$$cov(RC \times RH) = \Sigma_P \times (RC - e_C) \times (RH - e_H)$$

$$cov(RC \times RH) = 0.25(24 - 12)(28 - 14) + 0.50(12 - 12)(12 - 14) + 0.25(0 - 12)(4 - 14)$$

$$= 42 + 0 + 30$$

$$= 72$$

As correlation $r = \dfrac{cov(RC \times RH)}{\sigma_C \times \sigma_H}$

$$r = 72/(8.49 \times 8.72) = 0.97$$

Because the correlation coefficient r is positive and very close to 1 this means that the returns on the two investments are almost perfectly positively correlated. Based on the information given PLT plc cannot make a decision as to which is the best investment without first obtaining further information.

When there is perfect negative correlation between returns from S and T, $r = -1$.

$$\sigma_p^2 = (0.5^2 \times 40) + (0.5^2 \times 160) + (2 \times 0.5 \times 0.5x -1 \times \sqrt{40} \times \sqrt{160})$$

$$= 10 + 40 - (0.5 \times 6.325 \times 12.649)$$

$$= 10$$

The standard deviation or risk of the portfolio is $\sqrt{10} = 3.16\%$

When there is zero correlation between returns from S and T, $r = 0$.

$$\sigma_p^2 = (0.5^2 \times 40) + (0.5^2 \times 160) + (2 \times 0.5 \times 0.5 \times 0 \times \sqrt{40} \times \sqrt{160})$$

$$= 10 + 40 + 0$$

$$= 50$$

The standard deviation or risk of the portfolio is $\sqrt{50} = 7.07\%$

These are exactly the same standard deviations we calculated in Worked Example 5.8.

Markowitz's portfolio theory

🔒 We will use Worked Example 5.11 to illustrate Markowitz's portfolio theory (Markowitz H (1952) 'Portfolio selection' *Journal of Finance*, 6, 815–33). This theory deals with the way in which investors can diversify away unsystematic risk through investing in portfolios of shares in different companies. It considers sets of investors' portfolio choices of different combinations of risky investments.

Worked Example 5.11

Let's look at a portfolio of two investments with different risks and returns. We can assume that the two investments may be combined in any proportions with an infinite number of possible combinations of risk and return. We will consider whether one individual investment is the 'best' option or whether some combination of proportions of the two investments is a 'better' option.

The two investments are K and L and their expected returns and risks are as follows:

Investment	Return expected %	Risk (standard deviation) %
K	11	6.7
L	14	7.5

The correlation coefficient of KL is −0.3

The covariance KL is therefore $-0.3 \times 6.7 \times 7.5 = -15.075$

We can use the formulae shown on pages 195 and 199 to calculate the weighted average returns expected from different risk-return combinations of proportions of the two investments and their corresponding risks (standard deviations), as follows:

K %	L %	Return expected %	Risk (standard deviation) %
100	0	11.0	6.7
80	20	11.6	5.1
60	40	12.2	4.2
40	60	12.8	4.5
20	80	13.4	5.7
0	100	14.0	7.5

At the outset, if we were totally risk averse we may invest exclusively in K because it has a lower standard deviation and therefore risk than L. Alternatively, if we chose to combine proportions of K and L we can see that as the proportion of K reduces and the proportion of L increases then the standard deviation, or risk, of the portfolio reduces and the combined expected return increases. The combined risk continues to reduce as the proportion of L increases until a point is reached, as we can see in the table above, where the impact of the higher risk of L becomes greater than the benefit of negative correlation and the combined risk starts to increase. In this example, this is shown at around point C, which we can see from the ABC section of the graph illustrated in Fig. 5.4.

As proportions of L continue to be increased, and proportions of K reduce, we can see from the CDEF section of the graph that the combined expected return continues to increase but risk now increases. However, it can also be seen from the graph that any point on section CF is better than any point on section AC because a greater combined return may be obtained for the same level of risk. See, for example, combination Y, which gives a greater return than combination X for the same level of risk. The individual portfolios of combinations of investments that lie along the CF section of the graph are called efficient portfolios and the line itself is called the efficient frontier.

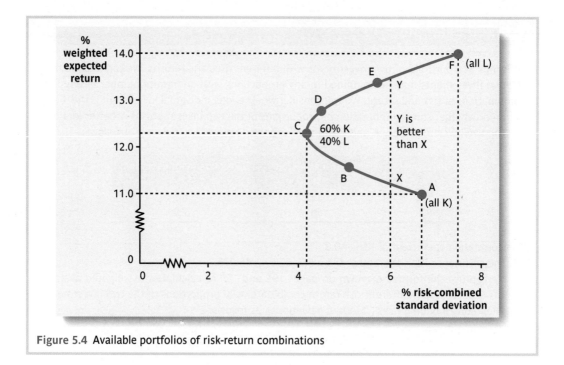

Figure 5.4 Available portfolios of risk-return combinations

We may conclude that:

- we cannot identify the 'best' investment option
- an investor wishing to minimise total risk would choose combination C (60% K, 40% L)
- an investor wishing to maximise return would choose F (100% L)
- any portfolio chosen by an investor along the CF line depends on the level of the investor's risk aversion – the amount of extra return they require to compensate for a particular level of extra risk.

The choice of combinations of investments all depends on an investor's attitude to risk. If we could quantify an investor's risk aversion and determine the premium they require on their return for a specific amount of additional risk then we may identify their 'best' portfolio. We will consider this later in this chapter when we look at investors' preferences.

Worked Example 5.11 considered possible combinations of just two investments to provide portfolios with different combinations of risk and return. If we include another possible investment M into the choice of portfolios then unsystematic risk may be further diversified (see Fig. 5.5).

An investor may consider K, L, or M alone as an individual investment, or may consider the following portfolios:

- K and L
- L and M
- K and M
- K, L, and M

which may provide a huge number of combinations of combined risk and return.

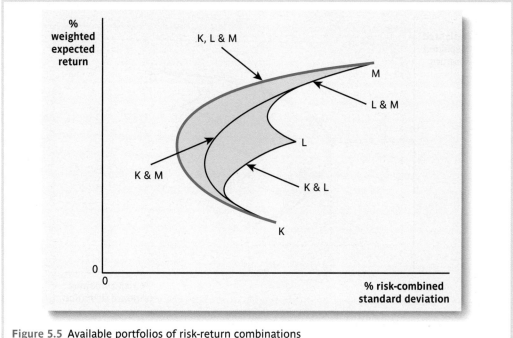

Figure 5.5 Available portfolios of risk-return combinations

'Better' portfolios may be obtained by combining all three investments. The coloured line KM in Fig. 5.5 represents all combinations of K, L, and M, which gives the investor a wider range rather than the two-investment portfolio combinations of K and L, L and M, or K and M.

Further investments may be included to give even greater opportunities to diversify away unsystematic risk. This is the basis of the portfolio theory developed by Markowitz, in which investor choice includes all risky investments. As we saw from the two-investment portfolio, identification of the optimum portfolio is dependent on investor attitude to risk, and this also applies to multi-investment portfolios together with our ability to quantify the premium required for specific levels of additional risk.

Markowitz's theory considers a large number of portfolio choices of risky investments available to investors. The shaded area KML that we saw in Fig. 5.5 is called the envelope curve and represents the range of combinations of returns and risks of risky investments (in that case relating to three investments). Figure 5.6 shows a similar curve relating to five risky investments for illustration, but which actually may be any number. Here, the shaded area KONML is the envelope curve.

All the possible investment combinations available to an investor is the range portfolios within the envelope curve. We saw in Fig. 5.4 that at point C the higher risk started to outweigh the benefit of negative correlation. The same effect occurs in Fig. 5.6 at point G. The efficient portfolios therefore lie along the line GO and GO is the efficient frontier. In the same way as in Fig. 5.4, in Fig. 5.6 investors will rationally invest only in portfolios along the coloured line GO. This is because they are better than all the other portfolios within the rest of the envelope curve, providing either the best return for a specific level of risk or the lowest risk for a specific return.

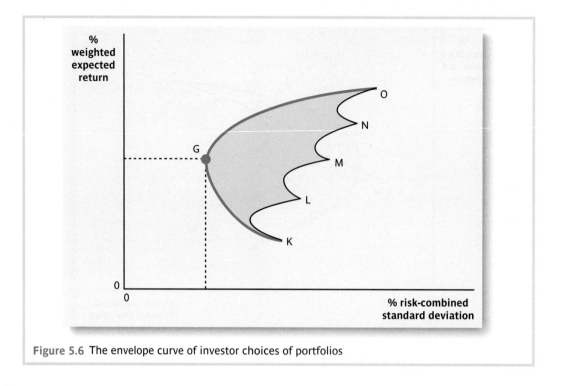

Figure 5.6 The envelope curve of investor choices of portfolios

Risk-free investments

All the portfolios we have looked at carry some degree of risk. So far, we have considered investor choices concerned only with risky investments. But some investments are risk-free. We know that investors may actually also lend and borrow at a virtually risk-free rate of return. It is extremely unlikely that the UK Government would default on any payment of interest and capital on its stocks, and therefore Government loans are generally assumed to be risk-free investments. As investors lend and borrow at higher rates of return then the corresponding levels of risk will also be higher. For the market as a whole we may assume a linear relationship between risk and return. We have superimposed a market risk-return line onto the graph in Fig. 5.6, which is shown in Fig. 5.7. It has been assumed that the risk-free rate of return R_f is known. The line has been drawn by starting at R_f and pivoting the line until it is tangential to the efficient frontier. This line is called the **capital market line (CML)** and the point of tangency H is known as the market portfolio, which is the optimal combination of risky investments, on the assumption that a risk-free rate of return exists.

Capital market line (CML)

The capital market line represents a combination of risk-free securities and the market portfolio of securities, and is drawn along the efficient frontier starting from the risk-free rate of return. It is an expression of the relationship between risk and return for a fully diversified investor. This means that if an investor is able to identify and invest in the market portfolio, and, borrow or lend at the risk-free rate of return, then the possible risk/return combinations for the investor would lie along a straight line, the capital market line (CML).

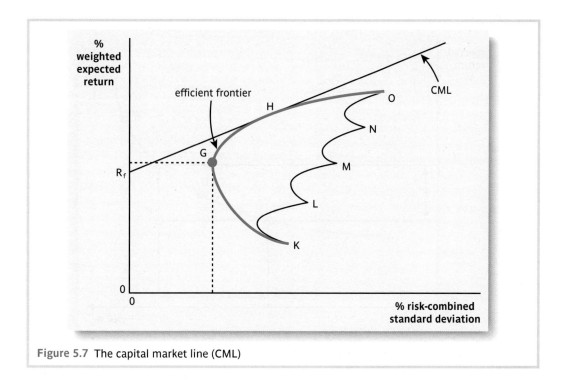

Figure 5.7 The capital market line (CML)

Assuming the existence of a risk-free rate of return, rational investors will always choose a portfolio that lies on the CML rather than the efficient frontier GO because the portfolios on the CML are better than those on GO. Point H, the market portfolio, is of course the same on both the CML and the efficient frontier. Risk-taking investors will choose portfolios lying on the CML to the right of point H – the further to the right, the higher risk-taking they are. Risk-averse investors will choose portfolios lying on the CML to the left of point H – the further to the left towards R_f, the more highly risk-averse they are. Investors who put all their investments into a market portfolio will choose point H.

The particular portfolio on the CML chosen by an investor will depend on their choice of maximum return for an acceptable level of risk. It is therefore dependent on investor preference.

Progress check 5.8

What is a capital market line (CML)?

Investors' preferences

Investors should rationally choose a portfolio of investments, which gives them a satisfactory balance between:

- expected returns from the portfolio
- risk that the actual returns from the portfolio will be higher or lower than expected, some portfolios being more risky than others.

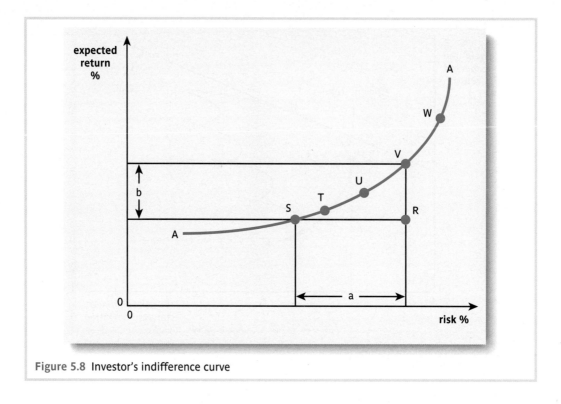

Figure 5.8 Investor's indifference curve

Rational investors wish to maximise return and minimise risk. If two portfolios have the same element of risk like V and R in Fig. 5.8, the rational investor will choose V, the one yielding b more return for the same level of risk. If two portfolios offer the same return, like S and R, the rational investor will select the portfolio with the lower risk, which is S. Portfolio S offers the same return as R, but with less risk amounting to a.

Therefore, portfolio V will be preferred to portfolio R because it offers a higher expected return for the same level of risk, and portfolio S will be preferred to portfolio R because it offers the same expected return for lower risk. But whether an investor chooses portfolio V or portfolio S will depend on the individual's attitude to risk – whether they wish to accept a greater risk for a greater expected return.

In Fig. 5.8 the choice of portfolio S, T, U, V, and W will depend on the individual investor's attitude to risk. Curve A is called the investor's **indifference curve** or utility curve. An investor is generally indifferent to the portfolios that give a mix of risk and expected return which lie on this curve. To the investor, the portfolios S, T, U, V, and W are all just as good as each other, and each of them is better than portfolio R.

Portfolio R lies on a separate indifference curve of return/risk combinations B (see Fig. 5.9), all of which may be equally acceptable to the investor, but their choice is dependent on their attitude to risk. However, these portfolios are all less acceptable than the portfolios on indifference curve A. The investor will prefer combinations of return and risk on indifference curve A to those on curve B in Fig. 5.9 because curve A offers higher returns for the same degree of risk (and less risk for the same expected returns). For example, for the same amount of risk x, the expected return for portfolio V on curve A is b more than portfolio R on curve B.

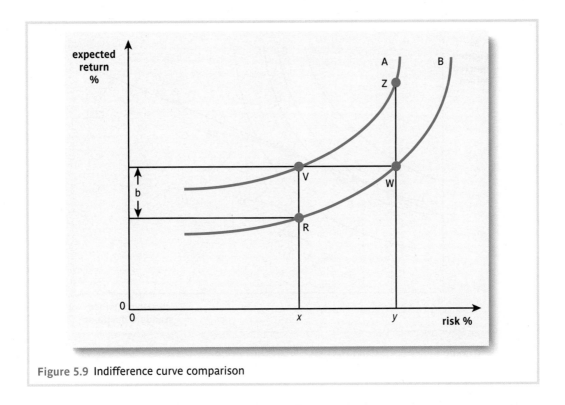

Figure 5.9 Indifference curve comparison

Similarly, an investor may move from point W, having a level of risk *y*, to point V which offers the same returns for a lower level of risk *x*. Alternatively, the investor may move to Z, which offers a higher return for the same level of risk *y*. A rational investor will always move either to the left or upwards in order to optimise their position in terms of return and acceptable level of risk.

The shape of an indifference curve indicates the extent to which an investor is a risk taker or is risk-averse. A steeply inclined indifference curve indicates a risk-averse investor, whereas a flatter curve indicates a risk-taking investor.

If we assume that an investor has indifference curves shaped as in Fig. 5.9 we can consider a range of indifference levels (or utilities) represented by curves A, B, C, and D, which are shown in Fig. 5.10 superimposed on the graphs we saw in Fig. 5.7. If the CML had not existed the investor would choose portfolio J, which is at the point where the investor's highest possible indifference curve (C) is tangential to the efficient frontier GO.

In Fig. 5.10 the CML is drawn at a tangent to the efficient frontier and cuts the y axis at the point of the risk-free investment's return R_f. As we saw in Fig. 5.7, because of the existence of a risk-free investment the CML (capital market line or securities market line) becomes the new efficient frontier.

More risk-averse investors will choose points on the CML closer to R_f, which means investing in a large proportion of risk-free investments. Risk-taking investors will choose points on the CML approaching point H, investing a higher proportion of their funds in the market portfolio.

Portfolio H in Fig. 5.10 is the same as point H in Fig. 5.7. It is the efficient portfolio which will appeal most to the risk-taking investor, ignoring risk-free investments. The only portfolio that consists entirely of risky investments, which a rational investor should want to hold, is portfolio H.

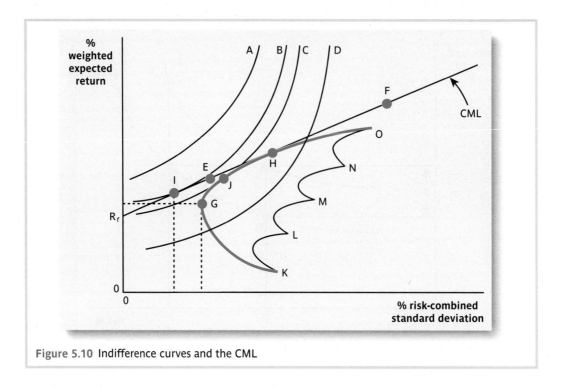

Figure 5.10 Indifference curves and the CML

Progress check 5.9

What are investors' indifference curves?

As with the curved efficient frontier line, one portfolio on the CML line is as attractive as another to a rational investor. One investor may wish to hold portfolio E, which lies between risk-free investment R_f and portfolio H.

Another investor may wish to hold portfolio F, which entails putting all their funds in portfolio H and borrowing money at the risk-free rate to acquire more of portfolio H. This investor, in order to meet their individual risk/return requirement, therefore uses a process of first selecting the market portfolio and then second, combining the optimal portfolio of risky investments with borrowing (or lending) at the risk-free rate. This two-stage process is known as the **separation theorem** (Tobin J (1958) 'Liquidity preference as behaviour toward risk' *Review of Economic Studies No 25*, February, 65–86). The separation theorem deals with the way that investors identify the market portfolio, which all rational investors should prefer, and how they combine a proportion of their funds in this together with either borrowing or lending at the risk-free rate of return to optimise their own individual risk-return preference. In this scenario the market portfolio may be considered as relating to the index of the Stock Exchange as a whole or a specific segment or part of it, so long as it is clearly recognised.

The portfolio that an investor will actually choose on the CML will be determined by their indifference curves. If we consider the indifference curves A, B, C, and D in Fig. 5.10 we can see that it is only curve B that can be tangential to the CML. Curves C and D represent lower levels of utility, and curve A, whilst it does represent higher utility, is above and beyond the CML. The investor with indifference curves A, B, C, and D will choose the portfolio at point I, where indifference curve B is tangential to the CML. This particular investor would invest most funds at the risk-free rate of return with the remainder invested in the market portfolio.

Why is point H the market portfolio? Well, rational investors will only want to hold one portfolio of risky investments, which is portfolio H. This may be held in conjunction with a holding of the risk-free investment (as with portfolio E). Alternatively, an investor may borrow funds to augment their holding of H (as with portfolio F). Therefore:

- since all investors wish to hold portfolio H, and
- we assume that all shares quoted on the Stock Exchange must be held by all these investors, it follows that
- all shares quoted on the Stock Exchange must be in portfolio H.

Portfolio H is the 'market portfolio' and each investor's portfolio will contain a proportion of it. (Although in the real world, investors do not hold every quoted security in their portfolio, in practice a well-diversified portfolio should reflect the whole market in terms of weightings given to particular sectors, high income and high capital growth securities, and so on.)

Actually, investors may be able to build up a small portfolio of shares that does better than the market, or they may end up with portfolios that perform worse than the market. Let's look at a worked example to illustrate this.

Worked Example 5.12

The following data relate to four different portfolios of shares:

Portfolio	Expected rate of return %	Standard deviation of return on the portfolio %
A	10	6
B	15	7
C	12	4
D	18	11

The expected rate of return on the market portfolio is 7% with a standard deviation of 2%. The risk-free rate is 4%.

We can identify which of these portfolios may be regarded as better than the market (efficient) or worse than the market (inefficient) by drawing a CML (see Fig. 5.11). When risk is zero the return is 4, and when risk is 2 the return is 7, so these points can be plotted and joined up, and the line can be extended to produce the CML.

The individual portfolios A, B, C, and D can also be plotted on the same chart and any portfolio which is above the CML, is said to be efficient and any portfolio which is below the CML is inefficient.

Portfolio C is very efficient, and portfolio B is also efficient, but portfolios A and D are both inefficient.

We can approach this in an alternative way, numerically instead of using graphs, by calculating the formula for the CML, assuming the standard deviation of a portfolio to be x, and the return from a portfolio to be y.

▶

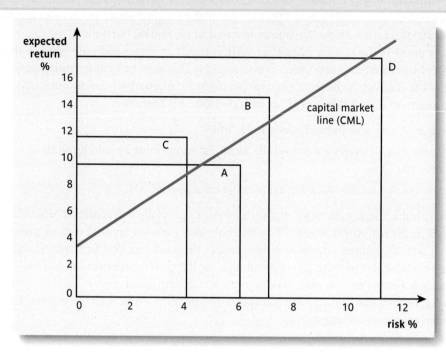

Figure 5.11 CML example

The CML formula is $y = R_f + bx$, where R_f is the risk-free rate of return, which in this example is 4.

If $x = 2$ then $y = 7$, and if $x = 0$ then $y = 4$

Therefore $\quad b = \dfrac{7 - 4}{2 - 0} = \dfrac{3}{2} = 1.5$

The CML therefore is $y = 4 + 1.5x$

Portfolio	Standard deviation x	CML return y	%	Expected return %	Portfolio type
A	6	$(4 + 1.5 \times 6)$ =	13.0	10	Inefficient
B	7	$(4 + 1.5 \times 7)$ =	14.5	15	Efficient
C	4	$(4 + 1.5 \times 4)$ =	10.0	12	Very efficient
D	11	$(4 + 1.5 \times 11)$ =	20.5	18	Inefficient

If the expected return exceeds the CML return for a given amount of risk, the portfolio is efficient. In this example B is efficient (15% > 14.5%) and C is even more efficient (12% > 10%), but D is inefficient (18% < 20.5%) and A even more inefficient (10% < 13%).

Progress check 5.10

When may a portfolio be considered as inefficient with regard to the CML?

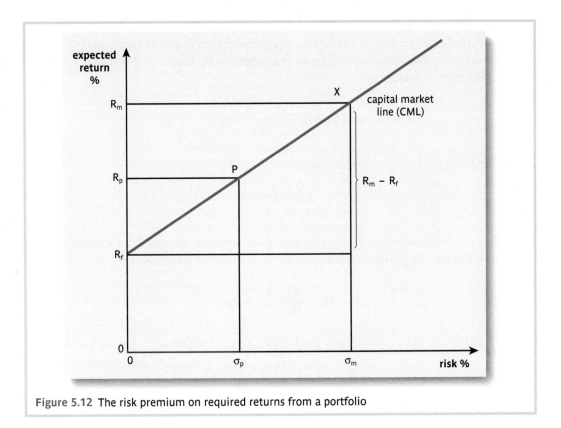

Figure 5.12 The risk premium on required returns from a portfolio

The return on the market portfolio

The expected returns from a portfolio will be higher than the return from risk-free investments because investors expect a greater return for accepting a degree of investment risk. The size of the risk premium will increase as the risk of the portfolio increases, and we can show this with an analysis of the capital market line (Fig. 5.12).

Let's assume that:

R_f is the risk-free rate of return

R_m is the return from the market portfolio X

R_p is the return on portfolio P, which is a mixture of investments in portfolio X and risk-free investments

σ_m is the risk (standard deviation) of returns from the market portfolio X

σ_p is the risk (standard deviation) of returns from portfolio P

The slope of the CML

$$b = \frac{(R_m - R_f)}{\sigma_m}$$

which represents the extent to which the investor's required returns from the portfolio should exceed the risk-free rate of return in compensation for the risk.

We can use the formula for the CML which was expressed in the $y = a + bx$ format in the previous worked example (where a is the risk-free rate of return R_f and bx represents the increase in the return as the risk increases). We know that when $y = R_p$, then $x = \sigma_p$ and so the equation of the CML can be expressed as:

$$R_p = R_f + \frac{(R_m - R_f)}{\sigma_m}\sigma_p$$

where the expression

$$\frac{(R_m - R_f)}{\sigma_m}\sigma_p$$

is actually the risk premium that the investor should require as compensation for accepting the risk of the portfolio σ_p. The portfolio risk σ_p may be determined by rearranging the formula above:

$$\sigma_p = \frac{R_p - R_f}{(R_m - R_f)} \times \sigma_m$$

The expected return of a portfolio lying on the CML can be written as:

$$R_p = (X \times R_m) + R_f \times (1 - X)$$

where X is the proportion invested in the market portfolio, and $(1 - X)$ is the proportion invested in risk-free securities.

Let's look at a worked example.

Worked Example 5.13

If an investor is told that R_f is 6%, R_m is 15%, and σ_m is 24%, we can determine the investor's return and risk if they hold a portfolio comprising 75% risk-free securities, and 25% market risk securities.

The portfolio return is:

$$\begin{aligned}
R_p &= (X \times R_m) + R_f \times (1 - X) \\
&= (25\% \times 15\%) + (6\% \times 75\%) \\
&= 3.75\% + 4.5\% \\
&= 8.25\%
\end{aligned}$$

The portfolio risk is:

$$\sigma_p = \frac{(R_p - R_f)}{(R_m - R_f)} \times \sigma_m = \frac{(8.25\% - 6\%)}{(15\% - 6\%)} \times 24\% = 6.00\%$$

We can also re-calculate to determine what the investor's return would be if they held a portfolio comprising 50% risk-free securities, and 50% market risk securities, and also 25% risk-free securities, and 75% market risk securities.

Portfolio type	Portfolio return %	Portfolio risk %
75% risk-free securities, and 25% market risk securities	8.25	6
50% risk-free securities, and 50% market risk securities	10.50	12
25% risk-free securities, and 75% market risk securities	12.75	18

The results are summarised in the table above and show that as the proportion of risk-free securities is reduced the overall risk to the investor is increased and the overall return to the investor is also increased.

In Chapter 6 we will further consider portfolio risks and returns when we take a more detailed look at CAPM.

Summary of key points

■ There is a positive correlation between risk and return – the higher the risk, the higher the return, and the lower the risk the lower the return.

■ Individuals display different attitudes to risk, and they may be risk taking, risk-averse, or indifferent to risk.

■ Companies face both business risk and financial risk.

■ Business risk comprises the general risks of companies not achieving satisfactory levels of operating profit.

■ Financial risk arises from the level of debt or loans held by companies and their ability to pay interest and repay the debt.

■ Business risk and financial risk together comprise systematic or market risk.

■ Systematic risk is inherent risk and cannot be diversified away.

■ Unsystematic risk is unique risk specific to a company or project, which may be mitigated through diversification.

■ Markowitz's portfolio theory deals with the mitigation or reduction of unsystematic risk through holding a range or a portfolio of investments.

■ Different investors have different preferences with regard to perceived risk and expected returns and their choices with regard to investments in risk-free and market risk securities and the proportions of both are shown on the capital market line (CML).

🔒 Glossary of key terms

beta factor (β) The measure of the volatility of the return on a share relative to the market. If a share price were to rise or fall at double the market rate, it would have a beta factor of 2. Conversely, if the share price moved at half the market rate, the beta factor would be 0.5.

capital market line (CML) A graphical representation of the linear relationship of the optimal risk-return trade-off of all rational investors' portfolios (i.e. the whole market) in which their funds are spread between the market portfolio and risk-free investments.

correlation coefficient A statistical measure that shows how one variable is linked with another variable, for example a measure of how closely the returns from two investments move in the same direction as each other.

diversification The 'real' or financial investment in more than one asset, or in more than one product group or industrial sector such that the returns are not perfectly correlated, in order to reduce exposure to unsystematic risk.

efficient frontier The range of optimum portfolios determined from the complete set of risk-return combinations of specific investments available to an investor.

indifference curve A graph which represents combinations of risk and return that provide equal utility or indifference for an investor.

portfolio theory A theory relating to risk and return developed by Markowitz in 1952, which considers how investors can diversify away from unsystematic risk by holding portfolios of different shares.

separation theorem The two-stage process in which unsystematic risk is diversified away by an investor by choosing the appropriate market portfolio of risky securities and then combining this with borrowing or lending at the risk-free rate in order to meet their particular risk-return requirement.

systematic risk (or market risk) Some investments are by their very nature more risky than others. This is nothing to do with chance variations in actual compared with expected returns; it is inherent risk that cannot be diversified away.

unsystematic risk Risk that can be diversified away.

❓ Questions

Q5.1 Describe the relationship between the return required by an investor and the perceived risk of the investment.

Q5.2 How may different individual attitudes to risk result in conflict?

Q5.3 Describe the types of risk that comprise systematic risk.

Q5.4 What are the main differences between systematic risk and unsystematic risk and what are their implications for an investor?

Q5.5 What is financial risk and what are its implications for highly geared companies?

Q5.6 How may a company and how may an investor reduce the impacts of unsystematic risk?

Q5.7 Explain what is meant by the efficient frontier.

Q5.8 What is a capital market line (CML)?

Q5.9 What do indifference curves tell us about investors' choices of the various risk-return combinations relating to a portfolio of investments?

Discussion points

D5.1 'It is not practical for individual investors to apply Markowitz's portfolio theory to their stock market investments.' Discuss the validity of this statement and whether or not and how Markowitz's portfolio theory may be applied by individual investors.

D5.2 'Inappropriate management of financial risk may result in a company going out of business.' Discuss.

Exercises

Solutions are provided in Appendix 2 to all exercise numbers highlighted in colour.

Level I

E5.1 *Time allowed – 15 minutes*

The level of risk for a market portfolio is 3% and the expected market return is 12%. The risk-free rate of return is 4%.

You are required to plot the capital market line (CML) from the above data.

E5.2 *Time allowed – 30 minutes*

The data in the table below relate to a portfolio of 30% of shares in Caldey plc and 70% of shares in Tenby plc.

Probability	Forecast return Caldey plc %	Forecast return Tenby plc %
0.20	10	12
0.50	12	18
0.20	14	24

The way in which returns from investments in portfolios of two or more securities vary together determines the riskiness of the portfolio. Ignoring the possibility of a zero correlation between the returns of Caldey plc and Tenby plc, you are required to calculate the portfolio returns and the risk of each if there is:

▶   (i)   perfect positive correlation
     (ii) perfect negative correlation.

E5.3 *Time allowed – 30 minutes*
The following data relate to four share portfolios A, B, C, and D

Portfolio	Expected return	Standard deviation
A	10%	4%
B	10%	7%
C	15%	3%
D	25%	5%

Required:

(i)   Explain what is meant by the term efficient portfolio.

(ii) Use the graph from Exercise E5.2 to plot the position of share portfolios A, B, C, and D, and state whether each portfolio is efficient or inefficient.

(iii) Assuming that an investor is using risk measurement to identify suitable shares in which to invest, use the graph in (ii) above to calculate what beta coefficient an investor would look for if they required a return of 11% on their investment.

(iv) Use the graph in (ii) above to calculate what rate of return a share should yield if it has a beta coefficient of 1.3.

Level II

E5.4 *Time allowed – 30 minutes*
French plc and Saunders plc are considering a variety of investment projects in a range of different industries, which are each expected to last for one year. The net cash flows and beta values of each project are shown in the table below:

Project	Beta factor	French plc net cash flow £000	Saunders plc net cash flow £000
I	1.3	300	
II	1.4		100
III	1.4		100
IV	0.8		200

The risk-free rate of return is 3% and the market rate of return is 8%.

Required:

(i)   Calculate the present values of each of the projects being considered by French plc and Saunders plc.

(ii) What will be the total beta factor of Saunders plc on the basis of all projects II, III, and IV going ahead?

(iii) Which company is likely to be valued most highly based on the above information?

E5.5 *Time allowed – 30 minutes*
Describe the characteristics of an efficiently diversified portfolio of equities and explain the reasons why diversification is used to reduce investor risk.

E5.6 *Time allowed – 45 minutes*

Abdul is an investor who has invested one quarter of his funds at the risk-free rate, which is 7%, and he has invested the remainder of his funds in a market portfolio of equities. The expected total return on his portfolio is 12% with a risk of 8%. Said is another investor who holds a similar market portfolio of equities to Abdul and his expected total return on his portfolio is 18%.

Both investors can lend and borrow at the risk-free rate, and both of their portfolios lie on the capital market line (CML).

Required:

(i) Provide calculations that illustrate the composition of the expected returns of Abdul's and Said's portfolios in terms of equity returns and fixed interest.

(ii) Draw the capital market line (CML) and show the position of both Adbul's and Said's portfolio.

(iii) Assume that Adbul wants to keep his portfolio on the CML and calculate the standard deviation he would have to accept in order to increase his expected return to 13% and show how the composition of his portfolio will change.

E5.7 *Time allowed – 45 minutes*

Bill Brownbridge is a UK-based investor who is currently considering making an investment in one or both of two listed companies, X plc, and Y plc. Information relating to expected returns from the two companies and the probabilities of their occurrence is shown below:

	Possible rates of return %	Probability of occurrence
X plc	30	0.3
	25	0.4
	20	0.3
Y plc	50	0.2
	30	0.6
	10	0.2

You may assume that there is no correlation between the expected rates of return from the companies comprising the portfolio, and that Bill Brownbridge is a risk averse investor.

Required:

(i) Calculate the expected return for each security separately and for the portfolio comprising 60% X plc shares, and 40% Y plc shares.

(ii) Using the standard deviation of returns from the expected rate of return as a measure of risk, calculate the risk of each share separately and of the portfolio as defined in (i) above.

(iii) Briefly outline the objectives of portfolio diversification and explain in general terms why the risk of individual securities may differ from that of the portfolio as a whole.

Chapter 6

Capital structure and the cost of capital

Chapter contents

LEARNING OBJECTIVES

Completion of this chapter will enable you to:

☑ Outline the capital asset pricing model (CAPM), and the importance of the β factor.

☑ Evaluate the cost of equity of a company using CAPM, and using the simple dividend growth model.

☑ Evaluate the cost of debt of a company.

☑ Calculate a company's weighted average cost of capital (WACC).

☑ Explain capital structure (or financial structure) and the concept of gearing or leverage of a company.

☑ Consider whether or not there may be an optimal capital structure.

☑ Explain the traditional approach, the Miller and Modigliani approaches, pecking order theory, and the WACC approach to capital structure.

Introduction

In Chapter 5 we saw how risk impacts on the returns from 'real' investments in value creating projects and also financial investments in shares. We also looked at how risk may be reduced through investment in a range, or portfolio, of diversified investments. We introduced CAPM and how β factors may be used to measure the volatility of the return of a share relative to the market. This chapter looks further at CAPM and how it may be used as a method of calculating cost of equity.

We will also look at other methods of calculating the cost of equity and cost of debt capital. A company's cost of equity and cost of debt may then be used to calculate its weighted average cost of capital, its WACC.

The proportion of debt of a company's total capital, its total debt plus equity, is called its capital structure (or financial structure). The chapter considers how a company's capital structure, its gearing or leverage, is measured. Any discussion about capital structure usually prompts the question 'what is a company's best (or optimal) capital structure?' The chapter closes with a review of a number of approaches to answering this question, including those proposed by Miller and Modigliani.

Capital asset pricing model (CAPM)

We saw in Chapter 5 that the risk premium that an investor should require as compensation for accepting the risk of a portfolio σ_p is:

$$\frac{(R_m - R_f)}{\sigma_m} \sigma_p$$

This risk premium may be rearranged into:

$$\frac{\sigma_p}{\sigma_m} \times (R_m - R_f)$$

and the expression $\frac{\sigma_p}{\sigma_m}$ is referred to as the beta factor β.

Therefore, an investor's required return from a portfolio:

$$R_p = R_f + \frac{(R_m - R_f)}{\sigma_m} \sigma_p$$

can be re-stated as:

Portfolio return $R_p = R_f + \beta \times (R_m - R_f)$

The beta factor β can be used to measure the extent to which a portfolio's return (or an individual security's return) should exceed the risk-free rate of return. The beta factor is multiplied by the difference between the average return on market securities R_m and the risk-free return R_f to derive a portfolio or security risk premium. The risk premium includes both a business risk and a financial risk element. This equation forms the basis of the capital asset pricing model (CAPM).

CAPM considers the market return, and also the risk-free return and volatility of a share. Shareholders expect returns that are in terms of dividends and capital growth. However, actual shareholder returns may be higher or lower than expected, because of risk.

As we have already seen in Chapter 5, diversified portfolios of investments may eliminate some unsystematic risk. Some companies may perform badly while others do well. But some risk cannot be diversified away – systematic risk. Systematic risk includes business or operating risks, for example those resulting from economic changes. Systematic risk also includes the financial risk in geared companies because of interest payable.

The return on risk-free investments (R_f), like Government securities, should be exceeded by the returns on other investments. Some investments have larger market (systematic) risk and some lower than the average market risk and so expected returns vary more or less than average. The relationship between the expected return on a company's shares, its **cost of equity** (K_e) and the average market return (R_m) may be measured by beta β (note that $\beta = 1$ for the stock market as a whole).

Investors can measure the beta factor of their portfolios by obtaining information about the beta factors of individual securities. β factors may be calculated using data collected in respect of periodic returns of market and individual company data using regression analysis. β values are also obtainable from a variety of sources such as investment analysts who specialise in the charting of the volatility of shares and markets, and their findings may regularly be found in the UK financial press. β values are also published quarterly by the London Business School's Financial Services.

It should be noted that CAPM recognises 'chance' returns and share price variations due to market risk. CAPM measures the β of individual shares by reliable statistical measures, but it does not take unsystematic risk into account, although it may be significant for an undiversified investor or a company with few products. But an investor may reduce or eliminate unsystematic risk through diversification.

CAPM may therefore be used to calculate the return on a company's shares while making some allowance for the systematic risk relating to that company.

CAPM can be stated as follows:

the expected return from a security = the risk-free rate of return, plus a premium for market risk, adjusted by a measure of the volatility of the security

If

R$_s$ is the expected return from an individual security
β is the beta factor for the individual security
R$_f$ is the risk-free rate of return
R$_m$ is the return from the market as a whole
(R$_m$ − R$_f$)   is the market risk premium

then

$$R_s = R_f + \{\boldsymbol{\beta} \times (R_m - R_f)\}$$

A variation of the above β relationship may be used to establish an equity cost of capital for use in project appraisal. The cost of equity K$_e$ equates to the expected return from an individual security R$_s$, and the beta value for the company's equity capital β_e equates to beta factor for the individual security β.

So, the returns expected by ordinary shareholders, or the cost of equity to the company = the risk-free rate of return plus a premium for market risk adjusted by a measure of the volatility of the ordinary shares of the company.

Therefore:

$$K_e = R_f + \{\boldsymbol{\beta}_e \times (R_m - R_f)\}$$

as represented in Fig. 6.1.

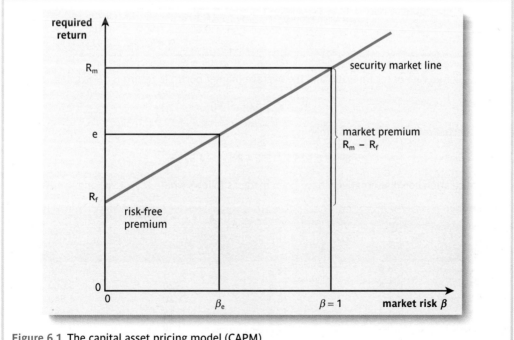

Figure 6.1 The capital asset pricing model (CAPM)

In Fig. 6.1 it should be noted that the linear relationship between risk and return is represented by the security market line (SML). Whereas the capital market line (CML) that we discussed in Chapter 5 represents the linear risk and return trade-off for investors in a portfolio of risky market-based assets and other risk-free assets, the SML represents the relationship between systematic risk (measured by β) and the required rate of return on capital assets.

CAPM assumes that the relationship between the return from a share and the average return for the whole market is a linear relationship. It should also be remembered that the CAPM considers systematic risk only. CAPM is a market equilibrium theory that was developed relating to the prices of shares, and their risks.

As we discussed in Chapter 5, just as an individual security or share has a beta factor, so too does a portfolio of securities. A portfolio consisting of a weighted proportion of all the securities on the stock market, excluding risk free securities, will have an expected return equal to the expected return for the market as a whole, and so a β factor of 1. A portfolio consisting entirely of risk-free securities will have a β factor of zero.

Worked Example 6.1

The β factor of an investor's portfolio is the weighted average of the β factors of the securities in the portfolio. Consider the following portfolio:

Security	Percentage of portfolio %	β factor of security	Weighted average
V	25	0.8	0.200
W	20	1.4	0.280
X	10	1.2	0.120
Y	15	1.3	0.195
Z	30	0.6	0.180
	100		Portfolio β_p = 0.975

If the risk-free rate of return is 8% and the average market portfolio return is 15%, using:

$$R_p = R_f + \beta_p(R_m - R_f)$$

the expected return from the portfolio is:

$$8\% + 0.975 \times (15\% - 8\%) = 14.825\%$$

The calculation could alternatively have been made as follows where R_m = 15%, and R_f = 8%:

Security	Expected return			
	Beta factor	$[R_f + \beta(R_m - R_f)]$ %	Weighting %	Weighted return %
V	0.8	13.6	25	3.400
W	1.4	17.8	20	3.560
X	1.2	16.4	10	1.640
Y	1.3	17.1	15	2.565
Z	0.6	12.2	30	3.660
			100	14.825

What are the practical implications of CAPM theory for portfolio management? Well, the conclusions we can draw from CAPM theory are that the investor should:

- decide on what β factor they would like to have for their portfolio – they may prefer a portfolio beta factor of greater than 1 in expectation of above-average returns when market returns are high and lower-than-average returns if market returns are low, or alternatively they may prefer a portfolio β factor below 1

- seek to invest in shares with a low β factor in a bear market, when average market returns are falling, and also sell shares with a high beta factor

- seek to invest in shares with a high β factor in a bull market, when average market returns are rising.

Limitations of CAPM

There are a number of limitations to the CAPM, including:

- it is a single factor model

- the model makes unrealistic assumptions, for example that the cost of insolvency is zero, and that markets are efficient

- the parameters of the model cannot be estimated precisely, for example those used in determining the risk-free rate of return and beta values

- the model assumes a linear relationship between its variables.

The CAPM is generally only useable where shares are traded on the open market. While the CAPM may be used to determine the value of a share, or determine the risk of a portfolio of shares, increasing doubt was expressed by Fama and French (Fama EF, French K (1992) 'The cross-section of expected stock returns' *Journal of Finance*, 47, June, 427–65) as to whether the SML exists, and whether beta has any impact on the level of returns earned on shares.

Cost of equity

In Chapter 5 we introduced the concept of risk and its correlation with returns on investments. The relationship between risk and return is also one of the key concepts relating to determination of the **cost of debt** and cost of equity capital. It is an important concept and so we will briefly explore risk a little further, with regard to investments in companies. We will discuss the cost of debt based on future income flows to the lender – interest payments. We shall similarly discuss the cost of equity based on future income flows to the shareholder – dividends. Dividends and dividend policy will be considered in more detail in Chapters 13 and 15.

The cost of equity to a company may be determined by looking at future cash flows. In the case of equity or ordinary shares these future cash flows are dividends. One difference between this method and the method applied to debt is that there is no tax relief for dividend payments. The value of an ordinary share may be simply expressed as the present value of its expected future dividend flows:

$$S = v_1/(1 + K_e) + v_2/(1 + K_e)^2 + v_3/(1 + K_e)^3 \cdots v_n/(1 + K_e)^n$$

where K_e = cost of equity capital
             $v_1 \ldots v_n$ = expected future dividends for each of 1 to n years
             S   = the current market value of the share

If dividends are expected to remain level over a period of time the formula may be simplified to:

$$S = \frac{v_1}{K_e}$$

Therefore, the cost of equity to the company would be:

$$K_e = \frac{v_1}{S}$$

This simple **dividend model** is based on the notion that shareholders value shares based on the value of their expected dividends. A disadvantage of the simple dividend model is that it assumes that shareholders are rational and consistent in their long-term dividend expectations.

Simple dividend growth model

A big assumption made in using the simple dividend model is that capital growth in share price is ignored because the share price at any time reflects expectations of future dividends at that time. Dividends payable on a particular share rarely stay constant from year to year. However, dividends may grow at a regular rate.

The so-called **dividend growth model** (or Gordon growth model) approach to cost of equity may be developed by revising the simple dividend model formula. The dividend growth model assumes a direct link between share price and expected future dividends and recognises the expected rate of dividend growth (G) achieved through reinvestment of retained earnings.

If K_e = cost of equity capital
v = current dividend
S = the current market value of the share

then

$$S = v/(1 + K_e) + v(1 + G)/(1 + K_e)^2 + v(1 + G)^2/(1 + K_e)^3 \cdots v(1 + G)^{n-1}/(1 + K_e)^n$$

If it is assumed that the share is held for an indefinite period then n can be assumed to tend towards infinity and if G is assumed to be constant the equation may be rewritten as:

$$\text{Current share price} \quad S = \frac{v(1 + G)}{(K_e - G)}$$

Therefore

$$\text{Cost of equity} \quad K_e = \frac{v(1 + G)}{S} + G$$

If the first year dividend v_1 is assumed to have grown at a rate of G so that $v(1 + G) = v_1$ then the cost of equity may be restated as:

$$K_e = \frac{v_1}{S} + G$$

Worked Example 6.2

Cher Alike plc has 3m ordinary shares in issue that currently have a market price (S) of £2.71. The board have already recommended next year's dividend (v_1) at 17p per share. The chairman, Sonny Daze, is forecasting that dividends will continue to grow (G) at 4.2% per annum for the foreseeable future.

What is Cher Alike plc's cost of equity?

$$K_e = \text{cost of equity capital}$$

$$= \frac{v_1}{S} + G = \frac{0.17}{2.71} + 4.2\%$$

$$= 0.063 + 0.042 = 10.5\%$$

Progress check 6.1

In what ways may a company's cost of equity be calculated?

Cost of debt

The interest rate paid on a loan is known almost with certainty. Even if the debt carries a floating or variable interest rate it is far easier to estimate than expected dividend flows on ordinary shares. Debt comprises debentures, loans etc., and may be corporate or Government debt. Their levels of risk are different, and some debt may be secured on specific assets or the assets of a company in general. The cost of debt is generally based on the current market rate for debt having a specific level of risk.

Two of the main differences between the cost of equity and the cost of debt are:

- the different levels of risk between debt and equity
- the tax shield is applicable to interest paid on debt, but not to equity dividends paid.

The cost of servicing debt capital is the yearly or half-yearly interest payment, which is an allowable expense for tax. The cost of repayment of a loan, or debt, depends on the type of loan. Loan capital, a debenture for example, may be irredeemable and traded, with a market value, or redeemable at a specific date. We will look at the calculation of the cost of a redeemable loan and also the cost of an irredeemable loan to a company.

If

K_d = cost of debt capital
i = annual loan interest rate
L   = the current market value of the loan.

If the loan is redeemable, and if R is the loan value at redemption after n years, then:

$$L = i/(1 + K_d) + i/(1 + K_d)^2 + i/(1 + K_d)^3 + \cdots + (i + R)/(1 + K_d)^n$$

The cost of debt in the above equation can be calculated by trial and error, by interpolation, or using the appropriate Excel function.

For an irredeemable loan the interest is payable in perpetuity (for ever), so:

$$L = i/(1 + K_d) + i/(1 + K_d)^2 + i/(1 + K_d)^3 + \ldots \text{ to infinity}$$

therefore:

$$L = i/K_d$$

Because interest payable on loans is an allowable deduction for corporation tax the cost of debt is normally calculated by adjusting the interest rate by the percentage of corporation tax to provide an after-tax rate of interest.

Therefore, if $t =$ the rate of corporation tax then

$$K_d = \frac{i \times (1 - t)}{L}$$

The expression $(1 - t)$ is called the tax shield.

By rearranging the formula it can be seen that market value of the debt is dependent on the level of future returns, the interest rate paid, which is determined by the level of risk associated with the investment, and the rate of corporation tax:

$$L = \frac{i \times (1 - t)}{K_d}$$

Worked Example 6.3

Owen Cash plc pays 12% interest (i) per annum on an irredeemable debt of £1m, with a nominal value of £100. The corporation tax rate (t) is currently 50%. The market value of the debt (L) is currently £90.

What is Owen Cash plc's cost of debt?

K_d = cost of debt capital

$$K_d = \frac{i \times (1 - t)}{L} = \frac{12\% \times (1 - 50\%)}{90}$$

$$K_d = \frac{12\% \times 50\%}{90} = 6.7\%$$

What would be the cost of debt if instead this loan were redeemable at par after three years?

If K_d is the cost of debt of the redeemable loan then

$$L = i/(1 + K_d) + i/(1 + K_d)^2 + i/(1 + K_d)^3 + \ldots + (i + R)/(1 + K_d)^n$$

$$90 = 6/(1 + K_d) + 6/(1 + K_d)^2 + (6 + 100)/(1 + K_d)^3$$

Solving this equation gives $K_d = 10.0\%$

Alternatively by interpolation, using a discount rate of 12% the NPV = −£4.59, and using a discount rate of 8% the NPV = £4.48

The difference between the two is £9.07, and therefore

$$K_d = 8\% + (£4.48 \times 4)/£9.97 = 9.98 \text{ or } 10\%.$$

Progress check 6.2

How can the cost of debt be determined?

Weighted average cost of capital (WACC)

Weighted average cost of capital (WACC) is the weighted cost of financing a company (equity, debentures, bank loans) weighted according to the proportion of each, based on their market valuations. Once the company's cost of debt (K_d) and cost of equity (K_e) have been calculated the individual costs of finance can then be weighted by the relative proportions of debt (D) and equity (E) within the existing capital structure to calculate its WACC.

The weighted average cost of capital (WACC) may be defined as the average cost of the total financial resources of a company, i.e. the shareholders' equity and the net financial debt. WACC may also be calculated on a marginal basis for additional incremental finance packages comprising debt and/or equity.

In practice, conditions within a company may change daily and so calculations of the cost of equity and the cost of debt may not be totally accurate. As the relative proportions of a company's equity and debt, its **gearing**, change, the returns required by investors and the levels of perceived risk may also change. It should be noted that the terms of a debt may require interest to be paid at a floating rate rather than a fixed rate, in which case an equivalent 'fixed' rate then has to be estimated.

If we represent shareholders' equity as E and net financial debt as D then the relative proportions of equity and debt in the company's total financing are:

$$\frac{E}{E+D} \quad \text{and} \quad \frac{D}{E+D}$$

The cost of equity is the expected return on equity, the return the shareholders expect from their investment. If we represent the cost of shareholders' equity as K_e and the cost of financial debt as K_d, and t is the rate of corporation tax, then we can derive the formula to calculate WACC.

$$WACC = \left\{ \frac{E}{E+D} \times K_e \right\} + \left\{ \frac{E}{E+D} \times K_d \right\} (1-t)$$

Interest on debt capital is an allowable deduction for purposes of corporate taxation and so the cost of share capital and the cost of debt capital are not properly comparable costs. Therefore this tax relief on debt interest ought to be recognised in any discounted cash flow calculations. One way would be to include the tax savings due to interest payments in the cash flows of every project. A simpler method, and the one normally used, is to allow for the tax relief in computing the cost of debt capital, to arrive at an after-tax cost of debt. Therefore, in order to calculate WACC, the cost of debt (K_d) must be adjusted for corporation tax (t), by $(1-t)$ the tax shield.

Worked Example 6.4

Fleet Ltd has the following financial structure:

K_e = 15%   return on equity (this may be taken as given for the purpose of this example)
K_d = 10%   lower risk, so lower than the return on equity
t = 30%   rate of corporation tax

$\dfrac{D}{E + D}$ = 60%   equity to equity plus debt ratio

$\dfrac{D}{E + D}$ = 40%   debt to equity plus debt ratio

We can calculate the WACC for Fleet Ltd, and also evaluate the impact on WACC of a change in capital structure to equity 40% and debt 60%.

Calculation of WACC for Fleet Ltd with the current financial structure:

$$\text{WACC} = \left\{ \frac{E}{E + D} \times K_e \right\} + \left\{ \frac{E}{E + D} \times K_d \right\} (1 - t)$$

$$\text{WACC} = (60\% \times 15\%) + \{40\% \times 10\% \ (1 - 30\%)\} = 11.8\%$$

If the company decides to change its financial structure so that equity is 40% and debt is 60% of total financing, then WACC becomes:

$$(40\% \times 15\%) + \{60\% \times 10\% \ (1 - 30\%)\} = 10.2\%$$

So it appears that the company has reduced its WACC by increasing the relative weighting from 40% to 60% of the cheapest financial resource, debt, in its total financing. However, this may not happen in practice because as the debt/equity ratio of the company increased from 0.67 (40/60) to 1.50 (60/40) the company's risk has also increased. There is a well-established correlation between risk and return; the providers of the financial resources will require a higher return on their investment. So, it is probably not correct to recalculate the WACC using the same returns on equity and debt, as both may have increased. This is one of the problems of trying to calculate an accurate WACC for a company, which is based on its relative proportions and costs of debt and equity capital.

As an alternative to the dividend models, the cost of equity of a company may be calculated by making an allowance for risk using the CAPM. This cost of capital may then be used to calculate a company's WACC.

Progress check 6.3

How is the weighted average cost of capital (WACC) calculated?

The uses of WACC

The market value of a company may be determined by evaluating its future cash flows discounted to present values by using its WACC. The lower the WACC then the higher the net present values of its future cash flows and therefore the higher its market value. The determination of the optimum D/E (debt/equity) ratio is one of the most difficult tasks facing the finance director. The risks and costs associated with debt capital and equity capital are different and subject to continual change, and may vary from industry to industry and between different types of business. Measurement of the D/E ratio may therefore not be a straightforward task, particularly for diversified groups of companies. Companies in different markets and indeed diversified companies that have trading divisions operating within different markets and producing different products face different levels of risk. If division A operates with a higher risk than division B then the required rate of return of A's investments should be higher than the hurdle rate of return of B's investments. The difference is 'paying' for the difference in risk. This is an important principle but very difficult to implement in practice.

There are many arguments for and against the use of WACC for investment appraisal. Its use is argued on the basis that:

- new investments must be financed by new sources of funds – retained earnings, new share issues, new loans, and so on
- the cost of capital to be applied to new project evaluation must reflect the cost of new capital
- the WACC reflects the company's long-term future capital structure, and capital costs; if this were not so, the current WACC would become irrelevant because eventually it would not relate to any actual cost of capital.

It is sometimes argued that the current WACC should be used to evaluate projects, because a company's capital structure changes only very slowly over time; therefore, the marginal cost of new capital will be roughly equal to the WACC. If this view is correct then by undertaking investments, which offer a return in excess of the WACC, a company will increase the market value of its ordinary shares in the long run. This is because the excess returns would provide surplus profits and dividends for the shareholders.

The arguments against the use of WACC are based on the criticisms of the assumptions made that justify the use of WACC:

- new investments have different risk characteristics from the company's existing operations therefore the return required by investors may go up or down if the investments are made, because their business risk is perceived to be higher or lower
- finance raised to fund a new investment:
  - may substantially change the capital structure and perceived risk of investing in the company
  - may determine the extent to which either debt or equity used to finance the project will change the perceived risk of the entire company, which must be taken into account in the investment appraisal
- many companies raise floating rate debt capital as well as fixed rate debt capital, having a variable rate that changes in line with current market rates; this is difficult to include in a WACC calculation, the best compromise being to substitute an 'equivalent' fixed debt rate in place of the floating rate.

Worked Example 6.5

Bittaboth plc has ordinary shares in issue with a market value four times the value of its debt capital. The debt is considered to be risk free and pays 11% (R_f) before tax. The beta value of Bittaboth's equity capital has been estimated at 0.9 (β_e) and the average market return on equity capital is 17% (R_m). Corporation tax is at 50% (t).

We can calculate Bittaboth plc's WACC.

$$K_e = \text{cost of equity capital}$$
$$K_e = R_f + \{\beta_e \times (R_m - R_f)\} = 11\% + \{0.9 \times (17\% - 11\%)\}$$
$$= 0.11 + (0.9 \times 0.06) = 0.164 = 16.4\%$$
$$K_d = \text{cost of debt capital}$$

which after tax is

$$i \times (1 - t) \text{ or } 11\% \times 50\% = 5.5\%$$

Any capital projects that Bittaboth may wish to consider may be evaluated using its WACC, which may be calculated as:

$$(4/5 \times 16.4\%) + (1/5 \times 5.5\%) = 14.2\%$$

14.2% is Bittaboth's weighted average cost of capital (WACC).

Progress check 6.4

What are some of the reasons why WACC is so important to companies?

Capital structure

We have already discussed the importance of the level of a company's debt with regard to its strategic financial decision-making. It is also very important with regard to its gearing, or financial (capital) structure. Strategic financing decisions on the appropriate levels of debt and equity at the lowest cost to the company have a big impact on shareholder wealth.

The financial structure of a company comprises both internal and external finance. If we first consider internal financing, then we can see that the aim of optimal investment in non-current assets results in profits that may be distributed in the form of dividends or retained for future investment. If the non-current assets are the engine of the business then working capital is the oil needed to lubricate it and enable it to run efficiently. The effective management of working capital is a further source of internal finance that supports the investment in non-current assets.

External finance is broadly comprised of debt (loans, debentures, etc.) and equity (ordinary shares). Examples of the broad range of different types of debt and equity are shown in Fig. 6.2, each of which will be discussed in detail in Chapter 7.

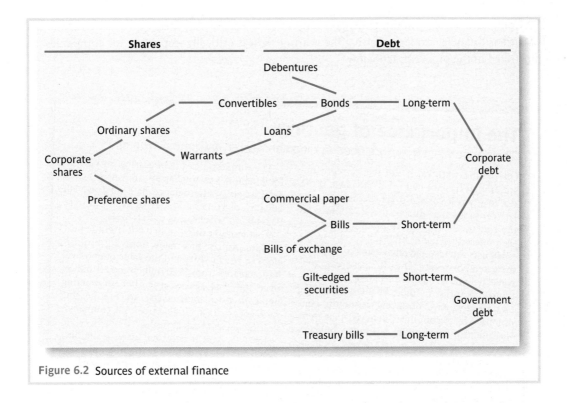

Figure 6.2 Sources of external finance

Gearing – debt and equity

Gearing is the relationship between debt and equity capital that represents the capital structure or financial structure of an organisation. The relationship between the two sources of finance, loans and ordinary shares, or debt and equity gives a measure of the gearing of the company. A company with a high proportion of debt capital to share capital is highly geared, and it is low geared if it has a high proportion of share capital to debt capital. We will consider the importance of gearing to companies and then consider worked examples that compare the impact of the use of debt capital compared with ordinary share capital.

Gearing (leverage, or debt/equity) has important implications for the long-term stability of a company because of, as we have seen, its impact on financial risk. The level of a company's gearing, its capital or financial structure is also very important with regard to its dividend policy. A company that is very low geared has a relatively high proportion of equity capital and may potentially have to pay out a high level of dividends. On the other hand, since its level of debt is relatively low then its level of interest payments will also be relatively low. A consequence of this is that it will also have a low tax shield relating to its interest payments.

A company that is very highly geared has a relatively low proportion of equity capital and therefore a low level of potential dividend payments. Consequently, since its level of debt is relatively high then its level of interest payments will also be relatively high. This will mean that it will also have a high tax shield relating to its interest payments. Specific dividend policies relating to companies at different stages in the life cycle are discussed in more detail in Chapter 13 and 15.

Companies closely monitor their gearing ratios to ensure that their capital structure aligns with their financial strategy. Getting the gearing right is critically important for companies, as illustrated in the press extract below.

The importance of gearing

'The dangers a company's gearing ratio can reveal', by John Kavanagh

One of the features of the recent reporting season that has not had much coverage is the rise in interest costs. Broker Goldman Sachs JB Were says that during the six months to the end of 2004, listed companies increased their interest payments by 7%.

Higher interest payments are a result of increased borrowing. Over the past year companies have taken on more debt to make acquisitions and invest in their businesses, hoping to take advantage of strong economic conditions. Most economists believed that there was underinvestment in Australian business in recent years. Higher debt levels could be accommodated comfortably on most balance sheets, which were geared pretty modestly.

But now the economy is slowing and interest rates are going up. Investors have become more sensitive to corporate borrowing levels and the impact higher interest charges might have on the bottom line.

Equity research group Lincoln Indicators has issued what it calls an 'early warning rating' on the packaging company Amcor. It says the company's gearing has moved beyond what it considers a prudent level.

Talk of a company's gearing is a reference to the ratio of assets and liabilities that make up the balance sheet. Too much gearing leaves a business vulnerable to rising interest charges. Too little gearing is also a problem; it means that the company is failing to take advantage of the leverage that debt provides to grow the business.

The simplest measure of gearing is to divide total liabilities by total assets. In Amcor's case, total assets at the balance date on June 30, 2004, were $10.3 billion. Total liabilities were $5.6 billion. The gearing ratio is 0.54.

That looks healthy enough but is a little misleading. Amcor has made some big acquisitions in recent years and the value of goodwill has increased from $720 million to $2.1 billion over the past two years. After subtracting goodwill from total assets, Amcor's gearing ratio goes to 0.68. On that basis, the company's gearing doesn't look as healthy.

In 2003, Amcor had total assets (excluding goodwill) of $7.6 billion and liabilities of $4.9 billion, giving it a gearing ratio of 0.64.

In 2002, total assets (excluding goodwill) of $8.1 billion and total liabilities of $4.3 billion gave it a gearing ratio of 0.5.

There is a clear rising trend in the gearing. Over that three-year period Amcor increased short-term debt from $362 million to $729 million and long-term debt from $1.7 billion to $2.1 billion.

Amcor investors should be comfortable with higher gearing as long as it leads to higher earnings. What's a little worrying is that earnings per share fell from 45 cents in 2003 to 44.5 last year. Amcor has some work to do to get its acquisitions producing returns for shareholders.

© *The Sun-Herald*, 20 March 2005

Various alternative actions may be taken by companies, as necessary, to adjust their capital structures by increasing or decreasing their respective levels of debt and equity. An example of one of the ways in which this may be achieved is to return cash to shareholders. In May 2004 Marshalls plc, the paving stone specialist that supplied the flagstones for the pedestrianised Trafalgar Square in London, announced that they were planning to return £75m to shareholders through a capital reorganisation. The reason the company gave for this was that it expected a more efficient capital structure as a result. The company was geared at only 6%, and had generated a £5.3m cash in its previous financial year, after dividends and £40m capital expenditure, which its chairman said had reflected its success in growing shareholder value and generating cash.

The extent to which the debt/equity is high or low geared has an effect on the earnings per share (eps) of the company:

- if profits are increasing, then higher gearing is preferable to benefit from the lower cost of debt and the tax shield
- if profits are decreasing, then lower gearing or no gearing is preferred to avoid the commitment to paying high levels of interest and because dividends do not have to be paid.

Similarly, the argument applies to the riskiness attached to capital repayments. If a company goes into liquidation, lenders have priority over shareholders with regard to capital repayment. So, the more highly geared the company the less chance there is of ordinary shareholders being repaid in full.

Progress check 6.5

What is gearing?

The many types of short- and long-term capital available to companies leads to complexity, but also the expectation that overall financial risks may be reduced through improved matching of funding with operational needs. The gearing position of the company may be considered in many ways depending on whether the long-term capital structure or the overall financial structure is being analysed. It may also be analysed by concentrating on the income position rather than purely on the capital structure.

Financial gearing relates to the relationship between a company's borrowings, which includes debt, and its share capital and reserves. Gearing calculations may be based on a number of different capital values. All UK plcs disclose their net debt to equity ratio in their annual reports and accounts.

The two financial ratios that follow are the two most commonly used (see also Chapter 8). Both ratios relate to financial gearing, which is the relationship between a company's borrowings, which includes both prior charge capital and long-term debt, and shareholders' funds (share capital plus reserves).

$$gearing = \frac{\text{long-term debt}}{\text{equity} + \text{long-term debt}}$$

$$debt\ equity\ ratio,\ or\ leverage = \frac{\text{long-term debt}}{\text{equity}}$$

Worked Example 6.6 illustrates the calculation of both ratios.

Worked Example 6.6

Two companies have different gearing. Company A is financed totally by 20,000 £1 ordinary shares, while company B is financed partly by 10,000 £1 ordinary shares and a £10,000 10% loan. In all other respects the companies are the same. They both have assets of £20,000 and both make the same profit before interest and tax (PBIT). ▶

▶

	A £	B £
Assets	20,000	20,000
less 10% loan	–	(10,000)
	20,000	10,000
Ordinary shares	20,000	10,000

$$\text{Gearing} = \frac{\text{long-term debt}}{\text{equity} + \text{long-term debt}} \quad \frac{0}{20,000 + 0} = 0\% \quad \frac{10,000}{10,000 + 10,000} = 50\%$$

$$\text{Debt equity ratio} = \frac{\text{long-term debt}}{\text{equity}} \quad \frac{0}{20,000} = 0\% \quad \frac{10,000}{10,000} = 100\%$$

Company B must make a profit before interest of at least £1,000 to cover the cost of the 10% loan. Company A does not have any PBIT requirement because it has no debt.

Company A is lower geared and considered less risky in terms of profitability than company B which is a more highly geared company. This is because the PBIT of a lower geared company is more likely to be sufficiently high to cover interest charges and make a profit for equity shareholders.

Gearing calculations can be made in a number of ways, and may also relate to earnings/ interest relationships in addition to capital values. For example:

$$\text{dividend cover (times)} = \frac{\text{earnings per share (eps)}}{\text{dividend per share}}$$

This ratio indicates the number of times the profits attributable to the equity shareholders covers the actual dividends paid and payable for the period. Financial analysts usually adjust their calculations for any exceptional or extraordinary items of which they may be aware.

$$\text{interest cover (times)} = \frac{\text{profit before interest and tax}}{\text{interest payable}}$$

This ratio calculates the number of times the interest payable is covered by profits available for such payments. It is particularly important for lenders to determine the vulnerability of interest payments to a drop in profit. The following ratio determines the same vulnerability in cash terms.

$$\text{cash interest cover} = \frac{\text{net cash inflow from operations} + \text{interest received}}{\text{interest paid}}$$

Progress check 6.6

Outline the ways in which financial gearing may be measured.

Worked Example 6.7

Swell Guys plc is a growing company that manufactures equipment for fitting out small cruiser boats. Its planned expansion involves investing in a new factory project costing £4m. Chief Executive, Guy Rope, expects the 12-year project to add £0.5m to profit before interest and tax each year. Next year's operating profit is forecast at £5m, and dividends per share are forecast at the same level as last year. Tax is not expected to be payable over the next few years due to tax losses that have been carried forward.

Swell Guys last two years' results are as follows:

	Last year £m	Previous year £m
Income statement for the year ended 31 December		
Sales	18	15
Operating costs	16	11
Operating profit	2	4
Interest payable	1	1
Profit before tax	1	3
Tax on ordinary activities	0	0
Profit after tax	1	3
Dividends	1	1
Retained profit	0	2

	Last year £m	Previous year £m
Balance sheet as at 31 December		
Non-current assets	8	9
Current assets		
Stocks	7	4
Debtors	4	3
Cash	1	2
	12	9
Creditors due within one year		
Bank overdraft	4	2
Creditors	5	5
	9	7
Net current assets	3	2
Total assets less current liabilities	11	11
less		
Long-term loans	6	6
Net assets	5	5
Capital and reserves		
Share capital (25p ordinary shares)	2	2
Profit and loss account	3	3
	5	5

Swell Guys is considering two options:

(a) Issue of £4m 15% loan stock repayable in five years' time.

(b) Rights issue of 4m 25p ordinary shares at £1 per share after expenses.

▶

▶ For each of the options the directors would like to see:

(i)   how the retained profit (derived from operating profit) will look for next year

(ii) how earnings per share will look for next year

(iii) how the capital and reserves will look at the end of next year

(iv) how long-term loans will look at the end of next year

(v)   how gearing will look at the end of next year.

(i)   **Swell Guys plc forecast income statement for next year ended 31 December**
      Operating profit £5m + £0.5m from the new project

	New debt £m	New equity £m
Operating profit	5.5	5.5
Interest payable [1.0 + 0.6]	1.6	1.0
Profit before tax	3.9	4.5
Tax on ordinary activities	0.0	0.0
Profit after tax	3.9	4.5
Dividends	1.0	1.5
Retained profit	2.9	3.0

(ii) **Earnings per share**

$$\frac{\text{profit available for ordinary shareholders}}{\text{number of ordinary shares}} \quad \frac{£3.9m}{8m} = 48.75p \qquad \frac{£4.5m}{12m} = 37.5p$$

(iii) **Capital and reserves**

	As at 31 December	
	New debt £m	New equity £m
Share capital (25p ordinary shares)	2.0 (8m shares)	3.0 (12m shares)
Share premium account	0.0	3.0
Profit and loss account	5.9	6.0
	7.9	12.0

(iv) **Long-term loans [6 + 4]**   10.0   6.0

(v)   **Gearing**

$$\frac{\text{long-term debt}}{\text{equity + long-term debt}} \quad \frac{£6m + £4m}{£7.9m + £6m + £4m} = 55.9\% \qquad \frac{£6m}{£12m + £6m} = 33.3\%$$

Progress check 6.7

Explain how a high interest cover ratio can reassure a prospective lender.

Return on equity (ROE) may be considered as a function of financial structure (debt/equity ratio), and return on assets (ROA).

If

D = debt capital
E = equity capital
t = corporation tax rate
i = interest rate on debt
ROA = return on assets

then

$$\text{ROE} = \{\text{ROA} \times (1 - t)\} + \{(\text{ROA} - i) \times (1 - t) \times \text{D/E}\}$$

In general, when ROA is greater than i then the higher the D/E, the higher the ROE; when ROA is less than i then the higher the D/E, the lower the ROE. These relationships are important with regard to a company's performance and its level of gearing. This should be of interest to shareholders and analysts, and particularly bankers who may not be too happy to allow the debt/equity to continue to increase even if profitability (ROA) exceeds interest.

Progress check 6.8

Why may a company not increase its debt/equity ratio indefinitely?

Optimal capital structure

A shareholder's return may be seen as comprising the return from a risk-free investment plus a return for the risk associated with that particular business. As the debt level of the business increases shareholders also require an additional premium for the financial risk relating to interest paid on debt. At high levels of gearing when debt levels are very large, shareholders will require a further additional premium to compensate for the risk of bankruptcy.

The debt-holder's return, or cost of debt, does not vary as levels of profit may vary, or generally as levels of gearing change. However, at very high levels of gearing when debt levels are very high, debt-holders may require an additional premium to compensate for some risk of bankruptcy, although perhaps not at the level of return demanded by shareholders.

We will consider whether or not an optimal capital structure exists and look at a number of approaches to the capital structure of a company including:

- the traditional approach
- the Miller and Modigliani (I) net income approach
- the Miller and Modigliani (II) market imperfections approach
- the Miller corporate and personal taxation approach
- pecking order theory
- the weighted average cost of capital (WACC) approach.

Traditional approach to capital structure (or financial structure)

The traditional approach to capital structure is based on a number of assumptions:

- taxation is ignored
- debt or equity can be simultaneously changed
- all earnings are paid out in dividends
- the business risk for the company is constant
- earnings and dividends do not grow over time.

If we assume that a company starts with its capital all in equity (see point U in Fig. 6.3). At that point the cost of capital is the risk-free rate of return plus a premium for the business risk of the company. If debt is increased in steps, the cost of equity (see the K_e line) increases steadily because of the additional premium required due to the financial risk arising from the increase in debt. The cost of equity continues to rise steadily until high levels of gearing are reached when it begins to rise steeply due to bankruptcy risk.

As levels of debt are increased in steps the cost of debt (see the K_d line) remains unchanged. However, at high levels of gearing the cost of debt also begins to rise, in the same way as the cost of equity, due to bankruptcy risk.

The WACC of the company is based on the cost of equity and the cost of debt. From point U, the company's WACC can be seen to decrease (see the WACC line) because of the increasing amount of low cost debt taken on by the company, compared to its fixed level of equity. WACC gradually drops as gearing increases to an optimal point V, after which WACC begins to slowly increase as the benefit of the low cost of debt is outweighed by the increase in the cost of equity.

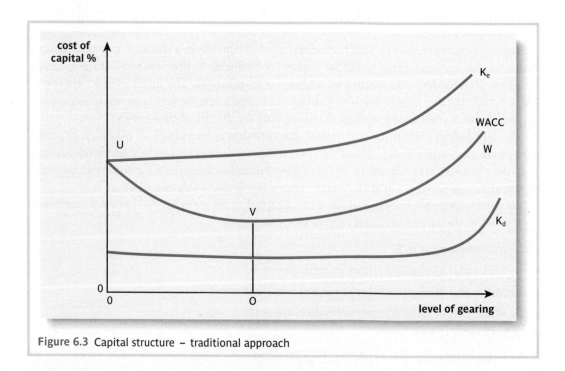

Figure 6.3 Capital structure – traditional approach

WACC increases sharply at very high levels of gearing (W) as the impact of higher costs of both equity and debt are felt, due to the risk of bankruptcy.

The traditional approach to capital structure is that there is an optimal point at the bottom of the WACC curve, the lowest cost of capital to the company. The company will aim for levels of equity and debt that gives the level of gearing at point O to achieve its lowest average cost of capital.

Miller and Modigliani (I) net income approach to capital structure

In 1958 Miller and Modigliani (MM) developed their first approach to capital structure (Modigliani F, Miller MH (1958) 'The cost of capital, corporate finance and the theory of investment' *American Economic Review*, 48, 261–97). Their approach assumed that there was no tax and that the capital markets were perfect so that there were no bankruptcy costs and therefore the cost of debt was constant at all levels of gearing (see the K_d line in Fig. 6.4). As the company increases its level of gearing, with equity being replaced by an equal amount of debt, the increased cost of equity (see the K_e line) is exactly offset by the increased total cost of debt and therefore the company's WACC remains constant (see the WACC line) at all levels of gearing.

MM therefore implied that there was no optimal capital structure in proposing that a company's WACC remains unchanged at all levels of gearing. This theory assumed that the cost of debt remains unchanged as gearing rises, but the cost of equity rises in such a way as to keep WACC constant.

MM defended their approach basing it on the behavioural proposition that investors would use arbitrage to keep WACC constant when gearing changed. Generally, arbitrage excludes the possibility of perfect substitutes selling at different prices in the same market. MM argued that

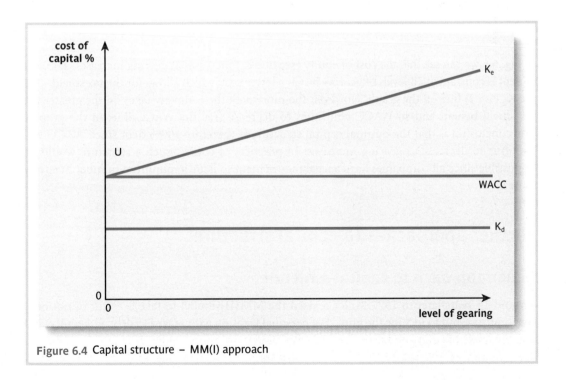

Figure 6.4 Capital structure – MM(I) approach

companies that were identical (apart from their gearing levels) should not have different costs of capital. Therefore, the valuations of these companies should also be the same.

Miller and Modigliani (II) market imperfections approach to capital structure

In 1963 MM revised their thinking and amended their earlier model by recognising the existence of corporation tax (a market imperfection) and its impact on the cost of debt (Modigliani F, Miller MH (1963) 'Corporate income taxes and the cost of capital: a correction' *American Economic Review*, 53, 433–43). Interest payable on debt is an allowable expense in computing the company's taxable profit. The tax deductibility of debt interest implied that the greater the debt the more the company would shield its profits from corporation tax. This so-called tax shield is illustrated in Worked Example 6.8.

Worked Example 6.8

A company pays interest on its loan at 10% per annum. The company pays corporation tax at a rate of 30% on its profits.

$$\begin{aligned}
\text{Cost of debt, interest payable} &= 10\% \text{ per annum} \\
\text{Actual cost of debt} &= 10\% \times (1 - 30\%) \\
&= 10\% \times 70\% \\
&= 7\%
\end{aligned}$$

The (1 – 30%) in the above example is referred to as the tax shield.

In Fig. 6.5 we can see that the cost of equity (see line K_e) increases as gearing increases. The cost of debt is constant at all levels of gearing but at a lower cost, which allows for the tax shield – see the $K_d (1 - t)$ line on the graph. However, the more debt the company takes on the greater the tax shield benefit and so WACC continues to decrease (see the WACC line on the graph). The conclusion is that the optimal capital structure is therefore 100% debt since WACC will continue to decrease as gearing increases. In practice, of course, such a structure would be impossible since all companies have a legal requirement to issue a minimum number of equity shares.

Further approaches to capital structure

Miller approach to capital structure

Around 15 years later in 1977 Miller revised the MM(II) model to take account of not only corporate tax, but to include the impact of personal taxation with regard to debt and equity, and also the levels of equity and debt that were available to investors (Miller MH (1977) 'Debt and taxes' *Journal of Finance*, 32, 261–75). Put very simply, Miller's model said that investors will

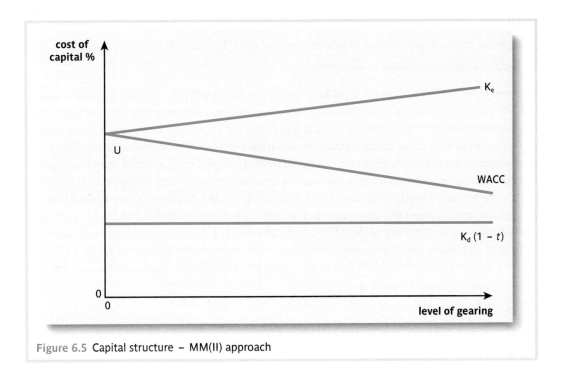

Figure 6.5 Capital structure – MM(II) approach

choose to invest in either the equity or debt of companies to suit their individual personal tax situations. Their choice will depend on their personal income tax and capital gains tax positions and the timings of such payments. Companies may prefer a higher level of gearing to take advantage of the tax shield relating to interest payments. This involves encouraging investors to move from equity investment to debt investment, which may result in a less favourable personal tax position. Investors may be induced to switch to debt from equity by companies offering a higher interest rate. Miller argued that the higher interest rate would be mitigated by the tax shield and the weighted average cost of capital would remain the same. The result is a horizontal WACC line, the same as in the MM(I) model shown in Fig. 6.4. Since Miller did not make any allowance for bankruptcy costs which may occur at very high levels of debt, then the WACC line remained horizontal at all levels of gearing. If bankruptcy costs were allowed for then the WACC line would curve upwards at the highest levels of gearing.

Pecking order theory

Baskin's research into gearing (Baskin J (1989) 'An empirical investigation of the pecking order theory' *Financial Management*, 18, 26–35) indicated that companies do not seek an optimal combination of debt and equity, but supported the alternative pecking order theories put forward by Donaldson in 1961 (Donaldson G (1961) 'Corporate debt capacity: a study of corporate debt policy and the determination of corporate debt capacity' Division of Research, Graduate School of Business Administration, Harvard University, Boston), and Myers in 1984 (Myers SC (1984) 'The capital structure Puzzle' *Journal of Finance*, 34, 575–92). Pecking order theory suggests that companies develop the following order of priorities relating to the alternative sources of financing:

1) internal sources of retained earnings generated by operating cash flow

2) external borrowing by way of bonds and bank loans if internal sources are exhausted

3) issue of new equity shares as a last resort.

Whereas Donaldson's reason for a pecking order was to do with the accessibility and costs of obtaining alternative sources of financing, Myer's reason for the existence of a pecking order was that directors and managers have much more internal knowledge about the financial status and future prospects of the company than the external capital markets. Such information asymmetry means that managers may have a more realistic view of the value of the business than the markets. Therefore, managers will only want to issue new shares if they believe that the market has overvalued the company. Managers will not want to issue new shares if they believe that the market has undervalued the company, and so will first consider retained earnings to finance a new project, and then choose debt finance if there are not sufficient earnings. A further disadvantage of a share issue by a company is that it may sometimes be seen as a signal that the shares are overvalued, which then results in a share price mark-down and therefore an increase in the company's cost of equity.

Is there an optimal capital structure?

We have seen that the MM(I), Miller, and pecking order theories suggest that an optimal capital structure does not exist for companies. However, the traditional approach to capital structure and MM(II) model suggest that it does exist. The WACC approach to capital structure considers the market imperfections of personal tax, corporation tax, and bankruptcy and agency costs, and may lead us to accept the existence of an optimal capital structure. There may be an agency problem because at high levels of gearing the shareholders have a lower stake in the business and they prefer high-risk projects, to provide a high return, and because they have less to lose. Debt-holders on the other hand are generally risk-averse.

The traditional approach to capital structure that we looked at earlier gave us the theoretical WACC line shown in Fig. 6.3 and reproduced in Fig. 6.6. In practice, companies may increase debt to sensible levels to enjoy the tax advantages and reduce WACC, so long as levels are not reached that cause investor concern about agency risk and possible bankruptcy. However, an optimal capital structure (O) obtained from a particular combination of debt and equity is unlikely. In reality, there is more likely to be a range of capital structures within which a company can minimise its WACC (between N and P on the WACC in practice line in the graph in Fig. 6.6) and so in practice the WACC graph is likely to be much flatter than the traditional graph.

While there appears to be no specific solution with regard to the 'best' capital structure it is possible to draw some broad conclusions from the various models and theories we have examined:

■ The capital structure decision is an important part of a company's financial strategy. Whether or not there is an optimal structure, an inappropriate structure may result in the destruction of shareholder wealth; for example, an untimely issue of shares.

■ As gearing continues to increase then generally a company's WACC will continue to fall because of the benefit from the relatively low cost of debt and the tax shield. Therefore shareholder value will be increased. However, at particularly high levels of gearing the market will react and equity shareholders will demand higher returns to compensate for the higher level of financial risk resulting from higher gearing. Therefore, the cost of equity will increase and WACC will increase and so shareholder value will fall.

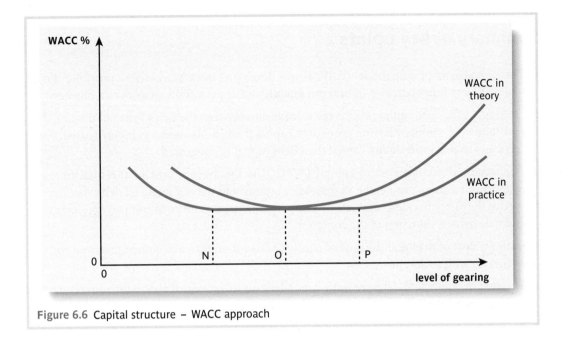

Figure 6.6 Capital structure – WACC approach

■ At very high levels of gearing the risk of bankruptcy is also very high. Financial risk is high because of the level of interest that has to be paid and the possibility of interest rates increasing. The power of debt-holders whose loans are secured on the assets of the company is such that they may force the company to cease trading, and sell its assets to repay the debt.

■ The tax benefits from borrowing are very real but this should not be the primary reason for borrowing. Tax benefits may be obtained in alternative ways, which therefore avoid the risk associated with high levels of gearing.

■ Many companies adopt the financial strategy of increasing debt to finance new investments to obtain tax benefits and reduce WACC, even though they may have cash surpluses. The decision to increase debt impacts on a company in a number of important ways, each of which should not be considered in isolation:

● financial risk – is future profitability sufficient to service and repay debt?

● dividends – can satisfactory levels of dividends be maintained at high levels of debt?

● WACC – at what point will an increase in gearing result in an increase in WACC?

● future interest rates – at what level will interest rates have a significant impact on profitability?

● banking relationships – it may be impractical and financially unfavourable to negotiate with and maintain relationships with a large number of banks.

Progress check 6.9

Outline the various approaches that have tried to answer the question 'Does a company have an optimal capital structure?'

Summary of key points

- The capital asset pricing model (CAPM) was developed from Markowitz's portfolio theory and considers systematic risk in order to establish a fair price for a security or a business.

- Gearing, or the debt/equity ratio, is the relationship between the two sources of finance, debt and equity – a company having more debt capital than equity capital is highly geared, and a company having more equity capital than debt capital is low geared.

- The weighted average cost of capital (WACC) is the average cost of the total financial resources of a company, i.e. the shareholders' equity and the net financial debt, that may be used as the discount rate to evaluate investment projects, a measure of company performance, and to provide a valuation of the company.

- Both the cost of debt and the cost of equity are based on future income flows, and the risk associated with such returns.

- The cost of equity and debt are both dependent on their level of risk, which therefore also impacts on the overall cost of a company's financing.

- A certain element of risk is unavoidable whenever any investment is made, and unless a market investor settles for risk-free securities, the actual return on investment in equity (or debt) capital may be better or worse than hoped for.

- Systematic risk may be measured using the capital asset pricing model (CAPM), and the β factor, in terms of its effect on required returns and share prices.

- The return on equity may be considered as a function of the gearing, or financial structure of the company.

- There are many approaches, for example the Miller and Modigliani approaches, which consider whether or not there may be an optimal capital structure for companies.

- Consideration of the WACC approach to capital structure suggests that perhaps a company's optimal capital structure may exist somewhere within a range of combinations of debt and equity.

🔒 Glossary of key terms

cost of debt The annual percentage rate of return required by long-term lenders to a company (loans and bonds), generally expressed net of tax as a cost to the company.

cost of equity The annual percentage rate of return required by the shareholders of a company.

dividend model A method of calculating the cost of equity that divides the current dividend by the current share price, which is based on the notion that shareholders value shares by the value of their expected dividends.

dividend growth model (or Gordon growth model) for calculating cost of equity assumes a direct link between the share price and expected future dividends and recognises the expected rate of dividend growth (G) achieved through reinvestment of retained earnings.

gearing Gearing calculations can be made in a number of ways. Financial gearing (or leverage) is generally seen as the relationship between a company's borrowings, which include both prior charge capital (capital having a right of interest or preference shares having fixed dividends) and long-term debt, and its ordinary shareholders' funds (share capital plus reserves).

security market line (SML) A linear graphical relationship between a security's return and its systematic risk, in an efficient market, measured by the company's beta, as defined in the capital asset pricing model (CAPM). It is effectively the capital market line (CML) adjusted for systematic risk.

tax shield A reduction in corporation tax payable due to the use of tax-allowable deductions against taxable income.

weighted average cost of capital (WACC) The average cost of the capital or financial resources of a company, which is its shareholders' equity plus its debt (debentures, bank loans, etc.) weighted according to the proportion each element bears to the total pool of capital. Weighting is usually based on market valuations, current yields and costs after tax.

Questions

Q6.1 Explain the capital asset pricing model (CAPM).

Q6.2 Describe the ways in which the costs of debt and equity capital may be ascertained.

Q6.3 How does risk impact on the cost of debt and equity?

Q6.4 What are the advantages and disadvantages for a company in using WACC as a discount factor to evaluate capital projects?

Q6.5 What is the beta β factor, and how may it be related to WACC?

Q6.6 What are the implications for a company of different levels of gearing?

Q6.7 How may a company's return on equity (ROE) be related to its financial structure?

Q6.8 Is there an optimal capital structure?

Q6.9 Explain the Miller and Modigliani I and II approaches to capital structure.

Q6.10 What is the WACC approach to capital structure?

Discussion points

D6.1 'In the real world the CAPM does not appear to be valid, therefore it is not a useful tool for dealing with required returns and systematic risk.' Discuss.

D6.2 The marketing manager of a large UK subsidiary of a multinational plc said 'Surely the interest rate that we should use to discount cash flows in our appraisal of new capital investment projects should be our bank overdraft interest rate. I don't really see the relevance of the weighted average cost of capital (WACC) to this type of exercise.' Discuss.

D6.3 In the long run does it really matter whether a company is financed predominantly by ordinary shares or predominantly by loans? What's the difference?

Exercises

Solutions are provided in Appendix 2 to all exercise numbers highlighted in colour.

Level I

E6.1 *Time allowed – 30 minutes*

A critically important factor required by a company to make financial decisions, for example the evaluation of investment proposals and the financing of new projects, is its cost of capital. One of the elements included in the calculation of a company's cost of capital is the cost of equity.

(i) Explain in simple terms what is meant by the cost of equity capital for a company.

The relevant data for Normal plc and the market in general is given below.

Normal plc	
Current price per share on the London Stock Exchange	£1.20
Current annual dividend per share	£0.10
Expected average annual growth rate of dividends	7%
β coefficient for Normal plc's shares	0.5
The market	
Expected rate of return on risk-free securities	8%
Expected return on the market portfolio	12%

(ii) Calculate the cost of equity capital for Normal plc, using two alternative methods:

    (a) the capital asset pricing model (CAPM)
    (b) a dividend growth model of your choice.

E6.2 *Time allowed – 30 minutes*

Normal plc pays £20,000 a year interest on an irredeemable debenture, which has a nominal value of £200,000 and a market value of £160,000. The rate of corporation tax is 30%.

You are required to:

(i) calculate the cost of the debt for Normal plc
(ii) calculate the weighted average cost of capital for Normal plc using the cost of equity calculated in Exercise E6.1 (ii) if Normal plc has share capital of £300,000
(iii) comment on the impact on a company's cost of capital of changes in the rate of corporation tax
(iv) calculate Normal plc's WACC if the rate of corporation tax were increased to 50%.

Level II

E6.3 *Time allowed – 45 minutes*

Adam plc is a publicly listed fashion retail company. The current market price of the company's shares is £25 (ex dividend), per share. The current dividend yield of the company's shares is 5%, and the current price/earnings ratio of the company's shares is 10.

Based on recently released information about the company and its future growth prospects, market dealers expect Adam plc to achieve a constant dividend growth rate of 3% per annum for the foreseeable future. We may assume that:

- the average return on the stock market is 10%
- the risk free rate of return is 4%
- the beta coefficient of Adam plc's shares is currently 1.25.

Required:

(i) Calculate the proportion of earnings paid out as dividends by the company.

(ii) Using the dividend growth model calculate the expected rate of return on the shares of Adam plc.

(iii) Using your results from requirement (ii) above, calculate by how much the share appears to be over- or under-valued according to the Capital Asset Pricing Model (CAPM).

(iv) Briefly explain why a difference between the dividend growth model share price and the share price calculated using CAPM may exist.

(v) Evaluate the principal assumptions of the CAPM, and the limitations of such assumptions in using the CAPM to value equities.

E6.4 *Time allowed – 30 minutes*

Lucky Jim plc has the opportunity to manufacture a particular type of self-tapping screw, for a client company, that would become indispensable in a particular niche market in the engineering field.

Development of the product requires an initial investment of £200,000 in the project. It has been estimated that the project will yield cash returns before interest of £35,000 per annum in perpetuity.

Lucky Jim plc is financed by equity and loans, which are always maintained as two thirds and one third of the total capital respectively. The cost of equity is 18% and the pre-tax cost of debt is 12%. The corporation tax rate is 40%.

If Lucky Jim plc's WACC is used as the cost of capital to appraise the project, should the project be undertaken?

E6.5 *Time allowed – 30 minutes*

Abey plc has a WACC of 16%. It is financed partly by equity (cost 18% per annum) and partly by debt capital (cost 10% per annum). The company is considering a new project which would cost £5,000,000 and would yield annual profits of £850,000 before interest charges.

It would be financed by a loan at 10%. As a consequence the cost of equity would rise to 20%. The company pays out all its profits in dividends, which are currently £2,250,000 a year. You may assume that Abey plc has a traditional view of WACC and gearing.

Required:

(i) Calculate the effect on the value of equity of undertaking the project.

(ii) Consider the extent to which the increase or decrease in equity value may be analysed into two causes:
  (a) the NPV of the project at the current WACC
  (b) the effect of the method of financing.

▶ E6.6 *Time allowed – 45 minutes*

The following financial information has been taken from the financial statements of Homeslore plc, a large national electrical equipment retailer.

All figures in £000s

Summary of profits and dividends for the year ended 31 December 2007

	2001	2002	2003	2004	2005	2006	2007
Profit before tax	1,600	1,800	1,800	2,000	1,900	1,800	2,300
Corporation tax	(550)	(600)	(600)	(750)	(550)	(620)	(980)
Profit after tax	1,050	1,200	1,200	1,250	1,350	1,180	1,320
Dividends	(570)	(600)	(600)	(700)	(800)	(850)	(900)
Transfer to reserves	480	600	600	550	550	330	420

Balance sheet as at 31 December 2007

Non-current assets		10,200
Investments		3,500
Current assets	4,500	
Current liabilities	(2,000)	
		2,500
		16,200
5% debentures	4,000	
Corporation tax	1,000	
		(5,000)
Net assets		11,200
Capital and reserves		
Share capital £1 ordinary shares issued		4,500
Reserves		6,700
Shareholders' funds		11,200

On 31 December 2007 the market value of Homeslore plc's ordinary shares was £4.60 per share cum dividend. Shortly after that date an annual dividend of £900,000 was due to be paid. The debentures are redeemable at par in five years' time. Their current market value at 31 December 2007 is £90. Annual interest has just been paid on the debentures. The company's capital structure has remained unchanged for the past seven years and there have been no issues or redemption of ordinary share capital or debentures during that period.

You may assume the rate of corporation tax is 30% and that no changes have been made to the system of taxation or the rates of tax during the past seven years.

Required:

(i) Calculate Homeslore plc's cost of equity.

(ii) Calculate Homeslore plc's cost of debt.

(iii) Calculate (to the nearest whole percentage) the weighted average cost of capital that Homeslore plc may use as a discount rate when appraising new investment opportunities.

E6.7 *Time allowed – 45 minutes*

An opportunity has arisen for Homeslore plc (see Exercise E6.6) to acquire a stock of specialised materials from an overseas supplier. The cost of the specialised stocks will be £700,000.

The sales manager of Homeslore plc has suggested that the net proceeds from the sale of these stocks will be influenced by a number of factors originating from outside the company, and has provided the following additional information:

	Possible net sales proceeds £	Probability %
Year 1	440,000	50
	200,000	40
	460,000	10
Year 2	600,000	60
	580,000	20
	350,000	20

The estimates for year 2 are independent of the estimates of year 1.

Required:

(i) Use the company's weighted average cost of capital (calculated in Exercise E6.6) to calculate the expected net sales proceeds each year, and the net present value of the project.

(ii) Briefly comment on the validity of the company using its weighted average cost of capital as a discount rate for the evaluation of investment opportunities.

E6.8 *Time allowed – 60 minutes*

Yor plc is a fast growing, hi-tech business. Its income statement for the year ended 30 September 2007 and its balance sheet as at 30 September 2007 are shown below. The company has the opportunity to take on a major project that will significantly improve its profitability in the forthcoming year and for the foreseeable future. The cost of the project is £10m, which will result in large increases in sales, which will increase profit before interest and tax by £4m per annum. The directors of Yor plc have two alternative options of financing the project: The issue of £10m of 4% debentures at par, or a rights issue of 4m ordinary shares at a premium of £1.50 per share (after expenses).

Regardless of how the new project is financed, the directors will recommend a 10% increase in the dividend for 2007/2008. You may assume that the effective corporation tax rate is the same for 2007/2008 as for 2006/2007.

Income statement for the year ended 30 September 2007
Figures in £m

PBIT	11.6
Interest payable	(1.2)
Profit before tax	10.4
Tax on profit on ordinary activities	(2.6)
Profit on ordinary activities after tax	7.8
Retained profit 1 October 2006	5.8
	13.6
Dividends	(3.0)
Retained profit 30 September 2007	10.6

▶

▶

Balance sheet as at 30 September 2007
Figures in £m

Non-current assets	
Tangible	28.8
Current assets	
Stocks	11.2
Debtors	13.8
Cash and bank	0.7
	25.7
Current liabilities (less than one year)	
Creditors	9.7
Dividends	1.6
Taxation	2.6
	13.9
Net current assets	11.8
Total assets less current liabilities	40.6
less	
Long-term liabilities (over one year)	
6% loan	20.0
Net assets	20.6
Capital and reserves	
Share capital (£1 ordinary shares)	10.0
Profit and loss account	10.6
	20.6

The directors of Yor plc would like to see your estimated income statement for 2007/2008, and a summary of share capital and reserves at 30 September 2008, assuming:

(i)   the new project is financed by an issue of the debentures
(ii) the new project is financed by the issue of new ordinary shares.

To assist in clarification of the figures, you should show your calculations of:

(iii) eps for 2006/2007
(iv) eps for 2007/2008, reflecting both methods of financing the new project
(v)   dividend per share for 2006/2007
(vi) dividend per share for 2007/2008, reflecting both methods of financing the new project.

Use the information you have provided in (i) and (ii) above to:

(vii) calculate Yor plc's gearing, reflecting both methods of financing the new project, and compare with its gearing at 30 September 2007
(viii) summarise the results for 2007/2008, recommend which method of financing Yor plc should adopt, and explain the implications of both on its financial structure.

E6.9   *Time allowed – 60 minutes*

Sparks plc is a large electronics company that produces components for MP3s and iPods. It is close to the current year end and Sparks is forecasting profits after tax at £60m. The following two years' post-tax profits are each expected to increase by another £15m, and years 4 and 5 by another £10m each.

The forecast balance sheet for Sparks plc as at 31 December is as follows:

	£m
Non-current assets	500
Current assets	
Stocks	120
Debtors	160
	280
Creditors due within one year	
Trade creditors	75
Overdraft	75
	150
Net current assets	130
Long-term loans	150
	480
Capital and reserves	
Share capital (£1 ordinary shares)	220
Share premium	10
Profit and loss account	250
	480

Sparks plc has a large overdraft of £75m on which it pays a high rate of interest at 15%. The board would like to pay off the overdraft and obtain cheaper financing. Sparks also has loan capital of £150m on which it pays interest at 9% per annum. Despite its high level of debt Sparks is a profitable organisation. However, the board is currently planning a number of new projects for the next year, which will cost £75m. These projects are expected to produce profits after tax of £8m in the first year and £15m a year ongoing for future years.

The board has discussed a number of financing options and settled on two of them for further consideration:

(1) a 1 for 4 rights issue at £3.00 a share to raise £150m from the issue of 50m £1 shares;
(2) a convertible £150m debenture issue at 12% (pre tax) that may be converted into 45m ordinary shares in two years' time.

The equity share index has risen over the past year from 4,600 to the current 5,500, having reached 6,250. Sparks plc's ordinary shares are currently at a market price of £3.37. Gearing of companies in the same industry as Sparks plc ranges between 25% and 45%. In two years' time it is expected that all Sparks debenture holders will convert to shares or none will convert.

The rate of corporation tax is 50%. Repayment of the overdraft will save interest of £5.625m a year after tax.

The board requires some analysis of the numbers to compare against the current position:

(i)   if they make the rights issue
(ii) if they issue debentures
(iii) if the debentures are converted.

The analysis should show:

(a) the impact on the balance sheet
(b) the impact on the profit after tax
(c) earnings per share
(d) gearing
(e) which option should be recommended to the board and why.

Sources of finance and the capital markets

LEARNING OBJECTIVES

Completion of this chapter will enable you to:

☑ Identify the different sources of external sources of finance available to an organisation and the internal sources, such as retained earnings, trade credit, and gains from more effective management of working capital.

☑ Compare the company's use of external short-term finance with long-term finance.

☑ Describe the unique characteristics and rights of equity (ordinary share) finance and debt (loan) finance.

☑ Outline the importance of dividends, rights issues, scrip (bonus) issues, share splits, scrip dividends, and share buy-backs to companies and investors.

☑ Explain the use of preference shares as a source of long-term share capital.

☑ Appreciate the range of debt finance available to companies, for example, loans, debentures, and bonds.

☑ Evaluate the difference between a redeemable debenture and an irredeemable debenture.

☑ Outline the growing importance of international debt finance and the use of Eurobonds.

☑ Explain what is meant by hybrid finance, which includes convertible preference shares, convertible bonds, warrants, and mezzanine debt.

☑ Consider how companies may use leasing as a source of long- and short-term finance.

☑ Outline the way in which UK companies may benefit from Government and European sources of finance.

☑ Explain what is meant by the primary and secondary capital markets, and their importance to companies and investors.

☑ Outline the various ways in which a company may issue new equity finance, and their advantages and disadvantages.

☑ Describe the role of the Stock Exchange and the Alternative Investment Market (AIM).

☑ Outline the roles of financial institutions, such as banks, merchant banks, pension funds, and insurance companies.

☑ Recognise the increasing growth of Islamic banking and Islamic finance in the UK and worldwide, as an alternative to traditional Western-style banking.

Introduction

This chapter begins with an outline of the types of finance available to businesses. Organisations require finance for both short and medium to long-term requirements and the types of financing should usually be matched with the funding requirement. Longer-term finance (longer than one year) is usually used to fund capital investment in non-current assets and other longer-term projects. Short-term finance (shorter than one year) is usually used to fund an organisation's requirement for working capital.

Financing may be internal or external to the organisation, and either short or long term. One of the sources of internal financing is derived from the more effective management of working capital, which is discussed in Chapter 10.

In Chapter 4 we dealt with decisions related to capital investment appraisal – the investment decision. This chapter will consider a number of alternative ways in which company investment

▶

▶ may be financed – the financing decision – and includes leasing and Government grants, but will focus on the main sources of long-term external finance available to an organisation: loans (or debt) and ordinary shares (or equity). We will also consider the various ways in which the different types of finance are raised. One of the fundamental differences between equity and debt financing is the risk associated with each, which has an impact on their cost, the determination of which we looked at in Chapter 6.

There are a number of sources of finance that are neither purely equity nor purely debt, but have characteristics that put them somewhere between the two. These are referred to as hybrid finance, which include, for example, convertible loans.

This chapter looks at the markets in which long-term financial securities are traded, and which are called the capital markets. Primary capital markets are the markets in which investors, both private individuals and financial institutions, provide funds for companies, which require new long-term finance by way of equity or debt. The secondary capital markets are the markets in which investors may sell and buy their securities, which are also a source of financial information for current and potential investors and for pricing information with regard to the primary markets. The main secondary markets are stock exchanges, the most important in the UK being the London Stock Exchange.

The chapter closes with a look at the range of financial institutions used by organisations and the roles they fulfil in corporate financing, and provides an introduction to the growing area of Islamic banking and Islamic finance.

Sources of finance internal to the business

The sources of finance available to a company may be regarded very broadly as being provided from within the company or provided from sources external to the company. These two sources are called internal finance and external finance.

Internal finance may be provided from retained earnings (or retained profit), extended trade credit, and cash improvements gained from the more effective management of working capital (see Fig. 7.1).

Retained earnings

Retained profit (retained earnings) is reported in a company's income statement as the residual profit for the year that remains after all costs, net interest charges, and corporation tax charges have been deducted, and ordinary share dividends payable and minority interests have been accounted for. This is the amount of profit that is then added to the equity of the company in the balance sheet under the heading retained profit. The accumulated retained profits of the company are increased by the net profit for the year less any dividends payable; they are part of the shareholders' funds and therefore appear on the balance sheet within the equity of the company. Similarly, losses will reduce the equity of the company.

The profit earned in a year is not the same as the cash flow for the year, because profit includes non-cash items like depreciation. It is also because the transactions from which profit is derived are generally not all realised in cash when they occur. These are the differences relating to changes in the working capital requirement of stocks (inventory), debtors (accounts receivable), and creditors (accounts payable). In addition, profit does not include items like purchases of non-current assets or funds received from loans or new share issues.

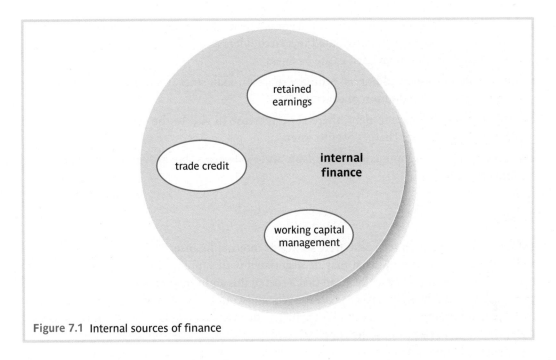

Figure 7.1 Internal sources of finance

Cash flow is represented by the movements in and out of cash (notes and coins), bank accounts, and bank deposits, the balances of which are shown as assets in the balance sheet. If cash is borrowed either by bank overdraft or bank loans then these are shown as liabilities in the balance sheet.

The retained earnings, or retained profit, shown in a company's balance sheet as a part of shareholders' equity is not totally represented by the cash and bank balances (less any loans and overdrafts) also shown in the balance sheet as assets (and liabilities). Retained profit includes the value of sales made and is surplus to deductions for:

- the operational costs of running the business
- net interest payable
- corporation tax payable
- dividends payable

but all sales may not yet have been received in cash and all operational costs, interest, tax, and dividends may not yet have been paid out of cash. In addition, retained profit does not include:

- cash paid to add to or replace non-current assets
- cash received from loans or equity capital

which are both items that are not related to the operational activities of the business.

It is the operational cash flow (minus interest, tax, and dividends actually paid out) that is the real internal source of finance rather than retained earnings. Companies may have high levels of retained profits and earnings per share, but little or no cash or borrowings. It is cash not profit that is required for investment.

There is statistical evidence which shows that through the 1990s the majority of capital funding of UK companies continued to be derived from internal sources of finance. 'Retained earnings' is the primary source of internal finance, and there are a number of reasons for this:

- it is the shareholders who approve at the annual general meeting (AGM) how much of the company's earnings will be distributed to shareholders as dividends, the balance being held as retained profit and reinvested in the business

- unlike with an issue of additional ordinary shares or loan stock, there are no administrative or legal costs, and no dilution of control

- unlike with an increase in debt, there is no increase in risk to the company arising from security required from charges over its assets

- retained earnings are immediately available and easily accessible provided the company has sufficient cash.

Trade credit

Trade creditors are often seen as a 'free' source of internal finance. This really is not the case, and extended payment terms that may be negotiated with suppliers inevitably include a cost. Extended credit terms will usually mean that a cost of this additional financing will already have been factored into the selling price charged. When discounts are offered by suppliers for early settlement, for example 1% discount for payment one month early (12% per annum), it immediately becomes apparent that the supplier's selling price must have included some allowance for financial charges. Therefore accounts payable are a source of finance but it is not free.

Large companies may employ the unethical policy of delaying payment to their suppliers, particularly small businesses or 'unimportant' suppliers, to enhance cash flow. While paying slower may occasionally be required to alleviate a short-term cash problem it really should be considered only as a last resort and regarded as a temporary measure. It is not only unethical, but it is not conducive to the development of good supplier relationships.

Working capital management

The more effective management of the company's operating cycle or working capital requirement as an additional source of internal finance is discussed in Chapter 10.

The choice between the use of external and internal finance by companies, for growth, new investment projects, and expansion of their operations, involves major policy decisions. The use of retained earnings as a means of internal financing, while immediately accessible, is not free. The cost of shareholders' equity is a reflection of the level of dividends paid to shareholders, which is usually dependent on how well the company has performed during the year. The profit or net earnings generated from the operations of the company belongs to the shareholders of the company. There is a cost, an opportunity cost, which is the best alternative return that shareholders could obtain on these funds elsewhere in the financial markets. The amount of earnings retained is dependent on a company's dividend and profit retention policy. A company which maintains a low level of dividend cover (earnings per share divided by dividend per share) is likely to require a lower proportion of external funding than a company with a high dividend cover.

In general, companies may have sufficient cash flow from their normal operations to be able to use retained earnings for small investments or, for example, for replacement of furniture and equipment. If companies do not have sufficient cash flow from operations, or if they are considering large new investment projects, then it is more likely that they will require a larger proportion of external finance in the form of debt or equity.

Regardless of whether external finance is in the form of debt or equity, issue costs will inevitably be incurred. While dividends do not have to be paid by the company, interest payment is a commitment for the company and this increases the level of financial risk faced by the company.

Progress check 7.1

What are the differences between the three main sources of internal finance available to a company?

Short-term external sources of finance

The decision by companies on the use of either short-term or long-term funding should really be made with regard to the uses for which the funding is required. The risk and return profiles of the uses of the funding should be matched with risk and return profiles of the funding. The financing of the acquisition of long-term assets, or non-current assets, should be provided from long-term funding. The financing of the acquisition of short-term assets, or net current assets or working capital requirements, should normally be provided from short-term funding. At a personal level, for example, it would not make economic sense to finance the purchase of one's house with short-term finance such as a bank overdraft, which is repayable on demand. House purchase is normally funded with a long-term mortgage.

The level of working capital requirement, or net current assets, comprises stocks (or inventory), debtors (accounts receivable), less creditors (accounts payable), which are all constantly changing. The funding of an investment in working capital therefore needs to be flexible in line with its changing levels. Short-term financial debt includes the elements of overdrafts, loans, and leases that are repayable within one year of the balance sheet date. Short-term finance tends to be more expensive, but more flexible than long-term debt and usually does not require any security. Short-term debt is therefore normally matched to finance the fluctuations in levels of the company's net current assets, its working capital.

Short-term finance generally incurs a higher interest rate than long-term finance, and it represents a higher risk for the borrower. Interest rates can be volatile, and an overdraft, for example, is technically repayable on demand. The company may finance its operations by taking on further short-term debt, as levels of working capital increase. Because of the higher risk associated with short-term debt, many companies adopting a conservative funding policy may accept a reduction in profitability and use long-term debt to finance not only non-current assets, but also a proportion of the company's working capital. Less risk-averse companies may use short-term debt to finance both working capital and non-current assets; such debt may be attractive because there is no commitment to pay a fixed level of interest over an extended period.

The main sources of external short-term finance are overdrafts, short-term loans, and leasing (see Fig. 7.2).

Overdrafts

A bank overdraft is borrowing from a bank on a current account, which is repayable on demand. The maximum overdraft allowed is normally negotiated and agreed with the bank

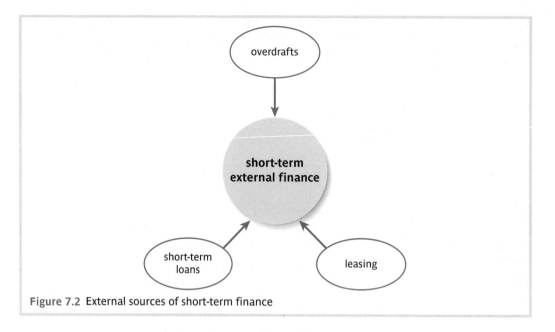

Figure 7.2 External sources of short-term finance

prior to the facility being made available. Interest, which is calculated on a daily basis, is charged on the amount borrowed, and not on the agreed maximum borrowing facility. In addition to overdraft interest, banks normally charge an initial fee for setting up an overdraft facility and an annual fee for its re-negotiation and administration.

Most businesses are regularly financed to some extent by overdrafts. They are flexible but are risky in terms of their being immediately repayable on demand by the bank. This may represent a problem to companies who are using overdrafts to finance other than working capital requirements, but who may be unable to easily obtain longer-term financing.

Short-term loans and leasing

Companies may occasionally obtain loans from banks or others, which are repayable within one year, in which case they are called short-term loans. However, loans and financial leases are generally sources of long-term finance (see the section on long-term external sources of finance below). The reason for including these topics in this section on short-term finance is to explain their appearance in the current liabilities section of company balance sheets.

In the *liabilities* part of a company's balance, within the section *current, or short-term, liabilities*, the heading *short-term financial debt* includes the elements of overdrafts, loans and leases that are payable within one year of the balance sheet date. An overdraft is technically repayable within one year of the balance sheet date and so only appears within *short-term financial debt*. Also within the *liabilities* part of a company's balance, within the section *long-term liabilities*, there is a heading *long-term financial debt*. Long-term financial debts are the elements of loans and leases that are expected to be payable after one year of the balance sheet date.

Progress check 7.2

Why do companies have overdrafts?

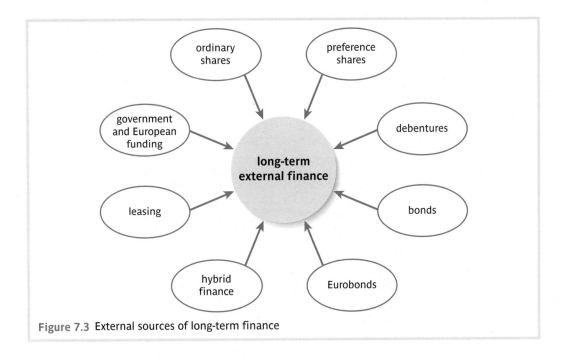

Figure 7.3 External sources of long-term finance

Long-term external sources of finance

As we discussed above, in matching the risk and return profiles of funding with the risk and return profiles of the uses of that funding, long-term funding should be used for the acquisition of long-term non-current assets. Long-term non-current assets include land, buildings, machinery, and equipment. External sources of long-term finance (see Fig. 7.3) include:

- **ordinary shares** (or equity shares)
- **preference shares**
- loan capital (financial debt that includes bank loans, **debentures**, and other loans)
- **bonds**
- **Eurobonds**
- **hybrid finance** (**convertible bonds**, **warrants**, and **mezzanine debt**)
- leasing
- UK Government funding
- European funding.

The two main primary sources of long-term finance available to a company, which are both external, are broadly:

- equity share capital (ordinary shares)
- debt (long-term loans and debentures).

Both types of financing have a unique set of characteristics and rights. The main ones are shown in the table in Fig. 7.4.

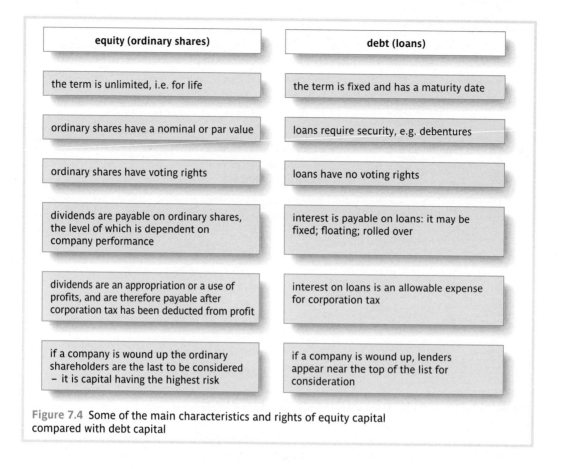

equity (ordinary shares)	debt (loans)
the term is unlimited, i.e. for life	the term is fixed and has a maturity date
ordinary shares have a nominal or par value	loans require security, e.g. debentures
ordinary shares have voting rights	loans have no voting rights
dividends are payable on ordinary shares, the level of which is dependent on company performance	interest is payable on loans: it may be fixed; floating; rolled over
dividends are an appropriation or a use of profits, and are therefore payable after corporation tax has been deducted from profit	interest on loans is an allowable expense for corporation tax
if a company is wound up the ordinary shareholders are the last to be considered – it is capital having the highest risk	if a company is wound up, lenders appear near the top of the list for consideration

Figure 7.4 Some of the main characteristics and rights of equity capital compared with debt capital

The choice by a company of which of the various types of long-term sources of external finance to use depends on a number factors, which include, for example:

- the type of company (plc or Ltd)
- the company's financial status
- the company's ability to provide security
- the cost of the individual source of finance
- the company's existing capital structure (which we discussed in Chapter 6).

Each of the factors influencing a company's choice of financing is likely to depend on the stage it has reached in its development. For example, a start-up company is unlikely to be making profits or generating high levels of operating cash flow. The original investors in a start-up company are usually unlikely to be able to provide all the cash required in the early years to cover start-up costs, research and development, investment, and operational requirements. Therefore, outside investors are usually sought. These may perhaps be venture capitalists who provide developing companies with either equity or debt capital for a relatively short period after which time they withdraw having usually received a very high return on their capital.

Growth companies, which have emerged from the start-up phase and established themselves in their particular markets, are likely to be making modest profits and have sufficient cash flows for operational requirements. However, they are still likely to have additional cash requirements for investment in future growth. This may be acquired from debt or equity, or a combination of the two, or from leasing, for example. The choice will depend on the company's individual circumstances, its growth prospects, and how it is perceived by potential investors.

Mature companies will be well established in their particular markets. They are likely to be making significant profits and cash flows, but with limited growth prospects. Shareholders in mature companies will expect high levels of dividends because there may be no scope for share price growth. Since the level of new, 'real', risky investment by a mature company may be low, it is unlikely to require additional equity financing. On the other hand, it may seek debt financing in order to reduce its WACC in order to increase shareholder value and deter hostile takeover bids by making the business too expensive.

The choice of financing will be considered in more detail in Chapters 13 and 14, when we will look at the financial strategies that may be adopted during each of the above stages in a company's life cycle, and in Chapters 16 and 17, which deal with mergers and acquisitions. The role of venture capitalists is considered in more detail in Chapter 13, and in Chapter 18 when we look at management buy-outs (MBOs).

Ordinary, or equity shares

The equity of a company includes its share capital and accumulated profits retained (or losses incurred) to date and since the business commenced trading. Share capital comprises ordinary shares and preference shares (see below). Ordinary shares entitle the shareholders to the remaining profits after all other prior charges, including interest on loans, corporate taxation, and for example preference share dividends, have been met. When a business is formed the maximum number of shares that the company is ever likely to need is determined at the outset in its memorandum of association and this level is called its authorised share capital. The number of shares actually in issue at any point in time is normally at a level for the company to meet its foreseeable requirements. These shares are called the company's issued share capital which, when all the shareholders have paid for them, are referred to as fully paid up issued share capital. Ordinary shares represent the long-term capital provided by the owners of a company.

Ordinary shares have a nominal value (or par value) of, for example, 25p or £1 or US$1 or 10 Riyals. The nominal value of the shares is decided when the level of authorised shares is decided. The shares cannot then be issued to shareholders for less than their nominal value. When shares are issued to shareholders they are usually issued at a premium. For example, 10,000 £1 shares may be issued for a total value of funds raised of £25,000. This means that share capital is raised amounting to £10,000 (nominal value) in addition to a share premium of £15,000. Both amounts are shown within the equity section of the company's balance sheet but under two separate headings: the ordinary shares account, and the share premium account.

After shares have been issued they may be bought and sold by investors between each other in the case of a private (Ltd) company, or via a stock exchange in the case of a public (plc) company. The subsequent sale and purchase of ordinary shares after the initial issue of shares provides no further funds for the company and has no impact on its balance sheet. The level of activity in the selling and buying of shares is a factor of their demand and depends on the view taken by investors of their future returns by way of an increase in share price and future dividend flows.

Ordinary shareholders receive a dividend at a level determined usually by company performance and not as a specific entitlement. The level of dividends is usually based on the underlying profitability of the company (Tesco plc actually advised their shareholders of this relationship in the late 1990s). In addition, ordinary shareholders normally have voting rights (whereas debt-holders and preference shareholders do not).

Ordinary shareholders have voting rights attached to their shares, which allows them to vote at the AGM. There is an additional class of shares called non-voting shares, which have no voting rights.

When a company goes into liquidation an administrator is appointed who draws up a list of creditors to which the company owes money including the Government, suppliers, employees, debt-holders, and ordinary shareholders. The ordinary shareholders are always last on the list to be repaid. Ordinary shareholders are paid out of the balance of funds that remains after all other creditors have been repaid. As ordinary shares therefore represent capital of the highest risk to investors, then ordinary shareholders expect the highest returns compared with the returns from other investments.

Additional equity capital may be raised through issuing additional shares up to the level of authorised share capital. A company may increase its number of shares through making scrip issues and rights issues. A scrip issue (or bonus issue) increases the number of shares with the additional shares going to existing shareholders, in proportion to their holdings, through capitalisation of the reserves, or retained profits, of the company. No cash is called for from the shareholders. In a rights issue, the right to subscribe for new shares (or debentures) issued by the company is given to existing shareholders.

Dividends

The return expected by investors in the highest risk securities, ordinary shares, comprises capital appreciation in the form of share price increases and income in the form of dividends. The dividend decision, or earnings retention decision, is strategically very important to a company with regard to five key areas:

- the views and expectations of shareholders
- the level of profits being made by the company
- the use of retained earnings for financing new investment
- the level of the company's cash resources
- the way in which surplus funds should be used should suitable investment opportunities be unavailable.

After a company has paid all its expenses, costs, interest, and corporate taxes, what is left is the net profit that effectively belongs to the shareholders. With regard to the five points above, a level of dividends may be proposed by the directors and declared for cash payment by the company in the UK usually every six months (USA every three months), with reference to its level of profitability. The interim dividend is paid halfway through the company's financial year, and the final dividend is paid after the end of the financial year. It is paid after the year-end because the shareholders need to approve the final dividend at the company's annual general meeting (AGM).

In general a company must be making profits in order to declare a dividend and it must have the cash available in order to pay a dividend. Profits include those for the current year and past profits so that according to the Companies Act 1985 dividends may be paid out of accumulated net realised profits. A dividend is not an expense but an appropriation of profit and as such is not an allowable deduction for corporation tax. Income tax is normally paid by shareholders on dividends received.

The level of a company's financial gearing, its proportion of debt compared with equity capital, has an effect on the level of dividends it may pay. If it is highly geared then it has a comparatively high proportion of debt and therefore a commitment to paying high levels of interest. A high level of interest payments means a lower level of profit and cash with which to pay dividends. The company's decision to pay dividends is also affected by its requirement for the funding of new capital investment projects. The cost of using its retained earnings may be cheaper for the company and so that cost should be compared with that of external sources of finance (see the sections in Chapter 6 about cost of capital). Before considering the use of retained earnings for new investment by paying a lower level of dividends to shareholders the company must also consider the effect that this may have on shareholders and the share price.

The declaration of a dividend has an impact on a company's share price. The share price may change immediately a dividend is announced and is called a cum dividend share price. The share price remains cum dividend during a period when whoever holds the shares will receive the dividend. At a given date the entitlement to the dividend ceases and the share price becomes ex dividend. Everything being equal, the difference between the cum dividend share price and ex dividend share price will be the amount of dividend per share.

We will further consider the effect of dividends on share prices in more detail in Chapter 15 when we look at the theories of dividend relevance and irrelevance.

Rights issues

Companies have a legal obligation to first offer any new shares that they decide to issue to their existing shareholders. The term rights issues is used to describe such issues of new shares, which are normally for multiples of the shares held, for example two new shares for every one share held.

The 'rights' to buy the new shares are usually fixed at a price discounted by around 10% to 20% below the current market price. A shareholder not wishing to take up a rights issue may sell the rights. Discounts are offered in order to attract existing shareholders. The announcement of the offer of a rights issue by a company may immediately change the share price of the company, which is then called the cum rights share price. The cum rights share price will initially increase to reflect the right to apply for new shares at a price less than the market price. The share price remains cum rights for the period up to when the rights issue offer closes, during which time whoever holds the shares will have the right to receive or sell their rights. At the offer close date the entitlement to the rights ceases and the share price becomes ex rights. Everything being equal, the ex rights share price will then drop.

The amount of discount on the current share price that is offered to existing shareholders is chosen by the company at a level that makes the rights issue attractive to investors. However, the resultant rights issue share price will have an impact on the earnings per share of the company (see Worked Example 7.1).

Worked Example 7.1

A company that achieves a profit after tax of 10% on capital employed has the following capital structure:

2,000,000 ordinary shares of £1	£2,000,000
Retained earnings	£500,000

▶ In order to invest in some new profitable projects the company wishes to raise £780,000 from a rights issue. The company's current ordinary share price is £1.50.

The company would like to know the number of shares that must be issued if the rights price is: £1.30; £1.25; £1.20.

Capital employed is £2.5m [£2m + £0.5m]

Current earnings are 10% of £2.5m = £250,000

$$\text{Therefore, earnings per share (eps)} = \frac{£250,000}{2,000,000} = 12.50p$$

After the rights issue, earnings will be:

10% of £3.28m [£2m + £0.5m + £0.78m] = £328,000

Rights price £	Number of new shares £780,000 divided by the rights price	Total shares after rights issue new plus old shares	eps £328,000 divided by total shares pence
1.30	600,000	2,600,000	12.62
1.25	624,000	2,624,000	12.50
1.20	650,000	2,650,000	12.38

We can see that at a high rights issue share price the eps are increased. At lower issue prices eps are diluted. The 'break-even point', with no dilution, is where the rights share price equals the current capital employed per share £2.5m/2m = £1.25.

A rights issue may also have an impact on shareholder wealth. If existing shareholders fully take up their rights entitlement and either hold the shares or sell them, in any proportion, their wealth position will be unaffected (see Worked Example 7.2). If existing shareholders do not exercise their rights the number of shares they hold will be unchanged but their wealth will have reduced because the ex rights share price is likely to be lower than the cum rights share price.

Worked Example 7.2

A company has 1,000,000 £1 ordinary shares in issue with a market price of £2.10 on 1 June. The company wished to raise new equity capital by a one for four share rights issue at a price of £1.50. Immediately the company announced the rights issue the price fell to £1.95 on 2 June. Just before the issue was due to be made the share price had recovered to £2 per share, the cum rights price.

The company may calculate the theoretical ex-rights price, the new market price as a consequence of an adjustment to allow for the discount price of the new issue.

The market price will theoretically fall after the issue

1,000,000 shares × the cum rights price of £2	£2,000,000
250,000 shares × the issue price of £1.50	375,000
Theoretical value of 1,250,000 shares	£2,375,000

Therefore, the theoretical ex-rights price is

$$\frac{£2,375,000}{1,250,000} = £1.90 \text{ per share}$$

Or to put it another way

Four shares at the cum rights value of £2	£8.00
One new share issued at £1.50	£1.50
	£9.50

Therefore, the theoretical ex-rights price is

$$\frac{£9.50}{5} = £1.90 \text{ per share}$$

Generally the costs of a rights issue are lower than any other method of issuing shares to the public. If all the rights are taken up by the existing shareholders then there is no dilution of their current shareholdings. However, if they do not take up all their rights then their holdings will be diluted. Existing shareholders may not have sufficient funds to take up all their rights if the issue is very large. For this reason, rights issues may be the most appropriate method for relatively small share issues.

Scrip, or bonus issues

We have discussed the way in which retained earnings may be used as a source of funding by a company. Retained earnings may also be converted into share capital and issued at little cost to existing shareholders on a *pro rata* basis. Such issues of new shares are called scrip issues, or bonus issues. No cash is required from shareholders. The number of issued shares increases but the total equity of the company remains unchanged; it is merely its composition that changes. Scrip issues may be made by companies whose share price is relatively high and therefore a trading constraint. However, the share price may fall because of earnings dilution.

Share splits

When a company makes a share split it increases the number of shares in issue but correspondingly reduces the nominal value of the shares. This is done in such a way that the total nominal value of ordinary shares in the balance sheet remains as it was before the share split.

The possible reasons for their use are similar for both scrip issues and share splits:

- a share reconstruction may signal confidence in the investments that profit retention has been used to fund
- a reduction in the value of each share may put them into a more marketable price range and theoretically increase their liquidity, an idea contradicted by some academic research because of higher transaction costs and lower trading volumes
- shareholders may feel that a share reconstruction has in some way increased their wealth and while some research has disputed this, other research has given some credibility to the idea

of share splits giving the perception by shareholders of a favourable impact regarding the company's greater capacity to pay dividends in the future.

Scrip dividends

A scrip dividend, or share dividend, is yet another way in which a company may issue new equity without raising additional finance. A company may give more shares in the company to existing shareholders, either partially or totally, instead of paying cash dividends. As a result of the company paying a scrip dividend the share price should not fall. However, scrip dividends are taxed in the same way as cash dividends, unless the shareholder is exempt from paying tax.

Scrip dividends have some impact on the company, the big benefit obviously being that no cash is required to pay out scrip dividends, and they may be issued at very little cost. The company's financial gearing may decrease slightly, because of the increase in shares, which may or may not be to the company's advantage.

Share buy-backs

In the UK, a company may buy back its shares from its shareholders so long as they have given their permission for this at a general meeting of the company. This may be made by the company via the market or by a tender to all its shareholders. It is a method of returning cash to shareholders, which is an alternative to paying dividends. However, legally the company can only pay for the shares it buys back out of distributable profit.

There are a number of possible reasons why a company may want to buy back its own shares:

- it is a method of returning capital to shareholders
- it is a method of increasing gearing
- if gearing is increased with little increase in financial risk, the share price should increase – and so share repurchase by the company is now a tactic used quite widely in the UK as a defence against a hostile takeover
- the number of shares is reduced and so earnings per share is increased
- capital employed is reduced and therefore the return on capital employed is increased.

A **share re-purchase** (or **share buy-back**) is an alternative method to dividends of returning value to shareholders. Share buy-backs benefit shareholders because the return of their funds enables them to reinvest or use their capital in a more effective way. The value per share of the reduced number of shares is also increased.

A company may use a share buy-back as a method of managing its capital structure, and its weighted average cost of capital (WACC). This may therefore provide the opportunity for investments in projects that may otherwise have been rejected because of inadequate net present values. A disadvantage may be the increase in gearing of the company. However, the main advantages to the company are that eps and ROCE will be increased.

Share buy-backs can therefore be seen to be very closely linked with dividend policy, which is discussed in more detail in Chapters 13 and 15.

Progress check 7.3

What are ordinary shares and what are their distinguishing features?

Preference shares

Preference shares receive a dividend at a level that is fixed, and subject to the conditions of issue of the shares, they have a prior claim to any company profits available for distribution and no ordinary share dividends may be paid until all preference share dividends have been fully paid. Preference shareholders may also have a prior claim over ordinary shareholders to the repayment of capital in the event of the company being wound up.

Preference shares are part of a company's share capital and the cost to the company of issuing preference shares is similar to the cost of issuing ordinary shares, but whereas ordinary shares have voting rights, preference shares do not. They do bear some risk for investors, which is higher than that of debt capital, but at a far lower level than that of ordinary shares. Debt capital has a lower risk than preference shares because:

- loan interest must be paid before preference dividends are paid
- debt holders have a prior claim over preference shareholders to the repayment of capital in the event of the company being wound up
- debt capital normally has security based on one or more of a company's assets, whereas preference shares have no security.

Preference shares are normally cumulative preference shares, which entitle the shareholders to a fixed rate of dividend, and the right to have any arrears of dividend paid out of future profits with priority over any distribution of profits to the holders of ordinary share capital. There are a further five classes of preference shares:

- participating preference shares entitle their holders to a fixed dividend and, in addition, the right to participate in any surplus profits after payment of agreed levels of dividends to ordinary shareholders has been made
- zero dividend rate preference shares receive no dividends throughout the life of the shares
- variable dividend rate preference shares have their dividend agreed at a fixed percentage plus, for example, LIBOR (London Interbank Offered Rate of interest), rather than receiving a fixed level of dividend, or they may have a variable dividend which is set at regular intervals to a market rate by means of an auction process between investors known as AMPS (auction market preferred stock) – auction market securities are money market financial instruments, created in 1984, which reset dividends at a rate that is fixed until the next auction date, when the securities adjust with a new yield to reflect market conditions
- redeemable preference shares are issued on terms which require them to be bought back by the issuer at some future date, in compliance with the conditions of the Companies Act 1985, either at the discretion of the issuer or of the shareholder
- convertible preference shares have terms and conditions agreed at the outset, which provide the shareholder with the option to convert their preference shares into ordinary shares at a later date.

There are advantages and disadvantages in the use of preference shares by companies and investors. As with ordinary shares, the company does not have to pay dividends on preference shares if there are insufficient profits, and for this reason preference shareholders may expect higher returns. However, if preference shares are cumulative, then dividends will eventually have to be paid. In the same way as ordinary share dividends, preference share dividends are not allowable for corporation tax. A disadvantage for the company is that because preference shares bear a higher risk than debt capital, and they have no tax shield, then the cost of preference share capital is likely to be higher than debt capital.

The use of preference shares has been particularly popular in situations where venture capitalists (VCs) are involved, for example in new business start-ups and management buy-outs (MBOs). We will discuss the way in which this may operate in Chapter 18. VCs may also consider convertible preference shares, which may be converted into ordinary shares at a later date, as a means of further benefiting from a successful new venture.

Progress check 7.4

In what ways do preference shares differ from ordinary shares?

Long-term loans

Generally, companies try and match their longer-term financing with the purpose for which it is required, and the type of assets requiring to be financed which include:

- non-current assets
- long-term projects.

Long-term debt is normally matched to finance the acquisition of non-current assets, which are long-term assets from which the company expects to derive benefits over several future periods. It is usually more expensive and less flexible than short-term debt but has, to some extent, less risk for the investor than short-term debt.

Whereas dividends paid on shares are an appropriation of profit and therefore paid out of the company's after tax profit, interest payable on long-term loans (and short-term loans and overdrafts) is an expense. Loan interest and overdraft interest is therefore deducted from profit before tax, and therefore the effective cost of interest is reduced by the amount of the corporation tax rate. For example, if corporation tax were at 30% per annum, a loan on which interest is payable at 10% per annum would actually cost the company 7%, that is {10% − (10% × 30%)}. The amount by which the interest is reduced because of the effect of corporation tax is called the tax shield.

Long-term financial debts are the elements of loans and leases that are payable after one year of the balance sheet date. Debt capital may take many forms: loans, debentures, mortgages, etc. Each type of long-term debt requires interest payment and capital repayment of the loan and, in addition, security or collateral is usually required. Loan interest is a fixed commitment, which is usually payable once or twice a year. But although debt capital is burdened with a fixed commitment of interest payable, it is a tax-efficient method of financing because interest payments are an allowable deduction for corporation tax whereas dividends are not.

Debentures

Debentures and long-term loans are both long-term debt, which have a nominal, or par value of normally £100 in the UK. They may also have a market price, which is determined by their market demand related to their level of risk, interest rate, and period of issue. Debentures, long-term loans, and bonds are terms that are often taken to mean the same thing and may be for periods of between 10 and 20 years or more. Long-term loans may be either unsecured, or secured on some or all of the assets of the company. Lenders to a company receive interest, payable yearly or half-yearly, at a rate called the coupon rate, which may vary with market conditions. A debenture, or bond, or loan stock, more specifically refers to the written acknowledgement of a debt by a company, usually given under its seal, and normally containing provisions as to payment of interest and the terms of repayment of the principal. A debenture may be secured on some or all of the assets of the company or its subsidiaries. Other long-term loans are usually unsecured.

The debenture trust deed includes details that relate to:

- period of the loan
- security for the loan
- power to appoint a receiver
- interest rate and payment terms
- financial reporting requirements
- redemption procedures
- restrictive covenants.

Security for a debenture may be by way of a floating charge, without attachment to specific assets, on the whole of the business's assets. A floating charge is a form of protection given to secured creditors, which relates to the assets of the company, which are changing in nature. Often current assets like stocks or debtors are the subject of this type of charge. In the event of default on repayment, in which the company is not able to meet its obligations, the lender may take steps to enforce the floating charge so that it crystallises and becomes attached to current assets like debtors or stocks. Floating charges rank after certain other prior claims if a company goes into receivership or liquidation.

Security for a debenture may alternatively, at the outset, take the form of a fixed charge on specific assets like land and buildings. A fixed charge is a form of protection given to secured creditors, which relates to specific assets of the company. The charge grants the lender the right of enforcement against the identified asset, in the event of default on payment, so that the lender may realise the asset to meet the debt owed. Fixed charges rank first in order of priority if a company goes into receivership or liquidation.

Debentures are relatively low risk investments for investors, and therefore returns will be much lower than those demanded by equity shareholders. They are a tax-efficient method of corporate financing, which means that interest payable on such loans is an allowable deduction in the computation of taxable profit. The cost of long-term financial debt to companies therefore tends to be relatively low. However, the higher the proportion of debt that a company has, the higher the level of financial risk it faces, as a result of its having to pay interest and the possibility that debt-holders may force the company to cease trading and realise its assets should it have difficulty in servicing (or repaying) the loan.

A company may buy back its debentures on the open market, whether they are redeemable or irredeemable, which may be an advantageous method of cancelling their debt if the market price is below its par value. However, if they are redeemable debentures then sufficient cash must be found by the company for their redemption at the due dates. The consequences of a company not being able to meet its redemption commitments may result in debt-holders exercising their right to call a creditors meeting and appoint a receiver. A company may try and ease the burden of redemption in a number of ways:

- inclusion in the trust deed of the option of early redemption by the company at any time up to the redemption date rather than on the redemption date, with or without compensation to the debt-holders

- refinancing through replacement of the redeemable debt with a new debt issue having a later redemption date, using what is called a rollover bond

- creation of a sinking fund, in which money is put aside periodically and invested in perhaps a bond to provide a return which together with the principal will produce the required sum at the redemption date.

Lenders may try and protect themselves from the consequences of the company failing to meet its interest and capital repayment commitments, by preventing changes to the company's risk profile, through the inclusion of restrictive covenants in the debenture trust deed, for example:

- a minimum current ratio (current assets divided by current liabilities) or quick ratio (current assets less stocks, divided by current liabilities) reflected in the company's balance sheet

- conditions relating to the disposal of non-current assets

- restrictions on taking on additional debt and/or equity and maintenance of a specific level of financial gearing

- restrictions on amounts of dividends payable

and if the company does not fulfil the covenant conditions, then the trust deed will provide lenders with the right to seek immediate repayment in full.

Interest – fixed and floating rates

Loans may be taken by companies, which require payment of interest at either fixed or floating rates. A floating interest rate is generally linked to LIBOR (London Interbank Offered Rate of interest); for example, interest may be payable at LIBOR plus 2%. If a company expects that interest rates in the future may rise then it may try and protect itself with a loan that has a fixed interest rate. However, if future interest rates actually fall then there is an opportunity cost to the company, which could have been paying lower interest charges had it not committed to a fixed rate loan. If the company expects that interest rates in the future may fall then it may try and protect itself with a loan that has a floating interest rate, so that it may take advantage of lower market rates.

If lenders fear that future interest rates may fall then they may prefer a loan with a fixed interest rate. If lenders expect that future interest rates may rise then they may prefer the flexibility of a loan with a floating interest rate, to be in line with market rates.

Progress check 7.5

What is long-term debt and what are its distinguishing features?

Bonds – medium and long-term debt capital

There are many different types of debt instruments, of which the bond is perhaps the most popular. It is defined as a debt instrument, normally offering a fixed rate of interest (coupon) over a fixed period of time, and with a fixed redemption value (par). A debenture is often referred to as a bond.

The level of the risk relating to bonds, in terms of future interest payments and principal repayment, is measured by a number of organisations with reference to a standard risk index. Companies like Standard & Poor's, and Moody's carry out detailed financial analyses of specific companies, which have issued bonds regarding their forecast financial performances, and also general economic analyses and analysis of the financial markets. The resultant ratings for such bonds are reported by giving them letters denoting their level of quality and risk. For example, Moody's highest rating for a particular bond is Aaa and its lowest rating is C. The rating, and perhaps more importantly any rating downgrading of a bond is likely to have a serious negative impact on its market value.

A bond is a negotiable debt instrument of which there are broadly three varieties:

- domestic bond
- foreign bond
- Eurobond.

A domestic bond is a bond issued in the country in which the borrower is domiciled. It is a negotiable debt instrument denominated in the home country currency and essentially available for domestic distribution only.

A foreign bond is a bond issued in the country other than that in which the borrower is domiciled. It is a negotiable debt instrument denominated in the local currency of the issuer, but available for international distribution.

A Eurobond is a bond issued outside the country of its currency (see the next section below). Such bonds can not only be issued by borrowers domiciled in almost any country, they can also be acquired by investors domiciled in almost any country.

Bonds and loans may be irredeemable or redeemable debt in which case the principal, the original sum borrowed, will need to be repaid on a specific date. Irredeemable bonds are not particularly common and so most bonds are redeemable. Irredeemable bonds are perpetual bonds and have no redemption date. The value of an irredeemable bond (V_0) may be calculated (see Worked Example 7.3) in the same way as one would value a perpetuity, by dividing the annual amount of interest payable on the debt (d) by the market rate of return on debt expected by investors (R_d):

$$V_0 = \frac{d}{R_d}$$

The value of redeemable debt (V_0) may be found (see Worked Example 7.4) by using the DCF method to calculate the present value of future interest plus the present value of the future redemption value of the debt after n years (V_n), which is usually its par value, using the market rate of return on debt expected by investors (R_d):

$$V_0 = d/(1 + R_d) + d/(1 + R_d)^2 + d/(1 + R_d)^3 \cdots + (d + V_n)/(1 + R_d)^n$$

There is a wide range of types of bond, some of which we have already described, the most popular being:

- fixed rate bonds
- zero coupon bonds
- floating rate bonds – bonds, issued at a deep discount on their par value, on which no interest is payable which are attractive to investors seeking capital gains rather than income from interest

- sinking fund bonds
- rollover bonds
- convertible bonds – debts which are convertible to equities at a later date.

Worked Example 7.3

A Government stock, which has a par value of £100, offers a fixed annual income of £5, but there is no obligation to repay the capital. The market return on debt expected by investors is 5.5%. We are required to calculate the market value of this irredeemable debt.

$$d = £5 \qquad\qquad R_d = 5.5\%$$

Using

$$V_0 = \frac{d}{R_d} \text{ the market value of the debt} = \frac{£5}{0.055} = £90.91$$

The market value is less than, or at a discount to, the par value of the debt, because the stock is paying less than the expected market rate.

Worked Example 7.4

A bond has a par value of £100 and pays 7% per annum and is redeemable at par in three years' time. The return expected by investors in this particular bond market is 6.5% per annum. We are required to calculate the market value of this redeemable bond.

$$d = £7 \qquad R_d = 6.5\% \qquad n = 3 \text{ years} \qquad V_n = £100$$

Using

$$V_0 = d/(1 + R_d) + d/(1 + R_d)^2 + d/(1 + R_d)^3 \cdots + (d + V_n)/(1 + R_d)^n$$

The market value of the bond is

$$7/(1.065) + 7/(1.065)^2 + (7 + 100)/(1.065)^3$$
$$= £6.57 + £6.17 + £88.58$$
$$= £101.32$$

The market value is more than, or at a premium to, the par value of the bond, because the bond is paying more than the expected market rate.

International debt finance and Eurobonds

As global trade and the need for international finance increases, the use of international debt instruments, and in particular debt instruments such as bonds, is an area of growing importance to international financial managers. A company may have a subsidiary company in a foreign country. It may finance its subsidiary by borrowing in the subsidiary's local currency or in some other currency if it feels that its lower interest rate gains outweigh any risk of losses through exchange rate fluctuations. A Eurobond is long-term debt that facilitates such foreign borrowing.

The Eurocurrency market is described by Buckley (Buckley A (2004) *Multinational Finance*, London: FT/Prentice Hall) as a market in which '. . . Eurobanks accept deposits and make loans denominated in currencies other than that of the country in which the banks are located'. A Eurobond is a type of bearer bond, issued in a eurocurrency, usually US$, with maturities of 5 to 15 years. A bearer bond is a negotiable bond or security whose ownership is not registered by the issuer, but is presumed to lie with whoever has physical possession of the bond. A Eurobond is denominated in a currency other than the currency in which the bond is issued. It is therefore outside the control of that country and may be bought and sold in different countries by governments and companies.

For the past 20 years or so, Eurobonds have become increasingly more attractive to lenders and borrowers for a number of reasons:

- existence of few regulatory requirements in the Eurobond markets
- increasing flexibility of such instruments
- relative ease with which such bonds may be raised.

As a consequence, the Eurobond market has grown substantially in size over the same period. The advantages of the Eurobond market for both borrowers and lenders arise because of the substantial size of the market, its ability to absorb frequent issues, and its now established institutional framework. Such advantages include the following:

- lower borrowing costs inherent in the Eurobond market
- higher deposit rates inherent in the Eurobond market
- the increased convertibility of Eurobonds
- the existence of not only a primary market but also an active secondary market for both lenders and borrowers (see the later sections in this chapter about capital markets).

The key factors that an international company should consider when exploring the possibility of raising international debt capital and determining a debt policy are the same as many of the factors relevant to a domestic company. However, these factors and the different types of debt capital available should be considered in an international context.

The key factors a company needs to take into account when developing a borrowing strategy or a debt policy can be divided into two groups:

- external factors, or factors related to external perceptions of the company
- internal factors, or factors related to the internal policy-making structure within the company.

The emphasis placed on the above external and internal factors will depend on the nature, level, and composition of borrowing the company is considering, and whether it is:

- short-term – less than one year
- medium-term – between one year and 10 years
- long-term – over 10 years

or a combination of each of these.

Generally, the external factors include:

- the overall business risk profile of the company
- the debt servicing ability of the company
- the borrowing constraints imposed on the company or industrial sector by lenders, or government regulation and legislation
- the perceived gearing norm for the particular industrial sector.

Factors which are more internal to the company would include:

- the maturity profile of the company's existing debt
- the impact of additional debt on its financial gearing
- the interest rate mix of existing debt and new debt
- the availability of security for additional debt
- the potential impact of interest rate changes and exchange rate changes on both existing debt and new debt.

When seeking to reconcile the conflicting pressures of all the above internal and external factors, the company should seek to ensure that:

- the debt maturity profile of its existing debt matches its asset maturity profile
- where possible it maintains a balanced combination of fixed and floating rate debt
- where possible debt maturity is overlapped to avoid excessive outflows of cash or near cash resources and any associated liquidity problems.

Progress check 7.6

Explain the use of Eurobonds as long-term debt.

Hybrid finance – convertibles, warrants, and mezzanine debt

Loans may sometimes be required by companies particularly as they progress through a period of growth, their growth phase. These loans are usually required by companies to finance specific asset acquisitions or projects. Some of the disadvantages of the use of loans rather than equity are:

- the increase in financial risk resulting from a reduction in the amount of equity compared with debt
- the commitment to fixed interest payments over a number of years
- the requirement of a build up of cash with which to repay the loan on maturity.

Alternatively, if an increase in equity is used for this type of funding, eps (earnings per share) may be immediately 'diluted'.

However, some financing is neither totally debt nor equity, but has the characteristics of both. Such hybrid finance, as it is called, includes financial instruments like convertible loans (and convertible preference shares which we mentioned earlier in the section about preference shares).

Convertible loans

A convertible loan is a 'two stage' financial instrument. It may be a fixed interest debt, which can be converted into ordinary shares of the company at the option of the lender. Eps will therefore not be diluted until a later date. The right to convert may usually be exercised each year at a pre-determined conversion rate up until a specified date, at which time the loan must be redeemed if it has not been converted. The conversion rate may be stated as:

■ a conversion price (the amount of the loan that can be converted into one ordinary share)

or

■ a conversion ratio (the number of ordinary shares that can be converted from one unit of the loan).

The conversion price or ratio will be specified at the outset and may change during the term of the loan. The conversion value equals the conversion price multiplied by the conversion ratio and is the market value of the ordinary shares into which the loan may be converted. Conversion values are below the issue values of loans when they are issued, and as the conversion date approaches they should increase if the ordinary share price has increased so that investors will want to convert. The difference between the conversion value and the market price of the loan is called the conversion premium. The market price of the loan, and therefore the market premium are determined by the:

■ likelihood of investors converting according to market expectation

■ current and expected conversion values

■ amount of time left to conversion.

There are two aspects to the valuation of a convertible bond:

■ the conversion value of a convertible bond after n years (V_n) must be at a level which makes conversion attractive to investors, and its value depends on an estimate of what the ordinary share price (S) will be at the conversion date

■ the current value of a convertible bond (V_0) depends on its future conversion value.

If the expected annual percentage growth rate of the share price is g, and the number of ordinary shares that will be received on conversion is N then the conversion value of the convertible bond may be calculated as:

$$V_n = S \times (1 + g)^n \times N$$

The current market value of the convertible bond (V_0) may be found (see Worked Example 7.5) by using the DCF method to calculate the present value of future annual interest (i) plus the present value of the bond's conversion value after n years (V_n), using the market rate of return on bonds expected by investors (R_d):

$$V_0 = i/(1 + R_d) + i/(1 + R_d)^2 + i/(1 + R_d)^3 \cdots + (i + V_n)/(1 + R_d)^n$$

When convertible debt is first issued its market value will be the same as its redemption value. The conversion value will initially be less than the redemption value, but as the ordinary share price increases over time the conversion value will become increasingly greater than the redemption value. During the period up to conversion, the market value of the debt will be greater than the conversion value, because investors will expect that the share price will increase even further in the future, but it converges towards the conversion value at the conversion date.

Worked Example 7.5

A convertible bond with a par value of £100 pays 6% per annum and on the redemption date in three years' time may be converted into 50 ordinary shares or redeemed at par. The current share price is £2 and it is expected to grow by 7% per annum. An investor requires a return of 6.5% per annum and we are required to advise the maximum price that they should be prepared to pay currently for the bond.

$$S = £2 \qquad g = 7\% \qquad N = 50$$

Using

$$V_n = S \times (1 + g)^n \times N$$

the conversion value of the bond $= £2 \times (1.07)^3 \times 50 = £122.50$

The conversion value is higher than the par value of £100 and so an investor would choose to convert.

The present values of the future cash flows can then be calculated to determine the current market value of the bond V_0.

$$R_d = 6.5\% \qquad i = £6 \qquad V_n = £122.50$$

Using

$$V_0 = i/(1 + R_d) + i/(1 + R_d)^2 + i/(1 + R_d)^3 \cdots + (i + V_n)/(1 + R_d)^n$$

the current market value of the bond is

$$6/(1.065) + 6/(1.065)^2 + (6 + 122.50)/(1.065)^3$$
$$= £5.63 + £5.29 + £106.38$$
$$= £117.30$$

The maximum price that should be paid currently for the bond is therefore £117.30.

Loans and bonds are generally lower risk investments for investors than ordinary shares. Therefore, an advantage for investors in convertible bonds is that initially they may make a lower risk investment in a company and monitor its performance over a period of time before deciding to convert their bonds at a later date into higher risk ordinary shares. If the company's performance has not been particularly good and the share price has not risen sufficiently then investors may decide not to convert. This may be a disadvantage for the company if the convertible bonds then run their term to their maturity at which time the company will have to redeem them for cash. If the company's performance has been good and the share price has increased then at the conversion date the convertible bondholders have the choice of deciding to convert their bonds into ordinary shares.

The big advantage for companies of convertible bonds compared with straight loans is that under normal circumstances they do not have to be redeemed with cash. Convertibles increase the company's gearing to a higher level than investors may wish, but which may be acceptable since they know that gearing will again be reduced to an acceptable level when conversion takes place.

Although convertible bonds may eventually be converted into equity capital, until that time the company has the use of capital by paying interest at a lower cost than the cost of equity and which is allowable for corporation tax, which lowers its effective cost of capital even further. If the company feels that at the time it is looking to raise new capital its shares are underpriced and the company is undervalued, then convertible bonds may be an ideal alternative to an issue of equity.

Convertibles tend to pay a lower rate of interest than straight loans, which is effectively charging lenders for the right to convert to ordinary shares. They also pay a fixed rate of interest. Therefore, they provide benefits in terms of the company's cash flow as well as cost of financing, and facilitate accurate forecasting of interest payments. However, any increase in the debt of a company increases gearing and interest payments, which reduce profits and therefore reduces earnings per share. The increase in gearing also increases the level of financial risk faced by the company during the period up to when conversion takes place. Dilution of earnings per share and the level of control of the existing ordinary shareholders will also occur on conversion.

Progress check 7.7

What makes convertible loans attractive sources of finance to both investors and companies?

Warrants

Bond issues are sometimes made that include what are called warrants, or the rights to buy new ordinary shares in the company at a later date at a fixed share price called the exercise price. A warrant is defined as a financial instrument that requires the issuer to issue shares (whether contingently or not) and contains no obligation for the issuer to transfer economic benefits (FRS 4).

The warrant itself may be considered separately from the bond and traded. The reason for the inclusion of warrants in bond issues is to try and make the issue even more attractive to investors, who may then be able to reduce the cost of their investments by selling off the warrants. Therefore, for investors a bond issue with warrants provides a cost-effective investment that is also less risky than ordinary shares.

An advantage gained by companies from the issue of bonds with warrants is that the interest rate will normally be lower than that paid on straight loans. The level of additional ordinary shares as a result of exercising the warrants will normally be less than with convertible bonds, which means less impact on gearing and earnings per share. Making the bond issue more attractive to investors by including warrants should make the issue successful. This may be the case even if the company is unable to provide the levels of security that may normally be required for similar straight loans.

The calculation of what is called the intrinsic value of a warrant (V_w) is the current price of the ordinary shares (S), minus the exercise price (E), multiplied by the number shares (N) provided by each warrant:

$$V_w = (S - E) \times N$$

The market value of a warrant is actually higher than its intrinsic value by what is called its time value, because of possible growth in the share price:

intrinsic value + time value = market value of warrant

Warrants also possess gearing, which relates to the relationship between the movement in warrant value and the movement in share price. This is best illustrated with a worked example.

Worked Example 7.6

A company's loan stock has warrants attached to it, which entitle their holders to purchase 10 ordinary shares at an exercise price of £3 per share. The current share price is £4. We will calculate the intrinsic value of the warrant and evaluate the gearing effects of a share price increase and decrease over a year to £5 and £3 respectively.

Using

$$V_w = (S - E) \times N$$

the intrinsic value of the warrant is

$$V_w = (£4 - £3) \times 10 = £10$$

If the share price rises to £5, the intrinsic value of the warrant becomes

$$V_w = (£5 - £3) \times 10 = £20$$

So a 25% increase in share price results in a 100% increase in warrant value. The gain from buying and holding the warrant is proportionately greater than the gain from buying and holding ordinary shares.

If the share price falls to £3, the intrinsic value of the warrant becomes

$$V_w = (£3 - £3) \times 10 = £0$$

So a 25% decrease in share price results in a 100% decrease in warrant value to zero. The loss from buying and holding the warrant is proportionately greater than the loss from buying and holding ordinary shares.

Mezzanine debt

Another type of hybrid finance is called mezzanine finance. Mezzanine finance is unsecured debt finance but its risk-return profile is somewhere between debt and equity. Its level of risk is higher than that of loans with security, but lower than ordinary shares, and it is lower on the list of priority payments than straight debt, should the company go into receivership or liquidation. Because of this the interest rate for mezzanine debt is relatively high, typically at around 5% plus LIBOR. Mezzanine debt is usually provided by banks and normally may be convertible into ordinary shares or includes warrants for the option to buy new shares.

Mezzanine debt is often used to finance company takeovers, and also MBOs (management buy-outs). The reason for this is that it gives investors the opportunity of capital gains from exercising warrants or convertibles if the buy-out successfully results in high performance and an increase in share price. However, the downside risk of mezzanine finance is faced by both the company and investors.

Leasing

Leases are contracts between a lessor and lessee for the hire of a specific asset. Why then is leasing seen as a source of long-term financing? There are two types of leases, **operating leases** and **finance leases**, and the answer to the question lies in the accounting treatment of the latter.

Under both types of leasing contract the lessor retains the ownership of the asset but gives the lessee the right to use the asset over an agreed period in return for specified rental payments in accordance with SSAP 21 (Statement of Standard Accounting Practice 21: Accounting for Leases and Hire Purchase Contracts). The lease term is the period for which the lessee has contracted to lease the asset and any further terms for which the lessee has the option to continue to lease the asset with or without further payment; which option the lessee will exercise is reasonably certain at the inception of the lease (see the Financial Reporting Standard for Smaller Entities (FRSSE) published by the ASB).

An operating lease is any lease other than a finance lease. It is a rental agreement for an asset, which may be leased by one lessee for a period, and then another lessee for a period, and so on. The lease period is normally less than the economic life of the asset, and the lease rentals are charged as a cost in the income statement of the lessee as they occur. The leased asset does not appear in the lessee's balance sheet, and so an operating lease is a method of off balance sheet financing. SSAP 21 requires a company to disclose in its balance sheet only the lease payments due to be paid in the next accounting period. The lessor is responsible for maintenance and regular service of assets like photocopiers, cars, and personal computers. The lessor therefore retains most of the risks and rewards of ownership.

A finance lease is a non-cancellable agreement between a lessor and a lessee and it relates to an asset where the present value of the lease rentals payable amounts to at least 90% of its fair market value at the start of the lease. The lessee is usually responsible for all service and maintenance of the asset. The term of a finance lease usually matches the expected economic life of the asset. The primary period of a finance lease relates to the main period of the lease during which the lessor recovers the capital cost of the asset, plus a return, from the lease payments made by the lessee. During the secondary period of a finance lease the lessee may continue to lease the assets for a nominal sum, which is called a peppercorn rent.

Under a finance lease the legal title to the asset remains with the lessor, but the difference in accounting treatment, as defined by SSAP 21, is that a finance lease is capitalised in the balance sheet of the lessee. A value of the finance lease is shown under non-current assets, based on a calculation of the present value of the capital part (excluding finance charges) of the future lease rentals payable. The future lease rentals are also shown in the balance sheet as long- and short-term creditors. A lessee in a finance lease, although not the legal owner, therefore has substantially all the risks and rewards of ownership of the asset transferred to them by the lessor.

The main differences between an operating lease and a finance lease are:

■ an operating lease is for the rental of an asset for a specific purpose over a short period of time, but a finance lease covers the economic life of the asset

- an operating lease can easily be terminated but a finance lease is non-cancellable
- obsolescence risk is borne by the lessor in an operating lease, but by the lessee in a finance lease
- an operating lease is typically more expensive than a finance lease.

In the UK prior to the mid-1980s the main factor in the growth in popularity of leasing was the benefit derived from its treatment for taxation. Before 1984 there was no distinction between a finance lease and an operating lease and both were seen as off balance sheet financing. In 1984 the taxation incentives were reduced but leasing continued to grow in popularity for other reasons. In April 1984 SSAP 21 distinguished more clearly between operating and finance leases, requiring finance leases to be capitalised in companies' balance sheets.

Both operating and finance leases provide a source of finance if a company has a liquidity shortage because it means that the company does not have to provide the whole of the funding for the purchase of an asset at the outset. Even if borrowing is an option, some companies, and particularly start-up companies, may lack assets of sufficient quality to provide security for borrowing. Leasing may also still provide taxation benefits if the tax situations of the lessee and lessor are different.

In addition to being a source of funding, leasing may also be used by a company to increase cash or alleviate a cash flow problem. Assets may be sold by a company to a leasing company and then leased back from them. In 2001 the international law firm Denton Wilde Sapte advised the board of Marks & Spencer plc on the structured sale and leaseback of 78 stores across the UK for a cash consideration of £348m to Topland Group Holdings Ltd, a privately owned real estate investment group. Under this deal, Topland would lease the stores back to Marks & Spencer over the next 26 years for £24.6m per year at an annual rental increase of 1.95%.

An operating lease may be an answer to the obsolescence problem because assets like personal computers may be leased for periods of, say, up to one year and then exchanged for the latest models and acquired under a new operating lease. An operating lease still remains off balance sheet with regard to there being no requirement for the asset and the liability to be disclosed in a company's balance sheet.

A company may buy an asset outright for cash. Its alternatives are borrowing funds for the purchase or leasing. The decision to invest in the acquisition of an asset is one decision, the investment decision; the borrowing or leasing as a source of finance is a separate decision, the financing decision.

The investment decision and the financing decision may be made separately in either order or they may form a combined decision, and should take account of a number of factors:

- the asset purchase price and its residual value
- the lease rental amounts and the timing of their payments
- service and maintenance payments
- tax:
  - capital allowances for purchased non-current assets
  - tax allowable lease rental expenses
- VAT (relating to the asset purchase and the lease rentals)
- interest rates (the general level of rates of competing financing options).

The leasing decision evaluation process involves appraisal of the investment in the asset itself, its outright purchase or lease, and an evaluation of leasing as the method of financing, and in order to achieve an optimal result the decision may be considered in three ways:

- first make the investment decision, then find the optimal financing method – but in this case an investment may be rejected which would otherwise have been accepted if low-cost financing had been considered
- evaluate both the investment and the financing method together – involving very advanced investment and financing appraisal techniques
- first make the financing decision, then evaluate the investment – the two decisions are separate and so to evaluate the financing it may be assumed that the investment decision has already been made

and then leasing and borrowing may then be compared using DCF, the appropriate discount rate being the lessee's cost of borrowing.

In the following worked example it has been assumed that the decision to invest has already been made. The example looks at the comparison between borrowing and lending as the method financing the investment.

Worked Example 7.7

Bollees Ltd wants to buy a machine, which it expects to have a useful economic life of five years. The cost of the machine is £100,000. Bollees Ltd does not have the surplus cash available and so it will have to borrow funds for outright purchase at 10% per annum, and since it would own the machine it would also have to pay maintenance costs of £1,500 per annum. Alternatively, the machine could be leased. The lease payments would be £25,000 per annum for five years, which are allowable for tax, and are payable at the beginning of each year, and maintenance costs would be borne by the lessor. Bollees pays corporation tax on its taxable profits for the year, but in the following year, at 30% per annum, but it claims 40% first year capital allowances and then 25% per annum on a reducing balance basis. It is assumed that an appropriate capital investment appraisal has been made and that this is a viable investment for the company.

We will evaluate each of the options to determine whether Bollees Ltd should borrow to buy, or lease the machine.

The two alternatives for the company are leasing and borrowing, and so the relevant cash flows of the two alternatives can be compared using Bollees Ltd's after-tax cost of borrowing, which is $10\% \times (1 - 0.30)$, or 7%.

The capital allowances on the machine over five years are:

Year			
1	£100,000 × 0.4	=	£40,000
2	£60,000 × 0.25	=	£15,000
3	£45,000 × 0.25	=	£11,250
4	£33,750 × 0.25	=	£8,437
5	balancing allowance		£25,313
			£100,000

Bollees Ltd's deductions allowed for tax – capital allowances and the maintenance costs. ▶

Year	Capital allowances £	Maintenance costs £	Total deductions £	30% tax relief £	Year tax relief taken
1	40,000	1,500	41,500	12,450	2
2	15,000	1,500	16,500	4,950	3
3	11,250	1,500	12,750	3,825	4
4	8,437	1,500	9,937	2,981	5
5	25,313	1,500	26,813	8,044	6

The present values of the costs of leasing and of borrowing can now be compared:

Cost of leasing present value

Year	Cash flow £		Discount factor at 7%	Present value £
0–4	lease payments	25,000	4.39	(109,750)
2–6	30% tax relief	7,500	3.83	28,725
				(81,025)

Cost of borrowing present value

Year	Loan £	Maintenance costs £	30% tax relief £	Net cash flow £	Discount factor at 7%	Present value £
0	(100,000)			(100,000)	1.00	(100,000)
1		(1,500)		(1,500)	0.94	(1,410)
2		(1,500)	12,450	10,950	0.87	9,527
3		(1,500)	4,950	3,450	0.82	2,829
4		(1,500)	3,825	2,325	0.76	1,767
5		(1,500)	2,981	1,481	0.71	1,052
6			8,044	8,044	0.67	5,389
						(80,846)

We can see that the cost of leasing present value of £81,025 is greater than the cost of borrowing present value of £80,846, and so on a DCF basis Bollees Ltd should borrow funds for purchase rather than lease.

Other factors should be considered, such as the impact of borrowing on Bollees Ltd's financial gearing and its cost of capital. If the investment were to be reappraised using a revised cost of capital then on a DCF basis it may be rejected.

Progress check 7.8

In what ways may a company use leasing as a source of finance?

UK Government and European funding

Businesses involved in certain industries or located in specific geographical areas of the UK may from time to time be eligible for assistance with financing. This may be by way of grants, loan guarantees, and subsidised consultancy. Funding may be on a national or a regional basis from various UK Government or European Union sources.

By their very nature, such financing initiatives are continually changing in format and their areas of focus. In the UK, for example, funding assistance has been available in one form or another for SMEs, the agriculture industry, tourism, former coal and steel producing areas, and parts of Wales.

This type of funding may include support for the following:

- business start-ups
- new factories
- new plant and machinery
- research and development
- IT development.

There are many examples of funding schemes that currently operate in the UK. For example, the Government, via the DTI (Department of Trade and Industry), can provide guarantees for loans from banks and other financial institutions for small businesses that may be unable to provide the security for conventional loans. Via the various regional development agencies, they may also provide discretionary selective financial assistance in the form of grants or loans for businesses that are willing to invest in 'assisted areas'. The DTI and Government Business Link websites, www.dti.gov.uk and www.businesslink.gov.uk, provide up-to-date information of all current funding initiatives.

The Welsh Assembly's use of European Structural Funds (ESFs) assists businesses in regenerating Welsh communities. For example, through a scheme called match funding, depending on the type of business activity and its location, ESFs can contribute up to 50% of a project's funding. The balance of the funding is provided from the business's own resources or other public or private sector funding. Websites like the Welsh European Funding Office website, www.wefo.wales.gov.uk, provide information on this type of funding initiative.

The capital markets

In principle, in the same way as estate agents bring together buyers and sellers in the property markets, the capital markets provide the means by which investors and companies, and national and local governments requiring long-term finance are brought together. This long-term finance may be debt (loans, debentures, bonds, Government securities) or equity (ordinary shares). The information available in the capital markets includes companies' announcements and press statements relating to, for example, dividends and profit forecasts, companies' interim and year-end reports and accounts, and general economic and financial information relating to, for example, inflation rates, current and forecast interest rates, and market indices.

The capital market in which new equity and debt capital is initially raised by companies from investors is called the primary capital market. The issue of shares by a company to obtain a listing on a stock exchange is done though what is called an **initial public offering (IPO)**. Investors include private individuals and financial institutions like pension funds, and insurance companies.

There are five other methods used in the UK (see the section on new share issues below) by which funds may be raised through the issue of ordinary shares:

- **placings, and intermediary offers**
- **offers for sale, and issues by tender**
- **introductions.**

The capital markets also provide the means by which equity or debt may be transferred between one investor and another. The secondary markets include stock exchanges and stock markets on a worldwide basis, which provide the marketplace in which local and international securities may be traded. Stock exchanges have a primary market role as well as a secondary market role.

In small, private companies with few shareholders, the mechanism by which shareholders are able to sell or dispose of their shares is quite cumbersome. They first need to find a buyer for their shares – an existing shareholder, or a relative or friend. They next need to obtain a valuation of the business in order to calculate a share price. This usually means that such shares are not easily transferable and this difficulty is usually reflected in a lower share price than if the shares had been easily transferable.

For larger companies with many shareholders this would obviously be impractical, and companies themselves do not hold reserves of cash in order to redeem investors' securities. The secondary market is therefore essential for investors to be able to readily sell their investments, and also for investors to buy additional investments to add to their holdings. This means that securities listed on a stock exchange therefore have a high degree of liquidity, which is reflected in their value. The secondary market also provides a marketplace of investors in which organisations may raise additional long-term finance.

The most important long-term securities, which are traded in the capital markets, were discussed in earlier sections of this chapter, and include:

- ordinary, or equity shares
- preference shares
- long-term loans
- debentures
- bonds
- Eurobonds
- convertible bonds.

Government securities, like gilt-edged securities and UK Treasury bills, are also traded in the capital markets.

Ideally the capital markets should reflect perfectly fair prices of securities; they should aim to be markets that are perfectly efficient. Market efficiency is measured in terms of the amount and quality of market data available to investors and potential investors and their impact on market prices. We discussed the various forms of market efficiency (weak, semi-strong, and strong forms) and the efficient market hypothesis in Chapter 5.

New issues

Initial public offerings (IPOs)

In start-up businesses the ordinary shares are usually owned by the founder(s) of the business, and by family and friends, or possibly by other investors (maybe venture capitalists, seeking a gain in their value as the business develops). As a company grows it may need to make important decisions with regard to:

■ raising further equity share capital, in order to finance its growth, at levels much higher than the founders of the business or their friends and family are willing or able to afford

or

■ offering its shares for sale by making them publicly available and freely traded, to realise gains in their value for the founders or other investors.

The way in which a business may action these decisions is to go from being an unquoted company to a quoted company. It does this by 'going public' – by making an initial public offering (IPO) of shares in the company. This means that shares are offered for sale to the general public and to financial institutions which are then listed and traded on stock exchanges – in the UK, the London Stock Exchange (LSE) or the Alternative Investment Market (AIM – see below). The Public Offer of Securities Regulations 1995 governs the new issue of shares of unlisted companies in the UK.

A company seeking an IPO requires an adviser, sponsor, or broker, for example a merchant bank, to manage the listing process. The responsibilities of the sponsor or broker (which in practice may be the same organisation) include:

■ advice regarding the offer price of the shares

■ the timing of the issue

■ preparing and issuing a prospectus

■ liaising with the stock exchange

■ marketing the share issue to individual and institutional investors.

There is no guarantee that 'going public' with a new share issue will be successful. It very much depends on the current state of the financial markets but also on the company's past record of sales and profitability, and its growth potential, and the credibility and experience of its managers and directors. A company seeking a full listing on the LSE must comply with a number of important criteria, which are included in what's called its Purple Book, the main ones being:

■ an issue of a prospectus that includes financial performance forecasts and other information required by prospective investors

■ a minimum of 25% of the shares must be owned by the public after the listing

■ any controlling shareholder must not interfere with the company's independent decision-making and operations

■ the company must have made sales for at least three years up to the listing date from an independent business activity

■ there should not have been any significant changes in directors and senior managers of the business over the previous three years

■ a minimum market capitalisation of £700,000

■ audited accounts of the company must be provided for the past three years.

Placings and intermediary offers

A company may offer to issue its shares to selected institutional investors like insurance companies and pension funds using a placing. The institutions are approached by the company's sponsor, a merchant bank or stockbroker, prior to the issue taking place when the shares are offered at a fixed price. The company's sponsor underwrites the issue and therefore takes up any unplaced shares. This method also has the advantage of lower costs than other issue methods.

Other institutional and individual investors and the general public are not able to buy shares that have been placed until after the listing and official dealing takes place. Placings are therefore used specifically by companies as a method of issuing their shares to institutions and so the spread of shareholding is narrower than with other share issue methods.

An intermediary offer is effectively the same as a placing, but in this case the shares are placed with financial intermediaries like stockbrokers. The brokers other than the ones advising the company may then receive an allocation of the shares, which they can then distribute to their clients. This method therefore enables a wider spread of the shareholding than a placing.

Offers for sale and issues by tender

If a company is seeking a listing for the first time and it is a large share issue then the issue method used is usually an offer for sale. It is the method that must be used for share issues worth £30m or more. The company's broker and sponsor advise the company about the issue price, which is fixed prior to the offer and needs to be at a level that will attract investors but also at a level sufficient to raise the level of funds required for a given number of shares. The shares are initially sold to the company's sponsor, which is an issuing house like a merchant bank, which also underwrites the issue. This means that they will take up any shares that may not be taken up by institutions and individual investors. The issuing house may also arrange for sub-underwriting of the issue with other financial institutions to ensure that the company receives the funds it requires and to avoid any risk of the issuing house having to take up large numbers of shares itself.

The shares are offered for sale at a fixed price by the issuing house to institutions and individual investors by sending out a prospectus and share application forms. In the UK the prospectus must be published in the national press and must include details of the company's past performance and future expectations and full details about the company as required by the LSE's rules according to the Yellow Book.

An issue by tender is a variation on an offer for sale and may be used as an alternative to an offer for sale. In this case there is no prior fixed share price. Potential investors comprising the general public and institutional investors are invited to bid for shares at any price of their choosing, which is above the minimum share price set and underwritten by the issuing house. A resultant striking price is the price at which the shares are then sold, which is determined by the volume of applications at various prices. The shares on offer are allocated to all the investors who have bid the striking price or higher in order to ensure that all the shares that have been offered are sold. Refunds are paid to those investors whose bids were higher than the striking price.

Issues by tender may be used if it is difficult to establish an appropriate share issue price. However, an issue by tender is the most expensive method of share issue.

Introductions

If a company has a very large and widely spread share ownership where the amount of shares held by the general public is more than 25% (and remains so after the flotation) then a listing may be obtained by a Stock Exchange introduction. No new finance is raised and no new shares in the company are sold. Therefore, an introduction is a method of obtaining a stock exchange listing rather than a method of issuing new shares.

The reasons for a company using a Stock Exchange introduction for a listing are to:

- gain access to the capital markets
- ascertain a market value for its shares
- increase and widen the marketability of the shares.

With a Stock Exchange introduction the shares do not have to be marketed, and do not need to be underwritten. An introduction is therefore the least expensive stock exchange listing method.

Bond issues

There are a number of ways in which debt finance may be raised by companies. Bonds may be issued directly to financial institutions and the public by advertising in the financial press. Alternatively, they may be sold as new issues in the primary market through a merchant bank acting as an issuing house. The company may also request that the bank uses placings (as with equity capital) by allocating bonds with a number of its larger institutional customers prior to the date of issue.

Progress check 7.9

What are the ways in which a company may make a new issue of equity or debt?

The Stock Exchange

A stock exchange is a registered capital market for dealing in securities; it is where the securities of plcs may be bought and sold. The Financial Services Authority (FSA), in its role as the competent authority for listing securities, is referred to as the UK Listing Authority (UKLA), which regulates the London Stock Exchange (LSE) under the Financial Services and Markets Act 2000. The UKLA is responsible for regulating sponsors for new issues and for the listing of all securities and maintaining the Official List. It may also, in exceptional circumstances, suspend listings.

The numbers of new issues of securities (securities being offered for sale by companies for the first time) on the LSE increased again throughout 2005 and 2006 after a slowdown in 2003 and 2004. Although the numbers dropped again in 2006 they recovered to a little below 2005 levels in 2007. They were not yet at the same levels as the late 1990s and early 2000s. The levels of further issues of securities fell successively during 2005, 2006, and 2007 (see Figs. 7.5 and 7.6 below, source: London Stock Exchange).

Year	Public Offer	Placing	Placing and Public Offer	Introduction	Total
2000	26	40	9	19	94
2001	18	21	8	9	56
2002	12	14	7	7	40
2003	3	3	2	7	15
2004	7	8	3	6	24
2005	23	13	7	11	54
2006	20	12	3	6	41
2007	21	17	2	11	51

Figure 7.5 London Stock Exchange new issues of securities for each year from July 2000 to 2007

Year	Public Offer	Placing	Placing and Public Offer	Rights Issues	Share Options	Total
2000	31	119	28	17	303	498
2001	130	94	22	18	243	507
2002	150	86	22	19	241	518
2003	101	54	11	6	155	327
2004	111	68	18	14	223	434
2005	255	58	18	8	193	532
2006	250	53	10	6	149	468
2007	128	61	13	2	134	338

Figure 7.6 London Stock Exchange further issues of securities for each year from July 2000 to 2007

Members of the public and institutions may buy and sell securities, but they may only do so through a member of the LSE. Members of the LSE are firms of stockbrokers, comprising brokers and jobbers, who up to the 1980s conducted transactions face-to-face on the 'floor' of the LSE. Since that time dealing has now become computerised, where the same dealing process takes place using the Stock Exchange Automated Quotations (SEAQ) system that enables securities prices to be displayed by members, which are updated continuously.

The Alternative Investment Market (AIM)

An alternative to the LSE and operated by the LSE is the Alternative Investment Market (AIM). Since 1995 the AIM has been in existence for small companies, with a market capitalisation of less than £100m and typically around £20m, to obtain a listing. The AIM is both a primary and secondary capital market for an organisation's securities. Its advantage is that when companies apply for a listing on the AIM they do not have to have 25% or more shares held in public hands and do not have to report on three or more years trading performance.

Floating on the AIM
'Shearings takes fast lane to market', by David Litterick

Shearings, the holiday company and coach operator, is to join the Alternative Investment Market with a potential value of more than £100m.

The company was founded almost 100 years ago. Although it started out as a coach firm, it has expanded to include hotel breaks and cruises.

It now carries more than 500,000 holiday makers to destinations across the globe every year, specialising in customers over 55.

Shearings has been conducting a strategic review since earlier this year.

Although several trade buyers are thought to have expressed an interest, majority shareholder Bridgepoint Capital is understood to favour a stock market listing.

It is being advised by Baird, the broker.

The company is just one of a handful which said yesterday they intended to float on AIM, giving a further boost to London's junior market.

AIM has played host to 80 new admissions since the start of the year, taking the total to more than 831 companies with a market capitalisation of around £22 billion.

The exchange said it had accounted for about 60pc of new listings in Western Europe last year.

Mat Wootton, deputy head of AIM, said the past six months had seen a strong level of activity in the market, with AIM being particularly attractive because of its light regulatory burden.

It has about 25 companies in the pipeline who have expressed their intention to seek admission. AIM celebrates its ninth birthday this month and Mr Wootton said his ambition for the next year would be to improve the efficiency of the secondary market and attract more international companies to the exchange. But Garry Levin, managing director at Altium, sounded a note of caution.

He said: 'The market is not open for opportunistic companies. The emphasis from fund managers is on quality companies with solid equity growth stories. Only if these are sensibly priced is there an appetite for it.'

Others intending to float include:

- Monkleigh, a new company seeking to develop an integrated event marketing services group
- Libertas Capital, a financial services firm
- US online bookmaker Betonsports
- Plusnet, an internet service provider focusing on broadband services
- Eurocastle Investment, a Guernsey-based investment company dealing primarily in European real estate
- Smallbone, a Devizes-based manufacturer of bespoke kitchens
- Sales technology firm XN Checkout.

However, Wagamama, the Japanese style noodle bar chain, said it was putting its planned initial public offering on hold to pursue discussions with possible-buyers. The company, controlled by private equity firm Graphite Capital, said it had already had a number of approaches. 'We will choose the route that will maximise value for shareholders,' a spokesman said.

© *Daily Telegraph*, 8 June 2004

The holiday company Shearings (see the press extract above) expanded from a coach business to a company providing hotel breaks and cruises to become a company with a value of over £100m. The company carried out a strategic review of its business and considered that its future development may be best served by obtaining a stock market listing on the AIM. The press extract also indicates that at the same time a further 25 companies were also interested in obtaining an AIM listing.

The fact that a company may not have been able to obtain a full listing on the LSE may imply for potential investors that such an investment may be more risky than an investment in a company with a full listing. However, the AIM has proved to be very successful for small, growing businesses, which were typically family-owned or MBOs (management buy-outs), to raise finance and create a market for their shares. The costs of obtaining a listing on the AIM is cheaper than an LSE listing and it provides a means for investors like venture capitalists to realise their investments (see Chapter 18).

Progress check 7.10

What are the roles of the London Stock Exchange and the Alternative Investment Market (AIM) and how do the two institutions differ?

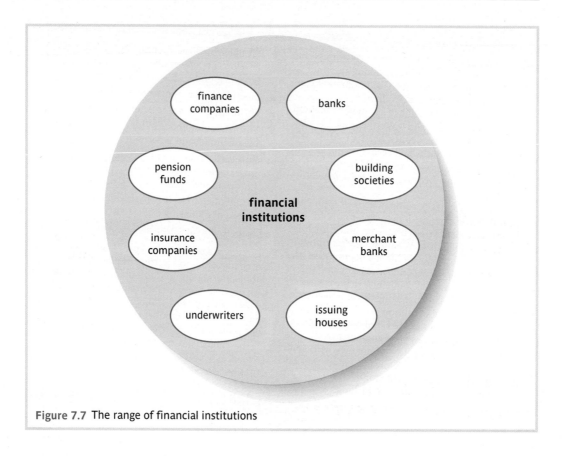

Figure 7.7 The range of financial institutions

Financial institutions

We have already discussed a number of financial institutions when we looked at the various sources of finance and new issues of debt and equity. The range of financial institutions is illustrated in Fig. 7.7.

Banks in the UK are part of the clearing system, which they use to clear cheques for payment and ensure that they are paid out of the payer's account and received by the payee's account. The UK banks provide one or more branches in most towns and cities for a range of banking services, including receiving cheques and cash into current accounts and interest-bearing deposit accounts, and making payments by cash, electronic transfer, mail transfer, Internet etc., or by whatever other means the customer requires.

A company must have a bank in order to process its financial transactions. Few businesses have only one bank and most companies use many banks. Large, multinational companies will have a large number of different banks, not just because of their size but because of their diversity of transactions and dealings. While this may be a necessity and good business practice it does impose an additional burden on the company having to manage such a large number of relationships.

Banks provide a wide range of services for companies, including overdraft facilities, long-term loans, interest and foreign exchange dealing facilities, but also advice and support. Banks do not like surprises and so it is important that good banking relationships are maintained by both small and large businesses. For the development of strong banking relationships it is necessary for the company to be completely open and honest with its bank managers. This requires regular face-to-face meetings and the provision of a regular supply of financial and non-financial information regarding the company's:

■ financial performance

■ financial position

■ strategic plans

■ budgets

■ new investment

■ progress of new projects.

It is important to provide regular information to the bank about bad news as well as good news. It is only from a position of trust that a bank can feel able to give help as necessary to a company should it perhaps encounter a temporary slowdown or a period of continuing recession.

When companies wish to raise new capital through equity or debt then various financial institutions may need to become involved. Loans may be made by banks with, or without, security. Small companies in the UK, for example, are able to obtain unsecured bank loans from banks with Government help in the form of loan guarantees. The main areas of lending by the UK high street retail banks are overdrafts, loans, and mortgages. Over recent years they have taken a large part of the mortgage lending business away from building societies, which were the institutions traditionally used for borrowing for property purchases, in addition to their role themselves as borrowers to provide investors with building society savings accounts. Following deregulation of the financial services sector, building societies also now increasingly provide most of the services provided by banks and so the distinction between themselves and banks is slowly disappearing.

We discussed earlier how issuing houses arrange new issues of equity or debt for companies. Issuing houses are normally merchant banks, which are part of the wholesale banking sector, and who are members of the Issuing Houses Association, which is responsible for Stock Exchange flotations. A merchant bank's role in new issues of equity and debt extends beyond that of acting as an issuing house, by also acting as a broker or adviser to a company in a new issue.

Merchant banks have other roles in addition to their responsibilities in new corporate financing. They are also increasingly active in developing derivatives like options and swaps (see Chapter 12), and providing advice in mergers and acquisitions (M&As) and corporate reorganisations and restructuring, and advice regarding strategic defences against hostile M&As (see Chapters 16, 17, and 18). Merchant banks also have a fund management role in managing the portfolios of investments of other financial institutions like, for example, insurance companies, investment and unit trusts, pension funds, and also some charities. A unit trust is a syndicate established under a trust deed, which pools investors' funds into an investment portfolio, and whose spread of buying and selling price reflects the value of the securities in the portfolio. An investment trust is usually a publicly quoted limited company, which invests in securities, whose share price reflects both the value of the portfolio of securities and the demand for its shares, and which is usually lower than the net asset values.

If a company's new issue is not successful in raising the funds the company requires, then the company may be left with unsold shares. This would be bad news for the company, not only because it will have raised insufficient funds, but because its credibility will have been dented and any subsequent issue will be even more difficult and more expensive. Companies therefore appoint underwriters to take up any shares, or debt, that are not sold during the new issue.

A company is therefore guaranteed to raise the funds required. An underwriter of new issues may be a merchant bank but is more likely to be a pension fund or insurance company.

The growth in the popularity of leasing in the UK up to the mid-1980s saw an increase in the establishment of finance companies, which specialise in various forms of leasing and hire purchase. As we have seen, leases provide the use of assets by lessees over varying periods of time where ownership of the assets remains with the lessor. With a hire purchase agreement legal title passes when the final instalment has been paid. Finance companies also provide a popular means of financing in the retail sector, for example for cars, computers, televisions and DVD recorders, and white goods. The finance companies themselves are generally specialist subsidiaries of banks.

Progress check 7.11

Explain the range of financial institutions that may be used by companies.

Islamic banking and Islamic finance

Over the past few years in the UK and worldwide there has been an increase in the use of Islamic banking, which is broadly based on the teachings of the Qur'an and forbids the charging of interest and engaging in businesses like alcohol and gambling. The first Islamic bank was opened in the early 1960s in Egypt and was called the Savings Bank of Mit Ghmar. In 1970, in the United Arab Emirates, the Dubai Islamic Bank was opened, which is one of the biggest and longest established Islamic banks. Since then, Islamic banks have been established in many other countries with the main centres being Saudi Arabia, Bahrain, Pakistan, and Malaysia.

Many Western banks now provide Islamic banking facilities within their own countries and overseas. Benefits of the Islamic financing system may be seen from its being less dependent on conventional company accounts than traditional systems, and in having a lower volume of documentation with less complexity. The UK's HSBC Amanah, HSBC's Islamic finance division, was launched in 1998. In July 2003 it introduced UK customers to the high street's first Shari'a home purchase scheme and current account. Since that time, HSBC has seen the UK Islamic banking market grow from strength to strength.

Currently, some supporters of Islamic banking feel that it is not growing quickly enough to compete with traditional banking, due mainly to a lack of general awareness and poor communication about its many advantages. However, it is nevertheless an important element of the financial sector. By 2005, Islamic banks worldwide were managing assets totalling about US$300bn. Standard & Poor's have estimated that by the end of 2006 this had risen to US$500bn.

The objective of traditional economics is the efficient allocation of resources while the objective of Islamic economics is the elimination of poverty. This is an important fundamental principle and must be considered whenever a new financial instrument is introduced to justify its existence. Islamic banking is based on economic legislation within the Shari'a, which represents the rules of God that came as a revelation from God to the prophet Mohamed. The sources of the Shari'a are the Qur'an (the Holy Book of Islam), the Sunnah (Ways of the Prophet), and Ijmaa (matters agreed by Islamic scholars), with the Qur'an being the primary influence. Since

Islam represents universality, the ideology of Islamic banking and financial institutions makes them universal institutions with no restrictions regarding locality and nationality. Islamic finance necessarily excludes the areas forbidden by Islamic economic teaching, for example: usury; gambling; speculation; deception; monopoly; extortion. But the focus of Islamic finance is the forbidding of usury and interest. It does this without undermining or contradicting other religions, cultures, economic and financial systems, and prevents injustice by separately identifying what is lawful from what is prohibited.

The Shari'a requires a redistribution of wealth and income to provide every Muslim with a guaranteed fair standard of living. This is achieved from a levy of an Islamic tax called a *zakat*, which each Muslim should calculate individually. The payment of a *zakat* is obligatory on every mentally stable, free, and financially able adult male and female Muslim, to support Muslims who are poor or in need. It is currently interpreted as a 2.5% levy on most valuables and savings held for a full lunar year, provided that the total value is more than a basic minimum known as *nisab* (3 ounces, or 87.48 gram of gold). Islamic banks maintain a *zakat* fund for collecting tax and distributing it to the people that need it either directly or through religious institutions.

The central theme of Islamic economics is the prohibition of *riba*, or interest. This is not dissimilar to the Christian and Jewish faiths that were also against usury, and many leading philosophers, like Aristotle, also rejected usury. Interest has harmful social implications because it encourages the accumulation of more and more money for its own sake rather than to support trade or real investment. Usury is absolutely forbidden by the Islamic faith.

The traditional properties of money are that it is:

- a unit of measurement
- a medium of exchange
- a store of value.

Islamic economists accept the first two properties but do not think of money as a store of value. Islamic economics says that money itself doesn't have a value, but holding it just enables purchases at some time in the future. The Islamic system identifies a number of implications with regard to the charging of interest:

- interest does not reflect real wealth creation and only increases money capital without a similar increase in the supply of goods – Islamic economics requires new capital to come from real commercial activities rather than simply monetary transactions
- interest interferes with markets forces
- prohibition of interest means that non-commercial borrowing is eliminated because lenders have no incentive to lend money
- if the financing of non-commercial activities is eliminated, inflationary pressures are reduced resulting in less volatility and more stability in the value of money
- since public sector borrowing is considered both unjustified and unethical unless it is to acquire physical assets, then current expenditure must be held within available national resources
- if Governments are prohibited from borrowing unlimited funds to meet current expenditure then deficit financing is prevented (in theory)
- if financing is only backed by the assets of commercial transactions then it does not create a debt burden for future generations because assets may be liquidated to repay debt.

In the Islamic economic system, returns are generated through the trading of assets from commercial activities, and are normally shared on a predetermined basis between parties. While Islamic banks aim to safeguard the assets of their clients and maximise investment returns, they are under no obligation to pay fixed returns on deposits or charge clients fixed costs of borrowing. Their primary objectives are:

- attracting funds by providing competitive returns on investment
- promoting economic growth by directing funds to production and commercial activities
- ensuring that investments result in an equitable distribution of wealth, through the provision of ethical and just financial support, and technological and management expertise for value-creating opportunities
- encouraging the emergence and development of entrepreneurs through requiring technical expertise instead of security as the basis for financing, resulting in employment, wealth creation, and growth, but also eliminating the need for large conglomerates
- efficiently providing other banking services to clients that conform with Islamic Shari'a.

Traditional banks exploit market imperfections to maximise shareholder wealth. Islamic banks are only intermediaries, and they provide a balance between the interests of shareholders, depositors, borrowers, and society in general. Islamic banks carry out trust and advisory functions and their client funds are all fiduciary, except for demand deposits. Because of their relationship with their depositors Islamic banks are relatively less risky than traditional banks for a number of reasons:

- deposits other than demand deposits do not count as bank liabilities, therefore they are lower geared than traditional banks
- there is no guarantee of repayment of a loan principal plus a profit
- clients who deposit funds are closely involved in its operations, so if there is an economic downturn the bank is unlikely to experience a run on deposits
- direct lending does not take place – loans are made in the form of prepayments and so there is no impact on debt to equity and debt to assets ratios.

This is all very different from traditional banking systems, which normally have the following disadvantages:

- constraints placed on customers because of their liabilities and gearing levels
- reserves not always sufficient to avoid a run on a bank because its liabilities are short term, whereas a large proportion of its assets are longer term
- repayment of a loan principal plus a return guaranteed at a future date, which are both therefore liabilities of the bank, and therefore the lender takes a risk that the bank's assets will provide sufficient value to make repayment at the maturity date.

Islamic banks are organised and operate in line with all appropriate company legislation that applies wherever they are operational. They are organised with a board of directors to which the chief executive and management committee report, but also an audit committee and a religious board, which is the ultimate authority. Each operation, documentation, product, and service is submitted to the Shari'a board by the bank's management for approval before they may be used or offered to clients. The religious board therefore has mandatory power to ensure that all operations, products, services, and documentation comply fully with Islamic Shari'a.

Because Islamic banks prohibit interest, they are expected to undertake activities only on the basis of various types of profit and loss sharing arrangement. The following financial instruments principally comprise two of the main pillars of Islamic banking:

Mudaraba (trust financing)

This is an agreement made between two parties: one provides 100% of the capital for the project and another party, known as the *modarib*, manages the project using his entrepreneurial skills. Profits arising from the project are distributed according to a pre-determined ratio but are not guaranteed. Any losses are borne by the provider of capital, who has no control over the management of the project.

Musharaka (partnership financing)

This is a financing technique involving a partnership between two parties who both provide capital towards the financing of a project. Both parties share profits based on a pre-agreed ratio, but losses are shared on the basis of equity participation. Management of the project may be carried out by both the parties or by just one party. This is a very flexible partnership arrangement where the sharing of the profits and management can be negotiated and pre-agreed by all parties.

The *mudaraba* concept has been expanded in practice to include three parties:

- the depositor as financier
- the bank as an intermediary
- the entrepreneur who requires funds.

When the bank receives funds from depositors it acts as an entrepreneur. When the bank provides funds to entrepreneurs it acts as financier. The bank therefore operates a two-tier system in which it acts with regard to both savings and the investment portfolio. For the depositors, an Islamic bank manages their funds to generate profits subject to the rules of *mudaraba*. The bank may then use the depositors' funds on a *mudaraba* basis in addition to other methods of financing, including mark-up, lease purchase, and benevolent loans (see below).

Both the *mudaraba* and *musharaka* comply fully with Islamic principles and are the main ways in which funds flow out of the banks. However, there are other important methods of uses of funds applied by Islamic banks, which include the following.

Istisna'a (manufacturing)

Istisna'a is a contract for purchase of goods by specification or order, where the price is paid progressively in accordance with the progress of completion of a job. It is used, for example, for the purchases of houses to be constructed where the payments made to the developer or builder are based on the stage of work completed. In the case of *bai al salam* (described below) the full payment is made in advance to the seller before delivery of goods.

Bai al Salam

Bai al salam is a contract for the purchase of goods, where the price is paid in advance and the goods are delivered in the future.

Murabaha (mark-up or cost plus financing)

This is a contract of sale for a profit and loss sharing arrangement between the bank and its client for the sale of goods at a price that includes a profit margin agreed by both parties. As a financing technique it involves the purchase of goods by the bank as requested by its client. The goods are sold to the client with a mark-up. Repayment, usually in instalments, is specified in the contract.

Bai bithaman ajil

This contract refers to the sale of goods on a deferred payment basis. Equipment or goods which have been requested by a client, are bought by the bank, which subsequently sells the goods to the client at an agreed price that includes the bank's mark-up (profit). The client may be allowed to settle by instalments within a pre-agreed period, or in a lump sum. *Bai bithaman ajil* is a credit sale and similar to a *murabaha* contract.

Qard ul hasan (a benevolent or good loan)

Qard ul hasan is an interest-free, benevolent loan that is given either for welfare purposes or for bridging short-term funding requirements. The borrower is required to pay back only the amount borrowed.

Ijara (leasing)

Ijara is a contract under which the bank buys and leases equipment to a client for an agreed rental and an agreed duration. Ownership of the equipment remains in the hands of the bank.

Ijara wa-iqtina (lease/hire purchase)

Ijara wa-iqtina is very similar to *ijara*, except that it is agreed in advance that the client commits to buy the equipment from the bank at an agreed price at the end of the lease period. The rental fees that have been paid constitute part of the price.

Sukuk

One of the most widely used Islamic financial instruments is the *sukuk*, which is effectively the Islamic equivalent of a traditional bond.

Sukuks are securities that comply with the Shari'a and its investment principles, which prohibits the charging, or paying of interest. Shari'a requires that financing should only be raised for trading in, or construction of, specific and identifiable assets. Trading in 'indebtedness' is prohibited and so the issue of traditional fixed income, interest-bearing bonds would not be compliant.

Originally, *sukuk* referred to any document representing a contract or conveyance of rights, obligations or monies done in conformity with Shari'a. It is believed that the *sukuk* was extensively used during medieval Islam for the transferring of financial obligations originating from trade and other commercial activities. In today's Islamic finance, the essence of the *sukuk* is in the concept of asset monetisation, or securitisation achieved through the process of issuing a *sukuk*. *Sukuks* are structured in parallel with the acquisition of a physical asset. Revenue streams from, for example, roads, airports, seaports, utilities, new buildings, power plants, and oil facilities are used to pay a profit on the *sukuk*. All *sukuk* returns and cashflows are linked to assets purchased or those generated from an asset once constructed and not simply considered as income that is interest based. A *sukuk* may be issued on existing assets as well as assets that may become available at a future date.

Shari'a-compliant products must be approved by a Shari'a scholar certified for issuing a *fatwa* (Islamic decree). There are currently apparently fewer than 20 scholars with such skills worldwide, which therefore increases the time taken to approve products like *sukuks*. Currently most *sukuks* are bought and held, and so to date there has tended not to be an active secondary market.

In addition to the HSBC, many Western banks, including Deutsche Bank, Barclays Capital and Citi, are all involved in Islamic banking. BNP Paribas has recently completed the second largest *sukuk* issue in Saudi Arabia for the Saad Trading Contracting and Financial Services Company. BNP Paribas acted as sole managing underwriter for the US$650m, 5-year *sukuk*. It was also the first *sukuk* issued in Saudi Arabia for a private business.

According to Standard & Poor's, London – as one of the major financial hubs to handle Islamic transactions – has become the sole non-Muslim competitor of natural Islamic markets in Dubai, Kuala Lumpur, and Bahrain. The UK government demonstrated its commitment in the 2007 budget by introducing new measures for *sukuks*, enabling them to be issued, held and traded in the same way as corporate bonds.

The above Islamic financial instruments are contracts on which commercial transactions may be based. International transactions normally use letters of credit, as do traditional banks. The difference is that the Islamic banks own the goods until full payment is received from the importer during which time the importer is given rights for the clearing of goods or products as agreed in the contract. Islamic banks actually deal with the goods whereas traditional banks only deal with documents. In cases of default, Islamic banks are in a much better legal position to recover losses since title has not yet passed on to the importer so they are better able to control credit. In traditional banking legal title to goods would have been passed to the importer, and so recovery of losses would depend on security or insurance cover.

Islamic banks have their own capital and rely on two main sources of funds:

- transaction deposits, which are free of risk but yield no return
- investment deposits, which carry the risks of capital loss in exchange for the promise of variable returns.

There are four main types of Islamic bank account:

- current accounts – depositors are guaranteed repayment of their funds, but they do not receive a return because the funds will not be used for profit and loss sharing ventures as these funds can only be used to balance the liquidity needs of the bank
- savings accounts – depositors earn an income, which is a premium paid by the bank at its discretion, dependent on the bank's financial results
- investment accounts – the provider of the funds, the *mudarib* or active partner, has absolute freedom in the management of the investment. Investment accounts are different from savings accounts because:
  - they have a higher fixed minimum amount of deposit
  - they have a longer duration of deposit,
  and most importantly
  - the depositor may lose some of or all their funds should the bank make losses
- special investment accounts – the depositors are usually large investors or institutions, and the accounts operate under the *mudaraba* principle. The differences between these accounts and investment accounts are that:
  - the funds are related to specific projects
  - investors have the choice to invest directly in projects carried out by the bank.

Because the relationship with their depositors is based on profit sharing, Islamic banks need to have fuller financial disclosure than traditional banks. The development of accounting standards for Islamic banks has therefore been of paramount importance. In the early 1990s a set of published accounting guidelines was established by the Accounting and Auditing Organisation for Islamic Financial Institutions (AAOIFI), which has up until 2007 issued 56 standards on accounting, auditing, governance, ethical, and Shari'a compliance, including a statement on capital adequacy. These standards are either mandatory or used as a guideline by the regulators in countries like Bahrain, Sudan, Jordan, Malaysia, Qatar, Saudi Arabia, United Arab Emirates, Lebanon, and Syria, and their widespread use continues to increase.

We have seen that there are a number of advantages and benefits provided by Islamic banking. However, it should be noted that there are also a number of issues and challenges faced by the Islamic banking system because it has:

- no lender of last resort
- highly liquid positions maintained by most banks
- no secondary capital market
- no conventional money markets
- little product innovation
- no pricing benchmark other than LIBOR or local equivalent (which is used only as an indicator rather than an interest rate).

Progress check 7.12

What are the major differences between traditional banking and Islamic banking, and what are their similarities?

Summary of key points

- Sources of finance internal to a company are its retained earnings, extended credit from suppliers, and the benefits gained from the more effective management of its working capital.

- Short-term, external sources of finance include overdrafts and short-term loans, which are used primarily to fund companies' working capital requirements.

- The main sources of long-term, external finance available to a company are equity (ordinary shares), preference shares, and debt (loans and debentures).

- Long-term finance is used to fund new businesses, companies that wish to 'go public', and to fund the acquisition of long-term non-current assets and new investment projects.

- Equity (ordinary shares) and debt (loans) have a number of unique characteristics and rights. For example, ordinary shares receive dividends and votes at the AGM, and loans receive interest and have no votes at the AGM.

- Dividends form part of the wealth of shareholders and are an important method of giving money back to shareholders, as are rights issues and share buy-backs.

- There is a range of debt finance available to companies, for example, loans, debentures, and bonds, which may be redeemable at a specific date, or irredeemable and never have to be repaid.

- As internationalisation increases there is a growing importance of international debt finance and the use of Eurobonds.

- Hybrid finance is neither purely debt nor equity, and includes convertible preference shares, convertible bonds, warrants, and mezzanine debt.

- Other sources of long-term, external finance available to UK companies include leasing, which companies may use as a source of long- and short-term finance, and UK Government and European funding.

- The primary capital markets are markets in which new equity and debt capital is initially raised by companies from investors.

- There are many methods that companies may use to issue new equity and debt finance.

- Stock exchanges, and in the UK the London Stock Exchange and the Alternative Investment Market (AIM) comprise the secondary capital markets.

- Financial institutions: banks; merchant banks; pension funds; insurance companies; finance companies, each play an important role in corporate financing.

- Islamic banking, as an alternative to traditional Western-style banking, is a fast-growing element of the financial sector, and Western banks have now established Islamic banking facilities within their own countries and overseas.

🔑 Glossary of key terms

bond A debt instrument, normally offering a fixed rate of interest (coupon) over a fixed period of tine, and with a fixed redemption value (par).

convertible bond A loan which gives the holder the right to convert to other securities, normally ordinary shares, and at a predetermined price and time.

debenture The written acknowledgement of a debt by a company, usually given under its seal, and normally containing provisions as to payment of interest and the terms of repayment of principal. A debenture may be secured on some or all of the assets of the company or its subsidiaries.

Eurobond A Eurobond is a type of bearer bond, which is a negotiable bond whose ownership is not registered by the issuer, but is presumed to lie with whoever has the physical possession of the bond. Specifically, a Eurobond is issued in a currency other than the currency of its country of issue, usually Eurodollars.

finance lease A lease is a contract between a lessor and a lessee for the hire of a specific asset. The lessor retains ownership of the asset but gives the right to the use of the asset to

▶

▶ the lessee for an agreed period in return for the payment of specified rentals (SSAP 21). A finance lease transfers substantially all the risks and rewards of ownership of the asset to the lessee.

hybrid finance A financial instrument that has the characteristics of both debt and equity.

initial public offering (IPO) The process by which a company may obtain a listing on a stock exchange. An IPO is a company's first public sale of its shares. Shares offered in an IPO are often, but not always, those of young, small companies seeking outside equity capital and a public market for their shares. Investors purchasing shares in IPOs generally must be prepared to accept considerable risks for the possibility of large gains.

intermediary offer An intermediary offer is effectively the same as a placing (see below), but in this case the shares are placed with financial intermediaries like stockbrokers.

introduction A Stock Exchange introduction may be used to obtain a listing, rather than issue new shares, if a company has a very large and widely spread share ownership where the amount of shares held by the general public is more than 25% (and remains so after the flotation).

Islamic banking A banking system based on economic legislation within the Shari'a, which represents the rules of God that came as a revelation from God to the prophet Mohamed.

Islamic finance Islamic finance focuses on the forbidding of usury and interest. It also excludes the areas forbidden by Islamic economic teaching, for example: usury; gambling; speculation; deception; monopoly; extortion.

issue by tender An issue by tender is a variation and alternative to an offer for sale (see below), where there is no prior fixed share price. The general public and institutional investors are invited to bid for shares at any price above the minimum share price set and underwritten by the issuing house. The shares on offer are then allocated at the striking price, which is determined by volume of applications at various prices, to all investors who have bid the striking price or higher ensuring that all shares that have been offered are sold.

mezzanine debt A non-traded debt which has risk and return characteristics somewhere between debt and equity, and attracts a high rate of interest. It is unsecured debt finance with a higher level of risk than that of loans with security, but lower than ordinary shares, and lower on the list of priority payments than straight debt.

offer for sale An invitation by a party other than the company itself to apply for shares in the company based on information contained in a prospectus.

operating lease A lease is a contract between a lessor and a lessee for the hire of a specific asset. The lessor retains ownership of the asset but gives the right to the use of the asset to the lessee for an agreed period in return for the payment of specified rentals (SSAP 21). An operating lease is a lease other than a finance lease, where the lessor retains most of the risks and rewards of ownership.

ordinary share Shares which entitle the holders to the remaining divisible profits (and, in a liquidation, the assets) after prior interests, for example creditors and prior charge capital, have been satisfied.

placing A method of raising capital in which there is no public issue of the shares or bonds. Instead they are issued in 'blocks' to individual investors or institutions who have previously agreed to purchase at a predetermined price.

preference share Shares carrying a fixed rate of dividend, the holders of which, subject to the conditions of issue, have a prior claim to any company profits available for distribution. Preference shares may also have a prior claim to the repayment of capital in the event of a winding up.

rights issue The raising of new capital by giving existing shareholders the right to subscribe to new shares or debentures in proportion to their current holdings. These shares are usually issued at a discount to the market price. A shareholder not wishing to take up a rights issue may sell the rights.

scrip issue (or bonus issue) The capitalisation of the reserves of a company by the issue of additional shares to existing shareholders, in proportion to their holdings. Such shares are normally fully paid-up with no cash called for from the shareholders.

share re-purchase (or share buy-back) An arrangement where a company buys its own shares on the stock market. UK companies may purchase their own shares so long as the shareholders have given permission in a general meeting of the company. It is a way of returning cash to shareholders. The number of shares in issue decreases and so the earnings per share increases as does the value of the shares.

striking price See issue by tender above.

warrant A financial instrument that requires the issuer to issue shares (whether contingently or not) and contains no obligation for the issuer to transfer economic benefits (FRS 4).

Questions

Q7.1 What are retained earnings and why are they an important source of corporate internal finance?

Q7.2 (i) What are the main sources of long-term, external finance available to an organisation?
(ii) What are their advantages and disadvantages?

Q7.3 Describe the key characteristics of ordinary share capital and the rights of ordinary shareholders.

Q7.4 Explain the various types of preference shares and their uses.

Q7.5 Describe the key characteristics of debt capital the rights of debt holders.

Q7.6   Why in recent years have Eurobonds become an important source of international finance?

Q7.7   What are the advantages and disadvantages of convertible loans and warrants to companies and investors?

Q7.8   Why may leasing be considered as a long-term source of finance?

Q7.9   Why may the shareholders of a private limited company seek a listing on the Stock Exchange, and in what circumstances should they consider the AIM as an alternative?

Q7.10 Explain the various roles of merchant banks in the areas of corporate finance and fund management.

Discussion points

D7.1   The ex-owner/manager of a private limited company recently acquired by a large plc, of which he is now a board member, said: 'This company has grown very quickly over the past few years so that our turnover is now over £20m per annum. Even though we expect our turnover to grow further and double in the next two years I cannot see why we need to change our existing financing arrangements. I know we need to make some large investments in new machinery over the next two years but in the past we've always operated successfully using our existing overdraft facility, which has been increased as required, particularly when we've needed new equipment. I don't really see the need for all this talk about additional share capital and long-term loans.' Discuss.

D7.2   'The growth in the use of various forms of hybrid finance has complicated the financing process, and has provided no real benefit to companies or investors.' Discuss.

D7.3   'The only gain I can see from the use of leasing for our company is that it is a method of off balance sheet financing.' Discuss.

D7.4   Discuss the factors that an international company should consider in the raising of international debt capital and in determining its debt policy.

D7.5   'All banks operate using the same rules and regulations.' Discuss.

Exercises

Solutions are provided in Appendix 2 to all exercise numbers highlighted in colour.

Level I

E7.1   *Time allowed – 30 minutes*

Vine plc is a UK retail company that has been trading successfully for a number of years. The management of the company has, however, become increasingly concerned because there has been a substantial reduction in the company's bank balance for the year ending 31 December 2006, even though the company has continued to generate profits.

The Vine plc financial statements for 2005 and 2006 are as follows:

Income statement for the year ended 31 December

	2005 £000	2006 £000
Turnover	7,000	9,000
Cost of sales	(3,500)	(4,200)
Gross profit	3,500	4,800
Operating expenses	(1,400)	(2,100)
Profit before tax	2,100	2,700
Taxation	(1,000)	(1,000)
Profit after tax	1,100	1,700
Dividends	(600)	(700)
Retained profit for the year	500	1,000

Balance sheet as at 31 December

	2005 £000	2006 £000
Non-current assets	3,800	6,500
less Depreciation	(1,700)	(1,400)
	2,100	5,100
Current assets		
Stocks	3,200	4,200
Trade debtors	2,800	5,100
Other debtors	900	500
Bank and cash	1,500	100
	8,400	9,900
Current liabilities		
Trade creditors	2,000	3,000
Other creditors	500	500
Taxation	1,000	1,000
Dividends	600	700
	4,100	5,200
Long-term liabilities		
Debentures	(2,000)	(3,800)
	4,400	6,000
Capital		
Share capital	2,000	2600
Profit and loss account	2,400	3400
	4,400	6000

Required:
Vine plc's retained profits have increased in 2006 compared with 2005 but to what extent has the business generated sufficient retained earnings to provide the financing it may require for the internal funding of new investment projects in the near future? Provide the appropriate analysis to support your explanation about the retained earnings of the company.

E7.2 *Time allowed – 30 minutes*
Lamarr plc is an established UK based manufacturing company, which currently generates profits of 16% on shareholders' funds. The company's current capital structure is as follows:

▶

▶

	£
Ordinary Shares (£1)	400,000
Share premium account	175,000
Profit and loss account	225,000
	800,000

The company is currently expanding its European operations and is considering raising £200,000 from a rights issue to fund a new investment project. As a result of its investment the company expects its return on total shareholders' funds to increase to an average of 16.5%. The current ex-dividend market price of Lamarr plc's shares is £2.20. The finance director of Lamarr plc has suggested three alternative prices for the rights issue:

£2.00

£1.80

£1.60

Required:

Which rights issue share price should Lamarr plc use if the company wishes to maximise its eps?

Level II

E7.3 *Time allowed – 45 minutes*

The directors of Emlyn plc are considering three methods of raising external finance of £5.5m by issuing either:

(a) 6% unsecured bonds at par

(b) new ordinary shares by a one for four rights issue at an issue price of £2.20 per share

(c) 7% preference shares of £1 at par.

The current share price at 18 December 2006 is £2.50. The income statement for the year to 30 September 2006 and balance sheet as at 30 September 2006 are shown below.

Income statement for the year ended 30 September 2006

	£m	£m
Turnover		45.5
Cost of sales		(29.6)
Gross profit		15.9
Distribution costs	3.1	
Administrative expenses	1.4	
		(4.5)
Operating profit		11.4
Net interest		(2.0)
Profit before tax		9.4
Tax		(3.3)
Profit after tax		6.1
Dividends		(3.8)
Retained earnings		2.3

Balance sheet as at 30 September 2006

	£m
Non-current assets	26.7
Current assets	29.9
Current liabilities (less than one year)	
Bank overdraft	(6.3)
Other creditors	(13.2)
Net current assets	10.4
Total assets less current liabilities	37.1
less	
Long-term liabilities (over one year)	
4% debentures	(13.5)
Net assets	23.6
Capital and reserves	
Ordinary shares 50p	5.0
Share premium account	3.9
Profit and loss account	14.7
	23.6

Required:

Evaluate each of the sources of external finance that are being considered by Emlyn plc and recommend which should be used by the company, ignoring issue costs. You should clearly state any assumptions that you make.

E7.4   *Time allowed – 45 minutes*

Globe plc has issued share capital of 500,000 £1 ordinary shares, and the current share price is £3.80, in a market in which there is currently a general upward movement in share prices. Globe plc's eps have been increasing at a relatively stable rate and were reported at 50p in the most recent annual report and accounts. Globe plc is planning to redeem £400,000 5% redeemable bonds by making a one for four rights issue of ordinary shares. However, the company does not want to dilute its eps by more than 12%. The company also wants the rights issue shares to be priced around 10% below the current share price. The company's rate of corporation tax is 35%.

Required:

(i)   How many shares would be required and what is the lowest market price at which the company would consider making the issue?

(ii) In theory what would be the resultant ex rights price of the shares, and the corresponding P/E (price earnings) ratio?

(iii) Outline the reasons generally why a company may prefer to make a rights issue of ordinary shares as a way of raising new capital rather than long-term debt, and explain whether there are circumstances in which a resulting dilution of earnings per share would be acceptable to shareholders.

E7.5   *Time allowed – 45 minutes*

Recently Wiltel plc issued £5m of convertible 8% debenture. The debentures have a nominal value of £100 and a current market value of £106. An interest payment was recently made. The debentures will be convertible into equity shares in three years' time at a rate of four shares per £10 debenture. The shares are expected to have a market value of £3.50

▶ each at that time, and all the debenture holders are expected to convert their debentures. You may assume that Wiltel plc pays an average rate of corporation tax of 25%, and tax savings occur in the same year as the interest payments.

Required:
Calculate the cost of capital of the convertible debenture.

E7.6 *Time allowed – 45 minutes*

(i) Distinguish between the nature and functions of the primary and secondary capital markets, and illustrate with examples.

(ii) Comment briefly on the suggestion that there is not enough new investment generally in industry because funds are otherwise used for speculation in secondary markets.

(iii) Explain the role of financial intermediaries as the financial institutions that help overcome the problems in ensuring that funds are put into economically desirable projects, by explaining the nature of the problems, the ways in which financial institutions help to overcome them, and why the large size of such financial institutions may be so beneficial.

E7.7 *Time allowed – 45 minutes*
The board of Nimrod plc, a medium-sized UK based retail company, is seeking to raise additional equity finance. They are not sure about which market they should seek a listing – the London Stock Exchange, or the Alternative Investment Market (AIM).

Required:
Explain the advantages and disadvantages of a market listing, and the differences between a listing on the London Stock Exchange and a listing on the AIM.

E7.8 *Time allowed – 45 minutes*
Curtis E. Carr & Co specialises in hiring out executive-type cars. It is expanding its operations and is currently seeking to acquire a new fleet of four new cars. Purchase of the fleet of cars would cost the company £150,000. Alternatively, leasing the cars would cost the company £30,000 per annum for seven years. If the fleet of cars is purchased it is estimated that the net residual value after seven years would be £5,000. Curtis E. Carr & Co currently has a cost of capital of 10%.

Required:
(i) Calculate and compare the costs of purchase and leasing.
(ii) Advise Curtis E. Carr & Co with regard to lease or purchase and identify the additional factors that should be considered and their potential impact on this decision.

Chapter 8

Financial analysis

Chapter contents

LEARNING OBJECTIVES

Completion of this chapter will enable you to:

☑ Carry out a performance review of a business, including the use of SWOT analysis.

☑ Identify the limitations of the performance review process.

☑ Differentiate between divisional manager performance measurement and economic performance measurement.

☑ Analyse business performance through the use of ratio analysis of profitability; efficiency; liquidity; investment; financial structure.

☑ Use both profit and cash flow in the measurement of business performance.

☑ Identify the relationship between return on equity (ROE), return on assets (ROA), and gearing, using the Du Pont system of ratios.

☑ Carry out a horizontal analysis of the income statement and the balance sheet.

☑ Carry out a vertical analysis of the income statement and the balance sheet.

☑ Interpret the information provided by segmental reporting.

☑ Compare the use of cash flow versus profit as the best measure in the evaluation of financial performance.

☑ Use earnings before interest, tax, depreciation, and amortisation (EBITDA) as a close approximation of a cash flow performance measure.

☑ Explain the use of economic value added (EVA™) and market value added (MVA) as performance measures.

☑ Outline some of the multivariate discriminant analysis (MDA) methods of predicting corporate financial failure.

Introduction

This chapter is concerned with how the performance of a business may be reviewed through analysis and evaluation of the balance sheet, the income statement, and the cash flow statement. Business performance may be considered from outside or within the business for a variety of reasons. The performance review process provides an understanding of the business which, together with an analysis of all the relevant information, enables interpretation and evaluation of its financial performance during successive accounting periods and its financial position at the end of those accounting periods.

The chapter begins with an outline of the steps involved in the performance review process and also considers the limitations of such a process. The main body of this chapter is concerned with ratio analysis. Financial ratio analysis looks at the detailed use of profitability, efficiency, liquidity, investment, and financial structure ratios in the evaluation of financial performance. We also look at three further tools of analysis. Horizontal analysis, or common size analysis, provides a line-by-line comparison of the accounts of a company (income statement and balance sheet) with those of the previous year. Vertical analysis considers each item in the income statement and balance sheet, which are expressed as a percentage of, for example, total sales and net assets (or total equity). Segmental reporting by large companies discloses information by each class of business, and by geographical region. Segmental analysis provides users of financial information with much more meaningful financial analysis of companies, which are comprised of diverse businesses supplying different products and services, rather than being engaged in a single type of business.

There is an ongoing debate as to whether cash flow or profit represents the best basis for financial performance measurement. The use of earnings per share (eps) and cash flow in performance measurement are discussed along with the measurement of earnings before interest, tax, depreciation, and amortisation (EBITDA) as an approximation of cash flow. Economic value added (EVA™) has become increasingly important in its use by companies as a performance measure, being an even closer approximation of a cash flow.

The chapter closes with an outline of some of the methods of multivariate discriminant analysis (MDA) that have been developed to try and predict corporate financial failure.

The performance review process

The availability of accurate and timely accounting and financial information is very important in support of the corporate finance function. Analyses of accounting and financial information is of interest to the various stakeholders of companies, both internal and external to the organisations, and for a variety of reasons. For example, shareholders, lenders, suppliers, customers, and banks are interested in analysing a company's financial performance and position from the perspective of safeguarding their interests and ensuring that objectives are being met with regard to their own particular requirements.

At the strategic level, a company will be interested in analysing:

- its own financial performance
- the performance of other companies.

Companies' annual and interim reports and accounts, which include their financial statements, provide a wealth of financial and non-financial information. The reasons for the analysis by a company of the performance of other companies may be to determine:

- the financial stability of potential new suppliers
- the financial health of customers
- the financial policies and cost structures of its competitors
- identification of possible takeover targets
- valuation of shares of Ltd companies
- valuation of companies in mergers and acquisitions,

and banks and other financial institutions will be particularly interested in using financial analysis to try and predict corporate failure and identify companies that may represent a poor lending risk.

A performance review and analysis by the company of it own accounting, financial, and non-financial information may be undertaken for a number of reasons, for example to:

- support the planning and budgeting process
- assist in investment decisions
- monitor manager performance against targets
- monitor company performance against standards
- identify areas where there is room for improvement
- assist in the management of working capital
- support the cash management and treasury function.

The main aim of a performance review is to provide an understanding of the business, and, together with an analysis of all the relevant information, provide an interpretation of the results. A performance review is generally undertaken using a standard format and methodology. The most effective performance review is provided from a balanced view of each of the activities of the organisation, which necessarily involves the close cooperation of each role: marketing; research and development; design; engineering; manufacturing; sales; logistics; finance; human resources management.

The performance review process begins with a SWOT analysis and works through a number of steps to the conclusions, as outlined in Fig. 8.1. A SWOT analysis includes an internal analysis of the company, and an analysis of the company's position with regard to its external environment.

SWOT is shorthand for strengths, weaknesses, opportunities, and threats. The first look at a company's performance usually involves listing the key features of the company by looking internally at its particular strengths and weaknesses, and externally at risks or threats to the

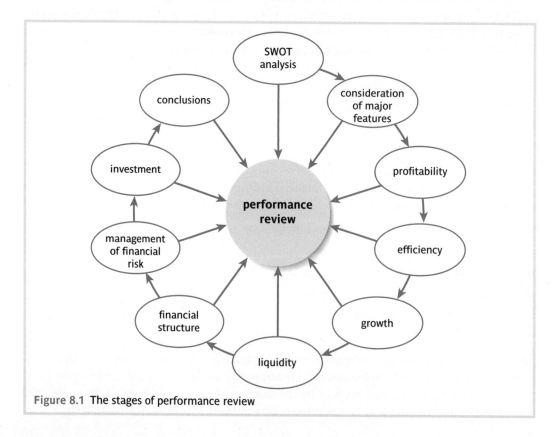

Figure 8.1 The stages of performance review

STRENGTHS Market share Part of a large diversified group	**WEAKNESSES** Slow product development Products designed not easy to manufacture
OPPORTUNITIES European joint ventures Market share of Japanese manufacturers	**THREATS** Japanese transplant manufacturers European economic recession

Figure 8.2 An example of a SWOT analysis

company and opportunities that it may be able to exploit. The SWOT analysis may give some indication of, for example, the strength of the company's management team, how well it is doing on product quality, and areas as yet untapped within its marketplace.

To keep the analysis focused, a cruciform chart may be used for SWOT analysis. An example is outlined in Fig. 8.2, relating to a UK subsidiary of a French multinational company in the 1990s which manufactured components for supply to automotive manufacturers.

The consideration of major features relates to the increasing amount of information now provided in published financial statements, which enables the analyst to look in detail at the various industrial and geographical sectors of the business, the trends within these and the business in general. Further background information may be extracted from the accounting policies, the auditors' report, chairman's report and details of any significant events that have been highlighted.

Profitability and investment performance may be assessed by considering a number of financial indicators and ratios of the company, which include:

- ROCE (return on capital employed), or ROI (return on investment)
- return on sales (ROS)
- gross margin to sales
- asset turnover
- earnings per share (eps)
- dividend cover
- dividend yield
- price earnings ratio (P/E).

The efficiency of the company may be considered in terms of:

- its operating cycle – its debtor days, creditor days, and stock days
- its operating gearing
- vertical analysis of its income statement.

In a vertical analysis of the income statement (which may also be applied to the balance sheet) each item is expressed as a percentage of the total sales. The vertical analysis provides evidence of structural changes in the accounts such as increased profitability through more efficient production.

Growth of the organisation may relate to sales growth and gross margin growth. Horizontal analysis, or common size analysis, of the income statement allows a line-by-line analysis of the accounts compared with those of the previous year. It may provide a trend of changes over a number of years showing either growth or decline in these elements of the accounts by calculating annual percentage growth rates in profits, sales, stock, or any other item.

Liquidity is concerned with the short-term solvency of the company. It is assessed by looking at a number of key ratios:

- current ratio
- acid test
- defensive interval
- cash ROCE
- cash interest cover.

The financial structure aspects of performance review are concerned with how the company is financed with regard to the long-term solvency of the company. It is assessed by looking at a number of other key ratios:

- gearing – the proportion of capital employed financed by lenders rather than shareholders, expressed in a number of ways, for example the debt/equity ratio (long-term loans and preference shares/ordinary shareholders' funds)
- dividend cover (eps/dividend per share)
- interest cover (profit before interest and tax (PBIT)/interest payable)
- various forms of off balance sheet financing.

Off balance sheet financing is defined as the funding or refinancing of a company's operations in such a way that, under legal requirements and existing accounting conventions, some or all of the finance may not be disclosed in its balance sheet. The Accounting Standards Board (ASB) has tried (and continues to try) to introduce recommendations for the inclusion of this type of financing.

Management of financial risk is concerned with how companies now increasingly trade multinationally, in an increasingly global market, with greater levels of sophistication in products, operations, and finance. Risk assessment and the management of risk are therefore now assuming increasing importance. The main areas of financial risk are the areas of investment, foreign currency exchange rates and interest rates, and levels of trade credit.

Investment ratios examine whether or not the company is undertaking sufficient investment to ensure its future profitability. These ratios include, for example:

- capital expenditure/sales
- capital expenditure/depreciation
- capital expenditure/gross non-current assets.

The conclusions of the performance review will include consideration of the company's SWOT analysis and the main performance features. They will consider growth and profitability and whether or not this is maintainable, as well as levels of finance and investment, and whether there is sufficient cash flow, and the future plans of the business.

All performance reviews must use some sort of benchmark. Comparisons may be made against past periods and against budget; they may also be made against other companies and using general data relating to the industry within which the company operates. Later in this chapter we will look in more detail at the use of profitability, efficiency, liquidity, and investment ratios, and ratios relating to financial structure.

> **Progress check 8.1**
>
> Describe each of the stages in a business performance review process.

Limitations of the performance review process

There are many obvious limitations to the above approach. In comparing performance against other companies (and sometimes within the company in comparing past periods), or looking at industrial data, it should be borne in mind that:

- each item in a balance sheet, except for cash and bank items, is a matter of opinion and not fact
- each item in an income statement is a matter of opinion and not fact
- there may be a lack of uniformity in accounting definitions and techniques
- the balance sheet is only a snapshot in time, and only represents a single estimate of the company's position
- there may actually be no standards for comparison
- changes in the environment and changes in money values, together with short-term fluctuations, may have a significant impact
- the past should really not be relied on as a good predictor of the future.

Diversified companies present a different set of problems. Such companies by their very nature are comprised of companies engaged in various industrial sectors, each having different market conditions, financial structures, and expectations of performance. The notes to the accounts, which appear in each company's annual report and accounts, invariably present a less than comprehensive picture of the company's position.

As time goes by, and accounting standards and legislation get tighter and tighter, the number of loopholes which allow any sort of window dressing of a company's results are reduced. Inevitably, however, there will always remain the possibility of the company's position being presented in ways that may not always represent the 'truth'. We will now look at the type of information that may be used and the important financial ratios and their meaning and relevance.

> **Progress check 8.2**
>
> What are the main limitations encountered in carrying out the performance review of a business?

Economic performance measurement

Most large organisations are divided into separate divisions in which their individual managers have autonomy and total responsibility for investment and profit. Within each division there is usually a functional structure comprising many departments. Divisionalisation is more appropriate for companies with diversified activities. The performance of the managers of each division may be measured in a number of ways, for example return on investment (ROI) and residual income (RI).

The relationships between divisions should be regulated so that no division, by seeking to increase its own profit, can reduce the profitability of the company as a whole. Therefore, there are strong arguments for producing two broad types of performance measure. One type of measure is used to evaluate managerial performance and the other type of measure is used to evaluate economic performance. In the current chapter, rather than divisional performance measurement, we are primarily concerned with the performance of the organisation as a whole. We will look at ratios that measure economic performance, which focus not only on profit and profitability, but on a range of other areas of performance that include, for example, cash and working capital.

Ratio analysis

The reasons for a performance review may be wide and varied. Generally, it is required to shed light on the extent to which the objectives of the company are being achieved. The company's primary objective is of course the maximisation of shareholder wealth. Further corporate objectives in support of the primary objective may include:

- earning a satisfactory return on capital employed (ROCE)
- maintaining and enhancing the financial position of the business with reference to the management of working capital, non-current assets and bank borrowings
- achieving cost targets and other business targets such as improvements in labour productivity.

Ratio analysis is an important area of performance review. It is far more useful than merely considering absolute numbers, which on their own may have little meaning. Ratios may be used:

- for a subjective assessment of the company or its constituent parts
- as a more objective way to aid decision-making
- to provide **cross-sectional analysis** and **inter-firm comparison**
- to establish models for loan and credit ratings
- to provide equity valuation models to value businesses
- to analyse and identify under-priced shares and takeover targets
- to predict company failure.

As we saw in our examination of the performance review process, the key ratios include the following categories:

- profitability
- efficiency
- liquidity
- investment
- financial structure.

Flatco plc
Balance sheet as at 31 December 2007

Figures in £000

	2007	2006
Non-current assets		
Intangible	416	425
Tangible	1,884	1,921
Financial	248	248
	2,548	2,594
Current assets		
Stocks	311	268
Debtors	573	517
Prepayments	589	617
Cash	327	17
	1,800	1,419
Current liabilities (less than one year)		
Financial debt	50	679
Creditors	553	461
Taxation	50	44
Dividends	70	67
Accruals	82	49
	805	1,300
Net current assets	995	119
Total assets		
less current liabilities	3,543	2,713
less		
Non-current liabilities (over one year)		
Financial debt	173	–
Creditors	154	167
	327	167
less		
Provisions	222	222
Net assets	2,994	2,324
Capital and reserves		
Share capital	1,200	1,000
Share premium account	200	200
Retained earnings	1,594	1,124
	2,994	2,324

Figure 8.3 Flatco plc balance sheet as at 31 December 2007

We will use the financial statements of Flatco plc, an engineering company, shown in Figs. 8.3 to 8.9, to illustrate the calculation of the key financial ratios. The income statement and cash flow statement are for the year ended 31 December 2007 and the balance sheet as at 31 December 2007. Comparative figures are shown for 2006.

Profitability ratios

We may assume that in general the managers of a business accept that the primary objective is to maximise the wealth, in line with objectives of the owners of the business. To this end there are a number of other objectives, subsidiary to the main objective. These include:

Flatco plc
Income statement for the year ended 31 December 2007

Figures in £000

		2007		2006
Turnover				
Continuing operations		3,500		3,250
Discontinued operations		–		–
		3,500		3,250
Cost of sales		(2,500)		(2,400)
Gross profit		1,000		850
Distribution costs	(300)		(300)	
Administrative expenses	(155)		(160)	
Other operating costs				
Exceptional items: redundancy costs	(95)		–	
		(550)		(490)
Other operating income		100		90
Operating profit				
Continuing operations	550		450	
Discontinued operations	–		–	
		550		450
Income from other fixed asset investments		100		80
Profit before interest and tax		650		530
Net interest		(60)		(100)
Profit before tax		590		430
Tax on profit on ordinary activities		(50)		(44)
Profit on ordinary activities after tax		540		386
Dividends		(70)		(67)
Retained profit for the financial year		470		319

Additional information
Authorised and issued share capital 31 December 2007, 1,200,000 £1 ordinary shares
(1,000,000 in 2006).
Total assets less current liabilities 31 December 2005, £2,406,000.
Trade debtors 31 December 2005, £440,000.
Market value of ordinary shares in Flatco plc 31 December 2007, £2.75 (£3.00, 2006).
Tangible fixed assets depreciation provision 31 December 2007, £1,102,000 (£779,000, 2006)

Figure 8.4 Flatco plc income statement for the year ended 31 December 2007

- survival
- stability
- growth
- maximisation of market share
- maximisation of sales
- maximisation of profit
- maximisation of return on capital.

Each group of financial ratios is concerned to some extent with survival, stability, growth, and maximisation of shareholder wealth. We will first consider ratios in the broad area of profitability (see Fig. 8.10), which give an indication of how successful the business has been in its achievement of the wealth maximisation objective.

Flatco plc
Cash flow statement for the year ended 31 December 2007
Reconciliation of operating profit to net cash flow operating activities

Figures in £000

	2007	2006
Operating profit	550	450
Depreciation charges	345	293
Increase in stocks	(43)	(32)
Increase in debtors and prepayments [−573 + 517 − 589 + 617]	(28)	(25)
Increase in creditors and accruals [553 − 461 + 82 − 49 + 154 −167]	112	97
Net cash inflow from operating activities	936	783

Figure 8.5 Reconciliation of operating profit to net cash flow from operating activities

Cash flow statement

Figures in £000

	2007	2006
Net cash inflow from operating activities	936	783
Returns on investments and servicing of finance (note 1)	40	(20)
Taxation	(44)	(40)
Capital expenditure (note 1)	(299)	(170)
	633	553
Equity dividends paid	(67)	(56)
	566	497
Management of liquid resources (note 1)	–	–
Financial (note 1)	373	290
Increase in cash	939	787

Figure 8.6 Cash flow statement

Reconciliation of net cash flow to movement in net debt (note 2)

Figures in £000

	2007	2006
Increase in cash for the period	939	787
Cash inflow from increase in long-term debt	(173)	–
Change in net debt	766	787
Net debt at 1 January [17 − 679 − 0]	(662)	(1,449)
Net funds/net debt at 31 December [327 − 50 − 173]	104	(662)

Figure 8.7 Reconciliation of net cash flow to movement in net debt

Note 1 to the cash flow statement – gross cash flows

Figures in £000

	2007	2006
Returns on investments and servicing of finance		
Income from investments	100	80
Interest received	11	–
Interest paid	(71)	(100)
	40	(20)
Capital expenditure		
Payments to acquire tangible non-current assets	(286)	(170)
Payments to acquire intangible non-current assets	(34)	–
Receipts from sales of tangible non-current assets	21	–
	(299)	(170)
Management of liquid resources		
Purchase of treasury bills	(200)	–
Sale of treasury bills	200	–
	–	–
Financing		
Issue of ordinary share capital	200	300
Debenture loan	173	–
Expenses paid in connection with share issues	–	(10)
	373	290

Figure 8.8 Note 1 – gross cash flows

Note 2 to the cash flow statement – analysis of change in net debt/funds

Figures in £000

	At 1 January 2007	Cash flows	At 31 December 2007
Cash in hand and at bank	17	310	327
Overdraft	(679)	629	(50)
Debenture	–	(173)	(173)
Total (debt)/funds	(662)	766	104

	At 1 January 2006	Cash flows	At 31 December 2006
Cash in hand and at bank	–	17	17
Overdraft	(1,449)	770	(679)
Total (debt)/funds	(1,449)	787	(662)

Figure 8.9 Note 2 – analysis of change in net debt/funds

$$\text{gross margin \%} = \frac{\text{gross margin}}{\text{sales}} = \frac{\text{sales} - \text{cost of sales (COS)}}{\text{sales}}$$

This is used to gain an insight into the relationship between production/purchasing costs and sales revenues. The gross margin needs to be high enough to cover all other costs incurred by the company, and leave an amount for profit. If the gross margin percentage is too low then sales prices may be too low, or the purchase costs of materials or production costs may be too high.

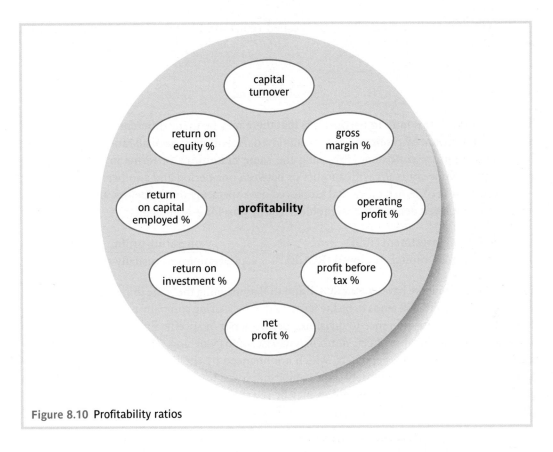

Figure 8.10 Profitability ratios

$$\text{operating profit } \% = \frac{\text{operating profit}}{\text{sales}} = \frac{\text{sales} - \text{COS} - \text{other operating expenses}}{\text{sales}}$$

The operating profit (or PBIT excluding other operating income) ratio is a key ratio that shows the profitability of the business before incurring financing costs. If the numerator is not multiplied by 100 to give a percentage, it shows the profit generated by each £1 of turnover.

$$\text{profit before tax (PBT) } \% = \frac{\text{profit before tax}}{\text{sales}} = \frac{\text{operating profit} +/- \text{net interest}}{\text{sales}}$$

This is the profit ratio that uses profit after financing costs, that is, having allowed for interest payable and interest receivable. It should be remembered that profit before tax (PBT) is a profit measure that goes further than dealing with the trading performance of the business, and because it allows for financing costs it provides an indication of pre-tax profit-earning capability from the sales for the period, given the company's financial structure.

$$\text{net profit } \% = \frac{\text{net profit}}{\text{sales}} = \frac{\text{profit before tax (PBT)} - \text{corporation tax}}{\text{sales}}$$

This is the final profit ratio after allowing for financing costs and corporation tax. The net profit (or profit after tax (PAT), or earnings, or net income (NI)), or return on sales (ROS) ratio is the profit available for distribution to shareholders in the form of dividends and/or future investment in the business.

We will next look at generally what is called return on capital employed, which may be expressed as:

$$\frac{\text{profit}}{\text{capital employed}}$$

The problem with this ratio in particular is that there may be many different interpretations of exactly what is meant by profit and capital employed. As with the use of all ratios, it is extremely important to ensure consistency by using the same definitions of terms in comparing the performance of one company with another or between one period and another.

One definition of return on capital employed uses operating profit (before interest and tax) and capital employed defined as shareholders' equity plus long-term debt.

$$\text{return on investment (ROI)} \atop \text{or return on capital employed (ROCE) \%} = \frac{\text{operating profit}}{\text{capital employed (usually averaged)}}$$

In the above formula we have shown ROCE and ROI as meaning the same thing. From experience we have found that ROCE tends to be the term used in measuring company performance, whereas ROI may be used with reference to divisional performance or specific investment projects.

In a company's balance sheet, non-current assets plus working capital (current assets less current liabilities) are the net assets, which are financed by the long-term funding of shareholders' equity plus long-term debt – the capital employed by the company. Non-current assets plus current assets less current liabilities may be rewritten as total assets less current liabilities. Therefore another way of representing ROI or ROCE is:

$$\text{return on investment (ROI)} \atop \text{or return on capital employed (ROCE) \%} = \frac{\text{operating profit}}{\text{total assets – current liabilities (usually averaged)}}$$

Capital employed may be total capital employed at the end of the year or it may be the average for the year. Similarly, total assets less current liabilities may be a total or it may be averaged.

This form of return on capital employed (using operating profit) compares income with the operational assets used to generate that income. Profit is calculated before financing costs and tax. This is because the introduction of interest charges introduces the effect of financing decisions into an appraisal of operating performance, and also tax levels are decided by external agencies (governments), and are therefore to a large extent costs that are uncontrollable.

The average cost of the company's finance (equity, debentures, loans), weighted according to the proportion each element bears to the total pool of capital, is called WACC, the weighted average cost of capital. The difference between a company's ROI and its WACC is an important measure of the extent to which the organisation is endeavouring to optimise its use of financial resources. In their 1999 annual report, Tomkins plc reported on the improvement in their ROI versus WACC gap and stated that 'to be successful a company must consistently deliver a return on investment (ROI) above its weighted cost of capital (WACC) and must actively manage both variables'. A company manages its ROI through monitoring its operating profit as a percentage of its capital employed. A company manages its WACC by planning the proportions of its financing through either equity (ordinary shares) or debt (loans), with regard to the relative costs of each, dividends, and interest (see Chapter 6).

In looking at acquisitions the importance of WACC is emphasised in the Tomkins plc 1999 annual report: 'Tomkins' strategy is to focus on strategic business activities and within this only to make acquisitions which add to shareholder value by enhancing earnings in the first year and deliver an ROI above the WACC hurdle rate (internal cost of capital) within three years.' This refers to the importance of WACC as a factor used in the evaluation of investment in projects undertaken (or not) by a business.

Another form of return on capital employed ratio is:

$$\text{return on assets (ROA)} = \frac{\text{profit after tax} + \text{interest}}{\text{total assets}}$$

In the above formula the total assets may be the value at the end of the year or may be the average for the year. Interest is added back to the profit before tax number in order to consider profitability that is not a function of the company's capital structure. However, it should be noted that this ROA measure is misleading if it is used to compare companies that have different capital structures. If two companies are geared differently then they will have different levels of interest payments and tax shields. If an operating performance comparison is required of such companies then variations on the above formula may be used.

Another form of return on capital employed, return on equity (ROE), measures the return to the owners on the book value of their investment in a company.

$$\text{return on equity (ROE)} = \frac{\text{profit after tax}}{\text{equity}}$$

This return on capital is measured using the profit earned after all expenses and charges have been made, and the equity is comprised of share capital and reserves.

We will return to ROA and ROE later in this chapter when we look at the linking of ratios in what is referred to as the Du Pont system of ratios.

$$\text{capital turnover} = \frac{\text{sales}}{\text{average capital employed in year}}$$

Capital turnover expresses the number of times that capital employed is turned over in the year, or alternatively the sales generated by each £1 of capital employed. This ratio will be affected by asset additions that may have taken place throughout a period but have not impacted materially on the performance for that period. Further analysis may be required to determine the underlying performance.

The profitability performance measures discussed above consider the general performance of organisations as a whole. It is important for managers also to be aware of particular areas of revenue or expenditure that may have a significant importance with regard to their own company and that have a critical impact on the net profit of the business. Companies may, for example:

■ suffer large warranty claim costs

■ have to pay high royalty fees

■ receive high volumes of customer debit notes (invoices) for a variety of product or service problems deemed to be the fault of the supplier.

All managers should fully appreciate such key items of cost specific to their own company and be innovative and proactive in identifying ways that these costs may be reduced and minimised.

Managers should also be aware of the general range of costs for which they may have no direct responsibility, but nevertheless may be able to reduce significantly by:

- improved communication
- involvement
- generation of ideas for waste reduction, increased effectiveness and cost reduction.

Such costs may include:

- the cost of the working capital operating cycle
- costs of warehouse space
- project costs
- costs of holding stock
- depreciation (as a result of capital expenditure)
- warranty costs
- repairs and maintenance
- stationery costs
- telephone and fax costs
- photocopy costs.

The relative importance of these costs through their impact on profitability will of course vary from company to company.

Worked Example 8.1

We will calculate the profitability ratios for Flatco plc for 2007 and the comparative ratios for 2006, and comment on the profitability of Flatco plc.

Gross margin, GM

$$\text{gross margin \% 2007} = \frac{\text{gross margin}}{\text{sales}} = \frac{£1{,}000 \times 100\%}{£3{,}500} = 28.6\%$$

$$\text{gross margin \% 2006} = \frac{£850 \times 100\%}{£3{,}250} = 26.2\%$$

Profit before interest and tax, PBIT

$$\text{PBIT \% 2007} = \frac{\text{PBIT}}{\text{sales}} = \frac{£650 \times 100\%}{£3{,}500} = 18.6\%$$

$$\text{PBIT \% 2006} = \frac{£530 \times 100\%}{£3{,}250} = 16.3\%$$

Net profit, PAT (return on sales, ROS)

$$\text{PAT \% 2007} = \frac{\text{net profit}}{\text{sales}} = \frac{£540 \times 100\%}{£3{,}500} = 15.4\%$$

$$\text{PAT \% 2006} = \frac{£386 \times 100\%}{£3{,}250} = 11.9\%$$

Return on capital employed, ROCE (return on investment, ROI)

$$\text{ROCE \% 2007} = \frac{\text{operating profit}}{\text{average capital employed in year}} = \frac{£550 \times 100\%}{(£3,543 + £2,713)/2}$$

$$= \frac{£550 \times 100\%}{£3,128}$$

$$= 17.6\%$$

$$\text{ROCE \% 2006} = \frac{£450 \times 100\%}{(£2,713 + £2,406)/2} = \frac{£450 \times 100\%}{£2,559.5} = 17.6\%$$

Return on equity, ROE

$$\text{ROE \% 2007} = \frac{\text{PAT}}{\text{equity}} = \frac{£540 \times 100\%}{£2,994} = 18.0\%$$

$$\text{ROE \% 2006} = \frac{£386 \times 100\%}{£2,324} = 16.6\%$$

Capital turnover

$$\text{capital turnover 2007} = \frac{\text{sales}}{\text{average capital employed in year}} = \frac{£3,500 \times 100\%}{£3,128} = 1.1 \text{ times}$$

$$\text{capital turnover 2006} = \frac{£3,250 \times 100\%}{£2,559.5} = 1.3 \text{ times}$$

Report on the profitability of Flatco plc

Sales for the year 2007 increased by 7.7% over the previous year, partly through increased volumes and partly through higher selling prices.

Gross margin improved from 26.2% to 28.6% of sales, as a result of increased selling prices but also lower costs of production.

PBIT improved from 16.3% to 18.6% of sales (and operating profit improved from 13.8% to 15.7%). If the one-off costs of redundancy of £95,000 had not been incurred in the year 2007 operating profit would have been £645,000 (£550,000 + £95,000) and the operating profit ratio would have been 18.4% of sales, an increase of 4.6% over 2006. The underlying improvement in operating profit performance (excluding the one-off redundancy costs) was achieved from the improvement in gross margin and from the benefits of lower distribution costs and administrative expenses.

ROCE was static at 17.6% because the increase in capital employed as a result of additional share capital of £200,000 and long-term loans of £173,000 was matched by a similar increase in operating profit.

Return on equity increased from 16.6% to 18%, despite the increase in ordinary share capital. This was because of improved profit after tax (up 3.5% to 15.4%) arising from increased income from fixed asset investments and lower costs of finance. Corporation tax was marginally higher in 2007 than 2006.

Capital turnover for 2007 dropped to 1.1 times from 1.3 times in 2006. The new capital introduced into the company in the year 2007 to finance major new projects is expected to result in significant increases in sales levels over the next few years, which will see improvements in capital turnover over and above 2006 levels.

Progress check 8.3

How may financial ratio analysis be used as part of the process of review of business performance?

Efficiency ratios

The regular monitoring of efficiency ratios by companies is crucial because they relate directly to how effectively business transactions are being converted into cash. For example, if companies are not regularly paid in accordance with their terms of trading:

- their profit margins may be eroded by the financing costs of funding overdue accounts
- cash flow shortfalls may put pressure on their ability to meet their day-to-day obligations to pay employees, replenish stocks, etc.

Despite the introduction of legislation to combat slow payment of suppliers, the general situation in the UK is poor in comparison with other European countries (see the following extract from *Accountancy Age*).

Companies that fail to pay suppliers on time
'Late payment costs UK companies £20bn', by Damian Wild

UK businesses could be losing up to £20bn every year in unpaid invoices, according to a report out today.

Intrum Justitia's UK Payment Index estimates that almost half (47%) of UK invoices are overdue – on average 18 days late – and 1.9% of total revenues are never paid at all.

The credit management service provider said the results of the survey clearly illustrated that payment delays put British businesses at risk. The increasing debt-to-income ratios significantly reduced profitability for companies – particularly SMEs who are vulnerable to variations in cash flow and often rely on a limited number of customers, it said.

Compared with Europe, the UK ranked poorly for payment delays, according to the company. The average 18 day UK payment delay is two days longer than in Ireland or the EU.

The research also reveals that UK creditors believe that one of the principal reasons for late payment is a deliberate decision on the part of debtors to use them as a 'source of free finance'. Another key reason cited was 'debtors' financial problems'.

'The consequence of payment delays on the public purse is also worrying – the UK government could be losing up to £10bn each year in lost VAT and corporation tax – the equivalent of the entire UK transport budget,' the report found.

© *Accountancy Age*, 26 June 2004

The range of efficiency ratios is illustrated in Fig. 8.11.

Efficiency generally relates to the maximisation of output from resources devoted to an activity or the output required from a minimum input of resources. Efficiency ratios measure the efficiency with which such resources have been used.

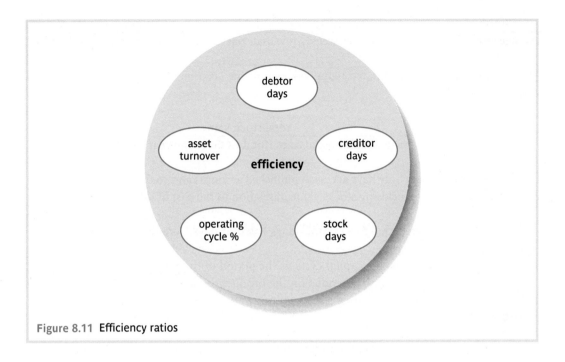

Figure 8.11 Efficiency ratios

$$\text{debtor days} = \frac{\text{trade debtors} \times 365}{\text{sales}}$$

Debtor days indicate the average time taken, in calendar days, to receive payment from credit customers. Adjustment is needed if the ratio is materially distorted by VAT (or other taxes). This is because sales invoices to customers, and therefore trade debtors (accounts receivable), include the net sales value plus VAT. However, sales are reported net of VAT. To provide a more accurate ratio, VAT may be eliminated from the trade debtors' figures as appropriate. (Note: for example, export and zero-rated sales invoices, which may be included in debtors, do not include VAT and so an adjustment to total trade debtors by the standard percentage rate for VAT may not be accurate.)

$$\text{creditor days} = \frac{\text{trade creditors} \times 365}{\text{cost of sales (or purchases)}}$$

Creditor days indicate the average time taken, in calendar days, to pay for supplies received on credit. For the same reason, as in the calculation of debtor days, adjustment is needed if the ratio is materially distorted by VAT or other taxes.

$$\text{stock days} = \frac{\text{stock value}}{\text{average daily cost of sales in period}}$$

Stock days (or stock turnover) are the number of days that stocks could last at the forecast or most recent usage rate. This may be applied to total stocks, finished goods, raw materials, or work in progress. The weekly internal efficiency of stock utilisation is indicated by the following ratios:

$$\frac{\text{finished goods}}{\text{average weekly despatches}} \qquad \frac{\text{raw materials}}{\text{average weekly raw material usage}} \qquad \frac{\text{work in progress}}{\text{average weekly production}}$$

These ratios are usually calculated using values but may also be calculated using quantities where appropriate.

$$\text{stock weeks} = \frac{\text{total stock value}}{\text{average weekly cost of sales (total COS for the year divided by 52)}}$$

Financial analysts usually only have access to published accounts and so they often use the stock weeks ratio using the total closing stocks value in relation to the cost of sales for the year.

$$\text{operating cycle (days)} = \text{stock days} + \text{debtor days} - \text{creditor days}$$

The operating cycle, or working capital cycle, is the period of time which elapses between the point at which cash begins to be expended on the production of a product or service, and the collection of cash from the customer. The operating cycle may alternatively be calculated as a percentage using:

$$\text{operating cycle \%} = \frac{\text{working capital requirement (stocks} + \text{debtors} - \text{creditors)}}{\text{sales}}$$

$$\text{asset turnover (times)} = \frac{\text{sales}}{\text{total assets}}$$

Asset turnover measures the performance of the company in generating sales from the assets under its control. The denominator may be the total assets at the end of the year or alternatively the average total assets for the year.

Worked Example 8.2

We will calculate the efficiency ratios for Flatco plc for 2007 and the comparative ratios for 2006, and comment on the working capital performance of Flatco plc.

Debtor days

$$\text{debtor days 2007} = \frac{\text{trade debtors} \times 365}{\text{sales}} = \frac{\pounds573 \times 365}{\pounds3,500} = 60 \text{ days}$$

$$\text{debtor days 2006} = \frac{\pounds517 \times 365}{\pounds3,250} = 58 \text{ days}$$

Creditor days

$$\text{creditor days 2007} = \frac{\text{trade creditors} \times 365}{\text{cost of sales}} = \frac{\pounds553 \times 365}{\pounds2,500} = 81 \text{ days}$$

$$\text{creditor days 2006} = \frac{\pounds461 \times 365}{\pounds2,400} = 70 \text{ days}$$

Stock days (stock turnover)

$$\text{stock days 2007} = \frac{\text{stock value}}{\text{average daily cost of sales in period}} = \frac{£311}{2,500/365}$$

$$= 45 \text{ days (6.5 weeks)}$$

$$\text{stock days 2006} = \frac{£268}{£2,400/365} = 41 \text{ days (5.9 weeks)}$$

Operating cycle days

$$\text{operating cycle 2007} = \text{stock days} + \text{debtor days} - \text{creditor days}$$
$$= 45 + 60 - 81 = 24 \text{ days}$$

$$\text{operating cycle 2006} = 41 + 58 - 70 = 29 \text{ days}$$

Operating cycle %

$$\text{operating cycle \% 2007} = \frac{\text{working capital requirement}}{\text{sales}}$$

$$= \frac{(£311 + £573 - £553) \times 100\%}{£3,500} = 9.5\%$$

$$\text{operating cycle \% 2006} = \frac{(£268 + £517 - £461) \times 100\%}{£3,250} = 10.0\%$$

Asset turnover

$$\text{asset turnover 2007} = \frac{\text{sales}}{\text{total assets}} = \frac{£3,500}{£4,348} = 0.80 \text{ times} \qquad [2,548 + 1,800]$$

$$\text{asset turnover 2006} = \frac{£3,250}{£4,013} = 0.81 \text{ times} \qquad [2,594 + 1,419]$$

Report on the working capital performance of Flatco plc

The major cash improvement programme introduced late in the year 2007 began with the implementation of new cash collection procedures and a reinforced credit control department. This was not introduced early enough to see an improvement in the figures for the year 2007. Average customer settlement days actually worsened from 58 to 60 days.

The purchasing department negotiated terms of 90 days with a number of key large suppliers. This had the effect of improving the average creditors' settlement period from 70 to 81 days.

A change in product mix during the latter part of the year 2007 resulted in a worsening of the average stock turnover period from 41 to 45 days. This is expected to be a temporary situation. An improved just in time (JIT) system and the use of vendor managed inventory (VMI) with two main suppliers in the year 2008 are expected to generate significant improvements in stock turnover.

Despite the poor stock turnover, the operating cycle improved from 29 days to 24 days (operating cycle % from 10.0% to 9.5%). Operating cycle days are expected to be zero or better by the end of year 2008.

Asset turnover dropped from 0.81 in 2006 to 0.80 times in the year 2007. The new capital introduced into the company in 2007 to finance major new projects is expected to result in significant increases in sales levels over the next few years, which will see improvements in asset turnover over and above 2006 levels.

Progress check 8.4

What do the profitability and efficiency ratios tell us about the performance of a business?

Liquidity ratios

The degree to which assets are held in a cash or near-cash form is determined by the level of obligations that need to be met by the business. Liquidity ratios (see Fig. 8.12) reflect the health or otherwise of the cash position of the business and its ability to meet its short-term obligations.

$$\text{current ratio (times)} = \frac{\text{current assets}}{\text{current liabilities}}$$

The current ratio is an overall measure of the liquidity of the business. It should be appreciated that this ratio will be different for different types of business. For example, an automotive manufacturer may have a higher ratio because of its relatively high level of stock (mainly work in progress) compared with a supermarket retailer which holds a very high percentage of fast-moving stocks and has no trade debtors.

$$\text{acid test (times)} = \frac{\text{current assets} - \text{stocks}}{\text{current liabilities}}$$

The acid test (or quick ratio) indicates the ability of the company to pay its creditors in the short term. This ratio may be particularly meaningful for supermarket retailers because of the speed with which their stocks are converted into cash.

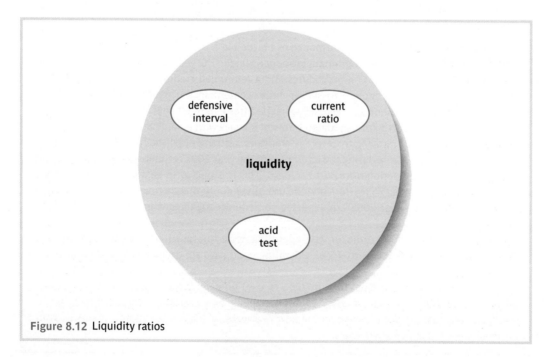

Figure 8.12 Liquidity ratios

$$\text{defensive interval (days)} = \frac{\text{quick assets (current assets} - \text{stocks)}}{\text{average daily cash from operations}}$$

The defensive interval shows how many days a company could survive at its present level of operating activity if no further inflow of cash were received from sales or other sources.

Worked Example 8.3

We will calculate the liquidity ratios for Flatco plc for 2007 and the comparative ratios for 2006, and comment on the liquidity of Flatco plc.

Current ratio

$$\text{current ratio 2007} = \frac{\text{current assets}}{\text{current liabilities}} = \frac{£1,800}{£805} = 2.2 \text{ times}$$

$$\text{current ratio 2006} = \frac{£1,419}{£1,300} = 1.1 \text{ times}$$

Acid test (quick ratio)

$$\text{quick ratio 2007} = \frac{\text{current assets} - \text{stocks}}{\text{current liabilities}} = \frac{£1,800 - £311}{£805} = 1.8 \text{ times}$$

$$\text{quick ratio 2006} = \frac{£1,419 - £268}{£1,300} = 0.9 \text{ times}$$

Defensive interval

$$\text{defensive interval 2007} = \frac{\text{quick assets}}{\text{average daily cash from operations}}$$
$$\text{(opening debtors + sales} - \text{closing debtors)}/365$$

$$= \frac{£1,800 - £311}{(£517 + £3,500 - £573)/365} = 158 \text{ days}$$

$$\text{defensive interval 2006} = \frac{£1,419 - £268}{(£440 + £3,250 - £517)/365} = 132 \text{ days}$$

Report on the liquidity of Flatco plc
Net cash flow from operations improved from £783,000 in 2006 to £936,000 in 2007. Investments in non-current assets were more than covered by increases in long-term finance in both years. Therefore, the operational cash flow improvement was reflected in the net cash flow of £939,000 (£787,000 in 2006).

The improved cash flow is reflected in increases in the current ratio (1.1 to 2.2 times) and the quick ratio (0.9 to 1.8 times). The increase in the defensive interval from 132 to 158 days has strengthened the position of the company against the threat of a possible downturn in activity.

Although there has been a significant improvement in cash flow, the increase in investment in working capital is a cause for concern. Actions have already been taken since the year-end to try and maximise the returns on investment: reduction in stock levels (noted above); further reductions in trade debtors and prepayments; investment of surplus cash in longer term investments.

Progress check 8.5

What are liquidity ratios and why are they so important?

Investment ratios

Investment ratios (see Fig. 8.13) generally indicate the extent to which the business is undertaking capital expenditure to ensure its survival and stability, and its ability to sustain current revenues and generate future increased revenues.

$$\text{earnings per share} = \frac{\text{profit after tax} - \text{preference share dividends}}{\text{number of ordinary shares in issue}}$$

Earnings per share, or eps, measures the return per share of earnings available to shareholders. The eps of companies may be found in the financial pages sections of the daily press.

$$\text{dividend per share} = \frac{\text{total dividends paid to ordinary shareholders}}{\text{number of ordinary shares in issue}}$$

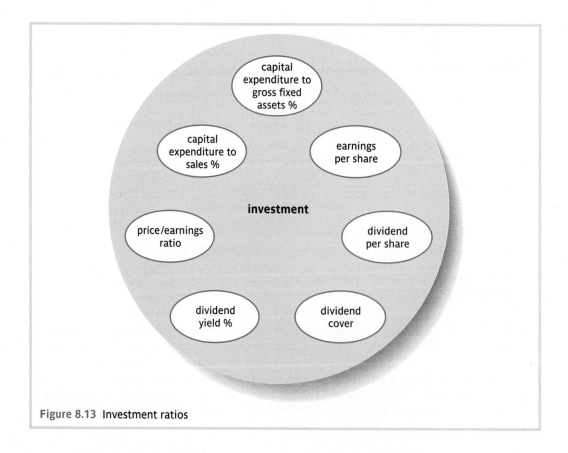

Figure 8.13 Investment ratios

Dividend per share is the total amount declared as dividends per each ordinary share in issue. It is the dividend per share actually paid in respect of the financial year. The amount must be adjusted if additional equity shares are issued during the financial year.

$$\text{dividend cover} = \frac{\text{earnings per share}}{\text{dividend per share}}$$

This shows the number of times the profits attributable to equity shareholders cover the dividends payable for the period. It also indicates the level of earnings retained by the company, its retention ratio.

$$\text{dividend yield \%} = \frac{\text{dividend per share}}{\text{share price}}$$

The dividend yield shows the dividend return on the market value of the shares, expressed as a percentage.

$$\text{price/earnings (P/E) ratio} = \frac{\text{current share price}}{\text{eps}}$$

The price/earnings or P/E ratio shows the number of years it would take to recoup an equity investment from its share of the attributable equity profit. The P/E ratio values the shares of the company as a multiple of current or prospective earnings, and therefore gives a market view of the quality of the underlying earnings.

$$\text{capital expenditure to sales \%} = \frac{\text{capital expenditure for year}}{\text{sales}}$$

This ratio gives an indication of the level of capital expenditure incurred to sustain a particular level of sales.

$$\text{capital expenditure to gross non-current assets \%} = \frac{\text{capital expenditure for year}}{\text{gross value of tangible non-current assets}}$$

This is a very good ratio for giving an indication of the replacement rate of new for old non-current assets.

Worked Example 8.4

We will calculate the investment ratios for Flatco plc for 2007 and the comparative ratios for 2006, and comment on the investment performance of Flatco plc.

Earnings per share, eps

$$\text{eps 2007} = \frac{\text{profit after tax} - \text{preference share dividends}}{\text{number of ordinary shares in issue}} = \frac{£540,000}{1,200,000} = 45p$$

$$\text{eps 2006} = \frac{£386,000}{1,000,000} = 38.6p$$

▶

Dividend per share

$$\text{dividend per share 2007} = \frac{\text{total dividends paid to ordinary shareholders}}{\text{number of ordinary shares in issue}}$$

$$= \frac{£70,000}{1,200,000} = 5.8\text{p per share}$$

$$\text{dividend per share 2006} = \frac{£67,000}{1,000,000} = 6.7\text{p per share}$$

Dividend cover

$$\text{dividend cover 2007} = \frac{\text{earnings per share}}{\text{dividend per share}}$$

$$= \frac{45\text{p}}{5.8\text{p}} = 7.8\text{ times}$$

$$\text{dividend cover 2006} = \frac{38.6\text{p}}{6.7\text{p}} = 5.8\text{ times}$$

Dividend yield %

$$\text{dividend yield 2007} = \frac{\text{dividend per share}}{\text{share price}}$$

$$= \frac{5.8\text{p} \times 100\%}{£2.75} = 2.11\%$$

$$\text{dividend yield 2006} = \frac{6.7\text{p} \times 100\%}{£3.00} = 2.23\%$$

Price/earnings ratio, P/E

$$\text{P/E ratio 2007} = \frac{\text{current share price}}{\text{eps}} = \frac{£2.75}{45\text{p}} = 6.1\text{ times}$$

$$\text{P/E ratio 2006} = \frac{£3.00}{38.6\text{p}} = 7.8\text{ times}$$

Capital expenditure to sales %

$$\text{capital expenditure to sales 2007} = \frac{\text{capital expenditure for year}}{\text{sales}} = \frac{£286 \times 100\%}{£3,500} = 8.2\%$$

$$\text{capital expenditure to sales 2006} = \frac{£170 \times 100\%}{£3,250} = 5.2\%$$

Capital expenditure to gross non-current assets %

capital expenditure to gross non-current assets 2007 =

$$\frac{\text{capital expenditure for year}}{\text{gross value of tangible non-current assets}} = \frac{£286 \times 100\%}{(£1,884 + £1,102)} = 9.6\%$$

net book value + cumulative
depreciation provision

$$\text{capital expenditure to gross non-current assets 2006} = \frac{£170 \times 100\%}{(£1,921 + £779)} = 6.3\%$$

Report on the investment performance of Flatco plc
The improved profit performance in 2007 was reflected in improved earnings per share of 45p from 38.6p in 2006. However, the price/earnings ratio dropped from 7.8 to 6.1 times.

The board of directors reduced the dividend for the year to 5.8p per share from 6.7p per share in 2006, establishing a dividend cover of 7.8 times. The dividend yield reduced from 2.23% at 31 December 2006 to 2.11% at 31 December 2007.

The increase in the capital expenditure to sales ratio from 5.2% to 8.2% indicates the company's ability to both sustain and improve upon current sales levels. The increase in the capital expenditure to gross non-current assets ratio from 6.3% to 9.6% demonstrates the policy of Flatco for ongoing replacement of old assets for new in order to keep ahead of the technology in which the business is engaged.

Progress check 8.6

What are investment ratios and what is their purpose?

Financial structure ratios

Financial structure ratios (see Fig. 8.14) are generally concerned with the relationship between debt and equity capital, the financial structure (or capital structure) of an organisation. This relationship is called gearing, or leverage. The ratios that follow are the two most commonly used. Both ratios relate to financial gearing, which is the relationship between a company's borrowings, which includes both prior charge capital and long-term debt, and its shareholders' funds (share capital plus reserves).

$$\text{gearing } \% = \frac{\text{long-term debt}}{\text{equity} + \text{long-term debt}}$$

and

$$\text{debt/equity ratio } \% \text{ or leverage} = \frac{\text{long-term debt}}{\text{equity}}$$

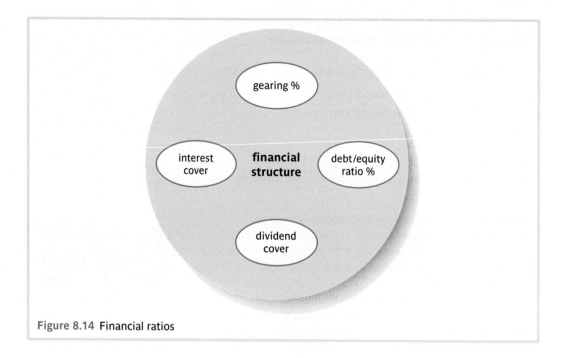

Figure 8.14 Financial ratios

Generally, in both the above equations preference shares are added to long-term loans because they are entitled to a fixed rate of dividend. However, preference dividends are only payable if sufficient profits have been earned and so if preference share dividends have not been declared the preference shares should be excluded from the calculations.

Convertible debt is treated as ordinary debt until it is converted. Provisions may sometimes be considered as liabilities included with long-term debt or they may be considered as part of equity. However, they may be excluded from the calculations because they are non-interest bearing and have no gearing implications for the profits available for shareholders.

Both the above ratios are equally acceptable in describing the relative proportions of debt and equity used to finance a business. They are ratios that compare debt to equity and they clarify the relationship between:

- funds requiring a fixed amount of interest
- funds provided by shareholders on which dividends may be paid each year.

The implications of these ratios are that:

- the higher these ratios are then the higher is the proportion of debt in the capital structure of the company, therefore
- the higher will be the amount of interest charges that may be expected, therefore
- the higher is the level of financial risk,

and the opposite will apply if these ratios are lower.

It is not possible to say exactly what level of gearing is appropriate for a particular company. However, a company may have an optimal capital structure, which may be used as a target. If it is not possible to determine this then a benchmark may be used by comparing similarly structured businesses within the same industry. Even then, the appropriate level of gearing for the company will depend on its particular circumstances, for example with regard to its level of business risk and therefore the level of financial risk it can 'afford' to accept (assuming total risk to be a combination of business risk and financial risk).

Some calculations of gearing include both long- and short-term debt. These are not the generally used ratios for gearing, but such ratios do recognise short-term financing as sources of finance, which are often automatically renewable.

We have so far considered gearing ratios that relate to a company's capital structure. Gearing calculations can be made in other ways that alternatively consider the company's income. So, in addition to the above ratios, ratios may also be based on earnings and interest relationships, for example:

$$\text{dividend cover (times)} = \frac{\text{earnings per share (eps)}}{\text{dividend per share}}$$

This ratio indicates the number of times the profits attributable to the equity shareholders covers the actual dividends paid and payable for the period. Financial analysts usually adjust their calculations for any exceptional or extraordinary items of which they may be aware.

$$\text{interest cover (times)} = \frac{\text{profit before interest and tax}}{\text{interest payable}}$$

This ratio calculates the number of times the interest payable is covered by profits available for such payments. It is particularly important for lenders to determine the vulnerability of interest payments to a drop in profit.

Worked Example 8.5

We will calculate the financial ratios for Flatco plc for 2007 and the comparative ratios for 2006, and comment on the financial structure of Flatco plc.

Gearing

$$\text{gearing 2007} = \frac{\text{long-term debt}}{\text{equity} + \text{long-term debt}} = \frac{\pounds 173 \times 100\%}{(\pounds 2{,}994 + \pounds 173)}$$

$$= 5.5\%$$

$$\text{gearing 2006} = \frac{\pounds 0 \times 100\%}{(\pounds 2{,}324 + \pounds 0)} = 0\%$$

Debt/equity ratio

$$\text{debt/equity ratio 2007} = \frac{\text{long-term debt}}{\text{equity}} = \frac{\pounds 173 \times 100\%}{\pounds 2{,}994}$$

$$= 5.8\%$$

$$\text{debt/equity ratio 2006} = \frac{\pounds 0 \times 100\%}{\pounds 2{,}324} = 0\%$$

▶

▶ **Dividend cover**

$$\text{dividend cover 2007} = \frac{\text{earnings per share (eps)}}{\text{dividend per share}} = \frac{45p}{5.8p}$$

$$= 7.8 \text{ times}$$

$$\text{dividend cover 2006} = \frac{38.6p}{6.7p} = 5.8 \text{ times}$$

Interest cover

$$\text{interest cover 2007} = \frac{\text{profit before interest and tax}}{\text{interest payable}} = \frac{£650}{£71}$$

$$= 9.2 \text{ times}$$

$$\text{interest cover 2006} = \frac{£530}{£100} = 5.3 \text{ times}$$

Report on the financial structure of Flatco plc

In 2006 Flatco plc was financed totally by equity, reflected in its zero gearing and debt/equity ratios for that year. Flatco plc was still very low geared in 2007, with gearing of 5.5% and debt/equity of 5.8%. This is because its debt of £173,000 at 31 December 2007 is very small compared with its equity of £2,994,000 at the same date.

Earnings per share increased by 16.6% in 2007 compared with 2006. However, the board of directors reduced the dividend, at 5.8p per share for 2007, by 13.4% from 6.7p per share in 2006. This resulted in an increase in dividend cover from 5.8 times in 2006 to 7.8 times in 2007.

Interest payable was reduced by £29,000 in 2007 from the previous year, but PBIT was increased by £120,000 year on year. The result was that interest cover was nearly doubled from 5.3 times in 2006 to 9.2 times in 2007.

Progress check 8.7

What are financial structure ratios and how may they be used to comment on the financial structure of an organisation?

Return on equity (ROE), return on assets (ROA), and the Du Pont system

Some companies and analysts like to link profitability, efficiency, and gearing ratios. This is illustrated in a number of relationships known as the Du Pont system of ratios. The first of these relationships considers another form of return on capital employed, return on assets (ROA):

$$\text{return on assets (ROA)} = \frac{\text{PAT + interest (or PBIT − tax)}}{\text{total assets}}$$

ROA may be rewritten as:

$$ROA = \frac{PBIT - tax}{total\ assets} = \underbrace{\frac{sales}{total\ assets}}_{\substack{asset\ turnover \\ ratio}} \times \underbrace{\frac{PBIT - tax}{sales}}_{\substack{profit\ margin \\ ratio}}$$

Asset turnover is an efficiency ratio, which is used to measure the performance of the company in generating sales from the assets under its control. The ability of a company to earn a higher return on assets is limited by competition. The profit margin ratio is a profitability ratio, and there is also a trade-off between the sales/assets ratio and profit margin. Companies in different industries may have the same level of ROA but different relationships between their asset turnover and profit margins. For example, a hotel chain may have a low asset turnover, which is compensated for by a high margin, whereas a fast food chain may have a high asset turnover but a lower margin.

We looked at return on equity (ROE) as a form of return on capital employed in the profitability ratios section earlier in this chapter.

$$return\ on\ equity\ (ROE) = \frac{profit\ after\ tax\ (PAT)}{equity}$$

Profit after tax (PAT) is the same thing as PBIT less tax and less interest. The second Du Pont relationship is derived from an expanded version of the ROE equation above:

$$ROE = \frac{PBIT - tax - interest}{equity}$$

which may be rewritten as:

$$= \underbrace{\frac{total\ assets}{equity}}_{\substack{equity\ multiplier \\ (a\ gearing\ ratio)}} \times \underbrace{\frac{sales}{total\ assets}}_{\substack{asset\ turnover \\ ratio}} \times \underbrace{\frac{PBIT - tax}{sales}}_{\substack{profit\ margin \\ ratio}} \times \underbrace{\frac{PBIT - tax - interest}{PBIT - tax}}_{debt\ burden}$$

The middle two terms are the efficiency ratio and profitability ratio that combined represent the company's ROA, which is dependent on operations and marketing skills and not on the financial structure of the company. The first and fourth terms are dependent on the financial structure of the business.

The equity multiplier is a gearing ratio, which is a way of examining the extent to which a company uses debt or equity to finance its assets. This ratio shows a company's total assets per £ (or unit of any other currency) of shareholders' equity. A high equity multiplier indicates that the company is relying on a relatively low level of equity to finance its assets, and *vice versa* if the equity multiplier is low. The debt burden is a measure of the extent to which the cost of interest reduces profits. If a company is financed totally by equity then terms one and four would both be 1. ROE would therefore equal ROA. If a company is geared then the first term would be greater than 1, because total assets are greater than equity; the fourth term would be less than 1, because the numerator now includes interest payable.

Worked Example 8.6

We will calculate and comment on the Du Pont ratios for Flatco plc for 2007 and the comparative ratios for 2006.

Return on assets (ROA)

$$\text{ROA \% 2007} = \frac{\text{PBIT} - \text{tax}}{\text{total assets}} = \frac{\text{sales}}{\text{total assets}} \times \frac{\text{PBIT} - \text{tax}}{\text{sales}}$$

$$= \frac{£650 - £50}{£4,348} = \frac{£3,500}{£4,348} \times \frac{£650 - £50}{£3,500}$$

$$= \quad 13.8\% \quad = \quad 0.80 \text{ times} \quad \times \quad 17.1\%$$

$$\qquad\quad \textbf{ROA} \qquad\quad \textbf{asset turnover} \qquad \textbf{profit margin}$$
$$\qquad\qquad\qquad\qquad\qquad\quad \textbf{ratio} \qquad\qquad\quad \textbf{ratio}$$

$$\text{ROA \% 2006} = \frac{£530 - £44}{£4,013} = \frac{£3,250}{£4,013} \times \frac{£530 - £44}{£3,250}$$

$$= \quad 12.1\% \quad = \quad 0.81 \text{ times} \quad \times \quad 14.9\%$$

$$\qquad\quad \textbf{ROA} \qquad\quad \textbf{asset turnover} \qquad \textbf{profit margin}$$
$$\qquad\qquad\qquad\qquad\qquad\quad \textbf{ratio} \qquad\qquad\quad \textbf{ratio}$$

Return on equity (ROE)

$$\text{ROE \% 2007} = \frac{\text{PBIT} - \text{tax} - \text{interest}}{\text{equity}} = \frac{£650 - £50 - £60}{£2,994} = 18.0\%$$

$$= \frac{\text{total assets}}{\text{equity}} \times \frac{\text{sales}}{\text{total assets}} \times \frac{\text{PBIT} - \text{tax}}{\text{sales}} \times \frac{\text{PBIT} - \text{tax} - \text{interest}}{\text{PBIT} - \text{tax}}$$

$$= \frac{£4,348}{£2,994} \times \frac{£3,500}{£4,348} \times \frac{£650 - £50}{£3,500} \times \frac{£650 - £50 - £60}{£650 - £50}$$

$$= \quad 1.45 \text{ times} \quad \times 0.80 \text{ times} \times \quad 17.1\% \quad \times \quad 0.90 \text{ times}$$

$$\textbf{equity multiplier} \qquad\qquad \textbf{ROA} \qquad\qquad\qquad \textbf{debt burden}$$

$$\text{ROE \% 2006} = \frac{£530 - £44 - £100}{£2,324} = 16.6\%$$

$$= \frac{£4,013}{£2,324} \times \frac{£3,250}{£4,013} \times \frac{£530 - £44}{£3,250} \times \frac{£530 - £44 - £100}{£530 - £44}$$

$$= \quad 1.73 \text{ times} \quad \times 0.81 \text{ times} \times \quad 14.9\% \quad \times \quad 0.79 \text{ times}$$

$$\textbf{equity multiplier} \qquad\qquad \textbf{ROA} \qquad\qquad\qquad \textbf{debt burden}$$

Report on the Du Pont ratios for Flatco plc

ROA has increased from 12.1% in 2006 to 13.8% in 2007. This shows an improvement, which was not apparent from the unchanged ROCE from 2006 to 2007. This was because the additional funding received in 2007 had not all been spent on new assets until 2008.

Asset turnover dropped from 0.81 in 2006 to 0.80 times in the year 2007. The new capital introduced into the company in 2007 to finance major new projects is expected to result in significant increases in sales levels over the next few years, which will see improvements in asset turnover over and above 2006 levels.

The profit margin increase was less than the increase in PBIT because of the greater impact of taxation in 2007. Return on equity increased from 16.6% to 18%, despite the increase in ordinary share capital. This was because of improved profit after tax (up 3.5% to 15.4%) arising from increased income from fixed asset investments and lower costs of finance. Corporation tax was marginally higher in 2007 than in 2006.

The debt burden of 0.90 times in 2007 increased significantly from 0.79 in 2006, reflecting increased gearing and therefore the requirement to pay additional interest in future years. This resulted from the issue of the debenture of £173,000 in 2007. The drop in the equity multiplier from 1.73 to 1.45 in 2007 indicated that the company had increased its equity financing of its assets, despite its increase in gearing.

We have seen how the level of gearing has the effect of either increasing or reducing ROE. We will examine this further by looking at another equation that represents the relationship between ROE and ROA, which can be determined by rearranging the company's cost of capital formula. We may assume that the company's cost of capital approximates to its ROA, adjusted for the tax shield. If E is the proportion of equity capital, D is the proportion of debt capital, i is the interest rate paid on debt, and t is the corporation tax rate:

$$\text{ROA}\,(1-t) = \frac{E \times \text{ROE}}{E+D} + \frac{D \times i \times (1-t)}{E+D}$$

$$\text{ROA} \times E \times (1-t) + \text{ROA} \times D \times (1-t) = (E \times \text{ROE}) + D \times i \times (1-t)$$

$$\text{ROA} \times E \times (1-t) + \text{ROA} \times D \times (1-t) - D \times i \times (1-t) = E \times \text{ROE}$$

$$\text{ROA} \times E \times (1-t) + (\text{ROA} - i) \times D \times (1-t) = E \times \text{ROE}$$

therefore

$$\textbf{ROE} = \{\textbf{ROA} \times (1-t)\} + \{(\textbf{ROA} - i) \times (1-t) \times \textbf{D/E}\}$$

which shows return on equity (ROE) as a function of return on assets (ROA) and the financial structure, leverage, or gearing of the company.

Worked Example 8.7 illustrates the use of this relationship and also gives a general rule derived from it.

Worked Example 8.7

A hospital equipment manufacturing company, Nilby Mouth plc, makes an operating profit (PBIT) of £12m on sales of £100m and with a total investment of £60m. The total assets are £60m, financed by equity (E) of £40m and debt (D) of £20m with an interest rate (i) of 10%. Assume the corporation tax rate (t) is 30%.

We will calculate:

(i)   the current return on equity (ROE)

(ii) the ROE if financing were changed so that debt was £40m and equity was £20m

▶

▶ **(iii)** the current ROE if operating profit were reduced to £4m

(iv) the ROE if operating profit were reduced to £4m and if financing were changed so that debt was £40m and equity was £20m.

Figures in £m

(i) Calculation of return on equity (ROE)

Profit before interest and tax, or operating profit PBIT = 12

PBT = 12 − (20 × 10%) = 10

Tax = 10 × 30% = 3

PBIT − tax = 12 − 3 = 9

Return on assets ROA = 9/60 = 15%

Debt/equity ratio D/E = 20/40 = 50%

$ROE = ROA \times (1 - t) + \{(ROA - i) \times (1 - t) \times D/E\}$

Return on equity ROE = {15% × (1 − 30%)} + {(15% − 10%) × (1 − 30%) × 50%}
= 12.25%

ROA is 15%, *i* is 10%, debt/equity is 50%, and ROE is 12.25%.

(ii) Calculation of ROE if financing is changed so that debt is £40m and equity is £20m

PBIT = 12; PBT = 12 − (40 × 10%) = 8; Tax = 8 × 30% = 2.4; PBIT − tax = 12 − 2.4 = 9.6

Return on assets ROA = 9.6/60 = 16%

Debt/equity ratio D/E = 40/20 = 200%

$ROE = ROA \times (1 - t) + \{(ROA - i) \times (1 - t) \times D/E\}$

Return on equity ROE = {16% × (1 − 30%)} + {(16% − 10%) × (1 − 30%) × 200%}
= 19.60%

ROA is greater than *i*, debt/equity ratio has increased, and ROE has increased,
16% > 10%   50% to 200%   12.25% to 19.60%

(iii) Calculation of ROE if the operating profit were reduced to £4m

PBIT = 4; PBT = 4 − (20 × 10%) = 2; Tax = 2 × 30% = 0.6; PBIT − tax = 4 − 0.6 = 3.4

Return on assets ROA = 3.4/60 = 5.67%

Debt/equity ratio D/E = 20/40 = 50%

$ROE = ROA \times (1 - t) + \{(ROA - i) \times (1 - t) \times D/E\}$

Return on equity ROE = {5.67% × (1 − 30%)} + {(5.67% − 10%) × (1 − 30%) × 50%}
= 2.45%

ROA is less than *i*, the debt/equity ratio is still 50%, and ROE has decreased,
5.67% < 10%   12.25% to 2.45%

(iv) Calculation of ROE if financing is changed so that debt is £40m and equity is £20m

PBIT = 4; PBT = 4 − (40 × 10%) = 0; Tax = 0 × 30% = 0; PBIT − tax = 4 − 0 = 4

Return on assets ROA = 4/60 = 6.67%

Debt/equity ratio D/E = 40/20 = 200%

$$ROE = ROA \times (1 - t) + \{(ROA - i) \times (1 - t) \times D/E\}$$

Return on equity ROE = {6.67% × (1 − 30%)} + {(6.67% − 10%) × (1 − 30%) × 200%}
                     = 0.007%

ROA is less than *i*, the debt/equity ratio has increased, and ROE has decreased,
  6.67% < 10%   50% to 200%   2.45% to 0.007%

The general rule apparent from the relationships outlined in Worked Example 8.7 is:

- when ROA is greater than *i* the higher the D/E, the higher the ROE
- when ROA is less than *i* the higher the D/E, the lower the ROE.

However, even if the ROA is greater than debt interest the company's bankers may not automatically allow the D/E to increase indefinitely. The company's risk increases as the D/E or leverage increases, in terms of its commitment to high levels of interest payments, and bankers will not tolerate too high a level of risk; they will also be inclined to increase the debt interest rate as D/E increases. Shareholders will have the same reaction; they are happy with an increase in ROE but realise that they also have to face a higher risk, and will therefore demand a higher return.

When a plc is seen to embark on a policy of increased borrowings and increasing its gearing ratio and therefore increasing its ROE, the financial press is usually quick to alert its readership to the increased financial risk. Plcs are usually prepared and ready for such comments in order to respond with their defence of such a policy.

Progress check 8.8

Why may bankers refuse additional lending to a company as its debt/equity ratio increases?

Horizontal analysis

Growth of a company, which may be considered in terms of sales growth and gross margin, may be looked at using income statement horizontal analysis, which presents all numbers in the income statement as a percentage using a base year, which is 100, for year-on-year comparison. Financial commentators usually begin articles on the performance of plcs by comparing the current year performance with the previous year, and then attempt a forecast of future performance. This is an example of a basic horizontal analysis that focuses on turnover and profits. In practice, only a few companies actually succeed in growing year on year, over an extended period (for example, 10 years).

CONSOLIDATED INCOME STATEMENT
for the year ended 31st March 2007

	Notes	2007 £ million	2006 restated £ million
Revenue	1,2	**6,151.7**	4,573.7
Cost of materials sold		**(5,300.0)**	(3,842.3)
Net revenues		**851.7**	731.4
Other cost of sales		**(413.7)**	(358.7)
Gross profit		**438.0**	372.7
Distribution costs		**(81.8)**	(75.3)
Administrative expenses		**(103.8)**	(84.0)
Impairment costs	3	**–**	(6.0)
Operating profit	1,4	**252.4**	207.4
Finance costs	6	**(36.0)**	(31.5)
Finance income	7	**9.2**	15.8
Share of profit / (loss) of associates		**0.9**	(0.2)
Profit before tax		**226.5**	191.5
Income tax expense	8	**(64.7)**	(54.7)
Profit for the year from continuing operations		**161.8**	136.8
Profit for the year from discontinued operations	40	**43.7**	14.5
Profit for the year		**205.5**	151.3
Attributable to:			
Equity holders of the parent company		**206.5**	152.1
Minority interests	33	**(1.0)**	(0.8)
		205.5	151.3

	Notes	pence	pence
Earnings per ordinary share attributable to the equity holders of the parent company			
Continuing operations			
Basic	10	**76.5**	64.2
Diluted	10	**75.3**	63.9
Total			
Basic	10	**96.9**	70.8
Diluted	10	**95.4**	70.5

The notes on pages 58 to 97 form an integral part of the accounts.

NOTES ON THE ACCOUNTS
for the year ended 31st March 2007

1   Segmental information

By business segment

For management purposes, the group was organised into four operating divisions – Catalysts, Precious Metal Products, Pharmaceutical Materials and Ceramics. Their principal activities are described on pages 8 to 13. The group sold its Ceramics Division during the year (note 40) and so its results are reported as discontinued operations. Sales between segments are made at market prices, taking into account the volumes involved.

Year ended 31st March 2007

	Catalysts £ million	Precious Metal Products £ million	Pharmaceutical Materials £ million	Eliminations £ million	Total £ million
Sales to external customers	2,192.6	3,824.4	134.7	–	6,151.7
Inter-segment sales	21.9	1,162.6	0.3	(1,184.8)	–
Total revenue	2,214.5	4,987.0	135.0	(1,184.8)	6,151.7
External sales excluding the value of precious metals	1,035.6	290.0	128.6	–	1,454.2
Segment result	148.8	85.3	35.5	–	269.6
Unallocated corporate expenses					(17.2)
Operating profit					252.4
Net finance costs					(26.8)
Share of profit of associates		0.9			0.9
Profit before tax					226.5
Income tax expense					(64.7)
Profit for the year from continuing operations					161.8
Profit for the year from discontinued operations					43.7
Profit for the year					205.5
Segment assets	1,308.1	298.4	324.2	(52.1)	1,878.6
Investments in associates	–	4.8	–	–	4.8
Cash and deposits					73.2
Current and deferred income tax assets					15.9
Post-employment benefits net assets					49.2
Unallocated corporate assets					67.5
Total assets					2,089.2
Segment liabilities	329.8	92.1	18.4	(52.1)	388.2
Borrowings, finance leases and related swaps					438.0
Current and deferred income tax liabilities					89.2
Employee benefits obligations					48.3
Unallocated corporate liabilities					47.4
Total liabilities					1,011.1
Segment capital expenditure	91.5	11.2	10.7	–	113.4
Capital expenditure on discontinued operations					4.5
Corporate capital expenditure					1.9
Total capital expenditure					119.8
Segment depreciation and amortisation	46.0	13.4	10.5	–	69.9
Depreciation on discontinued operations					5.5
Corporate depreciation					2.1
Total depreciation and amortisation					77.5
Significant non-cash expenses other than depreciation	1.5	1.3	–	–	2.8

NOTES ON THE ACCOUNTS
for the year ended 31st March 2007

1   Segmental information (continued)
     By business segment (continued)

Year ended 31st March 2006 (restated)

	Catalysts £ million	Precious Metal Products £ million	Pharmaceutical Materials £ million	Ceramics £ million	Eliminations £ million	Total £ million
Sales to external customers	1,477.4	2,962.4	133.9		–	4,573.7
Inter-segment sales	17.4	676.9	1.2		(695.5)	–
Total revenue	1,494.8	3,639.3	135.1		(695.5)	4,573.7
External sales excluding the value of precious metals	786.4	245.4	127.2		–	1,159.0
Segment result before impairment costs	134.2	62.2	33.8		–	230.2
Impairment costs	–	(6.0)	–		–	(6.0)
Segment result	134.2	56.2	33.8		–	224.2
Unallocated corporate expenses						(16.8)
Operating profit						207.4
Net finance costs						(15.7)
Share of loss of associates		(0.2)				(0.2)
Profit before tax						191.5
Income tax expense						(54.7)
Profit for the year from continuing operations						136.8
Profit for the year from discontinued operations						14.5
Profit for the year						151.3
Segment assets	1,119.1	305.8	331.3	164.6	(26.7)	1,894.1
Investments in associates	–	4.3	–	–	–	4.3
Cash and deposits						133.0
Current and deferred income tax assets						8.0
Post-employment benefits net assets						75.0
Unallocated corporate assets						52.2
Total assets						2,166.6
Segment liabilities	207.0	117.1	24.1	38.0	(26.7)	359.5
Borrowings, finance leases and related swaps						545.0
Current and deferred income tax liabilities						115.7
Employee benefits obligations						56.2
Unallocated corporate liabilities						45.7
Total liabilities						1,122.1
Segment capital expenditure	89.2	13.7	9.9	6.5	–	119.3
Corporate capital expenditure						4.7
Total capital expenditure						124.0
Segment depreciation and amortisation	39.8	13.0	10.0	6.3	–	69.1
Corporate depreciation						1.7
Total depreciation and amortisation						70.8
Significant non-cash expenses other than depreciation	–	7.7	–	–	–	7.7

NOTES ON THE ACCOUNTS
for the year ended 31st March 2007

1   Segmental information (continued)

By geographical segment

Pharmaceutical Materials is located in Europe and North America. All of the other divisions of the group have a presence in each of the geographical segments.

Year ended 31st March 2007

	Europe £ million	North America £ million	Asia £ million	Rest of the World £ million	Eliminations £ million	Total £ million
External sales by geographical destination	2,654.5	1,496.3	1,339.8	661.1	–	6,151.7
Carrying value of segment assets by location	1,154.5	478.6	176.7	141.2	(72.4)	1,878.6
Capital expenditure by location of assets	61.7	29.8	17.5	10.8	–	119.8

Year ended 31st March 2006 (restated)

	Europe £ million	North America £ million	Asia £ million	Rest of the World £ million	Eliminations £ million	Total £ million
External sales by geographical destination	1,862.2	1,124.9	1,089.6	497.0	–	4,573.7
Carrying value of segment assets by location	1,322.7	294.1	170.4	162.9	(56.0)	1,894.1
Capital expenditure by location of assets	61.3	42.5	13.7	6.5	–	124.0

2   Revenue

	2007 £ million	2006 restated £ million
Sale of goods	6,021.5	4,482.7
Rendering of services	109.8	86.6
Royalties / licence income	20.4	4.4
Total revenue – continuing operations	**6,151.7**	4,573.7

3   Impairment costs

	2007 £ million	2006 £ million
Impairment of UK Pgm Refining assets (Precious Metal Products)	–	6.0
Total impairment costs	**–**	6.0

During the year ended 31st March 2006 the group decided to stop using parts of the pgm refining process and so fully impaired the associated plant and equipment.

Horizontal analysis, or common size analysis, of the income statement allows a line-by-line analysis of the accounts compared with those of the previous year. It may provide over a number of years a trend of changes showing either growth or decline in these elements of the accounts by calculation of annual percentage growth rates in profits, sales, stock, or any other item.

Worked Example 8.8 illustrates the technique applied to a summary of the Johnson Matthey plc income statement for the years to 31 March 2007 and 31 March 2006 (see the consolidated income statement of the Johnson Matthey group from page 50 of its Annual Report and Accounts 2007, shown below).

Worked Example 8.8

We can prepare a horizontal analysis using a summary of the income statement results for Johnson Matthey plc for 2006 and 2007, using 2006 as the base year.

Johnson Matthey plc
Summary consolidated income statement for the year ended
31 March 2007

Figures in £m	2007	2006
Turnover	6,151.7	4,573.7
Operating profit	252.4	207.4
Net interest	(26.8)	(15.7)
Share of profit/(loss) of associates	0.9	(0.2)
Profit before tax	226.5	191.5
Taxation	(64.7)	(54.7)
Profit after tax	161.8	136.8
Profit for the year from discontinued operations	43.7	14.5
Profit for the year	205.5	151.3

If we consider the two years and use 2006 as the base year 100, this means that:

if   turnover for 2006 of £4,573.7m = 100

then   turnover for 2007 of £6,151.7m $= \dfrac{£6,151.7m \times 100}{£4,573.7m} = 134.5$

The same principle is used for each other line of the income statement as follows:

Johnson Matthey plc
Summary consolidated income statement for the year ended
31 March 2007

Horizontal analysis	2006	2007
Turnover	100.0	134.5
Operating profit	100.0	121.7
Net interest	100.0	170.7
Share of profit/(loss) of associates	100.0	550.0
Profit before tax	100.0	118.3
Taxation	100.0	118.3
Profit after tax	100.0	118.3
Profit for the year from discontinued operations	100.0	301.4
Profit for the year	100.0	135.8

We can see from the above horizontal analysis how the net profit for the year has been derived compared with that for 2006. Sales in 2007 increased by 34.5% over 2006, and operating profit for 2007 was increased by 21.7% over 2006. Corporation tax in 2007 was 18.3% higher than 2006, and profit for the year was 35.8% higher than the previous year.

Subsequent years may be compared with 2006 as base 100, using the same sort of calculation. This technique is particularly useful to make a line-by-line comparison of a company's accounts for each accounting period over, say, five or ten years, using the first year as the base year. When we look at a set of accounts we may by observation automatically carry out this process of assessing percentage changes in performance over time. However, presentation of the information in tabular form, for a number of years, gives a much clearer picture of trends in performance in each area of activity and may provide the basis for further analysis.

Progress check 8.9

What can a horizontal analysis of the information contained in the financial statements of a company add to that provided from ratio analysis?

Vertical analysis

A company's financial performance (and position) may also be considered by looking at a vertical analysis of its income statement (and balance sheet). In a vertical analysis of the income statement (or balance sheet) each item is expressed as a percentage of the total sales (or total assets). The vertical analysis provides evidence of structural changes in the accounts such as increased profitability through more efficient production. Worked Example 8.9 uses total turnover as the basis for calculation. The following analysis confirms some of the conclusions drawn from the horizontal analysis.

Worked Example 8.9

We can prepare a vertical analysis using a summary of the consolidated income statement for Johnson Matthey plc for 2006 and 2007.

Johnson Matthey plc
Consolidated income statement for the year ended 31 March 2007

Vertical analysis	2007	2006
Turnover	100.0	100.0
Operating profit	4.1	4.5
Net interest	(0.4)	(0.3)
Share of profit/(loss) of associates	(0.0)	0.0
Profit before tax	3.7	4.2
Taxation	(1.1)	(1.2)
Profit after tax	2.6	3.0
Profit for the year from discontinued operations	0.7	0.3
Profit for the year	3.3	3.3

▶

▶ Operating profit decreased from 4.5% in 2006 to 4.1% in 2007. Net interest charges and other financial items for 2007 were about in line with the previous year, as was taxation as a percentage of sales, and so profit before tax was 2.6% for 2007 compared with 3.0% for 2006. However, profit from discontinued operations was higher at 0.7% for 2007 compared with 0.3% for 2006. As a result, net profit for both 2007 and 2006 was 3.3% of sales.

Progress check 8.10

What can a vertical analysis of the information contained in the financial statements of a company add to the information provided from a horizontal analysis and a ratio analysis?

Segmental reporting

The section headed 'Notes on the Accounts' in the annual report and accounts of companies contains information that must be reported additional to, and in support of, the financial statements. This includes segmental information, which is analysis by business and geographical area relating to turnover, operating profit, and net assets. The first note in the Notes on the Accounts in Johnson Matthey's Report and Accounts for 2007 is headed Segmental Information. International accounting standard IAS 14, Segment Reporting (replaced by IFRS 8, Operating Segments, with effect from 1 January 2009), requires large companies to disclose segmental information by each class of business, and by geographical region, unless the directors feel that by doing so they may seriously damage the competitive position of the company. Segmental reporting is required in order that users of financial information may carry out more meaningful financial analysis.

Most large companies are usually comprised of diverse businesses supplying different products and services, rather than being engaged in a single type of business. Each type of business activity may have:

■ a different structure
■ different levels of profitability
■ different levels of growth potential
■ different levels of risk exposure.

The financial statements of such diversified companies are consolidated to include all business activities, which is a potential problem for the users of financial information. For analysis and interpretation of financial performance, aggregate figures are not particularly useful for the following reasons:

■ difficulties in evaluation of performance of a business which has interests that are diverse from the aggregated financial information
■ difficulties of comparison of trends over time and comparison between companies because the various activities undertaken by the company are likely to differ in size and range in comparison with other businesses
■ differences in conditions between different geographical markets, in terms of levels of risk, profitability, and growth

- differences in conditions between different geographical markets, in terms of political and social factors, environmental factors, currencies, and inflation rates.

Segmental reporting analysis enables:

- the further analysis of segmental performance to determine more accurately the likely growth prospects for the business as a whole
- evaluation of the impact on the company of changes in conditions relating to particular activities
- improvements in internal management performance, because it may be monitored through disclosure of segmental information to shareholders
- evaluation of the acquisition and disposal performance of the company.

Worked Example 8.10

The information in the table below relates to global sales by Guinness plc for the years 2000 and 1999.

Figures in £m	2000	1999
Global Sales	4,730	4,681
Asia/Pacific – B	349	324
Asia/Pacific – S	454	426
North America – B	166	151
North America – S	491	551
Rest of Europe – B	1,025	954
Rest of Europe – S	723	741
Rest of the World – B	203	198
Rest of the World – S	402	384
UK – B	519	495
UK – S	398	457
S = spirits B = beer		

(i) Using the information provided we may prepare a simple table that compares the sales for 1999 with the sales for the year 2000.

(ii) We can also consider how a simple sales analysis can provide an investor with information that is more useful than just global sales for the year.

(i)

Global sales	2000 Spirits	2000 versus 1999	2000 Beers	2000 versus 1999	2000 Total	2000 versus 1999	1999 Spirits	1999 Beers	1999 Total
	£m	%	£m	%	£m	%	£m	£m	£m
UK	398	−12.9	519	+4.8	917	−3.7	457	495	952
Rest of Europe	723	−2.4	1,025	+7.4	1,748	+3.1	741	954	1,695
North America	491	−10.9	166	+9.9	657	−6.4	551	151	702
Asia/Pacific	454	+6.6	349	+7.7	803	+7.1	426	324	750
Rest of the World	402	+4.7	203	+2.5	605	+3.9	384	198	582
Total global sales					4,730	+1.0			4,681

▶

> ▶ **(ii)** Numbers that are blandly presented in a global format do not usually reveal trends.
>
> Analysis of information by area, for example, may reveal trends and may illustrate the impact of new policies or the changes in specific economic environments.
>   The analysis of the Guinness sales for two years shows:
>
> - in which geographical area sales have increased or decreased
> - for which products sales have increased or decreased.
>
> Analysis of the results over several years is usually needed to provide meaningful trend information as a basis for investigation into the reasons for increases and decreases.

Class of business is a part of the overall business, which can be identified as providing a separate product or service, or group of related products or services. A geographical segment may comprise an individual country or a group of countries in which the business operates.

If a company operates in two or more classes of business activity or two or more geographical segments, there should normally be separate disclosure of information for each segment, which should include:

- sales to external customers and sales to other segments within the business, according to origin, and also by destinations of the goods and services if they are substantially different from the geographical region from which they were supplied
- operating profit before accounting for finance charges, taxation, minority interests, and extraordinary items
- net assets.

There are a number of problems relating to the principle of disclosure of segmental information, some of which we have already identified:

- directors may be reluctant to disclose information that may damage the competitive position of the company – foreign competitors may not have to disclose similar data
- segmental information may not be useful since the total company results are what should be relevant to shareholders
- some users of information may not be sufficiently financially expert to avoid being confused by the segmental information
- conglomerates may choose not to disclose segmental information, whereas a single activity company by definition is unable to hide anything.

There are, in addition, some accounting problems concerned with the preparation of segmental reports:

- identification of business class and geographical segments is not defined in IAS 14 (IFRS 8), but is left to the judgement of the directors of the company
- a lack of definition of segments results in difficulties in comparison of companies
- difficulties in analysis and apportionment of costs that are common between activities and geographical regions
- difficulties in the treatment of costs of transfers of goods and services between segments.

Progress check 8.11

Describe what is meant by segmental reporting, and why and to whom it is useful.

Worked Example 8.11

If we refer to Note 1 in the Johnson Matthey plc Notes on the Accounts in their Annual Report and Accounts 2007 (see pages 342 to 345) we can identify sales to external customers for 2007 and 2006. This will enable us to present the data in both pie chart and bar chart format, and more clearly explain JM's sales results for 2007 and 2006.

The pie charts in Figs 8.15 and 8.16 give a broad indication of sales turnover by type of business, and show that for both years precious metals provide just below two thirds of the turnover, and catalysts provide around one third of the turnover. Pharmaceutical materials is a small sector that provides the balance, 2.9% in 2006 and 2.2% in 2007. The bar chart in Fig. 8.17 is probably more useful in showing more clearly that turnover from the two largest sectors has increased in 2007 over 2006 but the smallest sector has remained at around the same volume.

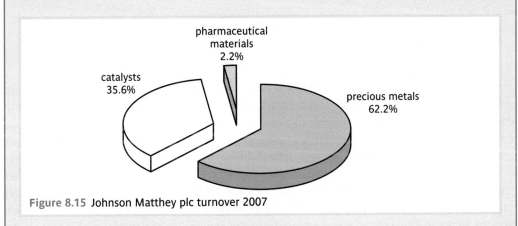

Figure 8.15 Johnson Matthey plc turnover 2007

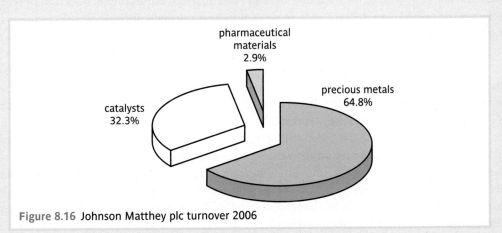

Figure 8.16 Johnson Matthey plc turnover 2006

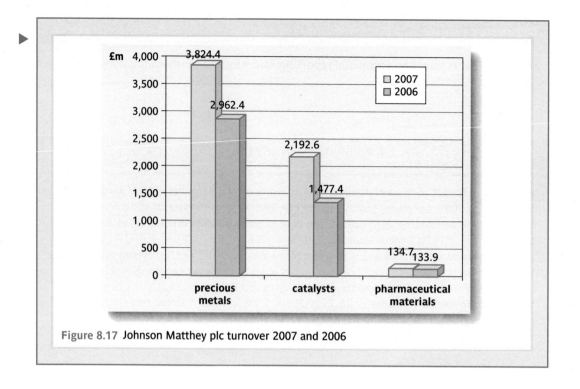

Figure 8.17 Johnson Matthey plc turnover 2007 and 2006

In this chapter we have looked at most of the key ratios and techniques for review of company performance and their meaning and relevance. However, the limitations we have already identified generally relating to performance review must always be borne in mind. In addition, it should be noted that the calculations used in business ratio analysis are based on past performance. These may not, therefore, reflect the current position of an organisation. Performance ratio analyses can also sometimes be misleading if their interpretation does not also consider other factors that may not always be easily quantifiable, and may include non-financial information, for example customer satisfaction, and delivery performance. There may be inconsistencies in some of the measures used in ratio analysis. For example, sales numbers are reported net of VAT, but debtors and creditors numbers normally include VAT. Extreme care should therefore be taken in any performance review to avoid reaching conclusions that may perhaps be erroneous.

If all the financial literature were thoroughly researched the number of different ratios that may be discovered would run into hundreds. It is most helpful to use a limited set of ratios and to fully understand their meaning. The ratios will certainly help with an understanding of the company but do not in themselves represent the complete picture.

Calculation of the ratios for one company for one year is also very limited. It is more relevant to compare companies operating in the same market and to analyse how a company has changed over the years. However, difficulties inevitably arise because it is sometimes impossible to find another company that is strictly comparable with the company being analysed. In addition, the company itself may have changed so much over recent years as to render meaningless any conclusions drawn from changes in ratios.

Cash versus profit, and EBITDA, EVA™, and MVA

The use of cash flow versus profit (or earnings per share) as a measure of company performance has become increasingly important. The advantages and disadvantages in the use of each are shown in Figs. 8.18 and 8.19.

Cash flow has assumed increasing importance and has gained popularity as a measure of performance because the income statement has become somewhat discredited due to the unacceptable degree of subjectivity involved in its preparation. Some of the financial ratios that we have already looked at may be considered in cash terms, for example:

$$\text{cash ROCE \%} = \frac{\text{net cash flow from operations}}{\text{average capital employed}}$$

and

$$\text{cash interest cover} = \frac{\text{net cash inflow from operations} + \text{interest received}}{\text{interest paid}}$$

which, in cash terms, calculates the number of times the interest payable is covered by cash available for such payments.

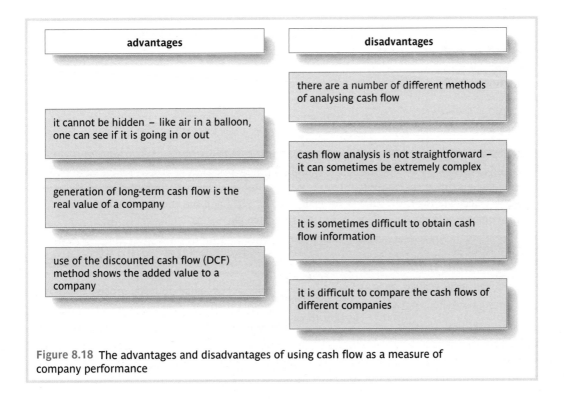

advantages	disadvantages
	there are a number of different methods of analysing cash flow
it cannot be hidden – like air in a balloon, one can see if it is going in or out	
	cash flow analysis is not straightforward – it can sometimes be extremely complex
generation of long-term cash flow is the real value of a company	
	it is sometimes difficult to obtain cash flow information
use of the discounted cash flow (DCF) method shows the added value to a company	
	it is difficult to compare the cash flows of different companies

Figure 8.18 The advantages and disadvantages of using cash flow as a measure of company performance

advantages	disadvantages
	the 1980s boom led to some creative accounting, e.g. Coloroll, Polly Peck, Maxwell and more recently Enron and WorldCom, all based on abuse of accounting conventions
simple method to use	
	different bases are used from one company to another
easy to compare companies	
	use of the historical cost convention means that there is no account taken of expected growth or inflation
possible to see the company relative to the market	there is no account taken of market risk
	the numbers are too easy to manipulate
profit is easily identifiable	the imprecise area of the treatment of extraordinary items and provisions has now been resolved but there still remain grey areas such as acquisition accounting, and accounting for derivatives

Figure 8.19 The advantages and disadvantages of using earnings per share (eps) as a measure of company performance

Worked Example 8.12

We will calculate the cash ROCE % for Flatco plc for 2007 and the comparative ratio for 2006, and compare with the equivalent profit ratio for Flatco plc.

Cash ROCE %

$$\text{cash ROCE \% 2007} = \frac{\text{net cash flow from operations}}{\text{average capital employed}} = \frac{\pounds936 \times 100\%}{(\pounds3{,}543 + \pounds2{,}713)/2}$$

$$= \frac{\pounds936 \times 100\%}{\pounds3{,}128} = 29.9\%$$

$$\text{cash ROCE \% 2006} = \frac{\pounds783 \times 100\%}{(\pounds2{,}713 + \pounds2{,}406)/2} = \frac{\pounds783 \times 100\%}{\pounds2{,}559.5} = 30.6\%$$

Report on the cash and profit ROCE of Flatco plc

While the profit ROCE % was static at 17.6% for 2006 and 2007, the cash ROCE % reduced from 30.6% to 29.9%. Operating cash flow for 2007 increased by only 19.5% over 2006, despite the fact that operating profit for 2007 increased by 22.2% over 2006.

Operating profit before depreciation (EBITDA) was £895,000 [£550,000 + £345,000] for 2007, which was an increase of 20.5% over 2006 [£450,000 + £293,000 = £743,000]. If pre-depreciation operating profit had been used to calculate ROCE, it would have been 28.6% for 2007 compared with 29.0% for 2006, a reduction of 0.4% and more in line with the picture shown by the cash ROCE.

The chairman of Flatco plc expects that ROCE will be improved in 2008 as a result of:

■ increased profitability resulting from higher sales levels generated from the investments in new projects

■ reduction in levels of working capital, with more efficient use of company resources.

Progress check 8.12

What are the benefits of using cash flow instead of profit to measure financial performance? What are the disadvantages of using cash flow?

The increasing importance of cash flow as a measure of performance has led to new methods of measurement:

■ the Rappaport method, which uses DCF looking 10 years ahead as a method of valuing a company

■ the economic value added (EVA™) method

■ enterprise value, which is a very similar method to EVA, which excludes the peripheral activities of the company.

A profit-based measure of financial performance EBITDA, or earnings before interest, tax, depreciation, and amortisation, is used by some companies as an approximation to operational cash flow. Amortisation, in the same way as depreciation applies to tangible non-current assets, is the systematic write-off of the cost of an intangible asset. The way in which EBITDA may be used has been illustrated in the Flatco plc Worked Example 8.12.

Back in 1999, Tomkins plc, in their annual report and accounts for that year, commented on their use of EBITDA as a performance measure. 'Sophisticated investors increasingly employ a range of measures when assessing the financial health and value of a company, diversifying into cash-based yardsticks from a simplistic earnings per share test. EBITDA is becoming widely accepted as a reliable guide to operational cash flow.'

We have seen that the method of performance measurement is not a clear-cut cash or profit choice. It is generally useful to use both. However, many analysts and the financial press in general continue to depend heavily on profit performance measures with a strong emphasis on earnings per share (eps) and the price/earnings ratio (P/E). Maximisation of shareholder wealth continues to be the prime objective with which managers of companies are charged. The extent to which success in particular performance measures align with shareholder wealth is particularly relevant. Equally important are the ways in which managers are motivated to maximise shareholder wealth, and in most organisations managerial remuneration provides the link between the measures of financial performance and shareholder value.

Financial performance measures such as a company's share price are commonly used to indicate how well the company is doing. However, it may be questioned as to how directly the share price reflects decisions that have been taken by management. In the context of managers' performance against budget targets, and the company's overall financial performance, we have previously discussed the merits and otherwise of performance measures such as profit after tax, earnings per share, dividends, return on capital employed, and cash flow, etc. Each has its limitations, but cash flow based measures are now becoming accepted as perhaps better indicators than profit related measures.

During the mid-1980s, Rappaport developed shareholder value analysis, from which the American firm Stern Stewart Management Services evolved concepts known as economic value added (EVA), and **market value added (MVA)**. Through EVA, Stern Stewart attempted to reconcile the need for a performance measure correlated with shareholder wealth, and a performance measure, which was also responsive to actions taken by managers. By the mid-1990s over 200 global companies had been in discussion with Stern Stewart with regard to adoption of EVA; Lucas Varity in the UK and Coca-Cola in the USA were already successful users of EVA.

If we assume that the organisation's objective is to maximise shareholder wealth then this will be achieved if new projects are taken on and existing projects are allowed to continue only if they create value. Investment in capital projects should be made only on the basis of choosing those with a positive net present value (NPV). However, NPV cannot be applied to remuneration schemes because it is a summary measure based on projected cash flows and not realised performance.

Companies usually turn to company earnings and cash flow (which are termed flow measures) for management remuneration schemes. EVA supports the same sort of recommendations that NPV provides at the project level, but also provides a better measure of management performance because it rewards for earnings generated, whilst also including charges for the amount of capital employed to create those earnings.

If profit after tax = PAT

Weighted average cost of capital = WACC

Net assets = adjusted book value of net capital = NA

Then we may define EVA as:

$$EVA = PAT - (WACC \times NA)$$

Worked Example 8.13 illustrates the calculation of EVA and its relationship with NPV.

Worked Example 8.13

A manager has to choose between three mutually exclusive projects. The company may invest:

- £50,000 in project A, or
- £110,000 in project B, or
- £240,000 in project C.

Project A is expected to generate incremental profits after tax (PAT) of £50,000 in year 1, £40,000 in year 2 (total £90,000), after which the project is terminated.

Project B is expected to generate incremental PATs of £45,000 in year 1, £70,000 in year 2, £70,000 in year 3 (total £185,000), after which the project is terminated.

Project C is expected to generate incremental PATs of £55,000 in year 1, £75,000 in year 2, £80,000 in year 3 (total £210,000), after which the project is terminated.

The company's WACC is 10% per annum. Capital levels may be assumed to be maintained throughout the life of each project. That is, each year's new capital investment equals depreciation in that year.

Capital items are sold at their book value in the final year of each project, so free cash flow (operating cash flow less capital expenditure) will be equal to PAT each year except the final years when the capital costs are recovered.

We will assess which project the manager will choose if their remuneration is:

(i)   tied to the NPV of the project

(ii) based on IRR

(iii) based on project earnings

(iv) based on EVA.

Using a discount rate of WACC at 10% per annum, we will first calculate the NPVs of each project.

Year	Cash outflows £000	Cash inflows £000		Net cash flow £000	Discount factor at 10%	Present values £000
Project A						
0	−50			−50	1.00	−50.0
1		50		50	0.91	45.5
2		90	[40 + 50]	90	0.83	74.7
3		0		0	0.75	0.0
Total	−50	140		90		+70.2
Project B						
0	−110			−110	1.00	−110.0
1		45		45	0.91	40.9
2		70		70	0.83	58.1
3		180	[70 + 110]	180	0.75	135.0
Total	−110	295		185		+124.0
Project C						
0	−240			−240	1.00	−240.0
1		55		55	0.91	50.0
2		75		75	0.83	62.3
3		320	[80 + 240]	320	0.75	240.0
Total	−240	450		210		+112.3

The IRR is the rate of return that would give an NPV of zero.

The interpolation and extrapolation techniques covered in Chapter 4 may be used to derive the internal rate of return of each project.

For project C, if we assume a discount rate of 30%, we may calculate a revised NPV as follows:

Year	Cash outflows £000	Cash inflows £000	Net cash flow £000	Discount factor at 30%	Present values £000
0	−240		−240	1.00	−240.0
1		55	55	0.77	42.4
2		75	75	0.59	44.3
3		320	320	0.46	147.2
Total	−240	450	210		−6.1

We have already calculated the positive NPV for project C of £112,300 using a cost of capital of 10%. The IRR of project C must be at some point between 30% and 10% (difference 20%).

▶ Using a similar calculation to that used in Worked Example 4.12 (Chapter 4):

$$\frac{£6,100}{x} = \frac{£12,300}{(20 - x)}$$

$$(£6,100 \times 20) - £6,100x = £112,300x$$

$$£122,000 = £118,400x$$

$$x = \frac{£122,000}{£118,400}$$

$$x = 1.03$$

Therefore, interpolation gives us an IRR of 30% less 1.03%, which may be rounded to 29%.

The IRRs of projects A and B may be calculated in the same way.

The cash flows, NPVs, and IRRs of the three projects may be summarised as:

Project	PAT			Cash out	Cash in			Total cash flow	IRR	NPV
	Year 1 £000	Year 2 £000	Year 3 £000	£000	Year 1 £000	Year 2 £000	Year 3 £000	£000	%	£000
A	50	40		−50	50	90 [40 + 50]		90	93	70.2
B	45	70	70	−110	45	70	180 [70 + 110]	185	53	124.0
C	55	75	80	−240	55	75	320 [80 + 240]	210	29	112.3

(i) Based on the highest NPV, project B at £124,000 is best for the company shareholders.

(ii) But if the manager's remuneration is based on IRR then he or she will choose project A at 93%.

(iii) If the manager is remunerated on total project cash flow then he or she will choose project C at £210,000.

(iv) We can calculate the EVA for each project, which equals profit after tax for each period, less capital employed at the start of each period multiplied by the weighted average cost of capital.

Year	Project A		Project B		Project C	
	£000	EVA £000	£000	EVA £000	£000	EVA £000
1	50 − (50 × 10%)	45	45 − (110 × 10%)	34	55 − (240 × 10%)	31
2	40 − (50 × 10%)	35	70 − (110 × 10%)	59	75 − (240 × 10%)	51
3			70 − (110 × 10%)	59	80 − (240 × 10%)	56
Total		80		152		138

We may also calculate the NPV of the EVAs of each project, the present values of the EVAs:

Year	Discount factor at 10%	Project A		Project B		Project C	
		Cash flow £000	NPV £000	Cash flow £000	NPV £000	Cash flow £000	NPV £000
1	0.91	45	41.0	34	30.9	31	28.2
2	0.83	35	29.1	59	48.9	51	42.3
3	0.75			59	44.2	56	42.0
Total		80	+70.1	152	+124.0	138	+112.5

This illustrates that EVAs actually equate to cash flows because their present values are approximately the same as the NPV of each project. The small differences between the totals calculated for Project A and Project C are as a result of rounding differences.

We have seen from Worked Example 8.13 that earnings-based remuneration schemes may result in over-investment of capital, whereas return on net assets will result in under-investment of capital. Use of EVA as a basis for management remuneration takes account of the fact that the use of capital is charged for by using WACC; additionally, at the project level, the present value of the EVAs gives the same result as NPVs derived from free cash flows. Compare the results in the project NPV tables with the NPVs of the EVAs of each project in Worked Example 8.13.

Although the free cash flow NPVs give the same result as the present values of the EVAs, EVA is more appropriate for remuneration schemes because, as well as being fundamentally related to shareholder value, it is a flow measure of performance. The reason is that flow measures of performance are needed for periodic remuneration because remuneration is designed to provide a flow of rewards. The other flow measure is cash flow. EVA is a better measure than that because it takes into account the cost of capital invested in the project.

Worked Example 8.14

We will compute the EVA for 2005, 2006 and 2007 for a major plc from the following information.

Group cost of capital		5%
		£m
Adjusted net assets	2007	750
	2006	715
	2005	631
Profit after tax	2007	550
	2006	526
	2005	498
Equity	2007	100
	2006	48
	2005	115
Net debt	2007	800
	2006	802
	2005	546

Year	Profit after tax £m	Adjusted net assets £m	5% cost of capital × net assets £m	EVA £m	EVA % of net profit
2007	550	750	37.50	512.50	93%
2006	526	715	35.75	490.25	93%
2005	498	631	31.55	466.45	94%

Note how the profits are being earned using borrowed funds to finance the group. The plc can earn a very high EVA by using borrowed funds.

We have talked about EVA in respect of projects, and that the present value of future EVAs equals the NPV derived from future free cash flows. At a company level, the present value of EVAs equals the market value added (MVA) of a business. This is defined as the difference between the market value of the company and the adjusted book values of its assets.

EVA is a good financial performance measure because it answers the question of how well the company has performed in generating profits over a period, given the amount of capital tied up to generate those profits. However, the capital base is a difficult element to estimate in calculating EVA. The total net assets value on a balance sheet is not an accurate representation of either the liquidation value or the replacement cost value of the business. Stern Stewart consider more than 250 possible accounting adjustments to a balance sheet to arrive at a valuation of the company's assets. In practice most organisations find that no more than a dozen or so adjustments are truly significant, for example stocks, depreciation, goodwill, deferred tax, and closure costs.

Worked Example 8.15

We will compute the MVA for 2006 and 2007 from the following extracts from the annual report and accounts of a major plc, using the adjusted value of its net assets.

	2007	2006
Number of shares (5p)	950.2m	948.9m
Share price	278p	268p
Net assets	£1,097m	£1,437m

	2007	2006
Net assets	£1,097m	£1,437m
Market value	£2,641m	£2,543m
MVA	£1,544m	£1,106m

Progress check 8.13

What is economic value added (EVA) and what is it used for?

EVA probably does not change or add anything to the conclusions reached on the basis of conventional cash flow based valuation analysis. EVA is primarily a behavioural tool that corrects possible distortions. However, along with most other financial measures, it fails to measure on an *ex post* basis. EVA is undoubtedly a very useful concept for measuring and evaluating management and company performance. It is not a cure for poor management and poor investment decisions but it raises the profile and the awareness of the costs of capital involved in undertaking projects and in running the business.

Predicting corporate financial failure

One of the uses of ratio analysis is in the area of trying to predict corporate failure. The various groups of corporate stakeholders have an obvious interest in such predictions, for example:

- shareholders would like to know how risky their investments are
- employees would like to know how secure their jobs are
- suppliers would like to be sure that they will be paid
- lenders would like to be reassured that interest and loan repayments will be made.

If stakeholders are able to determine which companies are riskier than others then they may make better informed decisions. There has been a great deal of research that has resulted in the development of various **multivariate discriminant analysis (MDA)** models that are used to try and predict corporate financial failure, such as those developed by:

- Argenti (Argenti J (1976) *Corporate Collapse – the Causes and Symptoms*, London: McGraw-Hill)
- Datastream's model developed by Marais (Marais DAJ (1979) *A Method of Quantifying Companies' Relative Financial Strength*, Bank of England Discussion Paper, No. 4)
- Altman (Altman E (1983) *Corporate Financial Distress – A Complete Guide to Predicting, Avoiding and Dealing with Bankruptcy*, New York: Wiley)
- Taffler (Taffler RJ (1982) 'Forecasting Company Failure in the UK Using Discriminant Analysis and Financial Ratio Data', *Journal of Royal Statistical Society*, (A) 145, Part 3, 342–58, and (1995) 'The Use of the Z-Score Approach in Practice', City University Business School Working Paper 95/1).

Datastream is a commercial company, which provides a range of statistical and economic information, including Z-Scores, for selected companies based on their own model developed by Marais. The model is based on a sample of 100 UK companies, 50 of which failed and 50 of which did not, and is based on four independent measures of company performance:

- profitability
- liquidity
- gearing
- stock turnover.

Taffler's Z-Score is based on the four ratios:

- profit before tax/current liabilities
- current assets/total liabilities
- current liabilities/total assets
- liquid current assets/daily cash operating expenses,

each of which is multiplied by constant factors.

Taffler's Z-Scores range between negative (higher risk) and positive (lower risk); the higher or lower the Z-Scores indicate the level of potential failure or survival.

Edward Altman's model is based on a sample of 66 manufacturing companies, 33 of which failed and 33 of which did not, matched by size and industry and selected on a stratified random basis, and is based on the following ratios:

- working capital/total assets
- retained earnings/total assets
- earnings before interest and tax/total assets
- equity/total liabilities
- equity/total assets.

Altman's model may be used for prediction of corporate failure by calculating his Z-Score for public and private industrial companies. For a public industrial company Z equals:

$$1.2 \times \frac{\text{working capital}}{\text{total assets}} + 1.4 \times \frac{\text{retained earnings}}{\text{total assets}} + 3.3 \times \frac{\text{EBIT}}{\text{total assets}} + 0.6 \times \frac{\text{equity}}{\text{total liabilities}}$$

$$+ 1.05 \times \frac{\text{equity}}{\text{total assets}}$$

For a private industrial company Z equals:

$$6.56 \times \frac{\text{working capital}}{\text{total assets}} + 3.26 \times \frac{\text{retained earnings}}{\text{total assets}} + 6.72 \times \frac{\text{EBIT}}{\text{total assets}}$$

$$+ 1.05 \times \frac{\text{equity}}{\text{total liabilities}} + 0.0 \times \frac{\text{equity}}{\text{total assets}}$$

Altman's model predicts that public industrial companies with a Z-Score of less than 1.81 will become insolvent (private companies 1.1). Public industrial companies with a Z-score over 2.99 are considered to be healthy (private companies 2.60). Public industrial companies with a Z-Score of between 1.81 and 2.99 hover within the grey area between decline and recovery (private companies 1.1 and 2.60).

Worked Example 8.16

We can calculate the Z-Score for Flatco plc for 2007 as follows:

$$\frac{1.2 \times 995}{4,348} + \frac{1.4 \times 1,594}{4,348} + \frac{3.3 \times 650}{4,348} + \frac{0.6 \times 2,994}{1,354} + \frac{1.05 \times 3,500}{4,348}$$

$$= 0.275 + 0.513 + 0.494 + 1.327 + 0.845 = 3.454$$

So with a Z-Score greater than 2.99, Flatco plc may be considered to have a healthy financial position.

The many refinements to Altman's Z-Score, which are used by banks and by companies to assess creditworthiness, are kept highly secret because a successful method gives a business a significant competitive advantage in being able to identify good and bad borrowers. For example, the ability of banks to accurately identify good and bad credit risks has a big impact on their level of bad debt write-offs, and therefore their profitability. In 2006 the Royal Bank of Scotland reported an increase in its bad debts of 4.7% over the previous year to £887m. Compare this with the 50% and 20% increases for Barclays Bank and Lloyds TSB Bank respectively for the same period.

Caution should be exercised in the use of financial failure prediction models for a number of reasons. Such models are inevitably based on past data, business structure, and economic environment. For example, the 1990s and prior would not have included the significant presence of the 'hi tech' and dot.com companies that we have in the 2000s.

The use of MDA models may be augmented by statistical analyses of financial data to further assist in this area of prediction of corporate failure, using, for example, time series and line of business analyses. However, the use of any financial analysis is not an exact science because of the alternative application of financial standards and accounting policies adopted by companies.

We have assumed that the financial failure of a business means insolvency, but failure may have wider implications than the liquidation of a company. Models to predict financial failure are used extensively by banks, credit rating organisations, and financial analysts. Although there has been much research into the development of the MDA models themselves there has been less research and analysis into the validity and reliability of these models in practice.

Progress check 8.14

Who are the main users of Z-Scores and how do they use them?

Summary of key points

- The main aims of a business performance review are to provide an understanding of the business and provide an interpretation of results.
- Care must be taken in reviewing business performance, primarily because of lack of consistency in definitions, and changes in economic conditions.
- An important area of business performance review is the use of ratio analysis looking at profitability, efficiency, liquidity, investment and growth, and financial structure.
- The Du Pont system of ratios can be used to identify the relationship between return on equity (ROE), return on assets (ROA), and gearing.
- Horizontal analysis of the income statement (which may also be applied to the balance sheet) for two or more years starts with a base year 100 and shows each item, line-by-line, indexed against the base year, and is particularly useful in looking at performance trends over a number of years.
- Vertical analysis of the income statement (which may also be applied to the balance sheet) shows every item as a percentage of turnover (balance sheet–total assets), and is also particularly useful in looking at performance trends over a number of years.
- Segmental reporting provides a further dimension to the financial statements through analysis of turnover, operating profit and net assets, by business class, and geographical segments.
- Cash flow and cash ratios are becoming increasingly as important as profit and profitability ratios in the measurement of business performance.
- There is no best way of evaluating financial performance and there are advantages and disadvantages in using both earnings per share or cash flow as the basis of measurement.
- Earnings before interest, tax, depreciation and amortisation – EBITDA – is now commonly used as a close approximation of a cash flow performance measure.
- The technique of economic value added (EVA) is becoming widely used by companies as a performance measure that is very close to cash flow, and as a value creation incentive.
- There are a number of multivariate discriminant analysis (MDA) methods of predicting corporate financial failure used by banks, credit agencies, and financial institutions; the most well-known are the various versions of the Z-Score analyses developed by Taffler, Marais (Datastream), and Altman.

🔒 Glossary of key terms

acid test Quick assets (current assets excluding stocks) divided by current liabilities measures the ability of the business to pay creditors in the short term.

cash interest cover Net cash inflow from operations plus interest received, divided by interest paid, calculates the number of times the interest payable is covered by cash flow available for such payments.

creditor days Average trade creditors divided by average daily purchases on credit terms indicates the average time taken, in calendar days, to pay for supplies received on credit.

cross-sectional analysis Cross-sectional analysis provides a means of providing a standard against which performance can be measured and uses ratios to compare different businesses at the same points in time (see inter-firm comparison).

current ratio Current assets divided by current liabilities is an overall measure of liquidity.

debt/equity ratio A gearing ratio that relates to financial gearing, which is the relationship between a company's borrowings, which includes both prior charge capital and long-term debt, and its ordinary shareholders' funds (share capital plus reserves).

debtor days Average trade debtors divided by average daily sales on credit terms indicates the average time taken, in calendar days, to receive payment from credit customers.

defensive interval Quick assets (current assets excluding stocks) divided by average daily cash from operations shows how many days a business could survive at its present level of operating activity if no inflow of cash was received from sales or other sources.

dividend cover Earnings per share divided by dividend per share indicates the number of times the profits attributable to the equity shareholders cover the actual dividends payable for the period.

dividend yield Dividend return on the market value of a share shown as a percentage.

EBITDA Earnings before interest, tax, depreciation, and amortisation.

horizontal analysis (or common size analysis) An analysis of the income statement (or balance sheet) that allows a line-by-line analysis of the accounts with those of the previous year. It may provide a trend of changes over a number of years showing either growth or decline in these elements of the accounts through calculation of annual percentage growth rates in profits, sales, stock, or any other item.

interest cover Profit before interest and tax divided by interest payable, calculates the number of times the interest payable is covered by profits available for such payments. It is particularly important for lenders to determine the vulnerability of interest payments to a drop in profit.

inter-firm comparison Systematic and detailed comparison of the performance of different companies generally operating in a common industry. Normally the information distributed by the scheme administrator (to participating companies only) is in the form of ratios, or in a format that prevents the identity of individual scheme members from being identified.

just in time (JIT) The management philosophy that incorporates a 'pull' system of producing or purchasing components and products in response to customer demand, which contrasts with a 'push' system where stocks act as buffers between each process within and between purchasing, manufacturing, and sales.

market value added (MVA) The difference between the market value of the company and the adjusted book values of its assets.

multivariate discriminant analysis (MDA) MDA is a statistical technique which has been used to develop models that try to predict financial failure by: classifying samples of companies into two similar groups (one group in which all companies are predicted to survive and the other group in which all companies are predicted to fail) using a discriminant prediction equation of financial ratios; testing the theory by observing whether the companies are classified as predicted; investigating differences between or among the groups of companies; determining the optimum combination of discriminator ratios (for example a Z-Score) to best distinguish between the two groups of companies.

operating gearing The relationship of fixed costs to total costs. The greater the proportion of fixed costs, the higher the operating gearing, and the greater the advantage to the business of increasing sales volume. If sales drop, a business with high operating gearing may face a problem from its high level of fixed costs.

price earnings ratio (P/E) The market price per ordinary share divided by earnings per share shows the number of years it would take to recoup an equity investment from its share of the attributable equity profit.

return on capital employed (ROCE) ROCE, or return on investment (ROI), is the profit before interest and tax divided by average capital employed. It indicates the profit-generating capacity of capital employed.

return on equity (ROE) A form of return on capital employed which measures the return to the owners on their investment in a company. The return is measured as the residual profit after all charges and appropriations other than to ordinary shareholders have been made, and the equity is ordinary share capital plus reserves.

return on investment (ROI) See return on capital employed (ROCE).

segmental reporting The inclusion in a company's report and accounts of analysis of turnover, profits, and net assets by class of business and by geographical segments (Companies Act 1985/89 and IAS 14 (IFRS 8)).

▶

▶

stock days Stocks, according to SSAP 9, are goods held for future use comprising:

- goods or other assets purchased for resale
- consumable stores
- raw materials and components purchased for incorporation into products for sale
- products and services, in intermediate stages of completion (work in progress)
- long-term contracts
- finished goods.

SWOT analysis Performing a SWOT analysis is a means of gaining a clear picture of the Strengths, Weaknesses, Opportunities, and Threats, which made the organisation what it is. SWOT analysis can apply across diverse management functions and activities, but is particularly appropriate to the early stages of formulating strategy.

vendor managed inventory (VMI) The management of stocks on behalf of a customer by the supplier, the supplier taking responsibility for the management of stocks within a framework that is mutually agreed by both parties. Examples are seen in separate supermarket racks maintained and stocked by merchandising groups for such items as spices, and car parts distributors topping up the shelves of dealers and garages, where the management of the stocks, racking, and shelves is carried out by the merchandising group or distributor.

vertical analysis An analysis of the income statement (or balance sheet) in which each item is expressed as a percentage of the total. The vertical analysis provides evidence of structural changes in the business such as increased profitability through more efficient production.

❓ Questions

Q8.1 (i) Who is likely to carry out a business performance review?

(ii) Describe what may be required from such reviews giving some examples from different industries and differing perspectives.

Q8.2 (i) Outline how the business performance review process may be used to evaluate the position of a dot.com company like Amazon UK.

(ii) What are the limitations to the approach that you have outlined?

Q8.3 How is ratio analysis, in terms of profitability ratios, efficiency ratios, liquidity ratios, investment ratios, and financial structure ratios used to support the business review process?

Q8.4 Why should we be so careful when we try to compare the income statement of a plc with a similar business in the same industry?

Q8.5 (i) Why does profit continue to be the preferred basis for evaluation of the financial performance of a business?

(ii) In what ways can cash flow provide a better basis for performance evaluation, and how may cash flow be approximated?

Q8.6 In what way is company growth of such interest to shareholders?

Q8.7 Business performance may be evaluated to determine ways in which it can be improved upon. If managers are capable of delivering improved performance how can EVA be used to support this?

Q8.8 Explain how models that have been developed to predict corporate financial failure may be used in practice.

Discussion points

D8.1 In what ways may the performance review process be used to anticipate and react to change?

D8.2 'Lies, damned lies, and statistics.' In which of these categories do you think ratio analysis sits, if at all?

D8.3 'Economic value added (EVA) is nothing more than just flavour of the month.' Discuss.

Exercises

Solutions are provided in Appendix 2 to all exercise numbers highlighted in colour.

Level I

E8.1   *Time allowed – 30 minutes*

The information below relates to Priory Products plc's actual results for 2006 and 2007 and their budget for the year 2008.

Figures in £000

	2006	2007	2008
Cash at bank	100	0	0
Overdraft	0	50	200
Loans	200	200	600
Ordinary shares	100	200	400
Profit and loss account	200	300	400

You are required to calculate the following financial ratios for Priory Products for 2006, 2007, and 2008:

(i) debt/equity ratio (net debt to equity)

(ii) gearing (long-term loans to equity and long-term loans).

E8.2   *Time allowed – 60 minutes*

From the financial statements of Freshco plc, a Lancashire-based grocery and general supplies chain supplying hotels and caterers, for the year ended 30 June 2007, prepare a report on performance using appropriate profitability ratios for comparison with the previous year.

▶

▶

Freshco plc
Balance sheet as at 30 June 2007

	2007 £m	2006 £m
Non-current assets	146	149
Current assets		
Stocks	124	100
Debtors	70	80
Cash and bank	14	11
	208	191
Current liabilities (less than one year)		
Creditors	76	74
Dividends	20	13
Taxation	25	20
	121	107
Net current assets	87	84
Total assets less current liabilities	233	233
less		
Non-current liabilities (over one year)		
Debenture	(20)	(67)
Net assets	213	166
Capital and reserves		
Capital	111	100
General reserve	14	9
Profit and loss account	88	57
	213	166

Freshco plc
Income statement for the year ended 30 June 2007

	2007 £m	2006 £m
Turnover	894	747
Cost of sales	(690)	(581)
Gross profit	204	166
Distribution and administrative costs	(101)	(79)
Operating profit	103	87
Other costs	(20)	(5)
Profit before interest and tax	83	82
Net interest	(2)	(8)
Profit before tax	81	74
Tax on profit on ordinary activities	(25)	(20)
Profit on ordinary activities after tax	56	54
Retained profit brought forward	57	16
	113	70
Dividends	(20)	(13)
	93	57
Transfer to general reserve	(5)	–
Retained profit for the financial year	88	57

Additional information:

(i) Authorised and issued share capital 30 June 2007, £222m £0.50 ordinary shares (£200m, 2006).

(ii) Total assets less current liabilities 30 June 2005, £219m. Trade debtors 30 June 2005, £60m.

(iii) Market value of ordinary shares in Freshco plc 30 June 2007, £3.93 (£2.85, 2006).

(iv) Non-current assets depreciation provision 30 June 2007, £57m (£44m, 2006).

Freshco plc
Cash flow statement for the year ended 30 June 2007
Reconciliation of operating profit to net cash flow from operating activities

	2007 £m	2006 £m
Operating profit	103	87
Depreciation charges	13	10
Increase in stocks	(24)	(4)
Increase in debtors	(10)	(20)
Increase in creditors	2	4
Net cash inflow from operating activities	84	77

Cash flow statement

	2007 £m	2006 £m
Net cash inflow from operating activities	84	77
Returns on investments and servicing of finance	(2)	(8)
Taxation	(20)	(15)
Capital expenditure	(10)	(40)
	52	14
Equity dividends paid	(13)	(11)
	39	3
Management of liquid resources	–	–
Financing	(36)	7
Increase in cash	3	10

E8.3 *Time allowed – 60 minutes*
Using the financial statements of Freshco plc from Exercise E8.2, for the year ended 30 June 2007, prepare a report on performance using appropriate efficiency ratios for comparison with the previous year.

E8.4 *Time allowed – 60 minutes*
Using the financial statements of Freshco plc from Exercise E8.2, for the year ended 30 June 2007, prepare a report on performance using appropriate liquidity ratios for comparison with the previous year.

E8.5 *Time allowed – 60 minutes*
Using the financial statements of Freshco plc from Exercise E8.2, for the year ended 30 June 2007, prepare a report on performance using appropriate investment ratios for comparison with the previous year.

E8.6 *Time allowed – 60 minutes*
Using the financial statements of Freshco plc from Exercise E8.2, for the year ended 30 June 2007, prepare a report on performance using appropriate financial ratios for comparison with the previous year.

▶ *Level II*

E8.7   *Time allowed – 30 minutes*

You are required to compute the MVA for 2005, 2006, and 2007 from the estimated information for a large supermarket group.

	2007	2006	2005
Number of shares	6.823m	6.823m	6.776m
Share price	261p	169p	177p
Adjusted net assets	£5,000m	£4,769m	£4,377m

E8.8   *Time allowed – 60 minutes*

The summarised income statement for the years ended 31 March 2006 and 2007 and balance sheets as at 31 March 2006 and 31 March 2007 for Boxer plc are shown below:

Boxer plc
Income statement for the year ended 31 March
Figures in £000

	2006	2007
Turnover	5,200	5,600
Cost of sales	(3,200)	(3,400)
Gross profit	2,000	2,200
Expenses	(1,480)	(1,560)
Profit before tax	520	640

Boxer plc
Balance sheet as at 31 March
Figures in £000

	2006	2007
Non-current assets	4,520	5,840
Current assets		
Stocks	1,080	1,360
Trade debtors	640	880
Prepayments	40	80
Cash and bank	240	–
	2,000	2,320
Current liabilities (less than one year)		
Overdraft	–	160
Trade creditors	360	520
Tax payable	240	120
Dividend payable	280	384
	880	1,184
Net current assets	1,120	1,136
Total assets less current liabilities	5,640	6,976
less		
Non-current liabilities (over one year)		
Debentures	(1,200)	(1,200)
Net assets	4,440	5,776
Capital and reserves		
Ordinary share capital	4,000	5,200
Profit and loss account	440	576
	4,440	5,776

Required:

(i) Calculate the following ratios for the years 2006 and 2007:

    (a) gross profit percentage

    (b) profit before tax percentage

    (c) return on capital employed

    (d) debtor collection days

    (e) creditor payment days

    (f) stock turnover

    (g) current ratio

    (h) acid test ratio.

(ii) Comment on Boxer plc's financial performance over the two years and explain the importance of the effective management of working capital.

E8.9 *Time allowed – 90 minutes*

The chief executive of Laurel plc, Al Chub, wants to know the financial strength of Laurel's main competitor, Hardy plc. From Hardy's financial statements for the past three years he has asked you to write a report that evaluates the financial performance of Hardy plc and to include:

(i) a ratio analysis that looks at profitability, working capital, and liquidity

(ii) an identification of the top five areas which should be investigated further

(iii) details of information that has not been provided, but if it were available would improve your analysis of Hardy's performance.

Hardy plc
Balance sheet as at 31 March
Figures in £m

	2005	2006	2007
Non-current assets	106	123	132
Current assets			
Stocks	118	152	147
Debtors	53	70	80
Cash and bank	26	29	26
	197	251	253
Current liabilities (less than one year)			
Trade creditors	26	38	38
Other creditors	40	52	55
	66	90	93
Net current assets	131	161	160
Total assets less current liabilities	237	284	292
less			
Non-current liabilities (over one year)			
Debenture	(37)	(69)	(69)
Net assets	200	215	223
Capital and reserves			
Capital	50	50	50
Profit and loss account	150	165	173
	200	215	223

▶

▶

Hardy plc
Income statement for the year ended 31 March
Figures in £m

	2005	2006	2007
Turnover	420	491	456
Cost of sales	(277)	(323)	(295)
Gross profit	143	168	161
Distribution and administrative costs	(93)	(107)	(109)
Operating profit	50	61	52
Other costs	–	–	–
Profit before interest and tax	50	61	52
Net interest	(3)	(7)	(9)
Profit before tax	47	54	43
Tax on profit on ordinary activities	(22)	(26)	(23)
Profit on ordinary activities after tax	25	28	20
Dividends	(12)	(12)	(12)
Retained profit for the financial year	13	16	8

E8.10 *Time allowed – 90 minutes*

The following are the summarised financial statements of Dandy plc, a UK retailer. The company has been operating successfully for a number of years. Whilst over recent years, market opportunities have resulted in an expansion in trading operations, recent sales and profits have nevertheless fallen over the past three years. The company has had severe cash problems resulting in an increase in overall debt.

Income statement for the year ended 30 November

	2005 £000	2006 £000	2007 £000
Turnover	11,200	8,000	6,000
Cost of sales	(5,600)	(3,000)	(2,800)
Gross profit	5,600	5,000	3,200
Operating expenses	(4,000)	(2,600)	(2,000)
Profit before taxation	1,600	2,400	1,200
Taxation	(600)	(1,100)	(550)
Profit after taxation	1,000	1,300	650
Dividends	(600)	(200)	(300)
Retained profit for the year	400	1,100	350
Market price of shares at 30 November	£0.80	£0.90	£0.45

Balance sheet as at 30 November

	2005 £000	2006 £000	2007 £000
Non-current assets	3,600	2,700	6,500
Less: depreciation	(1,000)	(700)	(1,400)
	2,600	2,000	5,100
Current assets			
Stocks	1,700	1,800	2,200
Trade debtors	2,900	5,550	5,000
Debtors	300	1,800	500
Bank	400	50	400
	5,300	9,200	8,100
Current liabilities			
Trade creditors	1,300	1,200	1,000
Other creditors	1,000	1,000	1,500
Taxation	600	1,100	550
Dividends	600	200	300
	3,500	3,500	3,350
Total assets less current liabilities	4,400	7,700	9,850
less			
Non-current liabilities			
Debentures	(1,000)	(3,000)	(4,500)
Net assets	3,400	4,700	5,350
Capital and reserves			
Share capital (£1 ordinary shares)	2,000	2,200	2,500
Profit and loss account	1,400	2,500	2,850
	3,400	4,700	5,350

Required:

(i) Using the information provided, and stating all necessary assumptions, evaluate the past performance of Dandy plc and the future potential of the company.

(ii) Which other performance evaluation techniques (other than financial ratios) could be used to measure the performance of Dandy plc?

E8.11 *Time allowed – 120 minutes*

Locate the website for HSBC Bank plc on the Internet. Use their most recent annual report and accounts to prepare a report that evaluates their financial performance, financial position, and future prospects. Your report should include calculations of the appropriate ratios for comparison with the previous year.

E8.12 *Time allowed – 120 minutes*

Locate the websites for Tesco plc and Morrisons plc on the Internet. Use their most recent annual report and accounts to prepare a report that evaluates and compares their financial performance, and financial position. Your report should include calculations of the appropriate ratios for comparing the two groups, and an explanation of their differences and similarities.

Chapter 9

Financial planning

Chapter contents

LEARNING OBJECTIVES

Completion of this chapter will enable you to:

☑ Explain financial planning as part of the strategic management process.

☑ Outline the purpose of financial planning.

☑ Describe the financial planning process.

☑ Use financial modelling to plan the long-term activities of a business.

☑ Identify the ways in which a company may use alternative forecasting methods.

☑ Prepare cash flow forecasts as part of the financial planning process to determine a company's funding requirements.

☑ Explain the ways in which a business may plan for its future growth.

☑ Consider the financing options that a company may use to fund its future growth.

☑ Outline the ways in which a company's performance may be measured against its plans.

☑ Explain the ways in which the balanced scorecard may be used to translate a company's strategic plans into operational terms.

Introduction

Many companies have started up with very good ideas and good intentions with regard to their development and future sales growth. However, the corporate graveyard is full of companies who have been unsuccessful in these endeavours because they have failed to plan for such growth in terms of its impact on costs and planned levels of investment and funding.

This chapter considers financial planning, which is an important part of the strategic management process, concerned not with the absolute detail but taking a look at the big picture of the company as a whole. Strategic financial planning is not short term, but is concerned with periods of greater than one year, and looks at expected levels of a company's sales growth and how it may be financed.

In order to produce forecast long-term financial statements, financial plans are based on the company's planned growth rate, and its financial ratios relating to costs, working capital, tax, dividends, and gearing. Forecasts are not plans or budgets but are predictions of what may happen in the future. There are a variety of techniques, both qualitative and quantitative, which are used to forecast growth rates. Quantitative methods include use of the statistical techniques of exponential smoothing and regression analysis.

Cash flow forecasting is one part of the financial planning process and is used to determine a company's future funding requirements on a monthly and yearly basis. The company may use its own resources of retained earnings to support its plans for future sales growth. In some circumstances, additional external funding is a necessity for a company planning future growth. This chapter looks at how this additional funding may be acquired using debt and equity.

Two of the most widely used measures to compare companies' actual against planned performance are return on capital employed (ROCE) and earnings per share (eps). However, companies are now increasingly using non-financial measures in addition to financial measures to measure performance. This chapter closes with a look at such a technique, the balanced scorecard, which is a method used to link companies' long-term strategies into operational targets and key performance indicators.

The strategic view

The whole area of financial planning is questioned in the following article reproduced from *Accountancy Age*, with particular emphasis on the time spans over which financial plans may be realistic and therefore useful. This article, based on a survey of 258 finance directors, considers whether plans for large projects like the Olympics can be realistic when they are prepared so many years ahead of the events.

There are clearly different views as to whether or not the plans and budgets are effective and essential business tools. However, the majority of the world's most successful companies have attributed a large part of their success to their reliance on traditional formal planning systems. The long-term (strategic) and short-term (budget) planning processes are core management tasks that are critically important to the future survival and success of the business. The strategic plan and the budget prepared for planning purposes, as part of the strategic management process, are the quantitative plans of management's belief of what the business's costs and revenues will be over a specific future period. The budget prepared for control purposes, even though it may have been based on standards that may not be reached, is used for motivational purposes to influence improved departmental performance. Monitoring of actual performance against plans is used to provide feedback in order to take the appropriate action necessary to reach planned performance, and to revise plans in the light of changes.

How realistic are financial plans?

'FDs claim Olympic budgeting now is "unrealistic"', by Larry Schlesinger

We asked FDs two questions: Is the UK and London in particular capable of hosting the 2012 Olympic Games? AND Are budgets drawn up now unrealistic for an event to be held eight years later?

More than three-quarters of finance directors believe it is unrealistic for the 2012 London Olympic finance team to draw up budget plans eight years in advance of the event taking place.

As bid FD Neil Wood prepares the capital and operating budgets as part of the 600-page bid document to be submitted on 14 November, just 16% of the 258 FDs polled in the latest *Accountancy Age*/Reed Accountancy Big Question survey saw any value in doing this now.

Paresh Samat, finance director of Croner Consulting, said the bid team should 'learn the lessons from the rebuilding of the Wembley Stadium. The figures will end up 30% to 40% higher than estimates. Maybe we should go to

Japan and learn from their experiences of building an infrastructure from the last World Cup,' he said.

Another FD was even less convinced: 'Whatever you budget for now you need to double the figure that you ask for.'

FDs were, however, more supportive of the UK's and London's ability to host the 2012 Games, with more than two-thirds believing the capital will be able to stage the event. One FD said: 'Having hosted the Commonwealth Games successfully, I do not see why we should not host the Olympics.'

London 2012 says it will have access to £2.2bn of public funds if the bid succeeds – with £1.4bn coming from the National Lottery, £581m from London residents via a local tax and the rest coming from the London Development Agency.

© *Accountancy Age*, 3 June 2004

By the beginning of 2007 the UK Governments' estimates for the London Olympics had risen from an initial £2.35bn to £9bn. This was after the Culture Secretary, Tessa Jowell, had already admitted to Parliament, only a few months previously, an increase of 40% in the estimated cost to £3.3bn.

Currently, more and more companies are taking the view that the traditional planning and annual budgeting systems are unsuitable and irrelevant in rapidly changing markets. Further, they believe that budgets fail to deal with the most important drivers of shareholder value such as intangible assets like brands and knowledge. Some of these companies, like Volvo, Ikea, and Ericsson, have already revised their need for annual budgets as being an inefficient tool in an increasingly changing business environment. Volvo abandoned the annual budget ten years ago. Instead, they provide three-month **forecasts** and monthly board reports, which include financial and non-financial indicators. These forecasts and reports are supplemented with a two-year rolling forecast, updated quarterly, and four- and ten-year strategic plans updated yearly. It should also be noted that many of the dot.com companies that failed during the 1990s and early 2000s also felt that traditional budget methods were a little old-fashioned and irrelevant.

The broad purposes of budgeting include:

- planning and control, through
  - exception reporting of financial and non-financial indicators, which
  - economises on managerial time, and
  - maximises efficiency
- co-ordination, which
  - assists **goal congruence**
- communication, through
  - the feedback process, which should
  - reduce or prevent sub-optimal performance
- motivation and alignment of individual and corporate goals, through
  - participation of many people in the budget-setting process
- evaluation of performance, to facilitate control.

As a planning tool the budget is used to reflect the short-term outcomes from the use of a company's resources in line with its strategy. Planning is the establishment of objectives and the formulation, evaluation, and selection of the policies, strategies, tactics, and action required to achieve them. Planning comprises long-term **strategic planning**, and short-term operational planning. The latter usually refers to a period of one year. With regard to a new retail product, the strategic (long-term) plan of the business, for example, may include the aim to become profitable, and to become a market leader within three years. The short-term operational plan may be to get the product stocked by at least one leading supermarket group within 12 months.

Strategic planning is the process of deciding on:

- the objectives of the organisation
- changes in these objectives
- the resources used to attain these objectives
- the policies that are to govern the acquisition, use, and disposition of these resources.

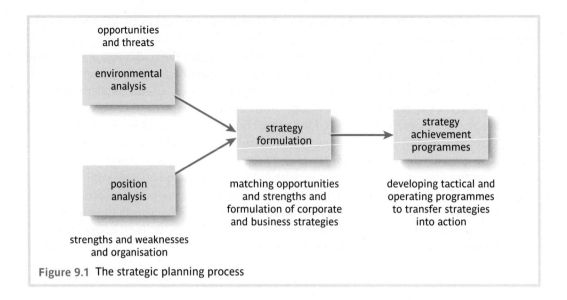

Figure 9.1 The strategic planning process

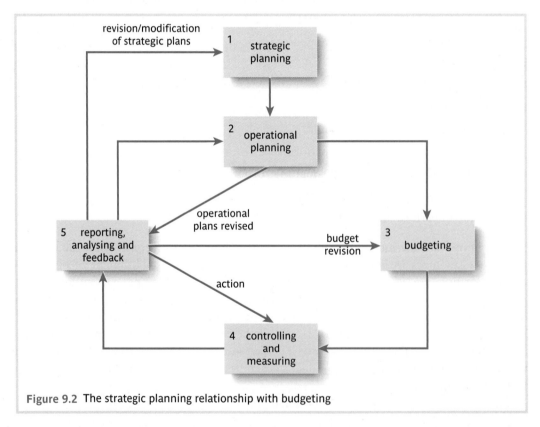

Figure 9.2 The strategic planning relationship with budgeting

The way in which a typical strategic planning process may be carried out in an organisation is illustrated in the flow charts in Figs 9.1 and 9.2. Strategic planning involves many ideas and options and lots of 'what-if' analysis. Its purpose is to try and provide a 'fit' between the company and its environment, and a focus on its main goals, and to assist in reaching those goals. The chart in Fig. 9.1 shows how analysis is linked to the development of strategies and actions.

The environmental analysis includes the opportunities and threats elements of a SWOT analysis of the business. It provides an audit of the company's external environment by considering political, economic, social, technological, environmental, and legal factors. It also considers the nature of the organisation's environment and its level of complexity. Environmental analysis provides a structural analysis of the competitive environment, and the company's competitive position and its market position.

Resources analysis looks within the organisation by considering the strengths and weaknesses elements of a SWOT analysis of the business. It uses value stream analysis, and an audit of its resources of people, materials, machinery and equipment, cash flow, and markets. Resources analysis includes financial analysis, and a comparative analysis of historical performance, industry norms, and the company's experience curve. It also includes an analysis of the company's levels of skills and flexibility, and an analysis of its various products and the stages in their product life cycles.

It is not correct to assume that planning is just an extension of budgeting, but there is a close relationship between these processes. A strategic plan is a long-term plan, which spans one or more years and is normally three to five years. The chart in Fig. 9.2 shows the sequences of each step in the process and the relationship between strategic planning and budgeting.

A budget is a quantified statement for a defined period of time, based on operational plans, which may include planned revenues, expenses, assets, liabilities, and cash flows. Strategy is expressed in broad conceptual terms, and for budgeting purposes it needs to be operationalised or translated into more detailed tactical and operational plans that can be understood at the functional level within the company. It must be translated into specific plans for functional areas such as:

■ marketing

■ research and development

■ purchasing

■ sales

■ production

■ human resources

■ information systems.

An important aspect of this operationalisation is:

■ the identification of required resources

■ the development of appropriate performance criteria

■ the implementation of appropriate control systems

■ the development of relevant operational budgets.

A budget provides a focus for the organisation, aids the co-ordination of activities, and facilitates control. To enable control of operations, actual performance may be compared with the budget. Differences between actual and budget are then reported, and analysed and feedback is used:

■ to provide information for appropriate remedial action to rectify 'out of control' operations

■ to enable necessary revisions of future short-term operational plans

■ to revise or modify long-term strategic plans, if necessary.

Financial planning is a part of the strategic planning process and includes:

- assessment of investment opportunities that will add value to the business
- consideration of the various alternative methods of financing new investment
- identifying the risks associated with alternative investment options
- ranking of alternative investment and financing options to optimise decisions
- measurement of performance of the financial planning process.

Although new capital investments may be proposed by a company's operational and administrative managers, the coordination of the total investment by the company is made by the directors of the business in line with their strategic objectives. In order to create corporate value it is essential that investments are made which return a positive net present value (NPV).

Investments that the company must ensure return positive NPVs include new projects or profit improvement projects within the business, or they may include acquisitions of other companies. The performance of group companies not meeting this criterion should be critically reviewed and, where appropriate, sold off or liquidated.

Financial planning at the company level is effectively capital budgeting at the top level dealing with each business sector rather than the detail of cost and revenue centre capital budgeting. It will include the five or ten year proposed financial plans submitted at departmental level consolidated to consider the growth expectations of the business as a whole and a consideration of the financial implications should the company not meet its growth expectations. Such plans will include the proposed capital expenditure and its alternative methods of financing. It will also consider working capital requirements, and the impacts of inflation, and taxation.

The purpose of financial planning

There are a number of reasons why companies devote considerable resources to the development of financial plans. They would not do this unless they anticipate that the benefits may be equally considerable.

There are differences between forecasts, budgets, and long-term financial plans. Forecasts look at what is likely to happen, and that information is used in budget preparation. Strategic financial plans consider what events may occur, but also look at potential problems that may arise, and their reasons and impact. Sensitivities may be looked at using scenario analysis and simulations to determine the impact on financial plans of various 'what-if' questions. For example, what would be the impact on a financial plan if costs were 10% higher, or if sales were 10% lower? Having determined the impact of possible deviations from the plan, the company may then make appropriate contingencies in the plan.

Financial plans should consider not only opportunities that the company may have which add value by providing a positive NPV, but also include other opportunities presented to the company, which are of more strategic interest. These include opportunities for developing new products, or new markets in ways that provide options for the company to make appropriate capital investments or not at some time in the future.

A company's financial plan should reflect its expected growth and how this may be financed. Growth may be financed internally through reinvestment of retained earnings. Alternatively, its capital investment for growth may require further external funding through either additional equity or additional debt. The plan itself will provide consistency in ensuring that growth is matched by whatever level of additional finance is required by the company.

The financial plan also provides consistency between the various corporate objectives. For example, a company may be planning levels of profit, sales, and costs. It is only by looking at the big picture of a financial plan that embraces all these objectives that it can be seen if these are consistent and mutually achievable. This applies to any corporate objectives that are in terms that relate to accounting ratios like, for example, return on capital employed, gross profit, or net profit. Such ratios that are stated as objectives must also consider the strategic decisions that need to be made to achieve them – for example, levels of investment, sales volumes, selling prices, and costs – and must be reflected in the financial plan.

Progress check 9.1

Explain the overall strategic planning process and the relationships between forecasting, budgeting, and planning.

The financial planning process

A company may have a number of alternative strategies, and these need to be translated into financial plans in order that they may be realistically compared. A simple model includes an income statement plan of sales and costs, and a balance sheet plan of assets, debt, and equity. More sophisticated models include a far greater number of variables and the relationships between them. These models are necessarily computerised, using spreadsheets such as Excel. There are three main elements in the financial planning process:

- input factors
- the financial model
- output factors.

The inputs are the company's financial statements and assumptions made about the future period to which the financial plan relates. The assumptions relate to, for example, estimated sales and levels of sales growth, costs to sales relationships, investment levels, and working capital ratios. The financial statements include the income statement, balance sheet, and cash flow statement.

Fig. 9.3 shows a financial planning income statement flow diagram and the input factors that the financial model may include. Fig. 9.4 shows a financial planning balance sheet flow diagram and the input factors that the financial model may include. The financial model comprises the relationships between each of the input factors, and the ways in which outputs are calculated and the consequences of changes to any of the inputs.

The outputs are the planned future financial statements based on the inputs and assumptions, and calculated by the financial model. These are referred to as *pro forma* financial statements. Outputs may also include a range of financial ratios that indicate the projected financial

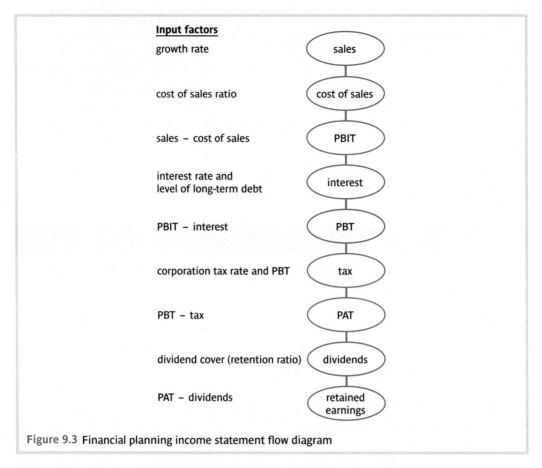

Figure 9.3 Financial planning income statement flow diagram

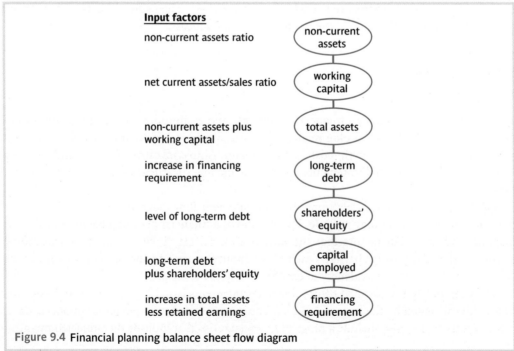

Figure 9.4 Financial planning balance sheet flow diagram

performance and financial position of the business which may be used to determine whether the plan is financially viable and acceptable to the company.

Financial modelling

Using the flow diagrams shown in Figs. 9.3 and 9.4 as the basis, we will illustrate the development of a company's financial planning models in the worked examples that follow.

Worked Example 9.1

Supportex Ltd's income statement for year 1 and its balance sheet at the end of year 1, appears as follows:

	A	B	C
1	Income statement	Year 1	
2	Figures in £000s		
3	Total sales	800	
4	Total costs	(600)	Costs are assumed to vary in line with sales
5	Net profit	200	
6			
7	Balance sheet	End Year 1	
8	Total assets	1,100	
9	Debt	(100)	10% debt/equity ratio
10		1,000	
11		———	
12	Equity	1,000	

Figure 9.5 Supportex year 1 simple income statement and balance sheet

Supportex has assumed that its total costs will vary directly in line with changes in its sales levels. It has also planned to maintain its debt/equity ratio at 10%.

Let's consider what will happen if in year 2 sales are increased by 20%.

▶   Because costs vary with sales then costs will also increase by 20%. If we assume that Supportex has no spare capacity, then for year 2 total assets also need to be increased by 20% to support the increased sales level. We may also assume that the increased assets level is financed by a similar 20% increase in long-term debt, and maintains the debt/equity ratio at 10%. The income statement and balance sheet for year 2 will appear as follows (year 1 is shown for comparison):

	A	B	C
1	**Income statement**	**Year 1**	**Year 2 dividend £40k**
2	**Figures in £000s**		
3	Total sales	800	960
4	Total costs	(600)	(720)
5	Net profit	200	240
6			
7	**Balance sheet**	**End Year 1**	
8	Total assets	1,100	1,320
9	Debt	(100)	(120)
10		1,000	1,200
11			
12	Equity	1,000	1,200

Figure 9.6 Supportex year 1 and year 2 simple income statement and balance sheet

We can see that equity has increased from £1m to £1.2m, an increase of £200,000. However, from the income statement, net profit is shown for year 2 as £240,000 not £200,000. Therefore, £40,000 dividends must have been paid out of net profit leaving retained earnings of £200,000, which has been added to equity. The planned sales growth of 20% and the decision by the company to maintain its debt/equity ratio of 10% have effectively determined the dividend level as a consequence of these decisions. Supportex's increase in total assets of £220,000 is financed by an increase in retained earnings of £200,000 and an increase in debt of £20,000.

Worked Example 9.2

Consider what would happen in Worked Example 9.1 if Supportex chose to pay £60,000 in dividends instead of £40,000. Retained earnings would then be £180,000 and equity would become £1.18m. The increase of £20,000 in dividends would have to be financed out of additional debt of £20,000. The level of gearing will therefore increase from 10% to 11.9% (£140/£1,180). Supportex's increase in total assets of £220,000 is financed by an increase in retained earnings of £180,000 and an increase in debt of £40,000. In such a model the level of debt can be seen to be the balancing item on the balance sheet.

Alternatively, if Supportex required its debt to be held at £120,000, then new equity of £20,000 would need to be issued, which would maintain its debt/equity ratio at 10%. Supportex's increase in total assets of £220,000 is then financed by an increase in retained earnings of £180,000, an increase in equity of £20,000, and an increase in debt of £20,000.

	A	B	C	D
1	Income statement	Year 1	Year 2 dividend £60k (debt increase)	Year 2 dividend £60k (equity increase)
2	**Figures in £000s**			
3	Total sales	800	960	960
4	Total costs	(600)	(720)	(720)
5	Net profit	200	240	240
6				
7	**Balance sheet**			
8	Total assets	1,100	1,320	1,320
9	Debt	(100)	(140)	(120)
10		1,000	1,180	1,200
11				
12	Equity	1,000	1,180	1,200

Figure 9.7 Supportex year 1 and year 2 simple income statement and balance sheet, with additional funding

The models shown in Worked Examples 9.1 and 9.2 show the ways in which the growth in sales of the business may be financed by retained earnings, and increases in debt and equity. The models do not tell us which is the best option. Dividend policy depends on a number of factors, as we shall see in Chapter 15, and may be interpreted by shareholders in many different ways. Although these models do not provide answers to these issues they do show us the impact on the balance sheet of the various options.

Worked Example 9.3 takes things a step further by looking at Supportex's financial statements in a little more detail. Worked Examples 9.3 and 9.4 illustrate a step by step approach to Supportex Ltd's five-year planning process.

Worked Example 9.3

The financial statements for Supportex shown below identify the various elements of cost in the income statement, and in the balance sheet separate total assets into non-current assets and working capital.

The income statement shows sales and costs for year 1 and the balance sheet shows the financial position of Supportex at the start of year 1 and the end of year 1, and states the assumptions which identify the relationships between the numbers.

With regard to Supportex's operating activities we can see that its cost of sales is 62.5% of sales and therefore its profit before interest and tax (PBIT) is 37.5% of sales. Its tax rate is 31% of

	A	B	C	D
1	Income statement		Year 1	Assumptions
2	Figures in £000s			
3	Total sales		800	
4	Cost of sales		(500)	62.5% of sales
5	Profit before interest and tax		300	total sales less cost of sales
6	Interest		(10)	10% of debt at start of year
7	Profit before tax		290	PBIT less interest
8	Tax		(90)	31% of profit before tax
9	Net profit		200	PBT less tax
10	Dividends		(30)	15% dividend payout ratio
11	Retained earnings		170	85% profit retention ratio
12				
13	Balance sheet	Start Year 1	End Year 1	Assumptions
14	Figures in £000s			
15	Non-current assets		700	87.5% of sales
16	Working capital		400	50% of sales
17	Total assets		1,100	
18	Debt	(100)	(100)	
19			1,000	
20				
21	Equity	830	1,000	

Figure 9.8 Supportex year 1 detailed income statement and balance sheet

profit before tax (PBT). Its working capital is 50% of sales. For modelling purposes it is reasonable to assume that these percentages will remain constant as sales levels change.

Supportex Ltd is currently financed by both debt and equity. Its interest payment is 10% of the debt balance at the start of the year. However, we cannot assume that the debt/equity ratio of 10% will remain constant as levels of sales change. The company may decide on various different levels of gearing (through issues of debt or equity), regardless of its operational activities.

The company has forecast that in year 2 sales will increase by 20%. It has also decided that the dividend payout and profit retention ratio will be maintained at 15% and 85% respectively, and has assumed that the interest rate of 10% will not change. It is assumed that non-current assets and working capital will increase at the same rate to support the 20% increase in sales.

We can see from Fig. 9.9 that, based on the above assumptions, net profit for year 2 is £241,000, and retained earnings are £205,000, which has been added to the equity from year 1.

	A	B	C	D
1	**Income statement**		Year 1	Year 2
2	**Figures in £000s**			
3	Total sales		800	960
4	Cost of sales		(500)	(600)
5	Profit before interest and tax		300	360
6	Interest		(10)	(10)
7	Profit before tax		290	350
8	Tax		(90)	(109)
9	Net profit		200	241
10	Dividends		(30)	(36)
11	Retained earnings		170	205
12				
13	**Balance sheet**	Start Year 1	End Year 1	End Year 2
14	**Figures in £000s**			
15	Non-current assets		700	840
16	Working capital		400	480
17	Total assets		1,100	1,320
18	Debt	(100)	(100)	(115)
19			1,000	1,205
20				
21	Equity	830	1,000	1,205
22				
23	Additional financing required			15

Figure 9.9 Supportex year 1 and year 2 detailed income statement and balance sheet

▶ We can see from the balance sheet at the end of year 2 that in order for net assets to be equal to equity, additional financing of £15,000 was required for the balance sheet to be in balance. This has been assumed to have been obtained through an increase in debt, shown in the increase in debt from £100,000 to £115,000 (debt/equity ratio 9.5%).

Alternatively, the additional external financing could have comprised equity or a combination of both debt and equity. If new equity of £15,000 had been issued instead of debt, then equity would be increased to £1,220,000 and debt would remain at £100,000 (debt/equity ratio 8.2%). If an increase in both debt and equity had been made, for example £10,000 debt and £5,000 equity, this would result in totals of £110,000 debt and £1,120,000 equity, which would result in gearing of 9.9% which would be closer to the original 10%.

The role of forecasting

A forecast is not a plan or a budget but a prediction of future environments, events, and outcomes. Forecasting is required in order to prepare plans and budgets. This should start with projected sales volumes and market share of current and new products. Examples of forecasts by product, or sector, can be found regularly in the press, for example car sales and mobile telephone sales.

Worked Example 9.4

We will use the year 1 financial statements from Worked Example 9.3 to calculate a five-year plan for Supportex Ltd. The five-year plan is based on sales growth of 20% per annum for each year. For planning purposes the model will use the assumptions shown in Worked Example 9.3 and will also assume that any additional financing is obtained by increasing debt. The results are shown in Fig. 9.10, and the numbers have been rounded to the nearest thousand.

The 20% growth in sales for each year has also resulted in an increase in total assets of 20% for each year. The increases in total assets in each year of £220,000, £264,000, £317,000, and £380,000 have been financed by increases in retained earnings of £205,000, £247,000, £296,000, and £356,000, and increases in debt of £15,000, £17,000, £21,000, and £24,000 for years 2 to 5. This has resulted from the dividend payout policy of 15% of net profit each year. Each year the debt/equity ratio has been reduced from 10% at the end of year 1 to 9.5%, 9.1%, 8.8%, and 8.4% at the end of years 2 to 5.

The model is also represented in the Excel spreadsheet shown in Fig. 9.11, which incorporates the forecast assumptions in columns A and B. The cell formulae for the calculations for year 4 in column I (which also apply to columns G, H, and J) are shown in column K. Setting up a planning model in a spreadsheet makes it a simple task to change the forecast growth rate and then review the impacts on both the income statement and balance sheet. The consequences may also be assessed for changes in financial strategy, for example dividend and gearing levels. They may also be assessed for changes in interest rates and tax rates and changes in strategy relating to investments in non-current assets and working capital.

Using the spreadsheet in Fig. 9.11 if we change the growth rate in cell B3 to 30% per annum the model will calculate different additional financing requirements, and therefore different debt/equity ratios for each year. We can summarise the results of changing the forecast growth rate for a range of values, for example 0% to 30%, which is shown in Fig 9.12.

	A	B	C	D	E	F	G
1	**Income statement**		**Year 1**	**Year 2**	**Year 3**	**Year 4**	**Year 5**
2	**Figures in £000s**						
3	Total sales		800	960	1,152	1,382	1,659
4	Cost of sales		(500)	(600)	(720)	(864)	(1,037)
5	Profit before interest and tax		300	360	432	518	622
6	Interest		(10)	(10)	(12)	(13)	(15)
7	Profit before tax		290	350	420	505	607
8	Tax		(90)	(109)	(130)	(157)	(188)
9	Net profit		200	241	290	348	419
10	Dividends		(30)	(36)	(43)	(52)	(63)
11	Retained earnings		170	205	247	296	356
12							
13	**Balance sheet**	**Start Year 1**	**End Year 1**	**End Year 2**	**End Year 3**	**End Year 4**	**End Year 5**
14	**Figures in £000s**						
15	Non-current assets		700	840	1,008	1,210	1,452
16	Working capital		400	480	576	691	829
17	Total assets		1,100	1,320	1,584	1,901	2,281
18	Debt	(100)	(100)	(115)	(132)	(153)	(177)
19			1,000	1,205	1,452	1,748	2,104
20							
21	Equity	830	1,000	1,205	1,452	1,748	2,104
22							
23	Additional financing			15	17	21	24

Figure 9.10 Supportex five-year plan income statement and balance sheet

	A	B	C	D	E	F	G	H	I	J	K
1	Model assumptions		Income statement			Year 1	Year 2	Year 3	Year 4	Year 5	Column I formulae
2			Figures in £000								
3	Growth	20.0%	Total sales			800.0	960.0	1,152.0	1,382.4	1,658.9	+H3+$B3*H3
4	% sales	62.5%	Cost of sales			(500.0)	(600.0)	(720.0)	(864.0)	(1,036.8)	-I3*B4
5	% sales	37.5%	PBIT			300.0	360.0	432.0	518.4	622.1	+I3+I4
6	% of debt	10.0%	Interest			(10.0)	(10.0)	(11.5)	(13.2)	(15.3)	-H18*B6
7			PBT			290.0	350.0	420.5	505.2	606.8	+I5+I6
8	% of PBT	31.0%	Tax			(89.9)	(108.5)	(130.4)	(156.6)	(188.1)	-I7*B8
9			Net profit			200.1	241.5	290.2	348.6	418.7	+I7+I8
10	% of net profit	15.0%	Dividends			(30.0)	(36.2)	(43.5)	(52.3)	(62.8)	-I9*B10
11	% of net profit	85.0%	Retained earnings			170.1	205.3	246.6	296.3	355.9	+I9+I10
12											
13			Balance sheet								
14			Figures in £000								
15	Growth	20.0%	Non-current assets			700.0	840.0	1,008.0	1,209.6	1,451.5	+H15+$B15*H15
16	% of sales	50.0%	Working capital			400.0	480.0	576.0	691.2	829.4	+I3*B16
17			Total assets			1,100.0	1,320.0	1,584.0	1,900.8	2,281.0	+I15+I16
18			Debt		(100.0)	(100.0)	(114.7)	(132.1)	(152.6)	(176.9)	+H18-I23
19						1,000.0	1,205.3	1,451.9	1,748.2	2,104.1	+H18-I23
20											
21			Equity			1,000.0	1,205.3	1,451.9	1,748.2	2,104.1	+H21+I11
22											
23			Additional financing required				14.7	17.4	20.5	24.3	+I17-H17-I11

Figure 9.11　Excel five-year planning model for Supportex

	A	B	C
1	Sales growth rate per annum %	Additional funding requirement Years 2 to 5 £000	Debt/equity %
2	0.0	– 742.6	0.0
3	10.0	– 394.7	0.0
4	20.0	76.9	8.4
5	30.0	696.9	34.0

Figure 9.12 Supportex five-year plan external funding requirement and debt/equity ratios

Large companies need to be very sensitive to trends and developments within their forecasting process as mistakes can prove very expensive. For example, a major UK chocolate manufacturer made too many eggs for Easter 2000, which did not sell; its forecasts and therefore its financial plans were proved to be very wide of the mark, and the impact on the business was extremely costly.

Forecasting usually relies on the analysis of past data to identify patterns used to describe it. Patterns may then be extrapolated into the future to prepare a forecast. There are many different methods of both qualitative forecasting and quantitative forecasting, and there is no one best model.

Qualitative techniques

Qualitative forecasting techniques do not use numbers or probabilities but use non-numeric information and consider trends in demand and behaviour. The following are examples of these techniques:

- the Delphi method – use of a panel of recognised experts, a group of wise men
- consumer market surveys – using questionnaires, surveys, etc.
- sales force estimates – the views of the people who may be closest to the customers and the market
- executive opinion – expert views of professionals in specific areas
- technological comparisons – independent forecasters predicting changes in one area by monitoring changes in another area
- subjective curve-fitting – using demand curves of similar products that have been launched in the past, for example similar product life cycles for similar products like CD players and DVD players.

Quantitative techniques

Quantitative forecasting techniques use numerical data and probabilities, and use historical data to try to predict the future. These techniques rely heavily on statistical analysis to project, for example, sales demand and relationships between the factors impacting on sales. Qualitative forecasting includes both univariate time series models and causal models. The following are examples of both these techniques.

Univariate time series models:

- moving averages
- exponential smoothing
- trend projections.

Causal models:

- regression analysis
- multiple regression.

Causal models involve the use of the identification of other variables related to the variable being predicted. For example, linear regression may be used to forecast sales, using the independent variables of sales price, advertising expenditure, and competitors' prices. Major retailers have been seen to be highly pro-active in revising their sales prices and their advertising activities (and expenditure) as a result of changes in the marketplace.

The use of such statistical models is usually a question of fitting the pattern of historical data to whichever model best fits. It could be argued that it is easier to forecast the sales of ice-cream than the sales of CDs by a new band. Apparently, the major music-based groups have also found this a mystery over the years. Whichever method is used it is important that the basis and the methodology of the forecasting is understood. All assumptions made and the parameters of time, availability of past data, costs, accuracy required, and ease of use must be clearly stated to maintain any sort of confidence in the forecasts.

Progress check 9.2

What is the role of forecasting and what are qualitative and quantitative techniques?

Cash flow forecasting and planning

Cash flow forecasting and planning is an area which, in practice, may use a number of methods of calculation. It is an important part of financial planning because in addition to the funding requirements projected on an annual basis, the company also needs to consider its monthly cash requirements. A company may have healthy year-by-year projected cash positions, which indicate that it requires no additional funding. However, because the sales and operational activities of the business may not be spread evenly over each year, then monthly phasing of the planned cash flow may reveal that additional funding within each year may be required.

The cash flow financial statement reported in a company's annual report and accounts uses a technique called the indirect cash flow method to determine operating cash flow. The indirect cash flow method starts with the company's operating profit and then adds back depreciation, which is not a cash outflow, and then adjusts for changes in working capital, and the result is operating cash flow. The working capital adjustment is required because profit is rarely realised in cash at the same time that transactions take place: inventory is not used immediately it is acquired; suppliers are not paid immediately goods or services are provided; customers do not pay immediately sales are made. The operating cash flow is then used as the basis from which to calculate the company's total cash flow, which is shown in a statement like the example shown in Fig. 1.11, which we saw in Chapter 1.

Planning and forecasting of cash requirements may also be made using the indirect method described above. However, either as an alternative to this or to support its results, monthly cash plans may be prepared using the direct cash flow method. An actual direct cash flow statement for the year details the actual receipts from customers and payments to suppliers, employees, and other payments. The same technique may be used for cash planning. The advantage of this is that it may benefit from the experience of the finance director or financial planner preparing the plan.

Let's look at an example, which, for simplicity, just considers the first three months of the first year of the financial plan of a business.

Worked Example 9.5

Dubai Dreams is a retailing outfit that has prepared a financial plan for its operations over the next five years. The company's finance director expects the next three months from January to March to demand some cash requirements beyond the normal operational outflows.

A monthly cash forecast must therefore be prepared from the following information, which has been made available by the company.

1. Dubai Dreams has a cash balance of Dhs28.7m at the end of December and a balance of at least Dhs20,000 must be available at the end of each month.

2. Sales forecasts are: December Dhs180m; January Dhs240m; February Dhs200m; March Dhs240m. The company has recently introduced a credit card system which relates to 40% of sales for each month and which is received in cash by the middle of the following month.

3. Cost of goods sold averages 75% of sales. Inventory (or stocks) purchased during each month is at a level that ensures that stocks of 1.5 times the value of the next month's cost of sales are held at the end of each month. The value of inventory on hand on 31 December amounted to Dhs270m, Dhs200m having been purchased during December. Inventory is purchased consistently over each month and creditors are paid in the month following purchase.

4. Operating expenses are forecast as follows:

   (a) Salaries and wages at 12% of sales, are paid in the month of sale.

   (b) Other expenses at an average 10% of sales, are paid in the month of sale.

   (c) Cash receipts expected from the repayment of a loan to a director of Dhs6m is due in March.

   (d) Repayment of a short-term loan of Dhs3m is due in February.

   (e) Repayments of a long-term loan are due at Dhs4m each in January and March.

   (f) New equipment was purchased for Dhs48m and four payments of Dhs12m each are due in February, March, April, and May.

   (g) Depreciation of all equipment is charged to the profit and loss account at the rate of Dhs5m per month.

   (h) Interest received from an investment of Dhs4.9m per month is expected.   ▶

▶ (i) Bonuses totalling Dhs52m are due to be paid to staff in January.

(j) A company tax payment of Dhs14m is due to be paid in March.

We can prepare a cash forecast for each month from the beginning of January to the end of March in order to identify possible cash needs for each month up to the end of March.

This example shows that Dubai Dreams requires short-term funding over the three months totalling Dhs95.2m. We can see from Fig. 9.13 that the levels of funding requirement are different for each of the three months. In practice, the company would expand this phased forecast to cover the five years of the plan to determine the level and pattern of the funding required throughout the entire period of the plan.

	A	B	C	D	E	F
1	**Cash forecast January to March**					
2	**Dirhams millions**	**January**	**February**	**March**		**Total**
3	**CASH RECEIPTS**					
4	Cash sales	144.0	120.0	144.0		408.0
5	Credit card sales	72.0	96.0	80.0		248.0
6	Loan repayment			6.0		6.0
7	Investment income	4.9	4.9	4.9		14.7
8	**Total receipts**	**220.9**	**220.9**	**234.9**		**676.7**
9	**CASH PAYMENTS**					
10	Suppliers	200.0	135.0	195.0		530.0
11	Salaries	28.8	24.0	28.8		81.6
12	Other expenses	24.0	20.0	24.0		68.0
13	Short-term loan repayment		3.0			3.0
14	Long-term loan repayment	4.0		4.0		8.0
15	Equipment payment		12.0	12.0		24.0
16	Staff bonuses	52.0				52.0
17	Company tax			14.0		14.0
18	**Total payments**	**308.8**	**194.0**	**277.8**		**780.6**
19	Month net cash flow	−87.9	26.9	−42.9		−103.9
20	Start month cash balance	28.7	−59.2	−32.3		28.7
21	End month cash balance	−59.2	−32.3	−75.2		−75.2
22	End month minimum cash balance	20.0	20.0	20.0		20.0
23	**Month funding required/(surplus)**	**79.2**	**−26.9**	**42.9**		
24	**Cumulative funding required**	**79.2**	**52.3**	**95.2**		**95.2**
25	New end month cash balance	**20.0**	**20.0**	**20.0**		**20.0**
26						

Figure 9.13 Dubai Dreams three-month cash forecast

Planning for growth

We have looked at fairly fundamental financial planning models. In practice, such models will necessarily be a little more sophisticated and allow for depreciation of non-current assets, and the interrelationship of variables like levels of debt, interest, working capital, and retained earnings. A more sophisticated model may allow for changes to many variables at one time and provide options with regard to their impact.

In the models we have considered we have assumed percentage changes that apply over each of the years in the plan. A more complex model will allow for different percentages applied to each year. It will also allow for changes in capital investment and working capital requirements resulting from the additional capacity required should particular sales levels be reached. However, it is also important to keep strategic financial plans as simple as possible so that a focus on the long-term objectives of the business is maintained.

The key relationship for a business that is planning for growth is the relationship between its growth, its internal funding, and its external funding requirements. The amount available from internal funding from retained earnings will depend on the company's dividend policy. It is possible to derive relationships that may determine how the company's growth may be achieved.

A company's ratio of its sales to its total assets (non-current assets plus working capital) tells us how much sales are currently being derived from each £, US\$, €, etc., of assets at its disposal. If the reciprocal of this ratio is multiplied by the company's planned sales increase, the result will therefore be the total amount of funding required for such growth. Therefore:

$$\text{funding requirement} = \text{planned sales increase} \times \frac{\text{assets}}{\text{sales}}$$

The funding may come from internal retained earnings or it may come from external sources.

If we assume that the planned sales increase is the same rate as the increase required in investment in assets, then

$$\text{planned sales growth rate} = \frac{\text{planned sales increase}}{\text{sales}} = \frac{\text{required new investment in assets}}{\text{assets}}$$

Therefore:

$$\text{required new investment in assets} = \text{planned sales growth rate} \times \text{assets}$$

and

$$\text{required new investment in assets} = \text{funding requirements}$$

and

$$\text{required new investment in assets} = \text{new external funding} + \text{funding from retained earnings}$$

If a company plans no growth at all there will be no requirement for additional capital and so any profits that have been retained are surplus to current requirements. As a company increases its projected growth rates then it will gradually use more and more of its retained earnings to fund this growth. At a particular level of planned growth the company will, in addition, require external funding. The growth rate where retained earnings are fully utilised and no external funding is required is the company's sales growth rate from internal funding. This may be expressed as:

$$\text{sales growth rate from internal funding} = \frac{\text{funding from retained earnings}}{\text{assets}}$$

Therefore it can be seen that if a company has a high earnings retention ratio then it can achieve a high rate of sales growth without needing additional external funding.

This ratio may be expanded into

$$\text{sales growth rate from internal funding} = \frac{\text{funding from retained earnings}}{\text{net profit}} \times \frac{\text{net profit}}{\text{equity}} \times \frac{\text{equity}}{\text{assets}}$$

or

$$\text{sales growth rate from internal funding} = \text{retention ratio} \times \text{ROE} \times \frac{\text{equity}}{\text{assets}}$$

From this relationship we can see that high sales growth may be achieved if the company pays a low level of dividends (high retention ratio), earns a high ROE, and has a high equity to assets ratio, or a low debt to assets ratio.

Financing growth

Companies may be very interested in how much growth they can achieve without taking on any additional external funding, by way of either debt or equity. They may also be interested in how much growth they can achieve by using retained earnings, plus additional equity but by not increasing debt; or, by using retained earnings, plus additional debt but by not increasing equity. These two scenarios will reflect the gearing level or financial structure that the company has targeted in its financial plan. If we consider the relationship

$$\text{sales growth rate from internal funding} = \text{retention ratio} \times \text{ROE} \times \frac{\text{equity}}{\text{assets}}$$

we can see that the maximum growth rate that the company can sustain if its gearing is not increased is

$$\text{sales growth rate from internal funding} = \text{retention ratio} \times \text{ROE}$$

which is dependent only on its retention ratio and its ROE.

Worked Example 9.6

In Worked Example 9.3 we saw that Supportex had a profit retention ratio of 85%, and was projecting an annual growth rate of 20% per year. The company has reported that its equity and debt at the start of year 1 was £0.83m and £0.1m respectively, and its assets were £0.93m. Its net profit for year 1 was £0.2m.

$$ROE = £0.2m/£0.83m = 24.1\%$$

$$equity/assets = £0.83m/£0.93m = 89.2\%$$

We can calculate the maximum growth rate for Supportex assuming that it maintains its total assets growth (non-current assets plus working capital) in line with its planned sales growth, and does not want to take on any additional external funding.

$$\text{sales growth rate from internal funding} = \text{retention ratio} \times ROE \times \frac{equity}{net\ assets}$$

$$= 0.85 \times 0.241 \times 0.892$$

$$= 0.18272 \text{ or } 18.3\%$$

This is lower than the company's planned growth rate of 20%. It can only achieve that growth by obtaining external funding. If Supportex was additionally prepared to maintain its gearing ratio of 12% (£0.1m/£0.83m) then using

$$\text{sales growth rate from internal funding} = \text{retention ratio} \times ROE$$

$$= 0.85 \times 0.241$$

$$= 0.20485 \text{ or } 20.5\%$$

we can see that the company could achieve a better growth rate of 20.5%, which is about in line with its financial plan.

If Supportex's sales growth from internal funding had been less than its planned growth rate then the company would either have to reduce its planned growth rate, or take on additional debt and increase its debt/equity ratio (gearing) in order to achieve its planned growth rate. In those circumstances, it is likely that the company would also eventually need to increase its level of equity.

A company's final, agreed financial plan should not be accepted until the projected financial position of the business has been reviewed in terms of the adequacy, or otherwise, of funding. In the determination of requirements for additional funding, and to safeguard the future of the business, risk analysis and risk assessment is essential to be carried out with regard to each of the uncertain areas of the plan.

Short-term additional funding may be obtained through extended overdraft facilities, but longer-term funding will be from loans, or debentures, or the issue of additional share capital. The appropriate funding decision should be made and matched with the type of activity for which funding is required. For example, major capital expenditure projects would not normally be funded by an overdraft; the type of longer-term funding generally depends on the nature of the project.

Strategic performance assessment

A company may measure financial performance against its long-term financial plan in many different ways. Each year of the financial plan may be translated into short-term budgets, which may be used for both planning and control. Performance may be considered using return on capital employed (ROCE), or earnings per share (eps). Such short-term performance measures focus only on the performance for that specific period.

ROCE is calculated as a percentage by dividing operating profit (pre-tax) by capital employed (total assets less current liabilities), which is usually averaged for the year. It is therefore a relative measure of profitability rather than an absolute measure of profitability. eps is calculated by dividing profit after tax by the number of ordinary shares in issue, and is therefore an absolute measure.

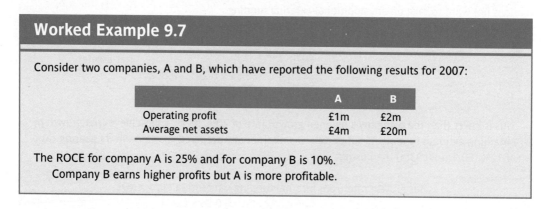

Worked Example 9.7

Consider two companies, A and B, which have reported the following results for 2007:

	A	B
Operating profit	£1m	£2m
Average net assets	£4m	£20m

The ROCE for company A is 25% and for company B is 10%.
Company B earns higher profits but A is more profitable.

Chief executive officers (CEOs) may, for example, be rewarded via a remuneration package, which is linked to a ROCE performance measure. Since ROCE tends to be low in the early stages of a company's business life cycle, CEOs may take a short-term view in appraising new investment proposals because they will be anxious to maintain their level of earnings. CEOs may therefore reject proposals for such investments even though they may provide a satisfactorily high ROCE over the longer term. The owners of the business, the shareholders, will of course be more interested in the longer-term ROCE of the business.

The divergence between the two points of view may occur because CEOs and shareholders are each using different assessment criteria. The views of CEOs and the shareholders may be brought into line if they both used the same criteria. This would mean abandoning the practice of linking a CEO's remuneration directly to short-term ROCE because it is likely to encourage short-term thinking.

It is sometimes claimed that eps is more likely to encourage goal congruence, but a similar lack of goal congruence to that resulting from the use of ROCE may occur if a CEO's performance is measured using eps. If performance is based on eps then a CEO may decide to replace old equipment (resulting in lower ROCE and worsened cash flow) to increase profit and therefore increase eps. The reduction in ROCE may therefore result in a sub-optimisation decision for the company as a whole. Alternatively, if CEOs' performances are based on ROCE then they may decide to make do with old equipment, resulting in a higher ROCE and improved cash flow, but which may result in a reduced eps. There have been many cases of UK manufacturers whose plant was much older than that used by overseas competitors, which may be as a direct result of the type of performance measure being used.

Worked Example 9.8

Let's consider two companies within a group, X and Y, which have an opportunity to invest in projects that both have an initial cost of £10m. The overall cost of capital for the group is 15% per annum. The expected operating profits from each investment and the current returns earned by the companies are shown below:

Company	X	Y
Investment cost	£10m	£10m
Expected operating profit	£2m	£1.3m
Current ROCE	25%	9%

The expected returns from each proposed project are 20% for company X and 13% for company Y. The CEO of company X would not be motivated to invest in the new project because 20% is less than the current ROCE. The CEO of company Y would be motivated to invest in the project because 13% is greater than the current ROCE. However, both decisions are incorrect for the group as a whole. This is because the company Y project returns 2% less, and the company X project returns 5% more, than the average cost of capital for the group of 15%.

Worked Example 9.9

Let's consider two companies within a group of companies, R and S, which have an opportunity to invest in projects that both have an initial cost of £10m. The overall cost of capital for the group is 15% per annum. The expected operating profits from each investment are shown below:

Company	R	S
Proposed investment	£10.0m	£10.0m
Expected profit before tax	£2.0m	£1.3m
Cost of capital charge (15%)	£1.5m	£1.5m
Residual income (loss)	+£0.5m	−£0.2m

The CEO of company R will be motivated to invest and the CEO of company S will not be motivated to invest.

If a great deal of pressure is placed on CEOs to meet short-term performance measurement targets, there is a danger that they will take action that will improve short-term performance but will not maximise long-term profits. For example, by skimping on expenditure on advertising, customer services, maintenance, and training and staff development costs, it is possible to improve short-term performance. However, such actions may not maximise long-term profits.

It is probably impossible to design performance measures which will ensure that maximising the short-run performance measure will also maximise long-term performance. Some steps, however, can be taken to improve the short-term performance measures so that they minimise the potential conflict. For example, during times of rising prices, short-term performance measures can be distorted if no attempt is made to adjust for the changing price levels.

The use of ROCE as a performance measure has a number of deficiencies. For example, it encourages CEOs to accept only those investments that are in excess of their current ROCE, leading to the rejection of profitable projects. Such actions may be reduced by replacing ROCE with eps as the performance measure. However, as we have seen, merely changing from ROCE to eps may not eliminate the short-term versus long-term conflicts.

Ideally, performance measures ought to be based on future results that can be expected from a CEO's actions during a period. This would involve a comparison of the present value of future cash flows at the start and end of the period, and a CEO's performance would be based on the increase in present value during the period. Such a system may not be totally feasible, given the difficulty in predicting and measuring future outcomes from current actions. Economic value added (EVA™) aims to provide a performance measure that is highly correlated with both shareholder wealth and divisional performance. EVA is calculated by deducting from profit after tax a financial charge for the use of the company's net assets. The net assets figure reported in the accounts is usually adjusted (in a variety of different ways) to reflect as realistic a valuation as possible of the company's net assets. The basis for the financial charge is usually the average cost of the capital used by the company (see Chapter 8).

ROCE and eps represent single summary measures of performance. It is virtually impossible to capture in summary financial measures all the variables that measure the success of a company. It is therefore important that accountants broaden their reporting systems to include additional non-financial measures of performance that give clues to future outcomes from current actions. This may include, for example, obtaining feedback from customers regarding the quality of service that encourages managers not to skimp on reducing the quality of service in order to save costs in the short term. Other suggestions have focused on refining the financial measures so that they will reduce the potential for conflict between actions that improve short-term performance at the expense of long-term performance.

As part of their strategic management process many companies now link their financial (and non-financial) plans with operations by using techniques like the **balanced scorecard**. In 1990 David Norton and Robert Kaplan were involved in a study of a dozen companies that covered manufacturing and service, heavy industry, and high technology to develop a new performance measurement model. The findings of this study were published in the *Harvard Business Review* in January 1992 and gave birth to an improved measurement system, the balanced scorecard.

The balanced scorecard concept had evolved by 1996 from a measurement system to a core management system. *The Balanced Scorecard* published by Kaplan and Norton in 1996 illustrates the importance of both financial and non-financial measures incorporated into performance measurement systems; these are included not on an *ad hoc* basis but are derived from a top-down process driven by the company's mission and its strategy.

An example of a balanced scorecard is shown in Fig. 9.14. It provides a framework for translating a strategy into operational terms. The balanced scorecard includes headings covering the following four key elements:

- financial
- internal business processes
- learning and growth
- customer.

The above four perspectives provide both a framework for measuring a company's activities in terms of its vision and strategies, and a measurement tool to give managers a comprehensive view of the performance of a business.

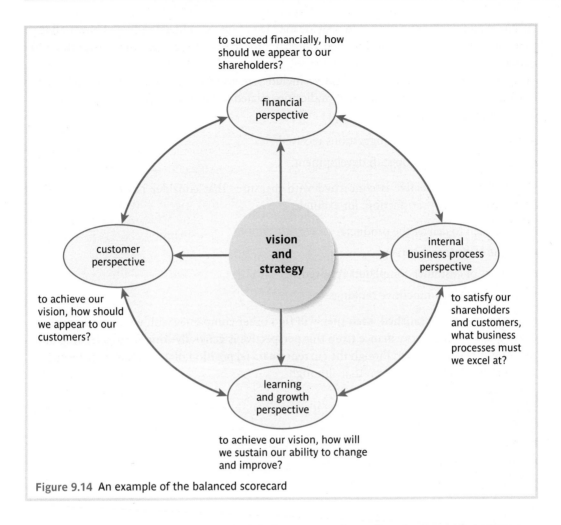

Figure 9.14 An example of the balanced scorecard

The financial perspective is concerned with measures that reflect the financial performance of a company. This is its ability to create wealth, and may be reflected in key performance indicators that include, for example:

- level of working capital
- cash flow
- sales growth
- profitability
- return on capital employed.

The emphasis placed on such financial indicators would depend on the position of the company within its business life cycle.

The internal business processes perspective is concerned with measures that reflect the performance of key activities, for example:

- the time spent prospecting new customers
- the cost of product processing
- number of units that require reworking.

Such measurements are designed to provide managers with an understanding of how well their parts of the business are running, and whether products and services conform to customer requirements.

The learning and growth perspective includes measures which describe the company's learning curve, and is concerned with indicators related to both individual and corporate self-improvement – for example:

■ the number of employee suggestions received

■ the total hours spent on staff development.

The customer perspective is concerned with measures that consider issues having a direct impact on customer satisfaction, for example:

■ time taken to deliver the products

■ results of customer surveys

■ number of customer complaints received

■ the company's competitive rankings.

If customers are not satisfied, then they will find other companies with which to do business. Consequently, poor performance from this perspective is generally considered a leading indicator of future decline, even though the current financial position of a company may be good.

From Fig. 9.14 it can be seen that although

■ objectives

■ measures

■ targets

■ initiatives

are implied within each of the elements, the financial element represents only one quarter of the total.

How the company appears to its shareholders is an important underlying factor of the balanced scorecard approach. But it is interesting to see that the measures that are considered by the company in satisfying shareholders go much further than just the financial measures:

■ To satisfy our shareholders and customers, what business processes must we excel at?

■ To achieve our vision, how will we sustain our ability to change and improve?

■ To achieve our vision, how should we appear to our customers?

Norton and Kaplan comment on the dissatisfaction of investors who may see only financial reports of past performance. Investors increasingly want information that will help them forecast future performance of companies in which they have invested their capital. In 1994 the American Certified Public Accountants (CPA) Special Committee on Financial Reporting in New York reinforced this concern with reliance on financial reporting for measuring business performance. 'Users focus on the future while today's business reporting focuses on the past. Although information about the past is a useful indicator of future performance, users also need forward-looking information.' The CPA committee was concerned on how well companies are creating value for the future and how non-financial measurement must play a key role. 'Many users want to see a company through the eyes of management to help them understand management's perspective and predict where management will lead the company. Management should disclose the financial and non-financial measurements it uses in managing the business that quantify the effects of key activities and events.'

Non-financial performance measures and concepts like the balanced scorecard illustrate the way in which financial-based measures are becoming less dominant in the measurement and evaluation of performance in most businesses.

Progress check 9.3

Describe the framework of the balanced scorecard approach and explain the ways in which this provides links with the financial plans of a company.

Summary of key points

- Financial planning is an integral part of a company's strategic management process.
- The main purpose of financial planning is to consider the big picture of a company's activities over the long term, five or ten years, with regard to its growth and how that growth may be financed.
- A company's financial planning process includes the development of a planning model that will produce long-term forecasts of its three main financial statements, which are based on input of the company's parameters and variables relating to its planned growth rate, and key financial ratios.
- Financial models may be used to plan the long-term impacts of a planned growth in the sales of a business.
- Forecasts are not plans or budgets but are predictions of future environments, events, and outcomes, and may be derived using both qualitative and quantitative techniques.
- Cash flow forecasts are part of the financial planning process and are used to determine a company's future funding requirements on a monthly and yearly basis.
- A company may plan for its future growth without necessarily using any additional external funding, but to use its own resources of retained earnings.
- A company that is planning future growth may require funding in addition to retained earnings, and may consider the financing options of debt and equity to fund such future growth.
- A company's performance may be measured against its financial plans using a range of financial ratios (see Chapter 8), with return on capital employed (ROCE) and earnings per share (eps) being the most widely used.
- Many companies, on a worldwide basis, have now adopted the balanced scorecard as a method of linking their long-term strategies into operational targets and key performance indicators.

🔑 Glossary of key terms

balanced scorecard An approach to the provision of information to management to assist strategic policy formulation and achievement. It emphasises the need to provide the user with a set of information which addresses all relevant areas of performance in an objective and unbiased fashion. The information provided may include both financial and non-financial elements, and cover areas such as profitability, customer satisfaction, internal efficiency and innovation.

budget A quantified statement, for a defined period of time, which may include planned revenues, expenses, assets, liabilities, and cash flows.

forecast A prediction of future events and their quantification for planning purposes.

goal congruence The state which leads individuals or groups to take actions which are in their self-interest and also in the best interest of the company. Goal incongruence exists when the interests of individuals or of groups associated with a company are not in harmony.

planning The establishment of objectives, and the formulation, evaluation, and selection of the policies, strategies, tactics, and action required to achieve them. Planning comprises long-term strategic planning, and short-term operational planning, the latter being usually for a period of up to one year.

qualitative forecasting Forecasting in terms that are not expressed numerically.

quantitative forecasting Forecasting in terms that are expressed numerically.

strategic planning A process of deciding on the objectives of an organisation, the resources used to attain these objectives, and on the policies that are to govern the acquisition, use, and disposition of these resources. The results of this process may be expressed in a strategic plan, which is a statement of long-term goals along with a definition of the strategies and policies, which will ensure achievement of those goals.

❓ Questions

Q9.1 (i) Why do businesses need to prepare financial plans?
 (ii) What are they used for?

Q9.2 (i) Give some examples of the ways in which forecasting techniques may be used to assess a company's future sales growth rates.
 (ii) What are the advantages and disadvantages in using each of these forecasting techniques?

Q9.3 Use diagrams to illustrate how the financial planning process may be used to produce long-term forecast financial statements.

Q9.4 Explain and illustrate the ways in which a business may plan for its future growth.

Q9.5 How may a business use a financial model to assess the levels of internal and external funding required to support its long-term growth?

Q9.6 What are the various financing options that a company may use to fund its planned future growth, and how may their levels be determined?

Q9.7 (i) How may a company's performance be measured and compared with its strategic financial plan?
 (ii) What are the advantages and disadvantages of these measures?

Q9.8 Outline the way in which the balanced scorecard links a company's strategy with its operational activities.

 ## Discussion points

D9.1 'Financial plans are not accurate because in general they do not differentiate between the behaviour of variable and fixed costs.' Discuss.

D9.2 'The area of financial planning is a minefield of potential problems and conflicts.' How should these problems and conflicts be approached to ensure that the performance of the business is aligned with its primary objective of shareholder wealth maximisation?

D9.3 'It is impossible to make accurate predictions about a company's activities even over a short-term period of say six months, therefore strategic financial plans of five and ten years have no value at all.' Discuss.

 ## Exercises

Solutions are provided in Appendix 2 to all exercise numbers highlighted in colour.

Level I

E9.1 *Time allowed – 15 minutes*

Hearbuy plc is a growth business, which assembles and sells mobile phones. They make and sell one model only and expect to sell 2,684,000 units during the next four years. The volume for each year is expected to be 20% above the preceding year. The selling price is £50 each. And the cost of sales is expected to be 70% of the selling price.

Hearbuy plc have prepared an estimated balance sheet as at the end of year 1 as follows:

	£m	£m
Non-current assets	13.50	
Stocks	10.47	
Trade debtors	4.01	
Cash and bank	3.55	31.53
Trade creditors	3.03	
Loans	4.50	
Equity	24.00	31.53

Interest is paid at 10% each year on the balance of its loans outstanding at the start of each year. The loans at the start of year 1 were £4.5m. Dividends are planned to continue at 60% of profit after tax. The company's corporation tax rate is expected to be 35%. The growth in investment in non-current assets is expected to be the same level as the growth in sales. Working capital is planned at 60% of sales.

Use an Excel spreadsheet to prepare a sales plan for Hearbuy plc in units and £m values for years 1 to 4.

E9.2 *Time allowed – 30 minutes*

From the data in E9.1 use an Excel spreadsheet to prepare an income statement for Hearbuy plc for year 1.

Level II

E9.3 *Time allowed – 30 minutes*

From the data in E9.1 and E9.2 use an Excel spreadsheet to prepare an income statement and balance sheet for Hearbuy plc for years 1 to 4, which show the levels of additional funding required, if any, by the company for each year.

▶ **E9.4** *Time allowed – 30 minutes*

From the income statement and balance sheet for Hearbuy plc from E9.3, identify and discuss the actions the company may take to eliminate the need for the additional funding in each year.

E9.5 *Time allowed – 30 minutes*

Using the income statement for year 1 from E9.3, and the relevant balance sheet data at the start of year 1, determine the level of growth that Hearbuy plc may achieve if it took on no additional external funding in years 2 to 4, assuming that the growth in total assets each year is expected to be at the same level as the planned growth in sales (that is, the ratio of total assets to sales remains constant).

E9.6 *Time allowed – 30 minutes*

Using the income statement for year 1 from E9.3, and the relevant balance sheet data at the start of year 1, determine the level of growth that Hearbuy plc may achieve if its growth in total assets each year is expected to be at the same level as the planned growth in sales (that is, the ratio of total assets to sales remains constant), and if it maintained its gearing ratio at the start of year 1 level for years 1 to 4.

E9.7 *Time allowed – 30 minutes*

An extract of the financial results for 2006 for three of the companies in the Marx Group plc is shown below:

	Company		
	Chico	Groucho	Harpo
Assets	£7.5m	£17.5m	£12.5m
Operating profit	£1.5m	£1.4m	£2.0m
Administrative expenses	£0.8m	£0.3m	£0.65m
Cost of capital per annum	7%	5%	10%

Required:

(i) Calculate the ROCE for each company for 2006.

(ii) Calculate the EVA each company for 2006.

(iii) Which measure provides the best performance measure for each company and why?

(iv) If each company is presented with an investment opportunity that is expected to yield a return of 9%.

(a) Which company(s) would accept and which company(s) would reject the investment opportunity if their performance is measured by ROCE, and why?

(b) Which company(s) would accept and which company(s) would reject the investment opportunity if their performance is measured by EVA, and why?

E9.8 *Time allowed – 45 minutes*

Ros Burns intends opening a new retail business on 1 October 2007, and intends investing £25,000 of her own capital in the business on 1 October 2007. The business, which will trade under the name of Arby Ltd, will sell fashion accessories.

The company intends purchasing non-current assets costing £80,000. These will be purchased in November 2007. They are estimated to have, on average, a five-year useful economic life with residual value of zero. They will be paid for in two equal instalments, one instalment due in December 2007, and one instalment due in February 2008.

Forecast sales from October 2007 to March 2008 are expected to be:

	£
October	200,000
November	205,000
December	180,000
January	200,000
February	205,000
March	200,000

30% of the total sales value is expected to be for cash, the remaining 70% being sold on credit terms of one month. Bad debts are estimated to be 5% of credit sales.

Wage costs are expected to be as follows:

	£
October	90,000
November	105,000
December	90,000
January	85,000
February	90,000
March	100,000

Materials costs are expected to be as follows:

	£
October	60,000
November	70,000
December	65,000
January	70,000
February	55,000
March	70,000

Wages will be paid in the month they are incurred, but materials will be purchased on the following basis:

- 50% of the material costs will be paid in one month following purchase
- 50% of the material costs will be paid in two months following purchase.

Overheads expenses, which are payable in the month in which they are incurred, are expected to be £35,000 each month.

Required:

(i) Prepare a monthly cash budget for Arby Ltd for the six-month period ending 31 March 2008. It should show the net cash flow for each month and the cumulative budgeted cash position at the end of each month to determine the level of additional financing required, if any.

(ii) Prepare a brief report for Ros advising her of the possible alternative sources of short-term and long-term finance available to the company, together with your recommendations, with reasons, of which types of financing she should consider using.

Case Study I: **Gegin**

Gegin is a UK-based high quality kitchen units manufacturer, which was launched in the late 1980s by Tim Imber. The business started its operations from one shop in Chester and grew substantially so that by 2006 the business operated from a total of 48 shops, located all around the UK. In addition, in 2003, a seven-year contract with a national chain of leading builders merchants was signed which gave Gegin wider market access in return for a flat fee and a percentage share of profits.

Originally, Tim Imber was the only full-time employee of Gegin. He was responsible for the design, construction, and marketing of the business's products as well as the day-to-day management of the company. The business, which required £190,000 to start, was funded 50% by Tim and 50% of the required capital was provided by Tim's brother-in-law, Len Graham. Len was an accountant by profession and acted in a part-time capacity as the company accountant and assisted Tim in certain aspects of management.

The company quickly expanded and problems emerged as supply could not keep pace with demand. It became necessary, therefore, to employ someone else to assist Tim in the construction of the furniture. As the business continued to grow, more people joined Gegin, so that as early as 1990, 25 people were employed by the company. At the same time, further shops were opened and a separate workshop and warehouse was established. Gegin's expansion was funded by a combination of re-investing profits and medium-term bank loans.

The result of all these changes was that by 1990, Tim Imber's time was almost exclusively given over to the management of the business. The following year the decision was made that Gegin would become a private limited company (Ltd), and it was at this point that Len Graham joined full-time employment as finance director. One of the first changes that Len brought about was the direct sourcing of the core materials used in Gegin's products. The timber now used was directly imported from Canada and Scandinavia.

On 31 March 2007, after 19 years of trading, the financial statements of the company showed a turnover of £60m, and a pre-tax profit of £14m.

The following financial statements relate to Gegin Ltd for the years 2005 to 2007:

Balance Sheet as at 31 March

	2005 £m	2006 £m	2007 £m
Non-current assets	36	27	55
less Depreciation	(10)	(7)	(14)
	26	20	41
Current assets			
Stocks	16	16	22
Trade debtors	28	27	20
Other debtors	3	16	5
Bank	5	7	8
	52	66	55
Current liabilities			
Trade creditors	18	15	10
Other creditors	15	7	16
Taxation	6	9	7
Dividends	3	4	2
	42	35	35

Net current assets	10	31	20
Total assets less current liabilities	36	51	61
less			
Non-current liabilities			
Debentures	(2)	(4)	(6)
	34	47	55
Capital and reserves			
Share capital (£1 ordinary shares)	20	22	25
Profit and loss account	14	25	30
	34	47	55

Income statements for the years ending 31 March

	2005 £m	2006 £m	2007 £m
Turnover	40	80	60
Cost of sales	(12)	(30)	(28)
Gross profit	28	50	32
Operating expenses	(10)	(26)	(18)
Profit before tax	18	24	14
Taxation	(6)	(9)	(7)
Profit after tax	12	15	7
Dividends	(6)	(4)	(2)
Retained profit for the year	6	11	5

Strategic review

In 2006, external consultants were asked to identify the strategic options open to Gegin. The review found that, although the middle to upper end of the fitted kitchen market was becoming increasingly competitive, there was still room for significant growth. Despite numerous shop openings, Gegin was still very much a regional operator. Expansion of the market was predicted to continue for many years, although Gegin's product and strategic positioning left the business vulnerable to changes in the business cycle. The company had been affected quite significantly by a fall in turnover in the mid to late 1990s. The consultants identified these issues and suggested a number of options for Gegin.

Option 1 – additional new shops

Initial investment cost   £86m
Potential annual income   £16m pa

The first option was for more shops to be opened, particularly in the south of England, where the company had little presence. This option had implications for the management and organisational structure of the company as at least two additional workshops, a warehouse, and distribution centres would be necessary to provide the required infrastructure. Such a centre was opened in the latter part of 1999, as a programme of shop openings had already been an idea that the management had been considering for some time. The company had previously considered franchising as a way to achieve this growth, and the company had already in 2003 entered into a seven-year contract that was signed with a large UK-based builders' merchants chain. However, subsequent market and business research regarding the UK market had suggested that franchising would not be a profitable proposition for a company like Gegin Ltd, and as a consequence the policy was abandoned.

Option 2 – diversification

Initial investment cost   £23m
Potential annual income   £6m pa

▶ The second option was diversification, because the company's significant experience of the import of quality timber from North America and Northern Europe was, the consultants suggested, not being exploited. The wholesaling of timber was therefore recommended. This had the added advantage of producing economies of scale, which would have the effect of reducing unit costs. Tim and Len together with their senior managers had not previously considered this proposal and felt that so long as they were not supplying major competitors this was a proposition that could and should be pursued.

Option 3 – lifestyle concept
Initial investment cost   £57m
Potential annual income   £10m pa rising to £15m pa in 4 years

The consultants suggested, as their third option, the development of the 'lifestyle concept' store format – shops that not only sold kitchen units, but also related accessories (such as kitchen furnishings and equipment) in a themed environment. Such shops had started to develop at the lower end of the market, but this format had not yet been rolled out in the market that Gegin Ltd occupied. This proposal found immediate favour with the directors of the company, although the size of each of the existing shops would not easily accommodate such a change. The movement to larger retail outlets, or the opening of new additional shops that could accommodate this format would be necessary, but costly.

Option 4 – move into the Asian market
Initial investment cost   £46m
Potential annual income   £6m pa rising to £14m pa in 6 years

The demand for English-designed quality kitchens had always been popular in Asia. The region as a whole was becoming potentially a more significant market and the consultants argued that a gradual move into this market would in time reduce Gegin Ltd's dependence on UK demand. The consultants, concerned about the risk associated with this option, felt that expansion in this way should be by way of a joint venture. This idea was one with which Tim, Len, and their senior managers readily agreed. The proposal suggested that, in the long term, furniture should be manufactured in Asia using designs and templates from the UK. In the short and medium term, however, in order to establish the viability of the market, furniture should be exported – a practice that the consultants suggested should continue until the market was sufficiently mature – for approximately five years.

Despite their caution, Tim and Len were very interested in each of the options identified by the external consultants. The question was how this growth should be financed. The consultants suggested the following alternative methods of funding:

1. The company may obtain a 'listing' as a public limited company (plc). This, the consultants suggested, would raise £40m from additional equity shares. The balance of any additional investment required could be provided from taking on additional debt capital, which was assumed would cost 10% per annum in interest.

2. Any new investment may be funded totally by taking on additional new debt, which was assumed would cost 10% per annum in interest.

It was assumed that Gegin Ltd's sales and profit performance for 2008 would be identical to 2007 if no new investment were undertaken. If one of the new investment options were to be undertaken then, regardless of which option, taxation as a percentage of PBT would be the same as 2007 and dividends as a percentage of PAT would be the same as 2007.

Required:

Prepare a report which:

(i) considers
- Gegin Ltd's financial status, and possible reasons for it
- the company's objectives
- why the company's directors may have engaged external consultants to carry out a strategic review of its activities

(ii) provides a short-term evaluation of the options suggested by the external consultants, assuming that one option is taken up by the company at the start of April 2007, showing:

(a) a summarised income statement and retained earnings for the year ended 31 March 2008

(b) capital and reserves at 31 March 2008

(c) medium and long-term loans at 31 March 2008

(d) gearing ratio at 31 March 2008

(e) earnings per share for the year ended 31 March 2008

for each option, and comparing the two funding options: a stock exchange listing and possible partial debt funding; total debt funding

(iii) advises the board which option the company should select, based on the information available, stating your assumptions, and giving appropriate reasons for the conclusions you have reached, and the recommendations you make.

Your report should identify some of the possible constraints the company may face, and give some consideration to non-financial factors that may affect the company, with regard to each option and in particular with regard to your proposed recommendation if implemented by the company.

(Note: a discounted cash flow approach is not required for this case study).

Management of working capital

LEARNING OBJECTIVES

Completion of this chapter will enable you to:

☑ Explain what is meant by working capital and the operating cycle.

☑ Describe the management and control of the working capital requirement.

☑ Explain the use of working capital management as a strategic tool, and its impact on profitability, ROCE, ROE, and liquidity.

☑ Outline how good working capital management releases resources that can be used to provide the internal finance to fund value-adding projects, or repay debt and reduce the interest burden.

☑ Outline some of the working capital policies that may be adopted by companies.

☑ Implement the systems and techniques that may be used for the management and control of stocks, and optimisation of stock levels.

☑ Outline a system of credit management and the control of debtors.

☑ Consider the management of creditors as an additional source of finance.

☑ Use the operating cycle to evaluate a company's working capital requirement performance.

☑ Action the appropriate techniques to achieve short-term and long-term cash flow improvement.

☑ Evaluate how the use of cash management models such as those developed by Baumol and Miller-Orr assist financial managers to manage their companies' cash flows.

Introduction

Strategy is a course of action that includes a specification of resources required to achieve a specific objective. The overall strategy of a company is *what* the company needs to do long term to achieve its objectives, and is primarily focused on maximisation of shareholder wealth. Working capital and its financing are important elements of these resources.

In previous chapters we have looked at the longer-term resources of capital investments in assets and projects, and the alternative sources of funds to finance them. This chapter considers the shorter-term elements of the balance sheet, the net current assets (current assets less current liabilities) or working capital, which is normally financed with short-term funding, for example bank overdrafts. The chapter begins by considering what is really meant by working capital, with an overview of its nature and its purposes.

Regular evaluation of the working capital cycle, or operating cycle, may be used to monitor a company's effectiveness in the management of its working capital requirement. Minimisation of working capital is an objective that reduces the extent to which external financing of working capital is required. However, there is a fine balance between minimising the costs of finance and ensuring that sufficient working capital is available to adequately support the company's operations.

▶

▶ An emphasis is placed on optimisation rather than minimisation and on the importance of good management of the working capital requirement (WCR) for the sustained success of companies. The techniques that may be used to improve the management of stocks (inventories), debtors (accounts receivable), and creditors (accounts payable) are explored in detail.

This chapter will close by linking working capital to the effective management of cash and by considering some of the ways that both long-term and short-term cash flow may be improved.

Working capital and working capital requirement

The balance sheet is sometimes presented showing assets on the one side and liabilities on the other. This may be said to be a little unsatisfactory since the various categories of assets and liabilities are very different in nature. Cash, for example, is a financial asset and has very different characteristics to non-current assets and stocks.

If we consider the following relationship:

$$\text{assets} = \text{equity} + \text{liabilities}$$

it may be rewritten as

$$\text{non-current assets} + \text{stocks} + \text{debtors} + \text{prepayments} + \text{cash}$$
$$= \text{equity} + \text{financial debt} + \text{creditors} + \text{accruals}$$

This may be further rewritten to show homogeneous items on each side of the equals sign as follows:

$$\text{equity} + \text{financial debt} - \text{cash}$$
$$= \text{non-current assets} + \text{stocks} + \text{debtors} - \text{creditors} - \text{accruals} + \text{prepayments}$$

Therefore

$$\text{equity} = \text{non-current assets} + \text{stocks} + \text{debtors} - \text{creditors} - \text{accruals} + \text{prepayments}$$
$$- \text{financial debt} + \text{cash}$$

Financial debt is comprised of two parts:

- long-term debt (payable after one year, in accounting terms)
- short-term debt (payable within one year, in accounting terms)

and so from substitution and by rearranging the equation we can see that:

$$\text{equity} + \text{long-term debt} = \text{non-current assets} + \text{stocks} + \text{debtors} - \text{creditors} - \text{accruals}$$
$$+ \text{prepayments} - \text{short-term debt} + \text{cash}$$

Therefore, equity plus long-term financial debt is represented by non-current assets plus working capital (WC)

$$\text{WC} = \text{stocks} + \text{debtors} - \text{creditors} - \text{accruals} + \text{prepayments} - \text{short-term financial debt} + \text{cash}$$

Stocks, of course, comprise raw materials, finished product and work in progress (including their share of allocated and apportioned production overheads).

The need for working capital – the operating cycle

The interrelationship of each of the elements within the working capital requirement may be represented in the operating cycle (see Fig. 10.1). The operating cycle, or working capital requirement cycle, is the period of time between when cash begins to be paid for the production of products or services and when cash is received from customers. It may be calculated in days by deducting accounts payable (trade creditors) days from stock (inventory) days plus accounts receivable (trade debtors) days, or in absolute value by deducting the balance sheet values of accounts payable from stocks plus accounts receivable.

The operating cycle includes:

- acquisition of raw materials and packaging, which are at first stored in warehouses prior to use, and are invoiced by suppliers and recorded by the company in trade creditors (or accounts payable), and then normally paid for at a later date

- use of materials and packaging in the manufacturing process to create partly completed finished goods, work in progress, stored as stock in the company's warehouses

- use of materials, packaging, and work in progress to complete finished goods, which are also stored as stock in the company's warehouses

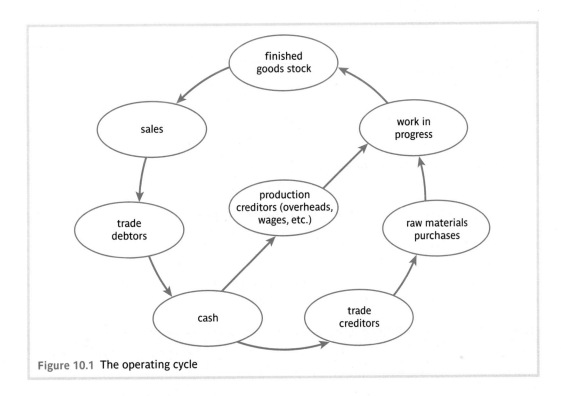

Figure 10.1 The operating cycle

- despatch of finished goods from the warehouses and delivery to customers, who accept the products for which they will pay
- recording as sales by the company its deliveries to customers, which are included in its trade debtors (or accounts receivable) and normally paid by customers at a later date
- use of cash resources to pay overheads, wages, and salaries
- use of cash resources to pay trade creditors for production overheads and other expenses
- use of cash resources to pay trade creditors for raw materials.

Worked Example 10.1

We can identify which of the following categories may be included within a company's operating cycle:

- plant and machinery
- trade creditors
- investments in subsidiaries
- cash
- work in progress
- patents
- accounts receivable
- fixtures and fittings.

Non-current assets are not renewed within the operating cycle. The following items extracted from the above list relate to non-current assets:

- plant and machinery
- investments in subsidiaries
- patents
- fixtures and fittings.

The remaining categories therefore relate to the operating cycle, as follows:

- trade creditors
- work in progress
- cash
- accounts receivable (trade debtors).

A company therefore uses some of its funds to finance its stocks, through the manufacturing process, from raw materials to finished goods, and also the time lag between delivery of the finished goods or services and the payments by customers of accounts receivable. Short-term funds, for example bank overdrafts, are needed to finance the working capital the company requires as represented in the operating cycle. Many companies use the flexibility of the bank overdraft to finance fluctuating levels of working capital.

Progress check 10.2

How is a company's need for investment in operations explained by the operating cycle?

Working capital requirement (WCR)

We have seen that:

> equity + long-term debt = non-current assets + stocks + debtors − creditors − accruals
> + prepayments − short-term debt + cash

From this equation we can see that the total financial resources of the company are equity plus long- and short-term financial debt minus cash. This represents the total money invested in the company, and is called the total investment. Therefore:

> total investment = non-current assets + stocks + debtors − creditors − accruals
> + prepayments

The total investment in the company can therefore be seen to comprise broadly two elements:

- investment in non-current assets
- investment in operations

where the investment in operations is

> stocks + debtors − creditors − accruals + prepayments

which is called the working capital requirement (WCR).

Stated in words, the WCR is telling us something very important: the company has to raise and use some of its financial resources, for which it has to pay, to invest in its operating cycle. These financial resources are specifically for the company to purchase and create stocks, while it waits for payments from its customers. The impact of this is decreased by the fact that suppliers also have to wait to be paid. Added to this is the net effect of accruals and prepayments. Prepayments may be greater than accruals (requiring the use of funds) or accruals may be greater than prepayments (which is a source of funds).

In most manufacturing companies the WCR is positive. The smaller the WCR, the smaller are the total financial resources needed, and the stronger is the company. Some businesses, for example supermarkets, may have limited stocks and zero accounts receivable, but high accounts payable. In such cases WCR may be negative and these companies are effectively able to finance acquisition of non-current assets with funds payable to their suppliers.

Worked Example 10.2

From the balance sheet of Flatco plc for 2007 and the comparatives for 2006 (see Fig. 10.2), we may calculate the working capital requirement for 2007 and the working capital requirement for 2006.

Working capital requirement:

WCR = stocks + debtors − creditors − accruals + prepayments
WCR for 2007 = 311 + 573 − 553 − 82 + 589 = 838
WCR for 2006 = 268 + 517 − 461 − 49 + 617 = 892

Flatco plc
Balance sheet as at 31 December 2007

Figures in £000

	2007	2006
Non-current assets		
Intangible	416	425
Tangible	1,884	1,921
Financial	248	248
	2,548	2,594
Current assets		
Stocks	311	268
Debtors	573	517
Prepayments	589	617
Cash	327	17
	1,800	1,419
Current liabilities (less than one year)		
Financial debt	50	679
Creditors	553	461
Taxation	50	44
Dividends	70	67
Accruals	82	49
	805	1,300
Net current assets	995	119
Total assets		
less current liabilities	3,543	2,713
less		
Non-current liabilities (over one year)		
Financial debt	173	–
Creditors	154	167
	327	167
less		
Provisions	222	222
Net assets	2,994	2,324
Capital and reserves		
Share capital	1,200	1,000
Share premium account	200	200
Retained earnings	1,594	1,124
	2,994	2,324

Figure 10.2 Flatco plc balance sheet as at 31 December 2007

We will use the financial statements of Flatco plc, an engineering company, shown in Figs 10.2 and 10.3, throughout this chapter to illustrate the calculation of the key working capital ratios. The income statement is for the year ended 31 December 2007 and the balance sheet is as at 31 December 2007. Comparative figures are shown for 2006.

Progress check 10.3

What is meant by working capital requirement (WCR)?

Working capital (WC)

Working capital (WC) is normally defined as:

current assets − current liabilities

Flatco plc
Income statement for the year ended 31 December 2007

Figures in £000

		2007		2006
Turnover				
Continuing operations		3,500		3,250
Discontinued operations		–		–
		3,500		3,250
Cost of sales		(2,500)		(2,400)
Gross profit		1,000		850
Distribution costs	(300)		(330)	
Administrative expenses	(155)		(160)	
Other operating costs				
Exceptional items: redundancy costs	(95)		–	
		(550)		(490)
Other operating income		100		90
Operating profit				
Continuing operations	550		450	
Discontinued operations	–		–	
		550		450
Income from other fixed asset investments		100		80
Profit before interest and tax		650		530
Net interest		(60)		(100)
Profit before tax		590		430
Tax on profit on ordinary activities		(50)		(44)
Profit on ordinary activities after tax		540		386
Dividends		(70)		(67)
Retained profit for the financial year		470		319

Figure 10.3 Flatco plc income statement for the year ended 31 December 2007

or

$$\text{WC} = \text{stocks} + \text{debtors} - \text{creditors} - \text{accruals} + \text{prepayments} - \text{short-term debt} + \text{cash}$$

Therefore

$$\text{WC} = \text{WCR} - \text{short-term debt} + \text{cash}$$

The difference between WC and WCR can be seen to be cash less short-term financial debt (or overdraft).

The financial analyst considers the definitions of long and short term in a different way to the accountant, thinking of long term as 'permanent' or 'stable', and so will consider WC in an alternative way by calculating the difference between the stable financial resources of the company and its long-term use of funds, its non-current assets.

Since

$$\text{equity} + \text{short-term debt} + \text{long-term debt} - \text{cash} = \text{non-current assets} + \text{stocks} + \text{debtors}$$
$$- \text{creditors} - \text{accruals} + \text{prepayments}$$

and

$$\text{WC} = \text{stocks} + \text{debtors} - \text{creditors} - \text{accruals} + \text{prepayments} - \text{short-term financial debt} + \text{cash}$$

an alternative representation of working capital is

$$WC = \text{equity} + \text{long-term debt} - \text{non-current assets}$$

As a general rule, except in certain commercial circumstances, WC should always be positive in the long run because if it were negative then the company would be financing its (long-term) non-current assets with short-term debt. Renewal of such debt represents a major liquidity risk. It is the same thing as, say, financing one's house purchase with an overdraft. Since WC has to be positive and the aim should be for WCR to be as small as possible, or even negative, there is a dilemma as to the acceptability of either positive or negative cash. The answer really depends on the quality of the WCR.

If net cash is negative then short-term debt is higher than the cash balance and so WCR is financed partly with short-term debt. So the question may be asked 'will the company suffer the same liquidity risk as with a negative WC?' If stocks are of high quality champagne, the value of which will probably rise year by year, or if the debtors (accounts receivable) are, say, blue chip companies with no credit risk, then a bank is likely to finance such WCR with no restrictions. If the quality of the WCR is poor the bank is unlikely to finance the WCR with short-term debt. The management and control of each of the elements of WCR – stocks, debtors, creditors, which we will look at in the following sections – must be considered in terms of both their quality and their level.

Progress check 10.4

What is meant by working capital (WC)? How may it differ in a manufacturing company compared with a supermarket retailer?

Working capital management as a strategic tool

In Chapter 4 we saw how strategically important capital investment decisions are to companies for their survival and growth in the future value of the business. We also saw that in addition to initial capital investment costs it is essential to include investments in working capital requirements in the appraisal of new projects. To ignore working capital requirements in the appraisal of an investment project is likely to result in subsequent under-funding and possibly a failure to provide an increase in corporate value.

Capital investment decisions are usually long-term strategic decisions, and in Chapter 7 we saw the various choices of long-term sources of finance that may be used by companies to fund such investments. The long-term sources of external finance include loans, debentures, bonds, and new equity. However, capital investment projects may also be financed internally, which may be cheaper and more easily accessible than external finance. In Chapter 7 we considered retained earnings as an internal source of finance and how good management of working capital may augment this.

There are conflicting objectives in the management of working capital with regard to a company's profitability and liquidity. Increased profitability is required in support of the company's primary objective of maximisation of shareholder wealth. The net current assets (working capital) of the company are a part of its capital employed. A company's capital employed comprises its non-current assets plus its net current assets. The company's return on capital employed

(ROCE) equals its profit before tax divided by capital employed. The lower the denominator, the higher will be the ROCE. Therefore, as the level of working capital is reduced the level of ROCE is increased.

Further to this, a reduction in working capital means reductions in either or both accounts receivable and stock levels, and increases in levels of accounts payable. This results in the requirement for lower levels of short-term financing (for example, overdrafts or short-term loans), which result in lower levels of interest payable. A reduction in levels of interest payable results in an increase in both profit before tax and profit after tax. Therefore, since

$$\text{ROCE} = \frac{\text{profit before tax}}{\text{capital employed}}$$

the level of ROCE is further increased as a result of a reduction in working capital. Also, since

$$\text{return on equity, ROE} = \frac{\text{profit after tax}}{\text{equity}}$$

then the level of ROE is also increased as a result of a reduction in working capital.

A reduction in the level of working capital and an increase in profit after tax may therefore release resources that can be used to provide the internal finance to fund further investments in productive assets (generating returns greater than the cost of capital), which may be used to reduce any existing interest burden, repay debt, and value to the business.

From the above we can see that the lower the level of working capital and the higher the return obtained from it, the greater will be the increase in corporate value.

In addition to the objective of increased profitability, appropriate levels of liquidity are required for the company to meet its operational cash requirements and to stay in business. The higher the level of cash, and therefore the higher the level of working capital, the more comfortable the company's managers will feel in meeting their day-to-day cash requirements, and the more able they will be to meet any unforeseen cash requirements. However, a high level of cash held by the company, while a comfort to managers, is not good news for shareholders. At worst, cash held as cash will earn no returns at all. At best, cash held in a bank deposit account may earn some interest, which will be added to both profit and cash flow. Bank deposit interest is unlikely to be anywhere near the returns from the type of investment projects that will generate value at the levels expected by shareholders.

In addition to higher levels of cash, a higher level of working capital also means increases in either or both accounts receivable and stock levels, and reductions in levels of accounts payable. These result in the requirement for higher levels of short-term financing (for example, overdrafts or short-term loans), which result in higher levels of interest payable. An increase in levels of interest payable results in a reduction in both profit before tax and profit after tax. Therefore, since

$$\text{ROCE} = \frac{\text{profit before tax}}{\text{capital employed}}$$

the level of ROCE is reduced as a result of an increase in working capital. Also, since

$$\text{ROE} = \frac{\text{profit after tax}}{\text{equity}}$$

then the level of ROE is also reduced as a result of an increase in working capital.

Worked Example 10.3

The financial statements for Supportex Ltd shown in Fig. 10.4 for years 1, 2 and 3 are an extract from the five-year plan model in Fig. 9.10 in Chapter 9. The income statement shows sales and costs for each year and the balance sheet shows the financial position of Supportex at the end of

	A	B	C	D	E
1	Income statement	Year 1	Year 2	Year 3	Assumptions
2	Figures in £000s				
3	Total sales	800	960	1,152	20% growth
4	Cost of sales	(500)	(600)	(720)	62.5% of sales
5	Profit before interest and tax	300	360	432	total sales less cost of sales
6	Interest	(10)	(10)	(12)	10% of debt at start of year
7	Profit before tax	290	350	420	PBIT less interest
8	Tax	(90)	(109)	(130)	31% of profit before tax
9	Net profit	200	241	290	PBT less tax
10	Dividends	(30)	(36)	(43)	15% dividend payout ratio
11	Retained earnings	170	205	247	85% profit retention ratio
12					
13	Balance sheet	End Year 1	End Year 2	End Year 3	Assumptions
14	Figures in £000s				
15	Non-current assets	700	840	1,008	87.5% of sales
16	Working capital	400	480	576	50% of sales
17	Total assets	1,100	1,320	1,584	
18	Debt	(100)	(115)	(132)	
19	Net assets	1,000	1,205	1,452	
20					
21	Equity	1,000	1,205	1,452	
22	ROCE	26.5% (290/1,100)	26.5% (350/1,320)	26.5% (420/1,584)	
23	ROE	20.0% (200/1,000)	20.0% (241/1,205)	20.0% (290/1,452)	

Figure 10.4 Supportex working capital 50% of sales

each year. The assumptions are stated, which identify the relationships between the numbers. The company's level of working capital is assumed to be 50% of sales. ROCE and ROE are 26.5% and 20.0% respectively.

Let's consider what happens if working capital is reduced to 30% of sales (see Fig. 10.5).

	A	B	C	D	E
1	Income statement	Year 1	Year 2	Year 3	Assumptions
2	**Figures in £000s**				
3	Total sales	800	960	1,152	20% growth
4	Cost of sales	(500)	(600)	(720)	62.5% of sales
5	Profit before interest and tax	300	360	432	total sales less cost of sales
6	Interest	(10)	–	–	10% of debt at start of year
7	Profit before tax	290	360	432	PBIT less interest
8	Tax	(90)	(112)	(134)	31% of profit before tax
9	Net profit	200	248	298	PBT less tax
10	Dividends	(30)	(37)	(45)	15% dividend payout ratio
11	Retained earnings	170	211	253	85% profit retention ratio
12					
13	**Balance sheet**	End Year 1	End Year 2	End Year 3	Assumptions
14	**Figures in £000s**				
15	Non-current assets	700	840	1,008	87.5% of sales
16	Cash surplus	60	83	111	
17	Working capital	240	288	345	30% of sales
18	Total assets	1,000	1,211	1,464	
19	Debt	–	–	–	
20	Net assets	1,000	1,211	1,464	
21					
22	Equity	1,000	1,211	1,464	
23	ROCE	29.0% (290/1,000)	29.7% (360/1,211)	29.5% (432/1,464)	
24	ROE	20.0% (200/1,000)	20.5% (248/1,211)	20.4% (298/1,464)	

Figure 10.5 Supportex working capital 30% of sales

In Fig. 10.5 we can see the consequences for Supportex Ltd of a reduction in working capital from 50% of sales to 30% of sales. These are summarised in Fig. 10.6.

	A	B	C	D
		Year 1	Year 2	Year 3
2	**Figures in £000s**			
3				
4	Working capital has been reduced for each year by	160	192	231
5	Therefore it has been possible to repay the debt of			
6	£100,000 and provide a cash surplus for each year of	60	83	111
7	The profit for Year 1 remains the same, but			
8	for Years 2 and 3 there is no interest and so			
9	Profit before tax is increased to		360	432
10	Tax is increased to		(112)	(134)
11	Net profit is increased to		248	298
12	Dividends are increased to		(37)	(45)
13	Retained earnings are increased to		211	253
14	Therefore			
15	Debt has been reduced to zero and			
16	Equity has been increased by retained earnings to		1,211	1,464

Figure 10.6 Consequences of Supportex's working capital reduction to 30% of sales

We can see from Fig. 10.6 that the reduction in the level of working capital has resulted in an improved cash position for Supportex, enabling it to repay its debt in year 1 and generate a cash surplus in years 1, 2, and 3. (It should be noted that the cash surpluses should strictly speaking be included as part of working capital – they have been separately identified here for illustration purposes). In practice, the company would invest the cash surpluses either on deposit to earn interest or in new investment projects to earn returns. The benefits of such investments have not been included in this model. Even so, the company is showing increased profitability because of its reduction in interest because of its debt repayment. This is reflected in increased dividends and also in retained earnings, which have consequently increased the total equity of the company.

In this example, because we have not included any returns on investments from the cash surpluses the improvement in profitability is small. Nevertheless, as a result of the reduction in working capital from 50% to 30% of sales both ROCE and ROE have increased from 26.5% and 20.0% to 29.5% and 20.4% respectively.

Worked Example 10.4

Let's use the same financial statements for Supportex Ltd shown in Worked Example 10.3 and consider what happens if working capital is increased from 50% to 70% of sales (see Fig. 10.7).

	A	B	C	D	E
1	Income statement	Year 1	Year 2	Year 3	Assumptions
2	Figures in £000s				
3	Total sales	800	960	1,152	20% growth
4	Cost of sales	(500)	(600)	(720)	62.5% of sales
5	Profit before interest and tax	300	360	432	total sales less cost of sales
6	Interest	(10)	(26)	(32)	10% of debt at start of year
7	Profit before tax	290	334	400	PBIT less interest
8	Tax	(90)	(103)	(124)	31% of profit before tax
9	Net profit	200	231	276	PBT less tax
10	Dividends	(30)	(35)	(41)	15% dividend payout ratio
11	Retained earnings	170	196	235	85% profit retention ratio
12					
13	Balance sheet	End Year 1	End Year 2	End Year 3	Assumptions
14	Figures in £000s				
15	Non-current assets	700	840	1,008	87.5% of sales
16	Working capital	560	672	806	70% of sales
17	Total assets	1,260	1,512	1,814	
18	Debt	(260)	(316)	(383)	
19	Net assets	1,000	1,196	1,431	
20					
21	Equity	1,000	1,196	1,431	
22	ROCE	23.0% (290/1,260)	22.1% (334/1,512)	22.1% (400/1,814)	
23	ROE	20.0% (200/1,000)	19.3% (231/1,196)	19.3% (276/1,431)	

Figure 10.7 Supportex working capital 70% of sales

	A	B	C	D
1		**Year 1**	**Year 2**	**Year 3**
2	**Figures in £000s**			
3				
4	Working capital has been increased for each year by	160	192	230
5	Therefore debt has been increased each year by	160	201	251
6	As a consequence, interest has been increased by		16	20
7	The profit for Year 1 remains the same, but			
8	for Years 2 and 3 because of the increase in interest			
9	Profit before tax is reduced to		334	400
10	Tax is reduced to		(103)	(124)
11	Net profit is reduced to		231	276
12	Dividends are reduced to		(35)	(41)
13	Retained earnings are reduced to		196	235
14	Therefore			
15	Debt has been increased and			
16	Equity, because of reduced retained earnings, is		1,196	1,431

Figure 10.8 Consequences of Supportex's working capital increase to 70% of sales

In Fig. 10.7 we can see the consequences for Supportex Ltd of an increase in working capital from 50% of sales to 70% of sales. These are summarised in Fig. 10.8.

We can see from Fig. 10.8 that the increase in the level of working capital has resulted in a worsened cash position for Supportex requiring it to increase its debt in years 1, 2, and 3. The company is also showing reduced profitability because of its increase in interest resulting from its increase in debt. This is reflected in lower dividends and retained earnings, which have consequently reduced the total equity of the company. As a result of the increase in working capital from 50% to 70% of sales both ROCE and ROE have decreased from 26.5% and 20.0% to 22.1% and 19.3% respectively.

Working capital policy

As we saw in Chapter 7, companies usually adopt a policy of matching financing with the type of investment being made in new assets and projects. Such a policy finances the long-term investment in non-current assets with long-term funding such as loans, bonds, equity, and retained earnings. The financing of its investment in operations, its short-term working capital requirement (WCR), offers a number of options to a company. Choices may be made between internal and external finance. The external financing of the WCR is usually provided by bank overdraft. This is because of its flexibility in accommodating the fluctuating nature of net current assets. However, this incurs a relatively high cost – short-term interest rates are normally higher than long-term interest rates.

The servicing costs of bank overdrafts, and other short-term funding, are not insignificant and so it is of obvious benefit for companies to maintain their overdraft facility requirements at minimum levels. Such requirements may be reduced by the adoption of appropriate policies with regard to the level of investment in working capital that a company chooses to operate.

The working capital policy adopted will be dependent on individual company objectives that may often be influenced by the type of business and the commercial or industrial sector in which it operates. The choice of policy inevitably presents a conflict between the goals of profitability and liquidity, and there is a range of working capital policies that may be chosen that lie somewhere between the following two approaches:

- aggressive
- conservative.

If the company adopts an aggressive working capital policy then for a given level of activity it will aim to operate with low levels of stocks, accounts receivable and cash. This type of policy is adopted in order to increase profitability as illustrated in Worked Example 10.3. However, it is a high-risk strategy that provides little flexibility for the company, and may result in:

- an inability to meet customer demand because of stock-outs
- poor customer relationships or loss of customers because of tight credit terms
- an inability to meet current commitments or pay suppliers because of cash shortages, and therefore a danger of interrupted supply of materials or services.

If the company adopts a conservative working capital policy then for a given level of activity it will aim to operate with higher levels of stocks, accounts receivable, and cash. This type of policy is adopted in order to increase liquidity as illustrated in Worked Example 10.4. It is a policy that provides greater flexibility, but its higher levels of stocks, accounts receivable, and cash will result in reduced profitability because of:

- the high costs of holding stocks (see the later section about stocks management)
- extended credit terms means that cash is received from customers later and therefore has to be funded by short-term overdraft, which incurs high interest costs
- the opportunity cost of holding cash, which is the returns that could otherwise have been earned from investment in profitable projects (which may be mitigated to some extent with interest earned from short-term lending of cash surplus to immediate requirements).

A conservative working capital policy presents lower levels of risk for the company because of:

- customer demand being easier to meet with less likelihood of stock-outs
- good customer relationships and customer retention because of favourable credit terms
- the ability to meet current commitments and pay suppliers and therefore avoiding interrupted supply of materials or services.

Any working capital policy adopted that lies between the two extremes of conservative and aggressive may be tailored to suit the requirements of the business and its particular market. A company cannot determine the 'right' working capital policy with absolute precision. However, it may benchmark similar companies in its particular industrial sector. For example,

	2005 £m	2004 £m
Barratt Developments plc		
Sales	2,513	2,516
Working capital	1,442 (57.4% of sales)	1,194 (47.5% of sales)
Johnson Matthey plc		
Sales	4,756	4,626
Working capital	417 (8.8% of sales)	389 (8.4% of sales)
Tesco plc		
Sales	37,070	33,557
Working capital	−2,615 (−7.1% of sales)	−2,391 (−7.1% of sales)

Figure 10.9 Illustrations of the range of working capital ratios in the construction, chemical, and supermarket industrial sectors

companies like automotive manufacturers, house builders, and retailers of fashion items and non-perishable goods will inevitably need to hold relatively high levels of materials, work-in-progress, and finished products, and will therefore have relatively higher levels of working capital (see Fig. 10.9). On the other hand, companies like supermarkets, food companies, and retailers of fast-moving and perishable goods will hold relatively lower levels of stocks and therefore lower levels of working capital. Additionally, supermarkets have only cash customers and therefore zero accounts receivable, and are also able to extend their credit with suppliers, and so their working capital tends to be extremely low or negative, or highly negative as seen in Tesco plc (see Fig. 10.9).

Working capital is the 'lubricant' of the investment in operations, enabling the 'engine' of the business, its investment in non-current assets, to be most effectively exploited. An under-utilisation of non-current assets can produce extra stocks, which increases the working capital requirement, and therefore the requirement for additional short-term financing and its associated costs. Reductions in levels of WCR reduce the requirement for financing and its associated costs. Maintenance of optimal, and therefore more manageable, levels of WCR increase levels of efficiency and effectiveness and, as we have seen above, additionally contribute to increased profitability and a reduction in the requirement for external financing.

Regardless of the policies adopted, the improved management of working capital may have a significant impact on the level of requirement for external and internal financing. Good management of their working capital requirement by companies can therefore be seen to be crucially important to both their short- and long-term success.

Progress check 10.5

Why is the good management of the working capital requirement (WCR) crucial to company success?

Stocks management

A lean enterprise uses less of everything to provide more, which results from the control and elimination of waste in all its forms. The Japanese quality expert Taiichi Ohno identified seven main areas of waste (called *muda* by Ohno), which relate to stocks to a large extent in terms of their handling, their movement, and their storage, in addition to the levels held and the proportion of defective and obsolete stocks (see Ohno T (1988) *The Toyota Production System*, Portland, OR: Productivity Press).

Areas of waste in stocks

The areas of waste or *muda*, identified by Ohno, emphasise the importance for companies of identifying and taking the appropriate action for improvement in this aspect of the management of working capital. Ohno's seven areas comprise:

- overproduction
- waiting
- transportation
- inappropriate processing
- unnecessary stocks
- unnecessary motion
- product defects.

Overproduction

Overproduction is the most serious area of waste, which discourages the smooth flow of goods and services and inhibits quality, productivity, communication, and causes increases in stocks, and leads to excessive lead and storage times, lack of early detection of defects, and product deterioration. Overproduction also creates artificial work rate pressures, and the build up of excessive work in progress. The further effects of overproduction can be seen in the dislocation of operations and poor communications. It also encourages the push of unwanted products through the system, for example, when encouraged through the use of bonus systems. The implementation of pull systems and *kanban* provide opportunities to overcome overproduction.

Waiting

Waiting occurs when there is no work or movement taking place, and it affects materials, products, and people. Waiting time should be used for training, maintenance, or *kaizen* activities but not overproduction.

Transportation

Transportation includes all unnecessary movement and double-handling and may result in damage and deterioration of materials and products. An example was seen in the UK during 1999 and 2000 where car manufacturers Rover and Vauxhall found themselves with unsold and excess stocks being stored for too long in the open air, and were then forced to cut back production because of storage and damage problems. Increased distances between processes causes unnecessary transportation which results in slower communication or feedback of poor quality, therefore slower corrective action.

Inappropriate processing

Inappropriate processing means providing complex solutions to simple procedures. This includes the use of large inflexible machines instead of small flexible ones, which encourages overproduction to recoup investment costs, and poor layout leading to excessive transportation and poor communications. The ideal is the smallest machine for the required quality located next to the preceding and succeeding operations. Inappropriate processing also includes the provision of insufficient safeguards, and the lack of these leads to poor quality. These may be provided through the use of, for example, *poka yoke* and *jidoka* techniques.

Unnecessary stocks

The holding of unnecessary stocks or inventories leads to longer lead times, which therefore results in increased holding costs, and the requirement for more space, resulting in high storage costs. It also prevents rapid identification of problems, and discourages communication, which all leads to hidden problems that may only be uncovered by reducing stock levels.

Unnecessary motion

Unnecessary motion refers to the importance of ergonomics for quality and productivity. Quality and productivity are both ultimately affected by operators stretching unnecessarily, bending, and picking up, leading to undue exertion and tiredness.

Product defects

Product defects result in a direct money cost for the business. Their existence is therefore an obvious opportunity for improvement, and is therefore an immediate target for the implementation of *kaizen* activity.

An example of the problems of overproduction resulting in excessive stocks can be seen from the Matalan press extract below. Its immediate effect is to increase the length of the operating cycle and increase the need for further funding, the cost of which has a negative impact on profitability. The other further effects of high stock levels have an additional downward impact on profit from the cost of increased waste in the ways we have examined above.

The result of Matalan being unable to clear its excess stocks following a disastrous Christmas 2004, was fear of a cut in the dividend paid to its shareholders. Many financial analysts downgraded their 2005 profit forecasts for Matalan, and the company saw a large drop in its share price.

The problem of too much stock

'Matalan given a dressing down', by Neil Hume

Matalan came under pressure yesterday after a leading broker cut its profit forecasts in the light of a year-end round-up meeting with the discount retailer.

After a disastrous Christmas, Matalan warned the City last month that it would make profits of only between £60m and £70m in the year ended February 28.

Yesterday, German bank Dresdner Kleinwort Wasserstein moved its estimate to the lower end of that range, citing concerns that Matalan had been unable to clear excess stock despite heavy discounting.

Dresdner said it had cut its pre-tax profit forecast by 8% to £60.4m and had advised clients to switch into JJB Sports, off 2.5p at 294.

'On our revised estimates, the stock trades on 13.9 times 2005 earnings. This looks expensive relative to the rest of the sector and we therefore maintain our reduce recommendation,' Dresdner said. The bank said it was concerned that the company might have to cut its dividend. Last year Matalan paid a dividend of 8.1p.

Other analysts were not so gloomy. Nick Bubb at Evolution Beeson Gregory said that although he had reduced his profit forecast by a couple of million pounds Matalan had made a good start to the new season. He believes it is possible that he will be upgrading his 2005 forecast when the company reports the full-year figures in May.

Matalan shares closed 7.25p lower at 164p – one of the biggest fallers in the FTSE 250.

© *The Guardian*, 26 February 2004

Stock levels should be optimised so that neither too little is held to meet orders nor too much is held so that waste occurs. The forecasting of stock requirements must be a part of the management process. In addition, stock level optimisation requires the following:

- establishment of robust stock purchase procedures
- appropriate location and storage of stocks
- accurate and timely systems for the recording, control, and physical checks of stocks
- monitoring of stock turnover performance
- implementation of effective stock management and reorder systems.

Progress check 10.6

Briefly explain how stock turnover performance may be monitored and the ways in which it may be improved.

Stock purchase

For cash flow (and operational efficiency) purposes it is crucial that efficient and effective sales order, materials procurement, and stock control systems are in place and operated by highly trained staff. Authority levels for the appropriate purchasing and logistics managers must be established for both price and quantities, for initial orders and reorders.

Stock location

A variety of options exists for the location of stocks and the ways in which they may be stored. Related items of stocks may be grouped together, or they may be located by part number, or by frequency of pick, or located based on their size or weight.

Stock recording and physical checks

Ideally, all stock transactions should be recorded simultaneously with their physical movement. Stock turnover must be regularly reviewed so that damaged, obsolete, and slow moving stock may be disposed of, possibly at discounted sales prices or for some scrap value.

In cash terms, holding on to unsaleable stocks is a 'waste' of the highest order. It uses up valuable space and time and needs people to manage it. It clogs up the system and reduces efficient order fulfilment, and represents money tied up in assets of little or no value. Businesses need to move on and dispose of old, obsolete, and slow-moving stocks.

Progress check 10.7

What are the ways in which improvements in a company's management of stocks may contribute to achievement of optimisation of its level of working capital requirement (WCR)?

It is inevitable that stocks will be required to be physically counted from time to time, to provide a check against stock records. This may be by way of a complete physical count two or three times a year, with one count taking place at the company's financial year end. Alternatively, physical cycle counts may take place continuously throughout the year. This system selects groups of stocks to be counted and checked with stock records in such a way that all stocks are checked two, three, four or more times up to maybe 12 times a year, dependent on such criteria as value or frequency of usage.

Stock ratios

You may recall from the sections in Chapter 8 about financial ratios that one of the efficiency ratios related to stock turnover is a measure used to monitor stock levels:

$$\text{stock days} = \frac{\text{stock value}}{\text{average daily cost of sales in period}}$$

Stock turnover (or stock days) is the number of days that stocks could last at the forecast or most recent usage rate. This may be applied to total stocks, finished goods, raw materials, or work in progress. The weekly internal efficiency of stock utilisation is shown in the following ratios:

$$\frac{\text{finished goods}}{\text{average weekly despatches}} \qquad \frac{\text{raw materials}}{\text{average weekly raw material usage}} \qquad \frac{\text{work in progress}}{\text{average weekly production}}$$

Stock ratios are usually calculated using values but may also be calculated for individual stock lines using quantities where appropriate:

$$\text{stock weeks} = \frac{\text{total stock value}}{\text{average weekly cost of sales (total COS for the year divided by 52)}}$$

Financial analysts usually only have access to published accounts and so they often calculate the stock weeks ratio using the total closing stocks value in relation to the cost of sales for the year.

Worked Example 10.5

From the balance sheet and income statement for Flatco plc for 2007 and the comparatives for 2006 (see pages 418 to 419), we may calculate the stock turnover for 2007 and the stock days (stock turnover) for 2006.

$$\text{stock days 2007} = \frac{\text{stock value}}{\text{average daily cost of sales in period}} = \frac{£311}{£2,500/365}$$

$$= 45 \text{ days (6.5 weeks)}$$

$$\text{stock days 2006} = \frac{£268}{£2,400/365} = 41 \text{ days (5.9 weeks)}$$

The performance for 2006, 2007, and future years may be more clearly presented in a trend analysis. If 2006 was the first year in the series, then 41 days may be expressed as the base of 100. The 45 days for the year 2007 is then expressed as 110 [45 × 100/41], and so on for subsequent years. Comparison of 110 with 100 (a 10% deterioration) more clearly shows its significance than the presentation of the absolute numbers 45 and 41 days.

ABC and VIN analysis

The appropriate level of control of stocks may be determined through assessment of the costs of control against the accuracy required and the potential benefits. Use of a Pareto analysis (80/20 analysis) allows selective levels of control of stocks through their categorisation into A items, B items, and C items. The ABC method uses Pareto to multiply the usage of each stock item by its value, ranking from the highest to the lowest and then calculating the cumulative result at each level in the ranking.

A items, for example, may be chosen so that the top five stock items make up 60% of the total value. Such items would then be continuously monitored for unit-by-unit replenishment. B items, for example, may be chosen from say 60% to 80% of the total value. Such items would be subject to automated systematic control using cycle counts, with levels of stocks replenished using economic order quantities (see below). C items, for example, may be identified as the 20% of stocks remaining – 'the trivial many' in financial terms. These stocks may be checked by sample counting; because of their low value, more than adequate levels may be held.

Other important factors impact on the choice of stock levels. Total acquisition costs must be considered rather than simply the unit purchase price. There may be requirements to provide items of stock using a just-in-time (JIT) approach (see the section dealing with JIT later in this chapter). The cost of not having a particular item in stock, even though it may itself have a low cost, may be significant if it is an integral part within a process. Consequently, in addition to ABC categories, stocks are usually allocated to vital/important/nice to have (VIN) categories, indicating whether they are:

- vital (V) – out of stock would be a disaster
- important (I) – out of stock would give significant operational problems or costs
- nice to have (N) – out of stock would present only an insignificant problem.

Progress check 10.8

Describe how stock turnover may be regularly monitored.

Economic order quantity (EOQ)

A simplistic model called the economic order quantity (EOQ) model, aims to reconcile the problem of the possible loss to a business through interruption of production, or failure to meet orders, with the cost of holding stocks large enough to give security against such loss. EOQ may be defined as the most economic stock replenishment order size, which minimises the sum of stock ordering costs and stockholding costs. EOQ is used in an 'optimising' stock control system.

If

P = the £ cost per purchase order

Q = order quantity of each order in units

N = annual units usage

S = annual £ cost of holding one unit

Then

the annual cost of purchasing
= cost per purchase order × the number of orders to be placed in a year
(annual usage divided by quantity ordered per purchase)

or

$$P \times N/Q$$

or

$$PN/Q$$

annual cost of holding stock
= annual cost of holding one unit in stock × average number of units held in stock
= $S \times Q/2$ or $QS/2$

The minimum total cost occurs when the annual purchasing cost equals the annual holding cost, or

$$PN/Q = QS/2$$

Cross multiplication gives

$$2PN = Q^2S$$

or

$$Q^2 = 2PN/S$$

Therefore when the quantity ordered is the economic order quantity:

$$EOQ = \sqrt{2PN/S}$$

Let's look at a simple example.

Worked Example 10.6

E.C.O. Nomic & Sons, the greengrocers, buy cases of potatoes at £20 per case.

£ cost of one purchase order	P = £5 per order
Number of cases turned over in a year	N = 1,000 cases (units)
Annual £ cost of holding one case	S = 20% of purchase price

Then, S = 20% × £20 = £4

$EOQ = \sqrt{2PN/S} = \sqrt{2 \times 5 \times 1,000/4}$

$EOQ = \sqrt{2,500}$

Economic order quantity EOQ = 50 cases of potatoes per order

EOQ illustrates the principle of stock ordering and stock holding optimisation but it is extremely limited. In practice, significant divergences from the EOQ may result in only minor cost increases:

- the optimum order quantity decision may more usually be dependent on other factors like storage space, storage facilities, purchasing department resources, logistical efficiency, etc.

- costs of purchasing and holding stock may be difficult to quantify accurately so the resultant EOQ calculation may be inaccurate

- in periods of changing prices, interest rates, foreign currency exchange rates, etc., continual recalculation is required that necessitates constant updates of all purchasing department and warehouse records of purchases and stocks – computerised systems can assist in providing the answers to some of the financial 'what-ifs' presented by changes in the business environment.

The emphasis over the past couple of decades on stock minimisation or stock elimination systems through the implementation of, for example, JIT, *kanban*, and vendor managed inventory (VMI) has reinforced the disadvantages of holding large stocks. High stock levels reduce the risk of disappointing customers, but it is a costly process not only in the inherent cost of the stock itself, but in the cost resulting from the 'wastes' identified by Ohno.

Progress check 10.9

Outline the basic conflict that might arise between the marketing department and the finance department when discussing the practical application of an economic order quantity (EOQ) system.

Just in time (JIT), materials requirement planning (MRP), and optimised production technology (OPT)

Just in time (JIT)

Just in time (JIT) is sometimes incorrectly referred to as a stock reduction or a zero stock system. JIT is a management philosophy that is a response to two key factors: the reduction in product life cycles; and the increase in levels of quality required from demanding customers.

JIT incorporates a 'pull' system of producing or purchasing components and products in response to customer demand. In a JIT system products are pulled through the system from customer demand back down through the supply chain to the level of materials and components. The consumer buys, and the processes manufacture the products to meet this demand. The consumer therefore determines the schedule.

The JIT system contrasts with a 'push' system where stocks act as buffers between each process within and between purchasing, manufacturing, and sales. In a push system, products are produced to schedule, and the schedule may be based on:

- a 'best guess' of demand

- last year's sales

- intuition.

Some of the key principles and techniques of waste elimination, which in turn support improved stock management, are embraced within the implementation of the JIT process:

- total quality control (TQC), which embraces a culture of waste elimination and 'right first time'

- *kanban* which is a system of signals used to control stock levels and smooth the rate of production, for example using cards to prompt top-up of materials or components driven by demand from the next process

- set-up time reduction for reduced manufacturing batch sizes

- *heijunka*, which is the smoothing of production through levelling of day-to-day variations in schedules in line with longer-term demand

- *jidoka*, or autonomation, where operators are empowered to stop the line if a quality problem arises, avoiding poor quality production and demanding immediate resolution of the problem

- improved production layout

- *poka yoke* (mistake proofing) fail-safe devices, supporting *jidoka* by preventing parts being fitted in the wrong way, so that poor quality is not passed to the next stage in the production process

- employee involvement including self-quality and operator first-line maintenance

- multi-skilling of employees for increased flexibility

- supplier development for higher quality and greater reliability of supply – in the UK, M&S, for example, have publicised their adoption of this practice.

Two other approaches to stock management:

- materials requirement planning (MRP), its development into manufacturing resource planning (MRPII)

- optimised production technology (OPT)

are sometimes seen as alternatives to JIT, but in fact may be used to complement JIT systems.

> ## Progress check 10.10
>
> Explain briefly what benefits might be gained by both supplier (manufacturer) and customer (national retailer) if they work jointly on optimisation of stock levels and higher quality levels.

Materials requirement planning (MRP)

MRP is a set of techniques, which uses the bill of materials (BOM), stock data and the master production schedule to calculate future requirements for materials. It essentially makes recommendations to release material to the production system. MRP is a 'push' approach that starts with forecasts of customer demand and then calculates and reconciles materials requirements using basic mathematics. MRP relies on accurate BOMs and scheduling algorithms, EOQ analyses, and allowances for wastage and shrinkage.

Optimised production technology (OPT)

OPT is a manufacturing philosophy, combined with a computerised system of shop-floor scheduling and capacity planning, that differs from a traditional approach of balancing capacity as near to 100% as possible and then maintaining flow. It aims to balance flow rather than capacity. Like JIT, it aims at improvement of the production process and is a philosophy that focuses on factors such as:

- manufacture to order
- quality
- lead times
- batch sizes
- set-up times,

and has important implications for purchasing efficiency, stock control, and resource allocation.

OPT is based on the concept of throughput accounting (TA), which was developed by Eli Goldratt and vividly portrayed in his book *The Goal* (Gower, 1984). The aim of OPT is to make money, defined in terms of three criteria: throughput (which it aims to increase), and inventory and operating expense, which should at the same time both be reduced. It does this by making better use of limited capacity through tightly controlled finite scheduling of bottleneck operations, and use of increased process batch sizes, which means producing more of a high priority part once it has been set up on a bottleneck machine.

Progress check 10.11

In the UK there are several low volume car manufacturers, for example Morgan Cars of Malvern and TVR of Blackpool. How would you relate the optimised production technology (OPT) philosophy to their operations.

Factory scheduling is at the root of OPT and the critical factor in OPT scheduling is identification and elimination or management of bottlenecks. OPT highlights the slowest function. This is crucially important in OPT: if one machine is slowing down the whole line then the value of that machine at that time is equivalent to the value of the whole production line. Conversely, attention paid to improving the productivity of a non-bottleneck machine will merely increase stocks.

Progress check 10.12

What are some of the systems and techniques that may be used to optimise the levels of stocks held by a manufacturing company?

Debtors and credit management

All companies that sell on credit to their customers should maintain some sort of system of credit control. Improved debt collection is invariably an area that produces significant, immediate cash flow benefits from the reduction of debtor balances. It is therefore an area to which time and resources may be profitably devoted.

Cash flow is greatly affected by the policies established by a company with regard to:

- the choice of customers
- the way in which sales are made
- the sales invoicing system
- the speedy correction of errors and resolution of disputes
- the means of settlement
- the monitoring of customer settlement performance
- the overdue accounts collection system.

These are all areas that can delay the important objective of turning a sale into a debtor and a debtor into cash in the shortest possible time. Each area of policy involves a cost. Such costs must be weighed against the levels of risk being taken.

Customers and trading terms

Sales persons are enthusiastic to make sales. It is important that they are also aware of the need to assess customer risk of the likelihood of slow payment or non-payment. If risks are to be taken then this must be with prior approval of the company and with an estimate of the cost of the risk included within the selling price. Similar limits and authorisations must be in place to cover credit periods, sales discounts, and the issue of credit notes.

Credit checks should always be made prior to allowing any level of credit to a potential new customer. Selling on credit with little hope of collection is a way of running out of cash very quickly and invariably resulting in business failure. The procedure for opening a new account must be a formal process that shows the potential customer that it is something that the organisation takes seriously. Many risky customers may thus be avoided.

Before a new account is agreed, at least three references should be obtained: one from the customer bank and two from high profile suppliers with whom the customer regularly does business. It is important that references are followed up in writing with requests as to whether there are any reasons why credit should not be granted. A credit limit should be agreed that represents minimum risk, but at a level that the customer can service. It should also be at a level within which the customer's business may operate effectively.

A copy of the latest annual and interim accounts of a potential customer should be requested from the Registrar of Companies. These will indicate the legal status of the company, who the owners are, and its financial strength. These accounts are by their nature historical. If large volumes of business are envisaged then details of future operations and funding may need to be discussed in more detail with the potential customer. If such large contracts involve special purchases then advance payments should be requested to reduce any element of risk.

Having established relationships with creditworthy customers a number of steps may be taken to further minimise risk associated with ongoing trading:

- sale of goods with reservation of title (Romalpa clause) – the goods remain in the ownership of the selling company until they are paid for, and may be recovered should the customer go into liquidation
- credit insurance cover in respect of customers going into liquidation and export risk
- passing of invoices to a factoring company for settlement; the factoring company settles the invoices, less a fee for the service, which therefore provides a type of insurance cover against non-payment – a factoring company can be used as a source of finance enabling short-term funds to be raised on the value of invoices issued to customers.

The measures adopted should be even more rigorous in their application to the supply of goods or services to businesses abroad. This is because of the inevitable distance, different trading conditions, regulations, currencies, and legislation.

Progress check 10.13

What are the ways in which improvements in the management of debtors and credit management may contribute to achievement of optimal levels of working capital requirement (WCR)?

Settlement methods

Payment collection methods should be agreed with all customers at the outset. The use of cheques, though still popular, is becoming a costly and ineffective collection method. Cash, credit card receipts, and automated electronic transfers are the main methods used by retailers, and regular speedy banking is the cornerstone of efficient use of funds. Bankers drafts are the next best thing to cash but should be avoided because of the risk involved through their potential for accidental or fraudulent loss. Mail transfers are frequently used for settlement by overseas companies. These tend to be costly and have been known to 'get lost' in the banking systems. Letters of credit together with sight drafts are frequently used for payments against large contracts.

Extreme care needs to be taken with letters of credit, which are a minefield of potential problems for non-settlement. Letters of credit must be completed providing full details and with the requisite numbers of copies of all supporting documentation. The conditions stipulated must be fully complied with and particularly regarding delivery of goods at the right time at the right location and in the quantity, quality, and condition specified.

Electronic collection methods continue to increase in popularity. Direct debit payments are an option where settlement may be made on presentation of agreed sales invoices to the bank. Personal banking is now a feature of the Internet. As its use and level of sophistication continues to be developed, corporate banking transactions conducted through the Internet will inevitably become a major feature. Absolute control is required over both sales and purchase ledger transactions, and all businesses benefit from the strict adherence to administrative routines by the staff involved. Successful control of cash and cheques requires well-thought-out procedures. Examples may be seen in the formal recording that takes place in the systems adopted in high volume businesses.

One of the most acceptable methods for many years has been payment through BACS (bankers automated clearing services). The BACS method requires customers to register as BACS users and to specify the type of payment pattern they wish to adopt for settlement of their creditor accounts (or payroll). Every week, or two weeks or every month, companies supply details of payments to be made – names of payees and amounts. These are then settled by BACS exactly on the day specified and with only one payment transaction appearing on the bank statement. This means that the problems of cost of individual cheques and the uncertainty of not knowing when each payment will be cleared are avoided.

Cash takings must be strictly controlled in terms of a log and the issue of receipts. Regular physical counts must be carried out and cash banked twice daily or at least once daily. Cheques may be lost in the post, or bear wrong dates, or wrong amounts, or the customer may have forgotten to sign. One person should be nominated to receive and bank cash and cheques. A separate person should maintain the sales ledger in order to maintain internal control.

Sales invoices

The sales invoicing system must ensure that prompt, accurate invoices are submitted to customers for all goods and services that are provided. A control system needs to be implemented to prevent supply without a subsequent sales invoice being issued. An invoicing delay of just one day may result in one month's delay in payment. Incorrect pricing, VAT calculations, invoice totalling, and customer names and addresses may all result in delay. A customer may be unlikely to point out an undercharged invoice.

Sales invoices may be routinely followed up with statements of outstanding balances. The credit period offered to customers should obviously be as short as possible. Care should be taken in offering cash discounts for immediate or early payment. This is invariably a disadvantage. Many customers will take the discount but continue to take the extended credit. This is something that may not even be spotted by staff responsible for checking and processing receipts from customers, which effectively results in an unauthorised cost being incurred by the business.

Debtor ratios

Another of the efficiency ratios from the sections in Chapter 8 about financial ratios relates to debtor days, which is a measure used to monitor customer settlement performance.

$$\text{debtor days} = \frac{\text{accounts receivable} \times 365}{\text{sales}}$$

Debtor days indicate the average time taken, in calendar days, to receive payment from credit customers. Adjustment is needed if the ratio is materially distorted by VAT or other taxes. Currently, UK sales for exports to countries abroad are not applicable for VAT. Other forms of sales tax may be applicable to sales in those countries.

Worked Example 10.7

From the balance sheet and income statement for Flatco plc for 2007, and the comparatives for 2006, we may calculate the debtor days for 2007 and the debtor days for 2006.

$$\text{debtor days 2007} = \frac{\text{trade debtors} \times 365}{\text{sales}} = \frac{£573 \times 365}{£3,500} = 60 \text{ days}$$

$$\text{debtor days 2006} = \frac{£517 \times 365}{£3,250} = 58 \text{ days}$$

A similar trend analysis to that described in Worked Example 10.5 may be used for greater clarification of performance.

If in 2006, 58 days = 100, then the year 2007 debtor days would = 103.

Progress check 10.14

Describe how customer settlement performance may be regularly monitored.

Collection policy

As a great many experienced businessmen may confirm, perhaps the key factor underlying sustained, successful collection of accounts receivable is identification of 'the person' within the customer organisation who actually makes things happen and who can usually speed up the processing of a payment through the company's systems. Payments are usually authorised by the finance director or managing director or the accountant. However, 'the person' is the one who prepares payments and pushes them under the nose of the appropriate manager for signature. Cultivation of a good relationship with 'the person' within each customer organisation is an investment that usually results in massive benefits.

The benefit of issue of regular monthly statements of account to customers may be questioned. Most companies pay on invoice and so a brief telephone call to confirm that all invoices have been received, to check on the balance being processed for payment, and the payment date, usually pays greater dividends. Issue of a statement is usually of greater benefit as an *ad hoc* exercise to resolve queries or when large numbers of transactions are involved.

A routine should be established for when settlement of invoices becomes overdue. This process should include having a member of staff who has the specific responsibility for chasing overdue accounts – a credit controller. Chasing overdue accounts by telephone is usually the most effective method. It allows development of good working relationships with customers to enable problems to be quickly resolved and settled.

It is absolutely essential that accurate debtor information is available, up-to-date in terms of inclusion of all invoices that have been issued and allowing for all settlements received, before calling a customer to chase payment. It is also imperative that immediately errors are identified, for example errors in invoicing, they are corrected without delay. This is one of the commonest areas used by customers to stall payment and yet the remedy is within the hands of the company!

Customer name	Hannagan plc Aged debtors As at 30 September 2007				
		·· ageing ··			
	total balance	up to 30 days	over 30, up to 60 days	over 60, up to 90 days	over 90 days
	£	£	£	£	£
Alpha Chemicals Ltd	16,827	7,443	8,352	635	397
Brown Manufacturing plc	75,821	23,875	42,398	6,327	3,221
Caramel Ltd	350,797	324,776	23,464	2,145	412
.	.	.	.	.	.
.	.	.	.	.	.
.	.	.	.	.	.
.	.	.	.	.	.
Zeta Ltd	104,112	56,436	43,565	3,654	457
Total	4,133,714	2,354,377	1,575,477	184,387	19,473
% ageing		56.96%	38.11%	4.46%	0.47%

Figure 10.10 Example of an aged debtors report

An indispensable information tool used by the credit controller should be an up-to-date aged debtors report giving full details of all outstanding invoices (see Fig. 10.10). This shows the totals of accounts receivable from all customers at a given date and also an analysis of the outstanding invoices in terms of the time between the date of the report and the dates on which the invoices were issued.

In addition, it is useful to have available the full details of each customers' payment record showing exactly what has been paid and when, going back perhaps one year. To provide a historical analysis and assist in resolving possible customer disputes, computerised systems may be used to hold customer data going back many years, for future retrieval. The friendly agreement of the facts on a customer account on the telephone usually goes a very long way towards obtaining settlement in accordance with agreed terms.

Perhaps one of the most effective methods of extracting payment from an overdue account is a threat to stop supply of goods or services. If a debt continues to be unpaid then the next step may be a chasing letter that shows that the organisation means business and will be prepared to follow up with legal action. Prior to sending any such letter the facts should be checked and double-checked – people and computers make mistakes! This letter should clearly explain what is expected and what the implications may be for non-compliance with agreed terms. A solicitor's letter should probably be considered, as a rule of thumb, not before an invoice is, say, 60 days overdue from its expected settlement date.

The last resort is to instruct a solicitor to take action against a customer for non-payment. Small debts may be recovered through the small claims court. The costs are low and the services of a solicitor are not necessarily required. Large debts may be recovered by suing the customer for non-payment. This is an expensive and very time-consuming business. The use of the last resort measures that have been outlined should be kept to a minimum. Their use may be avoided through a great deal of preliminary attention being paid to the recruitment of excellent staff, and the establishment of excellent systems, robust internal controls, and a formal credit control system.

Progress check 10.15

What are some of the ways in which the settlement of accounts receivable from customers may be speeded up?

Creditors management

The balance sheet category of creditors payable within one year in the UK comprises taxes, National Insurance, VAT, etc., and accounts payable to suppliers of materials, goods, and services provided to the company (trade creditors). Payments to the Government are normally required to be made promptly, but trade creditors are sometimes considered a 'free' source of finance. This really is not the case, and accounts payable are not free debt, as Worked Example 10.8 illustrates.

Worked Example 10.8

A supplier may offer Justin Time Ltd payment terms of 90 days from delivery date. If Justin Time Ltd alternatively proposes to the supplier payment terms of 60 days from delivery date the supplier may, for example, offer 1% (or 2%) discount for settlement 30 days earlier.

Annual cost of discount:

$$\text{At 1\% discount } \frac{365 \times 1\%}{30} = 12.2\% \text{ per annum}$$

$$\text{At 2\% discount } \frac{365 \times 2\%}{30} = 24.3\% \text{ per annum}$$

A discount of 1% for settlement one month early is equivalent to over 12% per annum (and a discount of 2% is over 24% per annum). Consequently, it becomes apparent that the supplier's selling price must have included some allowance for financial charges; accounts payable are therefore not a free debt.

Many companies habitually delay payments to creditors, in order to enhance cash flow, either to the point just before relationships break down or until suppliers refuse further supply. Creditors may be paid slower than the agreed terms to gain a short-term cash advantage but even as a short-term measure this should only be regarded as temporary. It is very short-term thinking and obviously not a strategy that creates an atmosphere conducive to the development of good supplier relationships. A more systematic approach to the whole purchasing and payables system is the more ethical and professional means of providing greater and sustainable benefits. This is an approach followed by the majority of UK plcs, which is now supported by changes in legislation that were introduced during 1999/2000.

With regard to suppliers, overall business effectiveness and improved control over cash flow may be better served by establishment of policies, in much the same way as was suggested should apply to customers, with regard to:

- the choice of suppliers
- the way in which purchases are made
- the purchase invoicing system
- the speedy correction of errors and resolution of disputes
- the means of settlement
- the monitoring of supplier payment performance.

Progress check 10.16

Explain whether or not trade creditors are a 'free' or even a cheap source of finance for a company, and why.

Suppliers and trading terms

New suppliers should be evaluated perhaps even more rigorously than customers with particular regard to quality of product, quality and reliability of distribution, sustainability of supply, and financial stability. Appropriate controls must be established to give the necessary purchasing authority to the minimum of managers. This requires highly skilled buyers who are able to source the right quality product for the job at the best total acquisition price (base price, delivery, currency risk, etc.), in the delivery quantities and frequencies required and at the best possible terms. Their authority must be accompanied by rules governing:

- which suppliers may be dealt with
- acceptable ranges of product
- purchase volumes
- price negotiation
- discounts
- credit terms
- transaction currencies
- invoicing
- payment methods
- payment terms.

Terms of trading must be in writing. Most companies print their agreed terms on their purchase orders.

Payment methods

Traditional supplier payment methods include:

- cash – very little used now by large businesses, because of its impracticality and issues of security and fraud
- bill of exchange – a negotiable instrument drawn by a supplier on the company, who by accepting (signing) the bill acknowledges the debt, which may be payable immediately (sight

draft) or at a future date (time draft), is a method of guaranteed payment and an instrument which may be discounted to raise cash

- cheque – a common form of payment, which is a bill of exchange drawn on a banker and payable on demand
- sight draft – a bill of exchange payable on presentation to a bank.

However, electronic payment methods are now increasingly used by companies. Electronic funds transfer (EFT) is a system used by banks and financial institutions for the movement of funds between accounts and for the provision of information. EFT is an electronic bulk clearing system used by the banks for relatively low value, high volume automated payments. An early form of EFT adopted by the UK banking system was BACS (discussed earlier), which has been used by companies for transactions such as payroll and supplier payments.

There are significant supply chain benefits of EFT, for example global activity 24 hours a day, 365 days a year, and control over cash flow through being able to determine exactly when payments will be cleared through the banking system. Potential risks arise from the use of EFT if EDI (electronic systems interchange) systems are unable to guarantee the transmission of complete and accurate transmission of data together with its verification of their authenticity. It is essential the EFT users ensure appropriate procedures for limiting authorised access to the systems.

Payments to suppliers should be made in line with terms of trading, but advantages may be gained from cheaper payment methods and providing better control than through the issue of cheques. For example, the payables system may automatically prepare weekly payment schedules and trigger automated electronic payments directly through the bank. Alternatively, submission of correct supplier invoices directly to the company's bank may also be used to support automatic payment in line with agreed terms. Provided that adequate controls are put in place to check and monitor such transactions these methods provide a cost-effective method of controlling cash outflows and may be an invaluable aid to cash planning.

International trade

In international trade there is a range of methods that may be used for international payments that includes:

- payment in advance
- irrevocable letter of credit
- counter-trade
- documentary collection
- open account payment
- payment on consignment.

Each of the payment strategies that may be adopted by companies trading internationally has its own advantages and disadvantages and varying types and level of risk. The decision on which method of payment to use will often depend on a range of interrelated issues, for example:

- perceived risk associated with the transaction
- terms generally on offer within the marketplace for similar products and services
- terms offered by competitors
- requirements of the supplier.

Payment in advance

With payment in advance, payment is expected by the supplier in full before goods are shipped. This method is normally used where a supplier has serious doubts about the company's ability to pay, or where the supplier's bank will not finance the transaction or extend existing credit arrangements. The advantage of this method of payment is that it eliminates the risk of payment default. However, the disadvantage is it may have a negative impact on the overall demand for a company's goods or services, especially where competitors offer more favourable terms of payment.

Irrevocable letter of credit

An irrevocable letter of credit may be used as an alternative to payment in advance. However, because the associated bank charges of a letter of credit can be high, its use is often restricted to transactions of a substantial nature. A letter of credit is an internationally accepted financial instrument generally issued in the form of an undertaking by the issuing bank (the importer's bank) to an exporter, through an advising bank (normally in the exporter's country). The undertaking is that the issuing bank will pay on presentation of documents, provided that the terms of the credit are strictly complied with. A second assurance of payment (usually a bank) prevents surprises and means that the issuing bank has been deemed acceptable by the confirming bank.

There are various types of letters of credit of which the confirmed irrevocable credit is the most secure. The advantages of using letters of credit are:

- the contract is with the bank
- the responsibility for ensuring all conditions on both sides are complied with rests with the bank
- they provide a contract of sale during manufacture
- they provide certainty of sale making the possibility of arranging borrowing easier for the exporter.

A disadvantage of using letters of credit is that they are usually legally and administratively complex. They are also expensive to arrange, which imposes extra cost on the supplier.

Counter-trade

Counter-trade can take many forms, some of the more popular being:

- counter-purchase – an agreement where the exporter undertakes to purchase goods and services from the country concerned (very common in Eastern Europe and developing countries)
- barter or compensation trade – the direct exchange of goods without any exchange of funds
- buy-back – an agreement where the exporter receives payment for the future output of goods or services supplied
- offset – the incorporation of components, materials etc., from the importing country into the exporter's finished product
- switch trading – an agreement where an importer utilises credit surpluses accumulated in another country to finance exports from a third country
- evidence accounts – the exporter maintains accounts which demonstrate matching counter-purchases from a particular market in which it has a continuing involvement.

The relative advantages and disadvantages of counter-trade really depend on the precise nature of the counter-trade agreement.

Documentary collection

Documentary bank collection is less secure than a letter of credit and involves sending shipping documents through the banking system to a bank in the buyer's country. These documents are only released to the buyer upon payment or acceptance of a bill of exchange, depending on the terms agreed in the sales contract.

The advantage of a documentary collection is that it minimises the risk of payment default. However, a disadvantage is that the bank charges for handling a bill of exchange can be fairly high, especially in some EU countries.

Open account payment

This is the international version of most domestic transactions where companies generally offer 30, 60, or 90 days to pay, and invoice the customer accordingly. In an open account arrangement the customer is trusted to ensure payment is made by the agreed method on or before the agreed date. Open account payment should be used only when the supplier is sufficiently confident that the company can be trusted to make full payment by an agreed date, and so the integrity of the company must therefore be beyond question or else the supplier has no security against non-payment.

An advantage of open account payment is that it is simple, and administratively cost effective to use. The big disadvantage is the high level of trust required between the supplying company and the purchasing company; the risk and therefore cost of payment default can be high.

Payment on consignment

Payment on consignment is in principle the same as payment on open account, but ownership of the goods remains with the supplier until the payment is made. The advantage of consignment payment is that it is often easier to repossess the goods in the event of non-payment.

International trade risk

The risks involved in international trade may be divided into three main types:

- country risk, (or political risk)
- property risk
- credit and commercial risk.

Country risk

The country risk (or political risk) associated with international trade can be considerable. While such risks can develop in a number of different ways, they are generally related to government actions and policies that seek to:

- expropriate company assets and profits
- impose foreign exchange currency controls
- impose price intervention policies that discriminate between domestic and non-domestic companies
- impose tax laws that offer preferential treatment to domestic companies
- impose social or work-related regulations that offer preferential treatment of domestic companies

- impose regulations that restrict access to local finance
- restrict the movement of company assets and resources.

The impact of such policies on a company's ability to undertake commercial activities, generate profits, and repatriate or reinvest such profits for future growth can be substantial. Therefore the recognition, assessment, and management of such risk is an important aspect of a company's international trading activities. However, given that international competitive advantage can only be attained by trading off higher levels of risk for higher overall returns, in general, companies tend to adopt management strategies and policies that seek to minimise company risk rather than eliminate it altogether. Such policies include:

- obtaining insurance against the possibility of expropriation of assets
- negotiating overseas government concessions or guarantees to minimise the possibility of creditor default or the expropriation of company assets
- structuring the company's financial and operating policies to ensure they are acceptable to, and consistent with regulatory requirements
- developing close social and political relationships with overseas country institutions
- integrating international production of products to include the overseas country and home country companies to ensure that overseas country companies are dependent on home country companies.

Property risk

Property risk relates to the risks involved in the transit of goods and services and the possibility that, during the transfer, loss or damage may occur before the completion of the sales contract. To minimise such risks it is important that a company involved in international trade should ensure that:

- agreed protocols are in place
- agreed procedures and documentation are followed and completed

and such trade protocols and procedures may include agreement on the following:

- responsibility for the transport of the goods and services
- responsibility for obtaining customs clearance
- requirement for insurance
- requirement for letters of credit
- currency of payment
- requirement for documentary evidence of receipt and collection
- nature and timing of payment.

There may also be a need to establish the import requirements of a particular country well before date of shipment to ensure the required documentation, for example number of copies of invoices, bills of lading, and certificates of origin. Procedures and documents may include use of the following:

- transport documents, including bills of lading, or airway bills
- commercial documents, including invoices, packing lists, and inspection certificates

■ government documents, including certificates of origin, export and import licences, and health certificates.

Credit and commercial risk

Credit and commercial risk relates to the risks associated with payment default by the buyer as a consequence of solvency problems or liquidation. The management of this risk, regardless of whether trade is domestic or international, should always commence at the quotation stage of the trade agreement or contract and continue through to the contract for sale. Such procedures underpin the whole export transaction from receipt of the order to final settlement, and can include the following:

■ credit assessment of the buyer prior to agreement to trade

■ regular revision of the level of trade contracts with the buyer

■ regular updating of credit arrangements.

Companies can also try and minimise credit and commercial risk by insuring against non-payment, or using letters of credit, or bank drafts, to help secure payment for the goods and service supplied.

Purchase invoices

Integrated purchase order, stock control, and payables systems, preferably computerised, should be used to control approval of new suppliers, trading terms, prices, etc. When supplier invoices are received by the organisation they must match completely with goods or services received and be matched with an official order. An efficient recording system should allow incorrect deliveries or incorrect invoices to be quickly identified, queried and rectified. The recording system should verify the credit terms for each invoice.

Progress check 10.17

What are some of the ways in which payments to suppliers may be improved to the mutual benefit of the company and its suppliers?

Creditor ratios

Another of the efficiency ratios, from the sections in Chapter 8 about financial ratios, relates to creditor days, which is a measure used to monitor supplier payment performance.

$$\text{creditor days} = \frac{\text{accounts payable} \times 365}{\text{cost of sales (or purchases)}}$$

Creditor days indicate the average time taken, in calendar days, to pay for supplies received on credit. Adjustment is needed if the ratio is materially distorted by VAT or unusual trading terms.

Worked Example 10.9

From the balance sheet and income statement for Flatco plc for 2007, and the comparatives for 2006, we may calculate the creditor days for 2007 and the creditor days for 2006.

$$\text{creditor days 2007} = \frac{\text{trade creditors} \times 365}{\text{cost of sales}} = \frac{£553 \times 365}{£2,500} = 81 \text{ days}$$

$$\text{creditor days 2006} = \frac{£461 \times 365}{£2,400} = 70 \text{ days}$$

A trend analysis may also be calculated in the same way as discussed in Worked Examples 10.4 and 10.7.

Payment policy

The priority for the accounts payable manager must be to maintain the level of payables and cash outflows in line with company policy, but at all times ensuring absolutely no interruption to any manufacturing processes or any other operations of the business. Fundamental to this is the development of good working relationships with suppliers so that problems may be quickly resolved and settled, thus avoiding any threats to supply.

The accounts payable manager must have accurate accounts payable information that is up to date in terms of all invoices received, invoices awaited, and payments made. In the same way as the credit controller deals with customer queries it is also imperative that the accounts payable manager requests corrections of invoice errors, immediately errors are identified. The accounts payable manager should have access to an up-to-date **aged creditors report** (see Fig. 10.11).

Hannagan plc
Aged creditors   As at 31 December 2007

Supplier name	total balance	up to 30 days	over 30, up to 60 days	over 60, up to 90 days	over 90 days
	£	£	£	£	£
Ark Packaging plc	9,800	4,355	2,555	445	2,435
Beta Plastics plc	45,337	32,535	12,445	144	213
Crown Cases Ltd	233,536	231,213	2,323	.	.
.	.	.	.	.	.
.	.	.	.	.	.
.	.	.	.	.	.
Zonkers Ltd	89,319	23,213	21,332	12,321	32,453
Total	**3,520,811**	**2,132,133**	**1,142,144**	**123,213**	**123,321**
% ageing		60.56%	32.44%	3.50%	3.50%

Figure 10.11 Example of an aged creditors report

This shows the totals of accounts payable to all suppliers at a given date and also an analysis of the balances in terms of the time between the date of the report and the dates of the invoices from suppliers.

The accounts payable manager should also have available detailed reports of all unpaid invoices on each account, and full details of each supplier's payment record showing exactly what has been paid and when, going back perhaps one year. The availability for use of correct, up-to-date information goes a long way to ensuring the avoidance of the build-up of any potential disputes.

Progress check 10.18

Describe how supplier payment performance may be regularly monitored.

Operating cycle performance

The operating cycle, or working capital cycle, which was illustrated in Fig. 10.1, is the period of time that elapses between the point at which cash begins to be expended on the production of products and the collection of cash from the customer. It determines the short-term financing requirements of the business. For a business that purchases and sells on credit, the cash operating cycle may be calculated by deducting the average payment period for suppliers from the average stock turnover period and the average customer's settlement period.

$$\text{operating cycle (days)} = \text{stock days} + \text{debtor days} - \text{creditor days}$$

The operating cycle may alternatively be calculated as a percentage using:

$$\text{operating cycle \%} = \frac{\text{working capital requirement (stocks} + \text{debtors} - \text{creditors)}}{\text{sales}}$$

Worked Example 10.10

From the working capital requirement calculated in Worked Example 10.2 and the stock days, debtor days, and creditor days calculated in Worked Examples 10.5, 10.7, and 10.9, we may calculate the operating cycle in days and % for Flatco plc for 2007 and 2006.

Operating cycle days:

Operating cycle 2007 = stock days + debtor days − creditor days

$$= 45 + 60 - 81 = 24 \text{ days}$$

Operating cycle 2006 = 41 + 58 − 70 = 29 days

▶ Operating cycle %:

$$\text{operating cycle \% 2007} = \frac{\text{working capital requirement}}{\text{sales}}$$

$$= \frac{(£311 + £573 - £553) \times 100\%}{£3,500} = 9.5\%$$

$$\text{operating cycle \% 2006} = \frac{(£268 + £517 - £461) \times 100\%}{£3,250} = 10.0\%$$

From this example we can see that Flatco plc's operating cycle has improved by five days from 2006 to 2007, an improvement of 0.5%. The deterioration in debtor days and stock turnover in this example has been more than offset by the increase in creditor days. Despite the overall improvement, this must be a cause for concern for the company who should therefore set targets for improvement and action plans to reduce its average customer collection period and reduce its number of stock days.

Overtrading

We have seen how important to a company is its good management of WCR. Personal judgement is required regarding choice of optimal levels of working capital appropriate to the individual company and its circumstances. This generally leads to the quest for ever-reducing levels of working capital. However, there is a situation called overtrading which occurs if the company tries to support too great a volume of trade from too small a working capital base.

Overtrading is a condition of a business that enters into commitments in excess of its available short-term resources. This can arise even if the company is trading profitably, and is typically caused by financing strains imposed by a lengthy operating cycle or production cycle. Overtrading is not inevitable. If it does occur then there are several strategies that may be adopted to deal with it:

- reduction in business activity to consolidate and give some breathing space
- introduction of new equity capital rather than debt, to ease the strain on short-term resources
- drastically improve the management of working capital in the ways which we have outlined.

This chapter has dealt with working capital, and the working capital requirement (WCR). We have looked specifically at management of the WCR. The appreciation by managers of how working capital operates, and its effective management, are fundamental to the survival and success of the company. Cash and short-term debt are important parts of working capital, the management of which we shall consider in the section that follows.

Progress check 10.19

How may a company's investment in operations, its operating cycle, be minimised? What are the potential risks to the company in pursuing an objective of minimisation?

Cash improvement techniques

We have already discussed how profit and cash flow do not mean the same thing. Cash flow does not necessarily equal profit. However, all elements of profit may have been or will be at some time reflected in cash flow. It is a question of timing and also the quality of each of the components of profit:

■ day-to-day expenses are usually immediately reflected in a company's cash book as outflows of cash

■ non-current assets may have been acquired with an immediate outflow of cash, but the cost of these assets is reflected in the income statement through depreciation which is spread over the life of the assets

■ sales of products or services are reflected as revenue in the income statement even though cash receipts by way of settlement of sales invoices may not take place for another month or two or more

■ some sales invoices may not be paid at all even though the sales revenue has been recognised and so will subsequently be written off as a cost to bad debts in the income statement

■ purchases of materials are taken into stock and may not be reflected in the income statement as a cost for some time after cash has been paid to creditors even though credit terms may also have been agreed with suppliers.

Cash flow is therefore importantly linked to business performance, or profit, which may fluctuate from period to period. There is also a significant impact from non-profit items, which may have a more permanent effect on cash resources.

The non-profit and loss account items that affect short-term and long-term cash flow may be identified within each of the areas of the balance sheet (see Fig. 10.12).

The short-term cash position of a business can be improved by:

■ reducing current assets

■ increasing current liabilities.

The long-term cash position of a business can be improved by:

■ increasing equity

■ increasing non-current liabilities

■ reducing the net outflow on non-current assets.

We shall consider each of these actions for improvement in the cash position of the business.

Progress check 10.20

Profit and cash do not always mean the same thing. In what way therefore does profit impact on cash flow?

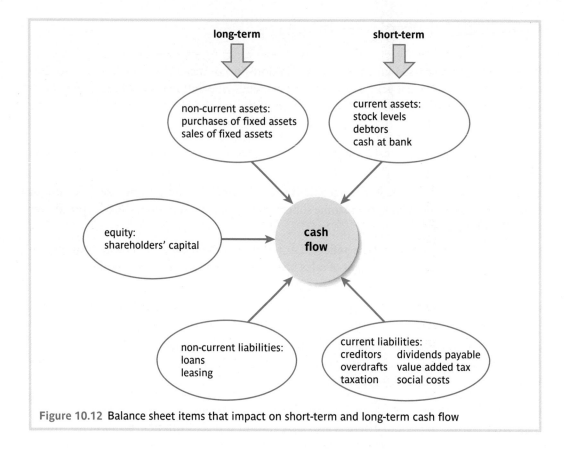

Figure 10.12 Balance sheet items that impact on short-term and long-term cash flow

Short-term cash flow improvement

Stock levels

Stock levels should be optimised so that neither too little is held to meet orders nor too much held so that waste occurs. It is a fine balance that requires planning, control, and honesty. Many companies either hide or are prepared to turn a blind eye to stock errors, over-ordering or over-stocking because managers do not like to admit their mistakes, and in any case the higher the stock then the higher the reported profit!

For cash flow (and operational efficiency) purposes it is crucial to put in place:

- efficient sales order systems
- materials procurement systems
- stock control systems

operated by highly trained staff.

Stock turnover must be regularly reviewed so that damaged, obsolete, and slow-moving stock may be disposed of at discounted sales prices or for some scrap value if possible. In cash terms, hanging on to unsaleable stocks is a 'waste' of the highest order. It uses up valuable space and time and needs people to manage it. It clogs up the system, hinders efficient order fulfilment, and represents money tied up in assets of little value.

Debtors

Debtors, or accounts payable, arise from sales of products or services. The methods employed in making sales, the sales invoicing system, the payment terms, and the cash collection system are all possible areas that can delay the important objective of turning a sale into cash in the shortest possible time.

Cash at bank

Whichever method is used for collection from customers, debts will ultimately be converted into a balance in the bank account. It is important to recognise that the balance shown on the bank statement is not the 'real' balance in the bank account. It is very important for a company to frequently prepare a bank reconciliation that details the differences between its cash book records and its bank statement at a given date. However, it should be noted that the bank statement balance does not represent 'cleared' funds. Cleared funds are funds that have actually been cleared through the banking system and are available for use. It is this balance, if overdrawn, which is used to calculate overdraft interest. There are software packages which routinely monitor bank charges and many users have obtained a refund from their bank.

The difference between the bank statement balance and the cleared balance is the 'float' and this can very often be a significant amount. The cleared balance information should be received from the bank and recorded so that it can be monitored daily. Cash requirements should be forecast in some detail, say six months forward, and regularly updated. Cleared funds surplus to immediate requirements should be invested. This may be short term, even overnight, in an interest-bearing account, or longer term in interest-bearing investments or the acquisition of capital equipment or even other businesses.

Creditors

Creditors may be paid more slowly than the agreed terms to gain a short-term cash advantage, but even as a short-term measure this should only be regarded as temporary. A more systematic approach to the whole purchasing and payables system is a more ethical and professional approach that may provide greater and sustainable benefits.

Ordering anything from a third party by any individual within the organisation is a commitment to cash leaking out at some time in the future. Tight controls must be in place to give such authority to only the absolute minimum of employees. This authority must be accompanied by rules governing:

- which suppliers may be dealt with
- acceptable ranges of product
- purchase volumes
- price negotiation
- discounts
- credit terms
- transaction currencies
- invoicing
- payment methods
- payment terms.

A tightly controlled and computerised system of:

- integrated purchase order
- stock control
- payables

must also include countersigned approval of, for example:

- new suppliers
- terms
- price ranges.

When supplier invoices are received by the organisation they must match absolutely with goods or services received and be matched with an official order. The recording system should verify the credit terms for each invoice. If payment is made by cheque, these should always bear two signatures as part of the control systems.

Cash improvements may be gained from the purchasing and creditors' system in a number of ways. The starting point must be a highly skilled buyer or buyers who are able to source the right quality product for the job at the best total acquisition price (base price plus delivery costs plus an allowance for currency risk, for example), in the delivery quantities and frequencies required and at the best possible terms.

Further gains may be achieved from efficient recording systems that allow incorrect deliveries or incorrect invoices to be quickly identified, queried, and rectified. Payments should be made in line with terms, but advantages may be gained from less costly payment methods and better control than the issue of cheques. For example, the payables system may automatically prepare weekly payment schedules and trigger automated electronic payments directly through the bank.

Alternatively, submission of correct supplier invoices directly to the company's bank may also be used to support automatic payment in line with agreed terms. Provided that adequate controls are put in place to check and monitor such transactions, they provide a cost-effective method of controlling cash outflows and cash planning.

Overdrafts

If an overdraft facility is a requirement then the lowest possible interest rate should be negotiated. As with the purchase of any service, it pays to shop around to obtain the best deal. Bank interest charges should be checked in detail and challenged if they look incorrect – all banks make mistakes. Software packages are available to routinely monitor bank charges.

A bank statement should be received routinely by the company weekly, or daily, and should always be thoroughly checked. A detailed monthly schedule of bank charges should be requested from the bank and checked very carefully. These charges should be strictly in line with the tariff of charges agreed at the outset with the bank. In the same way as interest charges, bank charges should always be challenged if they look incorrect.

At all times minimisation of both bank interest and bank charges must be a priority. This can be achieved by cash-flow planning and optimisation of the methods of receipts into and payments out of the bank account. If several bank accounts are held they should be seriously reviewed and closed unless they are really essential and add value to the business.

Taxation

Taxation on corporate profit is a complicated and constantly changing area. Tax experts may be engaged to identify the most tax efficient ways of running a business. At the end of the day, if a business is making profits then tax will become payable. Obvious cash gains may be made from knowing when the tax payment dates are and ensuring they are adhered to. Penalties and interest charges for late and non-payment are something to avoid.

Value added tax (VAT)

Value added tax (VAT) is probably an area that is even more complicated than corporate taxation. VAT does not impact on the profit of the business. Businesses are unpaid collectors of VAT. If a business is registered for VAT (currently mandatory for businesses with a turnover of £58,000 or more) it is required to charge VAT at the appropriate rate on all goods and services that are vatable. Accurate records must be maintained to account for all such VAT. Such VAT output tax, as it is called, must be paid over to Her Majesty's Revenue and Customs (HMRC) every three months or every month, whichever has been agreed.

VAT charged by suppliers, or input tax, may be offset against output tax so that the net is paid over monthly or quarterly. If input tax exceeds output tax, the VAT is refunded by HMRC. It is important to note that VAT offices look very carefully at trends on VAT returns. A return that is materially different to the trend will usually result in a visit from a VAT inspector who will carry out an extremely rigorous audit of all accounting records.

It may benefit an organisation to choose to account either monthly or quarterly for VAT. In the same way as corporate taxation, great care must be taken to submit correct VAT returns, and pay VAT on the correct date to avoid any penalties or interest charges.

Pay As You Earn (PAYE) and National Insurance (NI)

Pay As You Earn (PAYE) taxation and National Insurance (NI) contributions in the UK must be deducted at source from payments to employees. Salaries net of PAYE and NI are paid to employees, and the PAYE and NI and a further contribution for employer's NI is then paid to HMRC. Employees may be paid weekly or monthly and then PAYE and NI is paid over to HMRC during the following month. In exceptional circumstances HMRC may allow an odd day's delay. However, as with all other taxes, payment on the due date without fail is the best advice to avoid unnecessary outflows of cash in penalties and interest for non-compliance.

Dividends payable

Dividends are payable to shareholders by companies as a share of the profits. They are not a cost or a charge against profits but are a distribution of profits. There are some factors for consideration regarding cash flow. The timing of dividend payments is within the control of the company. Dividends may therefore be paid on dates that are most convenient in terms of cash flow and it is important to remember to include them in cash planning.

Progress check 10.21

Which areas within the income statement and the balance sheet may be considered to identify improvements to the short-term cash position of a company?

Worked Example 10.11

An extract from Flatco plc's balance sheet as at 31 December 2007 and 2006 is shown below. From it we can see that trade debtors at 31 December 2006 were £517,000. Sales were £3,250,000 and so debtor days for 2006 were 58 days. Trade debtors at 31 December 2007 were £573,000, sales were £3,500,000 and debtor days for 2007 had worsened to 60 days. Although new cash collection procedures and a reinforced credit control department were introduced in the latter part of 2007, it was too early to see an improvement by December 2007. A report published on the industry for 2006 indicated that the average time customers took to pay was 35 days, with the highest performing companies achieving 25 days.

Flatco plc
Extract of the balance sheet as at 31 December 2007

	2007 £000	2006 £000
Current assets		
Stocks	311	268
Debtors	573	517
Prepayments	589	617
Cash	327	17
	1,800	1,419

We will calculate the range of savings that Flatco would expect if it were to implement the appropriate measures to achieve average performance, or if it improved enough to match the best performers. We may assume that sales are more or less evenly spread throughout the year. Flatco's profit before tax for 2006 was £430,000 (2007: £590,000). The average bank interest paid or earned by Flatco plc was 9% per annum.

	Flatco	Average (derived)		Best (derived)	
Debtors	£517,000		£312,000		£223,000
Sales	£3,250,000		£3,250,000		£3,250,000
Debtor days	58		35		25
Gain per annum		[517 − 312]	£205,000	[517 − 223]	£294,000
Interest saved or earned at 9% per annum			£18,450		£26,460
Improvement to profit before tax		[£18,450 × 100/£430,000]	+4.3%	[£26,460 × 100/£430,000]	+6.2%

Assuming that Flatco plc's new credit control procedures become effective, at current trading levels it should result in a profit improvement for 2007 of between £25,000 and £37,000 per annum.

Long-term cash flow improvement

Shareholders' capital

Shareholders' capital has many advantages in providing a means of improving long-term cash flow. Provision of additional equity by the shareholders immediately strengthens the balance sheet. It also indirectly strengthens the profit position because equity (ordinary shares) does not bear a commitment to pay interest. Additional equity is an investment in future business, which will ultimately result in dividends payable from successful trading.

When the owners of an organisation provide additional equity, a personal cost is imposed on them in that the funding is from their own capital. It also may dilute their own stake or percentage of the business. New shareholders or professional risk capitalists (for example venture capitalists and private equity firms) may be another source of equity. This carries the same advantages but also the expectation of rewards is much higher than those from interest-bearing loans.

Loans

Long-term loans have certain advantages, particularly for the acquisition of non-current assets, even though they carry a commitment to regular interest payments, which may bear a fixed or variable rate. The period of the loan may be matched with the life of the asset and the agreed repayment schedule may be included in the cash flow plan with reasonable certainty.

Borrowing is always a big decision regardless of the amount. It has a cost and always has to be repaid. The ability to service any borrowing and the ability to repay must be assessed before making the decision to borrow. The real payback on borrowing for investment in non-current assets and working capital should be calculated, and cheaper alternatives such as:

- re-use of equipment
- renovation of equipment
- renegotiated terms of trading

fully explored before borrowing.

A disadvantage of long-term loans is that they will invariably need to be secured by lenders on non-current assets to be acquired, or existing, or on other long-term or short-term assets. This reduces some flexibility for the organisation and may limit future short-term or long-term borrowing requirements.

If a company needs to acquire land and buildings in order to trade it has a choice of purchasing leasehold or freehold, or renting. Purchase of premises additionally takes an organisation immediately into the property business. While property prices are rising, this speculation may appear attractive. However, it does represent some risk to the organisation – property speculation has proved disastrous to many companies in the past – and it may result in a lack of flexibility. If a company needs to expand or relocate, it may not be able to achieve this quickly and may be hampered by the fixed cost of owning a property.

Renting or short leases may present lower risk and greater opportunities in terms of location and flexibility and with regular payments that may be included in the cash flow plan. It also gives the organisation further financing opportunities, by not having a fixed liability of a loan secured on property.

Leasing and hire purchase

Leasing or hire purchase may be used for financing acquisitions of non-current assets. These two sources of finance require a slightly different accounting treatment. Hire purchase requires a large initial deposit and has VAT included in repayments. Hire purchase and leasing incur interest charges and depreciation, which are charged against profits. The term of either hire purchase or leasing can be matched with the expected life of the assets acquired. Cash flow may be planned in advance whichever method is chosen.

Purchases of non-current assets

The acquisition of non-current assets may represent an immediate outflow of cash. Cash-rich organisations may see advantages in outright purchases. However, the majority of organisations generally need to seek alternative funding. The sources of such funding may be from shares, loans, or leasing, either within the UK or from overseas.

The use of an overdraft facility is not usually appropriate for the acquisition of non-current assets. Non-current assets by definition have a long life and may be permanent in nature. An overdraft is repayable on demand, which is suitable for working capital requirements but is a risk if used to finance, for example, some machinery which may have an expected life of, say, 15 years.

Sales of non-current assets

Sales of non-current assets are an obvious means of raising funds. However, the opportunity cost of disposal of an asset must be considered prior to disposal and this should be considered in real terms using discounted cash flows with some allowance for inflation and taxation. An alternative may be to consider the sale of the asset to a leasing company, which then leases it back to the company.

Cash management

The Baumol cash management model

The similarity between cash and stocks was recognised in the Baumol cash management model (Baumol WJ (1952) 'The transactions demand for cash', *Quarterly Journal of Economics* 66 (4), 545–556). Cash may be regarded as a type of stock, a minimum level of which is required for a business to operate. This is particularly so for the control and management of bank balances which are drawn on and replenished (as with the stocks EOQ model we saw earlier), and where surpluses are invested for interest in the short term. The EOQ model may be applied to the transaction costs incurred in selling short-term investments in securities in order to replenish and maintain cash balances.

In this case if

P = the £ cost for a sale of one security

N = annual cash payments

S = the cost of holding cash, or the annual interest rate

then, using $EOQ = \sqrt{2PN/S}$

economic amount of cash to be transferred = √2 × cost of the sale of a security × annual cash payments/annual interest rate

Let's look at a simple example.

Worked Example 10.12

The finance director of Nina plc regularly invests surplus funds very short term in organisations, which pay interest averaging 8% per annum. The transaction cost every time an investment is sold is £40. The cash payments for each month total £900,000, or £10.8m for the year.

We can use the Baumol cash management model to calculate the most economic amount to transfer to the bank account each time and how often these transfers should be made.

£ cost of the sale of one investment	P = £40 per order
Annual cash payments	N = £10.8m
Annual £ cost of holding cash	S = 8% interest rate

$$EOQ = \sqrt{2PN/S} = \sqrt{2 \times £40 \times £10,800,000/0.08} = £103,923$$

The most economic amount of cash to be transferred to the bank account is say £104,000.

The finance director should transfer cash £10.8m/£104,000, or 104 times a year, which is twice a week.

The Baumol model may be relevant if the pattern of a company's cash flows and the transfers from its bank accounts are fairly consistent. Irregular cash flow patterns are more usual in most companies. The Miller and Orr cash management model (Miller MM, Orr D (1966) 'A model of the demand for money by firms', *Quarterly Journal of Economics* 80, 413–435) suggests that daily bank balances cannot be predicted and regular cash payments should not be assumed.

The Miller-Orr cash management model

The Baumol cash management model may be used to determine the frequency with which cash transfers should be made if cash flow patterns are regular. However, it is fairly safe to assume that irregular or random cash flow patterns are usually the norm in most companies. The Miller-Orr cash management model is based on this assumption, and suggests upper and lower limits that prompt cash transfers by selling short-term investments, which maintain the balance at a pre-determined return point.

The Miller-Orr model deals with the setting of the upper and lower limits and the position of the return point. If a company's daily cash flows fluctuate widely then the upper and lower limits will be wider apart (compared with if cash flows were less variable) and short-term interest will be lower and transaction costs higher.

If

R = the range between the upper and lower limits

P = the £ cost for a sale of one security

V = statistical variance of daily cash flows

S = the daily interest rate cost of holding cash

RP = return point

LL = lower limit

Then the Miller-Orr model sets the range between the upper and limits as:

$$R = 3 \times (0.75 \times P \times V/S)^{1/3}$$

and the return point as:

$$RP = LL + R/3$$

We can see that the return point is not half way between the upper and lower limits, but at a point somewhere below that, which means that the average cash balance on which interest is charged is therefore lower.

Let's look at a simple example.

Worked Example 10.13

Let's assume that the cash flows of Nina plc (see Worked Example 10.12) have become extremely irregular and unpredictable. The finance director of Nina plc has determined that the minimum cash balance required by the company is £75,000, and the variance of daily cash flows on a historical basis is £12.25m (£3,500 standard deviation). The company continues to make regular short-term investments of surplus funds, which now pay interest averaging at 9.125% per annum. The transaction cost every time an investment is sold is now £30.

We can use the Miller-Orr cash management model to determine the cash return point and how the finance director may manage this.

$$Range = 3 \times (0.75 \times 30 \times 12,250,000/0.00025)^{1/3}$$
$$= £30,992$$

Since the lower limit is £75,000 then the upper limit

$$= £75,000 + range £30,992 = £105,992$$
$$Return\ point = LL + R/3$$
$$= £75,000 + £30,992/3$$
$$= £85,330$$

Once the cash balance drops to the lower limit of £75,000 the finance director should sell investments amounting to £10,330 to return the cash to £85,330. As soon as the cash balance gets up to the upper limit of £105,992 the finance director should buy investments amounting to £20,662 to return the cash to £85,330.

Whether it is assumed that a company's cash flows are predictable (the Baumol cash management model) or unpredictable (the Miller-Orr cash management model), in practice the finance director or treasurer of a company should be able to determine the minimum and maximum cash balances that the company requires to operate, from experience and through the use of continuously updated cash plans and forecasts.

Cash management in practice

Any cash improvement exercise should include the factors we have discussed in the sections above about short- and long-term cash flow improvement. Each of these factors should also be regularly reviewed, and in order to maintain control over cash flow it is crucial that cash flow plans and forecast are prepared on a month-by-month or week-by-week basis for, say, six months ahead.

The phased cash flow plan should be updated daily, weekly, or monthly as necessary. It may be continually reviewed and revised in the light of actual performance, and for advantage to be taken of opportunities for improvement through savings and re-phasing as a result of consideration of the factors we have discussed above.

The recruitment of honest and reliable staff to deal with the control of cash and working capital is extremely important. Insufficient attention to this point together with a lack of frequent, appropriate training in credit control and cash management is a common occurrence, much to the cost of many companies. Many customers may detect a weak system of credit control and take advantage, resulting in considerable delays in payment of invoices.

Effective, integrated, computerised purchasing, stock control, order processing, and sales invoicing systems are the tools necessary for trained and motivated staff to optimise the use of cash resources and safeguard the company's assets. It should be appreciated that until a customer has paid an invoice it remains an asset, which is effectively under the direct control of another business.

Progress check 10.22

Which areas within the income statement and the balance sheet may be considered to identify improvements to the long-term cash position of a company?

Cash shortage is a common reason for business failure. However, businesses that are cash-rich may also fail to take full advantage of opportunities to maximise the return on capital employed in the business. Such opportunities may include:

- acquisition of new businesses
- investment in research and development
- investment in new products
- lending to gain the most tax-efficient returns.

All investments should, as a matter of company policy, be appraised using one of the recognised discounted cash flow techniques. A realistic company cost of capital should be used to determine whether each project is likely to pay back an acceptable return.

If surplus funds are to be invested for short-term returns, the most tax-efficient investments should be sought. An understanding of the relationship between risk and reward is a prerequisite. High-risk investment strategies should only be undertaken if the downside risk is fully understood, and the consequences are what the business could bear and survive should the worst happen. In both the UK and the USA there have been some high profile failures of deposit-takers, resulting in massive losses by the depositors (note the collapse of BCCI in the UK, and the more recent impact of the 2007 'credit crunch' in the USA and UK).

Good banking relationships should be maintained at all times, with regular meetings and the provision of up-to-date information on company performance and new initiatives. The bank should ensure that information is provided to the company as frequently as is required on loans, interest and bank charges details, bank statements, and daily cleared balance positions, so that they may be thoroughly checked as part of the daily routine. All slow-moving or inactive accounts, particularly, for example, old currency accounts opened for one-off contracts, should be closed to avoid incurring continuing account maintenance charges.

Summary of key points

- The operating cycle of working capital (WC), the net of current assets less current liabilities, is the period of time which elapses between the point at which cash begins to be expended on the production of a product or service, and the collection of cash from the customer.

- The difference between working capital (WC) and working capital requirement (WCR) is cash less short-term financial debt (bank overdraft).

- The working capital requirement is normally financed by bank overdraft because of its flexibility in accommodating the fluctuating nature of net current assets.

- The cost of short-term borrowing is relatively higher than long-term borrowing.

- Effective management and control of stock requires its appropriate location and storage, establishment of robust stock purchase procedures and reorder systems, and accurate and timely systems for recording, control, and physical checks of stocks.

- Effective management and control of debtors requires establishment of appropriate policies covering choice of the way in which sales are made, the sales invoicing system, the means of settlement, and the implementation of a credit management and overdue accounts collection system.

- Although not free, trade creditors provide the company with an additional source of finance.

- Effective management and control of creditors requires the establishment of appropriate policies covering choice of suppliers, the way in which purchases are made, the purchase invoicing system, and the means of settlement.

- Regular measurement of the operating cycle, which determines the short-term financing requirements of the business, enables the company to monitor its working capital performance against targets and identify areas for improvement.

- The short-term cash position of an organisation may be improved by reducing current assets, and/or increasing current liabilities.

- The long-term cash position of an organisation may be improved by increasing equity, increasing long-term liabilities, and reducing the net outflow on non-current assets.

- Cash management models (for example Baumol and Miller-Orr) have been developed to try and optimise the levels of cash held by companies, but in practice it is usually the experience of financial managers using continuously updated cash plans and forecasts that enable businesses to effectively manage their cash flows.

🔒 Glossary of key terms

aged creditors report The amount owed by creditors, or accounts payable, classified by age of debt.

aged debtors report The amount owed by debtors, or accounts receivable, classified by age of debt.

algorithm A process or set of rules used for a mathematical calculation.

BACS (bankers automated clearing services) An electronic bulk clearing system generally used by banks and building societies for low-value and repetitive items such as standing orders, direct debits, and automated credits such as salary payments.

cleared funds Cleared funds are funds that have actually been cleared through the banking system and are available for use. It is the cleared funds balance, if overdrawn, which is used to calculate overdraft interest.

country risk (or **political risk**) The risk associated with undertaking transactions with, or holding assets in, a particular country. Sources of risk might be political, economic, or regulatory instability affecting overseas taxation, repatriation of profits, nationalisation, currency instability, etc.

cycle count The process of counting and valuing selected stock items at different times, on a rotating basis, so that all stocks are counted two, three, four or more times each year.

economic order quantity (EOQ) The most economic stock replenishment order size, which minimises the sum of stock ordering costs and stockholding costs. EOQ is used in an 'optimising' stock control system.

effectiveness The utilisation of resources such that the output of the activity achieves the desired result. In other words, efficiency alone is not enough – efficiency in areas from which optimised output is what is required to be effective (to avoid being a 'busy fool').

efficiency The achievement of either maximum useful output from the resources devoted to an activity, or the required output from the minimum resource input.

ergonomics The study of the efficiency of persons in their working environment.

heijunka The smoothing of production through the levelling of schedules. This is done by sequencing orders in a repetitive pattern and smoothing the day-to-day variations in total orders to correspond with longer-term demand.

jidoka Autonomation, which increases productivity through eliminating the non-value adding need for operators to watch machines, thus freeing them for more productive work, for example quality assurance.

kaizen An 'umbrella' concept covering most of the 'uniquely Japanese' practices, it is a technique used for continuous improvement in all aspects of performance, at every level within the organisation.

▶

kanban A signal, for example a card used in JIT production, to prompt top up of materials or components driven by demand from the next process.

letter of credit A document issued by a bank on behalf of a customer authorising a third party to draw funds to a specified amount from its branches or correspondents, usually in another country, when the conditions set out in the document have been met.

manufacturing resource planning (MRPII) An expansion of material requirements planning (MRPI) to give a broader approach than MRPI to the planning and scheduling of resources, embracing areas such as finance, logistics, engineering, and marketing.

master production schedule A time-phased statement (usually computerised) of how many items are to be produced in a given period (like a giant timetable), based on customer orders and demand forecasts.

materials requirement planning (MRP or MRPI) A system that converts a production schedule into a listing of the materials and components required to meet that schedule, so that adequate stock levels are maintained and items are available when needed.

optimised production technology (OPT) OPT is a manufacturing philosophy combined with a computerised system of shop-floor scheduling and capacity planning. It is a philosophy that focuses on factors such as manufacture to order, quality, lead times, batch sizes, and set-up times, and differs from a traditional approach of balancing capacity as near to 100% as possible and then maintaining flow. The aim of OPT is to balance flow rather than capacity. The goal of OPT is to make money by increasing throughput and reducing stocks and operating expenses, by making better use of limited capacity by tightly controlled finite scheduling of bottleneck operations.

poka yoke Failsafe devices, support *jidoka* by preventing parts being mounted or fitted in the wrong way and alerting operators by flashing lights, ringing buzzers – it is a method of spotting defects, identifying, repairing, and avoiding further defects.

property risk The risk of loss or damage occurring in the transit of goods and services before the completion of the sales contract.

pull system A system whose objective is to produce or procure products or components as they are required for use by internal and external customers, rather than for stock. This contrasts with a 'push' system, in which stocks act as buffers between processes within production, and between production, purchasing, and sales.

Romalpa clause A contractual clause, named after a case in which its effect was litigated in 1976, by which the ownership of goods is to remain with the seller until they have been paid for. This can provide a useful protection for the seller in the event of the buyer's insolvency. Its value may be questionable if the goods are mixed with other goods in a manufacturing process or if they are resold to a third party.

❓ Questions

Q10.1 Describe how a company's financing of its investment in operations may be different from its financing of its investment in non-current assets.

Q10.2 (i) Explain the differences between working capital (WC) and working capital requirement (WCR).

(ii) What are the implications for companies having either negative or positive WCs or WCRs?

Q10.3 Outline the policy options available to a company to finance its working capital requirement (WCR).

Q10.4 Outline the processes and techniques that may be used by a company to optimise its stock levels.

Q10.5 (i) Explain what is meant by economic order quantity (EOQ).

(ii) Describe some of the more sophisticated stock management systems that the EOQ technique may support.

Q10.6 Describe the areas of policy relating to the management of its customers on which a company needs to focus in order to minimise the amount of time for turning sales into cash.

Q10.7 Outline the processes involved in an effective collections and credit management system.

Q10.8 Describe the policies and procedures that a company may implement for effective management of its suppliers.

Q10.9 (i) What is meant by overtrading?

(ii) What steps may be taken by a company to avoid the condition of overtrading?

Q10.10 Describe

(i) the operating cycle

(ii) an appropriate action plan that may be implemented to improve the short-term cash position of a business.

Q10.11 (i) For what reasons may some companies require increases in long-term cash resources?

(ii) What sources are available to these companies?

Discussion points

D10.1 If working capital is the 'lubricant' of a company's investment in its operations that enables its investment in non-current assets to be most effectively exploited, how does the company choose the best method of lubrication and how often should this oil be changed?

D10.2 'Management of working capital is simply a question of forcing suppliers to hold as much stock as we require for order and delivery at short notice, and extending payment as far as possible to the point just before they refuse to supply, and putting as much pressure as possible on customers by whatever means to make sure they pay within 30 days.' Discuss.

D10.3 'A manufacturing company that adopts a policy of minimising its operating cycle may achieve short-term gains in profitability and cash flow but may suffer longer-term losses resulting from the impact on its customer base and its ability to avoid disruption to its production processes'. Discuss.

Exercises

Solutions are provided in Appendix 2 to all exercise numbers highlighted in colour.

Level I

E10.1 *Time allowed – 30 minutes*

Oliver Ltd's sales budget for 2007 is £5,300,000. Oliver Ltd manufactures components for television sets and its production costs as a percentage of sales are:

	%
Raw materials	40
Direct labour	25
Overheads	10

Raw materials, which are acquired at the start of production, are carried in stock for four days and finished goods are held in stock before sale for seven days. Work in progress is held at levels where products are assumed to be 25% complete in terms of labour and overheads.

The production cycle is 14 days and production takes place evenly through the year. Oliver Ltd receives 30 days' credit from suppliers and grants 60 days' credit to its customers. Overheads are incurred evenly throughout the year.

What is Oliver Ltd's total working capital requirement?

E10.2 *Time allowed – 45 minutes*

Coventon plc's income statement for the year ended 30 June 2007, and its balance sheet as at 30 June 2007 are shown below. The chief executive of Coventon has set targets for the year to 30 June 2008, which he believes will result in an increase in PBT for the year. The marketing director has forecast that targeted debtor days of 60 would result in a reduction in sales of 5% from 2007 but also a £30,000 reduction in bad debts for the year. The same gross profit percentage is expected in 2008 as 2007 but stock days will be reduced by four days. The CEO has set further targets for 2008: savings on administrative and distribution costs of £15,000 for the year; creditor days to be rigidly adhered to at 30 days in 2008. One third of the loan was due to be repaid on 1 July 2007 resulting in a proportionate saving in interest payable. (Note: Coventon plc approximates its creditor days and stock days using cost of sales at the end of the year rather than purchases for the year.)

Coventon plc
Income statement for the year ended 30 June 2007

Figures in £000

Turnover	2,125
Cost of sales	(1,250)
Gross profit	875
Distribution and administrative costs	(300)
Operating profit	575
Interest payable	(15)
Profit before tax	560
Tax on profit on ordinary activities	(125)
Profit on ordinary activities after tax	435
Retained profit 1 July 2006	515
	950
Dividends	(125)
Retained profit 30 June 2007	825

Coventon plc
Balance sheet as at 30 June 2007

Figures in £000

Non-current assets	
Intangible	100
Tangible	1,875
	1,975
Current assets	
Stocks	125
Debtors	425
Prepayments	50
Cash and bank	50
	650
Current liabilities (less than one year)	
Overdraft	50
Creditors	100
Accruals	150
Dividends	125
Taxation	125
	550
Net current assets	100
Total assets less current liabilities	2,075
less	
Non-current liabilities (over one year)	
Loan	(250)
Net assets	1,825
Capital and reserves	
Share capital	1,000
Profit and loss account	825
	1,825

You are required to calculate the following:

(i)   operating cycle days for 2006/2007
(ii) operating cycle days for 2007/2008
(iii) the expected value of stocks plus debtors less creditors as at 30 June 2008
(iv) the PBT for 2007/2008.

E10.3 *Time allowed – 45 minutes*

Trumper Ltd has recently appointed a new managing director who would like to implement major improvements to the company's management of working capital. Trumper's customers should pay by the end of the second month following delivery. Despite this they take on average 75 days to settle their accounts. Trumper's sales for the current year are estimated at £32m, and the company expects bad debts to be £320,000.

The managing director has suggested an early settlement discount of 2% for customers paying within 60 days. His meetings with all the company's major customers have indicated that 30% would take the discount and pay within 60 days; 70% of the customers would continue to pay within 75 days on average. However, the finance director has calculated that bad debts may reduce by £100,000 for the year, together with savings of £20,000 on administrative costs.

Trumper Ltd has an overdraft facility to finance its working capital on which it pays interest at 12% per annum.

▶   The managing director would like to know how Trumper may gain from introducing early settlement discounts, if it is assumed that sales levels would remain unchanged. The managing director would also like suggestions as to how the company may reduce its reliance on its overdraft, perhaps through better management of its debtors, and whether the overdraft is the best method of financing its working capital.

Level II

E10.4 *Time allowed – 45 minutes*

Josef Ryan Ltd has experienced difficulties in getting its customers to pay on time. It is considering the offer of a discount for payment within 14 days to its customers, who currently pay after 60 days. It is estimated that only 50% of credit customers would take the discount, although administrative cost savings of £10,000 per annum would be gained. The marketing director believes that sales would be unaffected by the discount. Sales for 2008 have been budgeted at £10m. The cost of short-term finance for Ryan is 15% per annum.

What is the maximum discount that Josef Ryan Ltd may realistically offer?

E10.5 *Time allowed – 45 minutes*

Worrall plc's sales for 2007 were £8m. Costs of sales were 80% of sales. Bad debts were 2% of sales. Cost of sales variable costs were 90% and fixed costs were 10%. Worrall's cost of finance is 10% per annum. Worrall plc allows its customers 60 days' credit, but is now considering increasing this to 90 days' credit because it believes that this will increase sales. Worrall plc's sales manager estimated that if customers were granted 90 days' credit, sales may be increased by 20%, but that bad debts would increase from 2% to 3%. The finance director calculated that such a change in policy would not increase fixed costs, and neither would it result in changes to creditors and stock.

Would you recommend that Worrall plc increase customer credit to 90 days?

E10.6 *Time allowed – 45 minutes*

Chapman Engineering plc has annual sales of £39m, which are made evenly throughout the year. At present the company has an overdraft facility on which its bank charges 9% per annum.

Chapman Engineering plc currently allows its customers 45 days' credit. One third of the customers pay on time, in terms of total sales value. The other two thirds pay on average after 60 days. Chapman believes that the offer of a cash discount of 1% to its customers would induce them to pay within 45 days. Chapman also believes that two thirds of the customers who now take 60 days to pay would pay within 45 days. The other third would still take an average of 60 days. Chapman estimates that this action would also result in bad debts being reduced by £25,000 a year.

(i)   **What is the current value of debtors?**

(ii) **What would the level of debtors be if terms were changed and 1% discount was offered to reduce debtor days from 60 days to 45 days?**

(iii) **What is the net annual cost to the company of granting this discount?**

(iv) **Would you recommend that the company should introduce the offer of an early settlement discount?**

(v)   **What other factors should Chapman consider before implementing this change?**

(vi) **Are there other controls and procedures that Chapman could introduce to better manage its debtors?**

E10.7 *Time allowed – 60 minutes*

Sarnico Ltd, a UK subsidiary of a food manufacturing multinational group, makes sandwiches for sale by supermarkets. The group managing director, Emanuel Recount, is particularly concerned with Sarnico's cash position. The financial statements for 2007 are as follows:

Income statement for the year ended 30 September 2007

	£m	£m
Sales		49
Less: Cost of sales		
Opening stock	7	
add: Purchases	40	
	47	
less: Closing stock	(10)	(37)
Gross profit		12
Expenses		(13)
Net loss for the year		(1)

Balance sheet as at 30 September 2007

	£m	£m	£m
Non-current assets			15
Current assets:			
Stock		10	
Debtors		6	
		16	
less			
Creditors due within one year			
Trade creditors	(4)		
Bank overdraft	(11)	(15)	1
			16
less			
Creditors due after one year			
Loans			(8)
			8
Capital and reserves			
Ordinary share capital			3
Retained profit			5
			8

We may assume that debtors and creditors were maintained at a constant level throughout the year.

(i)   Why should Emanuel Recount be concerned about Sarnico's liquidity?

(ii) What is the 'operating cycle'?

(iii) Why is the operating cycle important with regard to the financial management of Sarnico?

(iv) Calculate the 365-day operating cycle for Sarnico Ltd.

(v)   What actions may Sarnico Ltd take to improve its operating cycle performance?

► **E10.8** *Time allowed – 60 minutes*

Refer to the balance sheet for Flatco plc as at 31 December 2007, and its income statement for the year to 31 December 2007 shown on pages 418 and 419 in Chapter 10.

A benchmarking exercise that looked at competing companies within the industry revealed that on average debtor days for 2007 were 33 days, average creditor days were 85 days, and average stock days were 32 days. The exercise also indicated that in the best performing companies in the industry the time that customers took to pay was 24 days, with creditor days at 90 days and stock days at 18 days.

You are required to calculate the range of values of savings that Flatco may achieve in 2008 (assuming the same activity levels as 2007) if it were to implement the appropriate measures to achieve average performance or if it improved enough to match the best performers.

You may assume that sales are more or less evenly spread throughout the year. The average bank interest paid or earned by Flatco plc is 9% per annum.

International operations and investment

Chapter contents

LEARNING OBJECTIVES

Completion of this chapter will enable you to:

☑ Appreciate the nature of internationalisation, and importance of international markets.

☑ Explain what comprises the international financial marketplace, and its significance for international companies.

☑ Outline why it is that companies may wish to undertake overseas operations.

☑ Describe the various types of international operation that international companies may engage in.

☑ Explain foreign direct investment (FDI) in terms of an international company's investment in new or expanded facilities overseas.

☑ Compare the unique features of investment appraisal in a multi-currency, overseas environment with the appraisal of domestic investment projects.

☑ Evaluate international investment projects based on multi-currency cash flow forecasts.

☑ Describe the factors that may influence the taxation strategy of multinational companies.

☑ Describe the use of transfer pricing by multinational companies, and the impact of exchange controls.

☑ Consider the alternative discount rate options that may be used in international investment appraisal.

☑ Describe the main sources of finance for international investment.

☑ Explain what is meant by country risk or political risk and outline the strategies that international companies may adopt to mitigate the impact of such risk.

Introduction

In Chapter 4 we looked at investment appraisal and decisions relating to whether or not to invest in a project, or choices between investments in alternative projects, which are competing for resources. These investments were fundamentally related to projects undertaken by companies in their own home countries. In this chapter we will consider the appraisal of investments that companies may undertake in overseas countries.

Before looking specifically at international investment we set the scene by looking at internationalisation in the broader context. We will begin by looking at the meaning of internationalisation, and in particular how it relates to the activities of international companies, and how the international financial marketplace operates.

Companies engage in overseas operations for a variety of reasons and they may enter international markets in a number of ways. Companies may start with a basic export operation and then develop this through further options, which may ultimately result in the establishment of an overseas presence in the form of an overseas subsidiary company.

The appraisal of international investments such as an overseas subsidiary may be a little more complex than the appraisal of domestic investments, with a greater number of variables to consider, for example the volatility of foreign currency exchange rates and cash flows, and local taxation systems. When international investments are evaluated using net present value (NPV) there is inevitably a wider choice of cost of capital that may be used as a discount rate.

The choice of financing for international investments also requires the consideration of additional factors in comparison with domestic financing. These factors relate to the quality and types of relationship that the home country parent company has with its overseas contacts as well as the financial considerations of foreign currency and interest rate risks, taxation, and gearing. They also relate to the risk in general of engaging in business overseas.

The chapter closes with a section about country risk (or political risk) and the ways in which companies may adopt strategies to reduce or eliminate such risk. This topic is also explored further in Chapter 12, where we look at specific techniques for dealing with risks arising from international operations.

Internationalisation

Internationalisation means many different things, for example, in the context of business, education, training, IT, and finance. Internationalisation refers basically to the act of bringing something under international control and relates to the increasing geographical dispersion of economic, as well as cultural, social, educational, technological, and political activities across national borders. The economic phenomenon of internationalisation has an increasing impact on:

■ the role of the financial markets
■ the activities of international companies.

Financial and commodity markets are increasingly concerned with issues related to the growing impact of international market pressures on:

■ local cultures
■ traditional political boundaries
■ market structures.

These pressures affect the social, political, and economic framework within which international companies operate. They are at the root of many of the international financial management issues of concern to international companies, and also responsible for the continually changing nature of the international financial marketplace.

The world in the 21st century is a complex place in which the interrelationships and interdependencies of the emerging new-world orders are often dominated by the politics of competition, and the economics of the marketplace. Such increasing interrelationships and interdependencies may possibly reflect divergence into the development of separate economic, social, and political systems, or they may reflect convergence into the development of a 'single' world system, having the same sort of economic structures, social and institutional environments. On the other hand, these interrelationships and interdependencies may reflect the rejection of traditional systems and a complete change through the development of a post-modern economic, social, and political system.

There are important issues relating to internationalisation and many theories of internationalisation that are concerned with international finance and the increasing global mobility of capital within and between differing geographical sovereign territories. It is also important to consider areas other than, for example, economic rationality, corporate financial objectives, and shareholder returns, such as, for example, internationalisation in the social, cultural, and political context. The latter contribute greatly to the creation of the interconnections and interrelationships that are increasingly essential to the survival of the international company. They also act as counter balances against the potential excesses of the international financial marketplace, and potentially act as protective mechanisms against the possible exploitation of second and third world countries.

Progress check 11.1

What does internationalisation mean with regard to a company's international operations?

The international financial marketplace

The international financial marketplace is basically like any other market. It is an interrelated network of buyers and sellers in which exchange activities occur in the pursuit of profit and reward, and may be:

- open to the public with unrestricted assess
- private and semi-closed with access restricted to particular organisations
- private and semi-closed with access restricted to transactions related to particular commodities or assets.

Whichever it is, the international financial marketplace is a place where the legal title of an asset, commodity, or currency is exchanged for either:

- the legal title of another asset, commodity or currency

or

- the legal promise that such an agreed exchange will take place at an agreed time and at an agreed place in the future.

There is a growing significance and increasing level of efficiency of international financial markets and their participants, which also have an increasing social, political, and economic influence on the day-to-day transactions within the domestic marketplace.

There are a number of important characteristics unique to the international financial marketplace:

- it is one of the largest global markets in operation, and it is comprised of an interrelated but geographically dispersed network of many different and unrelated buyers and sellers
- in the absence of any politically imposed regulatory requirements, there is generally freedom of entry to, and freedom of exit from, the international financial marketplace

- information regarding commodities, assets, and currencies available on the international financial marketplace is widely available to most of the buyers and sellers, many of which undertake both buying and selling activities

- the majority of activities in the international financial marketplace takes place between commercial banks.

There is a diversity of buyers and sellers in the international financial marketplace, who may in general be assumed to be:

- rational

- predominantly profit driven, their primary motive being profit maximisation

- well informed

- able to access relevant and useful information

- risk-takers.

The international financial marketplace is an interconnected network of key participants of either individuals or groups (see Fig. 11.1), and the key interrelating transactions between them all is the buying and selling of securities, currencies, and other financial assets.

As an interconnected network of buyers and sellers, the foreign exchange market exists as a collection of geographically dispersed trading centres located around the world. From London to New York, Paris to Hong Kong, Tokyo to Dubai, each of these markets has grown considerably through the latter part of the 20th century and into the 21st century. As they continue to

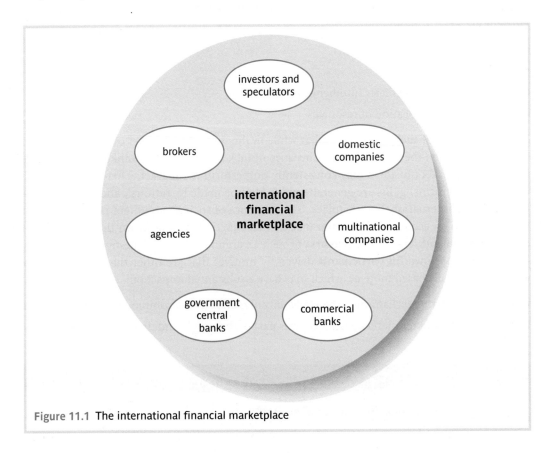

Figure 11.1 The international financial marketplace

grow at an increasing rate, the importance of the international financial marketplace is beyond doubt. Even the most minor fluctuations in the international financial markets now have a significant impact on companies and individuals worldwide, whether they are investors or not.

While the activities of any of the participants in the international financial marketplace affect the supply and demand of tradable commodities, assets, and currencies within the marketplace, by far the most influential group are the government central banks. The reasons for their influence may be:

- politically motivated and therefore structural in consequence
- economically motivated and therefore transactional or market-based in consequence.

Structural intervention is concerned with the establishment of exchange rate systems with:

- fixed exchange rates
- floating exchange rates
- managed exchange rates
- pegged exchange rates.

Transactional or market-based intervention is concerned with the need to protect or stabilise currency exchange rate movements relative to other currencies. The motivation for this is generally economic, but there may also be political reasons for intervention to protect or support a specific country's currency.

Modern sophisticated markets often exhibit some inefficiencies. However, the international financial markets are generally regarded as being fairly efficient. This is important because efficient markets promote:

- increased volumes of transactions
- greater mobility of funds
- the involvement of a greater number of participants
- a more efficient allocation of resources.

The implications of such efficiency is that while in the short term market outsiders may earn profits higher than the market average because of luck or chance, it is unlikely that over the longer term market outsiders may consistently outperform the market. Therefore, it may be argued that abnormal gains are generally unlikely to be made by rational, and honest, participants in the international marketplace. The relevance of such an argument is beyond doubt with regard to an economically driven market that functions primarily on the mechanics of supply and demand. The appropriateness of such an argument may be questioned. There may be a number of powerful participants driven by motives that are other than economic, for example politically based motives, which may have a substantial impact on:

- the overall market mechanisms – the availability of market assets, commodities, and currencies
- the activities of other market participants as part of the supply and demand mechanism.

Progress check 11.2

What is the international financial marketplace?

Why companies undertake international operations

There are many diverse economic, political, strategic, and personal reasons why companies may wish to engage themselves in operations overseas. It is likely that a combination of any number of reasons, rather than just one, stimulates companies' involvement in international operations. What may be strategically the most important reason is that such involvement gives companies access to overseas markets by enabling them to get closer to their customers, both final or intermediate customers. Note how the world's major motor vehicle manufacturers (through joint ventures) started to build plants in China in the 1990s, before even the basic road infrastructure had been constructed. This was in anticipation of the tremendous demand for cars expected in the 2000s by the whole Chinese population, following the country's unprecedented growth. At the same time, motor vehicle component manufacturers also started building plants to meet their expected demand from the motor vehicle manufacturer joint ventures.

Further motives and reasons why companies may undertake international operations include:

- home market saturation, leaving development of overseas markets as the only option
- the opportunity of higher returns for shareholders possibly obtained overseas
- utilisation of underemployed resources and spare capacity
- access to cheaper overseas financing
- keeping up with competitors
- exploitation of emerging and growing economies
- access to overseas government help with financing, grants, and development
- diversification of economic risk by trying to smooth out the boom-bust cycle relating to overseas countries' differing levels of economic growth
- lower overseas production costs, for example labour, plant, and machinery
- access to specialist overseas know-how and expertise
- economies of scale
- increasing and widening the exposure of companies' brand names and global strategies.

Companies undertake international operations in a variety of ways, and in some circumstances the route chosen may be related to the specific reason or reasons for their endeavours.

Progress check 11.3

Outline the reasons why companies may wish to develop international operations.

Types of international operation

When companies first begin to explore international markets they are faced with so many new situations and uncertainties. Initial forays into such unknown territories are usually on a small scale rather than making large-scale investments at the outset. Internationalisation by companies may be either through indirect means or by establishing a direct presence in the foreign country, and may take place in a number of ways, as shown in Fig. 11.2.

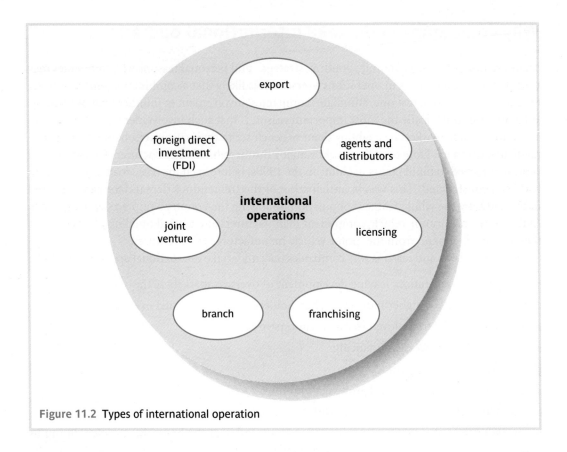

Figure 11.2 Types of international operation

Types of indirect international operations include:

- exporting
- appointment of an agent or distributor
- trademark licensing
- franchising.

Alternatively, a company may have a direct presence in a foreign country through:

- establishing a branch operation
- a joint venture
- foreign direct investment (FDI) – an outward investment in an overseas subsidiary by the domestic company.

Risk will be present whichever internationalisation strategy is adopted. Whether a business is a large, well-established multinational or a small business entering an international market for the first time, most companies will initially try to keep risk to a minimum and usually start with a small export operation. Buckley's incremental model of internationalisation (Buckley A (2004) *Multinational Finance*, 5th edn, London: FT/Prentice Hall) describes the route to establishing an overseas subsidiary as usually taking place incrementally, which may include all or some of the indirect and direct types of operation outlined above. This gradual exposure to a new international market is a process of risk-minimisation, familiarisation, and learning.

Exporting

Export activities offer a relatively low risk entry into the international marketplace. Exporting allows a company to expand its markets and its output, and at the same time most of the value-adding activities are maintained within the home country. Home market saturation may be the reason for expansion into new overseas markets, or it may be that higher shareholder returns may be achieved from such ventures.

Returns from exports need to be higher than those from domestic activities because distribution and selling costs will be higher. Although export activities do not require the initial investment that an overseas subsidiary requires, there will be the learning curve cost of familiarisation with the new market, the development and growth of the foreign customer base, and possible barriers to trade.

Appointment of an agent or distributor

The appointment of a local agent may be the answer to some of the difficulties involved with direct exporting by the home country company. This may require the services of an independent overseas agent or distributor who operates in a similar market and with an existing customer base that may also be accessed. Alternatively, a sole agent may be appointed for that specific country whose function it is to promote and sell only the home company's products and services.

Trademark licensing

In marketing-led businesses it may be beneficial for a home country company to allow its brand named products to be sold by overseas companies. A trademark licence may assign the manufacturing and selling rights for a product to an overseas company in return for payment of royalties. Licensing provides a means of:

- avoiding trade barriers that may be encountered with direct exporting activities
- overcoming possible problems of remitting profits to the parent company
- accessing rapidly expanding overseas markets without the need for an initial investment, and in circumstances where sufficient investment resources may not be available.

While licensing does not involve the cost of an initial investment, there are costs of negotiating, agreeing, and granting licences, and ongoing costs of monitoring their use and ensuring correct receipts of royalties. The granting of licences to overseas licensee companies may provide these companies with the opportunity to subsequently copy and compete with the home country company's products and steal customers and market share. The fact that they are based in foreign countries may make it difficult or impossible to enforce any non-competition agreements that may have been made.

Franchising

Companies may exercise a degree of control over an overseas company's use of its brands and trademarks through franchising. In this way the company licenses a complete business – for example, the McDonald's and KFC chains. As with trademark licensing, franchising involves similar administrative costs of set-up and monitoring. However, the threat of competition from overseas franchisees setting up on their own may be less than that posed by a company with a trademark licence.

Progress check 11.4

Outline the indirect ways in which a company may operate internationally.

Branch operation

A further low-cost step up from exporting may be the establishment of an overseas branch in a foreign country that may be run by local employees of that country, and possibly with some expatriate staff. An overseas branch provides a local presence overseas without requiring the large investment required to set up a subsidiary. However, any funding that is required must be provided by the parent company.

Joint venture

A home country company's involvement in a joint venture allows it an even greater level of control over operations than the granting of trademark licences or franchises. In general, a joint venture is a project undertaken by two or more persons or entities joining together with a view to profit, often in connection with a single operation. More specifically, a joint venture is defined as an organisation in which one entity holds an interest on a long-term basis and is jointly controlled by that entity and one or more other entities under a contractual arrangement (FRS 9).

In practice, the participants in a joint venture will each provide specific attributes and resources. In an overseas joint venture these may be, for example, knowledge of the particular country and markets, technical knowledge and expertise, financial resources, local connections and contacts such as customers, suppliers of materials, and distribution channels. Local partners in joint ventures may also be important in political lobbying, and providing the know-how with regard to finding the way through bureaucratic red tape, and dealing with legal and governmental regulation.

However, the advantages of joint ventures must be weighed against their disadvantages, which revolve around the issue of control and goal congruence. The joint venture may have too much flexibility and a lack of control, or it may be too inflexible and unable to adapt or change. A home country company, which has set up an overseas joint venture, may not be able to exercise an appropriate degree of direct control. It may also find that the attributes and resources promised by the other participants may not be at the levels expected.

The agency problem (see Chapter 3) is likely to appear in a joint venture through a lack of goal congruence. The joint venture may originally have been set up with specific policies relating to, for example, investment, choice of markets and customers, choice of suppliers, and levels of dividend. However, each of the participants in the joint venture may have different individual priorities. The levels of payment of royalties and management fees to the separate parent companies may also be a problem area, as may be the (transfer) prices paid for goods and services provided by each company which has invested in the joint venture (see the sections below about profit repatriation, transfer pricing, and royalties and management fees).

In some countries a joint venture is the only way of establishing an investment in a subsidiary or related company within a foreign country. For example, for many years this was pretty much the only method of investing in China, and investment regulations were heavily weighted in favour of local Chinese partners. That was because the Chinese government was keen to ensure that not too much control was left in the hands of foreign investors (even though it was keen to attract foreign money). More recently, the Chinese investment environment has changed significantly and most foreign investment is now in the form of wholly foreign-owned enterprises. However, in some cases it may still be necessary or advantageous for investments in China to take the form of joint ventures.

Investment in an overseas subsidiary

FDI may be inward (domestic investment by overseas companies) or outward (overseas investment by domestic companies). Here we are talking about outward FDI with regard to the establishment of new overseas facilities or the expansion of existing overseas facilities by a home country investor. It is a financial interest in perpetuity by an organisation in an overseas company in which it has effective control over its day-to-day management.

An investment in an overseas subsidiary is different from an investment in a non-related overseas business. The latter is what is called portfolio investment and relates to an organisation's acquisition of shares or loans in an unrelated overseas company, in which it has no control over day-to-day management.

An investment in an overseas subsidiary is also different from an investment in a home country subsidiary. Differences are due to problems arising out of, for example, movements in foreign currency exchange rates, exchange controls, differences in taxation systems, and transfer pricing (see the relevant sections below in which we discuss each of these issues).

The reasons for a direct investment in an overseas subsidiary may be summarised as:

- a possible means of ensuring maximisation of shareholder wealth
- natural progression from initial international involvement through exporting, use of agents, licensing, and franchising
- progression from a branch activity or a joint venture
- tax benefits
- alternative to unsatisfactory agency, licensing, or franchise arrangements
- requirements of local supply by overseas manufacturers
- lower distribution and transportation costs
- shorter supply chain and avoidance of time delays
- lower production costs
- intellectual property rights and patents protection
- after-sales customer service requirements
- the personal ambitions of individuals who wish to establish a business in a particular country.

Compared with exporting, an overseas subsidiary will derive obvious benefits from being closer to the customers, and through reduced distribution and selling costs, and the avoidance of bureaucratic inconvenience, import tariffs, and exchange controls (see the section on exchange controls below). After-sales service requirements will be better catered for by the local employees of an overseas subsidiary and so it is more likely to enhance the reputation and reliability of the product and achieve growth from repeat business and recommendation. This is illustrated in the press extract below which describes a Middle Eastern business, Dubai Aluminium Company's establishment of an overseas facility in Asia. Dubal's move was a progression from the use of local agents in order to ensure the highest levels of quality of customer service and to provide a platform for further growth in that area.

From agency to direct overseas presence
'Dubai Aluminium opens Seoul office', by staff reporter

Dubai Aluminium Company, Dubal, one of the largest producers of premium quality aluminium in the world, announced the opening of an office in Seoul, South Korea – the first-ever direct office in Asia.

Currently Dubal's exports to Asia amount to 450,000 tonnes, almost 40 per cent of its total production. Dubal's sales to South Korea alone stand at around 55,000 tonnes in 2006 against 45,000 tonnes in 2005.

The Dubal move is in line with the aluminium giant's strategic initiative to expand its high quality services overseas as approved by Shaikh Hamdan bin Rashid Al Maktoum, Deputy Ruler of Dubai and UAE Minister for Finance and Industry and Chairman of Dubal.

'Asian countries being our largest consumers, this is a natural evolution to the next level of our growth strategy. This will provide us the maximum leeway in ensuring our clients get the highest level of quality service besides enabling us to fully understand their requirements', said Abdulla bin Kalban, CEO, Dubal.

'Since 1994 Dubal had been working in Asia with dedicated agents who had played an excellent role in ensuring our reputation throughout the continent, especially in South Korea', added Bin Kalban.

© *Khaleej Times*, 9 June 2006

There are advantages in establishing an overseas subsidiary compared with a branch. As we have discussed above, branch funding is provided by the parent company, whereas an overseas subsidiary may be financed by debt or equity in its local currency. The parent company may also gain a tax advantage if the overseas subsidiary (rather than overseas branch) is in a relatively low corporate tax area. When overseas branch profits are remitted to a parent company they are normally taxed at the home country's tax rate, because a branch is not a legal entity separate from the parent company.

Setting up a new overseas subsidiary from scratch will obviously incur similar costs to the setting up of a domestic subsidiary. An advantage is that the business can be established exactly as the parent company wishes, without any costs of, for example, rationalisation and re-training of employees that may arise from the acquisition of an existing business. However, the acquisition of an existing reputable overseas company may incur such post-acquisition costs, but may also offer distinct advantages, such as an established supplier and customer base, and distribution network.

An overseas subsidiary may be set up in order to satisfy some personal requirements or ambitions of a parent company's chief executive or chairman, rather than the primary objective of maximisation of shareholder wealth. We discussed the possibility of the agency problem arising with an overseas joint venture, and this may also arise with an overseas subsidiary. We have already seen many examples in Chapter 3 of the serious impact of a lack of goal congruence and how company directors may pursue their own rather than shareholders' objectives. At an overseas subsidiary level the opportunities for this may be even greater because of distance, possible remoteness, and less direct control.

> ### Progress check 11.5
>
> Outline the direct ways in which a company may operate internationally.

International investment appraisal

Corporate investment appraisal is an area of corporate finance that is complex and sometimes controversial, and is particularly so with regard to international investment appraisal. The evaluation of an international investment may be considered from two perspectives:

- appraisal within the foreign country of the investment in that country's currency
- home country appraisal of the foreign investment by the parent company.

The perspective chosen will require a different treatment of the cash flows and other factors related to the international investment. Appraisal of a foreign investment within the context of the foreign country itself requires consideration of the following:

- initial investment
- additional working capital requirement (WCR)
- values of future cash flows
- timing of future cash flows
- profit repatriation
- local taxation
- transfer prices
- residual assets values.

Appraisal of a foreign investment from the home country's perspective by the parent company requires consideration of the following additional factors:

- forecasts of currency exchange rates and assessment of the impact of their changes
- differences between project cash flows and holding company cash flows due to the imposition of exchange controls
- differences in the tax systems and tax rates between the country of investment and the home country of the parent company
- the consequences of imposed royalties and management fees
- differences between project cash flows and holding company cash flows as a consequence of country risk (or political risk).

There may also be legal, ethical, and environmental constraints, for example pollution laws, and weekends occurring on a Thursday and Friday as in Muslim countries. Particular customs and practices may relate to specific countries, for example working practices, the rights of women, and perhaps the prohibition of alcohol. We will consider some of the factors outlined above relating to international investment appraisal, together with a discussion about how international transfer pricing may be used in the mitigation of exchange controls, and the influence of various different international taxation scenarios on international investment strategies. An overview of country risk and the strategies that international companies may use to minimise their impact is discussed in the final section of this chapter.

Initial investment

An estimate of the cost of an initial investment is likely to be no more accurate for an international investment than for a domestic investment. In fact, because of the greater number of variables involved it is likely to be less accurate, particularly where such expenditure may be made in a foreign currency (see the section about forecast currency exchange rates below). An overseas subsidiary's investment in non-current assets of land, buildings, plant, and equipment, may be provided by local debt or equity or may be provided by parent company debt or equity. Non-current assets may also be transferred to the overseas subsidiary by the home country parent company, which should be valued at their opportunity cost.

Working capital requirement

The working capital requirement of an overseas subsidiary will be ongoing throughout the life of the overseas subsidiary. It arises in the normal course of manufacturing and trading through accounts receivable, stocks of materials, work-in-progress, and finished products, and accounts payable. Materials and stocks may be acquired locally, and some may be provided by the parent company at agreed transfer prices (see the section about transfer pricing below).

Future cash flows

The estimation of future cash flows is likely to be even more precarious and subject to greater margins of error than estimates of initial investment costs. The further into the future one tries to estimate, the less accurate is the forecast. With future cash flows from an overseas investment there are the added complications of dealing with a foreign currency and the possible impact of overseas taxation.

The investment in an overseas subsidiary may be evaluated using the cash flows within the foreign country of the investment in that country's currency. On that basis, the investment appraisal may result in a positive net present value indicating an increase in shareholder value. This may or may not be truly accurate and is dependent on which particular cost of capital has been used in the calculation. Further to that, shareholder wealth is determined by the value added to the parent company and therefore the home country appraisal of the foreign investment by the parent company may be more relevant. The net present value of the investment in the overseas subsidiary should be calculated using the initial investment by the parent company and the future cash flows transferred to it, which may be restricted (see profit repatriation below).

Profit repatriation

If an overseas subsidiary has been financed by its parent company then the parent company will expect to receive dividends and possibly loan interest and loan repayments. In certain countries, profit repatriation may be restricted by government so that funds have to be retained for future investment in that country. Some countries possibly impose such constraints to limit any action by another country that may weaken their currencies, or to promote action themselves that may strengthen their currencies.

Worked Example 11.1

Wood Inc. is a company in the USA that is proposing to invest US$1.5m in a project in Spain. The project would be managed by Rono SA, a wholly owned Spanish subsidiary of Wood Inc. We will assume that:

- taxes will not be payable in either the USA or Spain
- foreign exchange rates will not change over the period of the project
- cash remittances from Spain are limited to 32% of the original investment in any one year.

The investment has the following cash flow profile:

Year	0	1	2	3
Project cash flows US$000	(1,500)	800	800	800

The project remittances to the holding company have the following profile:

Year	0	1	2	3	4	5
Receipts remitted US$000	0	480	480	480	480	480

We will consider whether the project should be accepted if Wood Inc. requires a 20% return on investments made in Europe.

For Rono SA, using a discount rate of 20% the project will have the following net present value:

Year	0	1	2	3		
Project cash flows US$000	(1,500)	800	800	800		
Discount factor	1.0	0.83	0.69	0.58		
Present value US$000	(1,500)	666	555	463	NPV + 184	

The NPV of the project is + US$184,000, therefore from the subsidiary's point of view the project is wealth creating.

For the Wood Inc. the project will have the following net present value:

Year	0	1	2	3	4	5	
Project cash flows US$000	(1,500)	480	480	480	480	480	
Discount factor	1.0	0.83	0.69	0.58	0.48	0.40	
Present value US$000	(1,500)	400	333	278	231	193	NPV − 65

The NPV of the project is −US$65,000, therefore from the holding company point of view the project is not wealth-creating, and clearly Wood Inc. should not undertake the project.

How should Wood Inc. resolve this apparent dilemma? If Wood Inc. is still keen to invest in the project then it may investigate a number of courses of action:

- review the project cash flows
- try and identify ways to reduce the initial investment
- attempt to re-negotiate the level of remitted cash flows from Spain.

Forecast currency exchange rates

The estimation of initial investments in a foreign currency, and the forecasting of cash flow values and timings in a country and currency that is not the home currency may be difficult because of different practices, behavioural patterns, and expectations within that country. If currency cash flows require translation into the home country's currency of the parent company, not only do the future foreign currency cash flows need to be forecast but so do the future expected exchange rates ruling at the appropriate future dates. In a perfect market the movement in exchange rates would not be a problem because in theory the purchasing power of the two currencies varies in the same proportion as exchange rate movements (see the exchange rate equivalency model which is discussed in Chapter 12). In practice, this may not be so and the risk of exposure to foreign currency exchange rate movements presents a very real problem to companies who have invested in overseas subsidiaries. Some of the methods used to address this problem are also discussed in Chapter 12.

Worked Example 11.2

Dale plc is a UK retail company, which is planning to invest £2m in a project in Germany that would potentially lead to the creation of a European-wide retail chain. As a result of investing in the project Dale plc will receive a single one-off payment of €3.5m at the end of year 4 of the project.

The current exchange rate (and the agreed exchange rate for the proposed investment) is £1 = €1.34. The management of Dale plc expects that over the next few years the € will strengthen against the £. The company expects that the £/€ exchange rate at the end of year 4 will be between £1 = €1.05 and £1 = €1.12. The company requires a return of 12% on European investments.

We will ignore taxation and assume there are no exchange controls between the UK and Germany, and consider whether Dale plc should undertake the project.

At an expected rate of return of 12% the equivalent value of £2m in four years would be:

$$£2m \times (1.12)^4 = £2m \times 1.5735 = £3,147,039$$

This means that in order to break even the project should generate an equivalent cash flow at the end of year 4 of £3,147,039.

If the expected receipt at the end of year 4 is €3,500,000, then the exchange rate would need to be 3,500,000/3,147,039 or £1 = €1.11. This exchange rate of £1 = €1.11 is within the range expected by the company and as a result Dale Plc may accept the project.

However, the range of exchange rates has been based on forecasts, and Dale plc may be a little concerned about their reliability. If Dale plc took out a Euro loan at 12% per annum to cover the original investment, the loan would be for £2m at the current exchange rate of £1 = €1.34, which equals €2.68m. The total cost of the loan including repayment of the principal would be:

$$€2.68m \times (1.12)^4 = €2.68m \times 1.5735 = €4,216,980,$$

which means a cash cost of €3.5m − €4.22m, or €0.72m to the company.

In practice, such a hedge is a logical option but in this particular case the cost of €0.72m may be prohibitive.

Exchange controls

The issue of exchange controls is a major concern for many companies trading and investing internationally. Exchange controls can have serious consequences because they can prevent the movement and restrict adequate management of assets and resources.

There are many types of exchange control that an international company may face and in response multinational companies have developed a range of techniques to mitigate some of their adverse impacts. Exchange controls relate to a wide range of regulations that may impact on both residents and non-residents of a country, and which prevent or restrict:

■ possession of assets denominated in a foreign currency

■ engagement in foreign currency transactions

■ acquisition, retention, and disposal of assets and liabilities located outside the country

■ acquisition, retention, and disposal of assets and liabilities denominated in a foreign currency.

The above restrictions are usually imposed by government central banks to contain or restrict the convertibility of foreign currency where a shortage of such a foreign currency may exist, and seek to restrict, prevent, or control economic activity. Such economic activity can include, for example, imports, exports, access to financial markets, the possession of foreign assets and foreign currencies, and repatriation of profits or cash flows.

Exchange controls that affect imports generally attempt to restrict imports to a level significantly less than that under free market conditions, because when a currency depreciates or devalues then imports increase. Exchange controls generally require resident overseas subsidiary companies to obtain strictly controlled licences for the importation of goods and services. The licences are then used to enforce import restrictions, and to restrict access to the foreign currency forward exchange market to their holders.

On the other hand, exchange controls that affect exports not only attempt to promote and encourage export activities, but more importantly seek to attract premium foreign currency exchange rates. However, these exchange controls may:

■ impose controls on payments related to exports

■ restrict export activities by the use of export licensing regulations

■ impose restrictions that limit access to foreign currency exchange markets.

With regard to borrowing, exchange controls may on the one hand seek to discourage or even prohibit local borrowing by non-residents, while on the other hand they may encourage overseas borrowing by residents by seeking to control loan terms and conditions of borrowing. Exchange controls may also seek to restrict possession of, and access to, foreign assets by subjecting the ownership and acquisition of such assets to government central bank permission. These exchange controls may also apply not only to the establishment and operation of foreign bank accounts, but also to the possession of foreign currencies.

While the above types of exchange control are very important, it is the imposition of exchange controls with regard to profit repatriation that may affect the movement of a company's cash flows, which is perhaps the most critical type. Many developed countries may allow free repatriation of investment capital and profit. However, other countries may impose severe restrictions on the repatriation of profit. These exchange controls are often complex, usually politically motivated, and frequently changed. Such restrictions may impose:

■ limits on the movement of all profits generated within a country

■ percentage restrictions on the level of profits available for repatriation

■ time limits on the repatriation of profits.

Companies may seek assurances on the imposition of such exchange controls but changes of government, particularly in politically unstable countries, often render such agreements worthless. Nevertheless, there are various means by which companies may release profits, which would otherwise be restricted by the imposition of exchange controls. Such methods include:

- use of transfer pricing
- establishment of fee and royalty agreements
- use of leading and lagging
- payment of dividends
- payment of management fees
- use of research and development fees
- use of currency invoicing
- use of parallel loans
- establishment of counter trade deals and agreements.

Worked Example 11.3

Gretchen AG is a German company that is considering investing €12.5m in a project in France. The company intends undertaking the project through Bondi SA, a partly owned French subsidiary. It has been assumed that:

- taxes are not payable in either Germany or France
- foreign currency exchange rates will not change over the period of the project
- no exchange controls exist between France and Germany to prevent the remittance of investment cash flows.

The investment has the following cash flow profile:

Year	0	1	2	3	4
Project cash flows €000	(12,500)	6,500	3,500	4,800	1,500

Because the project is to be managed through Bondi SA, a management fee of 10% on all project cash flows will be paid by Gretchen AG.

We will appraise the investment on the basis that Gretchen AG requires a 10% return on investments made in France.

Year	0	1	2	3	4	
Project cash flows €000	(12,500)	6,500	3,500	4,800	1,500	
Discount factor	1.0	0.909	0.826	0.751	0.683	
Present value €000	(12,500)	5,908	2,891	3,605	1,024	NPV + 928

The NPV of the project is + €928,000, and therefore the project is wealth-creating. However, we should also consider the impact that the management fees have on the net present value of the project. If we deduct 10% from the cash flows in years 1 to 4, we have the following cash flows and revised net present value:

Year	0	1	2	3	4	
Project cash flows €000	(12,500)	5,850	3,150	4,320	1,350	
Discount factor	1.0	0.909	0.826	0.751	0.683	
Present value €000	(12,500)	5,318	2,602	3,244	922	NPV − 414

> The revised NPV of the project is − €414,000, and therefore incurring the management fees results in the project being non-wealth-creating. Under the current arrangements Gretchen AG should reject the project. However, since this project is basically wealth-creating then negotiation regarding the level of management fees would clearly benefit both companies. If Bondi SA were to reduce its management fees by 4% to 6% then revised cash flows and net present value would be as follows:
>
> | Year | 0 | 1 | 2 | 3 | 4 | |
> |---|---|---|---|---|---|---|
> | Project cash flows €000 | (12,500) | 6,110 | 3,290 | 4,512 | 1,410 | |
> | Discount factor | 1.0 | 0.909 | 0.826 | 0.751 | 0.683 | |
> | Present value €000 | (12,500) | 5,554 | 2,718 | 3,388 | 963 | NPV + 123 |
>
> The NPV of the project would then be + €123,000, and therefore acceptable to Gretchen AG. It would also mean that Bondi SA would receive 6% × €16.3m (the total project cash flows) = €978,000 as opposed to nothing at all if Gretchen AG rejected the investment project.

Taxation

Taxation is political in origin while its effect is economic. It is as a consequence of such origins that international differences in rates of tax and schemes of assessment continue to exist, resulting in significant problems for international companies seeking to operate and invest internationally.

If a company seeks to maximise the wealth of its shareholders, a company operating and investing internationally will not only seek to:

■ minimise the impact and consequences of domestic and foreign taxes

but also to:

■ legitimate the means through which these taxes can be reduced.

An international company has a responsibility to its shareholders to try and minimise its global tax burden on its domestic and international profits, provided that such a strategy does not impact on its other business activities. One way of achieving this involves the use of tax havens, of which there are a number of types. They may be, for example, countries where no income or capital gains taxes are levied at all, or countries where tax rates are very low. They also include countries that do not tax foreign income as a means of trying to attract inward capital investment. For a tax haven to be acceptable to international companies the country would normally be required to have a:

■ stable political and economic structure
■ well-balanced social structure
■ structured and well-managed financial services sector
■ good communications network
■ stable long-term economic outlook.

Where possible, tax treaties should exist between the company's home country and potential tax haven countries, and few if any exchange controls should be in operation. The tax haven country should also levy low taxes on domestically generated income.

There are a number of problems and risks associated with companies' use of tax havens to minimise overall tax, which generally arise from changes in:

■ internal political structure of the country due to social or political unrest

■ economic alliances of the country due to negotiated trade agreements

■ tax changes due to changes to or the global harmonisation of taxation systems.

The various taxation schemes used in overseas countries may have an impact on international investment because of their different tax rates. They may also have an impact because of the availability or not of investment incentives, and whether or not overseas tax paid may be offset against domestic corporation tax through double taxation agreements. The following worked example considers some of these issues.

Worked Example 11.4

Dennis Ltd is a UK company, which is planning to invest in a project in Spain that is expected to generate the following net cash flows (and profits) over the three years of the project:

Year 1	€5m
Year 2	€4m
Year 3	€3m

Spanish corporation tax is expected to be:

Year 1	24%
Year 2	25%
Year 3	26%

Withholding tax is payable on all foreign dividends remitted to UK at the following estimated rates:

Year 1	15%
Year 2	15%
Year 3	20%

UK corporation tax is currently paid at 35%, and full tax credits are available for taxes paid in Spain.

It is assumed that foreign exchange rates will not change over the life of the investment, and that there are no exchange controls between the UK, Spain, and France to prevent the remittance of investment cash flows.

We will calculate the after-tax cash flows for each of the following scenarios:

■ all project profits remitted to the UK

■ all project profits reinvested in Spain

■ the investment is managed by a wholly owned French subsidiary with the dividends remitted to France for further investment outside the UK.

All project profits remitted to the UK

Figures in €000

Year	1	2	3
Cash flow/profit	5,000	4,000	3,000
Spanish corporation tax	1,200	1,000	780
at	24%	25%	26%
Dividend	3,800	3,000	2,220
Withholding tax	570	450	444
(% of dividend)	15%	15%	20%
Net dividend received	3,230	2,550	1,776
UK corporation tax (35% of profit)	1,750	1,400	1,050
Foreign tax credit (Spanish corporation tax plus withholding tax)	1,770	1,450	1,224
Residual tax (UK corporation tax less the tax credit, which is limited to the amount of UK corporation tax)	–	–	–
Net profit after tax (net dividend less residual tax)	3,230	2,550	1,776

Total profit after tax over the life of the project is €7.556m.

All project profits reinvested in Spain

Figures in €000

Year	1	2	3
Cash flow/profit	5,000	4,000	3,000
Spanish corporation tax	1,200	1,000	780
at	24%	25%	26%
Dividend	3,800	3,000	2,220

Total cash flow/profit after tax over the life of the project is €9.02m.

The investment is managed by a wholly owned French subsidiary with the dividends remitted to France for further investment outside the UK.

Figures in €000

Year	1	2	3
Cash flow/profit	5,000	4,000	3,000
Spanish corporation tax	1,200	1,000	780
at	24%	25%	26%
Dividend	3,800	3,000	2,220
Withholding tax	570	450	444
(% of dividend)	15%	15%	20%
Net cash flow/profit after tax	3,230	2,550	1,776

Total profit after tax over the life of the project is €7.556m.

Transfer pricing

A transfer price is the price at which goods or services are transferred between different units of the same company. If those units are located within different countries then it is referred to as international transfer pricing.

The extent to which the transfer price covers costs and contributes to profit is a matter of policy. A transfer price may, for example, be based on marginal cost, full cost, market price, or through negotiation. Where the transferred products cross national boundaries, then transfer prices used may have to be agreed with the governments of the countries concerned.

It can be seen that the whole issue of transfer pricing is potentially full of difficulties and conflicts, particularly in the area of international transfer pricing. Transfer pricing is a technique used by many multinational companies operating in a range of overseas countries. There is obvious potential for profit manipulation and tax evasion through the creative application of transfer pricing policies.

For a multinational company operating in a large number of countries there are factors that may influence the use of transfer pricing and determination of transfer pricing strategies and policies. Transfers of goods and services between companies may take place for a variety of reasons, for example transfer of:

- raw materials and components to assist in the production process
- sales and distribution facilities
- other services.

A multinational company may use transfer prices to:

- protect corporate funds
- minimise taxes
- minimise tariffs
- avoid exchange controls and quotas
- minimise exchange risk
- maximise profit
- optimise areas of inadequate financial performance.

In general, companies will set a transfer price at a minimum of the sum of the additional cost per unit incurred to the point of transfer, plus the opportunity costs per unit to the company as a whole. However, a wide range of factors may influence the actual level of transfer prices used by a company, for example:

- size of the company
- organisation structure
- managerial behaviour
- legal requirements
- social and cultural influences
- national and international fiscal requirements
- international pressures.

While each of the above factors are important influences their impact will ultimately be determined by:

- corporate objectives, the overriding objective being the maximisation of shareholder wealth
- the competitive position of the company
- government influence on the company's activities
- the profit distribution/retention policy of the company.

Royalties and management fees

Some international companies impose 'management fees' on their subsidiaries for services provided by senior managers and technical personnel, and may also make royalty charges on patents used by their subsidiaries. This is an area, which is usually very carefully monitored by tax authorities as such transfers of funds have often been a source of tax evasion.

The impact of charges made between companies within the same group, such as royalties and management fees, resulting from a company investing overseas may result in a wealth-creating project being rejected. This sort of issue is best dealt with by first establishing the viability of the proposal as a standalone investment project. The project may then be evaluated by calculating the impact of any additional fees and costs to determine its acceptability or not. Let's look at a worked example of this.

Worked Example 11.5

Hill Street Inc is a company based in Chicago, USA, which has the opportunity to invest US$20m in a project in Australia. The project would be managed by Everage Ltd, which is a subsidiary company based in Australia.

The estimated cash flows of the investment project are:

Figures in US$ million

Year	Cash flow
0	(20.0)
1	13.0
2	9.0
3	10.5
4	6.5

The estimated tax cash flows relating to the project are:

Figures in US$ million

Year	Cash flow
0	8.0
1	(9.0)
2	(3.0)
3	(3.5)
4	(2.5)

A management fee of 20% on all project cash flows is payable by Hill Street Inc to Everage Ltd in return for managing the project. It is assumed that:

- there are no exchange controls in the USA and Australia that may prevent the remittance of cash flows from the investment
- foreign currency exchange rates are not expected to vary over the period of the project.

▶ We will make the appropriate calculations, assuming that Hill Street Inc requires a 15% return on Australian investments, to determine whether or not the project should be accepted. The following cash flows are net of tax.

Year	Cash outflows US$ million	Cash inflows US$ million	Discount factor at 15%	Present values US$ million
0	−12.00		1.00	−12.00
1		4.00	0.87	3.48
2		6.00	0.76	4.56
3		7.00	0.66	4.62
4		4.00	0.57	2.28
			NPV	+2.94

The NPV of the project is + US$2.94m, and being positive is therefore wealth-creating.

If we deduct the 20% management fee from the cash flows years 1 to 4 we can re-calculate the NPV as follows:

Year	Cash outflows US$ million	Cash inflows US$ million	Discount factor at 15%	Present values US$ million
0	−12.00		1.00	−12.00
1		3.20	0.87	2.78
2		4.80	0.76	3.65
3		5.60	0.66	3.70
4		3.20	0.57	1.82
			NPV	−0.05

The revised NPV of the project is now − US$0.05m, and being negative indicates that the project is not wealth-creating and suggests that it should not be undertaken.

However, it should be noted that the opportunity of an otherwise good investment project that would increase shareholder wealth is being rejected because of the level of management fees paid between companies within the group. An alternative way of managing the project may therefore be considered.

Residual assets values

An investment in a new overseas subsidiary by a parent company must consider an estimate of the residual value of its assets, even though the company may be regarded as a going concern and may be assumed to exist in perpetuity. An estimate of the residual values of its assets at a point in time is required so that a realistic appraisal of the investment may be made, and also because the parent company may have plans to dispose of the subsidiary after so many years.

Progress check 11.6

What are the additional factors that need to be considered in international investment appraisal compared with appraisal of domestic investment projects?

International investment cost of capital

Many of the issues relating to the evaluation of domestic investments apply equally to international investment appraisal. There are in addition some unique factors relating to the evaluation of international investment. As with the appraisal of domestic investment projects, assuming that the NPV method is employed, international investment projects pose the same difficult question about which is the most suitable discount rate to use. For international investment projects there are a number of discount rate options that may be considered to calculate NPV, for example:

- a weighted average cost of capital (WACC)
- the WACC of the country parent company
- the WACC of the overseas subsidiary company
- the WACC of similar overseas companies
- a discount rate higher than a domestic discount rate to reflect the additional risk of an overseas investment
- the return required from similar risk overseas projects
- a required return specific to the investment.

In practice, the use of a company's WACC as the discount rate to evaluate an investment is inherently inaccurate because of the difficulties in its calculation and the fact that WACC may change because of the change in gearing as a result of additional financing of the new investment from either debt or equity. On the other hand, the arbitrary use of some discount rate that reflects the additional risk of an overseas investment is also unsatisfactory, as is a return required from similar risk overseas projects, because this type of risk (currency risk, interest rate risk, country or political risk) may be identified and managed.

The general consensus appears to be that the most appropriate discount rate for appraisal of an international investment should be a project-specific cost of capital that reflects the particular features and risk profile of the specific project. This discount rate may also allow for, for example, currency exchange rates, interest rates, and taxation specific to the individual overseas investment project. It may also take into account the type of financing, debt or equity, and their relevant risks.

The discount rate used will also depend on whether the investment is financed totally by equity or totally by debt or some combination of debt and equity. This then poses the additional questions about how the individual costs of financing should be determined. We have discussed the use of the CAPM to calculate cost of equity in Chapter 6. The CAPM does not require growth projections and while it is probably the best method of calculating a cost of equity its use in international investment appraisal is not without its problems. These include determination of, for example: the time period; which market portfolio to consider; the market premium; the beta value of the project. Some of these issues are considered by Buckley (*Multinational Finance*, 2004) in the development of an international version of the capital asset pricing model.

A possible alternative to NPV to evaluate an overseas investment project may be to use an **adjusted present value (APV)** described by Myers (Myers SC (1974) 'Interactions of corporate finance and investment decisions: implications for capital budgeting', *Journal of Finance* 29 (1), 1–25). This is based on the Miller and Modigliani II model (see Chapter 6), which assumes that WACC is reduced because of the debt tax shield. The APV method first requires the 'base case' NPV to be calculated. The 'base case' NPV is the present value of the cash flows of the investment, regardless of tax and financing, discounted at the rate of return that shareholders would require if the project were totally equity financed. This rate of return is the parent company's ungeared beta (β). Then the cash flows relating to the 'adjustments' of tax and financing are discounted using a risk-adjusted cost of debt. The two present values are then added to give an APV, which is acceptable to the company if it is above zero. It can be seen that the APV method may be particularly useful in dealing with international investments, which have diverse sources of finance, but it still has the problem of being able to estimate accurate and appropriate discount rates.

Progress check 11.7

Explain the significance of choice of discount factor in international investment appraisal.

In practice, international investment appraisal is a little more complex than the appraisal of a domestic investment. Some of the main issues are the volatility of foreign currency exchange rates, the estimated profitability of the project, the risks involved in an overseas investment, and the management of such risks. Let's look at an example that includes some of these issues.

Worked Example 11.6

Martin plc, a UK multinational company, has equity with a market value of £150m and debt capital with a market value of £100m. The company's current cost of equity is 12%, and its after tax cost of debt is 7%.

Martin plc has obtained a contract worth Aus$80m to supply and install plant and equipment for a company in Australia. The payment terms of the contract set by Martin plc, which are non-negotiable, are:

■ Aus$20m payment to be made on completion of stage one of the contract at the end of year 1

■ Aus$24m payment to be made on completion of stage two of the contract at the end of year 2

■ Aus$36m payment to be made on completion of stage three of the contract at the end of year 3.

The estimated cost of the supply and installation of the plant and equipment is Aus$70m.

Project cash outflows in respect to the project are expected to involve three currencies – Aus$, £ sterling, and euro – and cash flows are estimated as follows:

Year	0	1	2	3
Inflows Aus$	0	20	24	36
Outflows				
Aus$	6	3	7	4
UK £	3	3	1	3
€	3	3	4	5

The current exchange rates at the start of the project are:

$$£ = Aus\$2.50$$

$$€ = Aus\$1.67$$

At the start of the contract, foreign currency forecasts for each of the next three years have been made as follows:

- Aus$ will appreciate by approximately 5% against the £
- Aus$ will appreciate by approximately 10% against the €.

We are required to evaluate the investment using the base currency of £ sterling and advise Martin plc on the financial acceptability of the project. We should also point out the factors that may impact on the profitability of the project, the risks involved in the project, and make some suggestions as to how to hedge against these risks.

We can summarise the expected exchange rates based on the forecasts provided for the subsequent three years:

Year	0	1	2	3
Aus$/£	2.500	2.375	2.256	2.143
Aus$/€	1.670	1.503	1.353	1.217
therefore €/£	1.497	1.580	1.667	1.761

The estimated cash flows for the project can now be translated into a single currency, £ sterling:

Figures in £m

Year	0	1	2	3
Inflows				
Aus$ in £	0.000	8.421	10.638	16.799
Outflows				
Aus$ in £	2.400	1.263	3.103	1.867
£	3.000	3.000	1.000	3.000
€ in £	2.004	1.899	2.399	2.839
Total outflows	7.404	6.162	6.502	7.706
Net cash flow	−7.404	2.259	4.136	9.093

We can determine the current WACC of Martin plc:

$$WACC = \frac{(£150m \times 12\%) + (£100m \times 7\%)}{(£150m + £100m)} = 10\%$$

to use as an approximate discount rate to calculate the NPV of the project:

Year	Cash outflows £m	Cash inflows £m	Discount factor at 10%	Present values £m
0	−7.404		1.00	−7.404
1		2.259	0.91	2.056
2		4.136	0.83	3.433
3		9.093	0.75	6.820
			NPV	+4.905

▶

▶ Using £ sterling as the base currency, using the company's current cost of capital, and assuming the three-year currency exchange rate forecasts are correct, the positive NPV is acceptable in financial terms because it adds £4,905,000 to the value of shareholders' wealth. Therefore the project appears to be financially viable.

The company should also consider the potential risks of the project, for example:

- the reliability of the initial investment and cash flow forecasts, and therefore the profitability of the project
- the accuracy of the forecast future exchange rates
- the creditworthiness of the Australian customer.

To try and mitigate these risks Martin plc may, for example:

- obtain guarantees with regard to the cost estimates they have been given before agreeing to the project
- take out credit insurance with respect to the Australian customer
- use currency swaps, options, or forward contracts to try and cover the downside risk related to foreign exchange movements.

Financing international investment

Multinational companies with investments in overseas subsidiaries have the opportunity to access and exploit inefficiencies in the international capital markets, with regard to potentially lower costs of foreign equity and debt capital, and financial assistance from foreign governments. The lowest possible average cost of capital must be the objective but this has to be at an acceptable level of risk.

We discussed financing generally in Chapter 7, which was concerned mainly with sources of finance within a company's home country, and primarily the UK. As shown in Fig. 11.3, international financing requires the consideration of additional factors, which include:

- currency risk
- interest rate risk
- home country and overseas taxation
- financial gearing
- country or political risk.

An overseas subsidiary may be financed using the currency of the parent company's home country or the foreign currency of the subsidiary's country (see Chapter 7 – Eurobonds). The method chosen will form part of the group's foreign currency risk exposure strategy (see Chapter 12). Borrowing may take place in local foreign currency, in which case foreign exchange translation exposure may be managed by matching foreign currency interest and capital repayments with foreign currency operational cash inflows.

There will inevitably be differences between the tax regimes in the parent company's home country and the countries of overseas subsidiaries. There may be differences in the ways in which profits and losses, and dividends and interest are treated for taxation. In general, because interest is tax deductible whereas dividends are not, then it may be advantageous for overseas subsidiaries to maximise their use of debt finance rather than equity, up to the maximum levels of gearing that may be allowed by governments within specific countries.

Gearing considerations relate to the levels of debt and equity in the parent company, the overseas subsidiary, and other similar companies in the foreign country. For the parent company, equity investment in an overseas subsidiary is of higher risk than debt capital, and although interest payments must be made they may be far more stable and predictable than dividend payments. An overseas subsidiary's use of local equity capital, while risky for investors, may also be risky for the company depending on the efficiency of that particular country's equity market. An overseas subsidiary may have difficulties with access to local debt finance, which may involve costly bank fees and higher interest rates if the parent company is not known and does not have high creditworthiness in the foreign country.

The parent company may guarantee the overseas subsidiary's borrowing if its own overall level of gearing is acceptable, and then the subsidiary's borrowing may be treated independently as a separate issue. The borrowing strategy of the overseas subsidiary may then exploit local tax and interest rate benefits, and the possibility of foreign government subsidies and grants. If an overseas subsidiary is financed locally, using banks in that country, and using local foreign government support then political risk is mitigated since the likelihood of expatriation of the company's assets or interference in its affairs are less likely to happen. Overseas subsidiaries whose borrowings are not guaranteed by their parent company each need to independently consider optimisation of their own capital structures.

Progress check 11.8

What are the various types of financing that may be used to support international investment?

Risk and international investment

Buckley (Buckley A (2004) *Multinational Finance*, 5 the edn, FT/Prentice Hall: London) defines political risk as the exposure to a change in the value of an investment of a cash position resultant upon government actions. Political risk, usually described as country risk, is the level of exposure a company faces as a consequence of a change in government action. This exposure to such country risk may be seen in the potential change in value of an investment, project, or cash receipts following changes in government policy.

The country risk or political risk associated with international investment can be considerable. It is important for a company to not only recognise the existence of such risk, and its potential impact on the company's international activities, but also to be aware of the possible strategies available to try and eliminate, or mitigate, the consequences of such risk. While such risks can develop in a number of different ways, they are generally related to overseas government actions and policies that seek to:

■ expropriate company assets and profits

■ impose foreign exchange currency controls

■ impose price intervention policies that discriminate between the overseas country and home country

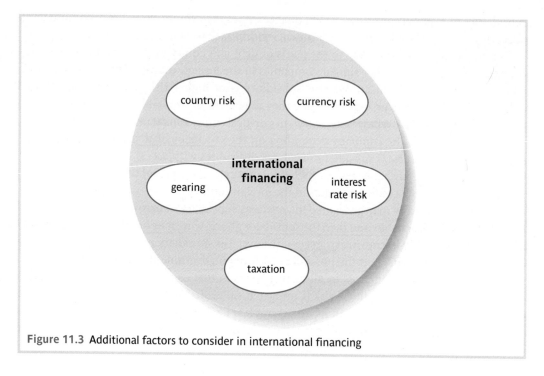

Figure 11.3 Additional factors to consider in international financing

- impose tax laws that offer preferential treatment to overseas country companies
- impose social and work-related regulations that offer preferential treatment of overseas country companies
- impose regulations that restrict access to local finance
- restrict the movement of company assets and resources.

These overseas government policies may impact on an international company's ability to:

- undertake commercial activities
- generate profits
- repatriate or reinvest such profits for future growth,

and their effects can be substantial. Therefore the recognition, assessment, and management of such risk is an important aspect of a company's international investment activities.

An international competitive advantage can only be gained by accepting some degree of country risk. Once a company has identified and recognised the existence of a potential country risk, it must then consider how this may impact on the company's activities. How can the company eliminate or mitigate the consequences of these risks? Companies may be willing to trade off higher levels of risk for higher overall returns. While the most extreme risk-averse strategy would be one of avoidance, that is the rejection of any investment projects in politically, socially, or economically uncertain countries, such an elimination strategy misses potential opportunities of investment projects that may yield high returns. In general, companies tend to adopt management strategies that seek to minimise country risk rather than eliminate it altogether. These management strategies may be either defensive, which protect or safeguard a company's overall position, or offensive, which aggressively consolidate a company's overall position, and include:

- obtaining insurance against the possibility of expropriation of assets

- negotiating overseas government concessions and guarantees to minimise the possibility of expropriation of company assets

- structuring the company's financial and operating policies to ensure they are acceptable to and consistent with regulatory requirements

- developing close social and political relationships with overseas country institutions

- internationally integrating operations to include overseas and home country companies to ensure that the overseas companies are dependent on home country companies

- locating research and development activities and any proprietary knowledge and technology in the home country to reduce the possibility of expropriation

- establishing global trademarks for company products and services to ensure such rights are legally protected domestically and internationally

- encouraging where possible the establishment of local participation in company activities

- encouraging local overseas shareholders to invest in the company's activities

- maintaining high levels of local overseas borrowing to protect against the adverse impact of exchange rate movements

- encouraging the movement of surplus assets from overseas country companies to the home country companies.

Progress check 11.9

Why is country risk so important to multinational companies?

Summary of key points

- Internationalisation, with regard to the increasing geographical dispersion of economic, cultural, social, educational, technological, and political activities across national borders, has an increasing impact on the role of the financial markets, and the activities of international companies.

- The international financial marketplace is an interrelated network of buyers and sellers in which exchange activities occur in the pursuit of profit and reward, and has obvious significance for international companies.

- Companies may wish to undertake overseas operations for a variety of reasons, but particularly to gain access to overseas markets by enabling them to get closer to their customers.

- Companies may engage in various types of international operations, for example through exporting, use of agents, licensing, franchising, or the establishment of a branch, joint venture, or an overseas subsidiary.

- International companies may consider foreign direct investment (FDI) in terms of investments in new or expanded facilities overseas.

▶ ■ There are additional, unique features associated with international investment appraisal in a multi-currency, overseas environment, compared with the appraisal of domestic investment projects, for example taxation, foreign currency cash flows, overseas interest rates, transfer prices, royalties, management fees, exchange controls, and country risk.

■ The evaluation of international investment using NPV requires the choice of a suitable cost of capital as a discount rate, the most appropriate of which may be the required return specific to the individual investment.

■ The choice of financing for international investments requires the consideration of currency risk, interest rate risk, taxation, gearing, and country or political risk.

■ Country risk, which is also called political risk, is the exposure a company faces as a consequence of a change in government action, against which it may protect itself through, for example, insurance, negotiation, development of close relationships, establishment of a local presence, and the use of local financing.

🔑 Glossary of key terms

adjusted present value (APV) A method of investment appraisal where the basic investment, excluding the impacts of tax and financing, is discounted using an ungeared cost of equity, the result of which is then added to the result of discounting the tax and financing cash flows, using an appropriate cost of debt.

expropriation of assets Expropriation refers to the action of a government taking away a business or its assets from its owners, which may occur mainly in countries where property laws are not concrete and well defined.

foreign direct investment (FDI) FDI may be inward (domestic investment by overseas companies) or outward (overseas investment by domestic companies).

joint venture A business entity in which a company holds an interest on a long-term basis and is jointly controlled by that company and one or more other venturers under a contractual arrangement (FRS 9). A joint venture may also refer to a project undertaken by two or more persons or entities joining together with a view to profit, often in connection with a single operation.

transfer price The price at which goods or services are transferred between different units of the same company.

❓ Questions

Q11.1 Explain the corporate financing implications of internationalisation.

Q11.2 Outline the roles of the key participants in the international financial marketplace.

Q11.3 Explain why companies may wish to engage in international markets.

Q11.4 Critically compare the different types of indirect international operations.

Q11.5 Critically compare the different types of direct international operations.

Q11.6 Describe the route by which a multinational company may ultimately establish a subsidiary company in a foreign country.

Q11.7 Outline the alternative methods of international investment appraisal.

Q11.8 Explain the advantages and disadvantages of the various discount rate options that may be used in the NPV evaluation of international investments.

Q11.9 Outline the risks associated with international investment.

Q11.10 Describe the strategies that may be adopted by multinational companies with regard to country risk.

Discussion points

D11.1 'Internationalisation is the only way that medium-sized and large companies can survive and prosper in the 21st century.' Discuss.

D11.2 'The cost of setting up an overseas subsidiary far outweighs any benefits.' Discuss.

D11.3 Chairman of a UK plc: 'The calculation of WACC is a straightforward matter and I don't see why it should be any more complicated if we are using it to evaluate an investment in an overseas subsidiary.' Discuss.

Exercises

Solutions are provided in Appendix 2 to all exercise numbers highlighted in colour.

Level I

E11.1 *Time allowed – 30 minutes*
Describe the main elements of the international financial marketplace.

E11.2 *Time allowed – 30 minutes*
Why do companies choose indirect methods like exporting rather than direct international operations like FDIs?

E11.3 *Time allowed – 30 minutes*
In what ways does international investment appraisal differ from domestic investment appraisal?

E11.4 *Time allowed – 45 minutes*
Explain the various ways in which an FDI may be evaluated, and compare the alternative choices of discount rate that may be used in such evaluations.

Level II

E11.5 *Time allowed – 45 minutes*
There is currently an economic recession throughout the continent of Indulosia, which has hit one of its countries, Zorbia, particularly hard. The UK Bank of Penderyn has

▶ made loans totalling £0.5bn to the government of Zorbia, for which it has received no repayments because of the widespread recession. Representatives of the Bank of Penderyn have had extensive discussions with officials of the Zorbian central bank and have now received a proposal. 'We acknowledge the Bank of Zorbia's debt with the Bank of Penderyn and, in order to satisfy its outstanding commitments to the Bank, the Zorbian government proposes that the outstanding debts of £0.5bn be exchanged for equity shares in a number of recently privatised Zorbian utility companies. The approximate current market value of these shares at today's exchange rate of £1 = 4.5 Zors is 1.35bn Zors.'

You are required to advise the Bank of Penderyn with regard to its overseas operation, and suggest how it may respond to the Zorbian government's proposal and recommend alternative courses of action that the bank may consider.

E11.6 *Time allowed – 45 minutes*

Explain and compare each of the alternative sources of financing an FDI, and their advantages and disadvantages to a multinational company.

E11.7 *Time allowed – 45 minutes*

Benjamin plc is a UK first tier supplier of integrated automotive systems to a number of French car manufacturers. Benjamin plc has issued share capital of 666,667 fully paid up £1 ordinary shares with a current *ex dividend* market price of £3 per share, and 1,000,000 £1, 5% preference shares with a current market price of £1 per share. A dividend of 10p per share has recently been paid to ordinary shareholders. The company also has £800,000 7% debentures redeemable at par in three years' time. The debentures have a current cum interest market value of £104.

Benjamin has recently received a proposal for a contract for £20m to supply some of its products to the French police.

The contract is expected to last four years and the estimated cash flows are:

Year	Cash flow
0	£(20.0m)
1	€11.0m
2	€13.5m
3	€10.0m
4	€3.5m

Benjamin plc is proposing the engagement of a UK-based management company to oversee the project. A management fee of £100,000 per annum is payable to the company in years 1 to 4 for their management of the French police contract. The UK corporation tax rate is assumed to be 35% on net profit payable in each year following the year in which the profit was derived. The £ sterling/euro exchange rates for the four years of the contract have been estimated at:

Year 1	£1 = €1.70
Year 2	£1 = €1.75
Year 3	£1 = €1.80
Year 4	£1 = €1.85

Required:

Benjamin plc uses its current weighted average cost of capital to evaluate overseas investments. On this basis, and ignoring French taxes, advise the company as to whether the contract should be accepted.

E11.8   *Time allowed – 45 minutes*

Provide a detailed explanation of country (or political) risk, and its relevance with regard to a multinational company's decision to establish a new overseas subsidiary in a fast-growing, low tax country. Outline the legitimate ways in which the multinational may minimise the risks you have described.

E11.9   *Time allowed – 45 minutes*

Lee Ltd is a UK company proposing to invest in a project in Singapore. The company expects the investment project to generate net profits of Singapore $ 2,000m per year. You may assume that:

- Singapore corporation tax is 18%
- a withholding tax of 10% is payable on all foreign dividend remittances
- UK corporation tax is 30% with full tax credits available for taxes paid in Germany
- foreign exchange rates will not change over the life of the investment
- no exchange controls exist between the UK, Singapore, and Germany to prevent the remittance of investment cash flows.

Required:

Calculate the after-tax cash flows in the following situations:

(i)   All the project profits are remitted to the UK.
(ii)   All the project profits are reinvested in Singapore.
(iii) The investment is managed by a wholly owned German subsidiary with the dividends remitted to Germany for further investment outside the UK.

E11.10 *Time allowed – 45 minutes*

Drex plc is a UK-based retail company with a market capitalisation of £800m. Because of increasing competition in the UK market, the company is considering two altern-ative mutually exclusive investment options:

- Option 1 is to invest £200m in the development of a range of new retail outlets in Norway.
- Option 2 is to invest £200m in a new subsidiary in Malaysia.

Because of financing constraints, the company can select only one of the options. The company is considering raising the required £200m from a combination of a rights issue and secured borrowing.

The risk/return profile of each option is as follows:

	Return	Standard deviation
New retail outlets in Norway	12%	0.04
New subsidiary in Malaysia	12%	0.05

▶

▶ The after-tax return on the capital invested in the existing UK business has been 10% per annum for the past few years with a standard deviation of 0.03. The correlation of project returns with the UK business is as follows:

- The correlation of the return on the Norway option with the average after-tax returns of the UK business is 0.8.
- The correlation of the return on the Malaysian project with the average after-tax returns of the UK business is 0.3.

Required:

Prepare a report for the board of Drex plc explaining which of the above two projects the company should undertake.

Chapter 12

Financial risk management

Chapter contents

LEARNING OBJECTIVES

Completion of this chapter will enable you to:

☑ Explain what is meant by financial risk and consider its implications.

☑ Describe the various types of financial risk.

☑ Explain the use of the exchange rate equivalency model in the context of alternative financial strategies.

☑ Analyse the issues relating to interest rate risk.

☑ Analyse the issues relating to exchange rate risk.

☑ Appreciate the importance of financial risk management.

☑ Consider the various methods used for the hedging of financial risks.

☑ Explain the use of some of the wide range of derivatives available for companies to hedge foreign currency exchange rate and interest rate risk.

☑ Evaluate the alternative financial risk management strategies.

Introduction

In Chapters 13 to 15 we will look at financial risk in general, as opposed to the business risk, faced by a business relating to the company's financial structure, or gearing, as it moves through its life cycle. Business risk relates to the variability of a company's operating profit or cash flow, dependent on levels of selling prices, demand volumes, cyclical trends, and the relationship between its level of fixed cost and total cost (operating gearing). The level of business risk varies from one industry to another. Financial risk with regard to a company's financial structure relates to the impact on profits of its commitment to and ability to pay interest, the level of interest rates, and possibility of bankruptcy.

More specific types of financial risk are considered in this chapter relating to movements in foreign currency exchange rates and interest rates. These are financial risks that may be faced by companies arising from:

- trade (selling or buying) with overseas organisations
- transactions (trade or investment) denominated in currencies other than £ sterling (for UK companies)
- investment in assets or businesses located overseas
- financial investment overseas.

This chapter introduces what is broadly called the exchange rate equivalency model, which can be used to explain relationships between exchange rates, interest rates, and inflation rates. It forms a basis on which a number of techniques of international financial management are based.

A company may previously have had very little experience of doing business outside the UK. However, international interest and demand for its products will lead to its involvement in trade and possibly investment in countries in, for example, Europe, Africa, Asia, North America, South America, and Eastern Europe. The development of such business may not only contribute to securing the longer-term future of the company, but also restore market confidence generally in the company's performance.

Companies may seek to establish a foothold in an increasingly competitive and unpredictable global marketplace to enhance shareholder value, but find that it is rarely risk-free. The volatility of global markets is seen in the pressures of international supply and demand, continuing deregulation of international markets, and the unremitting expansion of international corporate trading activities. The minimisation of risk, particularly the risk of financial loss, has become an increasingly important role for 21st century corporate financial managers.

The existence of the risk of financial loss may result from a range of interrelated social, political, and economic factors. In an international context the risk of financial loss may result from:

- the imposition of excessive legal restrictions
- restrictive exchange controls
- loss of goods in transit
- customer payment default
- failure to meet payment deadlines
- contractual obligations not being satisfied.

This chapter discusses the types of financial risk that companies may face when trading or investing internationally, and the various techniques that they may use to minimise the risks associated with those activities.

Risk and uncertainty

It is useful to clarify what is meant by risk as distinct from uncertainty, although both words are often used to mean the same thing. After a decision has been made the actual outcome may not be what was expected, but may be better or worse. The two approaches to analysing this are:

- uncertainty analysis, which is an unquantified approach that takes a view about how much actual outcomes may be better or worse than rational estimates
- risk analysis, which is a quantified approach about how future outcomes may vary expressed as probabilities.

The first approach, uncertainty analysis, in its simplest form considers the most likely outcome, and also the worst and best possible outcomes. A range of estimated outcomes may, for example, assist managers in assessing investment projects and rejecting those where the worst outcome might involve an unacceptable level of loss. This approach also enables a manager to compare alternative investment projects and choose the one offering attractive returns within acceptable levels of uncertainty.

The maximin, maximax, and minimax regret decision rules are forms of uncertainty analysis that may be applied where it is not possible to assign meaningful probabilities to alternative courses of action.

The maximin decision rule is used by a risk-averse decision-maker who wants to make a conservative decision. This type of decision-maker looks at the worst possible outcome of each decision alternative and chooses the one that has the least worse consequence. The decision is to select the option that offers the least unattractive worst outcome. This means choosing the option that maximises the minimum profit, or minimises the maximum loss (when it is then called the minimax rule).

The maximax decision rule is used by a risk-taking decision-maker who looks at the best possible outcome of each decision alternative and chooses the one that has the highest best consequence. The decision is to select the option that offers the most attractive best outcome. This means choosing the option that maximises the maximum profit.

The maximin and maximax decision rules are illustrated in Worked Example 12.1.

Worked Example 12.1

Right plc is considering three possible sales prices for a new product and has estimated the following sales volumes at each price over the life of the product:

Price per unit	£100	£105	£110
Expected sales volumes (units)			
Best	150,000	140,000	120,000
Likely	135,000	126,000	118,000
Worst	100,000	80,000	60,000

The costs over the life of the product are:

fixed costs £5m

variable costs £50 for each product

Which sales price should a company choose?

Price per unit	£100	£105	£110
Contribution per product	£50	£55	£60
Total profit/(loss)			
Best	£2.50m	£2.70m	£2.20m
Likely	£1.75m	£1.93m	£2.08m
Worst	£0.00m	£(0.60)m	£(1.40)m

Based on the *best sales volume*, the highest profit is at a price of £105 per product. Also, the likely profit at that price is slightly higher than at a price of £100, but the worst profit is a loss, which is lower than the break-even at a price of £100.

Based on the *likely sales volume*, profit at a price of £100 is almost as good as at a price of £105, but it is not as good as at a price of £110. However, although a price of £110 gives the highest profit at the likely sales volume, the profit at the best volume is the worst of the three prices and at the worst sales volume there is a loss, which is a higher loss than at the price of £105.

Based on the *worst sales volume*, a price of £100 guarantees that the company does not make a loss.

Using the maximin decision rule, a risk-averse decision-maker will choose a price of £100 because it is the least unattractive position estimated at break-even, even though at likely and best sales volumes the profits are the lowest and next lowest.

Using the maximax decision rule, a risk-taking decision-maker will choose a price of £105 because it is the highest best position estimated at £2.70m profit, although at a worst sales volume a loss is estimated and at a likely sales volume the profit is next lowest.

Whenever a decision is made there is likely to be subsequent regret by the decision-maker that an alternative decision had not been made. The extent of this regret is effectively a loss of opportunity, and a regret for any combination of actions and circumstances is equal to the benefit gained from the best action in those circumstances less the actual benefit gained in those circumstances. The minimax regret decision rule is that the decision option selected should be the one that minimises the maximum potential regret, for any of the possible outcomes. This is illustrated in Worked Example 12.2.

Worked Example 12.2

An investor is considering two investments A and B which have different expected returns dependent on whether the market is weak or strong, which are shown in the table below:

Investment	Return	
	Weak market	Strong market
A	£11,000	£15,000
B	£2,000	£21,000

Assuming it is not possible to assign probabilities to the likely market condition, we will consider which investment should be chosen.

Maximin rule – the payoff selected is the least unattractive worst outcome:
Worst outcomes

A = £11,000

B = £2,000

The decision is to choose A, which provides the least worse return.

Maximax rule – the largest payoff is selected assuming that the best possible outcome will occur:

A = £15,000

B = £21,000

The decision is to choose B, which provides the best maximum return.

Minimax regret rule – the payoff selected aims to minimise the maximum possible regret, for any of the possible outcomes. The regret table below shows the return that may be forgone for each project, depending on whether the outcome is a weak or strong market.

Choice	Regret table	
	Weak market occurs	Strong market occurs
A	£0 (i)	£6,000 (iii)
B	£9,000 (ii)	£0 (iv)

(i) 11 – 11   (ii) 11 – 2   (iii) 21 – 15   (iv) 21 – 21

The maximum regret for investment A = £6,000

The maximum regret for investment B = £9,000

The decision is to choose project A, because it provides the minimum maximum possible regret.

The outcome of a decision may be uncertain, but for some decisions it is possible to use risk analysis by assigning probabilities to various outcomes. Estimates of probabilities may be assessed from previous experience or from comparisons with similar situations. The probabilities are used to measure the likelihood that an event or state of nature will occur. A probability distribution lists all possible outcomes for an event and the probability of each one occurring, a very simple example of which is illustrated in Worked Example 12.3.

Worked Example 12.3

Two students, Janet and John, have just sat the same examination. Whether they have passed or failed the examination is called the outcome of the event (the examination). The probability of each outcome has been estimated by their teacher and the results are shown below in a probability distribution.

Outcome	Janet probability	John probability
Pass examination	0.8	0.6
Fail examination	0.2	0.4
	1.0	1.0

Because the probabilities each add up to one it means that one or other outcome will happen with certainty. The probability distribution provides more meaningful information than merely stating that the estimated outcomes are that both students are likely to pass.

In practice, probability distributions will include a great deal more data than illustrated in Worked Example 12.3. Instead of presenting huge probability distributions for many alternatives, it is more convenient to use summary measures of these data to assess risk. We illustrated the use of three of these – expected values, standard deviation, coefficient of variation – in some of the worked examples in Chapter 5.

Risk is both complex and subjective. In general, the risk of financial loss arises where the outcome of particular events, processes, and transactions are deemed to be uncertain. For example, a low-risk event is an event where the outcome is fairly predictable, whereas a high-risk event is an event where the outcome is fairly unpredictable. The term risk normally encapsulates notions of chance, speculation, and uncertainty.

Types of financial risk

Within the global trading environment, sources of financial risk for a UK company are:

- country – economic and social infrasructure, government policy, legal restrictions, exchange controls, trade restrictions
- property – products, services, businesses, financial investments, land, and buildings
- credit – terms of trading, method of settlement, and likelihood of non-payment
- interest rates – UK and overseas interest rates
- foreign currency exchange rates – the relative values of worldwide currencies.

We have considered credit risk in Chapter 10. In this chapter we will look in some detail at financial risk arising from movements in interest rates, and foreign currency exchange rates. Country risk is an area of risk which has significant influence on potential levels of property risk, credit risk, interest rate volatility, exchange rate volatility, and the alternative settlement strategies available to companies importing or exporting products or services overseas. Many alternative international settlement strategies exist: open account; consignment payment; payment in advance; documentary collection; letter of credit; counter-trade. However, their selection and use, whilst partly dependent upon mutual negotiation, is based on:

- perceived risk associated with the specific country
- perceived risk associated with the nature of the transaction
- terms generally on offer within the country for similar products or services
- terms offered by competitors trading within the specific country
- requirements and trading history of the importing or exporting company
- financial implications in terms of cash flow requirements and levels of financial charges for the importing or exporting company.

The strategic management of financial risk is clearly important to companies that use debt financing. Financial risk relating to changing levels of foreign currency exchange rates, and possibly both UK and foreign interest rates, is extremely important to multinational businesses, and companies operating in global markets.

In 1934 the United States Government fixed the rate at which the US$ was convertible into gold at US$35 per ounce. The Bretton Woods agreement of 1944 fixed £ sterling relative to the US$ at US$4.03 = £1. Therefore £ sterling also had a known 'gold parity'. All major world currencies were also fixed in value either to the US$ or the £, and therefore indirectly to gold. The UK Government devalued the £ in 1949 to US$2.80, and then in November 1967 to US$2.40. During this entire period up to 1971 foreign exchange remained relatively stable. From 1971 everything changed. In mid 1971 the United States suspended the convertibility of US$ into gold. During the following couple of years the Deutschmark and other European currencies were 'floated', and no longer fixed against the US$, and then subsequently re-fixed. The so-called 'Snake' Agreement in April 1972 allowed several European currencies to fluctuate by a small percentage around some agreed exchange rates. In June 1972 the £ sterling left the 'Snake', floated and fell in value. In February 1973 the US$ was devalued. In March 1973 the European currencies broke their links with the US$ completely, maintaining links only between each other, and then the Deutschmark was revalued again in June 1973.

Things came to a head in October 1973 when the members of the OPEC countries quadrupled the price of oil. The formal links that had previously held world currencies together, and had maintained their stability, had already been dismantled. Therefore, the first oil price crisis of 1973 was virtually impossible for the currency markets to absorb, and since that time the world has continued to experience repeated currency crises of increasing frequency and scale. Most currencies now float freely against each other, which means that their relative values are not fixed but vary from one minute to another for a variety of reasons.

Since 1971 exchange rates have moved much faster and more frequently than ever before. Even currencies that may be considered to be relatively stable can experience major movements on their exchange rates during the short term and over the longer term. It is not uncommon to see high levels of exchange rate volatility during a year, and exchange rates at the beginning and the end of a year may also be significantly different. During the period 1975 to 1993, for example, the year-on-year US$/£ exchange rate movements regularly ranged between 10 and 35%, although since 1993 and up to 2005 year-on-year movements have tended to be less than 10% (see Fig. 12.1). Timing is therefore the all-important factor in considering the appropriate actions required to eliminate or mitigate the impact of such foreign currency exchange rate

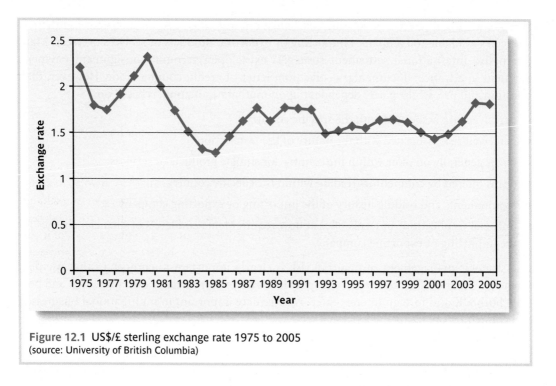

Figure 12.1 US$/£ sterling exchange rate 1975 to 2005
(source: University of British Columbia)

movements on the profits of a business. It is because companies undertake transactions and hold assets and liabilities denominated in currencies other than their local currency that they face exposure to movements in exchange rates.

Progress check 12.1

Why is financial risk particularly important to international companies?

The level of financial risk is greater the higher a company is geared financially. A company with high debt faces the risk that interest rates may rise, which will have a directly adverse impact on profit. The company also faces the risk that it may earn insufficient levels of profit over the term of a loan to ensure that it is able to service the loan. At very high levels of debt, a company may face the further risk of bankruptcy, actioned by a lender's lack of confidence that future interest commitments and loan repayments may not be capable of being met. The level of interest risk faced by a company may be measured by its income gearing (the reciprocal of income cover), which compares its interest payments as a percentage of profit before interest and tax. It may be argued that a low-geared company also faces the risk of lost opportunities of increased profits should future interest rates decrease. Interest rates were particularly volatile during the 1970s and 1980s, and as a consequence it became essential for companies to manage their exposures to interest rate risk.

There is obviously a need for companies to identify the types of financial risk that they face and to take the appropriate actions to mitigate such risks. The level of such actions (which are called hedging), with regard to interest rates depends on:

- the size and complexity of the company's borrowings
- the proportion of floating and fixed interest debt
- the volatility of interest rates
- the currencies in which loans are denominated.

In terms of foreign currency exchange rate risk the level and type of hedging depend on the type of transaction (buying or selling), number and values of transactions, and level of investments denominated in foreign currency, and the specific countries with which business is conducted. The increasing uncertainty surrounding foreign currency exchange rates, increasing globalisation, and the massive increase in international trade, means that exchange risk management has become critically important to companies. Their failure to insure or hedge against exchange rate movements may significantly impact on profits and may even result in the ultimate demise of the business. It is useful to regard interest and exchange rate management as a form of insurance. As individuals we insure ourselves against loss or injury. In the same way, companies insure themselves by hedging against adverse movements in interest rates and foreign currency exchange rates.

Since 1971 there has necessarily been an increased awareness by companies of the benefits of managing and hedging both their interest and exchange rate risk exposures. The importance of hedging to companies is related to size of the potential losses that may result from adverse movements in interest and exchange rates. In the next few sections we will look at the different types of interest rate and foreign currency exchange risk faced by companies and the hedging techniques available to control and manage such risk. There is a growing number of complex financial instruments, called derivatives, which are available for the hedging of exposure to the risk of movements in both interest rates and foreign currency exchange rates. The accounting rules covering the reporting of derivatives are currently a hot topic. Much discussion and disagreement continues both within the UK and between various other countries with regard to the control and reporting of derivatives by companies, particularly in the light of the various examples of their misuse (note Enron and see the section later about the use of derivatives).

Exchange rate equivalency model

In an increasingly global economy, the international financial environment is a complex network of social, political, and economic interrelationships in which the supply of, and demand for capital, commodities, currencies, and assets are continually affected by, for example:

- government controls and restrictions with regard to the international trade of goods and services
- government controls and restrictions on capital flows and currency movements
- the relative power of market players
- the general level of market expectations.

Within this dynamic setting, a number of theories and hypotheses have been developed to explain the relationships between:

- interest rate differentials
- inflation rate differentials
- movements in spot currency exchange rates
- movements in forward currency exchange rates.

The exchange rate equivalency model may be defined as a hypothetical relationship in which the nominal interest rate differential between two countries is assumed to be equal to the expected inflation rate differential between those two countries, the differential between the forward rate and the spot rate of the currencies over the given period, and any potential future change in the spot exchange rate. Moreover the inflation rate differential between two such countries is assumed to be equal to the rate of change of the expected spot exchange rate of those two countries. The expected change in spot exchange rates is also assumed to be equal to the differential between the spot exchange rate and the forward exchange rate.

The exchange rate equivalency model is a model that has been developed from a number of assumptions of market perfection, for example:

- the existence of no significant market imperfections
- the existence of no political or economic barriers to the mobility of capital and currencies
- the existence of no long-term sustainable arbitrage opportunities.

The exchange rate equivalency model may also be considered as a combination of the following theories and hypotheses:

- Fisher Effect (or Fisher's closed hypothesis)
- Interest Rate Parity Theory
- Purchasing Power Parity Theory
- Expectations Theory of exchange rates
- International Fisher Effect (or Fisher's open hypothesis).

In addition to the definition that we gave earlier, the exchange rate equivalency model may also be expressed in a diagrammatic representation, and also algebraically.

In diagrammatic format the exchange rate equivalency model can be represented as shown in Fig. 12.2.

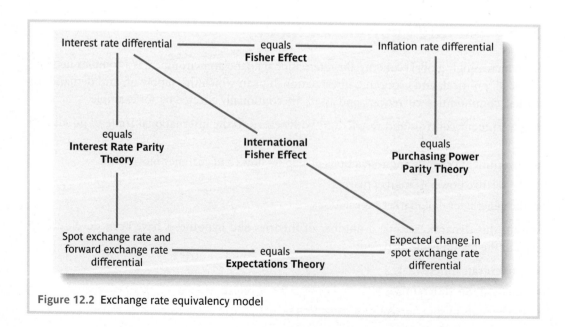

Figure 12.2 Exchange rate equivalency model

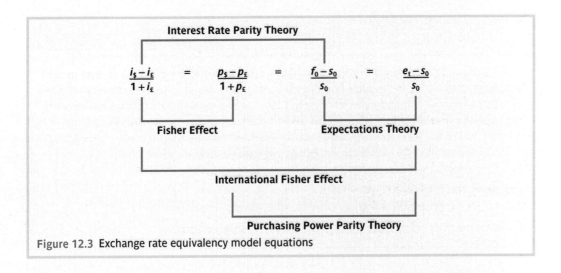

Figure 12.3 Exchange rate equivalency model equations

Each of the elements of the exchange rate equivalency model, and their algebraic equations and US$/£ sterling interrelationships may also be expressed as in Fig. 12.3.

Where

$i_\$$ = USA US$ interest rate f_0 = US$/£ forward exchange rate
$i_£$ = UK £ interest rate s_0 = US$/£ spot rate
$p_\$$ = USA inflation rate e_t = US$/£ expected spot rate
$p_£$ = UK inflation rate

Worked Example 12.4

The Interest Rate Parity Theory says that the ratio between the risk-free interest rates in two different countries is equal to the ratio between the forward and spot exchange rates. There is an opportunity to invest US$500,000 for a year, and obtain a one-year Japanese Yen bond paying 0.05% per annum or a one-year US$ bond paying 3% per annum. The spot rate is 115 ¥/US$, and the one-year forward rate is 111.706 ¥/US$.

We can determine if one bond is better than the other (ignoring transaction costs).

Value of the US$ bond after one year = US$500,000 × 1.03 = US$515,000
If US$ are exchanged for ¥   US$500,000 × 115 = ¥57,500,000
Value of the ¥ bond after one year   = ¥57,500,000 × 1.0005 = ¥57,528,750
And ¥ are then exchanged for US$ ¥57,528,750 @ 111.706 = US$515,000

They are the same (apart from rounding differences) as they should be by definition.

Worked Example 12.5

The Purchasing Power Parity Theory of exchange rates says that the expected change in spot exchange rates equals the expected difference in inflation rates. If inflation in the USA is forecast at 2% ($p_\$$) this year and Japan's inflation is forecast at a minus 0.92% (p_Y), we can calculate the expected spot rate one year ahead (e_t), given a current spot rate of 115 ¥/US$ (s_0).

$$\frac{p_Y - p_\$}{1 + p_\$} = \frac{e_t - s_0}{s_0}$$

therefore $e_t = [(p_Y - p_\$)/(1 + p_\$) + 1] \times s_0$

$\qquad = [(1 + p_Y)/(1 + p_\$)] \times s_0$

$\qquad e_t = [(1 - 0.0092)/(1 + 0.02)] \times 115 = 111.706$ (approximately)

Worked Example 12.6

The Fisher Effect says that the expected difference in inflation rates equals the difference in current interest rates and therefore real interest rates should be equal. If inflation in the US is forecast at 2% this year and Japan's inflation is forecast at minus 0.92%, and interest rates are 0.05% and 3% per annum in Japan and the USA respectively, we can illustrate that the real interest rate in each country is about the same.

$$\text{Japan real interest rate} = \frac{1.0005}{0.9908} = 1.0098 = 0.98\%$$

$$\text{USA real interest rate} = \frac{1.03}{1.02} = 1.0098 = 0.98\%$$

Worked Example 12.7

Nishanota can manufacture one of its passenger car models in the UK for a total cost of £11,200, including its profit margin. At a current exchange rate of 0.56 £/US$ the car sells for US$20,000 in the USA. If the US$ is expected to rise in value against £ sterling to an exchange rate of 0.60 £/US$, we can calculate what price the car may be sold at by Nishanota in the USA while still protecting its profit margin.

$$\frac{£11,200}{0.60} = US\$18,667$$

If the US$ had been expected to fall in value against £ sterling to an exchange rate of say 0.55 £/US$, the price would have to have been increased to over US$20,000 at US$20,364.

The exchange rate equivalency models' theories and hypotheses' explanations of movements in interest rates, inflation rates, spot currency exchange rates, and forward currency exchange rates form a basis for many international financial management techniques. However, the validity of these interrelationships is not beyond question, and evidence from research undertaken over the last 25 years remains inconclusive as to the precise nature of the relationship between interest rates, inflation rates, and exchange rate movements. There are concerns regarding the lack of empirical support with regard to both the short-term and long-term validity of many of the model's underpinning theories and hypotheses.

- Fisher Effect – some researchers have found a positive relationship between interest rate movements and inflation rate movements whilst other researchers have found little evidence of such a relationship.

- Interest Rate Parity Theory – empirical testing has suggested that an actual relationship between interest rate differentials and forward exchange rate premiums and discounts may exist in the shorter term, although substantial deviations were found in the medium to longer term.

- Purchasing Power Parity Theory – some researchers have found that purchasing power parity does hold in the medium to longer term. Other researchers have found significant deviations, leading to suggestions that other influential factors beyond the inflation and exchange rate relationship may impact differently on inflation rates and exchange rates.

- International Fisher Effect – some researchers have found Fisher's open hypothesis to hold well in the medium to longer term, whereas other researchers have found significant deviations.

- Expectations Theory – researchers have found conflicting evidence. Some have found that the forward rate is a good unbiased predictor of the future exchange rate, whilst other researchers have found this not to be the case.

Such criticisms imply that the assumption that market forces, underpinned by an implicit interrelationship between interest rates, inflation rates, and exchange rates freely determine the movements of currency exchange rates is clearly not the case. The reason for this is that often the largest player within the foreign exchange market, the government central bank, intervenes for reasons other than those of profit maximisation. The intervention of government central banks in the foreign exchange markets often occurs for other than primarily economic reasons.

Despite the criticisms, the exchange rate equivalency model is a useful model that has been deduced from the series of interrelationship between the relative levels of:

- interest rates
- inflation rates
- purchasing power,

which provides an approximation of how the interaction of inflation rates and interest rates may affect the movement of currency exchange rates.

In the absence of any significant market imperfections, arbitrage opportunities, political, and economic barriers to the mobility of international capital, the exchange rate equivalency model provides an opportunity to estimate and predict the effects and impact of changes in:

- inflation rates, on interest rates
- interest rates, on currency exchange rates
- inflation rates, on currency exchange rates
- spot exchange rates of a particular currency, on forward exchange rates of that particular currency.

Interest rate risk

Interest rate risk is faced by businesses, which may be either or both lenders or borrowers of funds. If a company borrows money at a specific rate of interest it faces a risk that market interest rates may subsequently fall and so it will have an opportunity cost of interest (and *vice versa* an opportunity gain should market interest rates increase). If a company lends by investing surplus funds at a specific rate of interest it faces a risk that market interest rates may subsequently increase and so it will have an opportunity cost of lost interest (and *vice versa* an opportunity gain of interest should market interest rates fall).

The way in which interest rates affect lenders or borrowers of funds depends on whether the agreed rates are fixed or floating rates. Floating rates of interest are usually stated as the LIBOR (London Interbank Offer Rate) rate of interest + or − a number of percentage points (for example, LIBOR + 2%). Therefore, interest paid or received will vary as LIBOR varies.

The impacts on lenders or borrowers of funds at fixed or floating rates may be broadly summarised as follows:

- A borrower of funds at a fixed interest rate faces the risk of a fall in general interest rates. This is because competitors who have borrowed at floating rates will benefit from lower interest payments, higher profit, improved cash flow, and lower financial risk and therefore a lower cost of capital.

- A borrower of funds at a floating interest rate faces the risk of:
  - a rise in general interest rates, resulting in higher interest payments, reduced profit, worsened cash flow, and higher financial risk and therefore a higher cost of capital
  - inaccurate and unreliable forecasts of future interest cash outflows
  - the possibility of bankrupty following large increases in interest rates, particularly if their level of gearing is high.

- A lender of funds at a fixed interest rate faces the risk of a rise in general interest rates. This is because competitors who have invested at floating rates will benefit from higher interest receipts, higher profit, and improved cash flow.

- A lender of funds at a floating interest rate faces the risk of:
  - a fall in general interest rates, resulting in lower interest receipts, reduced profit, and worsened cash flow
  - inaccurate and unreliable forecasts of future interest cash inflows.

In addition to the above situations, interest rate risk occurs when a business may be a lender and also a borrower of funds. It is unlikely that a company will have loans and investments of the same level at floating or fixed rates of interest, but if they do then the financial risk of borrowing may offset to some extent the risk of lending. It is probably more likely that a company will have loans and investments at differing floating rates or at floating rates that may or may not both be linked to LIBOR.

- A company which is both the lender and borrower faces the risk of:
  - loans and investments which are not similar in size
  - different floating rates
  - floating rates that are inconsistently based (for example linked to LIBOR)
  - interest rate revisions at different dates.

Progress check 12.2

What is interest rate risk?

Exchange rate risk

In increasingly global markets, businesses are even more likely to be engaged in transactions denominated in currencies other than that of their own country. A foreign currency exchange rate is broadly the rate at which one unit of a currency may be exchanged for one unit of another currency. The rates at which currencies may be exchanged today are different from the rates at which currencies may be exchanged, for example, next week, next month, or next year.

The exchange rates at which currencies may be bought and sold today are determined by a number of factors but effectively reflect the demand and supply of the currencies. There is a spread between the rate at which a currency is bought and the rate at which it is sold. The spreads of rates for immediate buying or selling are called the **spot rates**. The spot rate actually means the exchange rate at which a currency is bought or sold today for value two working days later.

The exchange rates at which currencies may be bought and sold some time in the future are called **forward rates**. Forward rates are determined by the amount of time elapsing between now and the future transaction date and the differential between the core interest rates applicable to each currency. The table in Fig. 12.4 illustrates the spreads of exchange rates at which a customer may buy or sell euros from or to a bank in exchange for £ sterling, at the spot rates, and the rates in three months' time, six months' time, and one year's time. For example, a customer could buy €1 from the bank (bank sells) for spot £0.6793, or sell €1 to the bank (bank buys) for £0.6790 spot on 19 May 2006.

	Bank buys euros	Bank sells euros
Spot rate	0.6790	0.6793
One month forward	0.6800	0.6803
Three months forward	0.6819	0.6822
One year forward	0.6897	0.6900

Figure 12.4 Euro/£ sterling forward exchange rates at 19 May 2006

The table in Fig. 12.4 shows that each of the €/£ forward rates are higher than the spot rates. The forward rates are said to be at a **discount** to the spot rates. This is because at 19 May 2006 the € interest rate would have been higher than the UK £ sterling rate of interest. If forward exchange rates are lower than the spot rates they would be described as being at a **premium** to the spot rates.

The table in Fig. 12.5 illustrates the way in which exchange rates are generally quoted in the financial media, as follows:

19 May 2006			
Spot	3 months	6 months	1 year
0.6790 – 0.6793	+10/10	+29/29	+107/107

Figure 12.5 Example of Euro/£ sterling forward exchange rate

The plus sign means that the forward rate is at a discount to the spot rate and the three months bank selling forward rate is $0.6793 + 0.0029 = 0.6822$ €/£. If the € interest rate was lower than the UK £ sterling interest rate then the € forward rates would be a premium to the £ and the appropriate premiums (for example – 10/10) would be deducted from the spot rates. Very often the + and – signs are not quoted in the media and it is assumed that it is known whether or not a forward exchange rate is at a premium or a discount.

Progress check 12.3

What is meant by describing a forward exchange rate as being at a premium or at a discount?

Exchange rate risk arises because the values of foreign currencies are not now fixed against some standard like gold but 'float' so that their comparative values vary from day to day due to the influence of, for example, economic and political factors. Economic risk, for example, relates to the risk of the impact of long-term movements in exchange rates on the competitive position of companies engaged in international markets. Economic risk may be avoided by not trading in such markets, but that does not avoid the economic risk of the company's home country. The exposure of businesses to exchange rate risk is broadly defined within two classifications, which are called transaction exposure and translation exposure. Transaction exposures relate to relatively short-term revenue transactions and translation exposures relate to the balance sheet and generally for periods in excess of one year.

Businesses may be engaged in transactions with suppliers or customers in countries other than their own country. A UK business may sell overseas or buy from overseas but may not necessarily invoice the customer or be invoiced by the supplier in £ sterling. An overseas customer may not accept an invoice in £ sterling because they require to be invoiced in their own domestic currency. An overseas supplier may insist on invoicing in their own domestic currency. The cost of selling or buying a currency on the day that a transaction takes place is related to the exchange rate on that day which is known by both parties to the transaction. If the transaction is paid and settled on that day then no risk or exposure arises.

Most business transactions are credit transactions, where goods or services are not paid for until some time after the original transaction. Foreign exchange rate risk arises precisely because such credit terms are given. If goods and services are purchased in the currency of the vendor then the business has a payables foreign exchange transaction exposure. If the business contracts to sell in the currency of the customer then the business has a receivables foreign exchange transaction exposure. Transaction exposure is therefore the risk of a difference occurring on a foreign currency transaction between the value of the transaction in local currency at the transaction date and the value of the transaction in local currency at the settlement date. The transaction exposure is due to a risk of a movement in the exchange rate between those two dates.

Worked Example 12.8

A customer in the USA insists on being invoiced for goods amounting to US$10,000 in US$ by Bruce plc, which is a UK company. At the time of delivery of the goods the value of the US$ sale in £ at the exchange rate on 13 May was £6,250 (£ = US$1.60). The US$10,000 sales invoice was issued a few days later and the exchange rate had changed to £ = US$1.62, which equals £6,173. The customer had agreed payment for two months later and the day they settled the invoice the exchange rate had moved again to £ = US$1.75, which equals £5,714. What is the value of the sale?

The value attributed to a sales invoice is its £ value on the day if invoiced in £ sterling. However, if a sales invoice is rendered in foreign currency SSAP 20 requires it to be valued at the exchange rate at the date of the transaction, or at an average rate for the period if exchange rates do not fluctuate significantly. In the above example the US$10,000 sale should be recorded at £1 = US$1.60 which equals £6,250. The US$10,000 was received two months later when £ sterling had appreciated to 1.75 against the US$ and so the US$10,000 was now worth only £5,714. Bruce plc therefore made a loss on exchange of £536 (£6,250 – £5,714).

Transaction exposure relates to transactions and current assets and current liabilities denominated in foreign currencies, generally occurring within one year. Assets and liabilities appearing on a company's year-end balance sheet must be translated using the company's local currency at the exchange rate at each balance sheet date. The precise exchange rate used for valuation may be, for example, the market closing rates on those dates or may be forward rates (which we shall discuss later). In addition, this issue arises particularly with regard to the translation of the assets and liabilities of overseas subsidiaries, which are denominated in the currencies of their country. For a holding company, at each year-end date the assets and liabilities of its overseas subsidiaries must be translated at the appropriate year-end exchange rates into its local currency for consolidation into its group accounts. Translation exposure relates to the risk that such translations may result in losses or gains as a result of movements in exchange rates.

Worked Example 12.9

A UK company has taken on a long-term loan of US$500m. In the first year at 31 December £1 = US$1.75 and in the second year at 31 December £1 = US$1.65. What is the translation loss to the company between years 1 and 2?

	US$m	31 December exchange rate	£m
year 1	500	1.75	285.7
year 2	500	1.65	303.0
year 2 translation loss			17.3

Throughout the life of the loan the company will have translation exposures because of the movements in the £/US$ exchange rate over the period of the loan.

The assets and liabilities of a company that has transactions in foreign currencies are originally valued using the exchange rates at the time that the original transactions took place. The assets and liabilities that have not been realised in cash by the date that the next balance sheet is prepared must then be revalued at the exchange rates effective at the balance sheet date. These revaluations will result in a foreign exchange gain or loss and will therefore affect reported profit, but because they are unrealised such translation exposures are effectively only 'paper' transactions and therefore do not affect cash flows. Gains and losses on exchange will affect cash flow only when the assets and liabilities are realised and valued at the exchange rates on the dates they are paid. Nevertheless, for public companies, translation exposures may have a significant impact on their market perception because of their effect on profit.

Financial risk management

Businesses may manage the types of financial risk we have described above, relating to exchange rates and interest rates, by matching and offsetting assets and liabilities and cash flows, or choosing particular types of assets and liabilities. The following are examples of the management of such risk exposure, which are concerned with balance sheet structure:

■ An export company may invoice customers in its own currency only, thus avoiding any foreign currency exchange rate risk, but at the same time incurring a business risk of lost sales opportunities from customers who prefer to be invoiced in their own currencies.

■ Interest rate risk may be mitigated if companies hold a mix of loans with both fixed and floating interest rates – an increase in interest rates provides a benefit from holding fixed interest loans, whereas a reduction in interest rates provides a benefit from having floating interest loans.

■ Foreign currency exchange rate transaction risk may be reduced if accounts payable denominated in specific foreign currencies are matched and offset against accounts receivable denominated in the same currencies.

■ Foreign currency exchange rate transaction risk may be reduced if accounts payable denominated in specific foreign currencies are paid perhaps earlier than the agreed settlement dates if exchange rates are expected to move unfavourably over the subsequent period.

■ Foreign currency exchange rate translation risk may be reduced by a company increasing its liabilities through borrowing in the same currency as the currency in which a non-current asset is purchased, the term of the loan being the same as the anticipated life of the asset.

Management of its assets and liabilities is not the only technique that a company may use to reduce or mitigate financial risk. The past 30 years or so has seen an enormous increase in the various types of **hedging** techniques that are available to businesses in the management of their risk exposure. These started with **foreign exchange forward contracts**, and **money market hedging** (of interest rates) and **forward interest rate agreements** (FRAs) through lending and borrowing in the money market. Since the early days hedging techniques have been developed into a huge range of what are called **derivatives** (see the section later on the use of derivatives). A derivative is defined in FRS 13 as a financial instrument that derives its value from the price or rate of some underlying item, which includes equities, bonds, commodities, interest rates, exchange rates, and stock market and other indices. Derivatives include **futures contracts**, **swaps**, **options**, and **swaptions**. Options (not to be confused with foreign exchange option forward contracts) may either be standard **traded options** or **over-the-counter** (OTC) **options**.

Hedging financial risks

Foreign exchange forward contracts

Foreign exchange forward contracts are used by businesses or individuals to buy or sell agreed amounts of currencies for delivery at specified future dates. Such contracts may be fixed foreign exchange forward contracts or option foreign exchange forward contracts. A fixed foreign exchange forward contract is a contract, for example, between a company and a bank, to exchange two currencies at an agreed exchange rate on a specific date (see Worked Example 12.10). A foreign exchange forward option contract extends this idea to allow the bank or the company to call for settlement of the contract, at two days' notice, between any two dates that have been agreed between the bank and the company at the time of agreeing the contract (see Worked Example 12.11).

Worked Example 12.10

A UK company, Broadcal plc expects to receive €100,000 from a customer at a specified date in three months' time. Today's spot rate against £ sterling is 1.4650 and the three-month fixed forward rate to sell € for £ is 1.4550. The company anticipates that £ sterling may strengthen against the € over the next few months in which case they would receive fewer pounds when they sell their €. They would prefer to 'fix' the amount now that they are going to realise in £ sterling in three months' time. They can do this by selling €100,000 to their bank at 1.4550 by promising to deliver €100,000 in three months' time, at which time they will receive £68,729 in return.

Alternatively, the company in Worked Example 12.10 may consider a foreign exchange forward option instead of a fixed foreign exchange forward contract.

Worked Example 12.11

Broadcal plc expects to receive €100,000 from a customer at any time over the next three months up to a specific date. Today's spot rate against £ sterling is 1.4650 and the three-month forward option rate to sell € for £ is 1.4600. The company anticipates that £ sterling may strengthen against the € over the next few months in which case they would receive fewer pounds when they sell their €. They would prefer to 'fix' the amount now that they are going to realise in £ sterling over the next three months. They can do this by selling €100,000 to their bank at 1.4600 by promising to deliver €100,000 at any time over the next three months (up to an agreed date), at which time they will receive £68,493 in return.

As we can see from Worked Examples 12.10 and 12.11, in forward contracts the cash flows occur not when an agreement is made but at the dates specified in the agreement. Forward contracts provide a hedge against downside risk through protection from adverse exchange rate (or interest rate) movements. However, such contracts, which are normally arranged through banks, are legally binding contracts and so any potential benefits from favourable movements exchange rates (and interest rates) are lost.

If a transaction is to be settled at a contracted exchange rate using a forward foreign exchange contract then the exchange rate specified in the contract should be used to value that purchase or sale in the accounts of the business. Such a trading transaction is then said to be covered by a matching forward contract.

At the end of each accounting period, all debtors denominated in a foreign currency should be translated, or revalued, using the rates of exchange ruling at the period-end date, or, where appropriate, the rates of exchange determined under the terms of any relevant forward contract currency agreements. Where there are related or matching forward contracts in respect of trading transactions, the rates of exchange specified in those contracts should be used.

A similar treatment applies to all monetary assets and liabilities denominated in a foreign currency, that is, cash and bank balances, loans, and amounts payable and receivable. An exchange gain or loss will result during an accounting period if a business transaction is settled at an exchange rate which differs from that used when the transaction was initially recorded, or, where appropriate, that used at the last balance sheet date. An exchange gain or loss will also arise on unsettled transactions if the rate of exchange used at the balance sheet date differs from that used previously. Such gains and losses are recognised during each accounting period and are included in the profit or loss from ordinary activities.

Progress check 12.4

UK International Ltd invoiced a customer in the USA for goods to the value of US$50,000 on 31 December. The US$ cheque sent to UK International by the customer was received on the following 31 January and was converted into £ sterling by the bank at US$1.7850 to £1. Discuss the two transactions, the invoice and its settlement, and their impact on UK International's income statement and its balance sheet as at 31 December 2005.

Money market hedging

A money market hedge may be used by companies, for example, who want to borrow funds for a specific period for an investment at some time in the future, but are also expecting an increase in interest rates by that time. Exposure to this risk may be hedged by borrowing funds now for the whole term until the end of the required specific period. The funds are then placed on deposit at market rates until the loan is actually required. If interest rates fall or rise in the period before when the loan is actually needed, the company will either pay more or less loan interest but also receive more or less deposit interest. Any loss would be considered a cost of hedging against the risk of paying a higher interest rate over the specific period of the loan.

Eurocurrency loans are another means of money market hedging. Eurocurrency is nothing to do with Europe or the euro. Eurocurrency refers to funds deposited in a bank when those funds are denominated in a currency differing from the bank's own domestic currency. A eurocurrency loan may provide a hedge against an exposure to foreign exchange rate risk.

The company in Worked Example 12.10 may consider a money market hedge as shown in Worked Example 12.12, instead of a fixed foreign exchange forward contract.

Worked Example 12.12

Broadcal plc expects to receive €100,000 from a customer at a specified date in three months' time and would like this settled at today's spot rate against £ sterling of 1.4650. The company anticipates that £ sterling may strengthen against the € over the next few months in which case they would receive fewer pounds when they sell their €. Broadcal plc can negotiate an immediate € loan from its bank, and it can immediately exchange the € for £ sterling at the spot rate of 1.4650. The proceeds may then be used to earn interest on deposit for three months. The €100,000 received in three months' time is then used to repay the € loan to the bank.

Assume that the € loan interest rate is 6.5% per annum (1.625% for 3 months), and £ sterling deposit interest rate is 5.0% per annum (1.25% for 3 months):

The value of the € to be borrowed is 100,000/1.01625 = €98,401

(€98,401 borrowed for 3 months is 98,401 × 1.01625 = 100,000)

The £ sterling value of €98,401 = 98,401/1.4650 = £67,168

The value of £67,168 in 3 months' time = 67,168 × 1.0125 = £68,008

Broadcal plc may not actually use this hedge since the amount of £ sterling received (£68,008) is less than that obtained from using the fixed foreign exchange forward contract (£68,729) as we saw in Worked Example 12.12.

Progress check 12.5

What is hedging?

Forward interest rate agreement (FRA)

A company may enter into agreements with a bank concerning interest rates relating to its future borrowing or lending. Such forward interest rate agreements (FRAs) are normally used only for very large sums of money (millions rather than thousands of pounds) and for periods of more than one year. An FRA, for example, may fix the interest rate on a loan at a specific date in the future. If interest rates rise and the actual rate on the specific future date is higher than the FRA rate then the bank will pay the difference to the company. If interest rates fall and the actual rate on the specific future date is lower than the FRA rate then the company will pay the difference to the bank.

An FRA may be used by a company to protect the downside interest rate risk on its borrowings. On the other hand, the company will not gain from any favourable interest rate movements.

The use of derivatives

Financial Reporting Standard 13: Derivatives and other financial instruments: disclosures, (FRS 13), defines a derivative as a financial instrument that derives its value from the price or rate of some underlying item, which include equities, bonds, commodities, interest rates, exchange rates, and stock market and other indices.

The use of derivatives has been a hot topic over the past few years and there are many *pros* and *cons* related to their use. Not least of these is the International Accounting Standards debate about their disclosure or not in the reports and accounts of public companies. Derivatives do represent financial commitments for a company, which may give rise to losses, and they may also present an opportunity for their misuse through unauthorised trading. Their proper use provides significant benefits for companies, but their misuse, as demonstrated by Nick Leeson, resulting in the downfall of Barings Bank, may be avoided through appropriate management controls, monitoring systems, and risk management. Management controls include:

- authorised limits on individual deals and positions
- limitations as to the types of derivatives used.

Monitoring systems include:

- regular valuation and monitoring of dealers' positions
- reporting on unauthorised dealing.

Risk management includes:

- setting the exposure policy for the treasury function: a profit centre or a cost centre
- a foreign exchange rate and interest rate exposure risk management strategy appropriate to the particular business
- identification and measurement of likely risk exposures
- selection of appropriate management techniques, hedging techniques, and derivatives.

The short-term aspect of the use of derivatives with regard to financing should be noted. They only have a relatively short life and are therefore only able to mitigate changes in the prices or rates of the underlying items, such as interest rates and exchange rates, for a limited period of time.

So, what are these derivatives, which are available to companies and have generated so much excitement? We will look at the following, which are some of the main financial instruments available to companies:

- options
- futures
- swaps
- swaptions.

Progress check 12.6

What is a derivative?

Options

Options are not the same as forward contract options, but are more similar to share options. Options are available as currency options and as interest rate options. A currency option is an agreement that enables a company to buy or sell an amount of foreign currency at a specified exchange rate at some future date. The agreement gives the right to the company to buy or sell but it is under no obligation to do so and may simply abandon the option. Similarly, share options provide an agreement with the right to buy or sell shares at a specific share price, and interest rate options provide an agreement with the right to borrow or lend at a specific interest rate, and again the company is under no obligation to buy or sell. Each of these types of option is used to reduce or eliminate risk exposure, by providing the flexibility to take advantage of favourable foreign currency exchange rate, share price, and interest rate movements.

Options are useful for companies who need to issue price lists for their goods or services in foreign currencies, or who make tenders for overseas contracts in foreign currencies. In both situations, companies do not have a certainty of receiving specific amounts of foreign currency at specific dates and therefore foreign currency forward contracts would not be appropriate. They need a financial instrument that provides flexibility to deal with variable and uncertain foreign currency cash flows. The cost of this flexibility is an **option premium**, which has to be paid when the option is bought and is non-returnable.

The right to borrow or lend a specific amount of money by a particular date at a guaranteed interest rate, the **strike rate**, can be provided with an interest rate option. The right must be exercised or not by the time the agreed date is reached. An interest rate option, for example, may guarantee the interest rate on a loan up to a specific date in the future. If interest rates fall and the actual rate by the date that the option expires is lower than the option rate then the company will not want to exercise the option. If interest rates rise and the actual rate by the date that the option expires is higher than the option rate then the company will want to exercise the option.

Variations of interest rate options are available which are called **interest rate caps** and **interest rate collars**. Interest rate caps are options in which there is a 'ceiling' interest rate (as opposed to a 'floor' interest rate). An interest rate collar enables a borrower to buy an interest rate cap and simultaneously sell an interest rate 'floor' which therefore fixes the minimum cost for the company, which is lower than if an interest cap only had been used. The trade-off for this cost minimisation is that the company will not derive the benefit from a fall in interest rates below the 'floor' level.

Worked Example 12.13

Jenkin plc currently borrows at 7% per annum. The finance director has advised that if interest rates were to rise above 8.5%, then this would represent a serious financial risk for the company at current gearing levels. Jenkin plc is therefore considering how it may benefit from a cap and collar agreement.

Jenkin plc may buy an interest rate cap at 8.5% from its bank, with a floor of 6.5%. The bank will have to reimburse Jenkin for the cost of any rise in interest rate above 8.5%. The bank pays Jenkin plc for agreeing to the floor of 6.5%, which Jenkin plc has effectively sold to the bank to partly offset the cost of the cap. If interest rates fall below the floor rate of 6.5% then the bank will benefit.

The premium for interest rate options is higher than FRA premiums. However, interest rate options may be standardised or tailor-made with regard to interest rates, amounts, currencies, and time periods.

Companies may obtain two different types of option:

- a traded option is available, for example, only for specific currencies, and is a standardised option with regard to its specified amount and term, and is bought and sold on an options exchange

- an over-the-counter (OTC) option is an option that is tailor-made by the bank to meet a company's specific requirements.

Traded options

Traded options are bought and sold on exchanges like LIFFE (the London International Financial Futures and Options Exchange). LIFFE is a London exchange for traded options (and futures contracts) and enables investors to hedge against the risk of movements in interest rates, gilt-edged securities prices, bonds prices, foreign currency exchange rates, and equity share prices. Similarly, for example, the New York Board of Trade (NYBOT) provides risk managers and investors with a marketplace for futures contracts and options in commodities such as sugar, cotton, coffee, and cocoa; and the Dubai Gold and Commodities Exchange (DGCX) is a marketplace for gold and silver, and also steel, cotton, and other commodities.

The standard sizes of options tend to be fairly large (for example, in units of the equivalent of millions of £ sterling), and they mature every quarter in March, June, September, and December. A traded option to buy currency or borrow funds is called a **call option** and an option to sell currency or lend funds is called a **put option**. A currency option may be agreed at the spot rate (termed **at the money**) or at a more or less favourable rate than the spot rate (termed **out of the money**). **American options** are options that can be exercised at any time within the specified option period. **European options** must be exercised at the end of the specified option period.

Disadvantages of traded options are that they are not negotiable and are not available for every currency. Traded option premiums are typically about 5% of the total transaction, and must be paid for when they are purchased, but the determination of actual premiums is a complicated process (in much the same way as applies to traded options in securities), which is dependent on:

- the movements and volatility of the foreign currency exchange rates and interest rates markets
- the strike price
- the time periods up to when the options expire.

An increase in interest rates, for example, will reduce the value of interest rate put options but increase the value of interest rate call options. Put options and call options, however, will both have a greater value in volatile currency and interest rate markets. The higher the volatility the more opportunity there is for the company having the option to gain; equally, the greater is the potential for a loss for the bank which is creating the option, and therefore the premium they charge is higher.

The higher the strike price of an interest rate option contract, the higher the price of a put option and the lower the price of a call option. An option becomes more valuable the longer the time there is until its expiry date, because it can continue to be used as a hedge by a company against adverse interest rate or currency exchange rates movements.

The value of an option can be divided into two parts: **time value** and **intrinsic value**. The time value of an option is a reflection of current interest rates. An option that is out of the money has no intrinsic value, but it can still have time value. The time value of an option is at its maximum at the start of the option period and proportionately decreases throughout the option period down to zero at the option expiry date.

The intrinsic value of the option is the difference between the strike rate and the current rate. It represents the value of an option if it is exercised immediately and only has a value if it is **in the money**. If it is out of the money it does not have an intrinsic value. For example, if a euro/sterling currency option is agreed with a strike rate of €1.55/£ and the current exchange rate is €1.45/£, then it is in the money and will have intrinsic value. However, if the option had been agreed with a strike rate of €1.35/£ it would be out of the money and would not have an intrinsic value.

Over the counter (OTC) options

Companies can obtain OTCs from banks and other financial institutions and they are tailor-made to meet the specific requirements of the company. An OTC agreement includes the name of the foreign currency or the interest rate, the amount, and the period of the term of the option. OTC options, as well as traded options, may also include floors, caps, and collars.

A foreign currency exchange rate or an interest rate floor provides a guaranteed rate of exchange, or a rate of interest, for a company to deal in at a future date should the exchange rate or interest rate move below this rate. A foreign currency exchange rate, or an interest rate, cap provides a guaranteed ceiling rate of exchange, or a rate of interest, for a company to deal in at a future date should the exchange rate or interest rate move above this rate. A collar combines the use of a floor and a cap by providing a lower and upper limit to an interest rate or exchange rate at which to buy or sell currencies, or borrow or lend funds. Worked Example 12.14 illustrates the use of a currency option.

Progress check 12.7

Describe put options and call options.

Worked Example 12.14

Dewdrop plc is tendering for a contract in US$ with a USA company called Snowdrop Inc. The expected cost of the contract is £1.85m but Dewdrop plc is prepared to accept a low margin in order to get the contract and is proposing a tender price of £2.0m. The contract will be awarded in six months' time. The current six-month forward US$/£ exchange rate is US$2.80 and so Dewdrop plc is prepared to bid a price of US$5.6m.

The board of Dewdrop plc is considering the use of using a currency option.

Let's first consider two possible loss-making scenarios. The first is where Dewdrop plc may arrange a forward currency contract and wait six months to see if it has been awarded the contract. The second is where Dewdrop plc arranges no forward cover but waits to see if it obtains the contract and then sells the US$ income at the spot rate in six months' time.

If Dewdrop assumes that it will be awarded the contract in six months' time then it may consider taking a six-month forward contract to sell US$5.6m at the six months forward rate of US$2.8/£. If after six months Dewdrop fails to get the contract then it will have to buy US$5.6m at the spot rate which we will assume has moved to US$2.5/£ to close out the forward contract.

▶

Dewdrop plc sale of US$5.6m six months forward at US$2.8/£	= £2.00m
Dewdrop plc purchase of US$5.6m at spot in six months' time at US$2.5/£	= £2.24m
Loss	= £0.24m

The second scenario is if Dewdrop does not take a six-month forward contract, but does nothing but wait six months to see if it is awarded the contract. Dewdrop may then be awarded the contract in six months' time when we will assume the spot rate may have fallen to US$3.2/£.

Dewdrop plc sale of US$5.6m at spot in six months' time at US$3.2/£	= £1.75m
Dewdrop plc cost of contract	= £1.85m
Loss	= £0.10m

Let's consider the situation if Dewdrop plc does neither of the above but instead arranges a currency option to sell US$5.6m at US$2.8/£ in six months' time at a fixed premium of £40,000.

If Dewdrop does not win the contract it can abandon the contract and its cost will be just the option premium of £40,000. But if at that time the US$ has weakened to say US$3.1/£ Dewdrop can make a profit by exercising the option contract and buying US$ at the spot rate:

Dewdrop plc sale of US$5.6m at the option rate in six months' time at US$2.8/£	= £2.00m
Dewdrop plc purchase of US$5.6m at the spot rate in six months' time at US$3.1/£	= £1.81m
Profit	= £0.19m

If Dewdrop wins the contract and the exchange rate is unchanged then Dewdrop can exercise the option:

Dewdrop plc sale of US$5.6m at the option rate in six months' time at US$2.8/£	= £2.00m
Option premium	= £0.04m
Dewdrop plc cost of contract	= £1.85m
Profit	= £0.11m

If Dewdrop wins the contract and the US$ has strengthened against £ sterling to, say, US$2.5/£ Dewdrop can abandon the option and sell its US$ at the spot rate:

Dewdrop plc sale of US$5.6m at the spot rate in six months' time at US$2.5/£	= £2.24m
Option premium	= £0.04m
Dewdrop plc cost of contract	= £1.85m
Profit	= £0.35m

There are a number of *pros* and *cons* for companies using options to cover interest rate or currency exchange rate exposure risk. The disadvantages are that:

- the premiums are high and so options are not a cheap method
- there is a difficulty in traded options being able to perfectly match both the duration and size of a company's exposure, because of their standardisation.

The advantages are:

- the opportunity to gain from favourable movements in exchange and interest rates
- that OTC options may be used to hedge non-standard interest rate and currency exchange rate exposures.

Futures

A futures contract is a contract like a forward contract, but with a futures contract an intermediary creates a standardised contract so that the two parties to the contract do not have to negotiate the terms of the contract. A financial future is an agreement between two parties on the future price of a financial variable at an agreed price. Futures on loans or deposits are used as a hedge against movements in interest rates. Similarly foreign currency futures are used as a hedge against movements in exchange rates. A futures contract is not an actual sale or purchase relating to loans or foreign currency. With a futures contract there is always a winner and a loser, which is unlike, for example, the sales and purchases of stocks and shares.

Financial futures contracts can be traded because they are standardised contracts. Forward contracts cannot be traded because they are not standardised. However, this disadvantage of forward contracts is balanced by the fact that they are not standardised and can be tailor-made in line with company requirements, with regard to their values and timespans. Futures are somewhat similar to traded options, as they are both standardised contracts, but futures require the payment of a **margin** rather than a premium. The margin is the percentage of a futures contract value that must be placed on deposit with a broker. Because a futures contract is not an actual sale, only a fraction of the value, the margin needs to be paid to open the contract.

If a company wants to protect itself against the risk of interest rates falling then it may buy interest rate futures contracts. If a company wants to protect itself against the risk of interest rates rising then it may sell interest rate futures contracts. Interest rate futures contracts generally have a standard size of US$1m and a period of three months. Interest rate futures contract prices are quoted by subtracting the interest rate from the nominal value of 100. For example, an interest rate futures contract nominal price of 91 means an interest rate of 9% (100 − 91). The minimum amount by which the price of an interest rate futures contract can move is called a **tick**. A tick is a movement of 0.01% of the contract price. Gains (or losses) on interest rate futures contracts are indicated by the changes in the nominal price.

The initial margin for a futures contract is usually around 1% to 3% of the contract value, payable to a futures exchange, for example the London International Futures and Options Exchange (LIFFE) in UK. LIFFE no longer offers currency futures, but these may still be traded on Far East and North American exchanges.

As with any other financial instrument, there are advantages and disadvantages with using currency and interest rate futures contracts. The advantages of futures contracts are:

- favourable movements in exchange rates and interest rates are credited immediately to the company's margin account
- futures contracts can be bought and sold on the futures markets which determine their prices
- an advance payment premium is not applicable to futures contracts.

The disadvantages with futures contracts are:

- because of their standardised contracts, futures contracts may not be a perfect hedge in terms of amounts and timing
- an advance premium does not have to be paid for futures contracts, but a margin must be paid
- futures contracts only hedge against downside risk – there are no opportunities of gains for companies from favourable movements in exchange rates and interest rates
- because markets are not totally efficient, basis risk exists where exchange rates and interest rates are not aligned with futures contracts prices and therefore futures contracts may not be 100% efficient.

Progress check 12.8

What are the differences between currency futures and forward foreign exchange contracts?

The way in which foreign currency exchange rate futures may be used is shown in Worked Example 12.15, and Worked Example 12.16 illustrates the use of interest rate futures.

Worked Example 12.15

Dewdrop plc is purchasing materials today, 28 February, in US$ from the USA company Snowdrop Inc. The cost is US$680,000 and payment has been agreed for 28 March. The spot rate to buy US$ is currently US$1.70/£ (which is also the 28 March futures price). The US$ can be bought forward at 28 March at US$1.58/£.

The board of Dewdrop plc is considering the use of currency futures, which may be bought and sold in blocks of £75,000 with a margin of 2%, compared with use of a forward exchange contract.

Dewdrop plc can use currency futures to hedge against the risk of £ sterling falling against the US$. The cost to buy US$680,000 at 28 March is £400,000 (US$680,000/1.70). The futures must be bought and sold in blocks of £75,000. Dewdrop plc, therefore, sells five US$ sterling futures contracts (which means the company takes delivery of US$ in return for £ sterling) at the rate of US$1.70/£. Dewdrop plc must also immediately deposit £1,500 (2% of £75,000) per contract with the futures exchange, a total of £7,500.

On 28 March Dewdrop plc must pay US$680,000 for the materials, at which time let's assume £ sterling will have weakened to spot rate US$1.60/£ to buy US$ and US$1.61/£ to sell US$.

Dewdrop plc has to 'close out' its futures contracts at US$1.61/£:

Giving a profit (US$680,000 @ 1.61 less US$680,000 @ 1.70) =	£22,360
Dewdrop plc buys US$680,000 @ 1.60 to pay Snowdrop Inc =	£425,000
Net cost to Dewdrop plc	= £402,640
Plus the margin	= £7,500
Total cost of materials using currency futures	= £410,140

We can compare this with the cost of a forward exchange contract US$1.58/£:

Dewdrop plc buys US$680,000 forward for delivery 28 March @ 1.58	= £430,379

If the board of Dewdrop plc believe there is a risk that the £ sterling may weaken against the US$ to around 1.60 by 28 March, then given the current spot and forward contract rates currency futures appear to be the cheapest option.

Worked Example 12.16

Dewdrop plc is taking a US$1m loan in three months' time for three months from 30 April. The current interest rate is 7% but the finance director is expecting that interest rates may rise over the next few months. The futures price is 92, and the interest rate is 8%.

If the interest rate at 31 July rose to 10%, what would be the benefit to Dewdrop plc of using an interest rate futures contract?

If the market were assumed to be inefficient, what would be the hedge efficiency if the futures price was 91, and the interest rate was still 8%?

Dewdrop plc would need to sell a US$1m interest rate futures contract at 92 to hedge against interest on the three-month loan required at 30 April.

At 31 July the contract price will have moved by the same amount as the interest rate, 90 and 10% respectively, which is 200 ticks [(10 − 8)/0.01]. One tick is

$$US\$1m \times 0.01\% \times 3/12 = US\$25.$$

At 31 July Dewdrop plc may close out its interest rate futures contract by buying a contract at 90 (100 − 10)

giving a profit (US$1m × 10% × 3/12 less US$1m × 8% × 3/12) = US$5,000
or 200 ticks × US$25   = US$5,000

Dewdrop plc may then offset the profit of US$5,000 against the higher cost of borrowing the US$1m at 10% at 31 July.

The cost of borrowing US$1m × 10% × 3/12   = US$25,000
compared with the cost at 8% of US$1m × 8% × 3/12 = US$20,000
an increase in interest of   US$5,000

The profit on closing out the futures contract is the same as the increase in cost of interest because the futures contract price is the same as the movement in interest rate and therefore it provides a perfect hedge with 100% efficiency.

If the interest rate was 8% but the futures price was 91, instead of the expected 92 in an efficient market, we now have an element of basis risk amounting to 92 − 91, or 1 percentage point. Basis risk gradually reduces over the period of the contract, which would be 0.33 percentage points over each of the three months. The level of basis risk indicates the level of efficiency of the hedge.

Dewdrop plc would need to sell a US$1m interest rate futures contract at 91 to hedge against interest on the three-month loan required at 30 April.

Now at 31 July Dewdrop plc gains only

[(10 − 9/0.01] or 100 ticks × US$25   = US$2,500

The additional higher interest cost of Dewdrop plc borrowing the US$1m at 10% at 31 July is

The cost of borrowing US$1m × 10% × 3/12   = US$25,000
compared with the cost at 8% of US$1m × 8% × 3/12 = US$20,000
an increase in interest of   US$5,000

The hedge effectively reduces the new interest cost by only US$2,500.

The efficiency of the hedge is therefore US$2,500/US$5,000 or 50%.

Swaps

The cash flows of some companies may vary as interest rates, exchange rates, commodity prices, etc. vary, resulting from particular risk profiles. Specific risk profiles may not be acceptable to companies. For example, a company may have a loan with a floating interest rate when in fact it would prefer a fixed interest rate. Or a company may have accounts receivable denominated in US$ when in fact it would prefer its receivables to be denominated in Japanese Yen. In 1981 swaps were devised to allow businesses to change their risk profiles to acceptable risk profiles.

Swaps can be arranged by companies as a hedge against currency exchange rates and interest rates exposures for relatively long time periods, at a relatively low cost compared with, say, options. Swaps are flexible not only with regard to the time period but are also flexible in terms of the amount, unlike standardised derivatives.

Swaps protect against downside risk but they don't enable companies to take advantage of opportunities arising from favourable currency and interest rate movements. There may also be a risk of default on, for example, payment of interest by one of the parties involved in the swap, and so it is crucial that swap agreements are only entered into with other parties who have only the highest credit status.

An interest rate swap is an agreement between two companies in which each company agrees to exchange the 'interest rate characteristics' of two different financial instruments of an identical loan. The mechanics of swaps are to effectively exploit the comparative advantages of a company's loans and currency dealings with another company's loans and currency dealings to provide both companies with a hedge against their exchange rate and their interest rate exposure risks. The companies do not normally deal directly with each other but deal through an intermediary, normally a bank, which receives a fee from both companies. Swaps are generally much longer-term derivatives than options and futures for periods of, for example, two years, five years, and even ten years. The interest rate swaps market is now much bigger than the currency swaps market, although currency swaps were the first swaps to be developed.

In a currency swap, two parties formally agree to swap amounts of currency and interest payments over an agreed period of time. A currency swap therefore also includes an interest rate swap. A currency swap between two companies can enable a company to borrow money in the particular foreign currency it requires while eliminating any exposure to exchange rate risk on the interest payments as well as exposure to exchange rate risk on the loan itself. Currency swaps can also facilitate, for example, a multinational group company's borrowing of money in international money markets through one of its companies based in a country (and currency) where interest rates are low, but which does not actually require the loan. The group company may then swap the loan into the currency in which they actually want to borrow at a lower rate than they would have paid if they had borrowed in that currency at the outset.

A currency swap procedure involves a number of steps, which may be summarised as follows:

- agree the currencies and the capital amounts to be included in the swap
- agree the period of the swap
- agree the exchange rate to be used in the swap (usually the current spot rate)
- exchange the agreed amounts of currencies between the two companies, for example £ sterling and French francs, at the agreed exchange rate
- exchange the interest payments between the two companies at agreed dates over the period of the swap
- at the maturity date of the swap, exchange back the swap amounts at the agreed exchange rate.

If they feel that it is to their advantage, companies may prefer to use variations of the currency swap described above. For example, companies may buy the required currencies at spot rates in the currency market and then exchange only interest payments and then at the maturity date of the swap, exchange the capital amounts at an agreed exchange rate.

As with interest rate swaps, currency swaps may comprise any combination of floating and fixed interest rates payable on the currency amounts to be swapped.

The following Worked Examples 12.17, 12.18, and 12.19 are examples of various types of currency swaps.

Worked Example 12.17

A German company has agreed to sell some large drilling equipment to a company in North America. It will be paid US$20m in three years' time in US$. The German company wants to arrange a currency swap to hedge its exchange rate risk exposure.

The German company may agree with another company to swap the US$ for Deutschmarks in three years' time at an agreed US$/£ exchange rate. The German company will give the other company US$20m in three years' time and receive Deutschmarks in return.

Worked Example 12.18

An American corporation has a subsidiary engineering company in the UK. The American group wants to purchase a small Scotch whisky distillery in Scotland (which is part of the UK). The USA group company needs a £1.32m loan to finance the purchase of the distillery. The US$/£ sterling spot rate is US$1 = £0.55.

The UK subsidiary of the US corporation also has a loan requirement. It wants to raise US$2.4m to purchase some state-of-the-art machine tools which it will import from the USA. For both companies to eliminate their foreign exchange exposure risk they could borrow in their own countries on behalf of each other. The USA parent company could borrow the US$2.4m, and the UK subsidiary company could borrow the £1.32m.

Worked Example 12.19

A French water company has agreed to buy some new water treatment equipment from a company in the UK, which will be paid for in £ sterling. The water company is considering the use of a currency swap to eliminate its foreign currency exchange rate exposure risk.

The water company can fund the £ sterling purchase of the equipment with a fixed interest £ sterling loan from a UK bank, on which interest is payable monthly. The water company's income is all denominated in French francs, and so its finance director has had discussions with a French bank about the possibility of a currency swap. The swap agreement will have an agreed exchange rate used to convert the £ sterling loan into a French francs loan, which will have a floating interest rate. The equivalent French francs capital sum will be used to calculate the French francs floating rate monthly interest payments which the water company will make to the bank, in return for the bank paying to the water company the £ sterling monthly interest payments on its £ sterling loan, which it will then pay on to the UK bank.

At the end of the period of the swap the water company will repay the French francs capital sum to the French bank and in return will receive a £ sterling payment, converted at the agreed exchange rate, which it will use to repay its £ sterling loan to the UK bank.

The currency swap will have enabled the French water company to make its £ sterling interest payments and repay its £ sterling loan in its own currency, French francs, and so avoid any exposure to exchange rate risk.

An interest rate swap is an arrangement whereby two companies contractually agree to exchange payments on different terms, one at a fixed interest rate and the other at a floating interest rate. With an interest rate swap it is the comparative advantages of each company's floating or fixed interest rates that provide the opportunity for both companies to gain.

The **plain vanilla swap**, or generic swap, is the commonest form of interest rate swap. The floating interest payments on a specific loan amount for a specific period are swapped with the fixed interest payments based on the same loan amount for the same period. In a plain vanilla swap there is:

- a fixed interest rate paying company
- a floating interest rate paying company.

One company may have a better credit rating and an absolute advantage over another company because it can borrow at a lower fixed rate and a lower floating rate. However, the other company may have a comparative advantage over the first company because its floating rate as a percentage of its fixed rate is lower than the same percentage for the first company. The swap gain is the spread of fixed rates less the spread of floating rates.

Progress check 12.9

What is an interest rate swap agreement?

The plain vanilla swap is best illustrated with an example.

Worked Example 12.20

Two companies, Lofix plx and Hifix plc, make their interest payments yearly.

	Lofix plc	Hifix plc
fixed rate	6.0%	7.0%
floating rate	LIBOR	LIBOR + 0.3%

Lofix borrows US$1m at its fixed interest rate of 6%, and Hifix borrows US$1m at its floating interest rate of LIBOR + 0.3%. The companies think that they can both gain by swapping interest payments. If LIBOR is 4.75%, and the bank's arrangement charge is 0.2%, what swap can be made and what is the gain for each company?

Lofix has an absolute advantage because it can borrow at a lower fixed rate and a lower floating rate than Hifix. But Hifix has a comparative advantage over Lofix because its floating rate is proportionately less expensive than Lofix at 72.1% (5.05/7) versus 79.2% (4.75/6).

If the two companies swap interest payments then:

- Hifix is better off by 1% because it is paying interest at 6% instead of 7%.
- Lofix is worse off by 0.3% because it is paying 5.05% (4.75 + 0.3) instead of 4.75%.
- If Hifix makes a payment of 0.3% to Lofix, then Lofix is neither better nor worse off.
- But, Hifix is still 0.7% better off.

The benefits of the swap need to be split evenly between Lofix and Hifix and so:

- Hifix will therefore have to make a 0.35% payment to Lofix so that Lofix will then have a floating rate of LIBOR − 0.35%, which is 4.4%.
- Hifix will then have a fixed rate of 7% − 0.35%, which is 6.65%.
- Both companies are better off by 0.35%.

In fact, Lofix plc and Hifix plc would not actually swap interest payments, but they would make balancing payments from one to the other for the difference between the fixed and floating rate. The balancing payments will vary as the floating rate varies. The swap would be arranged for the companies through their bank as an intermediary and the arrangement fee charged by the bank will reduce the benefit gained from the swap by both companies.

The bank's arrangement fee is 0.2% to be shared between Hifix plc and Lofix plc, 0.1% each, as follows:

- Lofix would therefore have a final floating rate of LIBOR − 0.25%, which is 4.5%.
- Hifix would have a final fixed rate of 7% − 0.25%, which is 6.75%.
- Both companies gain by 0.25% (and the bank will be better off by 0.2%).

There are other types of interest rate swaps besides plain vanilla swaps, for example basis swaps which involve the swap of two floating rate interest payments that have been determined on different bases.

Swaptions

A further variation on the swap is the swaption, which is really a combination of a swap and an option. Swaptions are like options but, although they may have lower premiums than options, they are not as flexible because companies cannot benefit from favourable exchange rate and interest rate movements.

Financial risk management strategy

We have discussed ways in which businesses may manage to reduce or mitigate particular types of financial risk relating to exchange rates and interest rates through:

- matching and offsetting assets and liabilities and cash flows
- choosing particular types of assets and liabilities
- hedging.

The hedging strategy adopted differs from one company to another. A company may, for example, hedge none of its exposures, or all of its exposures, or 70% of its exposures. The strategy relating to the level of hedging must be determined with regard to an assessment of the expected benefits from hedging or the potential losses that may arise from not hedging. Despite the many disadvantages of hedging, like high costs and the complex nature of derivatives, our own first-hand experience of treasury management in multinational companies has identified many benefits from hedging:

- protection of downside risk – an insurance policy to provide a 'guaranteed' income level over the short term

- avoidance of bankrupty resulting from large interest rate rises, where the company is highly geared
- smoothing of cash flows for more accurate forecasting and planning
- competitive advantage gained from reducing the risk from high gearing and high levels of foreign currency exposures
- opportunities for changing the nature of existing debt or increasing further borrowing resulting from interest rate hedging.

Hedging is used to reduce or mitigate risk, but the use of hedging itself is not without its own risks. In the mid-1990s the Barings Bank debacle saw losses of almost £1bn in futures on the Far East exchanges, which resulted in the bank going under. This happened as a result of the bank's inadequate internal control systems relating to the activities of their dealers, and in particular trader Nick Leeson. More recently in the 2000s during the investigations into the fall of Enron, the company's imaginative activities in the unregulated sector of the over-the-counter derivatives market illustrated the problems of such unregulated trading in derivatives (see the press extract below).

Derivatives – beware!

'As derivatives unravel, it's your lookout', by Edmond Warner

US power group Enron's collapse points to inherent dangers in the use of unregulated financial instruments.

I've always subscribed to the KISS principle of investing – Keep It Simple, Stupid. Not because I can't see the benefits offered by, say, derivative instruments, but because I recognise that, up against the collective intellect of the market, I am indeed stupid. The spectacular collapse of Enron at least reassures me that I am not alone.

A derivative need not be a complex financial instrument. It need not be a dangerous one. But in the hands of criminals and cretins it is often both. Whether Enron's management were one or the other – or both – will doubtless become clear over the years that it will take for litigation to work through its course.

What is certain is that derivative contracts formed a Gordian knot at the financial heart of a company that was once America's seventh largest and is now its biggest bust. Those who have chuckled at the regulators' apparent obsession with the threat posed by the phenomenal growth in the use of derivatives should recollect their jibes and blush. Not that regulation comes out of this affair with any credit.

Derivatives are nothing new. As the old textbook I used when first grappling with the concept of traded options tells us, 16th century merchants could buy and sell options on com-

modities while the ships carrying them were still at sea. Then, as now, the risk lover could bet aggressively on future price moves, the risk averse could hedge against possible price volatility.

I doubt whether, 400 years ago, merchants calculated an option price after consideration of its delta, gamma, theta, or rho, but the underlying principles are timeless. To bottom the risks involved in entering into an option or futures contract, one must model the dynamics of the relationship between the price of the contract and the underlying asset upon which it is based.

Much of the trade in plain vanilla derivatives based upon the most popular underlying assets – such as the big currencies, government bonds and equity indices – takes place through derivatives exchanges. In providing a standardised framework for contracts, exchanges are able to create a trading environment that encourages liquidity and hence fine pricing.

This 'on market' trading of derivatives allows regulators to sleep easy at nights. Foolish investors always need protecting from themselves – hence the more onerous requirements placed on private investors before they buy and sell derivatives than ordinary shares – but at least the regulatory audit trail through recognised exchanges is straightforward.

By contrast, 'off market' derivative transactions – in effect, non-standard direct contracts between bilateral parties – are the cause of much regulatory insomnia. Over the past decade or so, the volume of such transactions, across a wide swath of asset classes and instruments, has been extraordinary.

As with all markets in goods and services, this growth reflects an increase in both willing buyers and sellers. The end buyers are often 'real' businesses seeking to smooth their risk and revenue streams. The sellers are typically financial institutions, and particularly investment banks, eager to exploit higher margin opportunities to deploy their capital.

Industrial buyers of derivatives have risk management requirements specific to their own businesses. Hence the bespoke structuring of 'off market' contracts. The investment bank facilitating the transaction will typically assume some of the countervailing risk in the trade itself, and will lay the rest off with other investors. It will seek to build its own 'book' of contracts whose risks offset rather than compound each other.

Stark reminder

In this world of meaty, bilateral transactions, an assessment of counterparty risk is critical. The major derivative exchanges typically have some system of guarantees to protect the integrity of trade. But 'off market', you're on your own. It would certainly be foolhardy to rely on the authorities to concoct behind the scenes support should a counterparty collapse. Although they have been known to do so – remember Barings and LTCM.

Enron's implosion constitutes a stark reminder of counterparty risk.

The world's largest energy trader stood on the other side of vast numbers of derivative contracts. In many, many cases, the only guarantee behind the contract will have been Enron's own name and balance sheet. These are now revealed to be worth nothing.

It is at times of greatest stress in the financial system that derivatives-related disasters are most likely to occur. This is partly because it is then that asset prices tend to move outside the 'normal' ranges factored into the original derivatives price setting process. It is also because at extremes liquidity tends to dry up. Just when you need a buyer to close down a trade, everyone is a seller, or vice versa.

The seeds of Enron's downfall were sown over many years as it pursued its aggressive growth plans. It is surely no coincidence, though, that its collapse coincides with the sudden, juddering halt to the global economy. Its legacy – at least while memories last – will be a higher price for risk. And maybe a few New Year resolutions to keep it simpler.

© *The Guardian*, 1 December 2001

The report and accounts disclosure requirements and tax treatment of derivatives are uncertain and complex. Currently, there is not a consensus regarding the accounting treatment of derivatives and exactly what information should be disclosed. In 2005 the International Accounting Standards Board (IASB) issued IAS 39, which includes a number of complicated rules, and requires derivatives to be accounted for at market value. The world of derivatives continues to change constantly and is inevitably becoming even more complex.

Progress check 12.10

What are the risks associated with hedging foreign currency risk and interest rate risk?

Summary of key points

- Financial risk, as distinct from business risk, is crucially important to companies with regard to their levels of gearing and investment and trade in foreign currencies.

- There are various types of financial risk relating to a company's capital structure, its interest rate agreements, and foreign currency transactions.

- The exchange rate equivalency model explains relationships between interest rates, inflation rates, spot currency exchange rates, and forward currency exchange rates, and forms a basis of many international financial management techniques.

- An exposure to interest rate risk is faced by companies who lend or borrow money at either floating or fixed rates of interest.

- The economic risk element of exchange rate risk is faced by all companies; the other two elements, translation and transaction risk, are faced only by companies who trade, borrow, or invest overseas.

- The appropriate management of financial risk is important because of the volatility of both exchange rates and interest rates.

- Financial risk, relating to exchange rates and interest rates, may be managed by matching and offsetting assets and liabilities and cash flows; choosing particular types of assets and liabilities; or hedging.

- There are a number of methods that may be used for the hedging of financial risks:
  - foreign currency fixed or option forward contracts
  - money market hedging
  - forward interest rate agreements (FRAs)
  - derivatives.

- There is a wide range of derivatives available for companies to hedge foreign currency exchange rate and interest rate risk, including:
  - options – traded and over-the-counter (OTCs)
  - futures
  - swaps
  - swaptions.

- The financial risk management strategy adopted by a company must consider its attitude to risk; state its objectives; identify its exposures; value the exposures; assess the risk; assess the appropriate risk management techniques.

- There are many distinct benefits to be gained by companies who hedge financial risk, despite their complexity and cost.

- The problems with the use of derivatives relate to their accounting treatment and financial reporting, and also the lack of adequate internal controls to ensure their proper use.

🔑 Glossary of key terms

American option An option that can be exercised at any time within the specified option period.

at the money A currency option that is agreed at the spot rate.

basis swap A swap agreement which involves the exchange of two floating rate interest payments that have been determined on different bases.

call option An option to buy a specified underlying asset at a specified exercise price on, or before, a specified exercise date.

derivative A financial instrument that derives its value from the price or rate of some underlying item. Underlying items include equities, bonds, commodities, interest rates, exchange rates, and stock market and other indices (and for companies like Enron, the weather!).

discount The difference between the specified forward rate and the spot rate ruling on the date of a foreign exchange forward contract, where the forward rate is higher than the spot rate.

economic risk Economic risk relates to the risk of the impact of long-term movements in exchange rates on the competitive position of companies engaged in international markets, which may be avoided by not trading in such markets. Economic risk in a company's home country cannot be avoided.

European option An option that must be exercised at the end of the specified option period.

Expectations Theory The Expectations Theory of exchange rates regards today's forward foreign currency exchange rate as a reasonable expectation of the future spot rate.

Fisher Effect Also known as Fisher's closed hypothesis, the Fisher Effect describes the long-run relationship between expectations about a country's future inflation and interest rates. Normally, a rise in a country's expected inflation rate should eventually cause an equal rise in the interest rate (and *vice versa*).

foreign exchange forward contract A fixed forward contract is an agreement to exchange different currencies at a specified future date and at a specified exchange rate. The difference between the specified rate and the spot rate ruling on the date the contract was entered into is the discount (see above) or premium (see page 547) on the forward contract (SSAP 20). An option forward contract is an agreement to exchange different currencies on or before a specified future date and at a specified exchange rate.

forward interest rate agreement (FRA) An agreement which a company may enter into with a bank concerning interest rates relating to its future borrowing or lending of very large sums of money (millions rather than thousands of pounds) and normally for periods of more than one year.

forward rate The exchange rate at which a currency may be bought or sold some time in the future.

▶

▶ **futures contract** A contract relating to currencies, commodities, or shares that obliges the buyer (or issuer) to purchase (or sell) the specified quantity of the item represented in the contract at a predetermined price at the expiration of the contract. Unlike forward contracts, which are entered into privately, futures contracts are traded on organised exchanges, carry standard terms and conditions, have specific maturities, and are subject to rules concerning margin (see below) requirements.

hedging The use of transactions (hedges) to reduce or eliminate an exposure to risk.

interest rate cap A variation on an interest rate option in which there is a 'ceiling' interest rate, as distinct from a 'floor' interest rate.

interest rate collar An interest rate collar enables a borrower to buy an interest rate 'cap' and simultaneously sell an interest rate 'floor' which therefore fixes the minimum cost for the company, which is lower than if an interest 'cap' only had been used.

Interest Rate Parity Theory The theory that the lending and borrowing interest rates differential between two countries is equal to the differential between the forward foreign currency exchange rate of the two countries and the spot exchange rate.

International Fisher Effect Also known as Fisher's open hypothesis, the International Fisher Effect states that an expected change in a foreign currency spot exchange rate between two countries is approximately equivalent to the difference between the nominal interest rates of the two countries for that time.

in the money In the money refers to a situation when the strike price of an option is below the current market price for a call option or above the current market price for a put option. Such an option has an intrinsic value (see below).

intrinsic value The difference between the strike rate and the current rate of an option. It represents the value of an option if it is exercised immediately and only has a value if it is in the money. If it is out of the money it does not have an intrinsic value.

margin The percentage of a futures contract value that must be placed on deposit with a broker. Because a futures contract is not an actual sale, only a fraction of the value, the margin, needs to be paid to open the contract.

money market hedge A money market hedge is used by companies, for example, who want to borrow funds for an investment at some time in the future for a specific period, but are also expecting an increase in interest rates by that time.

option A right of an option holder to buy or sell a specific asset on predetermined terms on, or before, a future date.

option premium The cost of an option, which has to be paid when the option is bought and is non-returnable.

out of the money A currency option that is agreed at a more or less favourable rate than the spot rate.

over-the-counter (OTC) option An option that is tailor-made by the bank to meet a company's specific requirements. It is an option, which is traded directly between licensed dealers, rather than through an organised options exchange.

plain vanilla swap (or generic swap) The commonest and simplest form of interest rate swap. The floating interest payments on a specific loan amount for a specific period are swapped with the fixed interest payments based on the same loan amount for the same period. In a plain vanilla swap there is a fixed interest rate paying company, and a floating interest rate paying company.

premium The difference between the specified forward rate and the spot rate ruling on the date a foreign exchange forward contract, where the spot rate is higher than the forward rate.

Purchasing Power Parity Theory The theory that foreign currency exchange rates are in equilibrium when their purchasing power is the same in each of the two countries at the prevailing exchange rates. This means that the exchange rate between two countries should equal the ratio of the two countries' price level of a fixed basket of goods and services. When a country experiences inflation, and its domestic price level is increasing, its exchange rate must depreciate in order to return to purchasing power parity.

put option An option to sell a specified underlying asset at a specified exercise price on, or before, a specified exercise date.

spot rate In general, a spot rate is the rate of interest to maturity currently offered on a particular type of security. With regard to foreign currency, the spot rate actually means the exchange rate at which a currency is bought or sold today for value two working days later.

strike rate In an interest rate option, the strike rate is the right to borrow or lend a specific amount of money by a particular date at a guaranteed interest rate, which must be exercised or not by the time the agreed date is reached.

swap An arrangement whereby two organisations contractually agree to exchange payments on different terms, for example in different currencies, or one at a fixed interest rate and the other at a floating interest rate.

swaption A combination of a swap and an option. It is like an option but, although having a lower premium than an option, it is not as flexible because companies cannot benefit from favourable exchange rate and interest rate movements.

tick The minimum amount by which the price of an interest rate futures contract can move, and which is a movement of 0.01% of the contract price.

time value The time value of an option is a reflection of current interest rates, which is at its maximum at the start of the option period and proportionately decreases throughout the option period down to zero at the option expiry date. An option that is out of the money has no intrinsic value, but it can still have time value.

traded option A traded option is available, for example, only for specific currencies, and is a standardised option with regard to its specified amount and term, and is bought and sold on an options exchange.

transaction exposure The susceptibility of an organisation to the effect of foreign exchange rate changes during the transaction cycle associated with the export or import of goods and services. Transaction exposure is present from the time a price is agreed until the payment has been made or received in the domestic currency.

translation exposure The susceptibility of the balance sheet and income statement (profit and loss account) to the effect of foreign exchange rate changes.

Questions

Q12.1 Identify the sources of financial risk faced by companies and outline the reasons why such exposure to risk has increased so much in recent years and continues to increase.

Q12.2 What has been the impact of the 1973 oil crisis with regard to the world currency markets and foreign currency exchange rates.

Q12.3 What are the financial risks related to the level of a company's gearing?

Q12.4 Explain the implications of the financial risk faced by companies having fixed interest loans compared with those having floating interest rate loans.

Q12.5 Outline what is meant by the 'spread' of foreign currency exchange spot rates.

Q12.6 Describe the relationship between foreign currency spot rates and future rate (one month, three months, six months, etc.) premiums and discounts.

Q12.7 Explain, with regard to the foreign currency exchange rate risks faced by companies, what is meant by economic exposure; transaction exposure; translation exposure.

Q12.8 What are the main types of hedging techniques available to companies in their management of foreign exchange and interest rate risk exposures.

Q12.9 Briefly describe how the use of derivatives: options; futures; swaps; and swaptions, may be used to hedge both foreign exchange and interest rate risk.

Discussion points

D12.1 'Continuing economic instability worldwide has been inevitable ever since the USA suspended the convertibility of US$ into gold in the early 1970s.' Discuss.

D12.2 'Derivatives are not a new invention, but an unnecessary evil that have been with us for a very long time.' Discuss.

D12.3 'An interest rate swap agreement cannot really be a win–win situation for the two companies involved and the bank arranging the swap – someone must lose.' Discuss.

Exercises

Solutions are provided in Appendix 2 to all exercise numbers highlighted in colour.

Level I

E12.1 *Time allowed – 15 minutes*

Build-It-Fast plc is a UK company that exports a range of DIY products to Switzerland. On 1 July 2007 the company had recently agreed a large supply contract with a building retailer in Geneva. The supply contract is for goods and services worth Swiss francs 75,000,000. The treasurer of Build-It-Fast plc is concerned about the future of the £ sterling/Swiss franc exchange rate, and believes that over the next six months the value of the Swiss franc may fall significantly. The Swiss supply contract is due to be paid on 31 December 2007. The following exchange rate information is available:

Exchange rates quoted for 1 July 2007:

Spot rate (dealers buying rate)	£1 = SFr10.5155
Spot rate (dealers selling rate)	£1 = SFr10.5185
Forward rate – 3 months forward	0.0050–0.0075 discount
Forward rate – 6 months forward	0.0100–0.0125 discount

You are required to calculate:
- **(i)** the cost to Build-It-Fast of buying and selling Swiss francs on the spot market on 1 July 2007
- **(ii)** the spread on the 3-month forward rate, and the 6-month forward rate for the Swiss francs
- **(iii)** the forward rate for 3-month and 6-month contracts to buy and sell Swiss francs
- **(iv)** how much would be received in £ sterling if the treasurer of Build-It-Fast plc were able to sell the Swiss francs on 1 July 2007
- **(v)** how much the treasurer would receive in £ sterling were he to sell the Swiss francs 6 months forward on 31 December 2007.

E12.2 *Time allowed – 30 minutes*

Anthony plc is a UK company that exports high quality electronic components worldwide, and has contracted to sell a large order of components to Germany. The contract is worth €6,500,000. The electronic components were delivered on 1 September 2007, and the contract is due to be paid on 1 March 2008. The deal was organised by the company's marketing department, but the company's financial manager is very concerned because he believes the profit margin on the contract is very low. He suspects that the euro may fall substantially against the £ sterling over the next 6 months.

Spot rate on 1 September 2007	£1 = €2.25
Forward rate to sell euro 6 months forward	£1 = €2.30
UK – £ lending interest rate	10% pa
Germany – euro borrowing interest rate	8% pa

Required:

As the finance manager of Anthony plc, prepare a report to the board explaining what options are available to the company, and explain the implications regarding the relevant part of the exchange rate equivalency model.

▶

▶ E12.3 *Time allowed – 30 minutes*

The UK partnership, Ray & Co, is a worldwide importer and exporter of materials. On 30 September 2006 Ray & Co contracted to buy 2,000 tonnes of melinium from a vendor in Cambrasia at a price of Cam$7,000 per tonne, for immediate settlement on shipment. The 7,000 tonnes of melinium were to be shipped directly to a client in Pembolia, allowing one month's credit from shipment date, and Ray's selling price was PF300 per tonne. 1,000 tonnes of melinium were to be shipped during October 2006 and 1,000 tonnes were to be shipped during November 2006.

Ray & Co agreed cover with their bank for these transactions in sterling on the forward exchange market.

The £ sterling exchange rates at 30 September 2006 were as follows:

	Cambrasian dollars (Cam$)/£	Pembolian francs (PF)/£
Spot	200–201	7–7.75
1 month forward	1–2 cents discount	5–3 centimes premium
2 months forward	2–3 cents discount	8–6 centimes premium
3 months forward	3–4 cents discount	13–11 centimes premium

Commission on all transactions is payable at 0.05% with a maximum of £20 per transaction.

Required:

Calculate:

(i) The profit that Ray & Co would have earned on the complete deal.

(ii) The impact on Ray & Co's profit if:
  (a) the November 2006 shipment had been cancelled
  (b) the November 2006 shipment had been delayed until January 2007.

E12.4 *Time allowed – 30 minutes*

Blud Ltd sells small boats to customers in Spain. A delivery has just been made to a customer in Barcelona. Blud Ltd has invoiced €40,000, payable in three months' time. Blud's finance director has obtained the following information about €/£ foreign exchange rates and UK £ sterling and € interest rates:

€/£ sterling exchange rates

Spot	1.4648–1.4652
3 months forward	100–100 premium

Interest rates

	UK £ sterling		Spain euro	
	Deposit	Borrowing	Deposit	Borrowing
	4.5%	5.0%	1.9%	2.1%

Required:

(i) How should Blud Ltd's finance director maximise Blud Ltd's sterling receipt from the sale of the boat?

(ii) If, in addition to the above, Blud Ltd was required to make a payment of €20,000 to a Spanish supplier in three months' time, what may the finance director do to minimise the company's foreign currency exposure risk?

E12.5 *Time allowed – 30 minutes*

On 1 May 2007 Cookies plc needed to make a payment of US$730,000 in three months' time. The company considered three different ways in which it may hedge its transaction exposure – foreign exchange forward contract; money market; currency option – based on the following foreign currency exchange rate and interest rate data:

Exchange rates:

US$/£ sterling spot rate	1.8188–1.8199
Three month US$/ £ forward rate	1.8109–1.8120

Interest rates:

	Borrowing %	Lending %
US$	3.15	2.85
£ sterling	5	4.5

Foreign currency option prices in cents per US$ for a contract size of £25,000:

Exercise price	Call option (July 2007)	Put option (July 2007)
US$1.90/£	2.5	7.5

Required:
Calculate the cost of the transaction using each of the three different methods considered by Cookies plc to determine which is the cheapest for the company.

Level II

E12.6 *Time allowed – 45 minutes*

On 30 April 2006 Gleeson plc had a short-term borrowing requirement for £10m on 1 August 2006 for a period of three months. The borrowing rate of interest at 30 April 2006 was 7% and the board of directors was concerned that interest rates may increase over the next six months. The finance director was asked to look at the use of interest rate futures with regard to the following two scenarios:

(a) interest rates increase by 1% and the futures market price moves by 1%
(b) interest rates fall by 2% and the futures market price moves by 1.5%.

They also suggested the possibility of buying an interest guarantee at 7%, for which the cost would be 0.3% of the value of the loan.

At 30 April 2006 the price of July sterling three-month time deposit futures was 93.25. The standard contract size was £500,000, and the minimum price movement, one tick, was 0.01% of the loan per annum.

Required:
(i) Assess the impact of the use of interest rate futures for each of the scenarios (a) and (b) above and calculate each of hedge efficiencies.
(ii) Determine whether for each of the scenarios (a) and (b) above, the total cost of the loan would have been cheaper if the interest guarantee had been acquired.

E12.7 *Time allowed – 45 minutes*

Houses plc has a very good credit rating and is able to borrow funds at a fixed rate of 6.5%. Houses plc may also borrow funds at a floating rate of LIBOR plus 0.1% (LIBOR is currently 4.75%).

▶

▶ Thinice plc has a less favourable credit rating, being seen as a company with a slightly higher risk profile and so is able to borrow funds at a less favourable fixed rate of 7%. Thinice plc can borrow funds at a floating rate of LIBOR plus 0.2%.

Houses plc currently has a large fixed interest loan, and Thinice has a loan of the same size on which it pays a floating rate of interest. Houses plc would prefer to be paying a floating rate of interest but Thinice would like its loan to be at a fixed interest rate.

Required:

Make the unrealistic assumption that a bank will not be involved in an interest rate swap arranged between the two companies in which they have an equal share of any gain. Make the appropriate calculations to illustrate how both companies may benefit from such an agreement. Your calculations should show: the total gain of the swap; the gain to each company; the borrowing rates of each company after the swap has taken place.

E12.8 *Time allowed – 45 minutes*

The finance director of Privet plc wants to arrange a £5m six-month loan in three months' time, but is worried that the current borrowing interest rate of 8% may move adversely over the next few months. The finance director is considering various hedging options: an interest rate futures contract; a forward rate agreement (FRA); an interest rate cap.

Explain how each of these financial instruments may be used to benefit Privet plc, and discuss the disadvantages of their use.

Case Study II: **Millpot Ltd**

Millpot Ltd is a designer and manufacturer of fine pottery, aimed particularly at the mass market, via shops, large retail chains, and mail order companies. The company was founded many years ago by Martin Griffin, who was the managing director and was involved in the sales and marketing side of the business.

Towards the end of 2004 when Martin was due to retire, Emily Griffin, Martin's daughter, joined the company as managing director, along with Richard Higgins as marketing director. Emily had worked as a senior manager with Plato plc, a large UK designer and manufacturer of giftware, of which Richard had been a director. Emily and Richard capitalised on their experience with Plato to present some very innovative ideas for developing a new product range for Millpot. However, Emily and Richard's ideas for expanding the business required additional investment, the majority of which was spent during the financial year just ended on 31 March 2007.

The share capital of Millpot Ltd, 800,000 £1 ordinary shares, had all been owned by Martin himself. On retirement he decided to transfer 390,000 of his shares to his daughter Emily, and to sell 390,000 shares to Richard Higgins. Martin gifted his remaining 20,000 shares to Dennis Brown, who was the production director and had given the company many years of loyal service. Richard had used a large part of his personal savings and had taken out an additional mortgage on his house to help finance his investment in the business. This was, of course, paid to Martin Griffin and did not provide any additional capital for the business.

In order to raise additional share capital, Emily and Richard asked Martin's advice about friends, family, and business contacts who may be approached. Martin suggested approaching a venture capital company, Foxhole Ltd, which was run by a friend of his, Bill Fox. Foxhole already had a wide portfolio of investments in dot.com and service businesses, and Bill was interested in investing in this type of growing manufacturing business. He had known Martin and the Griffin family for many years, and was confident that Emily and Richard would make a success of the new ideas that they presented for the business. Additional capital was therefore provided from the issue of 800,000 new £1 shares at par to Foxhole Ltd, to become the largest shareholder of Millpot Ltd. Millpot Ltd also had a bank loan, which it increased during 2006/07, and had a bank overdraft facility.

The directors of the newly structured Millpot Ltd, and its shareholders were as follows:

Emily Griffin	Managing director	390,000 shares
Richard Higgins	Marketing director	390,000 shares
Dennis Brown	Production director	20,000 shares
Bill Fox	Non-executive director	
Foxhole Ltd		800,000 shares

As a non-executive director of Millpot Ltd, Bill Fox attended the annual general meetings, and review meetings that were held every six months. He didn't have any involvement with the day-to-day management of the business.

The new range at Millpot did quite well and the company also began to export in a small way to North America. Emily and Richard were pleased by the way in which the sales of the business had grown, and in the growth of their customer base. They had just received a large order from Potto, a German company, which was regarded as an important inroad into the European market. If Potto became a regular customer, the sales of the company were likely to increase rapidly over the next few years and would establish Millpot as a major player in the market.

In the first week of May 2007, the day that Millpot received the order from Potto, Emily also received a letter from the bank manager. The bank manager requested that Millpot Ltd immediately ▶

▶ and considerably reduce their overdraft, which he felt was running at a level which exposed the bank and the company to a higher level of risk than he was prepared to accept. Emily Griffin was very angry and felt very frustrated. Emily, Richard, and Dennis agreed that since they had just had such a good year's trading and the current year looked even better, the reduction in the overdraft facility was going to seriously jeopardise their ability to meet the commitments they had to supply their customers.

When they joined the company, Emily and Richard decided that Millpot, which had always been production led, would become a design and marketing led business. Therefore, a great deal of the strategic planning was concerned with integrating the product design and development with the sales and marketing operations of the business. Over the past three years Emily and Richard had invested in employing and training a young design team to help continue to develop the Millpot brand. The marketing team led by Richard had ensured that the enthusiasm of their key customers was converted into new firm orders, and that new orders were received from customers like Potto. The order book grew until it had now reached the highest level ever for the company.

In addition to his role as production director, Dennis had always tended to look after the books and any financial matters. Dennis wasn't an accountant and he hadn't had any formal financial training. But, as he said, he had a small and experienced accounts team who dealt with the day-to-day transactions; if ever there had been a problem, they would ask Millpot's auditors for some advice.

As soon as she received the letter from the bank, Emily called the bank manager to try and persuade him to continue to support the overdraft facility at the current level, but with no success. Emily also convened an urgent meeting of the directors, including Bill Fox, to talk about the letter and the draft accounts of the business for the year ended 31 March 2007. The letter from the bank was distributed to all the directors before the meeting.

Richard Higgins was very worried about his investment in the company. He admitted that his accounting knowledge was fairly limited. He thought that the company was doing very well, and said that the draft accounts for the year to 31 March 2007 seemed to confirm their success. Profit before tax was more than double the profit for 2006. He couldn't understand why the cash flow was so bad. He appreciated that they had spent a great deal of money on the additional plant and equipment, but they had already had a bank loan to help with that. He thought that the cash situation should really be even better than the profit because the expenses included £1.5m for depreciation, which doesn't involve any cash at all.

Emily Griffin, still appeared very angry at the lack of support being given by the bank. She outlined the impact that the overdraft reduction would have on their ability to meet their commitments over the next year. She said that the bank's demand to cut their overdraft by 50% over the next three months put them in an impossible position with regard to being able to meet customer orders. Millpot Ltd couldn't find an alternative source of such a large amount of money in such a short time.

Richard, Emily, and Dennis, had, before the meeting, hoped that Bill Fox would be prepared to help out by purchasing further additional new shares in the company or by making a loan to the company. However, it was soon made clear by Bill that further investment was not a possible option. Foxhole Ltd had made a couple of new investments over the past few months and so did not have the money to invest further in Millpot. As a venture capitalist, Foxhole had actually been discussing the possible exit from Millpot by selling and trying to realise a profit on the shares. Finding a prospective buyer for their shares, or floating Millpot on the alternative investment market (AIM), did not currently appear to be a realistic option.

Bill Fox had been so much involved in running his own business, Foxhole Ltd, that he had neglected to monitor the financial position of Millpot Ltd as often and as closely as he should have done. At the directors' meeting he realised that he should have been much more attentive and there was now a possibility that Millpot would not provide the returns his company expected, unless things could be drastically improved.

The financial statements of Millpot Ltd for the past two years are shown below:

Income statement for the year ended 31 March

	2006 £000	2007 £000
Turnover	7,000	11,500
Cost of sales	(3,700)	(5,800)
Gross profit	3,300	5,700
Operating expenses	(2,200)	(3,100)
Operating profit	1,100	2,600
Interest payable	(200)	(500)
Profit before taxation	900	2,100
Taxation	(200)	(400)
Profit after taxation	700	1,700
Dividend	(200)	(300)
Retained profit for the year	500	1,400
Retained profit brought forward	1,100	1,600
Retained profit carried forward	1,600	3,000

Balance sheet as at 31 March

	2006 £000	2006 £000	2007 £000	2007 £000
Non-current assets		4,300		7,200
Current assets				
Stocks	1,200		2,900	
Trade debtors	800		1,900	
Other debtors	100		200	
Cash at bank and in hand	100		–	
	2,200		5,000	
Current liabilities				
Trade creditors	600		1,300	
Other creditors	100		200	
Taxation	200		400	
Dividends	200		300	
Bank overdraft	–		2,100	
	1,100		4,300	
Net current assets		1,100		700
		5,400		7,900
Non-current liabilities				
Loan		(2,200)		(3,300)
		3,200		4,600
Capital and reserves				
Ordinary shares (£1)		1,600		1,600
Retained profit		1,600		3,000
		3,200		4,600

▶

Cash flow statement for the year ended 31 March 2007
Reconciliation of operating profit to net cash flow from operating activities

	£000
Operating profit	2,600
Depreciation charges	1,500
Increase in stocks	(1,700)
Increase in debtors	(1,200)
Increase in creditors	800
Net cash inflow from operating activities	2,000

Cash flow statement

	£000
Net cash inflow from operating activities	2,000
Returns on investments and servicing of finance (note 1)	(500)
Taxation – corporation tax paid	(200)
Capital expenditure (note 1)	(4,400)
	(3,100)
Dividends paid	(200)
	(3,300)
Financing (note 1)	1,100
Decrease in cash	(2,200)

Reconciliation of net cash flow to movement in net debt (note 2)

	£000
Decrease in cash for the period	(2,200)
Cash flow from increase in bank loan	(1,100)
Change in net debt	(3,300)
Net debt 1 April 2006	(2,100)
Net debt 31 March 2007	(5,400)

Note 1 to the cash flow statement – gross cash flows

	£000
Returns on investments and servicing of finance	
Interest paid	(500)
Capital expenditure	
Payments to acquire tangible fixed assets	(4,400)
Financing	
Increase in bank loan	1,100

Note 2 to the cash flow statement – analysis of change in net debt

	At 1 Apr 2006 £000	Cash flows £000	At 31 Mar 2007 £000
Cash and bank	100	(100)	–
Overdraft	–	(2,100)	(2,100)
Bank loan	(2,200)	(1,100)	(3,300)
Total	(2,100)	(3,300)	(5,400)

The directors of Millpot Ltd were unable to agree on a way of dealing with the financial problem faced by the company. Emily thought it best that she continue to try and negotiate with the bank manager, and believed that she could change the bank manager's mind if she:

■ presented him with the accounts for 31 March 2007, which showed such good results

and

■ made him fully aware of the implications of the reduction in the overdraft facility on the future of Millpot.

However, Richard and Dennis said that they were aware that Millpot Ltd had exceeded its agreed overdraft limit a few times over the past two years and so they were not confident that Emily could persuade the bank to change its mind. They suggested that they should try and find another investor prepared to provide additional funds for the business, to keep the business going. They really believed that the year-end accounts showed how successful Millpot had been over the past two years and that their track record was sufficient to attract a potential new investor in the business. Bill didn't agree. He felt that this would not be a practical solution. More importantly, Foxhole didn't want to have another large shareholder in the company because it would dilute its shareholding, and also reduce its influence over the future direction of the business. However, Bill agreed that immediate and radical action was necessary to be taken by the company.

After hours of argument and discussion, it became apparent that the problem would not be resolved at the meeting. Therefore, it was agreed by all present that expertise from outside the company should be sought to help the company find an acceptable and viable solution to the problem. The directors decided to approach Lucis Consulting, which specialises in helping businesses with financial problems, and to ask them to produce a plan of action for their consideration.

Required:
As a member of the Lucis team, prepare a report for the board of directors of Millpot Ltd which analyses the problems faced by the company and which sets out a detailed plan of action for dealing with its problems. Your report should include consideration of the following questions:

(i)   **What are the weaknesses in Millpot Ltd's current organisational structure?**

(ii) **What are some of the financial procedures and controls that Millpot Ltd lacks?**

(iii) **At which stage in its life cycle do you consider Millpot Ltd is currently at?**

(iv) **How does Millpot Ltd appear in terms of profitability and cash flow?**

(v)   **What are the weaknesses in Millpot Ltd's investment and growth plans and their financing?**

   Your report should be supported by appropriate analyses for the years ended 31 March 2007 and 31 March 2006.

Financial strategy

Part contents

Introduction to Part II

Part I of this book is about corporate finance, which is concerned with the effective use of financial resources to create corporate value. Part II is concerned primarily with how the use of appropriate financial strategies not only creates corporate value but reflects it in increased shareholder value.

Chapter 13 sets the scene by looking at the product life cycle (PLC) and how this may be reflected in a theoretical business life cycle (BLC) model that describes the stages through which businesses may typically progress from their initial start-up through to their decline and possible demise. The financial parameters particular to each stage of this simplified business life cycle will be identified and appropriate financial strategies will be discussed that may be used to exploit the specific circumstances in order to create shareholder value. It considers both financial risk and business risk and the relationship between them, and how these may change through each of the stages of the BLC. Each of the sources of external finance come with different levels of financial risk and the choice of these is considered with regard to the BLC, together with their corresponding levels of interest and dividends.

Chapter 14 focuses specifically on start-up businesses and their transition to their growth phase. These stages of company development are considered with regard to their risk profiles and options about how they may best be financed. This chapter also looks at how companies may finance new investment, and how they may move from private to public ownership and become quoted on a stock exchange.

Chapter 15 takes the development of the business a step further by looking at how companies, after experiencing a period of turbulence and market shakeout, enjoy a period of maturity, which may ultimately result in decline. These stages are considered with regard to their risk profiles and possible changes in their methods of financing. This chapter also looks at how mature companies may become takeover targets, and some of the strategies that may be employed to delay or avoid decline.

Chapters 16 and 17 look at specific strategies used by companies with regard to mergers and acquisitions (M&As). It considers the reasons, justifications, and motives for M&As, and how target companies may be valued. The financing of acquisitions may involve the use of additional debt or equity and alternative financial strategies. A number of defences against takeover are examined, applicable both before and after a takeover bid has been made. The post-takeover position of the acquiring company and the acquired company are considered with regard to each of the major stakeholders.

Chapter 18 is concerned with the way in which companies may be restructured or reorganised and the influences and reasons for these strategies. This chapter considers the strategies and techniques used in demergers, privatisations, management buy-outs (MBOs), and management buy-ins (MBIs).

The business life cycle and financial strategy

Chapter contents

LEARNING OBJECTIVES

Completion of this chapter will enable you to:

☑ outline the product life cycle (PLC) model

☑ explain the BCG matrix and its strategic implications

☑ explain a simple business life cycle (BLC) model

☑ explain the inverse correlation between business risk and financial risk

☑ consider business risk and financial risk throughout the life cycle of a business

☑ recognise the changing levels of earnings per share (eps) and cash flow during the different stages of the business life cycle

☑ identify the various sources of business finance throughout the business life cycle

☑ consider how dividend levels, the P/E ratio, and the share price may change during the different stages of the business life cycle.

Introduction

As a product moves through the various stages of its development from its conception, start-up, or launch to its decline and possible eventual demise, levels of sales, profits, and cash flow may be expected to change significantly. The **product life cycle (PLC)** model tries to identify the separate stages in this development.

The PLC model may be criticised for its oversimplification, the reasons for which will be considered in this chapter. However, in order to provide a framework in which to consider financial strategy, we will extend the PLC model to describe theoretically how a company may also develop and progress through its stages of growth, maturity and so on. Businesses in practice do not usually provide a single product or service; it is more likely that they may have a portfolio of many different products or services, each with a different life cycle. Businesses may also include a number of divisions or subsidiaries that also provide many different products or services, each with different life cycles. Diversified companies may be involved in an even greater range of industrial sectors, businesses, and products. We are assuming that the PLC model describes distinctly separate phases in the development of a product, which may or may not be strictly accurate. If we extend this principle as applying to a company it is certainly true that in practice a phase like the mature phase of a company will also include elements of, for example, growth or decline.

Despite its oversimplification and inherent weaknesses we will use this form of product life cycle model and broaden it into the context of the entire business to examine appropriate financial strategies that may be adopted by companies to create shareholder value. This chapter will introduce this type of life cycle as applied to a business, the stages of which will each be considered separately and in more detail in Chapters 14 and 15.

Product life cycle (PLC)

Products (and services) developed and provided by businesses may be considered at three different levels, examples of which are shown in Fig. 13.1. Generic products may be looked at the industry level, types of product at the sector of industry level, and branded versions of those products at the individual product level.

The life cycle of such products may apply in different ways at each of the different levels. At the industry level the mature stage tends to span a very long period. Whereas at the individual product level, which includes brands and makes of product, each stage in the life cycle may be of varying length with no common pattern. Each may be assumed to conform to the type of life cycle model illustrated by the curve in Fig. 13.2.

The product life cycle (PLC) looks at the tracking of movements of sales, and therefore profits and cash flows, where market share is changing throughout the entire cycle. The PLC

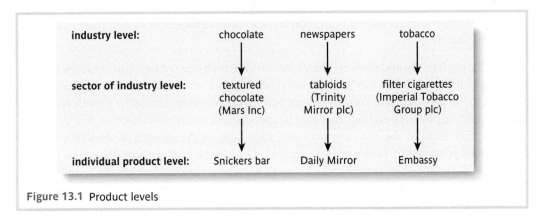

Figure 13.1 Product levels

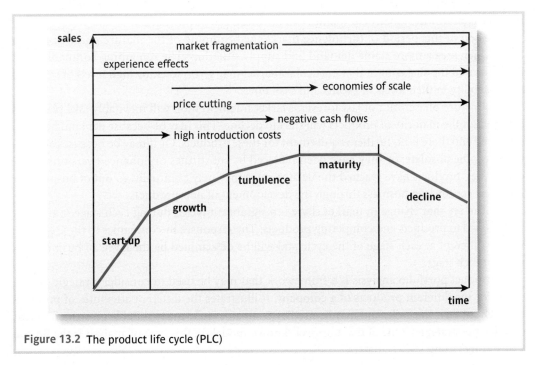

Figure 13.2 The product life cycle (PLC)

reflects what sales were over the life of the product, but the model may also be used to consider what future trends in sales, profits, and cash flows may be. At each stage of the cycle different levels of business risk will be faced at the industry level, sector of industry level, and individual product level with regard to political, economic, social, technological, environmental, and legal pressures, substitute and competing products, and competitors.

There are four separate stages in the product life cycle, separated by a period of instability or turbulence between the growth and maturity stages, and the effects of experience are seen throughout the entire cycle:

- start-up – which is the introductory phase of the launch of a product
- growth – in which new entrants are attracted into the market place
- turbulence – where increasing production capacity results in overcapacity, and then turmoil in the market resulting in shakeout
- maturity – where demand and supply are in balance
- decline – where there is market saturation and therefore replacement or new product development is required.

During the pre start-up and start-up phases there will be high costs of introducing a new product, during which time cash flows are likely to be highly negative, and this situation may also continue through to the growth phase. As the product becomes established during the growth phase, and into the mature phase, operating costs may be reduced as a result of economies of scale.

The parameters of the PLC are sales and time, and as the growth in sales of a product increases its prospects of future growth declines. During the high growth phase of a product, competitors are attracted into the market with the aim of taking market share and earning profits. This will provide increased capacity to meet increasing demand as the market grows. As the growth in demand slows down this will eventually result in overcapacity, followed by a period of competition and price-cutting. Continued competition and price-cutting will result in a shakeout in which many companies will be forced out of the market.

The end of this period of turbulence marks the beginning of the mature phase of the life cycle which sees a more stable demand and supply situation. The remaining companies that have survived the shakeout in that particular market may go on to enjoy high levels of sales and some stability in their levels of profits and cash flows.

The mature phase will not last forever. Market fragmentation will inevitably take place and demand for the majority of products will start to decline. This may be because demand has been saturated and there is no further requirement for these products. Or it may be because products have become obsolete, or they have been replaced by substitutes or enhanced versions. Once companies' products have reached the decline stage they may eventually go out of business, or they may continue in business through the development of new products.

We can see that change in market share is a significant factor during each stage in the PLC with regard to products and competing products. The responses by companies to these changes will be different at each stage of the cycle and will be determined by the levels of business risk faced at each stage.

A product portfolio analysis is a framework that may be used to consider strategic alternatives for the different products of a company. It illustrates the different attributes of products throughout their life cycle, and may be used by companies to identify suitable growth, maturity, and decline strategies. One of the most well-known models of this type of analysis is the Boston Consulting Group (BCG) matrix.

Progress check 13.1

Explain what is meant by the product life cycle (PLC) and how this may be applied to consider the life cycle of a business.

Boston Consulting Group (BCG) matrix

The BCG matrix shows the changing positions of portfolios of products within a company by considering the two dimensions of market share and market growth. This model looks at the rate of growth of the market and relative market share compared to largest competitor next up or down in the market. The relative market share of a company with a portfolio of products is illustrated in the BCG matrix in its comparison with the rate of market growth. These factors together with cash flows and profitability are important with regard to the successful development of any business. The relative market share rather than absolute market share is the significant factor. For example, a company achieving a market share of 40% may sound excellent. However, it would not be such a good position for the company if there was only one competitor, which had 60% of the market.

The BCG matrix can be used to determine how resource priorities may be allocated between products in the product portfolio of a company. To ensure sustainable long-term value creation, a company should have a portfolio of products that contains an appropriate balance of:

- growth products that may require the further investment of company resources
- low-growth products that may generate resources for investment by the company elsewhere.

The basic premise underpinning the matrix is that the greater the market share a product has, or the faster the market for a product grows, the better it is for the company.

The BCG matrix (see Fig. 13.3) shows a company with a number of different products, which may be grouped into categories called:

- problem children
- stars
- cash cows
- dogs.

Problem children

The products within this category have high growth potential, but a low market share, and provide low profit margins, and so need cash. If no cash is provided to support their development then their growth potential may not be achieved and they become dogs.

Possible strategies are to:

- invest sufficiently in product development and promotion to try and obtain a high share of new business and ensure that the products become stars
- acquire competing businesses as a way of obtaining products that are either actual or potential stars.

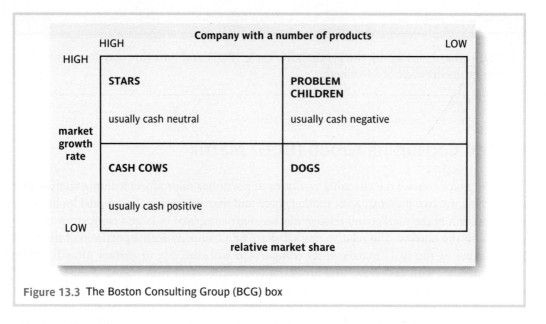

Figure 13.3 The Boston Consulting Group (BCG) box

Alternatively, if the company does not consider that either of these options is viable then it may get out of that market.

Stars

The products within this category are growing very fast, and so cash is needed to support this growth. The company aims to obtain high growth and a dominant market share with these products to make itself a market leader.

Possible strategies are to:

- protect market share through the creation of entry barriers to the market like the establishment of brand names, and the benefits of economies of scale
- reinvest earnings for future growth
- actively seek to try and take a share of new business from competitors
- seek out new products and markets to protect the company's future.

Cash cows

Products described as cash cows have low market growth, although a dominant market share. These products are very profitable and strongly cash positive.

Possible strategies are to:

- maintain their market dominance
- use elsewhere the cash generated by the cash cows and seek profitable reinvestment.

Dogs

When products become dogs they have a subordinate share of the market and have low market growth potential. Therefore, there are cost disadvantages and few growth opportunities.

Possible strategies are to:

- focus and dominate one segment, or develop a niche market (like that created by Rover, which extended the life of the Mini car to over 40 years)

- 'harvest' before the product 'withers on the vine' – reap the rewards without any further investment

- divest whilst there is still some value – sell off that part of the business

- abandon declining products and get out of the market.

A dog may possibly be revived through increased marketing. The life of products may also be continued by developing products like, for example, spare parts for products that are no longer in production in order to service customer requirements.

Generally, the BCG approach looks at cash rather than profit, but we may question whether the overall BCG rationale itself is sound. Although it may be difficult to define each of the variables, it may nevertheless be a little prescriptive. Does high growth result in high sales revenues and mean that there is little price competition? Does a high market share provide economies of scale, price-setting power, and result in the company achieving the role of market leader?

Companies are continually seeking ways to minimise risk, maximise revenue, and endeavour to increase market share. The basis of these strategies is the development of consistent and sustainable cash flows from sales of products and services. However, whilst the possession of cash cow products or services that command a large market share of an already mature market is important, future survival and success of a company cannot rest solely on such products and services. Future success is dependent upon having a balanced portfolio of products and services, represented by each of the boxes in the BCG matrix:

- problem children products or services occupying the introductory stage of the product life cycle

- star products or services occupying the growth stage of the product life cycle

- cash cow products or services occupying the maturity stage of the product life cycle

- dog products or services occupying the decline stage of the product life cycle.

Progress check 13.2

Describe the BCG matrix and its various components.

It is possible to use the BCG matrix to visualise the position of products, in order to assess appropriate strategies. It is the varying nature of a company's portfolio of products and services that directly affects the levels of risk faced by a company throughout their life cycle. Each of the boxes in the BCG matrix can be seen to be very similar to each of the phases in the PLC. The market growth rate in the BCG matrix relates to the sales volume growth of the PLC model, as products move from their start-up (problem children), to growth (stars), maturity (cash cows), and decline (dogs). Problem children effectively represent new start-up products requiring high levels of resources for market research, investment, research and development, operations, promotion, and advertising.

The business life cycle (BLC)

The concept of the business life cycle has many different meanings. A business life cycle may fall into an annual pattern like the seasonal activities of, for example, a farming business. Alternatively, businesses that undertake projects such as the construction of a water desalination plant or a nuclear power plant, may have business life cycles that span many years. The business cycle may also be considered at a macroeconomic level relating to cyclical changes in the economic environment in terms of growth, inflation, and interest rates.

From the BCG matrix in Fig. 13.3, which applies to a company having a portfolio of products, we can see how closely it imitates the PLC graph in Fig. 13.2, particularly if we assume that negative growth may be possible (as in the decline stage) when the company has a large proportion of dogs. We will apply this model of the life cycle to businesses or divisions, which may be active in particular industrial sectors. The four main phases of the PLC model: start-up or introduction phase; growth phase; mature phase; decline phase, will be used to describe the stages of corporate development and referred to the business life cycle (BLC).

We are using this business cycle approach because it is the time-tested way in which both industries and companies appear to have developed for hundreds of years right up to the present day. In the UK there are many good examples of this business life cycle pattern, and the ways in which the risks to which they were exposed shaped the future of industries, products, and companies. Look at, for example, the coal mining, shipbuilding, and pottery industries.

Worked Example 13.1

Coal had been used as a fuel for centuries but emerged as the main source of energy for the Industrial Revolution. Its use grew substantially in the early 19th century because of its abundance throughout the UK in Wales, Scotland, and the North of England. It was also able to be cheaply transported using canals and the railways. By the late 19th century there was enormous expansion of the coal industry and a great dependence on exports, and it became a mature industry throughout the 20th century. The coal industry declined by the end of the 20th century as its use was replaced with oil and natural gas, and because of social costs and political pressures. Despite its decline it remains one of the cheapest sources of energy, although it may still be environmentally unfriendly.

Worked Example 13.2

The UK as an island has a maritime history and so shipbuilding began a very long time ago but started seriously in the North of England in the 14th century and continued to grow up to the 18th century. During the 19th century shipbuilding was transformed into a modern hi-tech industry. Its boom years in the early 20th century were stimulated by the demand for warships and repair facilities. This was followed by a slump in the mid 1920s economic Depression but was revived briefly in the 1940s/1950s because of the Second World War demand. The industry again slumped in the 1960s because of reduced demand and an increase in foreign competition, and its decline continued throughout the late 20th century.

Worked Example 13.3

Traditionally, there has been an abundance of both coal and clay in the UK and particularly in the Staffordshire area. The pottery industry had very early beginnings, and a medieval pottery industry appeared to be thriving in the 13th century in some parts of the UK. Growth of the industry took place between the mid-17th century and mid-18th century through industrialisation. By the mid-18th century a substantial industry had been established which then matured through the 19th century. However, the pottery industry started to decline in the latter part of the 20th century because of changes in fashion, the availability of cheaper substitutes, and low cost foreign competition, to its virtual demise in the 21st century. The majority of pottery and ceramics production now takes place elsewhere than the UK in countries where production costs are considerably lower. Major companies like Wedgewood and Spode have now disappeared.

The business life cycles seen in industries have also been reflected in the life cycles of industrial sectors and in companies, the phases of each cycle tending to be shorter than those observed in industries. At both the sector of industry level and company level there is a wide range of good examples of the business life cycle, for example sporting newspapers (for example *The Sporting Life*), holiday camps (for example Butlins), family cars (for example Rover) and vinyl music records.

Worked Example 13.4

Mass production of shellac gramophone records began in Germany at the end of the 19th century and 78 rpm records continued to be produced worldwide throughout the first half of the 20th century. Magnetic tape recording emerged in the early 1940s and vinyl records developed in the late 1940s. 78s were then superceded by tape and vinyl 45 rpm and 33 rpm records in the 1950s. Many companies started up during this period of the 1950s producing vinyl records and enjoying rapid growth with the birth of rock music and then the Beatles phenomenon. These companies reached a period of maturity, which ran through the 1960s and 1970s. Then in the early 1980s the first CDs were marketed which saw the merging of the consumer music industry with the computer revolution. This signalled the imminent death of vinyl record (and tape cassettes), which disappeared by the 1990s (although there has been a recent revival of vinyl mainly as collector items). As the growth in demand for Internet digital downloads continues to increase throughout the early part of the 21st century, the CD is likely to become a relic of yet another bygone age.

We can see from the above examples that the types of risk and levels of risk faced by businesses are different during each phase of the business life cycle. Therefore different strategies should be adopted by companies at each stage of the cycle relating to, for example, marketing, human resources, operations, finance and so on. In this book we are concerned with financial strategy. This chapter and the chapters that follow consider the financial strategies that may be most appropriate for companies at each stage of the business life cycle. In this context we will look at financial strategy with regard to:

- approaches to financial risk
- levels of earnings, or profitability, and cash flow

- types and levels of investment

- sources of finance – debt and equity

- gearing, or capital structure

- levels of dividends

- levels of earnings retention

- share price,

and with the aim of maximisation of shareholder wealth through creation of shareholder value consistent with levels of perceived risk and returns required by investors.

In our use of the business life cycle we will consider a specific view of the development of a company through each of the phases we have described. Throughout the business life cycle (BLC), companies face continual change and the effect of their experience continues to influence the ways in which they behave and make decisions throughout the whole cycle.

New products and new businesses take some time to gain acceptance by potential customers and so initial sales growth is usually very slow. In the start-up phase, and as companies develop and grow, they inevitably incur high start-up and introduction costs. There are likely to be only a few companies in any new market. Since output is initially quite low then unit costs will be high, as will be the cost of advertising and promotion and costs of rectification of initial teething problems. Therefore, the start-up phase of the BLC is likely to see negative net cash flows which may continue right through into the growth phase. As a business develops through its growth phase and its output and sales increase, economies of scale may be achieved from which it may reap the rewards of increased profitability during its mature phase.

As output increases throughout the growth phase, unit costs will fall as a result of economies of scale. Strong demand will ensure some stability in sales prices. However, a strong market will also attract competitors, and so profitability will suffer from increased costs of product improvement, promotion, and distribution necessary for a business to try and maintain a dominant position in the market.

At the end of the growth phase the turbulence phase of the cycle normally sees a great deal of price-cutting by competitors. The turbulence phase is the period of uncertainty and change in the market that occurs towards the end of the growth phase from which only the strongest players survive to go on and enter the mature phase.

During the mature phase the rate of sales growth normally reduces to a level that is usually the longest and most successful period of the life cycle. In general, most products on the market at any point in time are in their mature stage, where the company's sales and profits are both good. In the mature phase new entrants may be tempted to enter such established and profitable markets, but to a lesser extent than during the growth phase. Increasing competition then inevitably leads to production overcapacity. Sales of products and businesses may start to decline and some players will leave the market. Eventually, total market demand may decline either quickly or slowly depending on the level of introduction of substitutes or replacement products. The businesses that remain in the market usually seek to 'harvest' the maximum possible return from a product before it eventually 'withers on the vine', or they may try to prolong the life of a product through modifications and development of niche markets. However, most businesses will leave the market during the decline phase because of falling profits. Those that remain in the market for too long in the decline phase before either getting out or seeking alternatives may simply go out of business.

There are a number of drawbacks that should be considered in the use of a business life cycle (and product life cycle):

- each stage is not clearly defined
- the length of each stage is not certain
- the location of a product or a business at a point in time is not accurate
- the shape of the curve outlined in the life cycle model may not always occur in actuality
- extrapolation of the life cycle graph may not be accurate
- the life cycle is not inevitable – it depends on what strategic decisions are made and which actions are taken
- some products and businesses may never decline (note the extremely long life span of a product like Kelloggs Corn Flakes)
- the strategic implications of the life cycle will depend on the nature of the competition
- the life cycle model may not necessarily be the case in the real world.

Life cycle analysis is therefore not an exact science. Businesses are usually never exactly clear about which stage in the cycle they are at any point in time. The business life cycle model we are using is therefore not a prescriptive model used to forecast the lives of products or businesses. We are using the business life cycle to describe generally how businesses and products may develop relative to the market, and to provide a framework that can be used to indicate which financial strategies may be most appropriate at each stage in the cycle.

Business risk and the life cycle

As we have seen in Chapter 5, businesses face both unsystematic risk and systematic risk. Unsystematic risk (or non-market risk) is risk unique to a company or a project that can be mitigated through diversification into other businesses or projects. Systematic risk (or market risk) is risk that cannot be diversified away. One element of systematic risk is business risk, and the other element is financial risk. Business risk is associated with systematic influences on a company's specific business sector. The level of business risk relates to the risk to a company's operating profits and varies from one industry to another. Different levels of business risk may be faced at different stages in its life cycle (see Fig. 13.4), examples of which we saw in Worked Examples 13.1, 13.2, 13.3, and 13.4.

Business risk relates to the variability of a company's operating profit or cash flow. During the start-up phase of the business life cycle sales are low and costs are very high. Profit and cash flow are dependent on the levels of sales made by a company, and on the levels and type of costs incurred by a company.

Sales are determined by selling price and sales volume, and the seasonal and cyclical trends of sales. It is possible to assess the risk to profits from changes in both selling price and demand volumes. The product may not succeed. Even if the product is very good, market demand may not be as high as expected when it reaches the mature stage of the life cycle, and may not be sufficient to warrant the initial investment. Competition and substitute or replacement products may curtail the length of the product's life. It may therefore be difficult to hold on to whatever market share is achieved, and demand for the product could fall off very quickly. For these reasons the risk to variability in the operating profit or cash flow can therefore be seen to be very high during the start-up phase of the life cycle.

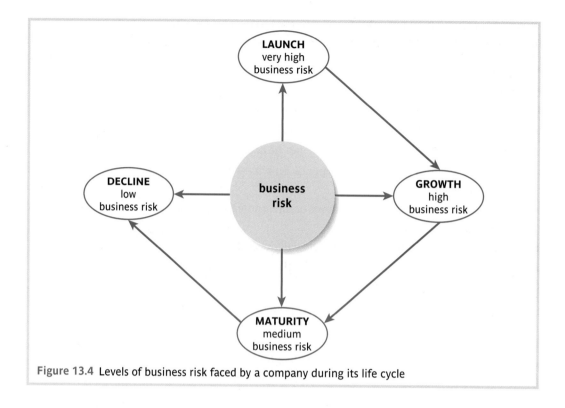

Figure 13.4 Levels of business risk faced by a company during its life cycle

If a product or a business survives the start-up phase of the cycle then the product is proven and has been accepted by the market. However, business risk is still faced by the company in terms of:

- sufficiently high market demand being maintained through to the mature stage of the cycle
- competition and substitute or replacement products, which may curtail the length of the product's life
- holding on to market share
- the potential for a rapid decline in demand for the product.

The risk to profits may be assessed by considering the company's level and structure of its costs, represented by its operating gearing (or leverage). Operating gearing may be considered simply as the relationship between fixed cost and total cost. A high proportion of fixed costs to total costs represents high operating gearing. The higher the operating gearing the greater is the advantage to the business of increasing sales volumes – the benefits of economies of scale. But, if sales are falling then a highly operationally geared business would find the high proportion of fixed costs a problem that may cause a swing from profit to loss. High operating gearing therefore indicates a high level of business risk.

Various operating gearing ratios may be used to assess the impact of fixed costs on a company. One example is the ratio that follows, which compares a company's contribution with its profit before interest and tax (PBIT):

$$\frac{\text{contribution}}{\text{PBIT}} = \frac{\text{sales} - \text{variable costs}}{\text{sales} - \text{variable costs} - \text{fixed costs}}$$

This relationship shows the extent to which fixed costs may be increased before the company gets into a loss-making situation. It also shows the relationship between a given increase in sales and the resultant impact on PBIT. Operating gearing increases as fixed costs rise and as variable costs fall. Unit contribution is the difference between the selling price and unit variable cost, measuring the incremental profit from one additional unit of a product or service. Since high fixed cost and low variable cost indicate a high contribution percentage, then high operating gearing indicates a high contribution percentage, and therefore high business risk.

The degree of operating gearing may be seen from the following ratio:

$$\text{degree of operating gearing} = \frac{\text{change in PBIT}}{\text{PBIT}} \times \frac{\text{sales}}{\text{change in sales}}$$

This relationship measures the percentage change in PBIT for a given percentage change in sales, and indicates a company's sensitivity to changes in its fixed costs. It may be used to measure the sensitivity of a business or a project to its fixed costs, and the impact of the cyclicality of its revenues.

We can see from the above relationship that during the growth phase the business risk of variability in the operating profit (PBIT) is not as high as during the start-up phase, but it is still high. The growth in the market generally during the growth phase means that a business is also likely to achieve high sales growth. Because of its high costs during the growth phase the company is unlikely to earn high profits until it gets towards the end of this phase and the benefits of economies of scale start to be seen.

Assuming that the business survives the shakeout period of the turbulence phase of the life cycle it is then able to move into its mature phase having established a relatively high market share. Because of this, the business faces a lower degree of business risk than in its growth phase. However, the business is still uncertain as to how long its mature phase will last and:

■ how competition and substitute or replacement products may still curtail the length of the product's life

■ how the business may hold on to its market share

■ whether there may be a rapid decline in demand for the product, for whatever reason.

Business risk due to variability in the operating profit or cash flow during the mature phase is therefore at a medium or moderate level. The only element of business risk remaining as the business moves into the decline phase is the speed at which demand for the product may fall. The level of business risk during this phase, therefore, is relatively low. The problem frequently met when products reach this phase is deciding exactly when to drop them, unless new life can be breathed into them, or whether they can be rejuvenated to produce further sales at reduced costs.

Financial risk and its inverse correlation with business risk

Financial risk is the risk of impact of interest on earnings measured by a company's financial gearing. Financial risk increases as levels of debt are increased and the company is committed to high levels of interest payments. The level of financial gearing therefore impacts on both the company's profits and its ability to pay dividends. The total of systematic or market risk faced by the company comprises the two elements of business risk and financial risk. We have seen how

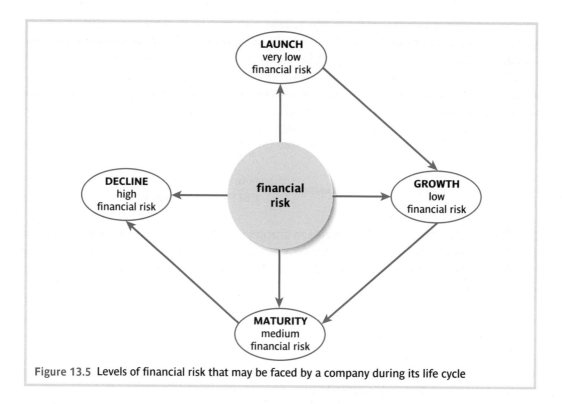

Figure 13.5 Levels of financial risk that may be faced by a company during its life cycle

business risk decreases as a company moves through its life cycle. Therefore, financial risk may be correspondingly increased throughout the life cycle without creating an unacceptable level of combined total systematic risk for the company, by increasing gearing through taking on higher levels of debt. A comparison of Figs. 13.4 and 13.5 illustrates this inverse correlation between business and financial risk.

During its start-up stage, a company normally makes no operating profit and there is a high risk of business failure. Therefore business risk is very high. Consequently, financial risk should be low which would normally mean that a start-up business is funded by equity rather than debt. However, this may not always be the case, and there are many instances of start-up companies being financed partly by debt, particularly by venture capitalists who may prefer this method of financing.

In the growth stage, operating profits should start to grow but will be volatile and there is likely to be some competition from new entrants to the market. Therefore, although lower than during the launch phase, business risk is nevertheless still likely to be high. If a small amount of debt is taken on in addition to equity then there will be some financial risk, although at a low level.

During the mature stage, a company's operating profits should be very high, with less volatility than during the growth phase, and therefore there is only a medium level of business risk. There is therefore scope for an increase in financial risk and so more debt may be taken on by the company without increasing total systematic risk. Financial risk is therefore likely to move to a medium level from the relatively low level seen in the growth phase.

In the decline phase the business has no growth prospects and so business risk is low. Debt levels are likely to be fairly high and so financial risk is high, not only because of interest payments, but at extremely high levels of debt there is also a risk of bankruptcy. However, it should be noted that not all mature and declining companies are necessarily saddled with huge debts. Some companies may have been able to repay all or most of their debt incurred during their mature phase and before going into decline.

An appropriate financial strategy may be developed for each stage in the business life cycle by exploiting the inverse correlation, which exists between financial risk and business risk. Although in theory this may appear quite logical it should be noted that in the real business environment the position is rarely so simple and straightforward. The relative levels of business risk and financial risk faced by a company will vary considerably. The weighting must generally be heavily towards business risk because it is a sound business strategy that provides the foundation for a successful business. If a company has adopted a poor business strategy then whilst its position may be mitigated, or its failure delayed, by using the best financial strategies, financial strategy alone cannot ensure success for a company.

A company may expect its business risk to continue to be reduced as it progresses over time through its life cycle. However, this may not happen if sudden changes occur in the market, such as increased competition, economic recession, or an introduction of substitute products. If in the meantime the company had increased its financial risk to exploit its inverse relationship with its business risk, a sudden increase in business risk would require total risk to be quickly reduced by reducing financial risk. This may involve repayment of debt, or an increase in equity, or both.

Progress check 13.3

Explain the inverse correlation between business risk and financial risk.

eps and net cash flow and the life cycle

During the start-up or launch phase of a product, or a business, sales may be expected to be very low or even non-existent, and therefore cash inflows will be zero or negligible. On the other hand, it is very likely that cash outflows will be very high because of high start-up costs. Because the inflow of cash from sales is low and cash outflows are high in respect of, for example, research and development costs, and marketing costs, net cash flow as well as eps may therefore be expected to be very highly negative (see Fig. 13.6).

During its growth stage, a business has an increasing inflow of cash from sales but cash outflows remain high because of working capital requirements, marketing costs, and continued investment in non-current assets for production, and possibly in cost reduction initiatives and new product development. The level of net cash flow is dependent on the rate of growth the company is achieving, but is likely to be neither highly negative nor highly positive. As sales increase eps will grow but may still be at relatively low levels because of high marketing costs, and because the benefits of economies of scale may not yet have been achieved.

The mature stage of a business usually sees cash inflows from sales at their highest levels and cash outflows are reduced because the company does not have to invest in new plant and machinery for future growth. In addition, since the product is now established then there is no need to continue to incur high levels of marketing cost. The net cash flow and eps at the mature stage of a business are therefore likely to be very highly positive.

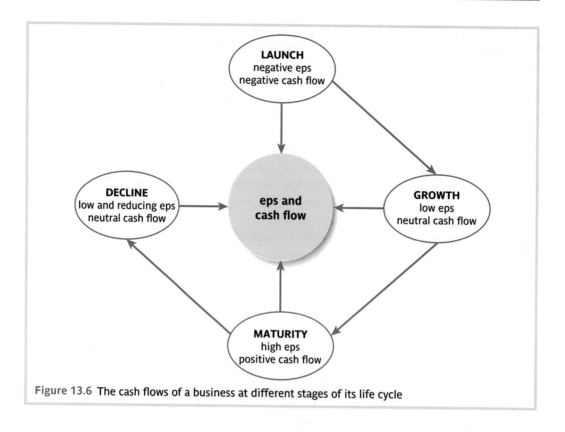

Figure 13.6 The cash flows of a business at different stages of its life cycle

During the decline stage of a business both cash inflows and cash outflows will be severely reduced. The eps of the business are likely to be low and reducing as sales levels fall. The net cash flow of the business is likely be low or negative, and its level is very much dependent on the rate of decline of the business.

Progress check 13.4

How may a company's net cash flow vary during each stage of the BLC?

Sources of funding and the life cycle

When a company is in its start-up phase, business risk will be very high and financial risk very low. Equity, very often provided by venture capitalists, is usually the source of financing for start-up companies rather than debt (see Fig. 13.7). This is because debt carries a fixed commitment for interest payments, which is difficult to meet during start-up when there are usually losses rather than profits, and negative cash flows. There is no such commitment with equity capital. During the start-up phase, the high returns required by equity shareholders will not be realised until funds are available for the company to pay dividends or unless shareholders dispose of their shares at a price higher than when they were acquired.

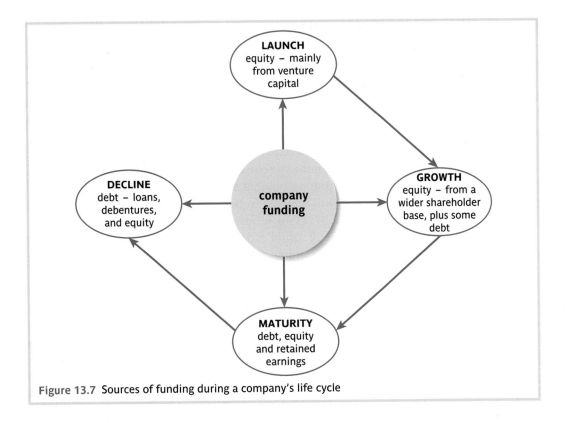

Figure 13.7 Sources of funding during a company's life cycle

During the growth stage of the company business risk is high and financial risk is low. Equity continues to be the main source of funds. But if business risk is reduced then a small amount of debt may be taken on. During this phase the original providers of equity capital may recover their investment at an increased value from:

■ sale of their shares to existing or new shareholders

■ public flotation of the company, which therefore widens the share ownership

■ buy-out of the company by its management, with or without the help of new external investors or lenders (see Chapter 18).

During the mature stage of the company business risk is at a medium level and financial risk is at a medium level. The company may continue to be funded largely by equity capital and also from its retained earnings, but financial risk may be increased to a medium level so the company's gearing may also be increased by taking on additional debt capital.

During the decline phase of the company business risk is low therefore financial risk may be increased. The level of debt may be increased because this cheap source of funding may 'help' declining profits because of its relatively low cost compared with other financing. Such debt may be secured on the residual value of the assets which remain tied up in the business.

Progress check 13.5

Why may equity be preferable to debt financing during a company's start-up phase?

Dividends and the life cycle

In this section we will consider the levels of dividends that may be paid by considering a company's financial performance throughout each of its phases in the business life cycle (see Fig. 13.8). The relationship between levels of dividends and each phase of the business life cycle is very much a generalisation and may not always be the case for all companies at all times and in every circumstance.

During its start-up phase the company has no distributable profits and negative cash flow and therefore the dividend payout ratio must be zero. During its growth phase as eps and cash flows start to increase there may be a nominal amount of dividend paid. The level of dividend payout will depend on the level of growth achieved by the company, with regard to the level of profit it has earned and conditional on its having sufficient cash flow.

During its mature phase the company would expect to maintain a high dividend payout ratio because there will be distributable profits even after debt interest, and there should be sufficient cash flow to pay high dividends. The company may now have little new investment opportunity. Therefore growth prospects are very limited, and so investors have less chance of capital gains and so will demand a high level of dividends. A possible agency problem may manifest itself here. Shareholders will generally require a high dividend payout during the company's mature phase but the directors or managers of the business may alternatively prefer to hold on to funds to give themselves increased operational flexibility.

In the decline stage the company may decide to use all the free cash flow that it has generated to pay dividends. This total dividend payout ratio means that dividends are likely to exceed profit.

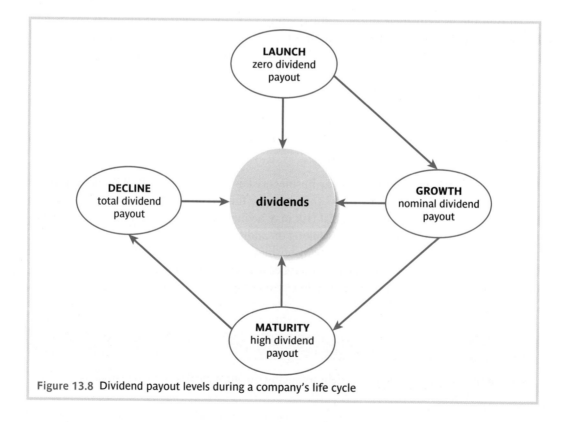

Figure 13.8 Dividend payout levels during a company's life cycle

In addition to consideration of the life cycle, there are a number of alternative theories relating to the dividend decision, which we will look at in Chapter 15, for example:

- residual theory – the company pays dividends only when all other investment opportunities have been exhausted
- Miller and Modigliani dividend irrelevancy theory – dividends are irrelevant to the market value of the shares
- traditional view – the company pursues a growth strategy from profitable reinvestment to maximise the market value of the company's shares.

Shareholders' returns and the life cycle

One of the strategic financial decisions that companies have to make is 'should we pay dividends now or retain earnings to reinvest in the company to provide future increased corporate value that will result in higher dividends in the future plus an increase in share price?'

Shareholders receive a return in two ways: dividends; capital appreciation from an increase in share price. The levels of dividend payments and capital growth are usually very different throughout each stage in the life cycle of the business as illustrated in Fig. 13.9.

During a company's start-up phase losses are likely to be made and cash flows will be highly negative. In addition, if the company is funded by debt as well as by equity then interest will also have to be paid. Therefore, dividends cannot be paid unless adequate cash is acquired by, for example, taking on more debt for that purpose. This is highly unlikely to happen, and so it is

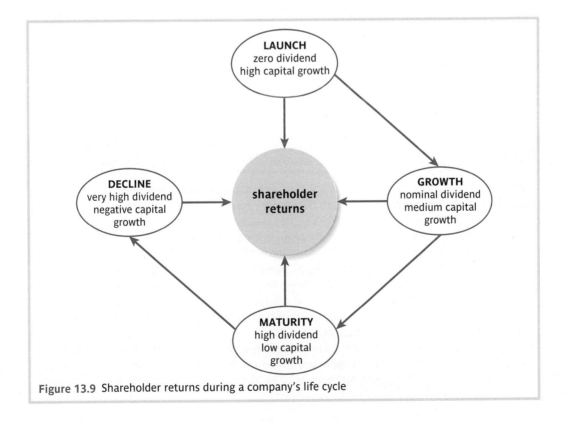

Figure 13.9 Shareholder returns during a company's life cycle

likely that during the start-up phase of a business no dividend will be paid. However, during the start-up phase there is likely to be a great deal of enthusiasm and optimism about the company's future prospects and expectations of growth, which should be reflected in an increase in value of the company's shares.

During the growth phase the business is likely to have started making modest profits, but will still have cash requirements for funding its operations and possibly investment in further growth. Therefore, it is unlikely to be able to pay more than a small amount of dividend. Because a large amount of the company's growth, which was anticipated during the start-up phase will already have been achieved by the time it reaches its growth phase then the expectation of future growth will reduce. Its level will depend on how innovative the company is in its investment, if any, in additional new projects.

When a company has reached its mature phase it will have reached a period of some stability in its life cycle in terms of its market share and sales levels. Its profit levels should be relatively high and less vulnerable to the fluctuations experienced during its growth phase. Costs will have been reduced through economies of scale, and investment levels will be lower unless it is preparing for another period of high growth. Cash flow is therefore likely to be high. High levels of dividends may therefore be paid, but the prospects for future growth will be low.

The decline phase of the company is the period when there is absolutely no expectation of growth and in which there may actually be negative growth. This may happen when the company may not even be maintaining its current level of non-current assets and may in fact be disinvesting by disposing of assets no longer required. During this phase, all cash flows received, including proceeds from asset disposals, may therefore be paid out in dividends, which may mean that the dividend level is even higher than the total expected shareholder return, if capital growth is negative.

There is an offsetting relationship between the dividend payout ratio and the expected level of capital growth. This relationship should be considered in the context of a company's decreasing overall risk profile as it matures and then moves into decline. The decreasing risk profile means that over time the rate of return demanded by investors will get lower and lower. The way in which this may apply at each stage in the business life cycle is illustrated in Worked Example 13.5.

Worked Example 13.5

During Grovidend Ltd's start-up phase the total annual return required by investors is represented wholly by expected capital growth because the future growth prospects of the company are high. We will assume that shareholders initially require a return of 30%, which at the start-up stage is all from capital growth, with no dividends being paid, as shown in Fig. 13.10.

During the growth phase of the company the total shareholder return (TSR) required by investors may have reduced to, say, 20% as overall risk levels fall. Most of this will still be expected from capital growth (for example 18%), and if the company is making some profit and has sufficient cash flow it may pay out a small dividend (for example 2%). As the company progresses through its growth phase the prospects of future growth will gradually reduce unless the product is exceptionally highly successful.

During the mature phase the overall return required by investors will have again reduced to say 12%, as the overall risk level continues to reduce, but the majority of this will now be expected from the dividend yield (for example 10%). The growth element of the return expected

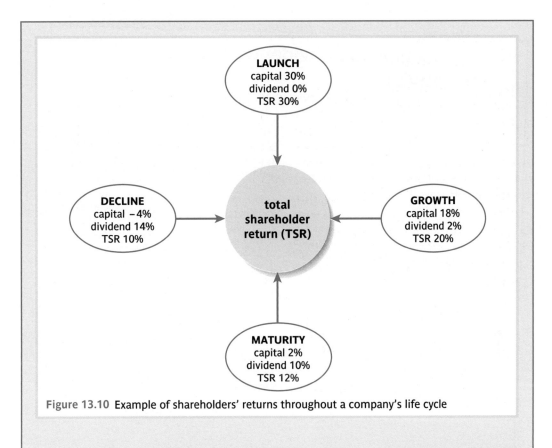

Figure 13.10 Example of shareholders' returns throughout a company's life cycle

by investors will be much reduced (to 2% for example), because the company's growth prospects are still reducing. However, this lack of future growth is more than offset by the dividend yield.

The decline phase shows a total dividend payout ratio of, say, 14%, which may be higher than the total annual return expected by investors, which has again reduced to, say, 10%. Therefore, capital growth may be negative during the decline stage at, for example, –4%.

For the shareholder, income tax is payable on dividends, and capital gains tax is payable on the share price gains when the shares are disposed of. In theory, if the after-tax returns from both were similar then shareholders should be indifferent as to whether a dividend is paid or not (but in practice this would also depend on their individual tax positions). If a dividend is not paid, then the value of shares should increase to reflect the present value of future cash flows generated from reinvestment of funds, which were available to be paid out as dividends. However, shareholders do actually like to receive dividends and achieve a growth in the share price, which is not always achievable as illustrated in the Pennon Group press extract on the next page. Pennon continued to maintain consistency in its levels of eps and dividend payouts. Despite a significant increase in Pennon's share price during 2004 water utilities remained a low risk industry, reflected in its lack of future growth prospects. However, this case should also be considered in the context of the more recent shortage of water in the UK. In the future, there will inevitably be a greater emphasis by utilities companies on cost reduction and the elimination of waste, and an increase in price of water.

The choice between dividends and capital growth

'Pennon's safe enough but doesn't hold water for growth prospects',
by Philip Aldrick

Investors seeking an interesting company with big growth prospects need not consider Pennon Group, the owner of the water and sewerage rights for Devon, Cornwall and parts of Dorset and Somerset, and Viridor Waste.

With assets of £2.6 billion and 2,300 staff, Pennon is a 'bog standard' utility with a waste disposal business bolted on the side. For investors this need not be a turn-off. Pennon generates oodles of cash relative to its size, and – like all utilities – gives most of it to shareholders in the form of dividends.

This is a business as predictable as the miserable English weather, which makes investors happy. Over the four past years, Pennon's operating profit has not varied outside a 7pc band and the amount paid in dividends has inched up from £49.4m to £51.1m.

As a result, Pennon shares have risen 44pc in value since the start of 2004, outperforming other UK utility stocks by about 13pc.

The price-earnings ratio is 14, and the forecast dividend yield is 4.4pc, low compared with its peers. Water is a low risk business, and the main threat to Pennon's profitability is the regulator of water utilities, Ofwat.

The statutory body decides how much Pennon is allowed to charge for water and sewerage, and in a decision a week ago called for operating expenditure efficiency improvements of 2.5pc a year for the next five years.

Releasing its interim results yesterday, Pennon said the decision presented a 'very tough' challenge, and consequently it will fire 100 staff and cut other costs. However, it promised to maintain the dividend, which some analysts are forecasting will grow 3pc above inflation up to at least 2010. This news helped Pennon shares rise 5p to 955p. Pennon offers a safe long-term investment but there are better water company picks for the income investor.

© *Daily Telegraph*, 10 December 2004

Pennon					
Market value: E1.19bn		Estyld: 4.5pc		Share price: 955p +5p	
Year to Mar	2001	2002	2003	2004	2005Gest
Turnover	£435.1m	£423.9m	£417.2m	£471.3m	£526m
Pre-tax profit	£74.2m	£77.4m	£74.2m	£78.8m	£81.0
Earnings per share	56.0p	53.0p	55.0p	57.7p	56.9p
Dividend per share	36.0p	37.5p	109.1p	41.0p	42.8p

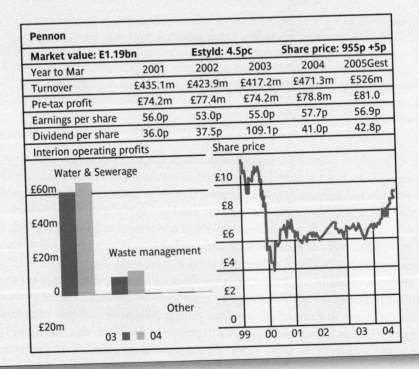

Price/earnings (P/E) ratio, the share price, and the life cycle

A company's share price is dependent on the level of activity in the market for its shares. The higher the demand is to buy the shares, the higher will be the share price because the supply in the short-term, the number of shares in issue, is fixed. The demand to buy shares partly reflects performance that the company has already achieved and partly reflects an expectation of future performance. Future performance relates to the expected present value of future net cash flows, which the market feels that the company is able to achieve. Because an element of the share price includes an expectation of value to be created from future opportunities, the prospects of capital growth of a company are reflected in its published price/earnings (P/E) ratio.

As we have already discussed, very high growth prospects at the start-up stage are likely to be followed by high growth during the growth phase, then medium growth during the mature stage, and no growth during the decline stage. Therefore, we can see that because the P/E ratio bears a direct relationship to expected future growth then it may be expected to fall over the company's life cycle (see Fig. 13.11).

A company's share price is its eps multiplied by its P/E ratio. During the start-up and growth stages nearly all shareholders' returns are generated from capital growth. As the rate of growth declines the share price may increase to a level that provides an acceptable level of shareholder return through a growth in eps, which takes account of the declining P/E ratio (applied to these earnings as they grow), and the changing dividend payout ratio which reduces expectations of future growth as the company matures.

We may generalise about how the P/E ratio and share price may change during the life cycle of a business. In the start-up phase of a business the P/E ratio may be very high because of the

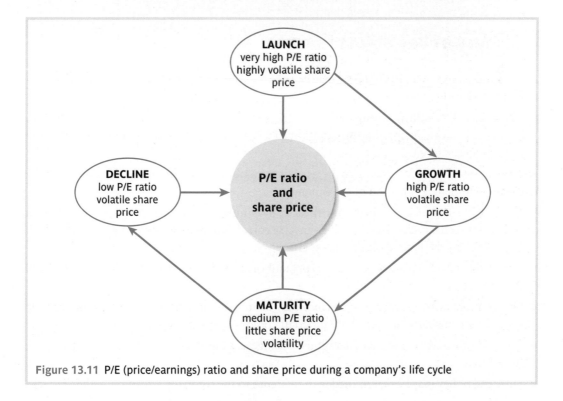

Figure 13.11 P/E (price/earnings) ratio and share price during a company's life cycle

expectation of high future levels of growth. The share price should increase but may be highly volatile because there is a high potential for failure of new businesses.

During the growth phase the P/E ratio may still be high, as growth expectations are still reasonably high. The share price may still be volatile because there will be continued uncertainty about whether the level of growth expected by investors will actually be achieved.

The P/E ratio will reduce to a medium to low level during the company's mature phase, because earnings should be high but growth expectations will be low. The share price should become fairly stable and with less volatility, because the largest part of total investor returns are now provided mostly from dividends.

During the decline stage of a company the share price normally declines and is also volatile because of the uncertainty surrounding how long the business may continue.

Progress check 13.6

In what ways do equity shareholders receive returns from their investment in a company and how does this differ from returns received by debt holders?

In Chapters 14 and 15 we will link together each of the parameters we have considered in this chapter for each of the phases in the business life cycle. By looking at the complete picture of the company with regard to risk, gearing, dividends, and so on, during its start-up, growth, maturity, and decline phases we can consider the financial strategies that may be adopted to achieve an increase in shareholder value. Chapters 16, 17, and 18 take this a step further by considering additional financial strategies related to diversification and reorganisation, achieved through mergers and acquisitions (M&As) and business restructuring.

Summary of key points

- The product life cycle (PLC) model may be used to describe the separate stages in the development of a product.

- The Boston Consulting Group (BCG) matrix may be used in a similar way to the PLC to assess the strategic financial implications at each stage in the development of a business and its products or services.

- The business life cycle (BLC) may be used as a framework describing the separate stages in the development and growth of a company.

- Levels of business risk and financial risk faced by companies change throughout the different stages in their life cycles, and there is an inverse correlation between these types of risk, which together comprise systematic or market risk.

- The levels of both earnings per share (eps) and cash flow vary during the different stages of the life cycle.

- One or more different sources of finance may be more appropriate throughout the separate stages of the business life cycle, with different combinations appropriate at each stage.

- The P/E ratio and total shareholder returns change as a business moves through each stage of its life cycle.

- Dividend policy may be determined with reference to the company's position in the life cycle.

> ### 🔑 Glossary of key terms
>
> **business life cycle (BLC)** The business life cycle has many different meanings, including:
>
> - an annual pattern, for example a business whose activities follow a seasonal cycle, or a business that undertakes a project which spans many years
> - changes in the economic environment, at a macroeconomic level, in terms of growth, inflation, and interest rates
> - the development of a company through a number of clearly defined phases, in the same way as the PLC.
>
> **product life cycle (PLC)** The period which begins with the initial product specification, and ends with the withdrawal from the market of both the product and its support. It is characterised by defined stages that include research, development, introduction, maturity, decline, and abandonment.

❓ Questions

Q13.1   Outline the disadvantages associated with use of life cycle models.

Q13.2   Compare the Boston Consulting Group (BCG) matrix approach with that of the life cycle model.

Q13.3   Why should a company not expect the level of business risk it faces to remain constant during its entire life cycle?

Q13.4   For each of the major stages in the life cycle of a typical company describe the main cash inflows and outflows, their likely magnitudes, and the resultant net cash flows.

Q13.5   Describe the factors that influence the level of financial risk faced by a company.

Q13.6   Explain the significance of financial risk to a company.

Q13.7   Outline the relationship between business risk and financial risk during the life cycle of a company and explain why the distinction between these two forms of risk is important.

Q13.8   Analyse the ways in which a company's financing needs change over its life cycle.

Q13.9   Discuss the reasons why companies may consider adopting different capital structures as they progress from their initial start-up through to maturity.

Q13.10 Why do companies pay dividends?

Q13.11 What are the key factors that influence a company in deciding the level of dividends it will pay?

👥 Discussion points

D13.1   'Every business should aim to maximise its number of BCG "cash cows".' Discuss.

D13.2   'Earnings per share (eps) tell shareholders everything they need to know about a company.' Discuss.

D13.3   'A shareholder is indifferent as to whether a dividend is paid or not.' Discuss.

Exercises

Solutions are provided in Appendix 2 to all exercise numbers highlighted in colour.

Level I

E13.1   *Time allowed – 30 minutes*
Outline a typical product life cycle (PLC) with reference to one specific industry.

E13.2   *Time allowed – 30 minutes*
Compare the BCG (Boston Consulting Group) matrix with the business life cycle approach. How do these two approaches assist in the development of appropriate financial strategies?

E13.3   *Time allowed – 30 minutes*
Outline the life cycle of a typical business, and explain the movements and net effects of its cash flows during each of the phases of its cycle.

E13.4   *Time allowed – 30 minutes*
In what ways does risk impact on a business as it moves through each phase of its life cycle? What strategies may a business adopt in response to such risks?

E13.5   *Time allowed – 30 minutes*
Explain the inverse correlation between financial risk and business risk, and how a company may use this to develop an appropriate financial strategy, during each stage of its life cycle.

E13.6   *Time allowed – 30 minutes*
Explain the circumstances necessary for a company to be able to pay dividends to shareholders.

Level II

E13.7   *Time allowed – 45 minutes*
Clearly explain why you would agree or disagree with the statement that 'a company's shareholders would never want the company to invest in projects with negative NPVs'.

E13.8   *Time allowed – 45 minutes*
Explain the ways in which a company may exploit the changing levels of business risk it faces to develop appropriate financial strategies in order to increase shareholder value.

E13.9   *Time allowed – 60 minutes*
The following is the capital structure of a company in the automotive industry:

	Number of units	Price per unit £	Market value
Ordinary shares	115,000,000	26.00	£2,990,000,000
Preference shares	10,000,000	32.50	£325,000,000
Warrants	14,400,000	13.50	£194,400,000
Bonds	2,000,000	650.00	£1,300,000,000

Due to large losses incurred during the past few years, the company had £2bn in carried forward tax losses. Therefore, the next £2bn of profit would be free from corporation tax. The consensus among financial analysts is that the company would not have cumulative profits in excess of £2bn over the next five years.

The majority of the preference shares are held by banks. The company had agreed to buy back the preference shares over the next few years, and needed to decide whether to issue new debt or equity shares to raise the funds needed to do this.

Analyse the company's financial structure and outline the implications of its funding options. Explain what would be the best funding option for the company and why.

E13.10 *Time allowed – 60 minutes*

In one of the back issues of Fortune magazine (4 May 1981) an article entitled 'Fresh Evidence That Dividends Don't Matter' relating to the largest 500 corporations in the USA, stated that: 'All told, 115 companies of the 500 raised their payout every year during the period 1970–79. Investors in this . . . group would have fared somewhat better than investors in the 500 as a whole: the median total annual compound return of the 115 companies was 10.7% during the decade versus 9.4% for the 500.'

Explain whether or not, in your opinion, the Fortune magazine article indicated evidence that investors prefer dividends to capital gains, and why this may be so.

Chapter 14

Financial strategies from start-up to growth

Chapter contents

LEARNING OBJECTIVES

Completion of this chapter will enable you to:

- ☑ Outline the key aspects in the profile of a start-up business.

- ☑ Identify the sources of financial and other support for start-up businesses.

- ☑ Explain the significant role that venture capitalists (VCs) may play in the support and development of new businesses.

- ☑ Describe the relationship between perceived risk and the return required by investors in a start-up business.

- ☑ Outline the key aspects in the profile of growth business.

- ☑ Explain how the transition from the start-up phase of a business to its growth phase may take place.

- ☑ Describe the relationship between perceived risk and the return required by investors in a growth business.

- ☑ Identify the various types of capital market.

- ☑ Outline the process by which a company flotation takes place, its initial public offering (IPO).

- ☑ Consider the ways in which a company may finance new projects.

- ☑ Explain the way in which a rights issue is made and the implications for a company and its shareholders.

Introduction

We saw in Chapter 13 how the PLC model (and also the BCG model) identifies the separate stages in the development of a business and its products. This chapter will focus on the start-up introduction phase and growth phase of products and the business life cycle.

During its early stages of start-up and growth a business usually requires additional external financing. The individuals who launch new businesses are inevitably optimistic and enthusiastic about their new ventures. However, the risks of not succeeding are high and so the returns expected from investments in such ventures are also necessarily high. The investment required to support new businesses may be provided by **venture capitalists (VCs)**, which specialise in providing funds for this type of investment.

We will consider the changes that take place when a company moves from its start-up phase to its growth phase, when it becomes much more market-orientated. During its growth phase a company may finance future growth by raising funds via financial institutions and private investors. A company may be floated on a stock exchange during its growth phase, through an initial public offering (IPO), before it reaches its mature stage when the opportunities for capital gains from increases in the share price may be limited.

Companies may finance new projects out of retained earnings or additional new project financing. Chapter 14 closes with a look at **secondary public offerings (SPOs)** such as rights issues, which are a source of new funding; existing shareholders are given rights to buy additional new shares at a discount to the market price in proportion to their existing shareholdings.

A profile of start-up businesses

Figure 14.1 provides a profile of a start-up business that summarises each of the variables that we considered in Chapter 13. Business risk is very high because of the uncertainty relating to both products (or services) and markets.

Start-up businesses are usually totally funded by equity, which is highly risky for the investors. Equity capital represents low financial risk for the business since it does not have to be repaid, and dividends do not have to be paid at all and may not be paid if the company is not making sufficient profits. Financial risk is also very low if there is no debt funding and therefore no commitments to interest payments.

One of the main providers of equity funding for a start-up business are venture capitalists (VCs). Venture capitalists are ideal investors for start-ups, because they are professionals who are well aware of the high level of business risk associated with businesses in their launch or start-up phase.

In order to keep financial risk as low as possible, start-up businesses may therefore aim to avoid the use of debt capital. VCs usually provide equity capital, and they are prepared to take high risks for which they expect high returns. Their returns are in the form of capital gains achieved from an increase in share price. VCs are not restricted to providing equity and may also provide debt and other types of capital.

Although high business risk is faced by start-up companies it is not necessarily so for VCs. VCs can mitigate the high business risks they face by developing a portfolio of investments. Consequently, sometimes VCs win and sometimes they lose. Once the growth phase is over, venture capitalists may want to cease to be investors in a business and realise their gains. This may then be the time for a public flotation on a stock exchange, or a management buy-out (MBO) of the company (see Chapter 18).

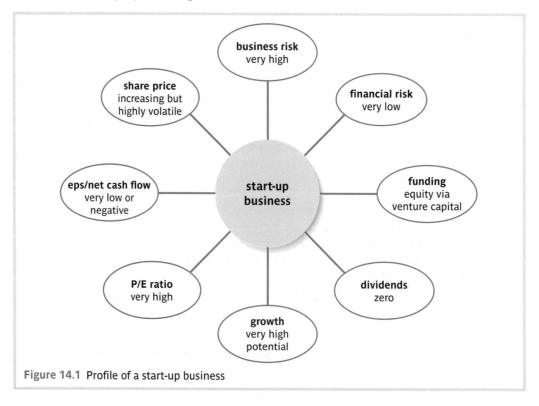

Figure 14.1 Profile of a start-up business

Sources of support for a start-up business

Start-up, high risk businesses are needed by the UK economy to replace declining industries. During the pre-launch stages of a new business there may be high costs of research and development (R&D) and costs of the development of new product concepts, which are generally sunk costs. Capital is necessary for these types of cost, which is termed seed capital. For products that still seem attractive for further development after the initial investment, further capital is required, which is called start-up capital, and is required to support operational requirements and marketing costs.

There is now an extremely wide range of support for new businesses in the UK. These include:

- the Department of Trade and Industry (DTI)
- trade associations
- regional development agencies such as the former Welsh Development Agency in Wales
- National Assemblies such as the Welsh Assembly
- knowledge networks such as Business Link (www.businesslink.gov.uk).

In the UK the DTI provides a great deal of help and support in the areas of:

- regulations and environmental issues
- innovation
- training
- exports
- European business
- investment
- Patent Office
- Companies House, for details of professional bodies, business contacts, etc.
- Small Business Service, for details of local support schemes.

Progress check 14.1

Outline the range of support available for start-up businesses and the types of support that they may provide.

Venture capitalists (VCs)

VCs are professional investors who provide funding for new businesses usually in return for an equity stake in the companies. The failure of some investments by VCs should be offset by the outstanding success of other investments, giving them an overall high return. VCs are actually generally risk-averse. They may specialise in particular industrial sectors but still maintain a portfolio of investments in that sector.

VCs have a short investment horizon (three to five years), and an important consideration for them is their 'exit' strategy of how to leave companies after success, making room for new investors with lower return expectations. The future growth prospects and the P/E ratios of start-up companies are very high, with an expectation of high capital gains. VCs usually sell out for capital gain before a company is cash positive and paying dividends. The re-financing of such businesses after exit by VCs is something we have already introduced and will discuss again later in this book.

Examples of venture capitalists are:

- Investors in Industry (3i)
- Equity Capital for Industry
- Business Expansion Scheme funds
- specialist areas, usually subsidiaries, within the clearing banks.

The press extract below includes a survey of deals undertaken by the top 10 VC firms in the UK during the period January to June 2004. It also provides an insight into the role of VCs in the USA, UK, and Europe over the past 20 to 30 years including the dot.com boom of 1999/2000. It explains the distinction between venture capital and private equity. Venture capital is a part of private equity, which also includes seed capital and start-up capital.

Survey into venture capital providers in 2004
'Venture Capital', by David Bain

The late-90s dot.com glory days of start-ups may be long gone, but VC firms are still funding new businesses on both sides of the pond – to the tune of 27 billion Euros in Europe alone.

TOP 10 VC FIRMS IN THE UK

	ASSETS INVESTED Euro (millons)	NUMBER OF DEALS Jan–Jun 2004
1 3i	11,109.00	18
2 Apax Partners	9,879.60	4
3 Accel Partners	2,691.90	5
4 Benchmark Capital	2,329.94	3
5 Atlas Venturers	1,728.93	3
6 Aberdeen Murray-Johnstone PE	746.35	6
7 Advent Venture Partners	678.30	4
8 Index Partners	509.80	3
9 Amadeus Capital Partners	447.81	5
10 Quester Capital Management	433.32	7

Source: VentureOne

In 1999, at the peak of the VC-fuelled dot.com boom, there were 133 listed Internet stocks in the US. Despite making combined losses of $3bn on sales of $15.2bn, the market valuation of these stocks was US$310 billion.

For most of us, the dot.com boom seems a million years ago, but cast your mind back to that extraordinary period in the history of business. Remember all those hugely trendy firms like boo.com, clickmango and Boxman? Well, apart from the Internet – and hopelessly optimstic management – all these firms had one thing in common: venture capital. Venture capital funds were as much an integral part of the tech boom as the Internet.

In the first year of the new millennium, private equity investment – venture capital and late-stage investments – swelled to $142.6 billion in the US and Europe (the European figure includes buy-outs). Four years earlier it had been just $1.8 billion. In 1999–2000, it was no great shakes to walk into a meeting with a venture capital firm and persuade them to sign a cheque for a couple of million dollars for a crazy business idea – as long as it involved the Internet. Wasn't everyone doing it at the time? Boo.com convinced French VC Europ@Web to do so in 20 minutes (so legend has it), before burning more than £100 million in 18 months. Yet it has not always been boom and bust for these firms and the companies they have funded.

In the US, where the industry is much more mature and ingrained within corporate financing methods, VCs played a crucial role in funding extraordinarily successful hi-tech companies in Silicon Valley. Iconic firms such as Apple, Cisco and Google relied on seed capital from Sequoia Capital, US Venture Partners and the like. Indeed, Silicon Valley would probably not have existed without VC funds. It's a measure of the maturity of the US venture capital market that the amount and depth of data on the sector is far more refined than in Europe. Across the Atlantic, the industry has a history of more than 30 years, whereas venture capitalism in Europe – including the UK – got under way in a significant form only in the late 1980s. US data tends to be more transparent, partly because of the clear divide made there between venture capital and private equity.

In European data, the distinction is often blurred. Not surprisingly, one of the best surveys on the main players in venture capital is based just down the road from Silicon Valley, in San Francisco. VentureOne has been researching the sector since 1986 and opened a London office in 2000 to bring its expertise to Europe. It teams up with Ernst & Young to produce quarterly and annual reports on the sector. In VentureOne's latest survey on European VCs, which looked at the number of deals done and assets under management in the first half of this year, the biggest player is the 3i Group – one of the few firms with a brand recognised outside its sector.

The London-based 3i has been a dominant player in venture capital and private equity for more than 20 years, where it has been at the top of most league tables. It's big across Europe and the US, but the group works across venture capital as well as private equity, and has investments in public companies. Firms like Quester Capital Management and Advert Venture Partners are known for their VC investments. Like 3i, they have pan-European businesses. German VC Techno Venture Management gets top billing in the annual Limited Partnership survey, which looks at VC firms from the point of view of the institutions –

such as pension funds and banks – that give them money. The survey is produced by Almedia Capital, a private equity and placement company, based in London. Apax Partners, whose chairman Sir Ronald Cohn is one of the founding fathers of the European VC industry, and Paris-based Sofinnova Partners also score well on this list. Last year in Europe, venture capital and private equity firms raised Euro 27 billion to invest in budding new businesses and buyouts, according to the annual survey by the Brussels-based European Private Equity and Venture Capital Association (EVCA). That's a little less than the year before, and a long way off the record level of Euro 48 billion raised in 2000.

The UK continues to be the leading venture capital centre in Europe, largely because of access to a large pool of funds from the City of London and a well-entrenched private-sector ethos. EVCA reckoned that in 2003 more than half of funds raised for VC and private equity deals were done from the UIC. Sweden accounted for the next-highest percentage, about 8%, followed by the Netherlands at 7%. Future surveys are likely to confirm the UK's dominance in venture capital firms, with names like 3i and Apax Partners doing the most deals across Europe. German, French and Scandinavian VC firms should also prosper, but a further shakeout in the sector – which began when the tech bubble burst in 2001 – is expected. And any return to the golden period of venture capital activity – year 2000 – is not around the corner.

WHAT IS VENTURE CAPITAL?

Venture capital and private equity are often seen as the same, and indeed firms like 3i and Advent Venture Partners work in both areas of financing. But venture capital forms only a part of private equity: the startup and seed capital bit. VCs sometimes become involved in late-stage and buyout investing, so some blurring in the data between the two kinds of funding is inevitable. This happens in Europe, where some larger private-equity firms operate at all levels, but rarely in the US. Organisations such as VentureOne and the European Private Equity and Venture Capital Association are improving the statistical output, and as the industry matures in Europe, firms should produce better data.

> ## Progress check 14.2
>
> What is a venture capitalist?

Risk and return in start-up

Start-ups are investment intensive, but also risk intensive. There is risk attached to the provision of seed capital to support:

- R&D costs in identifying new products
- applied research costs
- product development costs,

and risk attached to the provision of start-up capital to support the introduction of the launch stage of the business, which includes costs of operating facilities and marketing.

Systematic risk is reflected in the impact on the returns on a company's shares as a result of external factors like Government policy, interest rates, and economic cycles. In the initial period of a start-up business, this systematic risk does not exist. By definition, a start-up business has not been in existence long enough for such factors to have any significant impact on the returns on its shares. Systematic risk will start to increase as the start-up progresses. For example, a business selling fashion clothing is likely to suffer very quickly from an economic downturn. However, such systematic risk is difficult to measure if there is no share price history. A start-up business does face the unique or unsystematic risk of the company performing badly or failing.

During the start-up phase, earnings per share (eps) are usually negative or at best very low because of the high start-up costs and very low sales levels. Usually, there can be no dividends paid by a start-up business because:

- funds are needed for investment
- dividends are not legally payable if the company does not have distributable reserves.

Therefore, for a start-up company it is not possible to apply a dividend growth model to estimate the expected returns of investors. Also, it may not be possible to use the Capital Asset Pricing Model (CAPM) in a start-up situation because although there will be unsystematic risk, it is likely that there will be no systematic risk. It should be remembered that CAPM brings together portfolio theory, share valuation theory, the cost of capital theory, and gearing theory, and is concerned with:

- how systematic risk can be measured
- how systematic risk affects required returns and share prices

and so even if any systematic risk were present during the start-up phase it may not be possible to measure it because of the lack of a share price history.

A start-up company's share price may increase rapidly, but is likely to be very volatile because of the high potential for new business failures. How can the expected returns of a new business be estimated? Well, this may be estimated by using a probability-adjusted cash flow forecast, which allows for as wide a range of present value cash flows as possible, using a realistic discount rate, which is illustrated in Worked Example 14.1. It may also be estimated by using a much higher discount rate, reflecting a high level of risk, and unadjusted cash flows.

Worked Example 14.1

Helen Hywater is considering a start-up business, which requires an initial investment of £100,000, the returns on which are dependent on the outcomes of one of three opportunities, which may be available, one of which is certain to go ahead. It is not yet known with certainty which opportunity will go ahead and each of them generates different yearly net cash flows over two years, with a different likelihood of occurrence. The cost of capital for the business is 10% per annum.

The forecast probabilities and net cash flows for each year are:

Opportunity	Probability of occurrence	Per annum cash flow
1	0.5	£75,000
2	0.2	£25,000
3	0.3	£45,000
	1.0	

The total of the probabilities is 1, which indicates that one of the options is certain to occur. Even though one opportunity will definitely go ahead Helen needs to consider if she should make the investment at all.

We first need to use the probabilities to calculate the weighted average of the expected outcomes for each year.

Opportunity	Cash flow £	Probability	Expected cash flow £
1	75,000	0.5	37,500
2	25,000	0.2	5,000
3	45,000	0.3	13,500
Expected per annum cash flows			56,000

To calculate the expected NPV over the two years we need to discount the expected annual cash flows using the discount rate of 10% per annum.

Year	Expected cash flow £	Discount factor at 10%	Expected present value £
1	56,000	0.91	50,960
2	56,000	0.83	46,480
Total	112,000		97,440
Initial investment			100,000
Expected NPV			–2,560

The negative expected NPV of £2,560 indicates that Helen should not go ahead with the start-up. ▶

▶ It should be noted that the above technique of expected net present value has used an average cash flow, which:

– in the example is not actually capable of occurrence

– may not represent the real situation if the underlying risk of outcomes worse than the average are ignored.

If the expected per annum cash flow from opportunity 1 had been £150,000 instead of £75,000, giving an expected £62,690 positive NPV, Helen would have been keen to proceed with the investment. However, she should also consider the impact on the business if, for example, opportunity 2 had been the one that subsequently became available.

Worked Example 14.1 uses the technique of expected NPV in which financial estimates are very uncertain. In practice, it may be very difficult for a start-up venture, with unproven products and new markets, to use such an approach. In such cases, qualitative rather than quantitative information would be much more influential in guiding the decision to go ahead with the start-up. It should be noted that although the expected NPV approach is a useful method it may have more value when it is used for averaging repeated projects of a similar nature to make it a valid application.

With regard to Worked Example 14.1 it may be useful to consider the possible impact of additional information on the decision on whether or not to go ahead with the start-up, for example:

- viability of the products relating to each opportunity
- reactions of potential customers
- customer orders already received
- previous experience of starting a business
- previous experience within the industry
- the role of due diligence
- the role of VCs:
  - are they needed?
  - are they good or bad?
  - exit strategies
  - impact on other shareholders
- the consequences should the business fail
- financing.

In a start-up there is a need for as low a financial risk as possible, or preferably no financial risk. Therefore it is recommended that there is no use of debt at all. There is no advantage in the use of debt by a start-up company because debt only increases default risk, which mitigates any value of the tax shield, the tax benefit of loan interest (unlikely to be required during the start-up phase). Default risk is the risk of not being able to pay interest and the ultimate repayment of the loan. In a start-up business there is a high likelihood of default because of the relatively high premium of debt financing and the high cost of debt.

A profile of growth businesses

Figure 14.2 provides a profile of a business that has moved into its growth phase, and which summarises each of the variables that we considered in Chapter 13. Once a product has been successfully launched sales revenues should start to increase rapidly. A high degree of business risk continues to be faced until required sales levels and market share have been achieved. However, there is a reduction in business risk from the level during the start-up phase. Because of this a modification of business strategy may be required that should include:

■ an accent on marketing

■ a focus on increasing sales

■ an aim of increasing market share.

Most businesses during their growth phases that are seeking to finance investment, innovation, and growth are generally well served by a variety of private-sector sources of external finance. Equity finance, or debt finance secured on the assets of the business, may be neither suitable nor

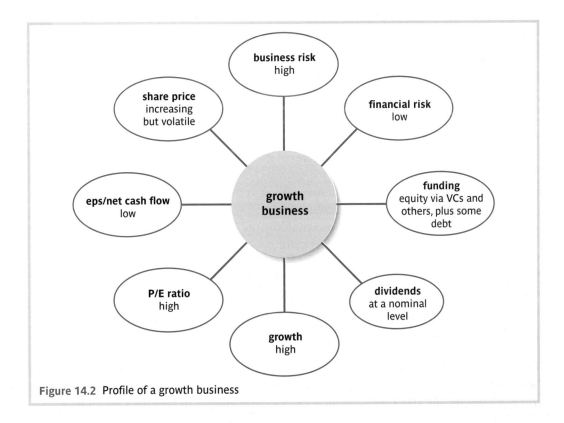

Figure 14.2 Profile of a growth business

available to all companies. Companies that have become too large or are in a fast-growing stage of their growth phase may find it difficult to obtain additional funds from existing individual shareholders. On the other hand, they may be insufficiently developed to obtain a stock market listing, or they may have insufficient assets to obtain adequate levels of debt finance. This difficulty in obtaining conventional financing results in what is often referred to as the funding gap or the financing gap.

To assist such companies, which are often SMEs (small and medium-sized enterprises) the UK government has instigated the following initiatives:

- establishment of a number of local, regional, and national agencies (including for example the Small Business Investment Taskforce) to offer advice to SMEs

- development of the Small Firms Loan Guarantee (SFLG) scheme which is operated by the government in partnership with 23 leading financial institutions, and is designed to enable loans to be made to SMEs that are unable to offer any security (collateral)

- promotion of the use of Venture Capital Trusts (VCTs) and the Enterprise Investment Scheme (EIS) by offering a number of tax reliefs to encourage individuals to invest in small companies which are facing a funding gap, either indirectly through a mediated fund such as a VCT, or directly by investing in a company through the EIS.

Another source of funding for companies is Business Angels (BAs). These are essentially wealthy individuals who invest in businesses with high growth potential, usually in return for equity. Some BAs invest their own capital, but there are also now many BAs who act on behalf of networks or investment syndicates.

In general BAs invest in businesses which:

- need an investment of between £10,000 and £250,000

- have a potential for a high rate of return

- are at an early stage of their development or expansion.

The main advantages of using a BA are that they often make quick investment decisions, and often without the need for complex business assessments. BAs are also able to bring valuable experience to a new business venture, because they often possess specialist local knowledge since most BAs tend to invest within 100 miles of their homes or offices.

A disadvantage in using BAs is that investments may be infrequent and irregular, and as a consequence, they may be difficult to locate, although the British Business Angels Association (BBAA) can be used to trace potential investors.

The BBAA is the national trade association for the UK's Business Angel networks and its associates and affiliates. The association seeks to:

- promote the recognition of Business Angel Networks (BANs)

- highlight the contribution that business angels can make to the entrepreneurial culture

- support member groups

- lobby the government to encourage a fair and equitable marketplace.

The BBAA (www.bbaa.org.uk) held its first AGM in June 2005, and is currently sponsored by Nesta (www.nesta.org.uk), and Kingston Smith LLP (www.kingstonsmith.co.uk). The BBAA is also supported by the DTI's small business service (www.sbs.gov.uk/sbsgov/action/home).

The transition from start-up to growth

The need to develop a sustainable competitive advantage is a good indicator of the level of business risk carried over from start-up to growth. In many companies we may see the construction of major entry barriers through factors such as learning curve cost reductions, economies of scale, and establishment of brand identities.

In the transition from start-up to growth there is a change of company focus from R&D, and the development of technology, to market-orientation. An example of this was seen in the pharmaceutical industry in the 1980s and 1990s where Glaxo, after their initial trials success and registration of patents, focused very heavily on marketing Zantac.

Consumers sometimes expect many new features in products, and sometimes companies may be guilty of 'over-engineering' products by providing too many unnecessary features. Despite the expectations of new features in products, commercial considerations may necessarily take precedence. A large number of new features and frequent design changes may result in delays in getting the product into the marketplace. Speed to the marketplace and the creation of appropriate barriers to entry are factors that are critical to the success of a growth business.

A change in the profile of investors

When a company moves from its start-up phase to its growth phase its financial risk remains low and the company is likely to continue to be financed by equity funding. Since VCs are unlikely to continue to fund businesses indefinitely, growth businesses are likely to seek a number of new investors. Additional new investors may also be required to finance further expansion of the business. Therefore, as a growth business develops and its prospects of future growth and its P/E ratio are still high, its VCs begin to implement their exit strategies. At this time current eps will be low but growth can be expected from an increasing market share. However, there is a lower expected return by investors since the product is now proven. There is lower business risk than during the start-up phase but it may still be high in periods of rapid sales growth.

There may be nominal dividends paid but cash is primarily required for further investment. The share price may be increasing but continues to be volatile because expected sales levels may still not actually have been achieved. New investors may need to be found to replace VCs and to fund additional investment for growth.

Because the VCs are seeking an exit, the company needs to consider the ways in which they may be replaced as investors. One option may be to remain as a limited (Ltd) company but increase the number of private investors from, for example, friends and family. Alternatively, the company may become a public limited company (plc) by inviting the public to buy its shares through obtaining a flotation on the stock exchange or the Alternative Investment Market (AIM).

The first option of remaining a limited company is the cheapest one, but it has a big disadvantage in the lack of marketability of the shares. The shareholders of a Ltd company have no easy route for selling their shares.

The second option, which is called 'going public' (rather than remaining private) has a number of important implications:

- the business must take appropriate measures for the protection of investors
- the costs of flotation of the company are very high
- there is a requirement for the disclosure of a large amount of financial and non-financial information to maintain the confidence of investors and the financial markets in the company.

Risk and return in growth

As we have already discussed, high business risk continues in the growth phase of a business because there is still a risk of expected growth that may not materialise. Major entry barriers can be constructed during rapid growth periods to keep out competitors, once a product's potential has been identified. These include branding, the costs of which may be justified in the anticipation of growing future sales. They also include economies of scale, leading to low cost production.

So, what returns will prospective investors require from IPOs of growth companies? Systematic risk is relevant for growth companies, which are sensitive to the changes in the external environment. Because a growth company faces systematic risk in addition to unsystematic risk, we can determine an estimate of the return required by investors using CAPM. Unsystematic risk is risk that can be diversified away. Systematic risk cannot be diversified away and, as we saw in Chapter 6, is reflected in CAPM in its basic form in the relationship:

$$R_s = R_f + \beta(R_m - R_f)$$

where:

R_s = the required return on a share

R_f = the risk free rate of return

β = the beta factor of the share – the measure of volatility of the security in terms of its systematic or market risk (where beta for the market as a whole is 1.0)

R_m = market rate of return.

The estimated return required by shareholders is implied by the β (beta) value of the company, the relative measure of its systematic risk compared to the whole market. If the company is a growth business where there is little or no company history, the β value for the company may be estimated from similar companies that are already publicly quoted. In order to use the CAPM for this purpose we need to consider betas in a little more detail. The beta of a company is really comprised of its equity beta and its debt beta. The beta that we have discussed so far is the equity beta, or geared beta, which reflects the total systematic risk faced by the company. Systematic risk comprises business risk and financial risk.

Business risk only is reflected in the company's ungeared beta, also called its asset beta. A company's ungeared beta reflects the weighted average of its equity beta and debt beta multiplied by the market values of its equity and debt, represented by the relationship:

$$\beta_u = \beta_e \times \frac{E}{E + D(1-t)} + \beta_d \times \frac{D(1-t)}{E + D(1-t)}$$

where:

E = market value of the company's equity

D = market value of the company's debt

β_u = ungeared beta

β_e = equity beta

β_d = debt beta

t = corporation tax rate

From the above equation we can see that if the company is financed totally by equity its ungeared beta will equal its equity beta. If the company has a mix of debt and equity financing then its equity beta will always be higher than its ungeared beta.

It is a big assumption, but if we assume that the companies we are considering always meet their interest payments and so there is no risk of default then in the short term we may assume that their debt betas are zero. The ungeared beta equation can therefore be rewritten and represented as:

$$\beta_u = \beta_e \times \frac{E}{E + D(1-t)}$$

or

$$\beta_e = \beta_u \times \frac{E + D(1-t)}{E}$$

Companies may be involved in more than one business sector, or in different investment projects, each of which will have different levels of business risk and therefore different ungeared betas. If we are trying to determine an approximate return expected from a growth company we can identify quoted companies which are involved in the same type of business, and therefore with the same risk profiles, and use the equity betas of these companies to provide an estimated return using CAPM.

The equity betas of these companies must first be ungeared to eliminate the impact of their different levels of gearing. Their gearing and levels of risk are likely to be different from the company whose return we are trying to evaluate.

In addition, the ungeared betas which we have calculated for these companies must be adjusted to eliminate the effects of any business sectors that they are involved in, which are not relevant to the business we are trying to evaluate. The average of the ungeared betas of these companies may then be used to provide an estimated, surrogate ungeared beta for the company we are evaluating. This surrogate beta may then be geared up, using the respective proportions of debt and equity, to provide an estimated equity beta for the company. Finally, the surrogate equity beta, along with the risk-free rate and market rate of return, may then be used in the basic CAPM formula to calculate the expected return for the company.

Let's look at an example of this.

Worked Example 14.2

Packtical is a UK company in the packaging industry, which is currently financed with 90% equity and 10% debt. The company is in its growth phase and requires additional capital. A prospective investor wants to determine what the current level of return should be for Packtical.

The prospective investor has identified four companies similar to Packtical, each with different beta values and levels of gearing. Three of the companies are involved wholly in the packaging industry. However, 40% of one of the companies, Pack & Carry plc, is involved in the logistics and distribution business, which is considered to be 60% more risky than packaging.

The most recent financial data provided for each of the four companies is as follows:

	Equity beta	Debt %	Equity %	Tax rate %
Happy Packers plc	1.20	40	60	30
Flopack plc	1.25	30	70	30
Packmaster plc	1.30	25	75	30
Pack & Carry plc	1.35	50	50	30

The risk-free rate of return is 3%, represented by the yield on UK Government Treasury stock. The packaging market sector average return is 8%. Packtical's tax rate is 30%.

We will assume that the debt for each of the companies is risk-free and therefore their debt betas are zero. The ungeared betas for each company can therefore be calculated using:

$$\beta_u = \beta_e \times \frac{E}{E + D(1 - t)}$$

Happy Packers plc:

$$\beta_u = 1.20 \times \frac{60\%}{60\% + 40\% \times (1 - 30\%)}$$

$$\beta_u = 1.20 \times \frac{60\%}{60\% + (40\% \times 70\%)}$$

$$\beta_u = 1.20 \times 0.68$$

$$\beta_u = 0.82$$

Flopack plc:

$$\beta_u = 1.25 \times \frac{70\%}{70\% + 30\% \times (1 - 30\%)}$$

$$\beta_u = 0.96$$

Packmaster plc:

$$\beta_u = 1.30 \times \frac{75\%}{75\% + 25\% \times (1 - 30\%)}$$

$$\beta_u = 1.05$$

Pack & Carry plc:

$$\beta_u = 1.35 \times \frac{50\%}{50\% + 50\% \times (1 - 30\%)}$$

$$\beta_u = 0.79$$

Because logistics represents 40% of Pack & Carry plc's business and is considered 60% more risky than the packaging business then its ungeared beta must be adjusted accordingly to calculate its packaging ungeared beta as follows:

$$\beta_u = 0.4 \times \text{logistics } \beta_u + 0.6 \times \text{packaging } \beta_u$$

and

$$\text{logistics } \beta_u = 1.6 \times \text{packaging } \beta_u$$

therefore

$$\beta_u = 0.4 \times 1.6 \times \text{packaging } \beta_u + 0.6 \times \text{packaging } \beta_u$$
$$0.79 = 1.24 \times \text{packaging } \beta_u$$

therefore

$$\text{Pack \& Carry plc's packaging } \beta_u = 0.64$$

The average of the Pack & Carry plc's adjusted ungeared beta and the other three ungeared betas is

$$\frac{0.82 + 0.96 + 1.05 + 0.64}{4} = 0.87$$

0.87 may be used as the surrogate ungeared beta for Packtical in order to calculate its surrogate equity beta by using the variation of the ungeared beta equation:

$$\beta_e = \beta_u \times \frac{E + D(1 - t)}{E}$$

$$\beta_e = 0.87 \times \frac{90\% + 10\% \times (1 - 30\%)}{90\%}$$

$$\beta_e = 0.94$$

We can now calculate Packtical's estimated return by using the basic CAPM formula:

$$R_s = R_f + \beta(R_m - R_f)$$
$$R_s = 3\% + 0.94 \times (8\% - 3\%)$$
$$R_s = 0.077$$

Packtical's expected return is therefore 7.7%.

Although the sort of data illustrated in Worked Example 14.2 may be used for comparison, it nevertheless uses historical information. It should also be remembered that CAPM assumes that the capital markets are perfect, when in fact they are not. Nevertheless, the capital markets may in fact reflect a fairly high level of efficiency. Although the results of the type of analysis shown in Worked Example 14.2 are therefore very much estimates and an indication of what actual returns may be, they may be reasonably accurate. Their accuracy will of course depend on the accuracy of the estimates of betas, risk-free and market returns, and the gearing of the companies being assessed.

Types of capital market

A market is a place of exchange, where the legal title and possession of an asset is exchanged for the legal title or possession of another asset, or the legal promise that such an exchange will take place in the future.

The assumed characteristics within such a market are that buyers and sellers:

- are rational
- are predominantly profit driven
- have access to relevant and useful information
- are well informed
- risk buying and selling in the market for a reward or a gain.

The capital markets are effectively no different from any other market, and possess the characteristics common to many other types of market. The main difference is that buyers and sellers deal in particular types of securities and other financial assets, and in a variety of different currencies.

In addition, there are many types of capital or financial markets, for example markets where the buyers and sellers meet face to face. In commodity or asset markets activity is restricted to the buying and selling of particular commodities and assets. Private markets have access restricted to buying and selling by particular organisations.

The main characteristics of the capital markets are that there are many buyers and sellers, and there is generally freedom of access. There are many buyers and sellers in the market who will undertake activities of both buying and selling. The information regarding commodities and assets available in the markets is widely available to all (or at least many) of the buyers and sellers.

Capital markets are markets that exist for the trading of long-term financial instruments or securities. The capital markets exist for companies, for public sector securities, and for Eurobonds. Eurobonds are nothing to do with Europe! In Chapter 7, we looked at a diagrammatic representation of all the different types of securities and financial instruments. It included Eurobonds which were described in some detail. They are bonds, which are denominated in currencies other than the currencies in which they are sold, for example a Japanese Yen bond that is sold in the USA.

Capital markets enable companies to raise funds via financial institutions and private investors. The most important capital markets for companies are those dealing with ordinary shares, preference shares, and debt in general, which includes debentures, unsecured loan stock, and convertible loan stock. Capital markets are comprised of what are termed **primary markets** (see Fig. 14.3), and **secondary markets** (see Fig. 14.4).

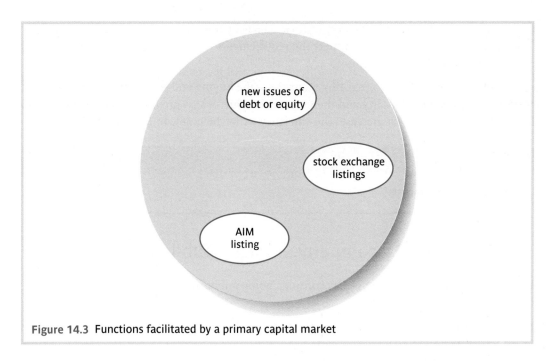

Figure 14.3 Functions facilitated by a primary capital market

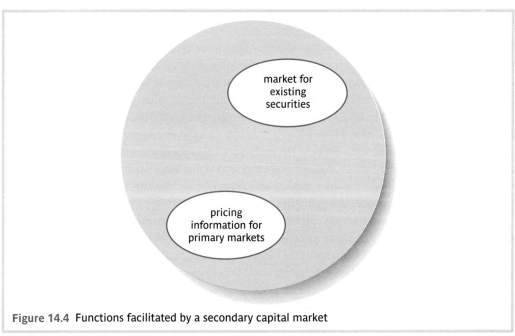

Figure 14.4 Functions facilitated by a secondary capital market

The London Stock Exchange (LSE) is the place that deals in both equity (shares) and bonds (debt) in the UK. The LSE acts in both the primary and secondary markets, and includes two key sections:

■ the Official List, comprising companies which are normally large and well established, and which have been trading for at least 3 years – the expected value of their shares after issue should exceed £700,000 and at least 25% of their share capital must be held by the public

■ the Alternative Investment Market (AIM), which opened in the UK in June 1995, is for smaller companies which do not meet the requirements of the Official List – its intention is to keep regulations to a minimum.

A secondary market is used for existing securities – the buying and selling of stocks and shares – which increases their liquidity and therefore their value. It also provides pricing information for primary markets, which increases the efficiency with which new funds may be allocated.

Progress check 14.4

What are capital markets?

The flotation of a company – initial public offering (IPO)

During its growth stage a business may consider 'going public' through an initial public offering (IPO), for a number of reasons:

■ the company may have big expansion plans for which it needs a large amount of new finance
■ the initial shareholders may want to dispose of their shares
■ the shareholders may include VCs who wish to exit the company and realise the gains in the value of their shares in the business.

In growth (and start-up) businesses the ordinary shares are usually owned by the founder(s) of the business, and by family and friends, and possibly by other investors. The shareholders may want to sell their shares for one of any number of reasons. As the business grows it may need to raise further equity share capital, or debt, in order to finance its growth, at levels much higher than the founders of the business, their friends, family, and maybe VCs, are willing or able to afford. Other investors include VCs who will certainly want to realise gains in the value of their shares as the business develops. Because the number of shareholders is likely to be quite small, the way in which they may sell or dispose of their shares is not straightforward. Their first problem is trying to find a buyer for their shares, which may be an existing shareholder, relative, or friend. Second, they must obtain a valuation of the business in order to calculate a share price.

During the growth (and start-up) phase, shares are not easily transferable because there is not a ready market for them. The share price is likely to be lower than if the shares could be easily sold or disposed of. Making the shares of the business publicly available and freely traded through an IPO, makes it possible for the shareholders and VCs to more easily realise their gains.

The way in which a business may obtain additional new financing, and make its shares more easily transferable and tradeable, is to go from being an unquoted company to becoming a company that is quoted on a stock exchange. As we discussed in Chapter 7, a company can do this by 'going public' by making an initial public offering (IPO) of shares in its company. This means that the shares are offered for sale to the general public and to financial institutions, which are then listed and traded on a stock exchange.

A flotation of a company must consider the rules of an initial public offering (IPO), some of the most important of which relate to the timing of the flotation and the issue of a prospectus. Potential investors must not become confused. The objectives of a flotation by a company must be clearly stated.

We can see from the following press extract about Umbro that floating a company during its mature stage may be difficult. Umbro had initially intended to float the company at 200p per share, which the market felt was far too high. The offer price was dropped to 100p per share to ensure that the issue would be successful. At that offer price it was expected to be more than twice oversubscribed.

During a company's mature stage its share price may be high, even though it may be offering higher dividends. The opportunities for large capital gains from the flotation of a company in its mature stage are therefore usually quite limited.

Flotation is very costly. It is also extremely time-consuming, and burdensome with regard to the high volume of regulations and disclosure required from companies obtaining a listing. Therefore, the company must be clear about the benefits of flotation. As well as providing an explanation of its reason for flotation the company should:

- indicate its target market
- state why the company is suitable for flotation
- outline the method of flotation.

Difficulties in setting the right price for an IPO
'Umbro marked down price', by James Moore

City institutions gave Umbro, England's football shirt supplier, a yellow card yesterday, forcing broker Cazenove to price the shares significantly below the 150p–190p range it was seeking.

It is understood that Umbro, being floated by its venture capitalist owner Doughty Hanson, will today announce that the stock has been priced at around 100p.

However, people with knowledge of the situation said yesterday that the company's capital structure had been tweaked, making the cut to the price look worse than it was.

It is thought the company's market value will be around £145m when the shares start trading. That is roughly 17pc lower than the £177m the company would have been worth had the shares been priced at the bottom of the original price range.

'It looks like a third lower than the bottom of the price range, but the structure has been altered so it's not quite that bad', said one City source.

It is believed that postponing the flotation was discussed. However, at the lower price enough institutions were tempted to enable the flotation to go ahead.

Today's pricing announcement is expected to say that the flotation has been more than two times oversubscribed.

Umbro is the second flotation that Doughty Hanson has had difficulties with this week. On Wednesday the IPO of German car parts and accessories group Auto-Teile-Unger was postponed.

Umbro is one of the most high profile listings scheduled for the summer and its failure could have knocked the IPO market's already fragile confidence.

However, one banker said: 'There have been some specific problems with this float. They were initially trying to get as much as 200p a share and that is just way too high'.

The difficulties with Umbro are not thought to have hit plans by CVC, another venture capitalist, to float Halfords. The retailer last night hosted a presentation to analysts with the shares expected to be priced on Wednesday as planned. The indicative price range was set at between 250p and 300p.

© *Daily Telegraph*, 28 May 2004

Financing new projects

Growth companies may want to invest in new high growth projects, which they may finance out of retained earnings. They may alternatively require additional new project financing.

But which new projects should be accepted by the company? Should new projects have the same risk profile or a different risk profile to the existing business? For new projects with similar risk profiles to the existing business the returns should be the same as the current investors' expected returns.

Should the returns from new projects be greater than the company's existing WACC? It really depends on the level of risk. Project risks must be considered against expected project returns.

Should WACC be used as a hurdle rate in the appraisal of investments in new projects? If it is, then many low risk, financially attractive projects may be missed. On the other hand, many unattractive, high-risk investments may be accepted.

We have discussed capital investment appraisal and the use of WACC in Chapter 4. The ways in which the investments in new projects are financed also have an impact on the company's risk profile. The way in which the risk profile of the company is adjusted is dependent on whether the additional funding is from debt or equity. The assessment of investment in new projects in terms of returns and risk must be considered along with the methods of financing. For most growth companies their WACC may actually be the same as their cost of equity.

Rights issues

High growth companies may finance new project investments from their retained earnings or from IPOs. New equity may also be obtained from secondary public offerings (SPOs). SPOs of shares in a company may be made at current market prices, or more usually at a discount to current market prices, which are called rights issues. Rights issues are share issues offered to existing shareholders who are given rights to buy additional new discounted shares in proportion to their existing holdings. If they do not wish to take them up, current investors may sell these rights options to other potential investors.

Let's look at an example that illustrates the use of a rights issue.

Worked Example 14.3

A company has share capital of 100,000 ordinary shares. The company needs to raise additional capital of £37,500 to fund an investment in a new project and decides to issue 25,000 new shares and offer them to existing shareholders at £1.50 each.

The market price of a share in the company is £2, which includes the rights.

Pre-rights number of shares   = 100,000

Number of new shares issued = 25,000

Rights issue share price   = £1.50

The theoretical value of new total 125,000 shares = $(100,000 \times £2) + (£1.50 \times 25,000)$

$$= £237,500$$

The theoretical ex-rights share price = £237,500/125,000 = £1.90

The price of the right is therefore £1.90 − £1.50 = 40p per share

In theory, the share price will fall to £1.90 for the old and new shares. This may or may not be so in practice. The level at which the share price may finally settle will depend on the stock market's reaction to the company's new investment opportunity and its methods of financing it.

If a company requires additional capital to invest in new projects it needs to consider its current return on capital and the expected returns on the new projects. In a rights issue the number of new shares issued and the issue price will have an impact on the company's post-issue eps. Rights issues are normally underwritten by merchant banks, who guarantee to take any unsold shares, which insures against the share price falling below the rights issue price.

If we assume that a company wishes to raise a specific amount of additional funding, then:

- at a high issue price the number of shares is less but eps is increased
- at a low issue price the number of shares is more but eps is 'diluted'.

It may be noted that dilution of percentage ownership will occur to those shareholders who do not take up the rights offer. Dilution of market value of the shares may occur if the rights issue results in a larger than expected fall in share price. The issue price should really make no difference to its attractiveness to existing shareholders. The 'break-even' point is the rights price that results in an eps equal to the current pre-rights eps, which is illustrated in Worked Example 14.4.

Worked Example 14.4

A company that achieves a profit after tax of 20% on capital employed has the following capital structure:

| 400,000 ordinary shares of £1 | £400,000 |
| Retained earnings | £200,000 |

In order to invest in some new profitable projects the company wishes to raise £252,000 from a rights issue. The company's current ordinary share price is £1.80.

The company would like to know the number of shares that must be issued if the rights price is £1.60; £1.50; £1.40; £1.20.

Capital employed is £600,000 [£400,000 + £200,000]

Current earnings are 20% of £600,000 = £120,000

Therefore, earnings per share (eps) = $\dfrac{£120,000}{400,000}$ = 30p

After the rights issue earnings should be 20% of £852,000, which equals £170,400.

Rights price £	Number of new shares £252,000/rights price	Total shares after rights issue	eps £170,400/ total shares pence
1.60	157,500	557,500	30.6
1.50	168,000	568,000	30.0
1.40	180,000	580,000	29.4
1.20	210,000	610,000	27.9

We can see that at a high rights issue share price the eps are increased. At lower issue prices the eps are diluted. The 'break-even point', with no dilution, is where the rights price equals the original capital employed per share £600,000/400,000 = £1.50.

Progress check 14.5

What is a rights issue?

In Chapter 15 we will be discussing the mature phase of a business. While rights issues may be used by growth companies it should also be noted that they are also widely used by mature companies as a method of obtaining additional new finance.

Summary of key points

- The regular introduction of new start-up businesses provides an important contribution to a country's economy.
- There is a wide range of sources of financial and other support for start-up businesses.
- Venture capitalists (VCs) play a significant role in providing financing for start-up and growth businesses because they are prepared to accept the high risks of such ventures for which they expect correspondingly high returns.
- During the transition from the start-up phase of a business to its growth phase there is a change of company focus from R&D and technology to market-orientation.
- Alternative types of capital market enable companies to fund future growth by raising funds via financial institutions and private investors.
- A company may be floated on a stock exchange during its growth phase, through an initial public offering (IPO), before it reaches its mature stage when the opportunities for capital gains for its initial investors may be limited.
- Whether companies finance new high growth projects out of retained earnings or additional new project financing, they need to consider whether new projects should have the same risk profile or a different risk profile to the existing business.
- New funding may also be obtained by a company from secondary public offerings (SPOs) such as rights issues in which existing shareholders are given rights to buy additional new discounted shares in proportion to their existing shareholdings.

🔈 Glossary of key terms

management buy-out (MBO) The purchase of a business from its existing owners by members of the management team, generally in association with a financing institution, for example a merchant bank or venture capitalist, who may buy part of the business, a division, or a subsidiary, or sometimes the whole group. Where a large proportion of the new finance required to purchase the business is raised by external borrowing, the buy-out is described as leveraged.

primary market A capital market in which securities are issued for the first time.

secondary market A capital market in which securities are traded once they have been issued.

secondary public offering (SPO) An issue of existing shares in a company at their market price, or possibly at a discount to current shareholders.

seed capital High risk equity investment into a new business by venture capitalists or other investors in order to finance the period of pre-start-up before launch.

start-up capital High risk capital that enables the new business to launch and become established, such that it can ultimately raise equity from other private investors or on an established stock exchange, at which time venture capitalists would expect to realise their holding of shares, and in so doing make a significant capital gain.

venture capitalist (VC) A provider of a specialised form of finance for new companies, buy-outs, and small growth companies which are perceived as carrying above-average risk.

Questions

Q14.1 What is the usual method of funding start-up companies, and how does this relate to their financial risk profiles?

Q14.2 Explain the main features of the investment behaviour of venture capitalists.

Q14.3 What are the features of unsystematic risk faced by a start-up business and how may the effects of these be mitigated?

Q14.4 Why is the profile of a company's investors likely to change as it moves from its start-up phase through into its growth phase?

Q14.5 Why are the capital markets important for growing companies, and how are primary markets different from secondary markets?

Q14.6 How can companies experiencing 'dynamic growth' react in terms of their financial strategy?

Q14.7 Outline the difficulties that may be faced by a company that is involved in an IPO.

Q14.8 In what ways may a growth company finance its investments in new projects and how are these linked to the way in which such investments may be evaluated?

Discussion points

D14.1 'The returns of 30% to 40% per annum expected by VCs are too high and restrict the growth potential of a business.' Discuss.

D14.2 'An IPO is inevitable if a company expects to grow indefinitely.' Discuss.

D14.3 'Shareholders always gain if they exercise their rights in a rights issue, and they always lose if they do not.' Discuss.

Exercises

Solutions are provided in Appendix 2 to all exercise numbers highlighted in colour.

Level I

E14.1 *Time allowed – 30 minutes*

Outline the various types of capital required for new businesses and their sources.

E14.2 *Time allowed – 30 minutes*

Explain the risk profile of a typical start-up business and the type of returns expected by investors.

E14.3 *Time allowed – 30 minutes*

Explain the risk profile of a typical growth business and the type of returns expected by investors.

E14.4 *Time allowed – 45 minutes*

Explain the role of venture capitalists and when and how they may become involved, and cease to become involved, in the development of a company.

Level II

E14.5 *Time allowed – 45 minutes*

What alternative methods of funding may be considered by a growth company that requires additional capital to finance new projects?

E14.6 *Time allowed – 45 minutes*

Outline why a company may consider an IPO, and explain the requirements for this. What are the advantages and disadvantages of an IPO to a company?

E14.7 *Time allowed – 60 minutes*

Gregor is a growing UK electrical component company financed by 20% debt and 80% equity. The provision of additional capital for expansion is currently being negotiated with an investor. The investor knows of three companies similar to Gregor, with the following financial data.

	Equity beta	Debt %	Equity %	Tax rate %
Pike plc	1.10	30	70	30
Rudd plc	1.15	25	75	30
Tench plc	1.25	20	80	30

Each of the companies is engaged in the electrical components industry. In addition, 50% of Pike plc's business is involved in computer repairs, which is considered to be 50% more risky than electrical components.

The risk-free rate of return is 4%. The electrical components market sector average return is 10%. Gregor's tax rate is 30%. The debt for each of the companies is risk-free and therefore their debt betas are zero.

Required:

Calculate Gregor's current level of return.

E14.8 *Time allowed – 60 minutes*

Rightlyso plc has 4 million ordinary £1 shares in issue, and the current share price is £8 per share. The company has announced a one for four rights issue by offering shares at £5.50 to all current shareholders. One shareholder, Mr Thomas, owns 1,200 shares and he is concerned that the value of his shareholding in Rightlyso plc will be diminished because the rights offer price is so much below the current market price of the shares.

Required:

Evaluate the impact of the following four options on the wealth of Mr Thomas as a shareholder of Rightlyso plc, assuming that the actual market value of the shares will be the same as the theoretical ex rights share price:

(i)   Mr Thomas exercises 100% of his rights.

(ii) Mr Thomas exercises 50% of his rights and sells 50%.

(iii) Mr Thomas sells all his rights.

(iv) Mr Thomas does not exercise his rights.

Case Study III: **Derlex Ltd**

Derlex Ltd is a new UK-based fashion start-up company created by two enthusiastic, confident, and ambitious undergraduate students, Alex Welch and Derek Kirby. Created in 2005, the company operates under the UK-registered 'Brown Circle' brand name, and produces a range of high quality sportswear products (polo shirts, bags, caps, etc.), which are sold over the Internet, and through a few selected retail outlets. With its products and services aimed at the proactive sports orientated 20 to 50 year old, the company's aim is to:

- produce and deliver a quality product and service
- develop customer loyalty for the 'Brown Circle' product portfolio
- create and maintain a financially viable and sustainable business.

The company's mission is to '. . . establish the Brown Circle brand as an inspirational symbol of style and class'.

The initial start-up costs of the company were fairly small and mainly administrative and management orientated, for example company registration costs, brand name registration costs, and product design costs.

The directors' financial projections indicated low cash inflows for 2006 but high and increasing cash inflows for 2007 and subsequent years. During early 2006, product manufacturing costs, distribution and marketing costs, and other retail development costs, for example website design fees, began to be incurred.

Additional funding was now required over and above that initially invested by the two directors, Alex Welch and Derek Kirby. Some start-up grants were available from a range of both government sponsored business agencies, and University-related agencies, but such funding was limited. The additional funding was required to finance:

- immediate short-term operational costs
- further product and service delivery plans.

The options available, in addition to the start-up business grants, were:

- short to medium-term debt, including loans and overdraft facilities
- additional equity capital.

Required:
Draft a report for Alex Welch and Derek Kirby, which outlines the current position of the business and the appropriate financial strategies that it may adopt. Your report should explain the differences between a start-up company, growth company, and mature company, and the financial strategies that each may follow. The advantages and disadvantages of alternative strategies should be explained, with recommendations of the financial strategies that are most likely to increase shareholder value and how they will achieve this.

Case Study IV: **Bircom plc**

Bircom plc is a large UK-based machine component manufacturing company in its growth phase. The company has six production facilities located in Glasgow, Birmingham, Leeds, York, Swindon, and Bristol, and four wholesale retail outlets located in Manchester, Bradford, Sheffield, and Cambridge. The company's head office is in Birmingham.

In 2005 the sales of Bircom plc's products accounted for approximately 27% of the total market for machine components in the UK, which was an increase of 5% each year since 2000. The company is now the single largest machine component manufacturer in the UK. Such rapid growth in market share has been due to the development and establishment of a market brand name by the management of Bircom plc for its range of products, a branding which has been made possible by extensive economies of scale and low cost and high quality manufacturing.

Over the past few years Bircom plc's performance has consistently exceeded market expectations. Currently, the company's shares have a β of 0.80. The expected return in the market in which Bircom is operating is 9% and the risk free rate of return is 4%.

The company is considering expanding its current production facilities during 2006 by investing in additional production facilities in Scotland and Wales. These additional production facilities would require a capital outlay of £40m. The company's directors have risk-assessed the revenues that may be generated from the new facilities associated with the expansion plan, and have estimated that cash flows could vary as follows:

Probability	Expected net cash flows £m
0.10	2
0.25	6
0.40	8
0.15	10
0.10	14

The directors of Bircom plc have also estimated that:

■ annual total net revenues will commence in Year 1 as soon as the new facilities are complete and on-line

■ annual fixed operational costs of the new production facilities are expected to be £2m per year and will be incurred from the commencement of the project

■ annual total net revenues will remain at the same level for the life of the production facilities, which is expected to be eight years

■ the production facilities are anticipated to be sold at the beginning of Year 9, when each is expected to realise £2m.

For project evaluation purposes, and to take into account the possible business risk associated with the expansion project, the directors of Bircom plc have decided to add a 2% risk premium to its current cost of capital. The company is currently totally financed by equity.

Required:

(i)   What are the advantages of using CAPM as the basis for calculating a company's cost of capital?

(ii) Why should a DCF-based method of investment appraisal be preferable to the accounting rate of return or payback?

▶

(iii) Calculate the expected value of the NPV of Bircom plc's expansion programme, and the minimum level of net revenues required to justify the investment.

(iv) Explain and evaluate the alternative methods of funding that may be used to finance Bircoms's project.

(v) Bircom plc is currently financed totally by equity, but we have not been told which of the various types of shareholders own the shares. Discuss the implications for the various possible types of investor in Bircom plc (which is in its growth phase), with regard to the alternative ways in which the investment in this project may be funded.

(vi) What other factors may have an impact on Bircom's investment decision?

(vii) Outline some of the actions that may be taken to assist in ensuring the viability of the project.

(viii) Recommend, giving reasons, which you feel may be the most appropriate financial strategies for Bircom plc in terms of creation of corporate value.

Financial strategies from growth to maturity to decline

Chapter contents

LEARNING OBJECTIVES

Completion of this chapter will enable you to:

☑ Identify the features of the turbulence phase of the business life cycle.

☑ Outline the key aspects in the profile of a mature business.

☑ Describe the transition from growth to maturity.

☑ Describe the relationship between perceived risk and the return required by investors in a mature business.

☑ Explain the way in which mature companies may be most appropriately financed.

☑ Consider the factors which impact on a company's dividend policy.

☑ Describe the situations in which companies may become targets for takeover.

☑ Outline the key aspects in the profile of declining business.

☑ Describe the transition from maturity to decline.

☑ Describe the relationship between perceived risk and the return required by investors in a declining business.

☑ Consider the ways in which a company may delay its decline.

☑ Explain the way in which a declining company may reduce its debt ratio.

Introduction

In Chapter 14 we looked in more detail at the start-up phase and growth phase of the BLC model. This chapter will look at the turbulence phase that occurs towards the end of the growth phase, during which time there is a great deal of activity with companies entering, and leaving the marketplace as they become unable to compete. The period of relative stability which follows this phase then sees the more successful businesses entering their mature phase, which they hope will continue for as long as possible until they move into the decline phase and eventual demise of products (and possibly companies).

The turbulence phase of the business life cycle

As companies move out of their growth phase but before they reach their mature phase they go through a period of turbulence. A period of fast growth in demand attracts many entrants into the market, despite the barriers that may have been constructed to deter their entry. The turbulence phase occurs towards the end of the growth phase of a company's life cycle.

Towards the end of the growth stage, risk will have reduced but growth indicates the opportunities for returns, which are attractive to new entrants to the market. An increase in capacity and the battles for market share, created by the new entrants, then result in price competition.

The period of turbulence and turmoil of overcapacity is followed by shakeout and then stability. The companies that lack the funding or the ability to compete are forced out of the market, with only the most successful companies moving on into their mature phase. The mature stage of the business life cycle cannot start until this position is resolved. The mature market is then one which becomes relatively stable.

The turbulence period and subsequent shakeout for businesses may be illustrated by what happens in the popular music industry. A singer or band may identify a new sound or unique way of delivering songs and music. If they are successful then many more similar artists appear on the scene who may copy and possibly improve on the original theme or idea. The inevitable shakeout that eventually occurs results in only very few of these artists standing the test of time and going on to become established names for an extended period of time.

A profile of mature businesses

Companies which have successfully completed and moved out of the growth phase will have survived the turbulence period resulting from aggressive price competition and the excess capacity built up in the growth stage. After the shakeout has occurred and surplus capacity has been removed the successful growth companies then move into the mature phase where their business risk exposure is much reduced as expected sales levels and market share are achieved.

During its mature phase a company's goal should be to maintain its market share and improve efficiency. We can see from Fig. 15.1 that earnings per share (eps) should be high during the mature stage and may increase as a result of gains from efficiency improvements. There

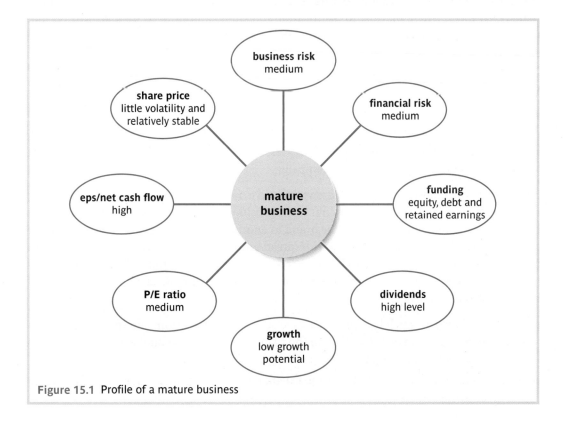

Figure 15.1 Profile of a mature business

is reduced business risk during a company's mature phase and so financial risk may be increased through an increase in debt levels, and benefits gained from additional tax shields. Overall financial risk may be maintained at a medium level through a mix of debt and equity financing.

A further source of funding now becomes available during the mature phase. This is retained earnings, which in addition to debt and equity may be used for investment in new projects. The amount of retained earnings available for investment is dependent on the company's dividend policy. Dividends are likely to be paid out at a high level in order to maintain a high level of total shareholder returns, since share price increases, reflected in a lower P/E ratio, will be low as future growth prospects will now be lower. The company's share price is likely to be fairly stable with little volatility since the largest part of shareholder returns are now in the form of dividends.

Progress check 15.1

What are some of the key differences in the profile of a mature company compared with a growth company?

The transition from growth to maturity

When a company moves into its mature phase a change in managerial focus is required in order to profitably maintain the high level of sales it has achieved. Management must recognise that their product will inevitably mature, and it may be a problem if they do not shift their managerial focus. There may be no justification to assume a prolonged high growth period. Consequently, management incentives based on growth should not be used during the mature stage of a business.

There are many examples of companies which, as a result of market pressure or lack of consumer demand, seek to reposition their product portfolios. Throughout 2006 we saw that:

- Coca-Cola continued to suffer from falling demand for soda-based drinks and as a result was forced to produce a raft of new products to reverse the slide

- McDonald's continued to suffer from bad press and was aiming to relocate its brand name with a new healthy-living marketing campaign.

Strong brands developed during a high growth period may not be capable of repositioning during the maturity stage, and to try and carry out such repositioning may prove very expensive. It may be better for the company to transfer the brand to another product, which is in or entering the growth stage. This is a practice that is widespread among large consumer goods companies. Marketing expenditure may need to be increased to maintain the existing market share.

In recent years, companies that have used their brand name to diversify their portfolio of successful products include:

- Procter & Gamble, which has made regular use of brand extension, and in particular with regard to the extension of its strongest brand names like Fairy Soap into new markets, such as the very successful Fairy Liquid, and then Fairy Automatic

- Armani, which extended its portfolio and expanded into everything from minimalist sofas to five-star holiday resorts

- Nike, which straddled both the casual fashion market and the hard-core athletic markets with innovative new products, marketing, and partnerships
- Kodak, which redefined its products and activities to become a major player in digital photography and printing.

Risk and return in maturity

As a company moves through its mature stage its unique, or unsystematic, risk level declines and cash flows become more predictable and stable. The demand of the product will have matured, and so profits are less volatile year-to-year, but they cannot be expected to grow dramatically.

During the mature phase business risk relates primarily to how long this stage may last and whether levels of profit and cash flow may be maintained, rather than risk associated with issues of growth and market share. Therefore, this reduction in the level of business risk means that investors may expect lower returns, which therefore results in a lower cost of equity to the company. The company should adopt the appropriate financial strategy to ensure that such reduced returns are acceptable.

We have seen from the CAPM that the beta (β) value for the market as a whole is 1. If a company has a β less than 1 it means that its returns are less volatile than the market as a whole. If a company has a β greater than 1 it means that its returns are more volatile than the market as a whole.

A growing company is likely to have a β greater than 1 (higher systematic risk and higher volatility). Stability of earnings and cash flows in the company's mature stage means that its unsystematic risk has reduced, and this also means therefore that its level of systematic (market) risk has increased as a percentage of total risk. However, the β of the company (which was high during its growth phase) is likely to move downwards towards 1 as it moves through its mature stage (although it may never actually reach 1). This is because the company's level of growth will have reduced and so it is now becoming less affected by the impact of external market changes. It therefore follows that the mature company's total returns will become much closer to that of the market as a whole. It should be noted that this may not always be the case; some utilities companies, which are generally companies in mature industries, often have very low beta values.

Communication by a mature company of its lower overall risk profile, due to lower unsystematic risk, is achieved by delivering less volatile results year on year. This is important to maintain stability in its share price and to avoid share price reductions.

Through the start-up and growth stages capital gains were high, but they decrease as maturity increases. Also, there is less need for the company to invest than there had been during the period of rapid growth.

Shareholders' reductions in capital gains may be mitigated by higher dividends. This is payable from higher profits and cash flows, which are helped by the value of the tax shield from increased debt. The inverse correlation may be noted as the reduction in business risk is offset by the higher financial risk as a result of increased debt funding.

Progress check 15.2

Outline the types of risk normally faced by a mature company.

Debt financing in maturity

There are, during a company's mature phase, high levels of earnings and cash flows accompanied by a high level of stability. The change in financial strategy from almost total equity to an increasing proportion of debt, can add considerable value for shareholders of a maturing company. The company is now a taxpayer because of its high earnings, which leads to:

- a relevance of the tax shield – the reduction in tax payable due to the use of the tax-allowable deduction of debt interest against taxable income
- a decrease in the probability of financial distress, as the company is able to service debt (pay interest), and repay its debt
- business failure becoming less likely.

Therefore debt financing is justified during a company's mature stage and is recommended.

> ### Progress check 15.3
>
> Why may debt financing be an appropriate financial strategy that may be used to add value to a mature company?

Dividends – why are they paid?

There are a number of reasons for paying dividends to shareholders, which are illustrated in Fig. 15.2 and discussed in the sections that follow.

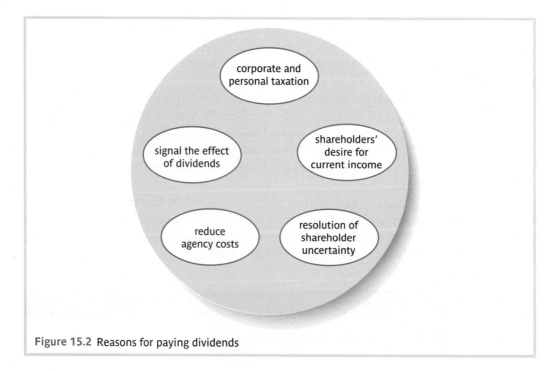

Figure 15.2 Reasons for paying dividends

Taxation

Dividend policies are greatly influenced by the tax systems under which businesses operate:

- corporate tax systems, because dividends are paid out of post-tax, distributable profits
- personal tax systems, because investors pay tax on the dividends they receive, with the amount of tax payable dependent on investors' individual tax positions.

Shareholders may, for example, prefer capital gains on the share price, which may be taxed at a lower effective rate for them as individuals, rather than dividends which may be taxed at a higher rate. Shareholders can choose when to realise a capital gain, because they may sell their shares whenever they want to. But shareholders do not have a choice about the timing of tax payable on dividends; companies pay dividends normally twice a year (and in practice, the timing of their payments is quite important for a company with regard to its cash flow planning).

Desire for current income

There is a huge demand for dividends from pension funds and other institutions, and from many trusts and endowments, which can only spend the dividend portion of their returns. These institutional investors, and many individual investors who have a current regular income requirement, want high dividend shares. Such investors cannot rely on gains from increases in share prices. Generally as salaries rise and the number of individuals requiring pensions increases, pension funds, for example, require a regular income flow provided by dividends to ensure that funds are consistently available to provide pension payments. This is not only to those pension holders who are in retirement, but also to the dependents of pension holders in accordance with their particular schemes.

The high level of increasing demand for high dividend shares created by institutional and other investors' requirements for current income from dividends will therefore push up the prices of such shares, particularly if dividends are rising. Equally, if a company's dividends are falling then its shares will be less in demand by these investors. The lack of demand for these shares following a fall in their dividends will effectively result in their share price falling.

In some circumstances, some types of institutional investors provide a demand for low-dividend shares that also have capital growth potential. These institutions provide investment packages at a low cost for individual investors. The institutional investors manage funds that are invested in low-dividend shares, from which they expect capital growth. These funds receive dividends, which together with their controlled sale of shares to realise gains, enable them to pay their investors specific levels of return.

Uncertainty resolution

£1 of dividend may be valued by investors more highly than £1 of retained earnings because investors regard future cash flows from new projects as being at a higher level of risk. Gordon (Gordon MJ (1963) 'Optimal investment and financing policy', *Journal of Finance* 18, 264–272) described this as an 'early resolution of uncertainty'. It may be argued that a current high-dividend policy benefits shareholders because it resolves uncertainty. Investors may evaluate the price of a share, or the value of the company, by forecasting and discounting future dividends. Forecasts of dividends to be received in the distant future have even greater uncertainty than forecasts of dividends in the shorter term; the greater the level of uncertainty then the higher the discount rate. Therefore, if companies pay small dividends now in order to invest retained earnings in new projects to provide higher dividends at a later date, then the current share price should be low.

Are short-term dividends less uncertain than dividends in the distant future? Well, the riskiness (uncertainty) of dividends depends on a company's business and financial risk. The bird-in-the-hand argument that dividends received now are worth more (just because they are received now) than dividends received in future years implies that the risk of the company may increase over time. However, this argument is fallacial as there is no reason to believe that risk increases over time for all companies.

Agency costs

There are agency theory implications that we may consider with regard to dividend payments. A company may have surplus cash but is unable to invest it in value-adding projects because its directors or managers may be reluctant to accept the high level of risk attached to them. In such circumstances, the alternative of payment of dividends to shareholders is seen as a positive sign of good corporate governance. If new investment projects are available for consideration then payment of surplus cash to shareholders may be seen as an automatic vetting system for the appraisal of investments in new projects. If managers reject these investment opportunities then it may be assumed that they have been appraised and considered unacceptable.

In Chapter 2 we saw the potential conflict between shareholders and directors, or managers, when ownership and control of a company is separated. The agency problem arises as a result of the directors not acting in the best interests of the shareholders. For example, a high retention of profits and cash by directors merely to provide a cushion for easier day-to-day management of operations means that a lower level of dividends may be paid out. Therefore the payment of dividends may be considered to be lowering the agency costs of equity. In this example, this results from reducing the amount of free cash flow available to managers, which therefore reduces the agency costs of holding on to cash that would otherwise have been paid out to shareholders in dividends (or invested in profitable new projects).

Companies that pay out dividends, may also periodically need to raise external funds rather than using retained earnings. The primary market to some extent therefore acts as a control against managers deviating from shareholders' best interests. The costs of issuing new equity shares may be offset by the lower agency costs of directors not acting in the best interests of shareholders.

We also saw in Chapter 2 that there may sometimes be an agency problem with regard to the relationship between debt holders and shareholders. For example, shareholders may prefer the use of debt for investments by the company in new, high-risk projects. Shareholders may subsequently receive the benefit of the rewards gained from the success of such investments from the receipt of dividends and an increase in share price, but it is the debt holders who bear the risk. A dividend may therefore be viewed as a transfer of wealth from debt holders to shareholders. Another example is a company, which, even if it is in financial distress, may be reluctant to cut dividends. This may impact on the ability of the company to repay debt. To protect themselves, debt holders can ensure that their loan agreements include provisions that dividends may only be paid if the company has positive earnings, cash flow, and working capital above pre-specified levels.

The dividend information content effect

There is an asymmetry of information between managers and shareholders, and so dividend decisions are seen by shareholders as providing information about the company and its performance. Also, when managers know more than individuals outside the business about a company's future prospects then they can signal this knowledge to investors through changes in dividend policy. Changes in dividends consequently have an information content and dividend policy is important in a semi-strong form efficient market. Increases in share price are generally observed to be associated with announcements of dividend increases. The rise in the share price following the dividend signal is called the information content effect.

Increases in dividends are not a credible signal about future performance if the higher level of dividends cannot be sustained at the company's current level of performance. If managers effectively lie about future performance by raising dividends, they may have to cut dividends in the future, which is something that very few managers are willing to do. Therefore, the information content effect implies that a share price may rise when dividends are raised if dividends simultaneously cause shareholders to upwardly adjust their expectations of future earnings.

We saw in Chapter 6 how, if a company's dividends grow at a regular rate, its share price and therefore its market value may be calculated using the dividend growth model, using the equation:

$$S = v_1/(K_e - G)$$

where S = share price
K_e = cost of equity
v_1 = expected dividend
G = expected growth rate

This formula implies that the share price may be increased by a company through an increase in its dividend payout. However, this assertion is not necessarily true. A company generates earnings, which may be retained for future investments or used to pay dividends, in any proportion it may choose. If we divide both sides of this equation by the company's eps we may re-write it as:

$$\frac{S}{eps} = \frac{v_1}{eps} \times \frac{1}{(K_e - G)}$$

S/eps is the company's P/E ratio and v/eps is the dividend payout ratio.
Therefore:

$$\textbf{P/E ratio} = \textbf{dividend payout ratio} \times 1/(K_e - G)$$

We can see that if the company were to increase its dividend then its dividend payout ratio would also increase. The company's cost of equity, e, is also likely to increase because of its increased dividend. In addition, less earnings would be available for future investment and so the growth rate, G, would decrease (unless further external funding was available to finance new projects, which may also increase the cost of equity). Therefore, $1/(K_e - G)$ would increase. This means that changes in the two elements in the right-hand side of the equation are likely to balance out. The P/E ratio may therefore remain unchanged or it may decrease. A weakness of the dividend growth model lies in its implicit assumption that a company's future dividend growth cannot be greater than the rate of increase of its cost of equity, which in practice is not necessarily true.

Dividend policy and payment of dividends

The strongest argument about how companies pay dividends is that they are seen as a signalling device to the market. This may say to shareholders of a growth company that future growth prospects are not as exciting as in the past.

For a mature company, paying out dividends may act as a signal that the company is doing well. An increase in levels of dividend indicates a stable level of post-tax profits. Reinvestment needs are covered from a lower profit retention ratio, in addition to the raising of debt funding in reasonable proportions. The P/E ratio decreases as the share price approaches a steady state value and the market will reassess the potential for future growth.

There are a number of different ways in which dividends may be paid. We will take a look at:

- cash dividends
- share dividends
- share re-purchase (or share buy-back).

Cash dividends

Companies, normally twice a year in the UK, declare so many pence payable as dividends per share held by each shareholder. The interim dividend is normally paid during the financial year, and the final dividend is paid after the financial year-end and after it has been approved by the shareholders at the company's AGM. These so-called cash dividends are therefore made by payments to shareholders twice a year for the appropriate amounts.

There are a number of alternative cash dividend policies that a company may adopt:

- fixed % payout, which is simple to operate and gives a clear signal to the financial markets about performance, but provides a straightjacket regarding reinvestment of earnings
- zero payout, which is unacceptable unless it is supported by a high expectation of future growth levels
- constant payout, which is used to create stability, and to avoid cuts in dividends and to maintain the share price level
- steadily increasing payout, which increases investor expectations, and may lead to future cuts in the dividend.

Let's look at two examples of companies' dividend policies.

Worked Example 15.1

Stanolly plc started as a two-man small business ten years ago. The company continues to be managed and controlled by its original proprietors, Stanley and Oliver. The company had grown slowly in the early years since its initial launch, but had then achieved much greater growth more recently. In 2006 the company was floated on the AIM. Whereas previously Stanley and Oliver had owned virtually all the ordinary share capital, around 45% of the shares are now owned by the general public.

Stanolly's performance over the five years to 2005 is shown below:

Year	Number of ordinary shares in issue	Profit before tax £000	Dividend £000
2001	2,000,000	440	220
2002	2,000,000	450	230
2003	2,000,000	470	240
2004	2,000,000	630	310
2005	2,500,000	825	410

In 2006 the number of shares in issue was increased to 3 million. The profit before tax was £1,005,000, and the directors considered paying a dividend of £480,000 for 2006.

The directors needed to determine whether their dividend policy was appropriate given their current status now that Stanolly was an AIM-quoted company.

The company's dividend policy in the past looks to have been based on paying dividends at a more or less fixed 50% of earnings, as illustrated in the table below:

Year	Earnings per share pence	Dividend per share pence	Dividend payout ratio %
2001	22.0	11.0	50.0
2002	22.5	11.5	51.1
2003	23.5	12.0	51.1
2004	31.5	15.5	49.2
2005	33.0	16.4	49.7
2006	33.5	16.0 (proposed)	47.8

A fixed percentage dividend policy may be appropriate when a company has moved from its growth phase to maturity when there is less volatility and some stability in the company's eps.

The dividend proposed for 2006 would mean a reduction in dividend per share from 2005, which would be unpopular with shareholders and may result in a drop in share price. The shareholders may be satisfied with the same level of dividend as 2005 at 16.4p per share which would give a higher payout ratio at 49%, which would still be slightly lower than 2005. This would create some stability and indicate the expectation of further capital growth. A higher dividend of say 20p per share would indicate that the company was approaching maturity with limited expectations of future growth.

Worked Example 15.2

Hammans plc expects to achieve earnings next year of £2.8m. These earnings are expected to continue in perpetuity without any growth unless a proportion of earnings is retained, which means that paying 100% of earnings as dividends will restrict the company to no growth. If Hammans plc were to retain 30% of its earnings, an annual growth rate in earnings (and hence dividends) of 2% in perpetuity could be achieved. If the company were to retain 70% of its earnings an annual growth in earnings (and hence dividends) of 3% could be achieved.

The return currently required by Hammans plc's shareholders is 10%. If Hammans plc retains 30% of its earnings, the required rate of return would probably rise to 12%. If Hammans plc were to retain 70% of earnings, the required rate of return would probably rise to as much as 14%.

We will determine an optimum retention policy for Hammans plc.

(a) No retentions, 100% dividend payout

The formula $S = v_1/(K_e - G)$ relates to share price (S), expected divided per share (v_1), cost of equity (K_e), and expected growth rate (G). This may be re-stated in total terms as:

$$P_0 = D_1/(r - G)$$

using the current market value of the shares (P_0), total expected dividends (D_1), and shareholders' expected returns (r).

$$P_0 = \frac{£2.80}{0.10 - 0.00}$$

$$P_0 = £28.0m$$

(b) 30% retention, 70% dividend payout

$$P_0 = \frac{£1.96m \times 1.02}{0.12 - 0.02}$$

$$P_0 = \underline{£19.99m}$$

(c) 70% retention, 30% dividend payout

$$\frac{£0.84m \times 1.03}{0.14 - 0.03}$$

$$P_0 = \underline{£7.86m}$$

The above calculations suggest an optimum dividend policy of 100% dividend payout ratio for Hammans Ltd, which would result in a market capitalisation of £28m.

Share dividends

Share dividends may be paid instead of cash dividends by capitalising the profits that would have been paid out in dividends and issuing shares instead. Dividends paid in shares are taxable in the same way as cash dividends. The company is effectively retaining its earnings and its cash for reinvestment. The difference for shareholders is that they may either hold on to the additional shares or sell them for cash.

Share re-purchase

It is the responsibility of the financial manager to use the resources of the company in the most efficient way in support of the objective of maximisation of shareholder wealth. During its mature phase, one of these resources, cash, is often surplus to the company's immediate requirements to maintain the business. Companies sometimes argue that their reason for holding on to surplus cash is just in case it may be required to finance acquisitions. However, there has often been increased pressure from institutional investors for companies to return their surplus cash rather than hold it for this purpose. The company may decide to return this cash to its investors either by paying special 'one off' dividends or by buying back some of its shares. The choice between paying dividends or buying back shares depends on many factors, including taxation.

A company's purchase of its own shares may take place where all shareholders accept the purchase on a *pro rata* basis. The company may use its excess cash to buy its own shares in one of two ways. The first, and most common, is when a company buys shares on the open market, just as private investors do when they buy shares through a broker. The company has to get authority from its shareholders in order to buy back the shares. This is usually done at a general meeting of the company. There have been many examples of share buy-backs by companies, particularly over the past 10 years or so. For example, in October 2005, Unilever plc and Unilever NV announced its commencement of an aggregate €500m share buy-back programme. The purchase of shares by the boards of directors on behalf of the companies was authorised in general meetings of shareholders of each company.

In the second and less common method a company may announce a tender offer. This involves all shareholders submitting a price they would be prepared to accept for their shares. In the UK, whichever of the two methods is used, the purchased shares are cancelled and the company's share capital is reduced. The company cannot then sell back the shares in the market at a later date. The P/E ratio should remain unchanged. Earnings per share (eps) will increase because the number of shares in issue decreases, and so the share price should increase to compensate for the non-receipt of dividends.

From the shareholders' viewpoint share buy-backs are generally good news. If there are fewer shares on the market then, unless demand for the shares changes for some other reason, the share price should rise. For the company, eps will be slightly reduced because of the reduction in interest received from the investment of its surplus cash, but this should be more than compensated by the increase in eps as a result of the reduction in number of shares.

We will look at an illustration of the use of a share buy-back in Worked Example 15.3.

Worked Example 15.3

Thriller plc is a company in its mature phase and makes profits after tax of £15m each year, which includes after-tax interest received of £1.5m per annum. Thriller currently has cash of £25m. Its number of equity shares in issue is 100m. The current share price is £1.

We will look at what may happen if the company uses all its cash resources of £25m to buy back its shares.

Thriller's current eps are £15m/100m = 15p

and its P/E ratio is £1.0/15p = 6.67 times

If Thriller uses all its £25m cash it can buy 25m shares (£25m/£1).

▶

▶ Because it will not now be receiving interest on its cash balances its profits after tax will fall to £13.5m (£15 − £1.5m).

The number of shares remaining will be 75m (100m − 25m), therefore eps will increase to 18p (£13.5m/75m).

If shareholders believe that the P/E ratio of 6.67 times is still appropriate, then they may be willing to pay £1.20 (18p × 6.67) for the shares. Therefore, in theory the share price should increase after the share buy-back. In practice, the share price will depend on how the market perceives a company's disposal of its cash, and its stage in its business life cycle.

If Thriller plc had any growth prospects shareholders may be willing to pay more than £1.20, because Thriller's potential profit growth would increase after returning the cash to share-holders, which was providing no more than average returns. However, in practice, as a mature company, investors are unlikely to see Thriller plc as having any growth prospects – it had not been able to invest its £25m surplus cash in new value-adding projects. Therefore, it is likely that investors may be not even willing to pay £1.20 per share.

Worked Example 15.4

Using the information from Worked Example 15.3, let's consider what would happen if the original share price had been lower than £1 at, say, 50p.

- £25m cash would have bought 50m shares (£25m/50p)
- eps would have been 27p (£13.5m/50m)
- the P/E ratio would have been 1.85 times (50p/27p)

If the original share price had been higher than £1 at say £2.50, then

- £25m cash would have bought 10m shares (£25m/£2.50)
- eps would have remained at the original 15p (£13.5m/90m)
- the P/E ratio would have been 16.67 times (£2.50/15p)

The share price of £2.50 is the 'equilibrium' price, which equals the original earnings level of 15p multiplied by the £25m cash divided by the annual interest of £1.5m. At any share price above £2.50 eps will fall, and the P/E ratio will increase. A company is therefore much more likely to buy back its shares when its P/E ratio is at a relatively low or medium level. Also, because it needs a lot of surplus cash to make a buy-back worthwhile, it is much more likely to be mature businesses that buy back their shares.

Worked Example 15.5 looks at a company, which is considering the choice between:

- a residual dividend policy in which its total free cash flow (operating cash flow less net invest-ment in non-current assets and working capital) is paid out in dividends
- paying dividends at a maintainable, regular growth rate each year, together with the possibility of share re-purchase.

Worked Example 15.5

Baker plc has 24m equity shares in issue, and has estimated its net operating cash flows (after interest and taxation) for the next five years as follows:

Year	Net cash flow £m
2007	4
2008	12
2009	5
2010	6
2011	4

which have been calculated before the deduction of additional investments in fixed capital and working capital as follows:

Year	Investment £m
2007	3
2008	2
2009	3
2010	3
2011	2

We can calculate the annual cash flows available and the dividend per share payable if a residual (or total) dividend policy is adopted, which are shown in the table below:

Year	Operating cash flow £m	Investment £m	Free cash flow £m	Dividend per share pence
2007	4	3	1	4.17 (£1m/24m)
2008	12	2	10	41.67 (£10m/24m)
2009	5	3	2	8.33 (£2m/24m)
2010	6	3	3	12.50 (£3m/24m)
2011	4	2	2	8.33 (£2m/24m)

Alternatively, the company may adopt a dividend policy based on maintainable regular dividend payments. We can calculate an appropriate annual dividend growth rate, the annual dividend payments, and the amounts that may be available for the company to purchase its own shares.

We may assume that to ensure an affordable and maintainable dividend the company could pay £1m in dividends in 2007, and the amount could increase each year up to £2m by 2011. To achieve this, the annual dividend percentage growth rate, G, can be calculated as follows:

$$(1 + G)^4 = £2m/£1m$$
$$1 + G = \sqrt[4]{£2m/£1m}$$
$$1 + G = 1.189$$
$$G = 18.9\%$$

▶

▶ The maintainable dividends payable for the years 2007 to 2011 are shown in the table below, calculated using the annual growth rate of 18.9%. The table also shows free cash flows, and the net cash available after dividends available for the company to purchase its own shares:

Year	Free cash flow £m	Maintainable dividends payable £m	Maintainable dividends per share pence	Net cash flow available for share purchase £m
2007	1	1.000	4.17 (£1m/24m)	0.000
2008	10	1.189	4.95 (£1.189m/24m)	8.811
2009	2	1.414	5.89 (£1.414m/24m)	0.586
2010	3	1.682	7.01 (£1.682m/24m)	1.318
2011	2	2.000	8.33 (£2m/24m)	0.000

It may be noted that if a share buy-back were not undertaken by the company then a special dividend may be paid in the years 2008, 2009, and 2010, calculated as follows:

2008 £8.811m/24m = 36.71p per share

2009 £0.586m/24m = 2.40p per share

2010 £1.318m/24m = 5.49p per share.

Progress check 15.4

What are the key factors that a company may consider in determining its dividend policy?

Dividend policy – some practical issues

If a company pays a dividend then less funds will be available within the company for reinvestment, and therefore there is likely to be a reduction in future earnings and dividends. In theory the fall in the *ex dividend* market price will not equal the amount of dividend because:

■ when the dividend is declared the shareholders' view of the riskiness of the company may change

■ the actual dividend may differ from the dividend declared.

Porterfield (Porterfield JTS (1965) *Investment Decisions and Capital Costs*, New Jersey: Prentice Hall) suggested that a dividend should only be paid if the market value of the share after the declaration of dividend (V_1) plus the declared dividend per share (D_0) is greater than or equal to the market value of the share before the declaration of dividend (V_0):

$$V_1 + D_0 > \text{or} = V_0$$

or

$$D_0 > \text{or} = V_0 - V_1$$

However, the situation is complicated by the fact that differential rates of tax may apply between personal income tax and capital gains tax. If we assume that dividend is D and the personal income tax rate is t, then when dividends are paid the net income to shareholders would be

$$D \times (1 - t)$$

If c is the rate of capital gains tax and we assume that V_0 is the current market value of the share without a capital gain, and V_1 is the future market value of the share with a capital gain then when earnings are retained in order to achieve capital growth, income to shareholders would be:

$$(V_1 - V_0) \times (1 - c)$$

Shareholders would prefer reinvestment by the company if

$$(V_1 - V_0) \times (1 - c) > [D \times (1 - t)]$$

Dividend policy should attempt to maximise the sum of

$$(V_1 - V_0) \times (1 - c) + [D \times (1 - t)]$$

If the rate of capital gains tax is less than the rate of personal income tax ($c < t$) then there should be a preference in favour of retained earnings, although there is no certainty that retaining the dividends will necessarily generate an equivalent amount of capital gains. In the UK both c and t are often scaled depending on the shareholder's overall income.

The dividend argument – relevancy and irrelevancy

We may question whether dividend policy is relevant or irrelevant. There are two schools of thought regarding the dividend argument:

- dividend policy is irrelevant to maximisation of shareholder wealth
- dividend policy is relevant to maximisation of shareholder wealth.

The dividend irrelevancy argument

The most well-known supporters of the irrelevancy argument were Miller and Modigliani (Miller MH, Modigliani F (1961) 'Dividend policy, growth and the valuation of shares', *Journal of Business* 34, 411–433), who suggested that in a tax-free world shareholders are indifferent between dividends and capital gains, and the value of a company is determined solely by the earnings power of its assets and investments. They argued that if a company with investment opportunities decides to pay a dividend resulting in retained earnings being insufficient to fund investment opportunities then the company would borrow funds. The loss in value in the existing shares as a result of borrowing instead of using internal funds would be exactly equal to the amount of dividend paid. They further suggested that the irrelevancy argument was valid whether the additional funds are raised by equity capital or debt capital.

The dividend relevancy argument

Supporters of the relevancy argument suggest that different levels of taxes on dividends and capital gains can create a preference for either a high dividend payout or a high retention policy. They therefore reject the irrelevancy argument and suggest that the existence of:

- imperfect markets
- imperfect information
- the inherent uncertainty of future outcomes

means that investors will prefer the early resolution of uncertainty and are willing to pay a higher price for the shares that offer the greater current dividends.

Gordon (Gordon MJ (1962) 'The savings investment and valuation of a corporation', *Review of Economics and Statistics* 44, 37–51) suggested that the higher the earnings retention rate, the greater was the required future return from investments to compensate for risk. He also suggested that the risk attitude of investors will ensure that shareholders' expected returns will rise for each successive year in the future to reflect growing uncertainty.

Takeover targets

Mature companies may run the risk of retaining profits for no 'profitable' use by investing in new projects with low returns. The result is a decline in the overall rate of return provided by the business. This may result from a disregard of the risk profile of new projects and possible agency problems.

If the transition from growth to maturity is not properly managed the share price may stay high for too long and then fall too sharply so then the company may become a takeover target (see Chapter 16). Business risk during the mature stage relates to how long the stable levels of profits and cash flow may be maintained. Enterprise Inns (see the press extract below) is a mature company that was floated in 1995, and which grew organically and by acquisition. Ten years later its business risk remained at a medium level. Its cash flows were stable, but it had little prospect of future growth.

Diversification of a business may result in destroying overall value. A mature company has low risk and share price volatility. If it diversifies into launch and growth products, its investors' perception of risk increases. They will then demand a higher return to compensate for the higher perceived risk. The company now has no significant competitive advantage and so it will not be able to deliver the increased return. The consequence is a reduction in shareholder value.

Maturity out of Enterprise
'Market miscellany', by Grant Ringshaw

Shares in Enterprise Inns (757p), the UK's largest pub company, have risen by 44 per cent after dipping to 525p in August. The price has been driven by a re-rating rather than upgrades to profit forecasts and relief that MPs cleared the industry of being anti-competitive.

Enterprise has been an extraordinary growth story. The company floated in 1995 with 489 pubs and a market value of just £58m – now it is worth £2.6bn and has almost 9,000 pubs. It has a rock solid business model – collecting rents from tenants who are also tied into beer

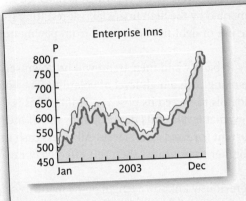

Enterprise Inns

the equivalent of 130p (after accounting for a two-for-one share split) and again in February 2003 at 273p. However, we did advise readers to take some profits at 461.75p in July 2003.

We now believe investors should look again at locking in part, but not all, of their profits. The shares are trading on a price/earnings ratio of about 13 – well above the historic multiple of 10.8. The current figure looks justified but any higher and the shares would start to look more than fair value. One factor that could drive the shares further would be a significant deal, but there are few opportunities, given that Enterprise and Punch have swallowed most rivals. Meanwhile, a merger between these two giants would face competition problems.

supply contracts – and a successful track record of integrating acquisitions, including its take-over of the 4,200-strong Unique pub estate last year.

We have long been supporters of Enterprise. We first tipped the shares in October 2000 at

Enterprise is still a very good company with a predictable income stream, but investors should bank some gains.

© *Daily Telegraph*, 9 January 2005

A profile of declining businesses

A summary of the financial parameters of a declining business is shown in Fig. 15.3. The strong positive cash flow of a mature company cannot continue forever, as product demand eventually dies away. Business risk continues to decrease from the maturity stage as a business moves into

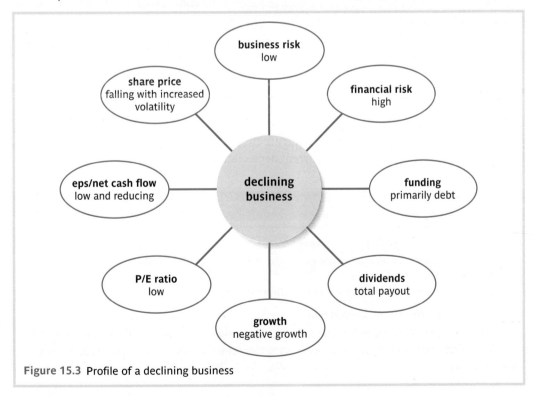

Figure 15.3 Profile of a declining business

decline because reinvestment is low and growth prospects are negative, which is reflected in its low P/E ratio. Low business risk may be complemented by the high financial risk resulting from the high level of interest payments to service the use of debt financing, and from paying out a high level of dividends.

In its decline phase a company's eps are likely to be low and their trend will be downwards, which will be reflected in a declining share price along with a high level of volatility. The company's dividend payout policy may allow its dividends to exceed its post-tax profits. This is due to inadequate financial justification to reinvest even at levels of its depreciation, which means that the company may fail to maintain its non-current (or fixed asset) levels. All excess cash may be paid out in dividends, and if dividends are higher than profits then this effectively means repayment of capital.

When the decline stage has been reached, the previously unknown length of the maturity stage is now known. The question that now arises is 'for how much longer can the business continue?'

Risk and return in decline

When a business reaches the decline stage the financial costs of the company require review. As sales reduce the company should reduce its fixed costs and get into short-term variable contracts on as much expenditure as possible. The increasing use of debt financing means that the company may benefit from the lower cost of capital due to the general lower cost of debt compared with equity and the benefit of whatever debt interest tax shield it can use.

In its mature phase the company could accept the operating gearing risk connected with fixed cost, because of its relatively high and stable levels of profits and cash flow. But, in the decline stage there is a risk that arises because of the company's exposure to sudden changes in the external environment. This can lead to large losses if the company still has a big proportion of fixed costs compared with its total costs.

In the decline stage of a business the focus must be on short-term financial impacts. This may be achieved through the use of the payback method for decision-making. During this stage this method should be used to justify expenditure, as opposed to the use of discounted cash flow (DCF) techniques.

The use of return on investment (ROI) as a performance indicator, in which depreciation is charged as an expense, must assume that a business intends maintaining its asset base by re-investing depreciation. This is not valid during the decline stage, at which time the business is very unlikely to be reinvesting at its current depreciation level.

Worked Example 15.6

Sleepers Ltd is an old established UK retail company. The shareholders of the company expect to receive a dividend of 30p per share each year into the foreseeable future. The current year's dividend is about to be declared.

The directors of the company are considering three options:

Option 1: retain the existing dividend policy

Option 2: increase the dividend to 35p this year – however, as a consequence of a potential reduction in retained earnings, it would be expected that future dividends would fall to 25p per share

Option 3: decrease the dividend to 25p this year – however, as a consequence of a potential increase in retained earnings, it would be expected that future dividends would increase to 35p per share.

The cost of shareholders' capital is 12%.
Let's determine which dividend policy may be recommended.

We will assume that the *cum dividend* share price (S) is represented by the current dividend (v_0) plus a value calculated from using the simple dividend model, which is the future annual dividend (v_1) divided by the shareholders' cost of equity (K_e) in perpetuity (see the section on cost of equity in Chapter 6).

Option 1
Using

$$S = v_0 + v_1/K_e$$

if a dividend of 30p is declared and shareholders' expectations of future dividends remain at 30p then the estimated price of the shares *cum dividend* would be:

$$30p + (30p/0.12) = £2.80$$

Option 2
If a dividend of 35p is declared and shareholders' expectations of future dividends fall to 25p then the estimated price of the shares *cum dividend* would be:

$$35p + (25p/0.12) = £2.43$$

Option 2 would reduce the estimated share price by 37p to £2.43, and therefore an increase in dividend to 35p per share is not recommended.

Option 3
If a dividend of 25p is declared and shareholders' expectations of future dividends increase to 35p then the estimated price of the shares *cum dividend* would be:

$$25p + (35p/0.12) = £3.17$$

Option 3 would increase the estimated share price by 37p to £3.17, and therefore a decrease in dividend to 25p per share may be recommended.

Strategies to delay decline

As we have seen, during a company's decline stage business risk is low and so financial risk may be increased through increased debt financing (borrowing against assets) and a very high dividend payout ratio, which may even be higher than profit levels (which is effectively a repayment of equity capital). The benefit to a company in its decline stage from an increase in its level of debt is illustrated in Worked Example 15.7.

Worked Example 15.7

Sailaway Ltd is a company that has been in business for over 100 years but is now in its twilight years. One of Sailaway's assets is a machine that it expects to be able to use productively over the next three years, after which time it believes it will be able to sell it for an estimated £200,000. The equity shareholders of the company currently expect a return of 12% per annum.

Sailaway Ltd is able to obtain a loan at 7% per annum. Given that its cost of debt is lower than its cost of equity, we can determine how the company may increase its debt in order to increase shareholder value.

In three years' time we may expect the disposal proceeds of the asset of £200,000 to be distributed to the shareholders. The value of these proceeds to the shareholders, in real terms, is the present value of the expected disposal value of the asset, which is:

$$\frac{£200,000}{1.12^3} = £142,356$$

The company could immediately borrow £163,260 (£200,000/1.07³) at 7% per annum, secured against the expected value of the machine after three years and these funds could be used now for distribution to shareholders. This sum is greater than the present value of the expected disposal value of the asset. Therefore, additional value will have been created for the shareholders as a result of Sailaway Ltd increasing its debt/equity ratio.

In practice, the actual amount that Sailaway may be allowed to borrow will depend on the lender's view of the accuracy of the estimate of the disposal value of the machinery after three years.

As a business moves into decline, there may be a conflict between shareholders and managers, who may want to avoid the final act of winding it up. This is one of the key issues in the agency problem.

In the decline stage, diversification is difficult due to lack of financing if the core business is already in decline. It is also not recommended because of the lack of increase in shareholder wealth derived from diversification.

The decline stage does not necessarily mean the depressing death of a business. A re-focus may result in the growth of a niche market and provide domination of a market segment that may be extended for an indefinite period. Note, for example, Rover's Mini car, which remained in production for over 40 years!

Worked Example 15.8

The Rover Mini was designed by Alec Issigoni and developed for mass production in the 1960s but was still selling volumes of around 30,000 per year in the 1990s, although mostly to Japan by that time. It was the first British-manufactured car to sell a total of 5,000,000 units. By the 1980s, a niche market had been established and the Rover company at that time considered that the market for the Mini could be further developed and expanded by enhancing the product and building on the success of the increased interest in smaller cars as a result of increasing fuel costs. Enhancement of the product also gave the opportunity to reduce costs and improve profitability throughout the whole value chain, through the use of value analysis, and kaizen to improve production efficiency. The success of the 'new' Mini in the late 1990s was so great that it became one of the few products that BMW chose to develop further into the BMW Mini following its takeover of that part of the Rover Group.

An examination of the reasons for the decline of a business may reveal opportunities that a company may consider. The following options may be looked at for adding value to a business in a decline stage that is expected to last for a while:

- split up the business
- acquire several small competitors
- make a **deep discount rights issue** to fund such acquisitions.

A large group may use the strategy of splitting a large group and running it as separate businesses. The company may acquire several of its small competitors within the industry at low cost and regain market share, so that:

- rationalisation by removing spare capacity may give an opportunity to increase selling prices
- the relative bargaining position with suppliers and customers may be improved
- decline may actually be turned round so that, in BCG terms, many small dogs may become one large cash cow.

Acquisition of competitors may be financed by further debt or by deep discount rights issues. A deep discount rights issue has a very low share issue price, and may be appropriate to finance such acquisitions. However, there is a risk that such a strategy might fail if investors have simply lost confidence in the company.

Progress check 15.5

How may the managers of a company try and extend the decline phase of its life cycle?

Reducing the debt ratio

We may consider a counter argument to that which supports an increase in debt during the decline stage of a business. A company in its decline stage may benefit from a reduction in its level of debt.

When a company is in decline it starts to see its sales volumes and values reduce. Unless it is able to radically reduce its level of fixed costs then its profits will also quickly start to decline. One of the company's fixed costs is the interest it may be paying on long-term debt, which is also a drain on the cash flow much needed by the company at this time to pay out dividends. Additionally, if profits are reducing then the company normally has less need for the tax shield provided by debt.

A declining business may try to increase shareholder value by reducing its debt/equity ratio. Reductions in debt, and therefore costs of debt, and reductions in shareholders' expected returns reduce risk perceptions and add value.

An increase of equity in a company's capital structure normally leads to an increase in WACC, because the cost of equity is generally greater than the cost of debt. A company in decline may currently be incurring higher costs of debt than its competitors by having to pay a substantial premium on its debt interest rate. If existing funding contains substantial risk premiums, then these can be removed by changing the financial strategy (by increasing equity), so that the inverse effect of a reduced WACC may be achieved. Therefore, an increase in shareholder value may be achieved due to the reduction in risk premium.

In Worked Examples 15.9 and 15.10 we look at the consequences of a company increasing its equity through a rights issue in order to repay debt and reduce its gearing.

Worked Example 15.9

Four Seasons plc had 25 million £1 ordinary shares in issue. It also had total debt capital of £50m. On 14 August 2005 the closing price of Four Seasons plc's shares was £2.39. The company had seen its market share decline slowly over the previous year or two. Due to even more adverse market conditions the period between 15 August 2005 and 29 August 2005 saw a further decline in the company's share price. On the 29 August the company's share price closed at £2.

On 30 August Four Seasons plc announced its intention to raise additional share capital through a £25m one-for-one rights issue at a deeply discounted price of £1 per share. The reason for raising this additional share capital was to drastically reduce its gearing ratio.

We will calculate the ex rights share price, and the value of the company and its gearing ratio after the rights issue. We can assume that no other external factors influence the share price of the company.

Original number of shares in issue 25m shares at a market value of £2 = £50m

One-for-one rights issue 25m shares at £1 per share   = £25m

Post-rights issue 50m shares at £1.50 (theoretical ex rights share price) = £75m

	Equity £m	Debt £m	Equity plus debt £m	Gearing ratio
Pre-rights value of Four Seasons plc (25m × £2)	50	50	100	0.5:1
Post-rights value of Four Seasons plc (50m × £1.50)	75	25	100	0.25:1

The deeply discounted rights issue means that to raise such a large amount of money a very large number of shares have to be issued but at the very low price. The low price is assumed to be in order to attract shareholders to invest more new funds.

Worked Example 15.10

In addition to the information given in Worked Example 15.9, we are told that Four Seasons plc's operating profit for the last financial year was £18m. The interest rate on its debt is 12% per annum before tax. Four Seasons' cost of equity is 15%. The corporation tax rate is 30%. Four Seasons plc has decided to distribute all profit after interest and tax in dividends and repay its debt.

We will consider the impact of the rights issue in Worked Example 15.9, and repayment of debt, on the company's cost of equity, share price, and the P/E ratio. We will also calculate the change in the company's WACC and how shareholder value will have been increased as a result of the reduction in Four Seasons' gearing.

Income statement before the rights issue

	£m		No of shares in issue	eps
Operating profit	18			
Interest	6	12% × £50m		
	12			
Corporation tax	4	30% × £12m		
Profit after tax	8		25m	32p (£8m/25m)

The share price at 29 August 2005 was £2 and so the P/E ratio was 6.25 (£2/32p).

If Four Seasons plc was in a steady state situation of zero growth then we may use the dividend growth model (with G being zero) to derive a cost of equity, which would be equal to the inverse of the P/E ratio = 1 × 100%/6.25 = 16%.

We are informed that the company's cost of equity is in fact 15%. The reason for this is that the company is not yet in a steady state situation when its dividend growth rate would be zero and so its cost of equity is somewhat lower at 93.75% of the steady state level.

Let's consider the income statement after the rights issue.

	£m	Number of shares in issue	eps
Operating profit	18		
Interest	3	12% × £25m	
	15		
Corporation tax	5	30% × £15m	
Profit after tax	10	50m	20p (£10m/50m)

If Four Seasons plc were at the steady state level of total decline then the growth rate G would be zero. We have calculated the theoretical ex rights share price at £1.50, therefore the steady state P/E ratio = 7.5 (£1.50/20p).

Four Seasons plc may still be assumed to be in the same state of decline and so we can again assume the cost of equity to be lower in the same proportion of 93.75% of the steady state level as before the rights issue, therefore

cost of equity would equal 93.75% of 1 × 100%/7.5 = 12.5%

therefore the P/E ratio would be approximately 10%/12.5% = 8

If the P/E ratio is 8 then with eps of 20p this would imply a share price of £1.60, instead of the theoretical share price of £1.50. The increase in share price reflects the likely reaction of the market because of the reduction in total interest and the reduction in shareholders' returns, resulting in an increase in value for shareholders.

WACC before the rights issue

debt D = £50m   equity E = £50m   corporation tax rate t = 30%

cost of debt K_d = 12%   cost of equity K_e = 15%

$WACC = K_e \times E/(E + D) + K_d(1 - t) \times D/(E + D)$

$WACC = 15\% \times 50/(50 + 50) + 12\% \times (1 - 30\%) \times 50/(50 + 50)$

$WACC = 7.5\% + 4.2\% = 11.7\%$

WACC after the rights issue

debt D = £25m   equity E = £75m   corporation tax rate t = 30%

cost of debt K_d = 12%   cost of equity K_e = 12.5%

$WACC = K_e \times E/(E + D) + K_d \times (1 - t) \times D/(E + D)$

$WACC = 12.5\% \times 75/(75 + 25) + 12\% \times (1 - 30\%) \times 25/(75 + 25)$

$WACC = 9.375\% + 2.1\% = 11.475\%$

WACC has been reduced following the rights issue and therefore the net present value of Four Seasons plc's future cash flows will be increased.

> ## Progress check 15.6
>
> Is there just one appropriate financial strategy that a business may usually adopt with regard to its capital structure during its decline phase?

During their mature phase, companies may have run out of ideas for new investment projects. The payment of special dividends and share buy-backs may do something to maintain share price levels. However, mature companies are often targets for acquisition, particularly if their shares appear to be underpriced compared with the value of their net assets. Chapters 17 and 18 look at mergers and acquisitions (M&As) and how they may be financed.

Summary of key points

- A period of market turbulence usually occurs towards the end of the growth phase of the BLC, and the resultant shakeout sees only the most successful companies moving on into their mature phase.

- During the transition from growth to maturity a change in managerial focus is normally required to maintain a high level of sales with increased profitability.

- The level of unsystematic risk reduces as a company moves through its mature stage as profits and cash flows become more stable and predictable.

- The existence of the tax shield is a key factor that may lead mature companies to change their financing strategy from total equity to an increasingly high proportion of debt.

- A company's dividend policy varies considerably as it moves through each of the phases of its life cycle, and is also influenced by both corporate and personal taxation systems.

- Mature companies may become targets for takeover possibly because of agency problems and if they run out of suitable new investment project ideas and so are unable to maintain their overall shareholder returns.

- Product demand does not last forever and so there is an inevitable move from the mature phase into the decline phase.

- As a company moves into a decline phase its managers must reassess the risk associated with its level of fixed costs, and identify ways in which they may be reduced.

- The decline phase does not necessarily mean the quick death of a business or product and there are many ways in which the decline phase may be extended.

- Shareholder value may be increased during the decline phase following a reduction in the company's debt ratio, or possibly as a result of an increase in its debt ratio.

> ## 🔒 Glossary of key terms
>
> **cash dividend** A dividend paid to shareholders in cash six-monthly and yearly.
>
> **deep discount rights issue** A rights issue in which the company's shares are offered to existing shareholders at a very large discount on the current market price.
>
> **share dividend** A share dividend (also called a scrip dividend) is a partial or total alternative to a cash dividend, where shareholders accept more ordinary shares in the company instead of cash.
>
> **value analysis/value engineering** Value analysis is the broad term usually used to include both value analysis and value engineering. Value engineering applies to products under development, whilst value analysis applies to products currently in production.
>
> **value chain** The sequence of business activities by which, in the perspective of the end user, value is added to the products or services produced by an organisation.

❓ Questions

Q15.1 Describe the period of turbulence that occurs between a company's growth phase and its mature phase.

Q15.2 How does a company's risk profile change after it has moved into its mature phase?

Q15.3 Outline the ways in which debt financing may benefit a mature company.

Q15.4 Explain the tax and cash flow planning implications with regard to a company's dividend policy.

Q15.5 Explain three of the reasons why companies pay dividends to shareholders.

Q15.6 Explain the dividend information content effect and the ways in which this impacts on shareholders.

Q15.7 Why do mature companies so often become the targets for hostile takeovers?

Q15.8 Explain how a conflict of interest between the shareholders and directors of a company may manifest itself during the decline stage of its life cycle.

Q15.9 Describe the financial strategies that a company may adopt in order to delay its decline.

👥 Discussion points

D15.1 Company chairman: 'If we continue to pay no dividends for the foreseeable future and reinvest all of the earnings of the business then shareholders will be happy because of the value that will be added to the company.' Discuss.

D15.2 'The ways in which dividends are paid is irrelevant to the company and its shareholders.' Discuss.

D15.3 'Once a company has moved into its decline phase then its inevitable demise is certain to occur very quickly.' Discuss.

Exercises

Solutions are provided in Appendix 2 to all exercise numbers highlighted in colour.

Level I

E15.1   *Time allowed – 30 minutes*
Explain the risk profile of a typical mature business and the type of returns expected by investors.

E15.2   *Time allowed – 30 minutes*
Explain the risk profile of a typical declining business and the type of returns expected by investors.

E15.3   *Time allowed – 30 minutes*
Why is a company's dividend policy likely to change over its life cycle?

E15.4   *Time allowed – 30 minutes*
Wane plc is an established retail company with retail outlets in South Wales and the North East of England.

The company is considering four alternative dividend policies:

- Option 1 – pay a dividend of 6.5p per share for each year in perpetuity.
- Option 2 – pay a dividend of 5.5p in 2007 with growth thereafter of 6% per year.
- Option 3 – pay a dividend of 5p in 2007 with growth of 9% for each of the next four years, and with 5% growth thereafter.
- Option 4 – pay a dividend of 5p in 2007 with growth of 10% for each of the next four years, and with 4% growth thereafter.

The company estimates that:

- if Option 1 is adopted the company's cost of equity will be 7%
- if Option 2 or Option 3 are adopted the company's cost of equity will rise to 10%
- if Option 4 is adopted the company's cost of equity will rise to 12%.

The company currently has an issued share capital of 785,000 ordinary shares.

Required:
Using the above information advise the company as to which dividend option would maximise the value of the company.

E15.5   *Time allowed – 30 minutes*
Wooden plc is an all equity financed company with the following history of annual dividend payments:

Year	Dividend per share
Current year	9.0p
1 year ago	8.5p
2 years ago	8.0p
3 years ago	7.8p
4 years ago	7.0p

The current year's dividend has recently been paid. Wooden plc has an opportunity to invest in a new retail facility, the cost of which would be funded from internal funds over the next three years. If the company invests in the new retail facility, dividends for the next three years will have to be reduced to 6.0p. Once the retail facility is complete, however, the company expects the dividend will increase to 10.0p and grow (as a result of the increased revenue benefits of the new retail outlet) by 8% pa for the foreseeable future.

The company requires a rate of return of 12% for its shareholders, and has an issued share capital of 1,650,000 ordinary shares.

Required:

(i) If the company does not develop the retail facility and dividends continue to grow at the historical rate, what would the value of the company be using the dividend valuation model?

(ii) If the company develops the retail facility and dividends are reduced for the following three years, what would the value of the company be, using the dividend valuation model?

Level II

E15.6   *Time allowed – 30 minutes*

Solva plc is a company that is financed by £1 ordinary share capital and redeemable debentures. The debentures carry a nominal rate of 12% per annum, and have a current market value at par. The company has paid an annual dividend of 15p per share in the past and is expected to continue to do so in the future.

The market value per share is currently £2.50 ex dividend. The total market value of the equity is £5,000,000 and the market value of the debentures is £2,500,000.

The company has a dividend policy of paying out all residual income as a dividend to shareholders.

The company has the option to redeem all the debentures in the next financial year. The finance director of the company has suggested that a rights issue of shares (at a price of £2.00 per share) could be used to raise the finance to repay all the outstanding debentures.

If the debentures are redeemed, the finance director expects the cost of equity to fall by 1%.

Required:

Determine the market value of Solva plc after the debentures have been redeemed and compare this with the company's current market value. You may ignore any possible impact of taxation.

E15.7   *Time allowed – 45 minutes*

Outline the alternative dividend policies for a company at each stage of its development. Explain the relationship between the dividend payout ratio and expected capital growth in share value.

E15.8   *Time allowed – 45 minutes*

Angle plc is a UK based manufacturing company. The company is currently financed by a combination of ordinary share capital and debentures. The ordinary shares have a current market value of £3.00 *ex dividend*. The total market value of the equity is £9,000,000. The debentures are 7% irredeemable debentures and have a current market value at par. The total market value of the debentures is £4,000,000. The company has ▶

▶ recently paid an annual dividend of 30p per share, and anticipates future dividends to remain at that level for the foreseeable future.

Angle plc is now considering a major new development that will cost the company £4,000,000. Annual net cash flows from the new development are expected to be £500,000 (before interest) in perpetuity. The company proposes to finance the new development using a new issue of 7% debentures at par.

The increase in debt is not expected to change either the market value or the cost of existing debentures. However, the increase in gearing will increase the financial risk for shareholders, and if the new development is undertaken and financed by debt, the company expects the company's cost of equity to increaseby 2%.

Assume the business risk of the company will be unaffected by the new development, and that all net earnings (earnings after the deduction of interest) will be paid out as dividends in the year they are received. The impact of taxation may be ignored.

Required:

Advise Angle plc if they should undertake the project, and calculate the impact of the method of financing the development on the value of the company.

E15.9   *Time allowed – 45 minutes*

Cresswell plc is a mature company making post-tax profits of £30m a year. Its profit includes after-tax interest received of £2m a year. Cresswell currently has a cash surplus of £20m. Its number of equity shares in issue is 100m. The current share price is £2. Cresswell plc is considering using its £20m cash surplus to buy back some of its shares.

Required:

(i)   Calculate Cresswell's eps and P/E ratio before and after the share buy-back.

(ii) Explain whether or not the share buy-back should be undertaken by Creswell and why.

E15.10 *Time allowed – 45 minutes*

Using the information from Exercise 15.9, discuss the implications for Cresswell plc and its shareholders if the original share price had been higher than £2 at, say, £3, or if it had been even higher.

Case Study V: **Kite Ltd**

Kite Ltd is a first-tier supplier to major passenger car and commercial vehicle manufacturers. As a first-tier supplier Kite provides systems that fit directly into motor vehicles, which they have manufactured from materials and components acquired from second, third, fourth-tier, etc., suppliers. During the 2000s, through investment in R&D and technology, Kite had come to be regarded as one of the world's leaders in design, manufacture, and supply of innovative automotive systems.

In the early 2000s, Kite started business in one of the UK's many development areas. It was established through acquisition of the business of Mayfly from the Nuthatch Group. Mayfly was a traditional, mass production automotive component manufacturer, located on a brownfield site in Fordmead, once a fairly prosperous mining area. Mayfly had pursued short-term profit rather than longer-term development strategies, and had a poor image with both its customers and suppliers. This represented a challenge but also an opportunity for Kite to establish a world-class manufacturing facility.

A major part of Kite's strategic plan was the commitment to investing £30m to relocate from Fordmead to a new fully equipped 15,000 square metre purpose-built factory on a 20-acre greenfield site in Dingfield, which was finally completed during the year 2006. At the same time, it introduced the changes required to transform its culture and implement the operating strategies required to achieve the highest level of industrial performance. By the year 2006 Kite Ltd had become an established high quality supplier and was close to achieving its aim of being a world-class supplier of innovative automotive systems.

In December 2006 a seven-year bank loan was agreed with interest payable half yearly at a fixed rate of 8% per annum. The loan was secured with a floating charge over the assets of Kite Ltd.

The financial statements of Kite Ltd for the years ended 31 December 2005 and 2006 are shown below, prior to the payment of any proposed dividend.

Income statement for the year ended 31 December 2006

	2006 £000	2005 £000
Turnover	115,554	95,766
Cost of sales	(100,444)	(80,632)
Gross profit	15,110	15,134
Distribution costs	(724)	(324)
Administrative expenses	(12,348)	(10,894)
Operating profit	2,038	3,916
Net interest	(868)	(972)
Profit on ordinary activities before taxation	1,170	2,944
Taxation	–	–
Profit for the financial year	1,170	2,944

The company has no recognised gains and losses other than those included above, and therefore no separate statement of total recognised gains and losses has been presented.

▶ **Balance sheet as at 31 December 2006**

	2006 £000	2005 £000
Non-current assets		
Tangible assets	42,200	29,522
Current assets		
Stocks	5,702	4,144
Debtors	18,202	16,634
Cash at bank and in hand	4	12
	23,908	20,790
Current liabilities	(23,274)	(14,380)
Net current assets	634	6,410
Total assets less current liabilities	42,834	35,932
Non-current liabilities		
Borrowings and finance leases	(6,000)	–
Provisions for liabilities and charges	(1,356)	(1,508)
Accruals and deferred income	(1,264)	(1,380)
Net assets	34,214	33,044
Capital and reserves		
Share capital	22,714	22,714
Profit and loss account	11,500	10,330
Shareholders' funds	34,214	33,044

Cash flow statement for the year ended 31 December 2006

	2006 £000	2005 £000
Net cash inflow from operating activities	12,962	3,622
Returns on investments and servicing of finance		
Interest received	268	76
Interest paid	(1,174)	(1,044)
Net cash outflow from returns on investments and servicing of finance	(906)	(968)
Capital expenditure		
Purchase of tangible fixed assets	(20,490)	(14,006)
Sale of tangible fixed assets	12	30
Government grants received	1,060	1,900
Net cash outflow from investing activities	(19,418)	(12,076)
Net cash outflow before financing	(7,362)	(9,422)
Financing		
Issue of ordinary share capital	–	8,000
Increase in borrowings	6,000	–
Net cash (outflow)/inflow from financing	6,000	8,000
Decrease in cash in the period	(1,362)	(1,422)
Note – reconciliation of net cash flows to the movement in net funds		
Decrease in cash in the period	(1,362)	(1,422)
Cash inflow from movement in borrowings	(6,000)	–
Opening net debt	(1,974)	(552)
Closing net debt	(9,336)	(1,974)

Note – analysis of changes in net debt during the year

	2005 £000	cash flow £000	2006 £000
Cash at bank and in hand	12	(8)	4
Overdraft	(1,986)	(1,354)	(3,340)
Borrowings due after one year	–	(6,000)	(6,000)
Net debt	(1,974)	(7,362)	(9,336)

Required:

(i)   Prepare a SWOT analysis for Kite Ltd and identify what you consider may be the main risks faced by Kite Ltd, both internally and external to the business.

(ii) Prepare a report for shareholders that describes Kite's financial status.

(iii) The company has stated that it has achieved high levels of quality and customer satisfaction but would you, as a shareholder, be satisfied with the financial performance and financial position of the business.

(iv) At what stage in its life cycle would you consider Kite Ltd to be at and what are your reasons?

(v)   What currently may be the appropriate financial strategies for Kite Ltd?

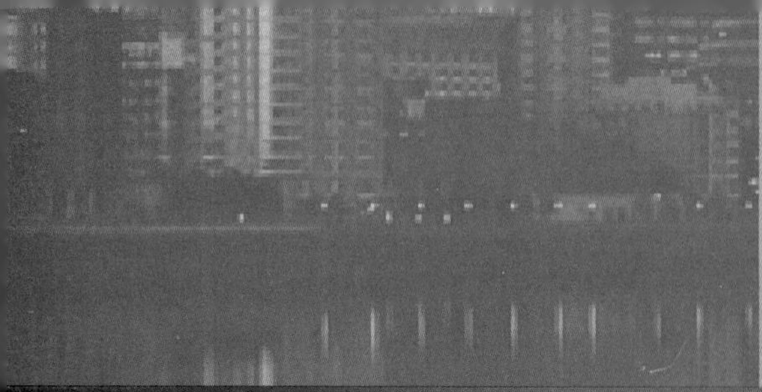

Chapter 16

Mergers and acquisitions (M&As)

Chapter contents

650

LEARNING OBJECTIVES

Completion of this chapter will enable you to:

☑ Describe what is meant by mergers, acquisitions, amalgamations, and takeovers.

☑ Outline the principles underlying mergers and acquisitions (M&As).

☑ Identify the various types of M&A.

☑ Explain how market imperfections may be used to identify potential takeover targets.

☑ Appreciate the differences between 'good' and 'bad' reasons used to justify M&As.

☑ Consider the financial motives in M&As.

☑ Consider the managerial motives in M&As.

☑ Compare the various methods used for the valuation of M&A target companies.

☑ Explain some of the further reasons for share valuation, and share valuation models.

Introduction

Mergers and acquisitions, which are also called amalgamations and takeovers, are generally referred to as M&As. This chapter explains what is meant by M&As and considers why M&As take place between businesses. The obvious reason why M&As should take place in a competitive market environment is because it may be felt that shareholder wealth may be increased as a result. We shall see that this may not necessarily be the case, and also how it may not be the only reason why they take place at all. In order for M&As to take place the businesses involved need to be valued in a way that is acceptable and agreed by all the parties involved. We will look at a range of methods used to value businesses and consider the circumstances in which they may be most appropriate.

This chapter closes by considering some of the reasons, other than for M&As, why businesses may need to be valued. We will also look at some further methods that may be used to value the shares of both quoted and unquoted companies.

What are mergers, acquisitions, amalgamations, and takeovers?

Companies need to grow in order to generate increased dividend flows and capital gains for their shareholders. This growth may be achieved organically which is usually slow and costly, although smaller companies can achieve dynamic growth organically much more easily than larger companies.

Companies may try to reverse or accelerate the business life cycle. A company in its decline stage or mature stage may try to reverse its business cycle through investment in new product areas in order to try and create a new growth phase. Alternatively, a company may try and accelerate its business life cycle, for example, to justify growth values already priced into its shares. They may try to achieve this through dynamic changes in the structure of the business, and such changes may be achieved through mergers or acquisitions.

Underlying principles of M&As

A merger or an acquisition occurs when two businesses combine into one. Companies A and B may merge to become company C, which becomes a new entity. A merger is therefore a meeting of two equals to form a new venture.

However, mergers are rare, and what occurs more commonly is the acquisition, or takeover, which involves one company A acquiring the share capital of another company B, without a new entity being formed. Usually, in an acquisition, the larger company is the acquirer and a smaller company is the target; but this is not always the case.

In M&As, the combined expected present values of future cash flows of the combination of the two companies involved should be greater than the sum of the expected present value cash flows of the two individual companies, in order to create additional shareholder value. This may not be the case if a large premium is paid to shareholders of the target company. If the price paid by the acquiring company for the target company is higher than the added value that is gained from future expected cash flows then there will be no increase in shareholder value.

The costs of a takeover or a merger may be very high indeed. The cost of a proposed takeover that does not subsequently take place may also be considerable, such as the legal and advisory costs incurred in Sir Philip Green's abortive attempt to acquire Marks & Spencer in July 2004, which is described in Worked Example 16.1. Such costs also include losses incurred by investors in share dealings in addition to the fees paid by the company to legal and financial advisers.

Worked Example 16.1

In June 2004 Philip Green proposed an offer of between 290p and 310p a share in cash for M&S, along with a 25% stake in his newly formed business Revival Acquisitions. This valued M&S at around £9bn. Later in June 2004, Green upped his offer to 370p per share.

To win back shoppers and to try and fend off Green, the M&S board appointed Stuart Rose as CEO. Rose, who had started his career with the company, reorganised some of M&S's cluttered stores, cut unpopular lines, and sold non-core businesses such as financial services. The M&S board had to decide whether they had done enough to convince shareholders to give the business the time needed to restore flagging sales. M&S's board of directors did persuade the shareholders that they could add more value for them and they rejected both of Green's offers.

In early July 2004, Green came back with an increased offer of 400p per share. It was then reported in the press that to persuade shareholders to reject this latest bid, Stuart Rose would unveil his rescue plans for M&S by offering them a sweetener in the form of a special dividend or share buy-back, which would come from the sale and leaseback of dozens of M&S properties.

On 12 July 2004, M&S's pension trustees dropped a bombshell into the battle for control of the company by warning Philip Green that he may have to inject hundreds of millions of pounds into the pension fund if his bid for M&S succeeded. This could be as much as an extra £785m a year over three years. Analysts said the trustees' statement could be the beginning of a 'poison pill' that could torpedo Green's £9.1bn takeover proposal for the company. (See more about the 'poison pill' in the section about equity restructuring in Chapter 17.)

On 14 July 2004 Philip Green dramatically dropped his £9.1bn bid for Marks & Spencer, blaming the retailer's board for blocking a formal offer. Green walked away after nearly 3,000 small shareholders offered almost total support to the board at the M&S annual meeting in London. At the time Green said 'we will see who is the best retailer; there is only one vote that counts and that is the customers'. Stuart Rose spelled out his plan to return £2.3bn to M&S shareholders, worth £1 per share, and announced the sale of the retailer's financial services off-shoot to HSBC. He also planned to buy the Per Una range of women's fashion from its creator George Davies and make savings of up to £320m a year.

During 2005, M&S started to show some signs of recovery. In November 2006, M&S reported that sales and profits before tax had increased significantly for the first half of 2006. The price of their shares soared to an all-time high of slightly over £7 per share at the news, which was £3 more than Sir Philip Green offered in 2004. Stuart Rose said that the company had gained market share in all areas in which it traded.

M&S's success continued in the second half of 2006 and in January 2007 Stuart Rose revealed that they had also had a good Christmas. Like-for-like sales for the third quarter ended 30 December 2006 rose 5.6%, and total sales gained 9.2%. Internet sales soared more than 70%, and international sales increased by 18.2%.

According to the City analysts, shareholders regarded the turnaround in M&S's fortunes a testament to Rose's skills and leadership abilities. With hindsight, the group's performance indicated that M&S's shareholders had made the right decision in rejecting Green's takeover bids.

Stuart Rose was rewarded with a knighthood is the 2008 new year honours list.

Progress check 16.1

What is a merger (amalgamation) and what is an acquisition (takeover)?

Types of M&A

Mergers and acquisitions take place in a number of ways and there are various types of M&A. The most common of these are shown in Fig. 16.1, and are discussed in the sections that follow.

Horizontal integration

One company A may take over or merge with another company B operating in the same industry at a similar level of production so that their operations may be combined. Horizontal integration relates to a merger or takeover involving a competing business and may be defined as:

- the merging of two or more companies at the same level of production

or

- the acquisition of a competitor or a number of competitors at the same level of production in pursuit of market power or economies of scale.

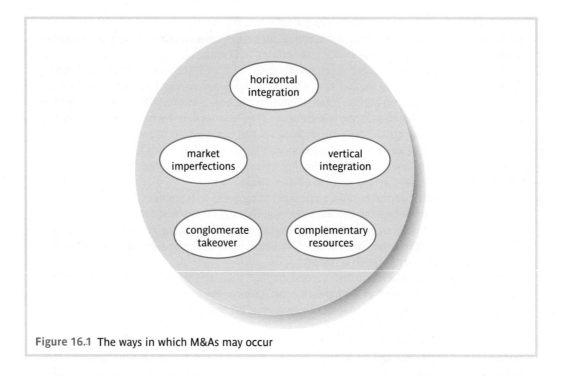

Figure 16.1 The ways in which M&As may occur

There are numerous examples of horizontal integration, which include Morrison plc's acquisition of Safeway plc, Walmart Inc's acquisition of Asda plc, and Granada plc's and Carlton plc's formation of ITV plc.

The main benefits of horizontal integration may be seen in:

- economies of scale – selling more of the same or a similar product
- economies of scope – sharing resources common to different products
- increased market power (over immediate suppliers and those further down the supply chain)
- reduced costs of marketing, selling, and distribution.

The main problems faced by companies involved in horizontal integration include:

- possible legal issues regarding the creation of market monopolies – horizontal integration by acquisition of a competitor may increase market share above a level that allows fair competition
- anticipated economic gains may not materialise (note Morrisons plc's poor results following its takeover of Safeway).

Vertical integration

Vertical integration relates to a merger or takeover involving another business that may be a customer or a supplier. The merger or takeover involves two companies who are active in different stages of production within the same industry.

Vertical forward integration involves a move forward down the supply chain by company A acquiring company B to secure an outlet for company A's products; company A merges with or may take over one or more of its customers. Vertical backward integration involves a move backward up the supply chain by company A acquiring company B to secure supply of raw materials; company A merges with or may take over one or more of its suppliers.

Examples of vertically integrated companies include Apple Computers Inc, BP plc, and Royal Dutch Shell plc.

The main benefits of vertical integration include:

- increased economies of scale
- greater economies of scope
- improved cost efficiency
- greater competitiveness
- reduced threats from suppliers or customers
- higher degree of control over the entire value chain.

The main disadvantages of vertical integration include:

- the limitation of a company's reaction to change
- the high cost to sustain such a company.

Complementary resources

A company A may acquire or merge with company B that uses, for example, similar materials or distribution channels. Company B may be a business that is using the same suppliers as the acquiring company A.

The combined operations of the companies can benefit from cost reductions from increased purchasing power and rationalisation of operations. There may be an increase in purchasing power derived from the larger size of the combined entity. There may also be rationalisation as a result of the pooling of knowledge and resources, and elimination of the duplication of processes and effort.

Conglomerate takeover

A conglomerate takeover involves the acquisition of a company B engaged in a totally different line of business to that of the acquiring company A. To the acquiring company A this means moving into new, unknown areas involving high risk, but also potentially high returns. However, this strategy is questionable with regard to whether it is able to add shareholder value.

An example of a conglomerate takeover was Vivendi Universal's diversification into film and music production and telecommunications in the 1990s. Another high profile conglomerate takeover was the food group Ranks Hovis McDougall's (RHM) acquisition by the multinational engineering conglomerate Tomkins plc in 1992, for which it has been suggested it paid much more than its fair value. Tomkins' massive growth had been achieved mainly through acquisition and prior to, and after the RHM acquisition, it continued to report continued year-on-year increases in earnings per share (eps). The problem with conglomerate takeovers, as Tomkins plc found, was that increases in eps were not necessarily reflected in a growth in share price. During the 1990s, as the Tomkins group ran out of ideas for investment in new growth projects, it returned cash to shareholders through buying back its shares and subsequatly sold off RHM and other significant parts of the group.

Market imperfections

A target company may be one that is for some reason undervalued in the market, which is therefore by definition an inefficient or semi-efficient market. The share price may not reflect the earning potential of the company or the value of its assets.

The participants in a proposed takeover may not agree on the price of the target company's shares. Very often, acquiring companies may 'overpay' for acquisitions as in the case of Tomkins and RHM. The benefits of the synergy effect (2 + 2 = 5) may be questioned. Is the whole new entity worth considerably more than the worth of the two separate entities, or considerably less?

Let's look at an example.

Worked Example 16.2

Oliver plc and Ramsey plc are rival food retail companies both operating in the UK.

The following information is available on each company:

	Oliver plc	Ramsey plc
Most recent dividends per share	£0.35	£0.15
Most recent earnings per share	£0.62	£0.25
Number of shares in issue	6m	3m
Current market price of shares	£8.80	£3.15
Current weighted average cost of capital	10%	10%

The management of Oliver plc is currently considering making a formal cash offer of £5.20 for each of Ramsey plc's shares.

The current management of Ramsey plc expect future dividends will grow by 5% each year in perpetuity. However, if the company is acquired by Oliver plc, the management of Oliver plc expect cost reductions and economies of scale will increase the growth rate to 7% each year in perpetuity. The transaction costs of the proposed acquisition are expected to be £1.2m.

We will use Gordon's dividend growth model (see Chapter 6) to calculate the value created by the acquisition. The market share price (S) is determined from the current dividend (v), the shareholders' required rate of return (K_e), and the expected dividend growth rate (G), as follows:

$$S = \frac{v \times (1 + G)}{(K_e - G)}$$

We will also calculate the value created for each group of shareholders if the cash offer of £5.20 is accepted by Ramsey plc's shareholders, and calculate the increase or decrease in value that would result if, due to integration problems, only 50% of the anticipated acquisition benefits were realised.

Value created by the acquisition
Ramsey plc – value before the acquisition

Using $S = \dfrac{v \times (1 + G)}{(K_e - G)}$

$£0.15 \times 1.05/(0.10 - 0.05) = £3.15$ per share

3 million × £3.15 = £9.45m

Ramsey plc – value after the acquisition

$$£0.15 \times 1.07/(0.10 - 0.07) = £5.35 \text{ per share}$$
$$3 \text{ million} \times £5.35 = £16.05m$$

		£m
£5.35 × 3m =		16.05
Costs		1.20
		14.85
Value prior to merger		9.45
Total value created		£5.40m

Cash offer of £5.20 per share
Ramsey plc

   3m × (£5.20 – £3.15)   £6.15m value gained by Ramsey shareholders

Oliver plc

   3m × (£5.35 – £5.20) – £1.20m   (£0.75m) value lost by Oliver shareholders

Total value created   £5.40m

Value created if only 50% of the anticipated acquisition benefits are realised

   Loss of acquisition benefits 50% × £5.40m = £2.70m

Ramsey plc

   3m × (£5.20 – £3.15)   = £6.15m value gained by Ramsey shareholders

Oliver plc

   3m × (£5.35 – £5.20) – (£1.20m + £2.70m) = (£3.45m) value lost by Oliver shareholders

Total value created   £2.70m

Progress check 16.2

Outline the different forms of M&A.

Reasons and justifications for M&As

The level of mergers and acquisitions increased worldwide over previous years to a very high level of activity in 2005. The chart shown in Fig. 16.2 gives an indication of the industrial sectors in which there was most M&As activity in Europe for the year to September 2005 in terms of value and volume of mergers and acquisitions. During 2005 the *Financial Times* was predicting that the total volume of M&As for the year in Europe would reach £532bn.

In February 2005 CNN reported that in the USA alone in January 2005 there had been 571 M&A deals amounting to US$144bn. This huge level of activity was forecast to continue throughout 2005. However, they also reported that 70% of the big M&A deals worldwide over the previous two years had failed to create value; 50% of M&A deals had actually destroyed shareholder value.

European Mergers and Acquisitions **Deal by Industry Sector – Year to September 2005**	**Value** **% of total**	**Volume** **% of total**
Industrials and chemicals	11	22
Financial services	9	11
Business services	3	11
Consumer	12	17
Energy, mining, and utilities	22	5
Technology, media, and communications	17	15
Leisure	3	5
Transport	3	4
Pharmaceuticals, medical and biotechnology	4	5
Construction	6	5

Figure 16.2 European mergers and acquisitions
(Source: Office of National Statistics, www.statistics.gov.uk)

However, we should not conclude that all M&As are failures and do not create value for shareholders. An example of what appears to be a huge success was the Royal Bank of Scotland's acquisition in March 2000 of the much larger NatWest Bank, which is illustrated in Worked Example 16.3.

Worked Example 16.3

NatWest Bank plc was very much in need of a turnaround (see Nohria N, Weber J (2003) *The Royal Bank of Scotland: Masters of Integration*, Harvard Business School Case N1-404-026, 15 August). In March 2000 it was acquired by Royal Bank of Scotland (RBS), which was a much smaller outfit. 70% of RBS's revenue growth had been organic. However, this reverse takeover dramatically improved the company's revenues, profits, and market capitalisation. The additional gains following the takeover, included:

- RBS's improved competitive position in all its businesses, giving them many market leader positions

- significantly improved cost-income ratio to make it one of the most efficient players in the banking industry

- the bringing of new customers to all segments of the bank

- an increase in the satisfaction of existing customers

- an increase in employee morale and pride they felt in being part of a winning organisation.

In January 2007, RBS's share price achieved its highest point ever at £20 per share. In 2006, Citigroup predicted that RBS was undervalued by £10bn because of a so-called 'management discount' based on the market's view of the bank's focus on acquisitions rather than generating shareholder value. However, RBS's chief executive, Sir Fred Goodwin, countered that by confirming that the bank was on track to exceed the market's expectation for profits of about £9.16bn in 2006, and stressed that there was no need for the bank to be looking at major acquisitions. One analyst commented that RBS was growing slightly faster than the rest of the banking sector, but its shares were still underpriced compared with the shares of the other UK banks. He predicted the 'management discount' on the shares would diminish further throughout 2007 and since the share price had gone through the £20 mark it should stay above that level and continue up towards what he felt the company was worth.

While the RBS/NatWest integration appears to have been a success, management sometimes may forget the underlying principles for justifying M&As. Directors and managers of businesses are employed by companies to manage their assets in the most effective way to maximise shareholder wealth. The main justification of M&As therefore must be that target companies really should be worth more than they will cost the acquiring companies. This means that the expected future present value cash flows of the combined companies, minus the costs of acquisition, must amount to more than the expected future present value cash flows of the two individual companies. However, many other reasons may be offered to justify M&As, some of which are 'good' and some of which are 'bad', a number of which are discussed in the article below reproduced from the December 2005 issue of *The Manufacturer*.

The secret to the success of M&As

'Target acquired', by Justin Pugsley

Mergers and acquisitions, often the quickest way for companies to grow or diversify, can be fraught with difficulties and pitfalls. Justin Pugsley discovers the secret to their success.

Driven by low borrowing costs and cash rich companies, mergers and acquisitions are booming again. According to the *Financial Times*, the volume of mergers and acquisitions across Europe is set to reach £532 billion this year. There is also likely to be a lot of disappointment once the current bidding fever subsides and managers are confronted with the reality of making their deals work.

According to Angus Knowles-Cutler, corporate finance partner with consultants, Deloitte, around 70 per cent of transactions fail to live up to expectations. 'Research has shown that about 35 per cent of managers leave after the deal is done with 50 per cent leaving if the takeover is hostile,' explains Knowles.

Christian Hasenoehrl, managing partner with Gallup Consulting says that companies formed out of an acquisition or merger can lose 16 to 49 per cent of their combined market within two to five years.

Usually, poor planning is to blame and because management greatly underestimates the task of integrating two organisations.

Daimler Benz's take-over of Chrysler is a classic example of a large takeover which went wrong. Many industry sources described it as a mismatch of management styles and culture. The solid hierarchical prestigious German company taking over an American entrepreneurial company used to operating by the seat of its pants lurching from crisis to crisis. The German company also upset many of Chrysler's talented managers by riding roughshod over them. They soon departed to the dismay of Chrysler's workers and Daimler's investors.

Fixing Chrysler came at a huge price for Daimler. It had to send in a large number of its own managers to turn the American acquisition

▶

around, thereby neglecting its very profitable core business – Mercedes Benz.

Throw in the problems with Daimler's Mitsubishi adventure and the troubled Smart car subsidiary and there is the perfect recipe for a distracted management engaged in fire fighting rather than managing.

Indeed, the image of Mercedes Benz has been damaged due to quality problems with its cars. It has also been losing ground to rivals such as Audi and Jaguar which have instead been focusing on innovative ways of building cars. Fortunately, not all mergers and acquisitions are subject to so many problems. Many do work creating an enterprise worth more than the sum of its parts.

'We tend not to stray outside our areas of competence,' explains Terry Twigger chief executive officer of UK aerospace, defence and electronics manufacturer, Meggitt PLC. The company last year bought Dunlop Standard Aerospace with private equity group Carlyle Group for $1.4 billion and Meggitt retaining Dunlop Aerospace Design and Manufacturing division. At the time, the deal was greeted with concern by some analysts due to its size.

However, integration appears to be going well thanks to Meggitt's advanced preparation and attention to detail. Indeed, Meggitt has been on the acquisition trail for many years, for example snapping up businesses from defence giant BAE Systems. 'We research companies extensively before buying them. It is not unusual for us to study a target business from a distance for five to six years,' explains Twigger. 'We also do a considerable amount of due diligence and work-out before-hand where the business will fit.'

He adds that familiarity with the industry helps considerably. 'We have a good understanding of the different corporate cultures in our industry,' says Twigger.

In integrating the Dunlop acquisition, Meggitt worked closely with Deloitte. Knowles-Cutler of Deloitte explains that the more the business is a 'people's business' the harder it can be to make integration work. 'At one extreme you've got an asset-based business such as a mining company, at the other end you've got say an advertising agency, which is all about people,' says Knowles-Cutler. 'I would say manufacturing usually falls somewhere in the middle of those two extremes.'

For businesses, which are heavily people orientated or brand- or location-based the strategy of the acquiring company is often to build brand portfolios, explains Knowles-Cutler. An example of that approach is beverages company Diageo.

For instance, re-locating a whisky distillery whose name is heavily associated with a particular part of Scotland could destroy the brand's name. 'These types of companies add value by focusing on marketing and distribution channels,' says Knowles-Cutler.

Nonetheless, he explains that the people side is still important with the value of manufactured products increasingly related to their intellectual property component. Also, in an increasingly competitive environment retaining and keeping good managers motivated is crucial.

He advises that management should communicate its intentions and objectives, and clarify the non-negotiables as soon as possible and tell people where they stand with their jobs. 'It's important to kill off speculation early, preferably before the deal closes,' he says.

Illustrating the importance of communicating clearly and openly, Knowles-Cutler says productivity tends to plummet around the time of a merger or an acquisition. In an organisation: 'Where people work eight hours, they'll spend 5.9 hours working productively, during a transaction that can fall to just two hours,' he explains.

Virginia Merritt with management consultants Stanton Marris talks of managing energy levels, which are at a particularly high level during a take-over and manifest themselves in the form of anxiety and concern among workers. She advises quickly managing that energy positively by engaging people within the target companies and communicating with them. 'Involve people in the acquired company in the integration process and show that everyone is working for the best result,' advises Merritt. She adds that if the acquiring company is perceived to be adding value to the acquired company it can substantially boost morale and relieve anxiety.

Another problem that can surface, is that competitors may use the uncertainty surrounding a take-over to poach valuable staff from the target company.

Describing the acquisition of Dunlop, Twigger explained that the managements of both entities engaged in intensive meetings about the future of the new group. In other words, the management of the acquired company were consulted and included in the details of the integration. 'We also did some social bonding to make the Dunlop management feel more part of a team,' says Twigger. Workers were also informed as quickly as possible over developments.

IT systems can pose a serious challenge and have been known to derail some mergers and acquisitions: 'With IT systems we're quite pragmatic. We don't insist they must use the same ERP system as us,' says Twigger. 'People can carry on using their same systems; we can create interfaces between theirs and our system or, in time, migrate them onto ours.'

With most companies being heavily reliant on IT, an audit in this area is absolutely essential.

For specialist radio frequency and sensing technology equipment manufacturer e2v technologies, corporate change has been a way of life for many years.

e2v is a spin off from Marconi; itself a refocused specialist telecoms manufacturer when BAE Systems bought the defence side of the business in 1999.

The management then bought out e2v in 2002 and listed it on the stock market in 2004. 'Our strategy is to buy businesses with solid product lines, established products within niche markets, which complement our own,' explains Peter Knowles, e2v's commercial director. In August this year, e2v acquired x-ray products manufacturer Gresham Scientific Instruments for €5.1 million. According to Knowles, e2v is intending to grow and gain a foothold in markets related to its business via acquisitions.

Other than undergoing the usual due diligence procedures, Knowles explains that it is particularly important to gauge the attitude of customers towards any potential take-over. 'With customers it's always a very sensitive area, there's a lot of confidentiality issues and you don't want to worry them,' says Knowles.

As an example he mentioned that Gresham's Japanese customers were relieved that e2v was in the same industry sector and could offer financial backing to their supplier. 'They were particularly worried that one of their rivals might buy the business and gain control over its proprietary technologies,' says Knowles. 'They welcomed e2v taking it over because it's a supplier company.'

Knowles heads up the company's mergers and acquisitions team and is supported by various technical experts within the business. They are brought in when needed with evaluating targets and helping with integration.

Before acquiring or merging, companies must know themselves, says Hasenoehrl from Gallup, so they can better understand how to make deals work or if they're even worth undertaking in the first place. Twigger, with Meggitt, emphasises that being upfront and honest with people is crucial to making a deal work.

Making a merger or an acquisition work is basically about common sense and doing thorough research. However, all too often the focus is too much on balance sheets and assets while synergies with the human factor are all too often too far down the list of priorities. Indeed, the term 'human audit' is relatively new and underused, despite the fact it is ultimately people who make or break deals.

© First published in the December 2005 issue of *The Manufacturer*

Very broadly, the good reasons a company may have for M&As are to:

- support value-creating growth – note from the above article the strategies of businesses that are brand-orientated, for example Diageo's acquisition strategy 'to build brand portfolios'
- complement business strategies in terms of products, market, technologies, etc. – note from the above article, e2V's strategy to 'buy businesses with solid product lines, established products within niche markets, which complement our own . . . and gain a foothold in markets related to our business via acquisitions'
- stop a competitor merging with or taking over a business.

The bad reasons a company may have for M&As are to:

- increase earnings per share (eps)
- build empires by buying companies rather than running them successfully.

The main justifications supporting the reasons for M&As are shown in Fig. 16.3, and are each considered in the sections that follow.

Economic factors

If company managers believe that shareholder wealth will be enhanced then that is a good reason for going ahead with an acquisition. The managers therefore believe that the two companies

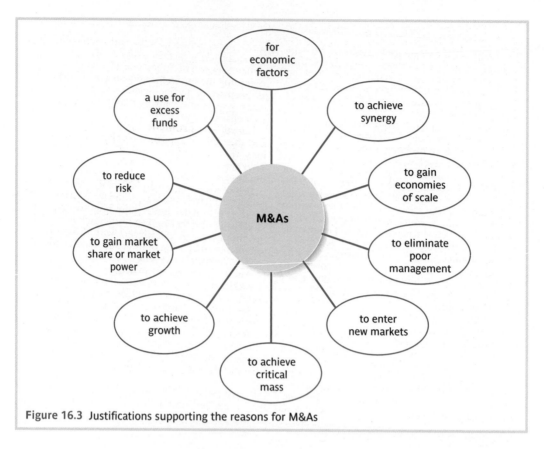

Figure 16.3 Justifications supporting the reasons for M&As

t and p will be worth more in combination than as separate entities. In other words, the present values (PV) of the future cash flows of the combined entity will be greater than the present values of the future cash flows of the individual entities, which may be represented as:

$$PVt\&p > PVt + PVp$$

Synergy

The assets of two companies, and the activities in which two companies are engaged, may complement each other. Synergy is the creation of wealth due to the increase in the output of the combined companies over the sum of outputs of the separate companies, using the same resources.

The shorthand commonly used to denote synergy is:

$$2 + 2 = 5$$

It may be noted that Rappaport's seven drivers of value may be used to quantify synergies derived from an acquisition (see Chapter 2).

Economies of scale

Economies of scale are similar to the synergy effect, but economies of scale are due to the benefits that occur because of the larger scale of operations after the merger or acquisition.

Economies of scale are most likely in horizontal mergers because of the higher level of sales achieved with a lower cost base. However, economies of scale may also occur in vertical mergers.

Elimination of inefficient management

A company may be poorly run because managers are satisfying their own requirements, instead of seeking to maximise shareholders' wealth (see the agency problem in Chapter 2). The share price may therefore decline and attract prospective buyers who believe that they may manage the company's assets more efficiently.

The elimination of ineffective management following a merger or an acquisition may be a more attractive option than a vote by shareholders to remove them. A vote by shareholders to remove ineffective management may also take a long time and may not be totally effective.

Entry to new markets

The achievement of growth by a company organically or internally may be too slow or too costly. Companies may want to develop new areas by product, business type, or geographically. To achieve these aims a merger or an acquisition may be a quicker option. It may also be a cheaper option because, for example, there will be no costs of acquiring new premises, and additional personnel and marketing costs.

This strategy is particularly popular in the retail trade where starting from scratch is particularly costly and time-consuming. An example was Iceland's acquisition of Bejam in 1987. Through that acquisition Iceland was able to break into the North of England geographical market instead of competing there with Bejam from a zero base.

Critical mass

Smaller businesses may merge to achieve critical mass. Small companies may lack credibility because of their:

- small size, which usually means they have a shortage of buying power, knowledge, etc.
- lack or resources for research and development, in terms of funding and specialist skills
- lack of investment in brands, with possibly no brands developed at all.

Merging companies can pool resources to provide a critical mass to finance the above requirements. Smaller companies involved in such mergers may then take advantage of an existing brand and an existing knowledge base.

Growth

When businesses have successfully moved through their start-up phase and are reaching the growth stage they may find it hard to grow further organically. A takeover provides a quick solution to provide further growth. Note British American Tobacco (BAT), which took over Allied Dunbar and Eagle Star, both financial institutions, as part of their growth strategy, using surplus cash.

An alternative for a cash rich mature company, as we have already discussed in Chapter 15, is to return funds to shareholders by a share repurchase or by paying shareholders a special dividend.

Market share or market power

Companies may use horizontal mergers or takeovers to increase their market share. Swallowing up the competition therefore gives such businesses the ability to earn monopoly profits.

Companies may use vertical integration to increase their buying power in raw materials and distribution resources. They may do this either through merger or takeover of customer or supplier companies (vertical forward or vertical backward integration).

However, a legislative obstacle of referral to the Monopolies and Mergers Commission may cause financial damage and damage to the reputation of a company. Time may therefore be lost and any advantages eroded or eliminated because the price of the deal may increase, and very high legal fees may be incurred.

Risk reduction

A company may acquire another company in a different line of business. Such diversification may be justified in terms of reducing shareholder risk. Note the example of a business that sells both ice cream and umbrellas in order to reduce total overall business risk. When the weather is hot and sunny, people will buy ice cream, but they will not need to buy umbrellas; when the weather is cold and rainy, people will need to buy umbrellas, but they are less likely to buy ice cream.

If a company is involved in many different businesses then the volatility in its levels of profits and cash may also be smoothed. An example is a conglomerate takeover. The many examples of conglomerate takeovers in the 1980s and 1990s showed tremendous growth in eps and cash flow. However, as we have already discussed earlier in this chapter, although eps may be increased it is not necessarily true that the share price will also increase. Conglomerates have historically not added value for shareholders and it is often the case that cash surpluses are returned to shareholders for their investment elsewhere, rather than being invested in new projects within the conglomerates themselves.

Excess funds

Some companies may build up large amounts of cash that may not be earning sufficient returns to meet the expectations of shareholders. GEC/Marconi, for example (see Worked Example 16.4), did just that through the 1980s and 1990 by building up cash excesses, which were surplus to their growth requirements.

Worked Example 16.4

GEC (re-named Marconi in 1999) during the 1980s and 1990s was a cash rich, mature company that City analysts felt should be returning funds to the shareholders. But Marconi wanted to reverse its mature position back into the growth phase by investing in the high-tech, fast growing dot.com and telecoms industry. It used its funds to make acquisitions in this industrial sector, rather than return them to shareholders. However, it went further than this and took on high levels of debt to finance further such acquisitions. In the early 2000s, the dot.com and telecoms industry collapsed and this also resulted in Marconi's gradual collapse and decline. Effective from 1 January 2006, the Marconi name and most of the assets were acquired by the

Swedish company Ericsson, with Marconi still used as a brand within Ericsson. The remainder of the Marconi company was renamed telent plc.

As a mature business, Marconi should not have been funded totally by equity, but then when it reversed its cycle into an industry with high business risk to become a growth company it should not have become highly geared by taking on such high levels of debt. It was perhaps an example of trying to do the right things, but doing them wrongly.

If companies are cash rich but sufficient numbers of appropriate value-adding new projects cannot be found in which to invest, then excess funds may be more usefully invested in the acquisition of other companies. Rather than following Marconi's example, acquisitions necessarily require consideration of the appropriate relationships between risk and return, and the matching of such investments with the appropriate types of funding.

Financial motives in M&As

There are some further motives for acquisitions, which may be divided into financial motives, and also managerial motives considered in the following section.

We will first consider four financial motives, which relate to:

- target company undervaluation
- corporation tax
- unemployed tax shields
- earnings per share – 'bootstrapping'.

Target company undervaluation

One justification of a takeover may be that the target company is considered to be a bargain. The target company may be perceived as being undervalued in the market because its share price is low. The implication of this may be that the capital markets are not totally efficient, or are viewed as inefficient, if the share price does not reflect the value or the potential value of the business.

Even if capital markets are generally seen as efficient, some companies may be difficult to value with certainty so there is a further possibility of undervaluation.

Corporation tax

A company may have run out of brought forward tax benefits to utilise against current and future years profits. Therefore, this may result in it paying out a high proportion of its profits in tax.

The tax benefits from unused capital allowances in a target company may therefore be considered for utilisation by a takeover company. The target company may, for example, be making losses or low profits but may have high levels of unused tax allowances.

Unemployed tax shields

A low geared company may have a high proportion of its capital in equity or it may be totally financed with equity. Such a company may therefore want to acquire a tax shield or increase its own tax shield to reduce its tax liability. It may achieve this by merging with, or taking over, a highly geared company. Such a highly geared target company will have a high level of debt and therefore be making high interest payments.

Bootstrapping

An acquiring company, which is seeking to take over another company, may have a higher P/E ratio compared with the company it is seeking to take over, the target company. The acquiring company may therefore increase its overall combined earnings by a greater proportion than its increase in share capital if the takeover is financed by a share-for-share issue (see Worked Example 16.5). This type of activity, where a company tries to boost its eps through acquisition, is called 'bootstrapping'.

Worked Example 16.5

The following data relates to the share capital of two companies A, the acquiring company, and B the target company:

Company	A	B
Number of ordinary shares	200m	25m
Earnings	£20m	£5m
eps	10p	20p

Company A has proposed a deal in which it may offer to the shareholders of company B 10m shares in company A for 25m shares in company B.
    The data relating to the combined entity AB will then be:

Company	AB
Number of ordinary shares	210m
Earnings	£25m
eps	11.9p

The post-acquisition eps is therefore higher than the pre-acquisition eps of company A, although it is lower than the pre-acquisition eps of company B.

Progress check 16.3

How would you generally distinguish between 'good' and 'bad' motives for M&As?

Managerial motives in M&As

There may be M&A situations in which the shareholders' wealth maximisation objective is secondary to managers' personal objectives in wishing to enhance their own positions. In such situations, the basis of such takeovers may therefore be a manifestation of the agency problem between shareholders and managers or directors. The motives behind such takeovers may be to increase managers':

■ emoluments – salary, car, bonus, pension, club membership, etc.

■ power – a seat on the main board of directors, and wider responsibility

■ security – creating a situation in which they are unlikely to lose their jobs – managers may believe, rightly or wrongly, that they will be more secure in a larger organisation.

From a shareholder perspective, of course, these types of takeover cannot be justified. If a takeover does go ahead on this basis then the underlying agency problem may be overcome through the introduction of an executive share option scheme. If directors and managers become shareholders then in theory they should have the same objective as all other shareholders – the maximisation of shareholder wealth.

Target company valuation

When a company is considering a takeover of, or a merger with another company, it must carry out an appraisal of the company in terms of what it may be worth, as well as what sort of fit and synergy effects the deal will provide. The takeover bid price offered may then be an estimated 'fair value' in excess of, for example, the current market share price. What the target company may be worth can be considered using one of many different approaches. There are a number of ways in which the estimated fair value may be determined. The three broad approaches to company valuation are:

■ stock market valuation of the company's shares

■ valuation of the company's assets

■ valuation of the company's future earnings or cash flows – a going concern valuation.

Stock market valuation

The valuation of a company's shares may be based on the stock market valuation at the current market price. This method is very simple to use. It involves the multiplication of the number of ordinary shares issued by the company by the current market share price. Whether or not the result is a 'fair price' depends on the efficiency of the stock market.

This method may be a useful starting point, but may not be a 'fair price' because:

■ the share price may reflect only infrequent trading in the shares, and the volume of trading in shares may greatly affect the share price

■ the company may be a private limited (Ltd) company and therefore not quoted on a stock exchange

■ post-acquisition benefits are ignored, which are based on the intentions of the acquiring company.

Worked Example 16.6 illustrates a stock market valuation of Flatco plc.

Worked Example 16.6

The 2007 financial statements for Flatco plc are shown in Figs. 16.4 and 16.5.

Flatco plc
Balance sheet as at 31 December 2007

Figures in £000

Non-current assets	
Intangible	416
Tangible	1,884
Financial	248
	2,548
Current assets	
Stocks	311
Debtors	573
Prepayments	589
Cash	327
	1,800
Current liabilities (less than one year)	
Overdraft	50
Creditors	553
Taxation	50
Dividends	70
Accruals	82
	805
	995
Net current assets	
Total assets less current liabilities	3,543
less	
Non-current liabilities (over one year)	
Loan	173
Creditors	154
	327
less	
Provisions	222
Net assets	2,994
Capital and reserves	
Share capital	1,200
Share premium account	200
Retained earnings	1,594
	2,994

Figure 16.4 Flatco plc balance sheet as at 31 December 2007

Predco plc is negotiating its acquisition of Flatco plc and its directors are considering its valuation using a variety of methods. The financial data relating to Predco plc for the same period is as follows:

Profit on ordinary activities after tax	£570,000
WACC	17%
P/E ratio	12.5

The directors of Predco plc believe that the company will continue to increase its profit on ordinary activities after tax by 3% per annum for the foreseeable future as a result of economies

Flatco plc
Income statement for the year ended 31 December 2007

Figures in £000	
Turnover	3,500
Cost of sales	(2,500)
Gross profit	1,000
Distribution costs	(300)
Administrative expenses	(155)
Other operating costs	
Exceptional items: redundancy costs	(95)
	(550)
Other operating income	100
Operating profit	550
Income from other non-current asset	
investments	100
Profit before interest and tax	650
	(60)
Net interest	
Profit before tax	590
	(50)
Tax on profit on ordinary activities	
Profit on ordinary activities after tax	540
Dividends (5.8p per share)	(70)
Retained profit for the financial year	470

Additional information
Authorised and issued share capital 31 December 2007 1,200,000
£1 ordinary shares (1,000,000 in 2006)
Market value of ordinary shares in Flatco plc 31 December 2007: £2.75 (2006: £3.00)
Earnings per share 2007: 45p (2006: 38.6p)
P/E ratio 2007: 6.11 times (2006: 7.80 times)

Figure 16.5 Flatco plc income statement for the year ended 31 December 2007

of scale and synergies obtained from the takeover. Many of Flatco plc's processes use identical equipment to Predco and so the directors also believe that they may sell off a number of assets for £250,000 during 2008.

We will consider Flatco plc in terms of its stock market valuation.

$$\text{number of ordinary shares in issue} = \frac{\text{balance sheet value of ordinary shares}}{\text{nominal value of each ordinary share}}$$

$$= £1,200,000/£1$$

$$= 1.2\text{m shares}$$

$$\text{stock market valuation of Flacto plc} = \text{number of ordinary shares in issue} \times \text{market price}$$

$$= 1.2\text{m} \times £2.75$$

$$= \underline{\mathbf{£3,300,000}}$$

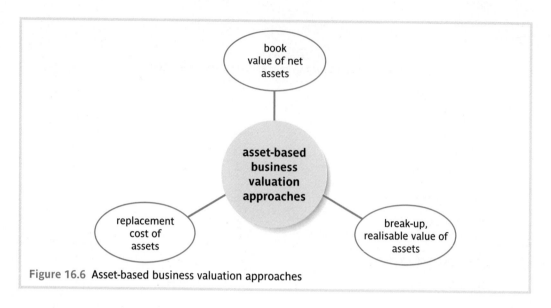

Figure 16.6 Asset-based business valuation approaches

The three main asset-based approaches to company valuation are shown in Fig. 16.6.

Book value of net assets valuation

If we consider the net book value of a company's non-current assets in its balance sheet, together with its working capital and then deduct the value of its loans, debentures, etc., the result is a balance sheet total of net assets. This may be represented as:

book value of net assets valuation = non-current assets + net current assets – long-term debt

There are a number of obvious limitations to this method of valuation. First, asset valuations based on historical costs, which may be factual and available directly from the balance sheet, do not necessarily reflect the current valuation of assets. There may also be prior charges on assets, made by lenders to the company.

Second, the valuation of stocks may be unreliable or unrealistic because of type of valuation method that may have been used, and it may not always be possible to recover the full cost of stocks (inventory) through sales.

Third, the valuation of debtors may be unreliable or unrealistic because of the particular doubtful debts policy adopted and the collectability of the accounts receivable at the values shown in the balance sheet.

Fourth, intangible assets such as goodwill, human capital, and brand names, are ignored, unlike some other models like those based on earnings or dividend yield, or the super profits model (see later).

Fifth, costs such as development expenditure would also have a value related to future profits, which may be much higher than their value as assets, currently stated in the company's balance sheet.

Sixth, not all liabilities may have been quantified and there may be hidden liabilities.

Even if the book value of net assets were totally reliable it would really be only a lower limit valuation. The net assets model may be used as a measure of security in a share value. The value of shares in a particular class is equal to the net tangible assets attributable to that class of share.

Worked Example 16.7

Using the data from Worked Example 16.6 the directors of Predco plc may calculate a book value of net assets valuation of Flatco plc.

	£000
total assets less current liabilities	3,543
less	
intangible non-current assets	(416)
	3,127
less	
long-term debt	(173)
	2,954
net asset value	**£2,954,000**
number of ordinary shares	1.2m
value per ordinary share	= £2,954,000/1,200,000
	= £2.46 per share

It can be seen from the above calculation that the valuation of the company based on the historical costs of its book assets is around 10% less than the market value calculated in Worked Example 16.6.

Break-up, realisable value of assets valuation

As an alternative to net assets valuation, assets may be valued according to their net realisable value. However, valuation is not necessarily a simple matter.

The realisable value of the target company's assets is the residual amount that could be realised if they were sold separately on the open market, after deducting any liquidation costs and other liabilities. If the market value, that is the total value of the shares, is below the break-up value, which is the market value of the individual assets within the company, then the company is undervalued.

Replacement cost of assets valuation

The costs of acquiring the separate assets of a target company may be determined on an open market basis. These are the costs to replace the assets, rather than what they could be sold for. The advantage of this method is that replacement cost valuations are more relevant than historical cost book valuations, or current realisable valuations.

Disadvantages are that this method ignores goodwill, and it is usually difficult to identify separate assets, like separate individual factories, machinery, etc., and determine their replacement cost. Assets may also be complementary and therefore their separate valuation may not be totally realistic; how much use is a left shoe to a two-legged person if they don't also have the right shoe to accompany it?

The five main earnings or income-based, or going concern, approaches to company valuation are shown in Fig. 16.7.

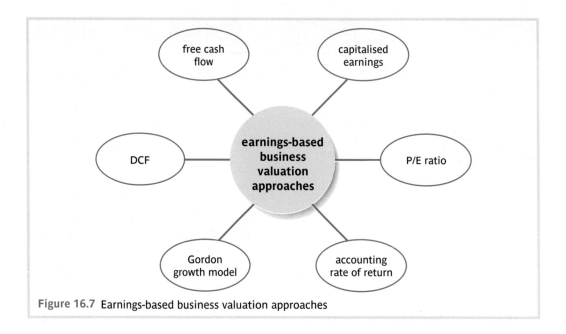

Figure 16.7 Earnings-based business valuation approaches

Capitalised earnings valuation

The capitalised earnings method calculates the value of a company by capitalising annual main-tainable expected earnings, using its earnings yield (earnings per share divided by the current share price, which is the reciprocal of the P/E ratio) or return on investment (ROI). Expected earnings may be estimated using average historical earnings and making an uplift for synergy and economies of scale. This, of course, is very subjective.

The required earnings yield used to capitalise earnings should reflect the size of the business and the type of industry. The choice of required earnings yield may also be an estimate, rather than a precise calculation.

Worked Example 16.8

Using the data from Worked Example 16.6 the directors of Predco plc may calculate a capitalised earnings valuation of Flatco plc.

$$\text{capitalised earnings value} = \frac{\text{annual maintainable expected earnings}}{\text{required earnings yield}}$$

required earnings yield = eps/share price

$$\text{Flatco plc required earnings yield} = \frac{£0.45 \times 100}{£2.75} = 16.364\%$$

(which is also the reciprocal of its P/E ratio: $1 \times 100/ 6.11$)

$$\text{Flatco plc capitalised earnings value} = \frac{£540,000}{0.16364} \quad \text{(assuming that current earnings are equal to its maintainable expected earnings)}$$

$$= \underline{\mathbf{£3,300,000}} \quad \text{(rounded up)}$$

Price/earnings (P/E) valuation

The P/E method of valuation multiplies the target company's distributable earnings by an appropriate P/E ratio (the company market valuation divided by distributable earnings).

Possible P/E ratios which may be used for this type of valuation include:

- the predator, or acquiring company, P/E ratio

- the target company P/E ratio

- a weighted average combination of the predator company P/E and the target company P/E ratio.

If the target company's P/E ratio is used, the resultant valuation will be the same as an earnings valuation of the target company. The P/E ratio used normally depends on who is making the valuation and for what purpose.

The P/E ratio model is a method of valuing a large controlling interest in a company or a whole company, where the owners can decide on the dividend and profit retention policy. It is an earnings-based valuation as can be seen from the relationship:

$$\text{P/E ratio} = \frac{\text{market value of shares}}{\text{earnings per share (eps)}}$$

This relationship can be rewritten as:

$$\text{market value} = \text{eps} \times \text{P/E ratio}$$

where

$$\text{eps} = \frac{\text{profit after tax (PAT)} - \text{preference share dividends}}{\text{number of ordinary shares in issue}}$$

and therefore

$$\text{market value} = \frac{(\text{PAT} - \text{preference share dividends}) \times \text{P/E ratio}}{\text{number of ordinary shares in issue}}$$

The growth component reduces during the life cycle of a company as expansion of the business slows down. The P/E ratio reflects any expected future growth of a company, which is already incorporated in the share price. The share price moves only with respect to changes in expectations of future growth.

A growth of the P/E ratio is not a guarantee of a rise of the share price. A high P/E ratio is a signal to company managers that investors expect a future growth of eps. Low dividends and high reinvestments mean that managers expect growth. A lower P/E ratio is a signal that prospects of growth are decreasing. Growing dividends per share and low reinvestment is not the basis for growth.

Worked Example 16.9

Using the data from Worked Example 16.6 the directors of Predco plc may calculate a price/earnings ratio valuation of Flatco plc. Predco plc must decide on a suitable P/E ratio and then multiply this by Flatco plc's eps. Flatco plc's eps may be its historical eps or its expected future eps.

Predco may also use one of a number of P/E ratios: Predco plc's P/E ratio; Flatco plc's P/E ratio; the weighted average of the P/E ratios of the two companies. We will consider valuations of Flatco plc using its historical (2007) eps and the three different P/E ratios.

Predco plc P/E ratio

Market value of Flatco plc = Flatco 2007 eps × Predco P/E × number of Flatco ordinary shares

$\qquad$ = £0.45 × 12.5 × 1,200,000

$\qquad$ = **£6,750,000**

Flatco plc P/E ratio

Market value of Flatco plc = Flatco 2007 eps × Flatco P/E × number of Flatco ordinary shares

$\qquad$ = £0.45 × 6.11 × 1,200,000

$\qquad$ = **£3,300,000**   (rounded up, and equal to the capitalised earnings valuation)

Weighted average P/E ratio

The combined earnings (profit on ordinary activities after tax) = £540,000 + £570,000

$\qquad$ = £1,110,000

Flatco plc P/E ratio weighted by combined earnings $= \dfrac{6.11 \times £540,000}{£1,110,000}$

Predco plc P/E ratio weighted by combined earnings $= \dfrac{12.5 \times £570,000}{£1,110,000}$

Weighted average P/E ratio $= \dfrac{6.11 \times £540,000}{£1,110,000} + \dfrac{12.5 \times £570,000}{£1,110,000}$

$\qquad$ = 2.97 + 6.42

$\qquad$ = 9.39

Market value of Flatco plc = £0.45 × 9.39 × 1,200,000

$\qquad$ = **£5,070,600**

Accounting rate of return model

The accounting rate of return (ARR) model may used with regard to takeovers to assess the maximum an acquiring company can afford to pay, because it considers the post-acquisition profits.

The ARR model is different from the P/E ratio method, which is concerned with a market rate of return required by investors. The ARR model considers the accounting rate of return (or ROCE) required from the company whose shares are to be valued:

$$\text{market value} = \frac{\text{estimated future profits}}{\text{required ROCE}}$$

For a takeover bid, profits will usually be adjusted for changed circumstances following the takeover, such as:

- directors' pay
- interest payable
- the impacts of post-takeover rationalisation and the engagement of new management.

Gordon growth model valuation

The Gordon growth model, or dividend growth model, may be used to value a company by calculating the present value of future dividends accruing to its shares, which are expected to grow each year. The company valuation is calculated using the formula:

$$\frac{v \times (1 + G)}{(K_e - G)}$$

where

v is the current dividend payment

G is an annual dividend growth percentage, calculated using the historical values of the target company's dividends

K_e is the cost of equity or shareholders' return of the target company using the CAPM.

In practice, there may be a great deal of difficulty in estimating an annual dividend growth percentage for the target company.

Discounted cash flow (DCF) valuation

The DCF valuation model is an appropriate method to use when one company intends to acquire another company, and to then provide further investment in order to improve future profits.

A DCF method of company valuation assumes that the maximum amount the predator company would pay for the target company is the difference between the present values of its pre- and post-acquisition cash flows. This may be represented as:

present values of the target (t) and predator (p) companies' post-acquisition cash flows

less

present values of the predator (p) company's pre-acquisition cash flows

or

$$\text{PVt\&p} - \text{PVp}$$

The model normally uses after-tax cash flows and an after-tax cost of capital (WACC). Cash flows net of tax, and ignoring any purchase consideration (acquisition price), are discounted to calculate the NPV. The NPV is then the maximum purchase price that should be paid.

If estimates of future cash flows are not readily available, they may be determined using an approximation of cash flow like EVA (economic value added). We discussed EVA in Chapter 8, which is calculated by deducting the cost of using the company's assets from its profit after tax. The cost of using the company's assets is calculated by multiplying its WACC by an evaluation of its net assets.

In theory, the DCF method is the preferred business valuation method. It is based on cash flows rather than profits, or earnings. The earnings valuation approaches we have looked at are based on accounting profit, which is an extremely subjective measure. This is because the determination of profit is reliant on the many accounting conventions and standards, and the various alternative asset valuation method choices available to companies. The capital markets are not totally efficient and even if they were a stock market valuation may rarely provide a 'fair' value of a company. A company's share price is based on many factors, including the information available about the company, the reports of financial analysts, the demand for its shares, and the volume of trading.

When we looked at investment appraisal in Chapter 4 we saw that if a company invests in a project that generates a positive NPV then it will increase the wealth of the business by that amount. Elsewhere in this book we have discussed how this increase in corporate value may be reflected in shareholder value. The value of a company may be considered in terms of the total NPV of each of its investment projects. The acquisition of another business is the same as an investment in any other project. It should be appraised using DCF in the same way as any other long-term project to determine the value being added to the business.

The accuracy of any valuation method is dependent on the accuracy and reliability of the data, and who is making the valuation, and for what purpose. Although DCF may be the preferred method it is not without its difficulties, which relate mainly to:

- quantifying the synergy and economies of scale effects on estimated future cash flows
- deciding on future cash flow time horizons – five years, or multiples of five years are usually used
- deciding on an appropriate discount rate – the predator's WACC may be used, but not if the target company has significantly different risk characteristics, in which case the CAPM may be used to allow for the systematic risk of the target company.

Worked Example 16.10

Using the data from Worked Example 16.6 the directors of Predco plc may use the DCF method to compare the present value of the future cash flows of the combined entity with the present values of its future cash flows if the acquisition did not go ahead.

Using distributable earnings (profit on ordinary activities after tax) as an approximation of cash flows:

Present value of future cash flows – no acquisition

Predco plc current distributable earnings = £570,000
Discount factor = Predco plc WACC = 17%

$$\text{Present value of future expected cash flows} = \frac{£570,000}{0.17}$$

$$= £3,352,941$$

Present value of future cash flows – with acquisition

$$\text{Predco plc post-acquisition distributable earnings} = £570,000 + £540,000$$

which it is assumed will increase in subsequent years by 3% per annum.

The present values of future cash flows can then be calculated using Predco plc's WACC, adjusted for the inflation rate of 3% applied to distributable earnings.

$$\text{Cash flow from the disposal of surplus assets during 2008} = £250,000$$

The present value of the disposal proceeds can be calculated by multiplying it by the discount factor for 2008 (year 1) using Predco plc's WACC rate of 17%, which is 0.855.

Present value of post-acquisition cash flows

$$= \frac{£1,110,000 \times 1.03}{(0.17 - 0.03)} + (£250,000 \times 0.855)$$

$$= \frac{£1,143,300}{0.14} + £213,750$$

$$= £8,166,428 + £213,750$$

$$= £8,380,178$$

The difference between the present values of the future cash flows assuming acquisition and no acquisition are:

$$£8,380,178$$

$$\text{less } £3,352,941$$

Maximum price that should be paid by Predco plc for Flatco plc = **£5,027,237**

Free cash flow model

Free cash flow is a widely used financial term that is used with many different meanings. In Chapter 1 we explored the differences between profit and cash flow. Operating profit differs from operating cash flow because:

- depreciation reduces profit but does not represent outflows of cash
- working capital is required because revenues (or sales or income), and expenses (or costs or expenditure) are not necessarily accounted for when cash transfers occur, and stocks are not always used as soon as they are purchased,

and at the net profit level there are further differences between profit and cash flow. This is because income statement revenues and expenses do not include all the events that impact on the financial position of the company, for example, investments in assets, interest, taxation, dividends, and the issue of new shares and loans.

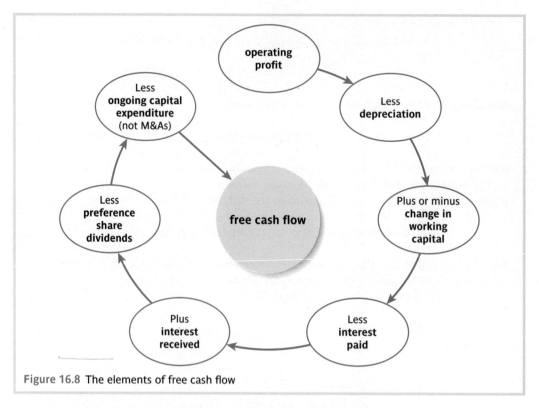

Figure 16.8 The elements of free cash flow

Here we will use a standard definition of free cash flow that is very similar to the cash flow example we saw in Fig. 1.11 in Chapter 1. This is illustrated in Fig. 16.8.

The present value of a company's free cash flows, calculated as shown in Fig. 16.8, may be used to provide a business valuation using an appropriate cost of capital, similar to the calculations we saw in Worked Example 16.10.

In practice, an actual valuation of a company may be determined using shareholder value analysis (SVA) developed by Alfred Rappaport (Rappaport A (1986) *Creating Shareholder Value: The New Standard for Business Performance*, London: Free Press). SVA is an extension of the use of free cash flows, and assumes that the value of a company may be determined from the NPV of its future free cash flows using an appropriate cost of capital. The SVA calculation usually involves the use of detailed estimates of a company's free cash flows for a planning period of say 5 or 10 years and a 'terminal' value. The terminal value may be taken as the value of the company's net assets at the end of the planning period. Instead of using a terminal value, the company's free cash flow for each year after the planning period may be estimated in detail. Alternatively, the terminal value may be based on the fifth or tenth year's free cash flow, and calculated using a similar formula to the Gordon growth model. The terminal value equals:

$$\frac{C_t \times (1 + G)}{(d - G)}$$

where

C_t is the free cash flow for the last year in the planning period (for example Year 10)

d is the discount rate

G is the long-term sustainable growth rate after the last year in the planning period.

SVA may be used for company valuation, but it may also be used to calculate additional value created from alternative strategies. Used in this way, which is very similar to the use of EVA (see Chapter 8), there is no need to determine a terminal value.

The use of SVA for the valuation of a business is illustrated in Worked Example 16.11.

Worked Example 16.11

Jalfreda plc has forecast its free cash flows for Years 1 to 10 as follows:

Year	1	2	3	4	5	6	7	8	9	10
£m	−1.0	−1.2	−1.1	0.5	0.7	0.9	2.5	4.7	6.8	7.2

Jalfreda has estimated its long-term sustainable growth rate after year 10 at 4% per annum. Its cost of capital is 12%, which may be used as a discount rate.

The terminal value based on Jalfreda's year 10 cash flow may be calculated as follows:

$$\frac{\text{free cash flow for year 10} \times (1 + \text{the long-term growth rate})}{\text{discount rate} - \text{long-term growth rate}}$$

$$= \frac{£7.2m \times (1 + 4\%)}{12\% - 4\%}$$

$$= \frac{£7.2m \times 1.04}{0.08}$$

$$= £93.6m$$

The present values of Jalfreda plc's free cash flows, including the Year 10 terminal value of £93.6m, can be calculated as follows:

Year	Free cash flows £m	Discount factor at 12%	Present value of free cash flows £m
1	−1.0	0.893	−0.893
2	−1.2	0.797	−0.956
3	−1.1	0.712	−0.783
4	0.5	0.636	0.318
5	0.7	0.567	0.397
6	0.9	0.507	0.456
7	2.5	0.452	1.130
8	4.7	0.404	1.899
9	6.8	0.361	2.455
10	100.8 (7.2 + 93.6)	0.322	32.458
Total present value			**£36.481m**

(Note: discount factors have been calculated to three decimal places instead of using the tables in Appendix 1.)

The total present value of Jalfreda plc's free cash flows is £36,481,000, which may be used as the basis for a valuation of the company.

Other reasons for share valuation

We have seen how a takeover bid price offered may be an estimated 'fair value' in excess of the current stock market share price valuation. Similarly, a proposed merger of companies may require an assessment of the share value of each company. The share prices of publicly quoted companies (plcs) may be quoted on a stock exchange or the Alternative Investment Market (AIM), in which case a stock market valuation of such companies is readily available.

However, both quoted and unquoted companies may need to be valued for a number of other reasons in addition to takeover and merger valuations:

- shares may need to be used to supply collateral, or security, for loans
- a private limited (Ltd) company may want to 'go public', that is floated on a stock exchange or the AIM, and therefore need to fix a share issue price for the initial public offering (IPO)
- since there is not a ready market for shares in a limited (Ltd) company, its shares may need to be valued to be sold
- individual holdings of shares may need to be valued for inheritance tax or capital gains tax purposes
- a subsidiary within a group of companies may need to be valued if it is to be sold off.

Some further share valuation models

One or other of the business valuation methods we have considered above may be used for reasons other than takeovers and mergers, as appropriate. There are also some further valuation methods, three of which are illustrated in Fig. 16.9.

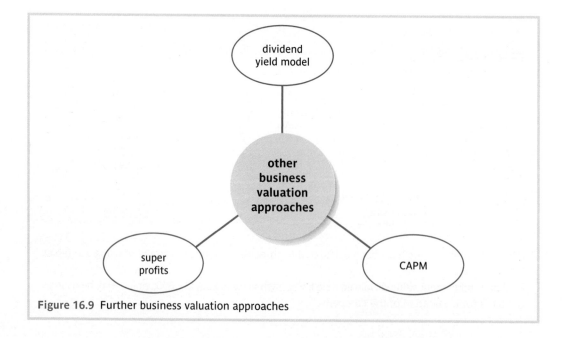

Figure 16.9 Further business valuation approaches

Dividend yield model

The dividend yield model is suitable for the valuation of small shareholdings in unquoted companies. It is based on the principle that small shareholders are mainly interested in dividends, rather than capital gains from the increase in value of their shares. The market valuation of a company's shares may be represented as:

$$\text{market value} = \frac{\text{dividend per share}}{\text{expected dividend yield \%}}$$

assuming a constant level of future dividends.

The multiplication of this value by the number of ordinary shares in issue gives a market valuation of the company.

Alternatively, the Gordon dividend growth model, discussed earlier, may be used if future dividend growth may be predicted. If a dividend method is used for shareholders who wish to sell their shares, the valuation offer price compensates them for the increases in future dividends they would be giving up.

Capital Asset Pricing Model (CAPM)

The CAPM (see Chapter 5) may be used to value shares for a stock market listing by establishing a required equity yield. The market valuation of a company's shares may be determined by dividing its cost of equity into its dividend (which may be adjusted for any expected future dividend growth).

$$\text{cost of equity} = \text{risk-free rate of return} + [\beta \times (\text{market rate} - \text{risk-free rate of return})]$$

or

$$K_e = R_f + \beta \times (R_m - R_f)$$

If we assume a current dividend of v and a future dividend growth rate of G% per annum then using the Gordon dividend growth model:

$$\text{market valuation} = \frac{v \times (1 + G\%)}{(K_e - G\%)}$$

Worked Example 16.12

Using the data from Worked Example 16.6 the directors of Predco plc may use the CAPM to value Flatco plc. The risk-free rate of return R_f is 1% per annum and the market rate of return R_m is 2.5% per annum. Flatco plc's beta factor $\beta = 1.13$.

Using $\qquad K_e = R_f + \beta \times (R_m - R_f)$

Flatco plc cost of equity $= 1\% + 1.13 \times (2.5\% - 1\%)$

$$= \underline{2.695\%}$$

▶

> Flatco plc market value $= \dfrac{\text{current 2007 dividend}}{\text{cost of equity}}$ (assuming no dividend growth)
>
> $\qquad = \dfrac{£70,000}{0.02695}$
>
> $\qquad = \underline{\textbf{£2,597,403}}$
>
> It should be noted that this valuation is higher than Flatco plc's book value of its net assets valuation of £1,486,000 at 31 December 2007, but lower than the valuation based on its share price 31 December 2007 of £2.75 × 1,200,000 = £3,300,000.

Super profits model

A rather out-of-fashion method, the super profits method applies a 'fair return' to the net tangible assets. But what is a fair return?

This model then compares the 'fair return' with expected profits. Any excess of fair return over expected profits, the super profits, is used to calculate goodwill. Goodwill is therefore taken to be a fixed number of years of super profits. The market value is then calculated by adding goodwill to the company's tangible assets valuation.

This method is now rarely used and has a number of disadvantages:

- difficulty and subjectivity of establishing a 'fair return'
- profit numbers are subjective and therefore not ideal
- the number of years of super profits used is arbitrary.

Progress check 16.4

Outline in general why there may be so many different methods used to provide a valuation of a business.

Worked Example 16.13 compares the market share price at 1 April 2006 of a major UK plc, Marks & Spencer, and compares this with a number of the alternative valuations, which we have discussed above.

Worked Example 16.13

The financial statements of Marks & Spencer plc for the years to 1 April 2006 and 2005 are shown in Figs 16.10 and 16.11.

Marks & Spencer plc valuations as at 1 April 2006
Market capitalisation

1 April 2006 £9.36bn = 1,682m shares × 556.50p, or **£5.57 per share**
1 April 2005 £5.72bn = 1,658m shares × 344.75p, or **£3.45 per share**

Marks & Spencer plc
Consolidated balance sheet

	Notes	2006 £m	2005 £m
ASSETS			
Non-current assets			
Intangible assets	13	163.5	165.4
Property, plant and equipment	14	3,575.8	3,586.2
Investment property	15	38.5	38.6
Investments in joint venture	16	9.0	8.7
Other financial assets	17	3.3	0.3
Trade and other receivables	18	242.8	211.2
Deferred income tax assets	25	35.5	24.6
		4,068.4	4,035.0
Current assets			
Inventories		374.3	338.9
Other financial assets	17	48.8	67.0
Trade and other receivables	18	210.5	213.8
Derivative financial instruments	22	76.4	–
Cash and cash equivalents	19	362.6	212.6
Assets of discontinued operation	7C	69.5	–
		1,142.1	832.3
Total assets		5,210.5	4,867.3
LIABILITIES			
Current liabilities			
Trade and other payables	20	867.8	717.9
Derivative financial instruments	22	8.0	–
Borrowings	21	1,052.8	478.8
Current tax liabilities		58.7	15.5
Provisions	24	9.2	25.2
Liabilities of discontinued operation	7C	20.5	–
		2,017.0	1,237.4
Non-current liabilities			
Borrowings	21	1,133.8	1,948.5
Retirement benefit obligations	11	794.9	676.0
Other non-current liabilities	20	74.8	71.8
Derivative financial instruments	22	9.5	–
Provisions	24	19.1	19.7
Deferred income tax liabilities	25	6.1	4.7
		2,038.2	2,720.7
Total liabilities		4,055.2	3,958.1
Net assets		1,155.3	909.2
EQUITY			
Called up share capital – equity	26,27	420.6	414.5
Called up share capital – non-equity	27	–	65.7
Share premium account	27	162.3	106.6
Capital redemption reserve	27	2,113.8	2,102.8
Hedging reserve	27	(8.0)	–
Other reserves	27	(6,542.2)	(6,542.2)
Retained earnings	27	5,008.8	4,761.8
Total equity		1,155.3	909.2

Figure 16.10 Marks & Spencer plc consolidated balance sheet as at 1 April 2006

Marks & Spencer plc
Consolidated income statement

	Notes	52 weeks ended 1 April 2006 £m	52 weeks ended 2 April 2005 £m
Revenue	2	**7,797.7**	7,490.5
Operating profit			
Before exceptional operating charges		**850.1**	648.7
Exceptional operating charges		**–**	(50.6)
	2,3	**850.1**	598.1
Interest payable and similar charges	5	**(134.9)**	(120.9)
Interest receivable	5	**30.5**	27.9
Profit on ordinary activities before taxation		**745.7**	505.1
Analysed between:			
Before exceptional operating charges and property disposals		**751.4**	556.1
Loss on property disposals	3	**(5.7)**	(0.4)
Exceptional operating charges	3	**–**	(50.6)
Income tax expense	6	**(225.1)**	(150.1)
Profit on ordinary activities after taxation		**520.6**	355.0
Profit from discontinued operations	7A	**2.5**	231.2
Profit for the year attributable to shareholders		**523.1**	586.2
Earnings per share	8A	**31.4p**	29.1p
Diluted earnings per share	8B	**31.1p**	28.9p
Earnings per share from continuing operations	8A	**31.3p**	17.6p
Diluted earnings per share from continuing operations	8B	**31.0p**	17.4p
Non-GAAP measure:			
Adjusted profit before tax (£m)	1	**751.4**	556.1
Adjusted earnings per share	8A	**31.4p**	19.2p
Adjusted diluted earnings per share	8B	**31.1p**	19.0p
Share price		**556.5p**	344.75p
Number of ordinary shares in issue		**1,682m**	1,658m

Figure 16.11 Marks & Spencer plc consolidated income statement for the year to 1 April 2006

Book value of net assets

	£m
Total net assets (£5,210.5m – £2,017.0m)	3,193.5
Less Intangibles	163.5
	3,030.0
Less long-term debt	1,133.8
	1,896.2

At 1 April 2006 Marks & Spencer had 1,682m shares in issue, therefore the value per share would be

£1,896.2m/1,682m = **£1.12 per share** (compared with the actual share price of £5.57)

Capitalised earnings valuation

Capitalised earnings value = annual maintainable expected earnings/required earnings yield

Required earnings yield = eps/market share price

At 1 April 2006 eps = 31.4p per share, and the quoted share price was 556.5p per share. Therefore the required earnings yield would be:

$$(31.4p \times 100)/556.5p = 5.64\%$$

Profits on ordinary activities after tax can be used as an approximation of the annual maintainable expected earnings, therefore the capitalised earnings valuation would be:

$$£520.6m/0.0564 = £9.23bn$$

£9,230m/1,682m = **£5.48 per share** (compared with the actual share price of £5.57)

Dividend growth model valuation

Growth may be estimated using past dividends (the total of interim and final dividend) obtained from prior years' reports and accounts:

2002	9.5p
2003	10.5p
2004	11.5p
2005	12.1p
2006	14.0p

The annual growth rate G may be calculated over the four years as follows:

$$(1 + G)^4 = 14.0p/9.5p$$
$$(1 - G) = {}^4\sqrt{14.0p/9.5p}$$
$$1 - G = 1.10$$
$$G = 0.10 \text{ or } 10\%$$

Using G – 10%, the market price of the shares 1 April 2006 mv = 556.5p, and the current dividend v = 14p, we can estimate the required shareholders' return K_e, as follows:

$$\text{market valuation mv} = \frac{v \times (1 + G)}{(K_e - G)}$$

$$K_e = \frac{v \times (1 + G)}{mv} + G$$

$$K_e = \frac{14p \times 1.10}{556.5p} + 0.10$$

estimated shareholder return K_e = 0.135 or 13.5%

Share valuation without growth using the dividend valuation model

14p/12.8% = **£1.09 per share** (compared with the actual share price of £5.57)

Share valuation with growth using the Gordon growth model

$$\frac{14p \times 1.10}{12.8\% - 10\%} = £5.50 \text{ per share} \text{ (compared with the actual share price of £5.57)}$$

Summary of key points

■ Mergers, or amalgamations, are now quite rare and what occurs more commonly are acquisitions, or takeovers.

■ In mergers and acquisitions (M&As) the combined expected present values of future cash flows of the combined companies should be more than the sum of the expected present values of future cash flows of the two separate companies.

■ M&As may occur as a result of horizontal integration, vertical integration, complementary resources, conglomerate takeover, and from the exploitation of market imperfections that have resulted in the market undervaluation of companies.

■ There are a number of 'good' and 'bad' reasons used to justify M&As.

■ The financial motives for M&As include taxation benefits, gains from target company undervaluation, and enhancement of eps.

■ Managerial motives for M&As result from managers' desire to enhance their own position with regard to emoluments, power, and security.

■ There are a large number of methods that may be used to value an M&A target company based broadly on the valuation of its shares, assets, future earnings or cash flows, and P/E ratios.

■ Businesses may need to be valued for a number of reasons other than M&As, for example for security for loans, or if a company wishes to be floated on a stock exchange.

🔑 Glossary of key terms

acquisition See takeover.

amalgamation See merger.

merger (or amalgamation) A merger (or amalgamation) is a business combination that results in the creation of a new reporting entity formed from the combining parties, in which the shareholders of the combining entities come together in a combination for the mutual sharing of the risks and benefits of the combined entity, and in which no party to the combination in substance obtains control over any other, or is otherwise seen to be dominant, whether by virtue of the proportion of its shareholders' rights in the combined entity, the influence of its directors, or otherwise (FRS6). A demerger takes place when the merger process is reversed, and separate entities emerge from the merged body.

takeover (or acquisition) A takeover (or acquisition) is the acquisition by a company of a controlling interest in the voting share capital of another company, usually achieved by the purchase of a majority of the voting shares.

Questions

Q16.1 Outline the ways in which a merger differs from a takeover.

Q16.2 How and why do mergers and acquisitions take place?

Q16.3 Explain the fundamental principles underlying M&As.

Q16.4 In what ways may market imperfections be exploited by takeover activity?

Q16.5 Outline the business and financial reasons for company mergers.

Q16.6 Describe six justifications for M&As.

Q16.7 Differentiate between the financial motives and managerial motives for M&As, and illustrate both with some examples.

Q16.8 Which Acts of Parliament and financial institutions monitor and control merger and acquisition activities in the UK?

Q16.9 Consider why a growth in eps may not necessarily be reflected in a growth in share price, and support this with examples.

Q16.10 Describe the motivation for takeovers and analyse why target companies often employ defence strategies in response to a hostile takeover.

Q16.11 Outline the reasons why shareholders may require valuations of their businesses.

Q16.12 Critically compare the use of net asset valuations and earnings valuations of companies.

Discussion points

D16.1 Discuss the likely winners and losers following the possible acquisition of Marks & Spencer plc by someone like Philip Green.

D16.2 Discuss the possible benefits to the economy of any country resulting from a high level of M&A activity.

D16.3 Discuss the possible behaviour of share prices during a merger, the impact of a merger announcement on the share prices of the two companies involved, and how this may be measured.

Exercises

Solutions are provided in Appendix 2 to all exercise numbers highlighted in colour.

Level I

E16.1 *Time allowed – 15 minutes*

A large group called Pitch plc has shown interest in acquiring the shares of Perfecto plc, a smaller company in the same industry. Perfecto plc is quoted on the AIM and its balance sheet as at 30 September 2007 is shown below:

Perfecto plc
Balance sheet as at 30 September 2007

	2007 £000
Non-current assets	
Intangible	203
Tangible	902
	1,105
Current assets	
Stocks	161
Debtors	284
Prepayments	295
Cash	157
	897
Current liabilities (less than one year)	
Creditors	187
Corporation tax	70
Dividends	20
Accruals	100
	377
Net current assets	520
Total assets less current liabilities	1,625
less	
Non-current liabilities (over one year)	
Creditors	77
Loan	85
Provisions	103
	265
Net assets	1,360
Capital and reserves	
Capital (600,000 £1 ordinary shares)	600
Share premium account	105
Profit and loss account	655
	1,360

The profits on ordinary activities after tax for the past five years have been:

	£000
2007	150
2006	140
2005	160
2004	150
2003	130

Perfecto plc has paid dividends of £40,000 for each of the past five years. The company has forecast that its dividends will increase by 4% over subsequent years.

Perfecto plc's share price at 30 September 2007 was £1.84, and its P/E ratio 7.36 times.

The directors of Perfecto had the tangible assets of the company valued at £1.8m at 30 September 2007 (not reflected in the balance sheet at that date).

Pitch plc's profit after tax for 2007 was £800,000, and its WACC 6%. Its P/E ratio at 30 September 2007 was 9 times. An investigation into the proposed takeover has determined incremental net cash flows, over and above that expected from the separate companies, may be achieved by the group following its acquisition of Perfecto plc, as follows:

	£000
2008	130
2009	130
2010	150
2011	100
2012	130

You are required to provide a valuation of Perfecto plc using the book value of its net assets.

E16.2 *Time allowed – 15 minutes*
Using the data from E16.1 provide a valuation of Perfecto plc using the replacement cost of its net assets.

E16.3 *Time allowed – 15 minutes*
Using the data from E16.1 provide a capitalised earnings valuation of Perfecto plc.

E16.4 *Time allowed – 15 minutes*
Using the data from E16.1 provide a P/E ratio valuation of Perfecto plc.

Level II

E16.5 *Time allowed – 15 minutes*
Using the data from E16.1 provide a DCF valuation of Perfecto plc.

E16.6 *Time allowed – 15 minutes*
Using the data from E16.1 provide a CAPM valuation of Perfecto plc.
   You may assume that Perfecto plc has a β factor of 1.2, and the risk-free rate of return is 1% per annum and the market rate of return is 6.5% per annum.

E16.7 *Time allowed – 15 minutes*
Horse plc is considering the acquisition of Cart plc. Horse plc has a current market value of £100,000,000. Cart plc has a current market value of £50,000,000. If the acquisition occurs expected economies of scale will result in savings of £2,500,000 per annum for the foreseeable future. The required rate of return on both companies and the proposed combination is 10%. The transaction costs will amount to £2,000,000.

Calculate:

(i) The present value of the gain from the merger.
(ii) The value that would be created for Horse plc's shareholders if a cash offer of £70,000,000 is accepted by Cart plc's shareholders.

E16.8 *Time allowed – 30 minutes*
The Burns Group plc is investigating the viability of acquiring Allen Ltd, which is currently earning profits after tax of around £1,000,000 per annum. Burns Ltd's financial advisers consider that Allen's post-tax profits may be increased to £1,200,000 per annum following the acquisition. Each company in the Burns group has a target of earning a post-tax return on capital employed of 8%.

▶

▶ Required:

(i) Calculate a valuation of Allen Ltd based on the accounting rate of return.
(ii) Indicate how the Burns Group may negotiate an acceptable takeover price.
(iii) What are the advantages to Burns of using an ARR valuation?

E16.9 *Time allowed – 30 minutes*

Morecambe plc is considering taking over Wise Ltd, which has net tangible assets of £850,000 and current earnings of £110,000 per annum. Morecambe's directors believe that 9% per annum is a fair return in their industry.

Required:

(i) Calculate a valuation of Wise Ltd based on the super-profits method and assuming goodwill is equal to four years super-profits.
(ii) What are the disadvantages to Morecambe plc's use of this method of valuation?

E16.10 *Time allowed – 30 minutes*

Porgy plc is a large electronics company. The company is currently undertaking a large expansion programme, and is considering the acquisition of Bess plc, a smaller retail company. Porgy plc currently has a stock market value of £90,000,000 while Bess plc has a stock market value of £40,000,000. The management of Porgy plc expects the acquisition of Bess plc to generate significant economies of scale and cost savings. They expect the market value of the combined company to be £158,000,000.

To secure the required share capital in Bess plc, the management of Porgy plc have decided to pay a premium of £20,000,000. Additional transaction costs are expected to be £5,000,000. The required rate of return on both companies and the proposed combination is 10%. Porgy plc has 45,000,000 shares in issue and Bess plc has 20,000,000.

Required:

(i) Calculate the present value that would be created by the acquisition.
(You can assume the management of both Porgy plc and Bess plc are shareholder wealth maximisers, and that the initial savings will continue in perpetuity).
(ii) If Porgy plc decides to purchase the shares of Bess plc with a cash offer, calculate the price Porgy plc would offer for each of Bess plc's shares.
(iii) If shares are offered in such a way that Bess plc's shareholders would possess 1/3 of the merged company, what value would be created for Porgy plc's shareholders?
(iv) If a cash offer of £60,000,000 was accepted by ALL Bess plc's shareholders what value would be created for Porgy plc's shareholders?
(v) Explain the reasons which the management of Bess plc may suggest as to why the offer made by Porgy plc should be rejected.
(vi) Outline the tactics the managers of Bess plc could employ to effectively contest the bid.

E16.11 *Time allowed – 45 minutes*

Black Ltd is a profitable company and the owners are also the directors. The directors have decided to sell their business, and have identified organisations interested in its purchase: White plc; Scarlet plc; Brown plc. Black Ltd's latest balance sheet and additional financial information are shown below:

Black Ltd financial position at the most recent balance sheet date

	£	£
Non-current assets		
Land and buildings	800,000	
Plant and equipment	450,000	
Motor vehicles	55,000	
		1,305,000
Current assets		
Stocks	250,000	
Debtors	125,000	
Cash	8,000	
Prepayment	2,000	
		385,000
Total assets		1,690,000
Current liabilities		
Creditors	180,000	
Taxation	50,000	
		230,000
		1,460,000
Non-current liabilities		
Secured loan		400,000
Net assets		1,060,000
Capital and reserves		
300,000 ordinary shares @ £1		300,000
Reserves		760,000
		1,060,000

Black Ltd's profit after tax and interest but before dividends over the previous five years has been:

	£
Year 1	90,000
Year 2	80,000
Year 3	105,000
Year 4	90,000
Year 5	100,000

Black Ltd's annual divided has been £45,000 for the past six years.

The company's five-year plan forecasts an after-tax profit of £100,000 for the next 12 months, with an increase of 4% per annum over each of the next four years.

As part of their preparations to sell the company, the directors of Black Ltd have had the non-current assets revalued by an independent expert, which is not reflected in the most recent balance sheet:

	£
Land and buildings	1,075,000
Plant and equipment	480,000
Motor vehicles	45,000

The average dividend yield and P/E ratio of three public companies in the same industry as Black Ltd over the past three years have been:

▶

▶

	White plc		Scarlet plc		Brown plc	
	Div Yield %	P/E	Div Yield %	P/E	Div Yield %	P/E
Most recent year	12.0	8.5	11.0	9.0	13.0	10.0
Previous year	12.0	8.0	10.6	8.5	12.6	9.5
Three years ago	12.0	8.5	9.3	8.0	12.4	9.0
Average	12.0	8.33	10.3	8.5	12.7	9.5

Large companies in the industry apply an after-tax cost of capital of about 18% to acquisition proposals when the investment is not backed by tangible assets, as opposed to a rate of only 14% on the net tangible assets.

The following is an estimate of the net cash flows which would accrue to a purchasing company, allowing for taxation and the capital expenditure required after the acquisition to achieve the company's target five-year profit plan:

	£
Year 1	120,000
Year 2	120,000
Year 3	140,000
Year 4	70,000
Year 5	120,000

Required:

The directors of Black Ltd have asked you for your assessment of the ordinary share price a potential purchaser may be willing to pay.

Using the above information prepare six alternative valuations which a prospective purchaser may consider.

E16.12 *Time allowed – 45 minutes*

Explain why companies may consider making mergers and acquisitions, and critically examine some of the 'good' reasons and the 'bad' reasons for these strategies.

E16.13 *Time allowed – 45 minutes*

Critically comment on six ways in which a company may justify the acquisition of another company.

Financial strategies in M&As

Chapter contents

LEARNING OBJECTIVES

Completion of this chapter will enable you to:

☑ Describe how cash, equity shares, and debt may be used to finance mergers and acquisitions (M&As).

☑ Recognise the differences between the use of debt and the use of equity in the financing of M&As.

☑ Explain the financial strategies relating to M&As and the ways in which suitable target companies may be identified.

☑ Outline the range of takeover defences that may be made by a company to avoid being taken over before a formal takeover bid has been made.

☑ Consider the range of takeover defences that may be made by a company to repel a takeover once a formal takeover bid has been made.

☑ Explain the impact of M&As on shareholders, directors, managers, employees, and financial institutions.

Introduction

This chapter looks at the ways in which M&As may be financed, involving the use of cash, debt, or equity in one way or another. We will consider the advantages and disadvantages of each method of financing and particularly the differences between the use of debt or equity.

Suitable target companies must be identified for acquisition or merger and appropriate financial strategies developed to derive the optimum benefits from such activity. The benefits from the synergies expected to result from M&As then need to be evaluated, before deals are completed.

There is a wide range of defences that may be used by companies to avoid being merged or taken over. Some of these defences may be used before a formal offer has been made, and, if these are unsuccessful, some other defences may be employed after a formal bid has been received.

This chapter closes by considering the impact of M&As on the major stakeholders in both target companies and acquiring companies. These include shareholders, directors, managers, employees, and financial institutions.

Financing acquisitions

Because of the sheer size of most mergers and acquisitions, the financing implications are extremely significant. The choice of the most appropriate financing method for M&As is therefore a very important decision for a board of directors.

The main methods used to finance M&As are shown in Fig. 17.1. We will discuss each of these methods, which includes a vendor placing, in the sections that follow. We will also discuss what is termed a mixed bid, and consider the use of debt compared with equity in the financing of M&As.

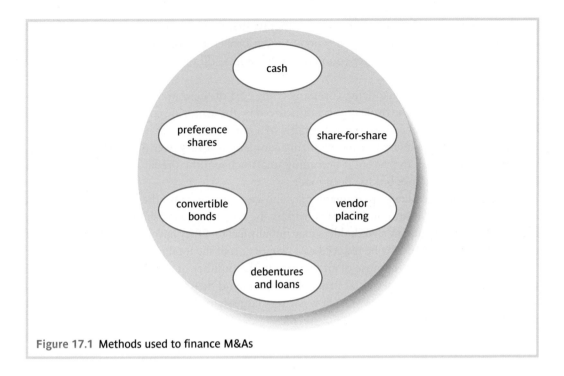

Figure 17.1 Methods used to finance M&As

Cash

The purchase of a target company's shares for cash is attractive to its shareholders because the value is certain. There is an advantage to the target company in that no share selling costs will be incurred. However, there is also a disadvantage in that there may be a capital gains tax liability for the shareholders of the target company. An advantage to the takeover bidding company is that the offer for the target company makes it clear that the number of shares will not be changed which would lead to dilution of earnings per share (eps).

The cash to fund a takeover may be provided from:

- cash provided internally from a company's retained earnings
- external use of mezzanine finance – debt, which has the risk and return characteristics somewhere between equity and debt
- external leverage, from high amounts of debt finance.

However, if a company making a takeover bid does not have sufficient cash to pay for the shares in the target company, it will be at a disadvantage if it has to borrow to fund the takeover.

A cash purchase of a business is classed as a takeover and so the rules of merger accounting may not be applied. Merger accounting is explained in more detail in the later section on vendor placings.

Share-for-share

A bidding company, or predator company, may offer a deal whereby the target company's shareholders receive a fixed number of shares in the predator company in exchange for the shares they hold in their own company.

The advantages to the target company are that its shareholders still retain an equity interest in the new combined business, and they do not incur brokerage costs or capital gains tax liabilities on their shares. So, the target company shareholders still remain part owners of the new business.

A disadvantage to the acquiring company is the cost of the share-for-share method compared with a cash offer. The brokerage costs incurred by the acquiring company are usually very high and may be a significant factor in appraisal of a potential takeover.

The value of shares offered by the acquiring company will vary over time so the offer needs to be generous enough to prevent it becoming unattractive if the predator's share price drops any time after the takeover bid has been made.

At a later date the takeover company may subsequently increase the number of shares in issue, resulting in a dilution of the shares held by the target company shareholders. Therefore, although the target company shareholders may initially feel that they have a reasonable number of shares, this may subsequently be reduced as a proportion of the total number of issued shares.

A decrease in gearing, because of an increase in the number of ordinary shares, may move the predator from its optimal capital structure in theory and therefore increase its cost of capital.

The AOL acquisition of Time Warner was a very large share-for-share deal, which is outlined in Worked Example 17.1.

Worked Example 17.1

The largest ever acquisition up to that time took place in the year 2000. It was AOL's takeover of Time Warner. The US$163bn deal announced on 10 January 2000 involved the issue of shares in a combined new entity, which would be valued at around US$350bn. For every share held in their respective companies, each AOL shareholder would receive 1 new share and each Time Warner shareholder would receive 1.5 new shares. The AOL shareholders would have 55% of the new entity and the Time Warner shareholders would end up with 45%.

We will consider the implications of this share-for-share deal for the shareholders of each company.

The announcement of the deal immediately pushed up the share prices of both companies. However, AOL was an Internet, new economy, dot.com business and very much larger than Time Warner, which was a traditional media group valued at around US$80bn. Before the announcement of the acquisition, Time Warner's share price and P/E ratio were relatively low, reflecting its position as a traditional media company. AOL's share price and P/E ratio were relatively high, reflecting the dot.com boom, which perhaps valued AOL higher than its real worth. It is likely that the high premium being paid to the Time Warner shareholders (1.5 shares for each share held, compared with 1 share to AOL shareholders) reflected this apparent over-valuation.

On 12 January 2000, the value of the takeover dropped as AOL's share price fell 8% after analysts downgraded its future performance prospects; Time Warner's share price fell by 5.5%. By 15 January, the value of the acquisition had fallen to US$145bn. Some analysts warned that the value of the deal may fall to as low as US$128bn; they felt that the acquisition was less than a perfect match, which may hamper AOL's growth, and was more to do with 'huge corporate egos, bloated investment banking fees and awesome executive bonuses' (see *Daily Telegraph* various media and business sections articles, 11 to 15 January 2000).

Vendor placing

A vendor placing is a variation on a cash offer, which allows the acquiring company to apply **merger accounting** rules rather than **takeover accounting** rules to the post-merger company. A cash offer is classified as a takeover and the accounting rules relating to mergers cannot be applied.

UK takeover, or acquisition, accounting rules require the following:

- a restatement of net assets to fair value at the acquisition date
- profits of the target company to be included from the acquisition date
- the difference between the purchase price paid for the target company and its net assets fair value to be accounted for as goodwill.

UK merger accounting rules require the following:

- no restatement of net assets to fair value
- profits of the target company to be included for the whole of the accounting period
- the difference between the purchase price paid for the target company and its net assets fair value to be added to or deducted from reserves.

Merger accounting is allowed if the two groups of shareholders continue their shareholdings as before the companies combine, but on a combined basis. The companies combine on an equal footing.

A vendor placing involves the acquiring company offering shares to the target company with the option to continue their shareholding, and at the same time arranging for the new shares to be placed with institutional investors and for cash to be paid to the target company's shareholders. The institutional investors, for example insurance companies and pension funds, are approached by the company's sponsor (a merchant bank or stockbroker), before the issue takes place and offer the shares at a fixed price. The company's sponsor underwrites the issue and therefore takes up any unplaced shares. Other potential investors (both institutional and the general public) cannot buy shares that have been placed until after the listing and official dealing takes place. Compared with other share issue methods, placings have lower costs, but because companies use them because they want to issue their shares to institutions the spread of shareholding is relatively narrow (see the section about new issues in Chapter 7).

Another variation on the cash offer is a vendor rights issue. A vendor rights issue is the same as a vendor placing, but instead the shares are offered to the acquiring company's shareholders.

Debentures and loans

A debenture, which is a type of bond, is a written acknowledgement of a debt that includes the terms regarding payment of interest and the principal. A debenture is normally secured on a specific asset, or the assets in general, of a company.

The use of securities other than the shares of the acquiring company as a means of paying the target company is now rare in the UK. It is not entirely clear why this should be so, but in the UK the use of debentures, preference shares, and loans in M&As fell from around 25% in the 1970s, to 15% in the 1980s, to 1% in the 1990s.

Debt is largely unacceptable to target company shareholders, who have previously shown their preference for higher risks and returns associated with their being equity shareholders.

However, the issue of debt by an acquiring company as a means of payment for a target company does not lead to dilution of eps. In addition, the interest payments on debt are tax efficient. These are potentially very big plusses for a predator company.

Bonds

A bond is a debt that offers a fixed rate of interest over a fixed period of time, and has a fixed redemption value.

The use of bonds leads to an increase in the predator company's gearing. A big disadvantage of bonds is that they require the build up of cash reserves by the company with which to pay off the loans on maturity.

Convertible bonds

To overcome some of the problems of using straight bonds, a company may issue convertible bonds. Convertible bonds, which are an example of hybrid securities, offer bond-holders a means of benefiting from future corporate growth.

Convertible bonds are 'two stage' financial instruments, which:

- start their life as a convertible debenture or a convertible preference share
- include an option to convert them into an ordinary share at a later date.

The predator company receives a number of advantages from the use of convertible bonds:

- dilution of eps will not occur until much later when the bonds are converted into ordinary shares – therefore, earnings increase without increasing the number of shares until a much later date
- convertibles tend to pay a lower coupon rate (or interest rate), which greatly benefits the cash flow of the company
- convertibles reduce the short-term carrying cost of company financing, that is interest rather than dividends.

There are a number of commonly used terms associated with convertibles, or convertible bonds, which are listed below:

- **coupon yield** is the interest paid on the nominal value of a bond (or a loan, or debenture)
- **straight bond value** is the market value dependent on the coupon rate relative to market interest rates
- convertible bonds issued at par (the nominal price of the bond used for setting the interest rate) normally have a lower coupon rate than straight bonds because the investor has to pay for the conversion rights – the bonds will become ordinary shares at a later date
- **conversion ratio** is the number of ordinary shares that will be obtained from the conversion of one unit of the convertible bond
- **conversion value** is the market value of the ordinary shares into which a unit of the convertible bond may be converted
- convertible bond value is the market value dependent on the straight bond value, current conversion value, time up to conversion, and the ordinary shares risk and return expectation.

Preference shares

Preference shares are shares rather than loans but do not constitute part of the ownership of the company. Preference shares carry a fixed rate of dividend, which is a prior claim on profits, and they may have a prior claim on capital. The use of preference shares as a means of payment in a takeover is even more rare than the use of debt.

In a takeover, preference shares are less attractive to the predator company than ordinary shares because they lack flexibility, and also because their dividends are distributed from post-tax profit and so are not allowable for tax.

In a takeover, preference shares do not offer ownership to the target company's shareholders, and neither do they provide the security of a cash offer.

Mixed bids

Mixed bids of share-for-share offers supported by a cash alternative have become increasingly popular in UK. There are two main reasons for this:

- mixed bids are acceptable to target company shareholders because they can choose the method that best suits their individual liquidity preferences and tax positions
- rule 9 of the City Code on Takeovers and Mergers 1988 (City Code) applies.

Rule 9 of the City Code requires companies, which are acquiring 30% or more of a target company's shares, to make a cash offer (or cash alternative if a share-for-share offer is being made) at the highest price paid by the predator company for the target company's shares over the previous 12 months.

The City Code is a set of rules and principles that governs the way in which takeovers and mergers of public companies are carried out in the UK. The code applies to all UK resident companies.

The City Code does not specifically concern itself with commercial aspects of a takeover or merger, or with the way a company conducts its business, but is designed to ensure the protection and equal treatment of shareholders in certain takeover and merger situations, and where there are changes in the individuals and groups that control that company.

The City Code also sets out a detailed timetable under which all such takeovers and mergers are conducted, and covers issues such as:

- the conditions of an offer
- information availability regarding target and predator company shareholders
- target company restrictions with regard to its directors
- how the approach to a target company should be made
- the announcement of the takeover bid
- obligations of the target company board of directors
- conduct of companies during the offer.

International Financial Reporting Standard IFRS 3 Business Combinations, and the Statement of Financial Accounting Standards SFAS 141 Business Combinations, published by the Financial Accounting Standards Board (FASB), provide further information on the requirements of mergers and acquisitions.

Progress check 17.1

Which method of financing an M&A may be preferred by the shareholders of a target company, and why?

Debt versus equity in financing acquisitions

The cost of debt to a company is generally lower than its cost of equity at low levels of gearing, because of the low risk and high risk respectively to investors, associated with debt and equity.

Financial leverage (gearing) is the use of debt finance to increase the return on equity by deploying borrowed funds in such a way that the return generated is greater than the cost of servicing the debt. The return must be greater than the debt interest rate.

If the return on deployed funds is less than the cost of servicing the debt, the effect of the leverage is to reduce the return on equity. That is, the return rate is less than the debt interest rate.

As we saw in Chapter 7 there are many different sources of finance available to businesses comprising various forms of debt and equity and combinations of the two. Debt and equity may be looked at in terms of their perceived risk and the return required from them. The range of types of financing and their attributes is shown in Fig. 17.2. Government debt (low risk, low return) and equity, or ordinary share capital (high risk, high return) represent the extremities of

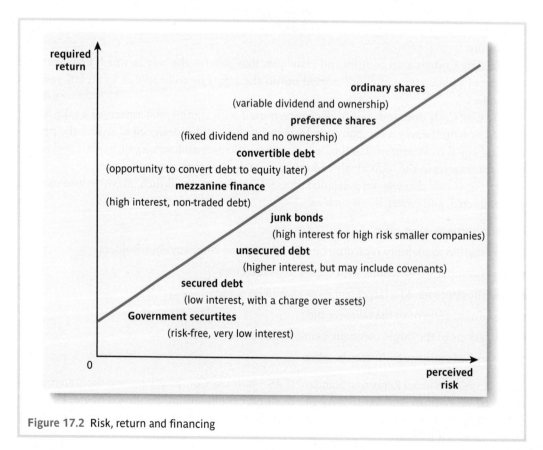

Figure 17.2 Risk, return and financing

a continuum of financial instruments, which includes secured and unsecured, long and short-term debt, and preference shares. Financial instruments are available with a range of combinations of risk and potential return. Sometimes in trying to distinguish between debt and equity the boundaries become blurred. There are literally hundreds of hybrid financial instruments on the market. They represent additional possibilities for further sophistication in company financing.

Financial strategy in acquisitions

There are a number of important strategic factors that relate to the financial aspects of acquisitions. There is a financial role in evaluating the value of potential synergies, the evaluation of $2 + 2 = 5$, rather than involvement in the achievement of the synergies themselves. Another financial role is to identify a potential target company which is not adopting an optimum financial strategy to maximise shareholders' wealth. Various alternative options may be considered from the valuation of potential target companies, in order to consider the maximum purchase prices that may be offered. It should be noted that the financial structure of the target company may also need to be changed, for example through leverage.

A financially astute takeover expert can identify companies that show signs of inappropriate financial strategies or some evidence of an agency problem. An example of a clear sign of an inappropriate financial strategy is a mature group that has very large net cash surpluses. This may indicate the group's reluctance to invest in new projects. A predator company may acquire such a group, and strip off the cash, then leverage the company, by taking on debt, on the basis of the cash generation capability of its core business.

We will consider a number of aspects related to the identification of suitable target companies for acquisition, including **greenmailing** and the **earn-out method**, which are summarised in Fig. 17.3.

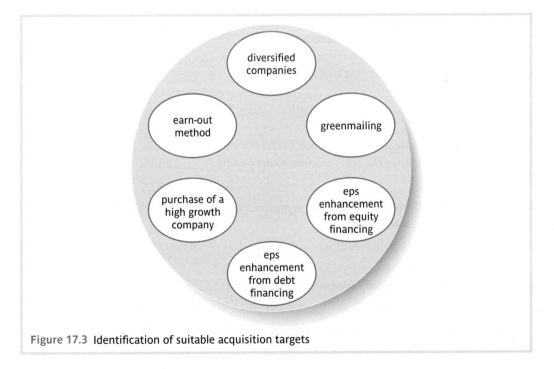

Figure 17.3 Identification of suitable acquisition targets

Diversified companies

A group that has diversified into growth areas with competitive advantages offers even greater opportunities for a predator to increase post-acquisition value. This is because parts of the business are still in the growth phase and have not yet reached maturity.

A diversified group should ideally be valued at a minimum of the weighted average P/E applicable to its component businesses. However, in practice this may be difficult to ascertain. If some of the newly acquired parts of the group company do not perform well after acquisition they may be sold for appropriately high P/E multiples.

Greenmailing

A corporate raid is a particular type of hostile takeover in which the target company is acquired and then broken up. Predator companies who are corporate raiders may have a significant impact on the strategies of targeted companies without taking complete control of them. This may be achieved by acquiring just a small part of target companies.

A corporate raider may buy a stake in a company, which is considered to be significantly undervalued, and in this way 'greenmail' the management, which is effectively accusing them of running the company to the detriment of the shareholders by not aiming to maximise shareholder wealth. The greenmail threat is to acquire the entire company, sack the management, and implement a new strategy.

In the USA, where companies have acquired shares in such a target company, this tactic has been used and has resulted in management offers to buy out the corporate raiders' stakes, with an inevitable large capital gain to the raider.

eps enhancement using equity financing

Most plcs see eps as their most important financial measure. However, it should be noted, as we have previously discussed, that enhancement of eps is not one of the 'good' reasons for an acquisition. Rightly or wrongly, even though cash measures are probably better, eps is a key element in maintaining share price levels, because:

$$\text{share price} = \text{eps} \times \text{P/E}$$

If equity rather than cash is used to finance a takeover deal then there will be an impact on the eps of the combined entity. The level of impact on eps will depend on the target company's P/E ratio, as follows:

- if the P/E ratio of the bidding company is greater than the P/E ratio of the target company – then eps will be increased

- if the P/E ratio of the bidding company is less than the P/E ratio of the target company – then eps will be diluted

- if the P/E ratio of the bidding company is the same as the P/E ratio of the target company – then eps will be unchanged.

Worked Examples 17.2 and 17.3 illustrate the impact on eps of an equity-financed acquisition at different levels of the target company's P/E ratio.

Worked Example 17.2

Presley plc wants to acquire Richard plc by offering shares to Richard's shareholders. The price that Presley plc will pay is the market capitalisation of Richard plc. To keep the calculations simple we will assume that they each have 1,000,000 ordinary shares in issue and their current share prices are both £4.

We will consider the impact of the takeover on Presley's combined company eps at different levels of P/E for Richard plc.

Presley plc's P/E ratio greater than Richard plc's P/E ratio

	Presley plc	Richard plc
Issued shares	1,000,000	1,000,000
Net profit after tax	£0.16m	£0.20m
eps	16p	20p
Share price	£4	£4
P/E ratio	25	20
Number of Presley plc shares in issue after the takeover	2,000,000	
Total net profit	£0.36m	
eps	18p	

The combined company's eps have increased to 18p from Presley's 16p.

Presley plc's P/E ratio the same as Richard plc's P/E ratio

	Presley plc	Richard plc
Issued shares	1,000,000	1,000,000
Net profit after tax	£0.20m	£0.20m
eps	20p	20p
Share price	£4	£4
P/E ratio	20	20
Number of Presley plc shares in issue after the takeover	2,000,000	
Total net profit	£0.40m	
eps	20p	

The combined company's eps are unchanged at 20p.

Presley plc's P/E ratio less than Richard plc's P/E ratio

	Presley plc	Richard plc
Issued shares	1,000,000	1,000,000
Net profit after tax	£0.20m	£0.16m
eps	20p	16p
Share price	£4	£4
P/E ratio	20	25
Number of Presley plc shares in issue after the takeover	2,000,000	
Total net profit	£0.36m	
eps	18p	

The combined company's eps have been diluted to 18p from Presley's 20p.

In Worked Example 17.2 if the numbers of issued shares and share prices of the two companies had been different then the solution would just require a recalculation of the price paid for the acquisition. Worked Example 17.3 illustrates the impact on eps and net assets of an equity-financed acquisition where the numbers of issued shares and share prices of the two companies are different.

Worked Example 17.3

Python plc is a UK manufacturing company, which has an issued share capital of 2 million £1 ordinary shares. The company's net assets (excluding goodwill) are £2.5m and the company's average annual earnings are £2m. Python plc currently has a P/E ratio of 10.

Pig Ltd is a UK manufacturing company, which has an issued share capital of 1 million £1 ordinary shares. The company's net assets (excluding goodwill) are £3.5m and the company's average annual earnings are £500,000.

The shareholders of Pig Ltd have recently accepted an all-equity offer from Python plc, and the offer values Pig Ltd's shares at £6 each.

We will calculate Python plc's earnings and net assets per share before and after the acquisition of Pig Ltd.

Python plc – before the merger:

$$\text{eps} = £2m/2m \text{ shares} = £1.00$$
$$\text{net assets per share} = £2.5m/2m \text{ shares} = £1.25$$

Python has a P/E ratio of 10, and therefore the current market value of Python's shares is £10 (10 × £1).

Pig Ltd – before the merger:

$$\text{eps} = £0.5m/1m \text{ shares} = £0.50$$
$$\text{net assets per share} = £3.5m/1m \text{ shares} = £3.50$$

Python plc's offer of £6 per share for Pig Ltd gives Pig a P/E ratio of 12 (£6/£0.50).

Because Python's P/E ratio is lower than Pig's P/E ratio, Python's earnings will therefore be diluted as follows:

The market value of Pig Ltd is £6 million (1 million × £6). Therefore Python plc would have to issue 600,000 shares to finance the deal (£6 million/(£1 × 10).

Python plc – after the acquisition:

$$\text{eps} = (£2m + £0.5m)/(2m + 0.6m \text{ shares}) = 96p$$
$$\text{net assets per share} = (£2.5m + £3.5m)/2.6m \text{ shares} = £2.31$$

Python plc's eps have been diluted to 96p from £1, but the company's net assets per share have increased to £2.31 from £1.25.

However, for Pig Ltd the opposite is the case. In total, Pig Ltd's shareholders would receive 600,000 shares in Python plc for the 1,000,000 shares they used to hold in Pig Ltd – 6 shares for every 10 shares they had each held.

Pig Ltd earnings:

10 old Pig shares would earn 10 × £0.50 eps = £5.00
6 new Python shares would earn 6 × £0.96 eps = £5.76,
which is an increase of 76p/6, or 12.7p per share.

Pig Ltd net assets:

10 old Pig shares would be worth 10 × £3.50 = £35.00
6 new Python share would be worth 6 × £2.31 = £13.86,
which is a decrease of £21.14/6, or £3.52 per share.

eps enhancement using debt financing

If debt instead of equity is used to finance a takeover deal then the interest rate paid on the debt will have an impact on the eps of the combined entity. The extent of the impact on eps will depend on the P/E ratio of the target company, as follows:

- if the post-tax interest rate is less than the inverse of the P/E ratio of the target company – then eps will be increased

- if the post-tax interest rate is greater than the inverse of the P/E ratio of the target company – then eps will be diluted.

This is similar to eps enhancement using equity financing, but in this situation the increased growth prospects are offset by increased financial risk due to increased debt and higher interest.

The impact of the use of debt financing for a takeover at different levels of interest rate is illustrated in Worked Example 17.4.

Worked Example 17.4

Presley plc (see Worked Example 17.2) wants to acquire Richard plc and finance the takeover totally by debt. The price that Presley plc will pay is the market capitalisation of Richard plc. The companies each have 1,000,000 ordinary shares in issue and the current share prices are both £4.

We will consider the impact of the takeover on Presley's combined company eps if it is able to finance the acquisition through borrowing £4m at 4%, 5%, or 6% per annum. The corporation tax rate is 20%.

Presley plc's cost of debt is 4%

	Presley plc	Richard plc
Issued shares	1,000,000	1,000,000
Net profit after tax	£0.20m	£0.16m
eps	20p	16p
Share price	£4	£4
P/E ratio	20	25
Cost of additional debt @ 4%	£0.128m	
£4m × 4% × (1 – 20%)		
Number of shares in Presley plc		
after the takeover	1,000,000	
Total net profit £0.36 – £0.128m	£0.232m	
eps	23.2p	

The combined company's eps have increased to 23.2p from Presley's 20p.

The after-tax cost of debt is 4% × (1 – 20%) = 3.2%, which is less than the reciprocal of Richard plc's P/E ratio 1 × 100%/25 = 4%

▶

▶   **Presley plc's cost of debt is 5%**

	Presley plc	Richard plc
Issued shares	1,000,000	1,000,000
Net profit after tax	£0.20m	£0.16m
eps	20p	16p
Share price	£4	£4
P/E ratio	20	25
Cost of additional debt @ 5% £4m × 5% × (1 − 20%)	£0.16m	
Number of shares in Presley plc after the takeover	1,000,000	
Total net profit £0.36 − £0.16m	£0.20m	
eps	20p	

The combined company's eps remain at 20p.

The after-tax cost of debt is 5% × (1 − 20%) = 4%, which equals the reciprocal of Richard plc's P/E ratio 1 × 100%/25 = 4%

Presley plc's cost of debt is 6%

	Presley plc	Richard plc
Issued shares	1,000,000	1,000,000
Net profit after tax	£0.20m	£0.16m
eps	20p	16p
Share price	£4	£4
P/E ratio	20	25
Cost of additional debt @ 6% £4m × 6% × (1 − 20%)	£0.192m	
Number of shares in Presley plc after the takeover	1,000,000	
Total net profit £0.36 − £0.192m	£0.168m	
eps	16.8p	

The combined company's eps have been diluted to 16.8p from Presley's 20p.

The after-tax cost of debt is 6% × (1 − 20%) = 4.8%, which is greater than the reciprocal of Richard plc's P/E ratio 1 × 100%/25 = 4%

As in Worked Example 17.2, if in Worked Example 17.4 the numbers of issued shares and share prices of the two companies had been different then the solution would just require a recalculation of the price paid for the acquisition.

Purchasing a high-growth company

The usual takeover or merger scenario is where a large company may bid for and acquire, for example, a smaller people-based, owner-managed company. The acquisition price will reflect the high expectation of synergy benefits and economies of scale achieved from the takeover of the target company. However, post-acquisition, the key asset of the business, its managers, may leave or may not be motivated to achieve the expected benefits, which have been paid for. In addition to this, the acquisition purchase price may have been too high, and the expected benefits may not be achieved.

Earn-out method

Very often, what is called an earn-out method is used to acquire small companies, which have very good future prospects. An earn-out method may also be used to resolve differences of opinion on the value and the potential of a target company.

The eventual price paid for an acquisition may be tied to the subsequent growth rate in the early years following transfer of ownership. The earn-out deal may be that the target company shareholders receive part payment on acquisition, with the balance deferred a couple of years until a specific agreed level of profits has been achieved.

Because the risk of future performance is transferred to the existing owners, the acquisition price will be higher than normally expected. For an earn-out to be effective the vendor shareholders should also be the key managers in the company, to guarantee their commitment.

Compensation, in terms of the acquisition price, must be adequate reward to the vendors for 'waiting' for payment.

Progress check 17.2

What are the key financial strategies that may be adopted in the identification of M&A target companies?

Takeover pre-bid defences

We may question why a proposed takeover bid may be opposed at all. The directors of a target company may oppose a takeover bid because:

- they want to retain their jobs and they think that avoiding a takeover will achieve this (the most usual reason)
- they believe that they can create more value than would be created following a takeover.

Companies may try and avoid being taken over before a formal takeover bid has been made. The purpose of this is:

- to make a company difficult and expensive to take over
- early detection of a bid is an advantage to get a defence in place quickly
- to maintain consistency with the shareholder wealth maximisation objective.

Companies may use one or more of a number of pre-bid defences, which are shown in Fig. 17.4.

Investor communication

Maintaining good relations with investors and analysts may make a potential takeover difficult and expensive. It may prove very costly for a potential acquiring company to persuade shareholders about the benefits of the takeover. It may also require an unacceptably high offer price to induce them to accept.

Managers need to keep investors well informed about policies, strategies and performance, and about their aim to satisfy their risk and return preferences. Target companies may also make commitments to shareholders that potential predator companies feel unable to support.

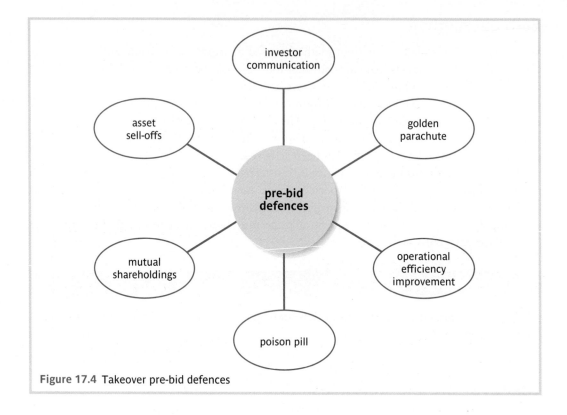

Figure 17.4 Takeover pre-bid defences

Golden parachute

'Golden parachutes' are extremely generous termination packages that may be contracted with senior managers, which effectively increase the cost of a takeover. These may be introduced into directors' contracts if there is a threat of a takeover.

For the predator company the removal of managers surplus to requirements after the takeover may then be very costly, because of the high cost of termination packages. This may be sufficient to make a takeover unattractive and therefore deter a potential predator company.

Operational efficiency improvement

The expense of a potential takeover may be increased by a target company raising its eps and share price (so reducing the likelihood of takeover) through:

- overheads cost reduction
- production rationalisation
- labour productivity improvement,

so that the takeover becomes more expensive and so less likely to proceed.

However, shareholders and others may be concerned at why it took a takeover bid threat for these initiatives to be put in place. Perhaps these should have been initiated by the directors regardless of the takeover bid.

Poison pill

A takeover target company may purchase its own shares, which reduces a predator company's ability to gain a controlling position. The share purchase reduces the equity of the target company as a proportion of its total capital.

Increased gearing (higher debt ratio) may make a takeover less attractive because of the ongoing high costs of interest payment commitments.

As illustrated in the press extract below, a target company may plant a 'poison pill' into the capital structure, for example rights of shareholders to buy future loan stock or preference shares, increasing the cost of possible acquisition. The potential future ongoing cost of interest payments makes the takeover look more expensive, and therefore less attractive, and therefore less likely to take place. This strategy has the same impact as the target company buying back its own shares.

PeopleSoft poison pill
'PeopleSoft defies $9.2bn Oracle bid', by Dominic White

American software giant PeopleSoft remained defiant against Oracle's hostile $9.2billion (£5billion) bid yesterday despite PeopleSoft shareholders backing the offer over the weekend.

The PeopleSoft board rejected Oracle's latest offer just hours after its investors tendered more than 60pc of their shares to its bitter rival. It is the fifth time PeopleSoft's directors have knocked Oracle back during an acrimonious 17-month campaign by the colourful Oracle chief executive Larry Ellison, sometimes described as 'the other software billionaire'.

However, some analysts said they are surprised that PeopleSoft is still holding out against the deal, which has received the blessing of the regulators.

In a statement, PeopleSoft director George 'Skip' Battle said: 'PeopleSoft's board of directors has met and considered the results of Oracle's unsolicited tender offer and unanimously reaffirmed its previous conclusion that Oracle's latest offer is inadequate'.

Mr Ellison added pressure by calling for PeopleSoft's directors to strike a quick deal, saying his $24-a-share cash and shares bid remained his best and final offer. 'The owners of PeopleSoft have spoken and overwhelmingly chosen to sell to Oracle', he said in a statement. 'It's time to bring this to a close'.

The battle may reach its climax this week when PeopleSoft returns to Delaware Chancery Court to see whether a judge will uphold its right to use a poison pill defence. Both software makers are scheduled to appear in the court on Wednesday to address PeopleSoft's shareholder rights plan, which Oracle says would flood the market with low-cost stock and make the bid prohibitively expensive.

Oracle, whose tender offer is conditional on the removal of the pill, hopes the result will prompt Vice-Chancellor Leo Strine to rule against the defence, the last hurdle to clinching the takeover. If he does, it would seemingly allow Oracle to close the deal, which could result in layoffs of between 6,000 and 10,000 PeopleSoft employees.

PeopleSoft, however, believes Mr Strine should uphold the pill in the face of a unanimous board holding out for a higher price for shareholders.

That would leave Oracle with an option of mounting a proxy fight early next year by nominating new PeopleSoft board members who might be more favorable to a buyout. Four of PeopleSoft's seven board members will be up for re-election in the spring at the firm's annual shareholder meeting. Oracle, already a PeopleSoft shareholder, said it has until the end of this week to submit nominations for new board members.

Some analysts have said PeopleSoft's board could try to drag out the takeover saga into a proxy fight to allow the company to post two quarters of results that could persuade shareholders its future remains bright. PeopleSoft recently forecast a rosy 2005 earnings outlook, but many Wall Street analysts said it was too optimistic.

Analysts have been speculating Oracle's offer might succeed since PeopleSoft fired its chief executive Craig Conway last month.

Mr Conway, formerly of Oracle, led the campaign to keep PeopleSoft independent, taunting his former mentor Mr Ellison along the way and referring to him as 'Ghenkis Khan'.

© *Daily Telegraph*, 22 November 2004

There are a number of other types of poison pill that may be effected by potential takeover target companies:

- staggering the retirement of directors, which may hinder rather than prevent a takeover
- issuing of new shares to 'friendly' shareholders to dilute the holding of a potential acquiring company
- changing the rules of the company so that a super-majority of, say, 75% is required, rather than the normal 50%, for a takeover to proceed.

Let's look at an example of another type of poison pill in Worked Example 17.5.

Worked Example 17.5

In September 2001, Royal Caribbean Cruises Ltd and P&O Princess Cruises plc announced their proposed 'merger of equals'. In December 2001, the Carnival Corporation launched a hostile takeover of P&O Princess. At first, Princess spurned the offer, then did an about-face, announcing that it would auction itself off to the highest bidder. In January 2002, the Carnival Corporation raised its offer in a final attempt to break up the UK cruise group's pre-arranged merger with Royal Caribbean. The value of the Carnival offer was now substantially greater than Royal Caribbean's. The management of P&O Princess continued to favour the pairing with Royal Caribbean, and advised investors of this through its website. Various governmental regulators in the USA, the UK, and Europe needed to consider their approval of any merger. The Carnival Corporation wanted the legitimacy of P&O's joint venture with Royal Caribbean to be tested in the UK courts because it would be a 'poison pill' and against the shareholders' interests according to the City Code. (See more about the City Code in the later section about equity restructuring.) Carnival said it would avoid paying the poison pill by delaying the completion of its takeover of Princess until January 2003. Approval for both deals was given by the European Commission, and by the UK and USA regulators. However, by early 2003 P&O Princess Cruises plc had agreed to its takeover by Carnival with a US$5.5bn agreement.

Mutual shareholdings

Some companies may have sufficient trust in each other to collude to prevent a takeover. Such collusion is a device that may ensure that a significant proportion of equity is kept within 'friendly hands'.

Target companies may arrange for other companies to take mutual shareholdings in each other to block potential takeover bids through such strategic alliances.

Asset sell-offs

The use of divestment as a pre-bid defence involves the disposal of some key assets, which would be particularly attractive to a predator company. Non-core, low growth businesses may be sold off by a potential takeover target company.

The divestment may then enable a concentration by the target company on markets in which the company is strong. This may then give the company some focus, in addition to helping to repel a hostile bid.

The result of such a strategic divestment by a target company should be an increase in profits, eps, and share price. This then achieves the objective of increasing the cost of a potential takeover, which as result becomes less likely to go ahead.

Progress check 17.3

Outline the pre-bid defences that may be used by a takeover target company.

Takeover post-bid defences

If none of the pre-bid defences have been successful then there are also a number of post-bid defences that may be used by target companies to repel a bid once one has been made. These are shown in Fig. 17.5.

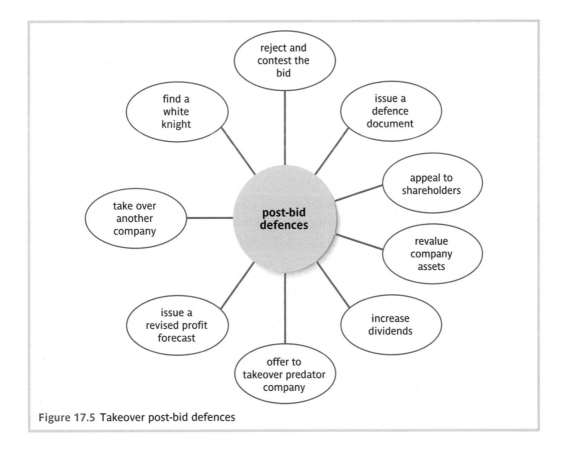

Figure 17.5 Takeover post-bid defences

Reject and contest the bid

The initial takeover bid may be attacked to signal to the predator that the target company will contest the takeover. This device is to let the predator know that the takeover bid is not welcome and will be defended.

This rejection may be enough to scare off the predator. But, why should the directors do this? It may be that the directors believe that the bid undervalues the company, or that synergies will not be achieved, or maybe they feel that the takeover is a threat to their own positions.

Issue a defence document

The board of directors of the target company may prepare a formal document, which is circulated to its shareholders praising its own performance and criticising the bidding company and its offer.

This document may criticise the bid by saying that:

- promised synergies are unlikely to be realised
- shareholder value will not be increased
- the takeover may represent a risk to shareholders,

and to be credible, such a document must be very carefully prepared, and it is important that its assertions are borne out by subsequent events.

Appeal to shareholders

Target companies may also make a pre-emptive appeal to their shareholders. The directors can do this by immediately circulating the shareholders.

The appeal to the shareholders should explain how the bid is not in the shareholders' favour from a logical and a price perspective. They should explain that shareholder value will be higher without the takeover than if the takeover were to go ahead.

Revalue company assets

A target company may revalue its assets, before or after a takeover bid. This can involve the revaluation of land and buildings (see an example of this in the following press extract), or the capitalisation of brand names that the company may have purchased, to make the company look stronger or more valuable.

The predator company may then need to make an increased offer, to up its bid following a revaluation of assets. However, if the capital markets are efficient, and since no new information is being provided, the existing share price may be a fair one. In that case, financial analysts will be aware of such assets even if they have not been revalued, so this will already be reflected in the company's share price. If the asset revaluation tactic is successful, and the target company's share price increases, then the predator may consider that the price required for the target company is too high and therefore withdraw.

The real value of a company's assets

'Green to bid £8.8bn as M&S considers selling flagship Lifestore',
by Edmund Conway

Retail entrepreneur Philip Green is this week expected to table a fresh bid for Marks & Spencer, as the high street giant considers ditching its flagship £15m homeware store.

Mr Green, who owns Top Shop and BHS, is preparing to raise his offer for M&S, following the board's near-instant rejection of his previous bid earlier this month.

Insiders expect the new offer – tabled through bid vehicle Revival – to be worth up to £8.8billion. It would value the company's shares at between 380p and 390p, and would offer current M&S shareholders the opportunity to hold equity in the new company, so as to reap any returns made by Mr Green.

The previous bid of 290p–310p in cash plus a 25pc stake in Revival was rejected within hours by the M&S board, under its newly appointed chief executive Stuart Rose. A number of M&S insiders, as well as city analysts, do not expect an offer below 400p to be accepted, although Mr Green has indicated that this is more than he regards the company is worth.

M&S is preparing to fight off a new bid by revaluing its portfolio of freehold property, which some reckon is worth up to £4billion – £2billion more than its valuation in the group's accounts. Mr Rose has brought in close adviser Charles Wilson to help mastermind the retail group's recovery.

Paul Myners has been drafted in as a temporary replacement for chairman Luc Vandevelde. It emerged yesterday that Mr Vandevelde's private equity fund, Change Capital Partners, is one of the bidders for £200m retailer Pets at Home.

Yesterday, Mr Rose was working at the company's Baker Street headquarters on a review of M&S's underperforming businesses. Top of the list is Lifestore, the home furnishings shop launched by ousted clothing chief Vittorio Radice. M&S has admitted that the pioneer Gateshead store is not meeting performance targets, but a spokesman warned yesterday that its fate may take some time to be decided.

'Stuart and Charles have only been at the company for 10 days', he said. 'It will take a certain amount of time for them to decide what needs changing and what doesn't. Lifestore is clearly not performing well at the moment so it is the subject of a review. Our revaluing of the property portfolio is already under way, and we should have the results in a matter of weeks'.

The spokesman played down suggestions that the value of the properties would be released and passed on to shareholders. 'We need to be able to point to the inherent value of the company if there is another bid', he said. 'For the moment, though, our main tactic here is to wait and see what Philip Green does next'.

Mr Green is expected to return from his home in Monaco this afternoon to put the finishing touches to the new bid. Yesterday he said: 'All I'm going to say at the moment is that we are considering our position. Other than that I can't make any comment'.

The M&S spokesman said Mr Rose was unavailable to talk to the press.

© *Daily Telegraph*, 14 June 2004

Increase dividends

A target company may announce an increase in dividend and its intention to pay future increased dividends. Again, there is the problem of a potential lack of credibility. It is reasonable for shareholders to question why current and future dividends should have suddenly been improved.

A dividend increase may persuade target company shareholders to reject a takeover offer. Or it may not, particularly if the shareholders remain unconvinced as to why increased dividends were not paid prior to a takeover offer. If promises of increased dividends are not kept, then the share price may fall. The company may then become an even easier target for takeover.

Offer to take over predator company – Pac-Man defence

The Pac-Man defence was named after the computer game in which the monster you are pursuing all of a sudden turns around and eats your monster instead. The idea is to counter an unwanted takeover bid by turning the tables and bidding yourself. A flaw in the strategy is that the moment the Pac-Man defence is deployed, the industrial logic of the deal has essentially been recognised. The only remaining question is who ends up eating whom.

Using the Pac-Man defence a target company may make a counter-bid for the shares of the predator company. This is also sometimes referred to as a reverse takeover. This usually involves a smaller more dynamic company attempting to acquire a larger company, but it is not always the case. This option is difficult and expensive but has occasionally been used successfully in the USA. The Pac-Man defence was used in the UK by Warner Music against EMI in June 2006 (see Worked Example 17.6).

Worked Example 17.6

EMI had been trying, on and off for more than six years, to acquire Warner Music, but one way or another they seemed incapable of pulling it off.

EMI's first attempt was thwarted by the competition regulators. Subsequently, the merger of BMG and Sony, and the way in which the industry had been structurally transformed by music downloads, encouraged Eric Nicoli, the EMI chairman, to believe that the regulators might prove more amenable. However, there had been a change of ownership at Warner Music, which was also headed by a new chairman. He recognised the synergies and cost cuts that could be derived by combining with EMI, but he was not amenable to being taken over by EMI or anyone else. He therefore countered EMI's US$31 per share bid for Warner Music with a £3.20 per share cash offer for EMI.

Both offers were dependent on board recommendation and due diligence, which neither party was willing to give, and so there was an impasse. In the majority of takeovers, it is shareholders in the company being taken over that gain most out of the transaction. Usually, the gains achieved by any synergies are less than the premium paid for the company being taken over and so the investors in the acquiring company are usually no better or worse off. On that basis, EMI shareholders should have been keen to accept Warner Music's cash.

Mr Nicoli, the EMI chairman, had difficulty in getting the City's support through a rights issue to fund his purchase of Warner Music. However, Mr Bronfman, the Warner Music chairman, appeared to have persuaded his backers that the whole deal could be financed with debt. His financing was therefore more secure, even if it was much higher risk.

Warner Music's Pac-Man defence was successful because its offer was rejected by EMI and EMI didn't make a further counter offer for Warner Music.

Issue a revised profit forecast

A report may be prepared by the target company indicating a forecast profit improvement at better than market expectations. Again, this must be prepared very carefully by the directors of the target company to maintain credibility. It may be quite reasonable for shareholders to question why profit forecasts have now suddenly been improved. If the market accepts the revised profit forecast, the share price will rise and make the proposed takeover more expensive. If the market does not accept the revised forecast then obviously this tactic will not work.

If, subsequent to the forecasts, the revised profit forecasts are not achieved then the share price will drop, bringing an increased risk of takeover and a loss of credibility in the repeat use of such a defence. This may also possibly make a takeover even cheaper and easier, which therefore defeats the initial aim of the profit announcement.

Take over another company

The target company may buy new assets or companies that are incompatible with the predator company's business. Alternatively, the target company may sell off the 'crown jewels', the assets in which the predator company is particularly interested. This is similar to the pre-bid takeover defence divestment strategy.

Both of these strategies are employed to make the potential takeover less attractive to the predator company, and to encourage it to withdraw. However, the City Code on M&As restricts such selling off of assets once a takeover bid has been made.

Find a white knight

A device that is sometimes seen as a last resort is for the target company to seek out a more acceptable company, a **white knight**, to take it over. An example of this is shown in the press extract below. The argument is that it is better for a company to be taken over by a company of its choice rather than some other hostile bidder. The City Code on M&As allows this tactic only if any information passed to the white knight is also passed to the initial predator.

Alternatively, the target company, with shareholders' prior approval, may issue new shares to a white knight to dilute the predator company's holdings. This again includes the involvement of a 'friendly pair of hands'.

It should be noted that the use of either of these options to defend against a takeover bid requires the approval of shareholders.

A white knight at Christmas

'Novar hopes for £750m white-knight rescue takeover before Christmas', by Andrew Murray-Watson

A 'white-knight' takeover of Novar, the building supplies group, could be announced before Christmas.

Bankers say that the company is in advanced talks to be bought for more than £750m by one of four possible trade buyers. A deal would save it from a hostile £745m takeover by Melrose, the Aim-listed investment vehicle.

The advanced nature of Novar's talks with potential white knights will come as a major blow to Melrose, which tabled a cash and shares deal originally valuing the group at £625m. At Melrose's current share price, the takeover is worth 173p per Novar share.

The leading contenders to make a white knight offer for Novar include Siemens, the German industrial giant, Schneider, Honeywell and General Electric. Cinven, the private equity group, is also understood to be interested in making an offer.

However, one of the major issues for any buyer is Novar's £270m pension fund deficit, as this could make a break-up of the group complicated.

Novar is planning to publish its bid defence document tomorrow. The defence is understood to raise the possibility of demerging Security Printing Services, the US-based cheque business, which could be valued at up to £600m on the New York stock market.

Stephen Howard, Novar's chief executive, is pursuing a twin-track approach that will see the company either broken up or sold.

Melrose is unlikely to raise its bid for Novar, despite the interest from other parties. However, analysts believe potential buyers will only be interested in buying the whole of Novar if this is the only way to gain control of Intelligent Building Systems, its highly regarded fire safety business.

Sir Graham Hearn, Novar's chairman, believes a defence can be successfully waged by proving the existing management can extract more value for shareholders than Melrose's cash and shares bid.

© *Daily Telegraph*, 12 December 2004

The position of shareholders, managers, employees, and financial institutions in M&As

M&As obviously impact on shareholders, and directors and managers of both the target and acquiring companies. They also impact on other stakeholders like employees, and on financial institutions like insurance companies, pension funds, and merchant banks.

In theory the economy should gain if assets are transferred from inefficient to efficient management. However, empirical research by Cowling *et al.* (Cowling K, Stoneman P, Cubbin J (1986) *Mergers and Economic Performance*, Cambridge: Cambridge University Press) in the 1980s suggested that in fact M&As at best had a neutral impact on the economy as a whole, and provided no great efficiency gains.

Shareholders

Target company shareholders generally appear to enjoy significant returns while predator company shareholders experience insignificant or negative returns.

A quantified look at both post-acquisition financial performance, and share price movement by the financial press leads them to conclude more often than not that merger and takeover activity is not wealth-creating but instead involves the transfer of wealth from predator to target company shareholders.

Managers and employees

The directors and managers in predator companies generally benefit from successful takeovers. This is because their power and security is further strengthened. Post-takeover, managers have increased power and status from running a larger company, often reflected in increased rewards. However, this may not necessarily be totally to the benefit of the shareholders. Directors' jobs become more secure since it is more difficult for a larger company to be subsequently taken over. This may be beneficial for the shareholders if the new larger company is value adding.

The directors and managers of target companies generally lose out after a takeover, because they may be deemed inefficient or surplus to requirements. There may be duplication of departments, and particularly duplication of senior management roles. Employees of target companies usually suffer in the same way, from the results of economies of scale, resulting in:

- redundancies from duplicated functions
- the closing down of unwanted parts of the acquired business.

After all, synergies and economies of scale are usually the very reasons and justifications of M&As, and so therefore there is usually a high chance of these outcomes.

Financial institutions

Financial institutions usually earn large fees from their advisory roles to target companies and acquiring companies in M&As. The financial institutions in M&As, such as merchant banks, investment banks, and M&A lawyers and accountants, are usually some of the really bigwinners, as well as the shareholders of the target companies.

Financial institutions are always one of the parties benefiting most from M&As because they are indispensable in a wide range of roles from advice on bid values, to organising pre- and post-bid defences, to arrangement of financing.

Progress check 17.4

What are the main impacts on the directors and managers of companies involved in M&As?

Summary of key points

- There are a number of ways in which mergers and acquisitions (M&As) may be financed which include the use of cash, equity shares, and debt.
- Cash may be the preferred option of the shareholders of a company being taken over, but both debt and equity are widely used in financing M&As.
- There are many advantages and disadvantages to shareholders that result from use of cash, debt, or equity in the financing of M&As.
- The accounting treatment of an M&A is dependent on the type of deal and how it is financed.
- There are a number of financial strategies relating to acquisitions and the ways in which suitable target companies may be identified and potential synergies evaluated.
- Many different types of takeover defences may be used by a company before a formal takeover bid has been made to try and avoid being taken over.
- Many different types of takeover defences may be used by a company to repel a takeover once a formal takeover bid has been made.
- M&A deals may have significant impacts on shareholders, directors, managers, employees, and financial institutions.

🔒 Glossary of key terms

conversion ratio The number of ordinary shares that will be obtained from the conversion of one unit of a convertible bond.

conversion value The market value of the ordinary shares into which a unit of a convertible bond may be converted.

coupon yield The interest paid on the nominal value of a bond (or a loan, or debenture).

earn-out method Target company shareholders receive part payment on acquisition, with the balance deferred a couple of years until a specific agreed level of profits has been achieved so that the eventual price paid for the acquisition may be tied to the subsequent growth rate in the early years following transfer of ownership. This arrangement gives a

▶

measure of security to the new owners, who pass some of the financial risk associated with the purchase of a new enterprise to the target company.

golden parachute An extremely generous termination package that may be introduced into a target company's directors' contracts if there is a threat of a takeover, which effectively increases the cost of a takeover.

greenmailing A corporate raider may buy a stake in a company, which is considered to be significantly undervalued, and in this way greenmail the management, accusing them of running the company to the detriment of the shareholders by not aiming to maximise shareholder wealth. The greenmail threat is to acquire the entire company, sack the management, and implement a new strategy.

merger accounting A method of accounting which treats two or more parties as combining on an equal footing. It is normally applied without any restatement of net assets to fair value, and includes the results of each for the whole of the accounting period. Correspondingly, it does not reflect the issue of shares as an application of resources at fair value. The difference that arises on consolidation does not represent goodwill but is deducted from, or added to, reserves (FRS 6).

mixed bid A share-for-share offer for a target company supported by a cash alternative, which means that its shareholders can choose the method that best suits their individual liquidity preferences and tax positions.

Pac-Man defence A reverse takeover, where a target company may make a counter-bid for the shares of the predator company.

poison pill A contractual obligation or a feature of the target company's capital structure that has the effect of increasing the cost of possible acquisition and make it less attractive to the predator company, and therefore less likely to take place.

reverse takeover See Pac-Man defence.

straight bond value The market value of a bond, which is dependent on the coupon rate relative to market interest rates.

takeover accounting A method of accounting which regards the business combination as the acquisition of one company by another: the identifiable assets and liabilities of the company acquired are included in the consolidated balance sheet at their fair value at the date of acquisition. The difference between the fair value of the consideration given and the fair values of the net assets of the entity acquired is accounted for as goodwill (FRS 6).

vendor placing A vendor placing involves the acquiring company offering shares to the target company with the option to continue their shareholding, and at the same time arranging for the new shares to be placed with institutional investors at a pre-determined price and for cash to be paid to the target company's shareholders.

white knight A more acceptable company which the target company may seek out to take it over with the rationale that it is better to be taken over by a company of its choice rather than some other hostile bidder.

Questions

Q17.1 Why is the method of financing important in M&As?

Q17.2 In what ways do a cash purchase of a business differ from a vendor placing?

Q17.3 How may eps be enhanced from a takeover?

Q17.4 Describe the various forms of equity restructuring that may be used by a target company to avoid its being taken over.

Q17.5 How may profit announcements, and changes in dividend policy, be used by target companies to provide defences after a takeover bid has been made?

Q17.6 Describe and explain the range of defence strategies used by companies facing a hostile takeover bid.

Q17.7 Outline the types of problem faced by employees and managers after their company has been taken over.

Discussion points

D17.1 'Takeovers merely satisfy the inflated egos of power-hungry company bosses.' Discuss.

D17.2 'The ways in which M&As are financed do not have any influence on their subsequent success.' Discuss.

D17.3 'There is no real defence against a takeover bid from a determined predator company.' Discuss.

D17.4 'The position of shareholders, managers, and employees in M&As is largely disregarded by both predator and target companies.' Discuss.

Exercises

Solutions are provided in Appendix 2 to all exercise numbers highlighted in colour.

Level I

E17.1 *Time allowed – 30 minutes*

Explain the advantages and disadvantages of using debt or equity in financing acquisitions.

E17.2 *Time allowed – 30 minutes*

Explain what is meant by a convertible bond and discuss the advantages from its use in financing a takeover.

E17.3 *Time allowed – 45 minutes*

Outline the alternative methods that may be used to finance an acquisition and the circumstances in which each method may be appropriate.

Level II

E17.4 *Time allowed – 45 minutes*

Explain some of the financial strategies that may be used in acquisitions and consider the possible impacts of these on both predator and target companies.

▶ **E17.5** *Time allowed – 45 minutes*

Discuss the reasons why a hostile takeover bid may be opposed by a target company. Outline how three pre-bid and four post-bid defences may be effectively employed to avoid a takeover.

E17.6 *Time allowed – 45 minutes*

Outline the differences between merger accounting rules and takeover accounting rules. What types of merger allow merger accounting rules to be used?

E17.7 *Time allowed – 45 minutes*

Explain the possible impact of M&As on shareholders, managers, and employees of both predator and target companies.

E17.8 *Time allowed – 45 minutes*

Blue Sky plc is a UK-based retail company. The company is considering expanding its retail operations and is considering the acquisition of a rival company White Cloud plc. Blue Sky plc has a current market value of £80m, and White Cloud plc has a current market value of £50m. Blue Sky plc expects the acquisition of White Cloud plc to result in substantial economies of scale, which will result in savings of £2.75m per year in perpetuity.

Blue Sky plc requires a rate of return on all investments of 10%, and has estimated that as a result of the acquisition transaction costs of £5m will be incurred.

Required:

(i)   Briefly explain the main reasons why a company would seek to acquire another company.

(ii) Calculate the present value of the gain to Blue Sky plc from the acquisition of White Cloud plc.

(iii) If a cash offer of £65 million is accepted by White Cloud plc's shareholders what value would be created for Blue Sky plc's shareholders?

(iv) If a share offer providing White Cloud plc's shareholders with a 30% holding in the Blue Sky plc after the acquisition what value would be created for Blue Sky plc's shareholders?

(v)   If White Cloud plc were to contest the offer, what possible defences could the company use to defend itself against the takeover bid?

E17.9 *Time allowed – 45 minutes*

Arkwright plc is a UK-based manufacturing company. The company has a weighted average cost of capital of 10%, and is financed partly by equity (cost 12%) and partly by debt capital (cost 8%).

The company is considering acquiring Granville Ltd, a design company. The acquisition of Granville Ltd would cost £10m, however the acquisition is expected to yield additional annual profits of £2m before interest charges.

The company expects to finance the investment with a further loan at a cost of 8% per annum. As a result of this additional borrowing, the company expects its cost of equity to rise to 15%.

The company pays out all profits as dividends, which are currently £3.6m a year.

You may assume the traditional view of WACC and gearing.

Required:

(i) Calculate the effect of acquiring Granville Ltd on the value of Arkwright plc's equity.

(ii) Calculate the extent to which the change in the value of Arkwright plc's equity is caused by:

   (a) the NPV of the project at the current WACC

   (b) the method of financing.

(iii) Briefly explain why the company's cost of equity would increase as the company increases its total borrowing.

Chapter 18

Reorganisations and restructuring

Chapter contents

LEARNING OBJECTIVES

Completion of this chapter will enable you to:

☑ Explain the reasons why company reorganisations and restructuring may take place.

☑ Outline the ways in which company reorganisations and restructuring may be made.

☑ Identify the financial strategies that may be adopted in response to issues internal to a company that may necessitate its reorganisation.

☑ Identify the financial strategies that may be adopted in response to issues external to a company that may necessitate its reorganisation.

☑ Appreciate the differences between the two forms of 'privatisation': sale by Government; return to private ownership.

☑ Consider the use of management buy-outs (MBOs) and management buy-ins (MBIs) as methods of restructuring and refinancing companies.

☑ Outline the problems that may be faced by MBOs and MBIs.

Introduction

As businesses grow and develop they inevitably face many challenges as well as opportunities resulting from changes in their internal operations and structures, and factors in their external environment. The development of a business may result in internal changes to its financial structure so that its gearing may be too high or too low. Alternatively, there may be external factors that impact on the company such as its shares trading at a price well below their fair value. This chapter will consider the reorganisations of companies that involve the adoption of appropriate financial strategies in response to both internal and external issues.

In the past, many UK businesses and some entire industrial sectors became Government-owned as a result of political decisions or because they may have suffered financial problems and therefore needed rescue. Subsequently, during the latter part of the last century, many businesses were restructured by being sold back by the Government to the private sector, through public flotation. Such sales by Government are examples of **privatisation**. The other type of privatisation dealt with in this chapter is a return to private ownership, moving from plc to Ltd company status. We will consider the reasons and the timings of these returns to private ownership, which are called **re-privatisations**.

Two other forms of company restructuring are management buy-outs (MBOs) and **management buy-ins (MBIs)**. This chapter will look at how a company may be purchased from its shareholders and managed by its existing managers (MBO) or managed by a new team of managers brought in from outside the company (MBI). We will also look at some of the problems encountered and to be overcome by MBOs and MBIs in order to ensure their success.

Reasons for reorganisations and restructuring

In the following sections we will look at how company restructuring takes place when:

- a company is in trouble due to internal issues, such as inappropriate financial strategies
- a company experiences a market underpricing of its shares, which is an example of an external issue.

The financial strategy of any business should generally change over time as it progresses through its business life cycle and in accordance with the development of its business strategy.

The financial strategy of a company may be wrong because:

- it has too little debt
- it may have too much debt

which are gearing problems and are issues that are internal to the company.

A company's shares may be trading at a market value considerably below a fair value. This is the market's perception of the share price, which may not be an efficient market. Major changes in business strategy may be stimulated by the threat of takeover. These are issues that are external to the company.

There are a number of ways in which a company may respond to these internal and external issues. We will consider financial strategies:

- in response to internal issues
- in response to external issues.

Reorganisation – financial strategies in response to internal issues

A mature company may, for example, have too little debt because it has remained equity financed for some time. This may have been deliberate company policy, even if it may have been misguided. Such a company can re-balance its levels of debt and equity in three ways, which are shown in Fig. 18.1.

If a company has a high level of equity compared to its level of debt, and assuming it has the cash available, it may pay out a special dividend far in excess of normal levels, which enables shareholders to reinvest their funds. Alternatively, it may undertake a share buy-back (see Chapter 15). In a share buy-back a company buys back its shares on the open market, and cancels them in its balance sheet (in the UK) and therefore reduces its equity and increases its gearing (assuming it is financed by both debt and equity). If a company has a comparatively low level of debt and therefore a high level of equity then it can use that equity to invest in value-enhancing new projects.

A company may have too much debt due to a misguided financial strategy, or because of a failure to adapt to changing circumstances, for example falling operating profits. Such a company may adopt one or more of the financial strategies shown in Fig. 18.2.

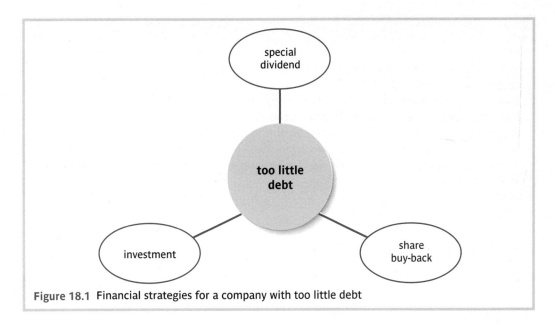

Figure 18.1 Financial strategies for a company with too little debt

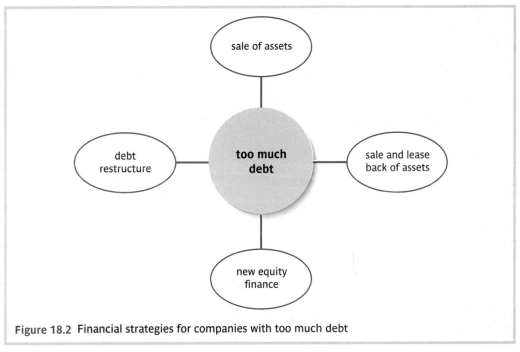

Figure 18.2 Financial strategies for companies with too much debt

Sale of assets

Companies may sell surplus assets to raise cash, and if the assets are non-core assets then this may be a simple method to action. A company may dispose of some of its assets for a number of reasons and in a number of ways. For example, core assets may be sold to a financing company and then leased back, to provide an immediate increase in cash flow. This is illustrated in Tesco's proposed split of its property portfolio in Worked Example 18.1.

Worked Example 18.1

In March 2006 the *Daily Telegraph* reported that the UK's biggest retailer, Tesco plc, was planning to place its £12bn (US$21bn) freehold property into a real estate investment trust (REIT) to enable it to use the money raised from selling shares in the REIT to buy back its own shares. After the report appeared saying that the company planned to unlock more value from its property assets, shares in the supermarket giant rose to a record high. Tesco denied that it had immediate plans to do this, but its finance director, Andrew Higginson said: 'We're obviously interested [in REITs] in the sense that we're a big property company. We've got people looking at whether it's a good idea.'

A sale of assets surplus to operational requirements requires:

- determination of non-core assets, which sometimes needs a fresh look at the business regarding:
  - which assets are really core assets
  - whether the core assets really need to be owned by the company to run the business properly
- finding a buyer, which may not be easy at a good price, particularly if it is generally known that the company is in difficulties – a situation we saw, for example, in the collapse of the telecoms industry in 2000
- acceptance of the accounting consequences (possibly disposal losses) – a company may not actually want to realise a loss on, for example, the disposal of a property in its financial statements.

Sale and lease back of assets

If a company has no assets surplus to its requirements then it cannot sell off its assets without affecting the company's operations. If the company has assets, which are being used for its core activities, it may still sell them to raise cash but then lease them back. This is illustrated in Marks & Spencer's property sale and lease-backs in Worked Example 18.2.

Worked Example 18.2

During 1999/2000 Marks & Spencer (M&S) had further increased its property portfolio through the acquisition of 19 Littlewoods stores. By 2001 M&S continued to suffer from the sales shortfalls that had impacted on the company over the previous three years. M&S needed to improve its cash flow and had already announced that it would be closing six of the Littlewoods stores. M&S also signed a number of sale and lease-back agreements relating to a significant proportion of its UK properties. In this way it could benefit from the immediate cash flow of selling the properties, in return for renting back the properties on an annual basis over subsequent years.

New equity finance

Cash may be raised from new investors through an issue of new equity, or from existing equity shareholders. A deep discount rights issue may be most appropriate for raising equity from existing shareholders (see Chapter 15). In this way, by offering shares to existing shareholders at such a huge discount on the current market price of its shares a company may be assured of raising the level of new finance it requires. The press extract below describes Morgan Crucible's plans to raise £50m from a one-for-four rights issue to provide the funds to cover most of the £70m cost of restructuring its business.

Morgan Crucible deep discount rights issue

'Crucible wants £54m for revamp', by Philip Aldrick

Engineer Morgan Crucible yesterday unveiled plans to raise £54m from shareholders to fund its restructuring as it posted deeper losses in the full-year results.

The company is launching a one-for-four rights issue at 100p a share, a 24.8pc discount to yesterday's closing price of 133p.

Chief executive Warren Knowlton plans to use the funds to cover much of the £70m cost of restructuring, which is expected to save between £35m and £50m annually from the end of 2006. The issue has been fully under-written by Cazenove, which will take a large share of the £4m advisers' fees.

Mr Knowlton said a rights issue had been preferred because he did not want 'to become reliant on the timing of the disposal programme [or] increase debt levels'.

At the year-end, Crucible had debt of £249m. It posted a £78m pre-tax loss against a £58.7m loss last time on sales 3pc lower at £850m.

For the underlying businesses, magnets for computer disk drives and medical implant ceramics, profits rose 26pc to £26.9m. The losses related to non-core businesses and asset write-downs.

Some manufacturing will be moved to eastern Europe and Asia and about 10pc of the 13,000 workforce will be made redundant.

© *Daily Telegraph*, 20 February 2004

An alternative to straight equity is a convertible debt, providing advantages with regard to the company's eps (earnings per share) and its cost of financing. Earnings per share are not immediately affected if such additional finance is provided, as there is no initial increase in the number of ordinary shares in issue. Since the cost of debt is generally lower than the cost of equity and has the benefit of the tax shield, then the cost of financing may also not be significantly increased, if at all. There is also the advantage of some downside risk protection for shareholders (if the share price should fall) and also an upside opportunity to make the risk worthwhile (if the share price should rise). In 2004 the hotel chain Accor restructured its business through an extension of its range of leisure products and casino interests, and its acquisition of 30% of the shares in the holiday village business Club Med. Accor issued a €280m convertible bond to pay for its 30% stake.

Debt restructure

A company's short-term survival may be aided if lenders can be convinced of the advantages of waiving interest payments or extending the term of a loan. Arrangements with creditors, for example the banks and other debt-holders, may be negotiated to restructure debt. This usually works only if the banks are owed significant sums by the company. It is sometimes said that 'If you owe the bank £1 million then you have a problem. If you owe the bank £1 billion then the bank has a problem'.

If a company is in financial difficulties, then to avoid the possible liquidation of the company, a debt-for-equity swap may be effected to release existing loans in exchange for an equity stake. If the debt-holders become shareholders then they may share in its recovery. If, on the other hand, the company's creditors force it to repay debt then the company may go bust. Therefore the creditors will lose out.

Debt renegotiation is always difficult because of the different interests of various stakeholders. Another disadvantage of a debt-for-equity swap is the dilution of existing shareholdings, which may result in a conflict between debt-holders and shareholders, as illustrated in the MyTravel press extract below. The company's existing bond-holders challenged in the High Court MyTravel's wish to action an £800m debt-for-equity swap without their consent. The financial reconstruction had been agreed by 98% of the shareholders. The bond-holders felt they were not getting a good deal, being offered 8% of the re-structured company. MyTravel threatened that the bond-holders would receive even less if they were forced to obtain permission through the court.

MyTravel bondholders challenge debt restructure

'MyTravel rescue faces new hurdle', by Alistair Osborne

MyTravel's attempt to force through a rescue restructuring faced another hurdle last night after the Court of Appeal ruled that the holiday company's bondholders could mount a fresh legal challenge.

The holders of £216m of subordinated convertible bonds will be allowed to put their case again at a High Court hearing on Monday that MyTravel has no right to implement a £800m debt-for-equity swap without their consent.

MyTravel initially offered its bondholders 8pc of the restructured company, with shareholders getting 4pc and the banks the rest.

However, when the bondholders opposed this, MyTravel said it would use a scheme of arrangement to force through the restructuring.

MyTravel added that it would cut the bondholders' stake to 4pc if it had to go to court to win permission for such a scheme and 2pc if it actually implemented it.

The bondholders include Fidelity, Société Générale, Lehman Brothers and New Star Asset Management.

MyTravel said that 97.8pc of shareholders and 99.9pc of creditors had voted in favour of the scheme, which it hoped to implement by the year end. MyTravel chief executive Peter McHugh will get a £2m bonus if the scheme goes through.

© *Daily Telegraph*, 14 December 2004

Progress check 18.1

What are the main financial strategies that may be adopted in response to internal restructuring issues?

Reorganisation – financial strategies in response to external issues

A company may be at a market value much lower than a fair value of its shares and therefore vulnerable to a possible takeover bid. To forestall an opportunistic takeover bid the company has a number of options:

- increase public relations activity to change market perception – the company may use public relations to explain its true value to shareholders and analysts
- demerger, or spin off some of the business units or divisions of the business, to demonstrate value
- go private – de-list the company from a public plc to a private Ltd company.

There are two meanings to the term 'going private':

- a sale by Government
- a re-privatisation.

Demergers

A company may have, in the past, diversified into areas where it had no real prospects of developing and so a successful core business may have developed into a larger group without providing any additional value. Both shareholders and analysts may find diversified groups very difficult to understand, which may lead to market under-pricing of the shares of such a group.

The splitting up of diversified groups, or conglomerates, may clarify individual investments. In general, the post-split sum of the market values of the separated companies is usually greater than the value of the whole group before the split.

Companies may be split in the following ways:

- demerger
- spin-off
- sale of a subsidiary.

A demerger is where one listed company becomes two or more listed companies, generally of equal size and initially with the same shareholders, although this is not always necessarily the case (see the press extract on the next page which reported GUS's planned demerger and sale of Burberry).

GUS sheds Burberry in demerger

'GUS prepares to ditch Burberry', by Mark Tran

The retail group GUS today set a date for selling the rest of its stake in the fashion house Burberry as it seeks to focus on its other businesses.

GUS will sever its links with Burberry on December 13 by distributing the remaining 65% stake in its luxury goods firm.

For every GUS share held, stockholders will receive Burberry and new GUS shares with the ratio being based on share prices at the time.

GUS said the demerger of Burberry will allow it to focus on Experian, its credit checking business and Argos retail, which includes Homebase, the DIY chain.

'The demerger of our remaining stake in Burberry is another major step in focusing GUS on fewer activities,' said Sir Victor Blank, the chairman of GUS. 'Distributing our stake to existing GUS shareholders will enable them to participate directly in the exciting growth opportunities we see at Burberry.'

GUS, which has been restructuring over the last few years, has steadily whittled down its businesses in the past year.

In May, the firm sold its remaining 50% stake in Lewis, raising £140m; in October, it agreed to dispose of Wehkamp, its Dutch home shopping business, for £265m.

Burberry was partially floated in 2002 and GUS's stake is worth about £1.2bn.

GUS unveiled details of its Burberry demerger as it reported pre-tax profits of £376m in the six months to September 30, a 7% drop from a year ago.

Profits fell in the half-year as Argos and Homebase suffered from weaker consumer spending, but both managed to gain market share and maintain or improve gross profit margins, the company said.

'Although profit at Argos has been impacted, as expected, by the tough UK retail environment, we have gained share and maintained or improved gross margin in the first half,' said John Peace, the chief executive of GUS.

Experian saw profits jump by a record £52m, or 36%, to £200m, while profits at Burberry were previously announced to be down 2%.

In the six months to September 30 2005, Burberry yesterday reported it made a pre-tax profit of £78.1m.

© *The Guardian*, 17 November 2005

A demerger may be contrasted with a spin-off, which is, for example, where a company divests itself of a division by distributing shares to its own shareholders usually in the form of a dividend. In a spin-off a subsidiary of a company may similarly be sold off in an IPO (initial public offering), or it may be actioned without any money changing hands (see the Weetabix press extract shown below).

Weetabix spins off

'Buy-out specialist spins off Weetabix', by Christopher Hope

The US buyout specialist Hicks, Muse, Tate & Furst yesterday formally spun off its European arm, owner of breakfast cereal maker Weetabix, as a separate stand-alone legal entity.

The move comes seven years after setting up in London. The new business, provisionally called Hicks Muse (Europe), is now controlled by three European partners, Lyndon Lea – who runs the operation – Neil Richardson and Robert Darment. They plan to drop the Hicks Muse name.

No money has changed hands in establishing the new entity, which concludes a process started last summer. Mr Lea said: 'It won't be that different – we have been a stand-alone business for quite a long time'.

He said all 11 dealmakers in the London office were taking equity in the new business.

© *Daily Telegraph*, 22 January 2005

The added value from the break-up of a company may be derived from:

- identification of the clearly defined segments of the business
- identification of the separate financial strategies of each business
- improved corporate governance
- better use of management incentives
- removal of the 'conglomerate discount', the reduced share price.

The size of a business is not necessarily a protection against takeover and the increasing power of corporate raiders. The current tendency is to reverse the trend of conglomeration. In this way, diversification strategies are reversed to concentrate on fewer core businesses.

As we have seen, demergers may be undertaken to improve the value attributed to the business by the financial markets. This was clearly illustrated by the break-up, or demerger, of British Telecom in 2001 into two separate businesses BT Group plc and mmO_2. BT Group plc retained the telecoms business and mmO_2 took up the wireless business. mmO_2 in particular has performed extremely successfully over the past couple of years.

Worked Example 18.3

A demerger relates to the division of a corporate entity into a number of independent corporate entities. Why would a company choose to demerge and what are the potential problems that may arise out of such a strategy?

The possible reasons for a company considering a demerger are that:

- specific parts of the business may represent a poor strategic fit
- one or more subsidiaries may no longer complement the business's core activities
- there may be unprofitable activities
- parts of the business may have high risk cash flows.

The potential problems that may arise from a demerger strategy are:

- economies of scale may be lost
- subsequent costs may be increased
- the company's asset backing may be reduced
- there may be a loss of operational synergies.

Privatisation – sale by Government

A public sector organisation (a nationalised industry) may be 'publicly' floated (in the private sector!). This is a sale by Government. We need to look at the reasons for such a privatisation and consider why and how the organisation came to be owned by the Government in the first place.

Some businesses may have been acquired initially by Government by historical accident or because they were in financial distress and then ended up being rescued and owned by Government. Subsequently, these businesses may then be returned to the private sector without subsequent controls, which it is argued that existing competition should provide. This argument says that controls may be exercised through the market. We have seen many examples like the rail network, the communications industry, and the motor industry, which may prompt us to question the effectiveness of market-driven controls.

Some businesses are effectively 'owned' by the UK Government, because of social policies or because of their strategic importance. Examples were the utilities and defence industries in the UK. A subsequent return to private ownership may require external regulation. An example of the type of control that may be put in place is a restriction to prevent foreign ownership of shares in the business of a defence contractor.

Privatisation through sale by Government may run the risk of abuse of monopoly power by new owners. Privatisation of a major utility creates a natural monopoly, the abuse of which may be a great economic threat.

The removal or control of monopoly power may be achieved through:

- competition, which is difficult to achieve and may prove very expensive

- the subsequent introduction of regulatory controls.

We may question whether the introduction of competition post privatisation really does provide the removal, or adequate control over, the abuse of monopoly power.

Privatisation – return to private ownership

A publicly quoted company (plc) may be returned to private ownership, which is called re-privatisation. A company may feel that plc status may no longer be appropriate and may wish to revert to a more restricted and closely held ownership. We have already discussed an example of this in Richard Branson's Virgin Group. Subsequently, however, Branson appeared to change his strategy by offering parts of his business back to the public as separate entities.

The reasons for re-privatisation are usually linked to the company's original reasons for 'going public' and its position in its life cycle when this occurred. The original flotation may have been a cash-in or a cash-out flotation. A cash-in flotation is used to raise funds for the continued expansion of the company. A cash-out flotation is used to obtain an exit route for existing shareholders rather than to raise any new money. An example is the exit of venture capitalists from a growth company.

A company that floated in its mature, cash positive stage should not want to re-privatise. If a mature company does want to re-privatise, it may be relatively easy to re-finance due to its strong cash position, the most common method being a management buy-out (MBO).

A reversal is more likely if the company was floated in its growth stage, when most of the initial financing was injected into the company. Then, as the company matured, cash flow would have become increasingly positive and so it would not have needed to raise additional funds. The main advantage that the shareholders of such a company would have from being public is the marketability of their shares. However, if shareholders still have high growth expectations, which the company may not be able to deliver, then the company may consider a reversal to private status.

Investors in a company that floated in its growth stage may no longer anticipate significant capital growth and the main advantage of plc status, the marketability of their shares, may not still apply. If only a small proportion of shares are publicly owned, a leveraged buyout may be used. This means that the existing equity shareholders, who own a very large majority of the shares may obtain a relatively small loan to finance the purchase of the small number of shares that are in public hands. There is not a huge number of examples of this strategy; a company called Caparo Engineering employed this technique in 1991.

A company that floated on very high growth expectations (perhaps resulting from a break-down of communications between the company and its investors), which it failed to deliver, may reverse its plc status as a part of a strategic repositioning. An example is where Andrew Lloyd Webber bought back his public Really Useful Group because of the pressure of other shareholders who required him to continually produce hit musicals.

A low share price and possibly insignificant dividends may lead to acceptance of any reasonable re-privatisation offer. Shareholders may be anxious to realise a realistic return on their investment. A change of management team and development of new strategies may also be necessary to avoid selling out at a heavily discounted share price. This strategy is called a management buy-in (MBI). An MBI is the same as an MBO except that the management team is a group of managers that is brought in from outside rather than from within the business.

Progress check 18.2

What are the main financial strategies that may be adopted in response to external restructuring issues?

Management buy-outs (MBOs)

A management buy-out (MBO) is the purchase of a business from its existing owners by members of the existing management team, generally in association with a financial institution, for example a merchant bank or a venture capitalist. The management team may buy a part of a group, a division, or a subsidiary, or sometimes the whole group.

If a large proportion of the new finance, required to buy the business, is raised by external borrowing then the 'buy-out' is described as a leveraged MBO. If the debt financing is greater than the equity then the MBO is said to be highly leveraged (or highly geared).

The impetus for an MBO

Where does the impetus for an MBO come from? Well, this may be seen from looking at:

■ the reasons why a holding company may favour a buy-out

■ the reasons why management may favour a buy-out.

A holding company may favour an MBO for a number of reasons:

■ to regain focus through disposal of a non-core business, because part of the business may have become non-core (for example the Chrysalis Group – see Worked Example 18.4)

- to release funds to support the rest of the group – the release of capital may be for potentially more profitable investments
- to pass on a family business following retirement of the owners.

Worked Example 18.4

LBC and Heart 106.2FM were London radio stations owned by the Chrysalis Group. In 2005 the group was in talks to sell off its books division in a £12.5m management buy-out. Chrysalis said that the business had reported 'extremely disappointing' full-year results and its write-downs related to the sale of the company to its management would create a significant exceptional loss. The chief executive of Chrysalis, Richard Huntingford, said the MBO deal would allow the group to start its new financial year in 'the right strategic shape', and referring to the books division he said 'it closes a chapter and one that has not been a happy experience for us'.

Management may favour a buy-out for a number of different reasons:

- to run the business autonomously without head office interference – ambitious management may see the potential for high growth
- fear that their division will be closed or outsourced, and so they will want to protect their jobs which may, for example, be threatened by outsourcing
- to run their own business rather than work for a new owner, therefore seeking independence and possible greater job security.

Whether the MBO is driven by the management or the owners of the business will influence the early stages of development of an MBO. The particular reason will be an important influence on the attitudes of potential financiers and other stakeholders.

If the owners of a business have indicated their approval for an MBO then the management team will be able to pursue this in their own way, without interference, and approach alternative providers of finance and funding. This is the simplest situation since there is no conflict if the shareholders have accepted in principle.

If it is the directors of the company that show initial interest in an MBO then their fiduciary duty may initially be questioned. Management should, by definition, be acting in the best interests of the shareholders. Management's interest in an MBO brings into question whose interests they are pursuing and is a further example of the agency problem.

An MBO may or may not be in the best interests of the shareholders. It may provide value for shareholders. It may be perceived as not providing value for shareholders, and therefore shareholders may strongly object to an MBO (see the Thorntons press extract on the next page). Management may therefore need to consider the feasibility of an MBO, before they approach the owners. This is a good approach because if the MBO is not feasible then the management team can drop the idea, and no-one is any the wiser. If the management team approaches the owners and then fail to obtain the necessary financing they will find themselves in a very weak position. If the MBO is feasible they may then seek to obtain the necessary funding and then approach the owners of the business in a much stronger position. It is a good idea to first see how the company feels about an MBO, but there may possibly be legal problems regarding disclosure of information.

Thorntons oppose chocolate buy-out

'Thorntons buyout under fire', by Jill Treanor

Plans for a management buy-out at Thorntons are being opposed by one of the chocolate firm's largest shareholders.

The Derbyshire-based company announced in mid-August that its executive chairman, Christopher Burnett, was considering making an offer at 185p. That values the group, still 24%-owned by the founding family, at just over £120m. However, Roger Morton, trustee of the Joseph Rowntree Charitable Trust, which owns 6% of the shares, believes the price is too low. 'I'm clear that these financial terms are seriously inadequate,' he said.

Mr Morton also opposed a possible takeover of Thorntons almost two years ago when the rumoured price was about 180p a share. He said that while the latest offer was only 5p more, the overall market had moved up 20% in the interim.

'It's a pity the company is being somewhat unsettled by another approach of this sort,' Mr Morton said.

The bid by the executive chairman is being evaluated by non-executive directors led by John Jackson. He was involved in rejecting the previous bids and is still being advised by Rothschild, the investment bank. The City believes Thorntons is trying to flush out trade buyers for the business.

The announcement of a possible buyout followed news from bookshop Ottakar's that its management was also considering a buy-out. While HMV, owner of Waterstone's, has admitted it might make a bid, Ottakar's revealed last week that its board had approved the buy-out plan.

John Thornton, former chairman of Thorntons, was the non-executive at Ottakar's who led the independent committee considering the bid. He is still on the chocolate firm's board.

© *The Guardian*, 30 August 2005

Alternatively, the management team may approach the owners before considering the MBO deal at all. This is the 'above the board' approach. The management team continue to respect their fiduciary duties by talking to owners before determining whether a deal can be done or not. However, if the owners of the business baulk at the idea then the management team could lose their jobs since they have no fall-back position.

Regardless of where the impetus for the buy-out originates, the management team need to approach the providers of finance, which may be venture capitalists (VCs), and consider the choice of debt or equity financing. Different financial providers may only get involved with deals up to a particular level, or only within particular industries. The management team also need to approach and engage professional advisers, such as lawyers, accountants, and bankers. Since the management team is likely to lack experience in all these areas, particularly in managing the MBO project itself, and the various options with regard to financing, they must also appoint an MBO project manager.

Worked Example 18.5

Management buy-outs have become increasingly popular over recent years. Which factors dictate whether the management buy-out will be successful?

Management buy-outs often occur as part of a corporate disinvestment strategy. The reasons for the disinvestment, together with the nature of the assets and liabilities of the business being divested, must be fully explored and understood by the buy-out team. The success of an MBO depends primarily on the skills of the management team and the price being paid for the MBO.

The stages of an MBO deal

Support for the deal must be secured before the MBO takes place, and the tax and legal implications must be fully considered. A fair price must be negotiated and agreed for the MBO, and a potential problem may be inadequate financing and asset backing. Following the MBO there may possibly be a loss of some employees if the business plans to relocate to another area. The maintenance of employee rights must be ensured for those employees that are retained.

Venture capitalists are the usual source of MBO funding, and normally provide a standard list of the stages of such a deal. The stages of a typical MBO deal are illustrated in Fig. 18.3.

Due diligence is undertaken by the venture capitalists on both the company and the management team through references obtained from individuals, banks, professional references, trade references, and other sources. It is necessary to determine whether the management team is capable of seeing the MBO deal through and running the business. An assessment must be made to ascertain whether the management team has any serious flaws, and normally appraisals are carried out to determine whether there is one or more of the management team that may need to be replaced.

The management team may also carry out due diligence on the venture capitalists (or any other providers of capital) to confirm that they are good, supportive, and trustworthy investors. It is important that VCs are hands-on and likeable, and able to get on well with the management team.

The structuring of an MBO requires a balancing of the needs of each of the parties by resolving the issues of:

- the requirements of each of the parties
- the amount that the business can afford to pay for the buy-out
- funding requirements.

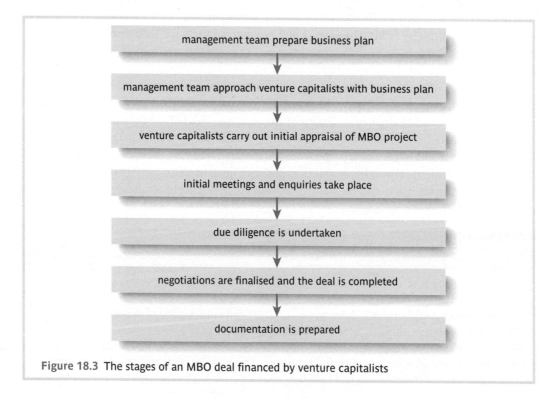

Figure 18.3 The stages of an MBO deal financed by venture capitalists

Each of the parties involved in an MBO will have different requirements. Lenders are generally looking for low risk investments, and require downside risk protection from, for example, covenants and security (leverage). Each of the members of the management team are usually motivated by wanting to be their own boss and the expectation of job security. They want to get a share in the equity of the business, and to get rich. Venture capitalists want a high return on equity, and a planned exit route out of the company, usually within a few years.

An MBO will have an impact on the cash flow of the business with regard to its being able to provide a return to both lenders and investors. Therefore, the amount that the management team can afford to pay for the business needs to be considered in terms of forecast profit levels, and its proposed levels of funding by debt and equity, and levels of interest cover and cash flow cover required (see Worked Example 18.5).

Worked Example 18.6

Jetrac Ltd is a well-established private company. The owners of the company are considering disposing of all their business interests, and have asked the senior management group of the company if they would be interested in buying the company. The owners of the company have suggested a market value of the company of £75m. The earnings of Jetrac Ltd for the year ending 31 March 2006 were £4m after interest and tax and dividends were £2.5m. Earnings and dividends are expected to grow at 4% per annum for the foreseeable future. We may assume that investments in similar companies to Jetrac Ltd currently achieve a return of 8%.

We are required to calculate what may be considered to be a fair value of the share capital of the company.

A fair value of the company may be calculated as follows:

$$\frac{\text{retained earnings} \times \text{annual growth rate}}{\text{expected return} - \text{annual growth rate}} = \frac{£2.5m \times 1.04}{(0.08 - 0.04)} = £65m$$

The company owners appear to be over-pricing the company by £10m.

Funding requirements must be considered to cover the purchase price that has been negotiated, the costs of further development of the business, and of course the professional fees, which are not insignificant. Professional fees usually amount to about 5% of the total deal.

The three issues considered above are really the constraints in considering determination of:

- the total funding is needed
- how much funding should be debt
- how much funding should be provided by the management team?

Funding needs to be determined with regard to how much is needed for the deal itself plus the professional fees, and also for working capital requirements. While debt is generally at a lower cost than equity, the level of gearing will affect the return on equity. Also, debt usually requires security and so debt levels are dependent on the asset backing that the business is able to provide and the quality and levels of cash flows the business can generate.

In addition to external funding for an MBO, the level of finance provided by the management team is also important. How much funding should the management team provide? In an MBO, each manager generally puts in the equivalent of one year's salary and maybe more. The MBO team needs to decide upon how much the relative ownership proportions should be. They also need to specify the level of returns they require and determine a dividend policy for the business.

Documentation for the MBO deal necessarily includes all sale and purchase agreements, loan agreements, covenants, new articles and memorandum of association for the new company, employment contracts, key employee insurance, etc.

Worked Example 18.7

The management of a plc are interested in making an offer to its shareholders for an MBO.

Assuming that the shareholders' approval to pursue the MBO in principle has been provided, we will consider some of the factors that the management team may need to consider.

Typically, the management team will agree as to who will become the managing director. The team will appoint a firm of financial consultants and together they will assess the viability and suitability of the buy-out. The consultants assist in the formulation of a business plan and an evaluation of the seller's asking price, and negotiation of the purchase of the business. The management team also needs to appoint legal consultants and select a firm of auditors, and ensure that due diligence tests are implemented.

If equity is required to fund the MBO then equity advisers must be selected and written offers obtained, followed by the selection of a lead investor and negotiation of the best equity deal. After all necessary debt, equity, and other finance has been secured then all necessary legal documents are prepared and legal ownership is passed to the management team.

Worked Examples 18.8, 18.9, and 18.10 illustrate how an MBO may be funded and the type of returns that may be expected by each of the parties involved in the deal.

Worked Example 18.8

During 2006 a large UK plc, the Nikos Group, agreed an MBO by the directors of one of its subsidiaries, Chance Ltd. To finance the MBO deal, the directors of Chance have established a relationship with the ITCD bank and engaged venture capitalists Siluc.

Chance's directors have agreed to buy the company for £18m and require a further £4m for working capital requirements and to cover the costs of the MBO. Between them the directors were able to invest a maximum of £500,000 in the MBO. They expected that the company's performance would immediately be greatly improved during the first year following the buy-out and they forecast an operating profit of £2.6m for the year ended 31 December 2007.

The ITCD bank agreed to provide loan capital at 6.5% per annum, but with two important conditions:

- Interest cover during the first year must be maintained at a minimum of 4 times.
- Gearing must not be greater than 45% of total funding.

To assist during the planning and roll-out of the MBO, Siluc and the directors of Chance employed a financial adviser specialising in MBOs, whose first task was to recommend an appropriate financial structure.

The limit of the funding by the ITCD bank first needed to be established:

Expected operating profit for 2007	= £2.6m
Interest cover	= 4 times
therefore the maximum interest at 6.5% per annum	= £650,000
which meant a potential maximum loan of	£10m

However, the total funding requirement was £22m, to cover the purchase of the company including costs and working capital requirement. ITCD imposed the condition that the loan may not exceed 45% of the total funding.

45% of the total funding of £22m = £9.9m

Therefore, the maximum bank loan must be restricted to £9.9m even though £10m appeared possible based on the interest cover restriction.

Since the maximum bank loan was £9.9m, then the balance of funding required of £12.1m must be provided by the directors of Chance Ltd and Siluc, the venture capitalists, as follows:

Chance Ltd directors =	£500,000	(4.1%)
Siluc	= £11,600,000	(95.9%)
Total	£12,100,000	(100.0%)

When the total funding requirements have been agreed, together with the level of debt and the contribution of the management team, then the balance required from venture capitalists can be assessed. The VC contribution may be in the form of ordinary shares, preference shares, or debt.

Worked Example 18.9

Using the information from Worked Example 18.8, we will consider the next issue that the financial adviser needed to address with Siluc and the directors, which was the terms of their investment in the MBO.

The directors indicated that they would feel disadvantaged and demotivated if they received only 4.1% of the ordinary share capital of the new business, compared to Siluc's 95.9%. They were expecting over 20% of the business.

The financial adviser suggested that this problem may be overcome by using preference gearing, where Siluc's investment would be partly in ordinary shares and partly in preference shares. He suggested £10m preference shares with a fixed dividend of 5% per annum.

The investments by Siluc and the directors of Chance would therefore be:

	Ordinary £1 shares	Preference £1 shares	Total
Chance Ltd directors	£0.5m (23.8%)	–	£0.5m
Siluc	£1.6m (76.2%)	£10.0m	£11.6m
	£2.1m (100.0%)	£10.0m	£12.1m

The decision about how much capital goes into ordinary shares and how much into preference shares is crucial in structuring the financing of an MBO. Preferential gearing is a method devised to give the management team proportionately more of the equity than their monetary contribution alone would deserve.

A convertible redeemable preference share is a particularly suitable financial instrument for MBOs. These are preference shares that are convertible into ordinary shares at a later date.

The terms of conversion into ordinary shares may be established so that preference shares can possibly start converting in three to five years, after it has been confirmed that a degree of success of the MBO has been achieved. This gives time for the MBO to establish itself.

Preferential gearing is used to motivate management with the option to enlarge its participation if the MBO is successful through greater equity participation.

Worked Example 18.10

Using the information from Worked Examples 18.8 and 18.9, we will consider the subsequent growth and future of the MBO. During the three years since the MBO the business was transformed and improved so that profit forecasts were exceeded and £7.1m of the original loan had been repaid. If we assume that three years after a successful MBO the Chance Ltd directors and Siluc, the venture capitalists, decide that they wish to sell the business, we may consider what sort of returns each may expect. The company still had growth potential and a prospective buyer had offered £27.5m for the business including taking over its remaining debt of £2.8m.

	MBO	Sale of business
Total funding of MBO	£22.0m	
Sale of business		£27.5m
less: Bank loan	£(9.9)m	£(2.8)m
	£12.1m	£24.7m
less: Preference share capital	£(10.0)m	£(10.0)m
Equity capital	£2.1m	£14.7m
Split of equity capital:		
Chance directors (23.8%)	£0.5m	£3.5m
Siluc (76.2%)	£1.6m	£11.2m
Total equity capital	£2.1m	£14.7m

The directors of Chance Ltd can be seen to have increased their initial investment of £0.5m by seven times to £3.5m over three years.

The venture capitalists made an initial investment of £11.6m (£1.6m being ordinary shares) and received dividends on their preference shares for three years at 5% on £10m, which at £0.5m per year is a total of £1.5m. Siluc's cash flows over three years may be summarised as follows:

Year	Cash flow £m	
0	(11.6)	initial capital investment
1	0.5	preference dividend
2	0.5	preference dividend
3	0.5	preference dividend
4	22.2	repayment of capital [£10.0m preference shares + £11.2m equity]

which in discounted cash flow terms represents a pre-tax internal rate of return of 27.5%.

Progress check 18.3

What is a management buy-out (MBO)?

Management buy-ins (MBIs)

A management buy-in (MBI) occurs when a group of experienced managers from outside the company, with a good track record, are brought into the company to run it. A buy-in may occur when a business runs into trouble and a group of outside managers sees an opportunity to take over the business and restore its profitability. An example of this was Gary Lineker's association with Leicester City football club in 2002. Adrian Wright's £30m bid for Moss Brothers is another example (see the press extract below).

A new look for Moss Bros following buy-in
'Former managers buy control of Moss Bros', by Simon Bowers

Adrian Wright, the former chief executive of Moss Bros, has led a £30m management buy-in to secure control of the company behind the Suits You, Racing Green, Young's Hire and Chester Barrie brands.

He is backed by private equity house Gresham. Speciality Retail Group has 80 stores – 68 of which trade under the Suits You name –

and for the year to January achieved sales of £74m.

Mr Wright plans 35 new stores over three years, most of which are likely to join the Racing Green chain. The vendors were managing director Brian Brick and his brother Alex.

© *The Guardian*, 28 November 2005

Progress check 18.4

What is a management buy-in (MBI)?

Problems with MBOs and MBIs

MBO and MBI financing is normally by debt and equity with high risk and an expectation of high returns. We have already seen the importance of assessing the correct proportion of debt and equity, and the proportions held by management and outside investors. The deal may be structured using, for example, founder shares so that managers take the risks but can gain effective control and become fully committed to the project.

Managers may not accept the board representation requirement that external financiers will insist upon. Alternatively, board representation by venture capitalists may demonstrate their commitment and a hands-on approach.

When an MBO takes place, there may be inadequate financing for new investment. This may be due to a lack of good advice leading to the lack of a realistic plan at the outset, which then results in a lack of funding. There may be difficulties in achieving a fair buy-out price. We saw this from looking generally at the variety of methods used in valuation of businesses in Chapter 16.

It should be noted that both MBOs and MBIs may result in tax and legal complications for the company and the management team. Managers who are involved in an MBO or MBI may have little accounting or financial management experience. Therefore, there may be a need to recruit a qualified accountant, which could significantly increase the costs of the MBO or MBI. The maintenance of the pension rights of previous employees may also result in high costs following the establishment of the MBO or MBI.

Following an MBO or MBI, employees may be unwilling to move geographically, or accept changes to work practices, remuneration, or other conditions. This, together with most of the other difficulties and problems, are really to do with the successful management of a large project and obtaining good advice regarding appropriate financing.

Summary of key points

- There is a number of reasons why companies may require reorganisation and restructuring, which may relate in particular to their levels of gearing and the market's perception of their share price.
- Company reorganisations may take place supported by a range of financial strategies.
- Changes to financial strategies may be introduced in response to issues both internal and external to a company that may necessitate its restructuring.
- Privatisation as a means of company restructuring may relate to a sale by Government to the public, for example UK utility businesses, or it may relate to the return of a company to private ownership (to Ltd from plc status).
- Management buy-outs (MBOs) and management buy-ins (MBIs) are two further methods that may be used to restructure and refinance companies.
- There are many advantages to be gained but also many problems that may result from the establishment of MBOs and MBIs.

🔑 Glossary of key terms

demerger A demerger is the separation of a company into several separate parts, particularly where the company may have grown by acquisition.

leveraged MBO A management buy-out (MBO) in which a large proportion of the new finance required is raised by external borrowing, and if the debt financing is greater than the equity financing then the MBO is said to be highly leveraged (or highly geared).

management buy-in (MBI) If there are insufficient skills and expertise within the management team, the business may be purchased from its existing owners by the members of an external management team, generally in association with a financing institution. As with an MBO, where a large proportion of the new finance required to purchase the business is raised by external borrowing, the buy-out is described as leveraged.

privatisation In the UK privatisation is the process of selling a nationalised industry to private owners (e.g. the general public).

re-privatisation The process of selling a publicly quoted company (plc), to private owners. The company may feel that plc status may no longer be appropriate and may wish to return to a more restricted and closely held ownership.

spin-off A company reorganisation in which a division or a subsidiary of the company becomes a separate and independent legal entity.

Questions

Q18.1 Outline the reasons why a company may consider reorganisation or restructuring.

Q18.2 How may debt restructuring be used as a financial strategy in response to an internal issue faced by a company?

Q18.3 Explain the differences between a spin-off and a demerger, and why a large group of companies may prefer one strategy to the other.

Q18.4 Outline the process followed in the privatisation of utilities in the UK.

Q18.5 Explain the goals of a typical management buy-out (MBO), and describe the business and financial strategies that may be used to achieve these goals.

Q18.6 Explain why a plc may wish to return to private ownership and become a Ltd company.

Q18.7 What are the advantages and disadvantages of the various ways in which an MBO may be financed?

Q18.8 Why may an MBO be popular with the managers of a business?

Discussion points

D18.1 'The financial restructuring of a company is really only a means of delaying the inevitable death of a business.' Discuss.

D18.2 Discuss and critically examine the procedure followed in the privatisation of a public company with which you are familiar.

D18.3 'MBOs generally meet the selfish aspirations of a handful of ambitious managers, whereas MBIs may provide a more professional and experienced approach to taking a business forward.' Discuss.

Exercises

Solutions are provided in Appendix 2 to all exercise numbers highlighted in colour.

Level I

E18.1 *Time allowed – 45 minutes*

Outline the internal issues relating to why companies may need to be restructured and how such reorganisations may be undertaken.

E18.2 *Time allowed – 45 minutes*

Explain the external strategic financial issues that may be faced by a business and the reorganisation strategies that may be used in response to these.

E18.3 *Time allowed – 45 minutes*

One of the meanings of 'privatisation' is the return of a public limited company (plc) to private ownership (Ltd). Explain why MBOs and MBIs are often used for such a 're-privatisation' and outline some of the problems that may be encountered.

E18.4 *Time allowed – 45 minutes*

Explain what is meant by a demerger and why a business may consider this strategy. How may value be added to a business as a result of a demerger?

▶

▶ *Level II*

E18.5 *Time allowed – 45 minutes*

What is a leveraged MBO and how is it implemented? What are the advantages to a venture capitalist and to the management team from using debt or preference shares to finance an MBO.

E18.6 *Time allowed – 45 minutes*

Explain some of the problems that might arise in an MBO or an MBI deal and provide some recommended courses of action that may eliminate or minimise the impact of such problems.

E18.7 *Time allowed – 60 minutes*

Pomfrit Ltd is a family-owned business and has an issued share capital of 1,500,000 ordinary shares. The shareholders have recently expressed their wish to sell all their shares in the company. As a result at a recent management meeting the company's managers decided to propose a management buy-out.

The earnings of the company over the next financial year are expected to be about £10m, and dividends are expected to be limited to £4m.

During the next financial year the company was intending to invest £12m in new capital projects. These were planned to be funded as follows:

- retained earnings £6m
- new share issue £6m.

Over the next three years the management of the company were expecting to limit dividends to 25% of earnings. No further new issues of capital were planned and it was expected that all investments after the next year would be financed from retained earnings.

While the expected rate of return from shares with similar risk is about 10%, the management of Pomfrit Ltd anticipate that an average rate of return of 15% on the planned new investments can be achieved in the first three years, although from year 4 onwards the return is expected to be 10% per annum. In addition, from year 4 onwards the management of the company expect to be able to establish and maintain a dividend payout ratio of 50%.

Required:

Calculate what you would consider to be an appropriate market price for Pomfrit Ltd's shares. You may ignore any impact of taxation.

E18.8 *Time allowed – 60 minutes*

Gillie plc is a UK-based manufacturing company. The company is currently financed by £1 ordinary share capital and irredeemable debentures. The debentures carry a nominal rate of 10%, and have a current market value at par. The company has paid an annual dividend of 40p per share in the past and is expected to continue to do so in the foreseeable future. The market value per share is £2 *ex dividend*.

The total market value of the company's equity is £6,000,000 and the market value of the debentures is £2,000,000.

The company is considering a major reorganisation of the company's operations infrastructure. The proposed reorganisation will cost the company £2,000,000, and is expected to return annual net cash flows of £525,000 (before interest) in perpetuity.

The company proposes to finance the reorganisation project with a new issue of 10% debentures at par. The rights of the existing debenture holders will be protected, so it is expected that the cost of existing debt will be unchanged and its market value will remain the same.

The higher gearing is expected to increase the financial risk for the shareholders. Assuming that the reorganisation proceeds and is financed by debt, the cost of equity is expected to increase by 5%.

Required:

Advise Gillie plc on whether they should undertake the reorganisation, and calculate by how much the choice in the method of financing affects the decision. You may ignore taxation and assume that all earnings before interest will be paid out as dividends in the year they are received.

Case Study VI: **Chamberlain plc**

Chamberlain plc is an electrical goods manufacturing company, and its shares are quoted on the London Stock Exchange. Its balance sheet as at 30 September 2007 is shown below:

Balance sheet as at 30 September 2007

	£m	£m
Non-current assets		350
Current assets		
Stocks	75	
Trade debtors	175	
Other debtors	50	
Cash at bank and in hand	200	
	500	
Current liabilities		
Trade creditors	150	
Other creditors	75	
	225	
Net current assets		275
		625
Non-current liabilities		
8% loan		(125)
		500
Capital and reserves		
Ordinary shares (£1)		50
Retained earnings		450
		500

The company is currently examining its future strategy by carrying out a strategic review of the business and considering diversification through acquisition. The board of directors of Chamberlain is looking at three possible takeover target companies:

- C-Price plc owns a number of electrical retail outlets throughout the UK and sells cut-price TVs, VCR, and DVD players to the general public. Chamberlain plc have sought the company's view regarding an offer and the indication is that they will sell at the right price. Chamberlain believes it may gain through re-branding C-Prices' products with its own brands.

- Packitin plc is a packaging company. If Chamberlain plc were to make a takeover bid, such a bid may be regarded as hostile by Packitin.

- Homefit Ltd is a mature unquoted company involved in manufacture and retail. It owns a number of well-established high street shops, and a factory in the Midlands area of the UK. It is a very mature family business. The major shareholder is due to retire soon and he has already discussed a possible sale of the business with Chamberlain's directors.

The following table includes publicly available information about Chamberlain and the three targeted takeover companies. A forecast growth rate is shown for each company and it is assumed that each company continues to operate independently and that dividend policies, capital structure, and risk characteristics will remain unchanged.

Financial information and forecast growth rates based on publicly available data

	Chamberlain	C-Price	Packitin	Homefit
Issued ordinary shares (m)	50	25	30	1.25
eps (pence)	100	70	32	155
Dividend per share (pence)	30	50	30	110
Share price (£)	17.50	7.00	6.25	n/a
Net assets book value (£m)	625	150	72.5	15
Cost of equity (%)	11	10	13	10.5
Forecast annual growth (%)	10	4	15	8

Chamberlain's accountants have produced the NPVs of the expected future post-acquisition cash flows of Chamberlain for each of the three acquisition options:

Chamberlain plus C-Price: £1,375m
Chamberlain plus Packitin: £1,146m
Chamberlain plus Homefit: £971m.

Required:

(i) Value each takeover option using four different methods and compare them.

(ii) Advise Chamberlain plc's board of directors as to what may be suitable cash offers for each company.

(iii) Explain some of the other factors, especially the non-financial factors, which should be considered by companies in general with regard to mergers and acquisitions, and particularly with regard to Chamberlain.

Appendix 1

Present value tables

Present value of £1

The table shows the value of £1 to be received or paid, using a range of interest rates (r) after a given number of years (n). The values are based on the formula $V_n r = (1 + r)^{-n}$

Rate r % After n years	1	2	3	4	5	6	7	8	9	10	11	12
1	0.99	0.98	0.97	0.96	0.95	0.94	0.93	0.93	0.92	0.91	0.90	0.89
2	0.98	0.96	0.94	0.92	0.91	0.89	0.87	0.86	0.84	0.83	0.81	0.80
3	0.97	0.94	0.92	0.89	0.86	0.84	0.82	0.79	0.77	0.75	0.73	0.71
4	0.96	0.92	0.89	0.85	0.82	0.79	0.76	0.74	0.71	0.68	0.66	0.64
5	0.95	0.91	0.86	0.82	0.78	0.75	0.71	0.68	0.65	0.62	0.59	0.57
6	0.94	0.89	0.84	0.79	0.75	0.70	0.67	0.63	0.60	0.56	0.53	0.51
7	0.93	0.87	0.81	0.76	0.71	0.67	0.62	0.58	0.55	0.51	0.48	0.45
8	0.92	0.85	0.79	0.73	0.68	0.63	0.58	0.54	0.50	0.47	0.43	0.40
9	0.91	0.84	0.77	0.70	0.64	0.59	0.54	0.50	0.46	0.42	0.39	0.36
10	0.91	0.82	0.74	0.68	0.61	0.56	0.51	0.46	0.42	0.39	0.35	0.32
11	0.90	0.80	0.72	0.65	0.58	0.53	0.48	0.43	0.39	0.35	0.32	0.29
12	0.89	0.79	0.70	0.62	0.56	0.50	0.44	0.40	0.36	0.32	0.29	0.26
13	0.88	0.77	0.68	0.60	0.53	0.47	0.41	0.37	0.33	0.29	0.26	0.23
14	0.87	0.76	0.66	0.58	0.51	0.44	0.39	0.34	0.30	0.26	0.23	0.20
15	0.86	0.74	0.64	0.56	0.48	0.42	0.36	0.32	0.27	0.24	0.21	0.18

Rate r % After n years	13	14	15	16	17	18	19	20	30	40	50
1	0.88	0.88	0.87	0.86	0.85	0.85	0.84	0.83	0.77	0.71	0.67
2	0.78	0.77	0.76	0.74	0.73	0.72	0.71	0.69	0.59	0.51	0.44
3	0.69	0.67	0.66	0.64	0.62	0.61	0.59	0.58	0.46	0.36	0.30
4	0.61	0.59	0.57	0.55	0.53	0.52	0.50	0.48	0.35	0.26	0.20
5	0.54	0.52	0.50	0.48	0.46	0.44	0.42	0.40	0.27	0.19	0.13
6	0.48	0.46	0.43	0.41	0.39	0.37	0.35	0.33	0.21	0.13	0.09
7	0.43	0.40	0.38	0.35	0.33	0.31	0.30	0.28	0.16	0.09	0.06
8	0.38	0.35	0.33	0.31	0.28	0.27	0.25	0.23	0.12	0.07	0.04
9	0.33	0.31	0.28	0.26	0.24	0.23	0.21	0.19	0.09	0.05	0.03
10	0.29	0.27	0.25	0.23	0.21	0.19	0.18	0.16	0.07	0.03	0.02
11	0.26	0.24	0.21	0.20	0.18	0.16	0.15	0.13	0.06	0.02	0.01
12	0.23	0.21	0.19	0.17	0.15	0.14	0.12	0.11	0.04	0.02	0.008
13	0.20	0.18	0.16	0.15	0.13	0.12	0.10	0.09	0.03	0.013	0.005
14	0.18	0.16	0.14	0.13	0.11	0.10	0.09	0.08	0.03	0.009	0.003
15	0.16	0.14	0.12	0.11	0.09	0.08	0.07	0.06	0.02	0.006	0.002

Cumulative present value of £1

The table shows the present value of £1 per annum, using a range of interest rates (r), receivable or payable at the end of each year for n years.

Rate r % After n years	1	2	3	4	5	6	7	8	9	10	11	12
1	0.99	0.98	0.97	0.96	0.95	0.94	0.94	0.93	0.92	0.91	0.90	0.89
2	1.97	1.94	1.91	1.89	1.86	1.83	1.81	1.78	1.76	1.74	1.71	1.69
3	2.94	2.88	2.83	2.78	2.72	2.67	2.62	2.58	2.53	2.49	2.44	2.40
4	3.90	3.81	3.72	3.63	3.55	3.47	3.39	3.31	3.24	3.17	3.10	3.04
5	4.85	4.71	4.58	4.45	4.33	4.21	4.10	3.99	3.89	3.79	3.70	3.61
6	5.80	5.60	5.42	5.24	5.08	4.92	4.77	4.62	4.49	4.36	4.23	4.11
7	6.73	6.47	6.23	6.00	5.79	5.58	5.39	5.21	5.03	4.87	4.71	4.56
8	7.65	7.33	7.02	6.73	6.46	6.21	5.97	5.75	5.54	5.34	5.15	4.97
9	8.57	8.16	7.79	7.44	7.11	6.80	6.52	6.25	6.00	5.76	5.54	5.33
10	9.47	8.98	8.53	8.11	7.72	7.36	7.02	6.71	6.42	6.15	5.89	5.65
11	10.37	9.79	9.25	8.76	8.31	7.89	7.50	7.14	6.81	6.50	6.21	5.94
12	11.26	10.58	9.95	9.39	8.86	8.38	7.94	7.54	7.16	6.81	6.49	6.19
13	12.13	11.35	10.64	9.99	9.39	8.85	8.36	7.90	7.49	7.10	6.80	6.42
14	13.00	12.11	11.30	10.56	9.90	9.30	8.75	8.24	7.79	7.37	6.98	6.63
15	13.87	12.85	11.94	11.12	10.38	9.71	9.11	8.56	8.06	7.61	7.19	6.81

Rate r % After n years	13	14	15	16	17	18	19	20	30	40	50
1	0.89	0.88	0.87	0.86	0.85	0.85	0.84	0.83	0.77	0.71	0.67
2	1.67	1.65	1.63	1.61	1.59	1.57	1.55	1.53	1.36	1.22	1.11
3	2.36	2.32	2.28	2.25	2.21	2.17	2.14	2.11	1.81	1.59	1.41
4	2.97	2.91	2.86	2.80	2.74	2.69	2.64	2.59	2.17	1.85	1.61
5	3.52	3.43	3.35	3.27	3.20	3.13	3.06	2.99	2.44	2.04	1.74
6	4.00	3.89	3.78	3.69	3.59	3.50	3.41	3.33	2.64	2.17	1.82
7	4.42	4.29	4.16	4.04	3.92	3.81	3.71	3.61	2.80	2.26	1.88
8	4.80	4.64	4.49	4.34	4.21	4.08	3.95	3.84	2.93	2.33	1.92
9	5.13	4.95	4.77	4.61	4.45	4.30	4.16	4.03	3.02	2.38	1.95
10	5.43	5.22	5.02	4.83	4.66	4.49	4.34	4.19	3.09	2.41	1.97
11	5.69	5.45	5.23	5.03	4.83	4.66	4.49	4.33	3.15	2.44	1.98
12	5.92	5.66	5.42	5.20	4.99	4.79	4.61	4.44	3.19	2.46	1.99
13	6.12	5.84	5.58	5.34	5.12	4.91	4.71	4.53	3.22	2.47	1.99
14	6.30	6.00	5.72	5.47	5.23	5.01	4.80	4.61	3.25	2.48	1.99
15	6.46	6.14	5.85	5.58	5.32	5.09	4.88	4.68	3.27	2.48	2.00

Appendix 2

Solutions to selected chapter-end exercises

E1.1 to E1.7

Please refer to the relevant sections in Chapter 1 to check your solutions.

E2.2 Shareholder value

The term shareholder value was introduced by Alfred Rappaport (1986). Although there is no uniform definition of the term, as it is used in a variety of contexts, shareholder value is often interpreted as the maximising of shareholder benefit and implies a primary focus on raising company earnings and the share price.

The most common methods of measuring shareholder value are:

- customer satisfaction and customer value-added (CVA)
- total cost analysis
- profitability analysis
- strategic profit model (SPM)
- economic value-added (EVA).

E2.5 Chancer Ltd – agency problem

The agency problem can be defined as a conflict of interest that may exist between the shareholders of a company (the principals) and the management of a company (the agents).

For Chancer Ltd the additional borrowing of £30m secured against the company's existing assets would have a dramatic impact on the company's gearing ratio. The additional debt would increase interest payments, and unless substantial savings can be generated by the new head office development, this could have a negative effect on the value of the company's shares. As a result whilst the development would undoubtedly raise the profile of the company in the short term it could mean a loss of value for shareholders. To eliminate such a problem is difficult and good investor relations are a useful starting point.

E2.7 Efficient market hypothesis (EMH)

Market efficiency is really a myth due to the complex and unpredictable interrelationships that now comprise the financial marketplace. Modern sophisticated capital markets often exhibit clear inefficiencies, usually at the strong form level.

However overall, in terms of pricing such markets are generally regarded as being partially efficient. But why are efficient markets important?

Efficient markets are seen as promoting:

- increased volumes of transactions
- greater mobility of funds
- the involvement of a greater number of participants
- a more efficient allocation and reallocation of resources.

The implications of such efficiency is that while in the short term market outsiders may profit at margins greater than the market average because of chance or luck, it is unlikely that over the longer term market outsiders could consistently outperform the market and earn profits over and above the market average.

Abnormal gains are generally not available to rational market participants. The relevance of such an argument to a wholly economically driven market (a market functioning primarily on the mechanics of supply and demand) is beyond doubt. Where there are a number of powerful participants driven by other than wholly economic motives, for example electoral pledges founded on politically based ideologies, the appropriateness of such an argument can have a substantial impact on:

- the overall market mechanisms – the availability of market assets, commodities, or currencies
- the activities of other market participants as part of the supply and demand mechanism.

E2.8 Crosby plc

Key issues are volatility and market confidence. Although profits are similar, trends differ.

Crosby has steady growth whereas Nash has growth but with a pattern that appears erratic and uncertain. Such growth patterns could indicate a lack of managerial competence and control. These problems could clearly reduce market confidence in the company and hence affect the value of the company.

It is, however, worth noting that other external conditions may well apply. These are conditions that may impact on either of the companies, for example potential growth opportunities, inherent goodwill within the companies, and the overall market conditions.

E2.9 Efficiency

In terms of stock markets and capital markets, pricing efficiency refers to the notion that prices rapidly reflect in an unbiased way all available information. Investment in financial assets should not on average produce abnormal returns.

Other types of efficiency include operational efficiency, which refers to the level of costs of carrying out transactions in capital markets. Allocational efficiency refers to the extent to which capital is allocated to the most profitable enterprise. This should be a product of pricing efficiency. Pricing efficiency emerges because the prices of assets are adjusted to reflect expected future cash flows.

Market efficiency is important because it:

- promotes investor trust in the market and thus encourages capital investment
- promotes allocational efficiency
- improves market information and therefore choice of investments.

E2.10 Implications of EMH

This is essentially a discussion on the context of the efficient markets hypothesis and the alternative forms of tested pricing efficiency: weak; semi-strong; strong.

There is no definitive answer but key issues that could be discussed may be:

- importance of information in market pricing
- relevance of past trends in market pricing
- levels of disclosure – public and private information.

E3.1 Accounting information and corporate governance

The role of accounting in corporate governance is wide and varied. The reports and financial statements, of companies should ensure:

- openness
- integrity
- accountability.

Accounting standards should be precise and strictly adhered to. External auditors should check and confirm that the company has complied with corporate governance requirement. Internal auditors may be responsible for the detection, minimisation and elimination of fraud.

E3.2 Effective corporate governance

Major participants in the corporate financial environment include:

- shareholders
- creditors
- employees
- directors
- trades unions
- banks and other financial institutions
- Government agencies
- auditors.

All the above participants have a role to play in corporate governance either directly (for example auditors and directors) or indirectly (for example employees).

With regard to corporate governance, directors' responsibilities are to ensure goal congruence between the objectives of the shareholders and managers of the company. The agency problem arises when directors (agents) do not act in the best interest of their shareholders (principals).

Relevant reports include:

Cadbury report (1992)

- Clarified key issues of corporate governance
- Defined corporate governance
- Provided a code of best practice
- Established roles of executive directors and non-executive directors
- Set standards of best practice in relation to financial reporting and accountability
- Establishment of audit committees for listed companies

Greenbury Code (1995)

- Made recommendations on directors pay

Hampel report (1996)

- Reviewed Cadbury and Greenbury reports

Combined code of practice

- Aim is to promote openness, integrity, and accountability
- Considers issues related to:
  - audit and the role of auditors
  - directors' obligations and responsibilities regarding:
    - duty of care
    - corporate manslaughter
    - insolvency
    - wrongful and fraudulent trading.

E3.3 Share options

Past UK governments have made managers' share option schemes tax efficient and therefore schemes are now very common amongst plcs.

Many plcs have found that their share prices react to specific management policies and decisions, for example takeovers and disposals of businesses. Users of financial information can assess these decisions, knowing of the options awarded to the directors.

Many plcs have found that they can only keep or attract high calibre managers by including share options in their remuneration packages.

Investing institutions demand more and more information regarding directors' remuneration. This can influence their basic hold or buy or sell decisions. The financial press frequently includes criticism of specific companies.

E3.4 Perks

Directors do not necessarily own the company they work for; the shareholders do.

Any monies (expenses) that a director takes from the company will affect the annual profit.

Annual dividends are paid from the annual profits. The shareholders approve the accounts at the AGM, which includes remuneration of the directors.

If the directors hide information regarding their remuneration and benefits from the shareholders, then that part of the accounts may not show a true and fair view of the company.

E3.5 Contracts

Before corporate governance codes of practice were introduced, shareholders found that their directors had powers that were increasing, especially regarding length of contract and compensation for loss of office. The financial press regularly commented on the compensation paid to a director, where company performance has been acknowledged to be poor, and the length of directors' contracts.

The Cadbury and Greenbury committees recommended that directors' contracts should be no longer than three years (Cadbury) and then one year (Greenbury). These committees had looked at the evidence presented to them. Hampel (1998) provided that the contracts should be one year or less.

UK financial institutions also became proactive regarding the length of directors' contracts issue. They noted that in the past too many highly paid directors were awarding themselves contracts in which compensation for loss of office was very high.

E3.9 Tomkins plc

Equity shareholders are the owners of the company, and the level of their dividends usually varies with levels of profits earned by the company.

Directors are appointed by the shareholders, and remunerated for their efforts. Major multinational companies are difficult to manage successfully over a long period of time. The remuneration of directors should reflect that difficulty.

The information that has been given about Tomkins plc shows that there is an executive director who earns a basic salary of just below £1m a year, an amount which most shareholders would like to see disclosed in the accounts and discussed at the AGM.

The bonus of £443,000 would also generate some interest amongst the institutions and individual shareholders. Institutions (and the UK Government) increasingly put pressure on directors if they feel that pay awards are excessive.

The consultancy agreement for a non-executive director may also be of interest to the various users of the notes to the accounts.

E4.3 Rainbow plc

(i) From a divisional point of view

Divisional managers are rewarded via a remuneration package which is linked to an ROI performance measure. Therefore they are likely to take a short-term view in appraising the investment proposals because they will be anxious to maintain their earnings. They would be interested in the short-term effect on ROI and perhaps on residual income (RI).

Project A	Year			
	1	2	3	4
	£000	£000	£000	£000
NBV of asset at beginning of year	60	45	30	15
Net cash inflow	21	21	21	21
Depreciation	(15)	(15)	(15)	(15)
Operating profit	6	6	6	6
Imputed interest at 15%	(9)	(7)	(5)	(2)
Residual income	(3)	(1)	1	4
ROI %	(6/60) 10.0	(6/45) 13.3	(6/30) 20.0	(6/15) 40.0

Project B	Year			
	1	2	3	4
	£000	£000	£000	£000
NBV of asset at beginning of year	60	45	30	15
Net cash inflow	25	20	20	15
Depreciation	(15)	(15)	(15)	(15)
Operating profit	10	5	5	–
Imputed interest at 15%	(9)	(7)	(5)	(2)
Residual income	1	(2)	–	(2)
ROI %	16.7	11.1	16.7	–

Project C	Year			
	1	2	3	4
	£000	£000	£000	£000
NBV of asset at beginning of year	60	45	30	15
Net cash inflow	10	20	30	40
Depreciation	(15)	(15)	(15)	(15)
Operating profit	(5)	5	15	25
Imputed interest at 15%	(9)	(7)	(5)	(2)
Residual income	(14)	(2)	10	23
ROI %	(8.3)	11.1	50.0	166.7

Red Division is likely to reject project A because of the potential adverse effect on the manager's remuneration in Year 1.

Similarly, project C is also likely to be rejected due to adverse results in the early years, despite the long-term profitability of the project.

Project B is the most likely to be accepted if the manager takes a short-term view to protect his or her remuneration in the coming year, although the decision will be affected by the division's current level of ROI.

(ii) From a company point of view

The company is likely to appraise the projects using discounted cash flow techniques.

Year	Discount factor at 15%	Project A		Project B		Project C	
		Cash flow £000	Present value £000	Cash flow £000	Present value £000	Cash flow £000	Present value £000
1	0.87	21	18.27	25	21.75	10	8.70
2	0.76	21	15.96	20	15.20	20	15.20
3	0.66	21	13.86	20	13.20	30	19.80
4	0.57	21	11.97	15	8.55	40	22.80
			60.06		58.70		66.50
Initial investment			60.00		60.00		60.00
Net present value			+0.06		−1.30		+6.50

From the company point of view project A may be acceptable although the NPV is very small and there is no room for possible error in the estimates and the risk of a negative return would be very great. The final decision will depend among other things on the risk premium built into the cost of capital.

Project B would be unacceptable whereas project C would be acceptable from a company point of view.

(iii) Probable decision

Project	Division	Company
A	Reject	Accept
B	Accept	Reject
C	Reject	Accept

The table shows that there is unlikely to be goal congruence between the company and the manager of Red Division.

The divergence between the two points of view has occurred because they are each using different assessment criteria. The views of the division and the company can be brought into line if they both use the same criteria in future. This would mean abandoning the practice of linking a manager's remuneration directly to short-term ROI because this is likely to encourage short-term thinking since ROI tends to be low in the early stages of an investment.

On the other hand it would be difficult to link remuneration to the net present value of individual projects because of the length of time before all the costs and benefits arise.

The specific problem with project A could be overcome through the use of annuity depreciation instead of the straight line method. The constant cash flows will then result in a smoother ROI profile over the life of the project. The manager would then be more likely to make the same decision as the company, although it depends to an extent on the division's current level of ROI.

The company may consider introducing the use of economic value added (EVA) as a measure of performance, which may be suitable for both divisional and economic performance.

E4.8 AAK

(i)

Year	Equipment £000	Running costs £000	Lighting, heating, etc. £000	Total outflow £000	Discount factor at 10%	Present value £000
0	120			120	1.00	120.000
1		40	15	55	0.91	50.050
2		44	15	59	0.83	48.970
3		48	15	63	0.75	47.250
4		52	15	67	0.68	45.560
5		56	15	71	0.62	44.020
Present value						355.850

We can assume that the annual sales at the full level is S. We first need to calculate the present value of each year's expected sales.

Year	Sales	Discount factor at 10%	Present value
1	0.4S	0.91	0.364S
2	0.7S	0.83	0.581S
3	1.0S	0.75	0.750S
4	1.0S	0.68	0.680S
5	1.0S	0.62	0.620S
Present value			2.995S

$$\text{contribution} = \text{sales} - \text{variable costs}$$

Because the prices of drinks are to be set at double their direct (variable) costs then half of the total present value of sales 2.995S must represent direct costs and the other half must represent contribution.

$$\text{Therefore contribution} = \frac{2.995S}{2} = 1.4975S$$

which is the present value of the contribution from the drinks.

To break even at an annual capital cost of 10% the present value of the contribution from drinks must equal the present value of the total outgoings, which is £355,850.

$$1.4975S = £355,850$$

$$S = £237,629$$

Therefore the required sales of drinks in each year are:

Year		£
1	£237,629 × 40%	95,052
2	£237,629 × 70%	166,341
3		237,629
4		237,629
5		237,629

(ii) Aspects of the proposals that require further investigation:

- Can the facilities be used outside normal licensed opening hours for alternative uses in order to increase the contribution?
- Has market research been carried out to support the belief that there will be additional future benefits?
- Will the proposed cost plus drinks pricing method result in competitive prices?
- Perhaps there is a better way for this project to utilise the space and the capital, and perhaps food may be an option.

E4.9 Lew Rolls

(i)

Year	10% DF	20% DF	Super CF £m	10% DCF £m	20% DCF £m	Superlux CF £m	10% DCF £m	20% DCF £m	Exec CF £m	10% DCF £m	20% DCF £m	Excel CF £m	10% DCF £m	20% DCF £m
0	1.00	1.00	−3	−3	−3	−7	−7	−7	−12	−12	−12	−15	−15	−15
1	0.91	0.83	1	0.91	0.83	2	1.82	1.66	0	0	0	10	9.10	8.30
2	0.83	0.69	1	0.83	0.69	2	1.66	1.38	0	0	0	10	8.30	6.90
3	0.75	0.58	1	0.75	0.58	2	1.50	1.16	7	5.25	4.06	0	0	0
4	0.68	0.48	1	0.68	0.48	2	1.36	0.96	7	4.76	3.36	0	0	0
5	0.62	0.40	1	0.62	0.40	2	1.24	0.80	7	4.34	2.80	0	0	0
Total			2	0.79	−0.02	3	0.58	−1.04	9	2.35	−1.78	5	2.40	0.20

(ii)
Calculation of IRR
From the table above calculate the IRR for each of the projects using interpolation/extrapolation as shown in Figs 4.3 and 4.4 in Chapter 4 to obtain:

	Super	Superlux	Exec	Excel
IRR	19.8%	13.6%	15.7%	20.9%
Ranking of projects (highest IRR ranked 1st)	2	4	3	1

(iii)
Net present value

	Super	Superlux	Exec	Excel
NPV of each project	£0.79m	£0.58m	£2.35m	£2.40m
NPV/£ invested	£0.263	£0.083	£0.196	£0.160
Ranking	1	4	2	3

NPV per £ invested is the more reliable evaluation method for appraisal of these alternatives. Therefore, given the £24m total constraint, the investment decision may be determined as follows:

	£m	NPV per £ invested	NPV £m
Super	3	£0.263	0.79
Exec	12	£0.196	2.35
Excel	9 (part)	£0.160	1.44
Superlux	0	£0.083	0
Optimum total NPV			**£4.58**

If IRR rankings were used to make the investment decision:

Excel	15	£0.160	2.40
Super	3	£0.263	0.79
Exec	6 (part)	£0.196	1.18
Superlux	0	£0.083	0
Total NPV			£4.37
			which is not optimal

(iv) and (v) Please refer to the relevant sections in Chapter 4 to check your solutions.

E5.1 CML

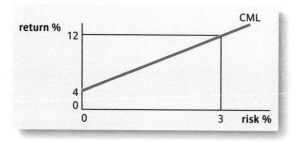

E5.2 Caldey plc and Tenby plc

(i) Perfect positive correlation

Probability	Caldey: 30% forecast return	Tenby: 70% forecast return	Combined portfolio return x			
p	%	%	%	$x \times p$	$(x - EV_x)$	$p(x - EV_x)^2$
0.20	3.0	8.4	11.4	2.28	(4.80)	4.61
0.60	3.6	12.6	16.2	9.72	–	–
0.20	4.2	16.8	21.0	4.20	4.80	4.61
				$EV_x = 16.20$		Variance = 9.22
						Standard deviation = 3.04

(ii) Perfect negative correlation

Probability	Caldey: 30% forecast return	Tenby: 70% forecast return	Combined portfolio return x			
p	%	%	%	$x \times p$	$(x - EV_x)$	$p(x - EV_x)^2$
0.20	3.0	16.8	19.8	3.96	3.60	2.59
0.60	3.6	12.6	16.2	9.72	–	–
0.20	4.2	8.4	12.6	2.52	(3.60)	2.59
				$EV_x = 16.20$		Variance = 5.18
						Standard deviation = 2.28

With perfect positive correlation the forecast returns from the shares of both companies are moving in the same direction, and this gives an expected return of 16.2% and a standard deviation or risk for the portfolio of 3.04%.

With perfect negative correlation the forecast returns from the shares of both companies are varying inversely, and this gives the same expected return of 16.2% and a standard deviation or risk for the portfolio of 2.28% which is lower than with perfect positive correlation.

If there is no correlation, the level of risk would lie between 2.28% and 3.04%.

E5.3 Efficient portfolios

(i) An efficient portfolio is one which lies on the securities market line, or capital market line. Its rate of return is as high as can be expected for the level of risk involved.

(ii)

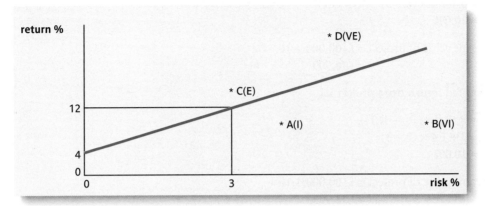

Portfolio A is quite inefficient as it lies below the capital market line (CML).
Portfolio B is very inefficient. It lies well below the CML.
Portfolio C is quite efficient lying above the CML and yielding 3% above the market portfolio for the same level of risk.
Portfolio D is very efficient, yielding around 7.5% more than the expected rate of return for the level of risk faced.

(iii)
We may calculate the beta value from a portfolio yielding a return of 11% from

$$R_p = R_f + \beta \times (R_m - R_f)$$
$$11 = 4 + \beta \times (12 - 4)$$
$$\beta = 7/8 = 0.875$$

(iv)
We may calculate the return on a portfolio with a beta of 1.3 from:

$$R_p = R_f + \beta \times (R_m - R_f)$$
$$R_p = 4 + 1.3 \times (12 - 4)$$
$$R_p = 14.4\%$$

E5.4 French plc and Saunders plc

(i)

French plc
Required return from project I

$$R_p = R_f + \beta \times (R_m - R_f)$$
$$= 3 + 1.3 \times (8 - 3)$$
$$= 9.5\%$$

Present value of project = £300,000/1.095
$$= £273,973$$

Saunders plc
Required return from project II

$$R_p = R_f + \beta \times (R_m - R_f)$$
$$= 3 + 1.4 \times (8 - 3)$$
$$= 10.0\%$$

Present value of project = £100,000/1.10
$$= £90,909$$

Required return from project III

$$R_p = R_f + \beta \times (R_m - R_f)$$
$$= 3 + 1.4 \times (8 - 3)$$
$$= 10.0\%$$

Present value of project = £100,000/1.10
$$= £90,909$$

Required return from project IV

$$R_p = R_f + \beta \times (R_m - R_f)$$
$$= 3 + 0.8 \times (8 - 3)$$
$$= 7.0\%$$

Present value of project = £200,000/1.07
$$= £186,916$$

(ii)
Total present value of Saunders plc's projects II, III, and IV
$$= £90,909 + £90,909 + £186,916$$
$$= £368,734$$

If Saunders plc goes ahead with its three proposed projects then its total beta factor will be

$$= \frac{£90,909}{£368,734} \times 1.4 + \frac{£90,909}{£368,734} \times 1.4 + \frac{£186,916}{£368,734} \times 0.8 = 1.1$$

(iii) Saunders plc has a higher present value and lower total systematic risk than French plc. Therefore in an efficient capital market Saunders plc would have a higher market value.

Saunders plc will be a diversified company and if investors were not themselves able to hold well-diversified portfolios and therefore reduce their unsystematic risk as much as possible, then this company may be more likely to be highly valued by investors. In a large and developed capital market such diversification by individual investors is feasible and so the apparent benefit derived by Saunders plc through its own diversification may not give it an advantage over French plc.

E5.5 Investor risk

The risk relating to an investment in a equity share comprises two elements:

- Systematic risk, or market risk is the element of total risk, which is generally common to all stocks and shares. It is market risk which is dependent upon general economic and market conditions. Systematic risk cannot be avoided and cannot be diversified away.

■ Unsystematic risk is that element of risk which is specific to type of industry or business in which the company is engaged. For example, ice cream sales are adversely affected by a cold and rainy summer. However, this unsystematic risk could be offset by diversifying into securities which are either negatively correlated (or to unrelated economic sectors of the market). A portfolio of shares in an ice cream company, for example, may be diversified to include a company which sells umbrellas, the sales of which are likely to move in the opposite direction to those of a company selling ice cream.

Unsystematic risk may be reduced by diversification, and research has shown that unsystematic risk accounts for around 70% of the risk of a security. In an efficiently diversified portfolio, different types of security are chosen with regard to markets, technology, geographical areas, product and service types, etc.

E5.6 Abdul and Said

(i)

Abdul's total returns $T = 12\%$

Risk-free rate of return $R_f = 7\%$

Adbul's return on his market portfolio of equities $= R_e$

One quarter (25%) of Adbul's funds are in risk-free investment and so three-quarters (75%) of his funds are invested in equities.
    Therefore

$$T = (0.25 \times R_f) + (0.75 \times R_e)$$
$$12 = (0.25 \times 7) + (0.75 \times R_e)$$
$$12 = 1.75 + (0.75 \times R_e)$$
$$R_e = 10.25/0.75$$
$$R_e = 13.67$$

The return on Adbul's equity investments is therefore 13.67%.
    Said's market portfolio of equities is similar to Adbul's market portfolio of equities and so we can assume also gives a return of 13.67%. Said is achieving a total return which is higher than this and so he also must be borrowing in funds at the risk-free rate.

Said's total returns $T = 18\%$

Risk-free rate of return $R_f = 7\%$

Said's return on his market portfolio of equities $R_e = 13.67\%$

Said's proportion of additional borrowed funds $= B$

$$T = (1 + B) \times R_e - (B \times R_f)$$
$$18 = (1 + B) \times 13.67 - (B \times 7)$$
$$18 = 13.67 + 13.67B - 7B$$
$$4.33 = 6.67B$$
$$B = 4.33/6.67$$
$$B = 0.65$$

Said has borrowed at the risk free rate of 7% to increase his funds by 65% which are all invested in equities, which may be illustrated as follows:

100 equities @ 13.67 % gives a return of	13.67
65 (addition of 65% to his own funds borrowed and invested by Said) @ 13.67% gives a return of	8.88
Cost of 65 borrowed at the risk-free rate of 7%	(4.55)
Total return	18.00

(ii)

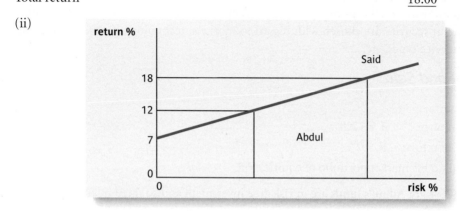

(iii) The capital market line is represented by

$$y = R_f + bx$$

where

Adbul's expected total return	$y = 12\%$
risk-free rate of return	$R_f = 7\%$
standard deviation or risk of Adbul's portfolio	$x = 8\%$
slope of the capital market line (CML)	$= b$

therefore

$12 = 7 + 8b$

$b = 5/8$

$b = 0.625$

The slope of the CML is 0.625 and this can be used to calculate the new risk (standard deviation) of the portfolio if Adbul increases his required return to 13%.

$y = R_f + bx$

$13 = 7 + 0.625x$

$x = 9.6$

Therefore for Adbul to increase his required return from 12% to 13% the risk will increase from 8% to 9.6%.

We can calculate Adbul's new portfolio as follows:

Abdul's total returns $T = 13\%$

Risk-free rate of return $R_f = 7\%$

Adbul's return on his market portfolio of equities $R_e = 13.67\%$

Adbul's proportion of funds invested in risk-free investments $= R$

$T = (1 - R) \times R_e + (R \times R_f)$

$13 = (1 - R) \times 13.67 + (R \times 7)$

$13 = 13.67 - 13.67R + 7R$

$-0.67 = -6.67R$

$R = 0.67/6.67$

$R = 0.10$

The proportion of funds invested in risk-free investments is therefore 10%. So in order to achieve an overall rate of return of 13%, Adbul would have to increase the proportion of his fund invested in equities from 75% to 90%, with a corresponding rise in the risk (standard deviation) of the portfolio to 9.6%,

E5.7 Bill Brownbridge

(i)

Probability	Company X				Company Y			
0.3	30	9	5	7.5				
0.4	25	10	0	0.0				
0.3	20	6	(5)	7.5				
0.2					50	10	20	80.0
0.6					30	18	0	0.0
0.2					10	2	(20)	80.0
	EV_x	25	Variance	15.0	EV_y	30	Variance	160.0

Expected return Company X = 25% $\sigma_x = \sqrt{15} = 3.87\%$

Expected return Company Y = 30% $\sigma_y = \sqrt{160} = 12.65\%$

Portfolio return $= (60\% \times 25\%) + (40\% \times 30\%) = 27\%$

(ii) $\sigma_p = \sqrt{[(\alpha_x^2 \times \sigma_x^2)(\alpha_y^2 \times \sigma_y^2) + (2 \times \alpha_x \times \alpha_y \times r \times \sigma_x \times \sigma_y)]}$

where $\sigma =$ standard deviation

$\alpha =$ proportion of investment in portfolio

$r =$ correlation coefficient of investment return, which for X and Y is zero

$\sigma_p = \sqrt{[(0.6^2 \times 3.87^2) + (0.4^2 \times 12.65^2)]}$

$= \sqrt{[(0.36 \times 15) + (0.16 \times 160)]}$

$= \sqrt{(5.4 + 25.6)}$

$= \sqrt{31}$

$= 5.57\%$

Risk company X = 3.87%

Risk company Y = 12.65%

Risk portfolio XY = 5.5%

(iii)

Portfolio and expected returns

A portfolio is a collection of different securities that make up an investor's total holding.

The expected return of a portfolio will be the weighted average of the expected returns of each of the securities in the portfolio.

The risk in a security or portfolio of securities is that the actual return will not be the same as the expected return.

The risk of a security or portfolio of securities can be measured as the standard deviation of the expected returns.

Risk and diversification

Portfolio theory suggests that the relationship of securities held in a portfolio is as important as the securities themselves.

Why does portfolio diversification appear to work?

The prices of different securities (equity or debt) do not move exactly together.

Diversification works best when investment returns are negatively correlated. If investment returns show negative correlation then by combining them in a portfolio overall risk will be reduced. In general investors choose a portfolio that balances expected return and risk. This is represented in the investor's individual indifference curve.

Traditional investment theory suggests that if two portfolios have the same return but different risks then the least risk option should be chosen, and if two portfolios have the same risk but different returns the greatest return option should be chosen. This is the risk averse assumption.

Does diversification affect all risk?

It depends on two key issues:

- size of the portfolio
- types of risk.

Size of portfolio: The risk-reducing impact of diversification is not linear but exponential. It works well with up to 20 or 30 investments, after which the impact becomes statistically minimal.

Types of risk include systematic and unsystematic risk. Systematic risk (sometimes called market risk) includes economy-wide (macroeconomic) sources of risk that affect the overall market and differs between types of investments with some industries riskier than others. Diversification can only assist in reducing unsystematic risk. Systematic risk must be accepted by the investor, the return being higher returns than the risk free rate of return.

Unsystematic risk (sometimes called unique risk) includes risk factors that only affect one company or investment (that is inherent risk).

Implications of systematic and unsystematic risk

To avoid risk altogether the investor must invest in risk-free investments. A small portfolio of investments will have both systematic and unsystematic risk. In a balanced portfolio the portfolio systematic risk will in theory be equal to the average systematic risk in the market as a whole.

E6.3 Adam plc

(i) Dividend yield = 5%, on share price of £25

Dividend per share therefore = £25 × 0.05 = £1.25
P/E ratio = 10, therefore earnings per share = £25/10 = £2.50
Dividend payout ratio = £1.25/£2.50 = 50%

(ii) Dividend growth model

$$K_e = \frac{v(1+G)}{S} + G = \frac{£1.25 \times 1.03}{£2.50} + 0.03 = 0.0815 \text{ or } 8.15\%$$

(iii) CAPM

$$K_e = R_f + \{\beta_e \times (R_m - R_f)\} = 4\% + \{1.25 \times (10\% - 4\%)\} = 11.5\%$$

From the dividend model:

$$S = \frac{v(1+G)}{(K_e - G)} = \frac{£1.25 \times 0.03}{(0.115 - 0.03)} = £15.15$$

The share price appears to be over-valued by £9.85 (£25 × £15.15).

(iv) Please refer to the relevant sections in Chapter 6 to check your solution.

(v) Assumptions for derivation of the CAPM:

- investors are risk averse
- everyone in the market has the same forecast
- investment opportunities are the same for all investors
- a perfect market and no transaction costs or taxation
- investors can borrow and lend freely at a risk free rate of return
- all investors have a single period planning horizon.

Theoretical implications:

- investors and companies require a return in excess of the risk free rate to compensate for systematic risk
- investors and companies should not require a premium for unsystematic risk since it can be diversified away
- systematic risk varies between companies and projects and therefore rates of return required by investors and companies will vary

- a linear relationship is assumed between the return on an individual investment or security (R_s) and the average return from all securities in the market (R_m), which will tend to be positively correlated
- differential returns between R_s and R_m may be due to systematic risk
- the relationship between R_m and R_s can be used to derive a beta factor (β) for individual securities
- unsystematic risk can be mitigated through diversification.

E6.4 Lucky Jim plc

If shareholders' equity is E and the net financial debt D then the relative proportions of equity and debt in the total financing are:

$$\frac{E}{E+D} \text{ and } \frac{D}{E+D}$$

$$\frac{E}{E+D} = 2/3$$

$$\frac{D}{E+D} = 1/3$$

Cost of equity $K_e = 18\%$

Return on financial debt $K_d = 12\%$

$$\text{WACC} = \left(\frac{2}{3} \times 18\%\right) + \left(\frac{1}{3} \times 12\%(1 - 40\%)\right) = 12\% + 2.4\% = 14.4\%$$

$$\text{The present value of future cash flows in perpetuity} = \frac{\text{annual cash flows}}{\text{annual discount rate}\%}$$

$$= \frac{\pounds 35{,}000}{0.144}$$

$$= \pounds 243{,}056$$

Net present value, NPV = £243,056 − £200,000 = +£43,056

Using WACC to discount the cash flows of the project, the result is a positive NPV of £43,056 and therefore the project should be undertaken.

E6.5 Abey plc

(i)   £

Current profits	2,250,000
Increase	
(£850,000 − extra interest 10% × £5,000,000)	350,000
New profits after project	2,600,000
New cost of equity	20%
New market value	13,000,000
Old market value	12,500,000 (earnings £2.25m/ cost of equity 18%)
Increase in shareholders' wealth	500,000

(ii)
NPV of the project using WACC 16%

$(£850,000/0.16) - £5,000,000 = £312,500$

The increase in the value of the equity is £500,000 (see above).
The +NPV of the project is £312,500 (see above).

Therefore the impact of financing the project is:

$£500,000 - £312,500 = £187,500$

E6.6 Homeslore plc

(i) Growth in dividends 2001 to 2007

$$= \sqrt[6]{(£900/£570)}$$
$$= \sqrt[6]{1.5789}$$
$$= 1.079, \text{ a growth rate G of } 7.9\%$$

current dividend $v = £900/4,500 = £0.20$ per share
current share price $S = £4.60 - £0.20 = £4.40$ *ex dividend*
using the dividend growth model

$$K_e = \frac{v(1 + G)}{S} + G = \frac{£0.20 \times 1.079}{£4.40} + 0.079 = 0.128$$

cost of equity $= 12.8\%$

(ii) Cost of redeemable debt

Year	Cash flow £	Discount factor at 5%	Present value £
0	(90)	1.000	(90.00)
1–5	5 – (5 × 0.30)	4.3295	15.15
5	100	0.7835	78.35
			3.50

Year	Cash flow £	Discount factor at 5%	Present value £
0	(90)	1.000	(90.00)
1–5	5 – (5 × 0.30)	4.2124	14.74
5	100	0.7473	74.73
			(0.53)

using interpolation $5\% + \{£3.50/(£3.50 + £0.53)\} = 5.87\%$ after tax
cost of debt $= 5.87\%$

(iii) Weighted Average Cost of Capital

Ordinary shares	£4.40 × 4.5m	£19,800,000	12.80%	£2,534,400
Debentures	£0.90 × 4.0m	£3,600,000	5.87%	£211,320
		£23,400,000		£2,745,720

$\text{WACC} = £2,745,720/£23,400,000 = 11.73\%$

E6.7 Homeslore plc

(i) Using WACC 11.73%, discount factor Year 1 = 0.895, Year 2 = 0.801

Year 1 {(£440,000 × 0.5) + (£200,000 × 0.4) + (£460,000 × 0.1)} × 0.895 = £309,670
Year 2 {(£600,000 × 0.6) + (£580,000 × 0.2) + (£350,000 × 0.2)} × 0.801 = £437,346

PV of benefits	£747,016
Cost – Year 0	£700,000
NPV	£47,016

(ii) Justification for using WACC is that by using WACC only those investments which offer a return in excess of WACC are accepted thereby contributing to the overall funds of the company.

It is assumed that WACC reflects the long-term future capital structure of the company. Problems are that:

- floating rate debt is difficult to incorporate into a WACC calculation
- the risk profile of prospective projects may differ from the risk profile of the company
- WACC does not consider the risk of individual projects.

E6.8 Yor plc

(i)

Yor plc
Income statement for the year ended 30 September 2008

Figures in £m	Debentures	Shares
PBIT	15.6	15.6
Interest payable	(1.6)	(1.2)
Profit before tax	14.0	14.4
Tax on profit on ordinary activities	(3.5)	(3.6)
Profit on ordinary activities after tax	10.5	10.8
Retained profit at 1 October 2007	10.6	10.6
	21.1	21.4
Dividends	(3.3)	(4.6)
Retained profit at 30 September 2008	17.8	16.8

(ii)

Yor plc
Capital and reserves as at 30 September 2008

Figures in £m	Debentures	Shares
Share capital (£1 ord. shares)	10.0	14.0
Share premium (4m × £1.50)		6.0
Profit and loss account	17.8	16.8
	27.8	36.8
Loans	30.0	20.0

(iii)

$$\text{earnings per share 2007} = \frac{\text{profit available for ordinary shareholders}}{\text{number of ordinary shares in issue}} = \frac{£7.8m}{10m}$$

$$= 78p$$

(iv) using debentures

$$\text{earnings per share } 2008 = \frac{\text{£10.5m}}{10m} = \text{£1.05}$$

using shares

$$\text{earnings per share } 2008 = \frac{\text{£10.8m}}{10m} = 77p$$

(v)

$$\text{dividend per share } 2007 = \frac{\text{total dividends paid to ordinary shareholders}}{\text{number of ordinary shares in issue}} = \frac{\text{£3.0m}}{10m}$$

$$= 30p$$

(vi) using debentures

$$\text{dividend per share } 2008 = \frac{\text{£3.3m}}{10m} = 33p$$

using shares

$$\text{dividend per share } 2008 = \frac{\text{£4.6m}}{14m} = 33p$$

(vii)

$$\text{gearing} = \frac{\text{long-term debt}}{\text{equity} + \text{long-term debt}}$$

2007	Using debentures 2008	Using shares 2008
$\dfrac{\text{£20.0m}}{\text{£20.6m} + \text{£20.0m}} = 49.3\%$	$\dfrac{\text{£30.0m}}{\text{£27.8m} + \text{£30.0m}} = 51.9\%$	$\dfrac{\text{£20.0m}}{\text{£36.8m} + \text{£20.0m}} = 35.2\%$

(viii) Summary of results

Figures in £m		Using debentures 2008	Using shares 2008
Profit after tax	7.8)	10.5)	10.8)
Dividends	(3.0)	(3.3)	(4.6)
Retained profit for year	4.8	7.2	6.2

The use of debentures to finance the new project will increase the 2007/2008 profit after tax, and available for dividends, by £2.7m or 34.6%, whereas if shares were used the increase would be £3.0m or 38.5%. Earnings per share will be increased to £1.05 (+27p) and decreased to 77p (−1p) respectively. However, retained profit would be increased by £2.4m (50%) and £1.4m (29.2%) respectively. The difference is because the gain from the lower interest cost in using shares is more than offset by the increase in dividends.

Dividend per share will be increased from 30p to 33p per share regardless of which method of financing is used.

Gearing at 30 September 2007 was 49.3%. If debentures are used to finance the new project then gearing will increase to 51.9%, but if shares are used to finance the new project then gearing will decrease to 35.2%. This represents a higher financial risk for the company with regard to its commitments to making a high level of interest payments. The company is therefore vulnerable to a downturn in business and also the possibility of its loans being called in and possible liquidation of the company.

E7.1 Vine plc

The reduction in the company's cash flow for 2006 is explained as follows:

	£
PBIT	2,700
Depreciaion	(300)
Stocks increase	(1,000)
Debtors increase	(1,900)
Creditors increase	1,000
Operating cash flow increase	500
Non-current assets	(2,700)
Tax paid	(1,000)
Dividends paid	(600)
Share capital increase	600
Debentures increase	1,800
Cash flow decrease	(1,400)

Bank and cash has been reduced by £1.4m in the year (£1.5m − £0.1m). The company is generating profits but much of the revenue from sales appears to be reflected in a high level of debtors, with the company investing heavily in increased stock levels.

E7.2 Lamarr plc

Current market value of Lamarr plc is

		£
Current ordinary share capital	400,000 × £2.20 =	880,000
Rights issue		200,000
		1,080,000

Expected earnings of Lamarr plc = £1,080,000 × 16.5% = £178,200

Current eps (before rights issue) = ((£880,000 × 0.16)/400,000) = £0.352 or 35.2p

Rights issue @ £2.00

Shares issued = £200,000/£2.00 = 100,000

Total shares in issue = 400,000 + 100,000 = 500,000

Theoretical ex-rights price £1,080,000/500,000 = £2.16

New eps £178,200/500,000 = 35.6p

Rights issue @ £1.80

Shares issued = £200,000/£1.80 = 111,111

Total shares in issue = 400,000 + 111,111 = 511,111

Theoretical ex-rights price £1,080,000/511,111 = £2.11

New eps £178,200/511,111 = 34.9p

Rights issue @ £1.60

Shares issued = £200,000/£1.60 = 125,000

Total shares in issue = 400,000 + 125,000 = 525,000

Theoretical ex-rights price £1,080,000/525,000 = £2.06

New eps £178,200/525,000 = 33.9p

E7.3 Emlyn plc

The company made a profit before tax of £9.4m in 2006, which was a return per share of 94p (£9.4m/10m shares). The share price is £2.50, and so the ratio of profit before tax to market value is 94p/£2.50, or 37.6%. This is the minimum return on new capital that should be expected, and so the assumption is that Emlyn plc will earn profit before additional interest and tax of 38% on the £5.5m that it raises.

(a) 6% bonds

(i) It may be difficult for the company to issue £5.5m bonds without having to provide security.

(ii) Earnings per share

Profit before additional interest is assumed to increase by 38% on new funds raised.

	£m
Profit before extra interest (£9.4m + 38% × £5.5m)	11.490
Less extra interest (6% of £5.5m)	(0.330)
Profit before tax	11.160
Tax @ 35% (£3.3m/£9.4m)	(3.906)
Profit after tax	7.254
Number of ordinary shares	10m
eps	72.5p

which is a big increase over the 2006 level of 61p (£6.1m/10m).

(iii) Debt/equity ratio

dividend payout ratio = £3.8m/6.1m = 62.3%
retained earnings = PAT £7.2m − dividends £4.5m (62.3%) = £2.7m

$$\frac{£13.5m + £5.5m}{£23.6m + £2.7m} = 72.2\%$$

Assuming dividends are paid at the same level as 2006 at 62.3% of PBT, the financial gearing, represented by the debt/equity ratio would rise to 72.2%, compared to the already high level of

57.2% (£13.5m/£23.6m) for 2006. This could have an adverse effect on the willingness of the bank, trade creditors and other investors to grant further credit.

(b) Ordinary shares

(i) The ordinary shares one for four rights issue is at a discount to the current market price at a price of £2.20 per share. This would result in the issue of 10m × 0.25 = 2.5m new shares, which at an issue price of £2.20 per share would raise £5.5m.

(ii) Earnings per share

Profit before additional interest is assumed to increase by 38% on new funds raised.

	£m
Profit before extra interest (£9.4m + 38% × £5.5m)	11.490
Tax @ 35%	(4.022)
Profit after tax	7.468
Number of ordinary shares	12.5m
eps	59.7p

which is a fall from the 2006 level of 61p.

(iii) P/E ratio

The P/E ratio on the basis of 2006 earnings is £2.50/61p = 4.1 times.

If this P/E ratio is applied to an eps of 59.7p, we would expect the share price to fall to about £2.44 (4.1 × 59.7p).

This compares with a theoretical ex-rights price of

	£
4 shares, market value £2.50	10.00
1 new shares issued at £2.20	2.20
5 shares theoretical value	12.20
Theoretical ex rights price £12.20/5	2.44

The share price after the rights issue may fall, but only to around its theoretical ex-rights price of £2.44 per share.

(iv) Debt/equity ratio

retained earnings = PAT £7.5m − dividends £4.7m (62.3%) = £2.8m

$$\frac{£13.5m}{£23.6m + £2.8m} = 51.1\%$$

Assuming dividends are paid at the same level as 2006 at 62.3% of PBT, the financial gearing, represented by the debt/equity ratio would fall to 51.1%, compared to 57.2% for 2006 and this would put the company in a slightly better position to raise further finance in the future, if required, by raising new debt capital.

(c) 7% preference shares

(i) Earnings per share

Profit before additional preference share dividends is assumed to increase by 38% on new funds raised.

	£m
Profit before extra interest (£9.4m + 38% × £5.5m)	11.490
Tax @ 35%	(4.022)
	7.468
Preference dividend 7% × £5.5m	(0.385)
Profit after tax	7.083
Number of ordinary shares	10m
eps	70.8p

which is a big increase over the 2006 level of 61p.

(ii) Debt/equity ratio

retained earnings = PAT £7.0m – dividends £4.4m (62.3%) = £2.6m

Preference shares are usually included with prior charge capital for gearing calculations, and so debt/equity would increase to

$$\frac{£13.5m + £5.5m}{£23.6m + £2.6m} = 72.5\%$$

Assuming dividends are paid at the same level as 2006 at 62.3% of PBT, the financial gearing, represented by the debt/equity ratio would rise to 72.5%, compared to 57.2% for 2006 and this is a level of gearing about which other creditors might have reservations about granting credit to the company.

Recommendations

The company should make either a rights issue of new equity or an issue of bonds. An issue of preference shares would improve eps, but not as much as an issue of bonds and so would not be as beneficial.

An issue of bonds would substantially increase eps, due to the low after-tax cost of the bonds, which an issue of new equity would not. However, because of the high level of gearing, the perceived risk of the company would rise, and the share price would probably fall to a lower P/E level.

In conclusion, a rights issue would probably be the most suitable method of financing since this would provide an extra injection of equity capital that would put the company in a good position for further growth in the future, without any harmful effects on eps or on the share price (allowing for the dilution with the issue).

E7.4 Globe plc

(i) We need to examine whether the company's requirements regarding the rights issue are viable.

(a) Total earnings after the redemption of the loan stock would be £263,000.

	£	£
Current earnings are 500,000 × 50p		250,000
Additional earnings after redeeming the bond		
Interest saved £400,000 × 5%	20,000	
Less tax on interest @ 35%	(7,000)	
		13,000
Earnings after redeeming the bond		263,000

If eps should be diluted by no more than 12%, they will be no less than 44p.

Therefore, the number of shares in issue will be:

$$\frac{\text{total earnings}}{\text{eps}} = \frac{£263,000}{£0.44} = 597,727$$

Therefore, the additional number of shares issued should not be more than 97,727.

The rights issue price will then be:

$$\frac{£400,000}{97,727} = £4.09$$

This is not viable because it is above the current market share price of £3.80.

(b) A rights issue price at 10% below the current share price would be £3.80 × 90% = £3.42. 116,959 shares would have to be issued to raise £400,000, and so the eps would be:

$$\frac{£263,000}{500,000 + 116,959} = 42.6\text{p, which is 14.8\% below the current eps 50p}$$

(c) If Globe plc makes a one for four issue, the number of shares issued would be 125,000 (500,000/4), and to raise £400,000 the issue price per share would be:

$$\frac{£400,000}{125,000} = £3.20$$

which is 15.8% below the current market value, and not 10% as required.

(ii) The theoretical ex-rights price of the shares would be:

	£
Market value cum rights of four shares (4 × £3.80)	15.20
Rights issue price of one share @ £3.20	3.20
Theoretical value of five shares	18.40

The theoretical ex rights price would be £3.68 per share (£18.40/5).

The eps would be:

$$\frac{£263,000}{500,000 + 125,000} = 42\text{p}$$

The P/E ratio would be $\dfrac{£3.68}{42\text{p}} = 8.8$ times

(iii) A rights issue of ordinary shares can be made to raise a substantial amount of new long-term capital.

If an issue of shares to new shareholders is chosen as an alternative to a rights issue, it is a Stock Exchange requirement that prior approval must have been obtained within the past

12 months, from the shareholders in a general meeting, for the issue of shares for cash other than as a rights issue. A rights issue is more likely to be successful than a public issue, because:

■ the offer is to existing investors who are familiar with the company

■ existing shareholders may wish to take up the rights offer in order to preserve their relative shareholdings in the company

■ the offer price, below the current market price, would be set in such a way as to attract shareholders into acceptance. The cost of a rights issue would also be less than that of an offer for sale.

The main drawback to a rights issue is its cost. Placings are cheaper, and would probably be preferred for smaller issues.

A rights issue would be preferable to raising long-term loan capital:

■ where the interest rate on the loan capital which must be offered to attract investors is unacceptably high

■ where the company's level of gearing would become unacceptably high, possibly causing a reduction in the market value of the ordinary shares as a result of the extra financial risk to shareholders

■ where the company wishes to reduce its level of gearing.

A dilution in net earnings per share would generally be expected as a result of a rights issue, at least in the short term. This should be acceptable to shareholders provided that the return obtained on their total investment is at least as high as it was before the rights issue.

Consider a company which has in issue 1 million ordinary shares with a market value of £2m and current annual earnings of £250,000 or 25p eps. It decides to make a one for four rights issue to finance a new investment. The offer price is £1.50 per share.

The current P/E ratio is 8 (share price £2 and eps 25p).
The theoretical market value of the 1,250,000 shares in issue after the rights issue is

4 × £2	£8.00
1 @ £1.50	£1.50
5	£9.50 = £1.90 per share × 1,250,000 = £2,375,000

If the P/E ratio is to be maintained at 8, then the market value of the 1,250,000 shares must be sustained by annual earnings of:

£2,375,000/8 = £296,875

eps would be £296,875/1,250,000 = 23.75p

Provided that the company pursues a consistent dividend policy by maintaining a constant dividend cover ratio then the shareholders would be happy with their return despite eps dropping from 25p to 23.75p.

E7.5 Wiltel plc

Redemption value of debt $V_n = £3.50 \times 4 = £14$ per £10 debt or £140 per £100 debt

Debt interest $d = £8$ pre-tax and $£8 \times (1 - 25\%) = £6$ after tax

Current market value of debt $V_0 = £106$

We want to find the market rate of return on bonds expected by investors (R_d), using:

$$V_0 = d/(1 + R_d) + d/(1 + R_d)^2 + d/(1 + R_d)^3 \cdots + (d + V_n)/(1 + R_d)^n$$

Therefore $£106 = £6/(1 + R_d) + £6/(1 + R_d)^2 + (£6 + £140)/(1 + R_d)^3$

This may be solved using the interpolation technique we saw in Chapter 4, and we will calculate NPV using estimated rates of 12% and 15%.

	Cash flows	Present values at 12%	Present values at 15%
Year 0	£106.00	−106.00	−106.00
Year 1–3	$£8 \times (1 - 0.25) = £6.00$	14.41	13.70
Year 3	$40 \times £3.50 = £140.00$	99.65	92.05
		+8.06	−0.25

Using interpolation the cost of convertible debt

$$= 12\% + \left[\frac{£8.06}{(£8.06 + £0.25)} \times (15\% - 12\%) \right] = 14.91\%$$

Therefore the company's cost of capital of the convertible debt is 14.9%.

E7.7 Nimrod plc

The advantages of a market listing include:

- easier access to capital
- the company will enjoy a higher profile and enhanced status with its customers and suppliers
- it may be a possible first step towards a full stock exchange listing
- it presents an opportunity for the company to create a market for its shares and widen its shareholder base
- it provides increased opportunities to make acquisitions.

The disadvantages of a market listing include:

- increased scrutiny by investors, analysts, and the press
- specific requirements for the company to keep investors informed
- the company may be subject to irrational market share price movements
- the company may be subject to short-termist pressure from shareholders.

The main differences between a listing on the London Stock Exchange and a listing on the AIM include:

London Stock Exchange

- there is a requirement for a minimum 25% shares to be in public hands
- normally a three-year trading record is required for the company
- shareholder prior approval is required for substantial acquisitions and disposals
- there is a minimum market capitalisation.

AIM

- there is no minimum number of shares required to be in public hands
- there is no minimum trading record requirement
- there is no prior shareholder approval required for acquisitions and disposals
- a nominated adviser is required at all times
- there is no minimum market capitalisation requirement.

E7.8 Curtis E Carr & Co

(i) PV of purchase

$$£150,000 - (£5,000/(1.10)^7) = £150,000 - (£5,000 \times 0.5132) = (£150,000 - £2,566) = £147,434$$

The equivalent annual cost of the purchase would be:

£147,434/7 year annuity factor @10%

£147,434/4.8684 = £30,283

The annual lease payment is less than the equivalent annual purchase cost therefore the company should lease.

(ii) Please refer to the relevant section in Chapter 7 to check your solution.

E8.1 Priory Products plc

(i) **Net debt to equity**

Net debt	100	250	800
Equity	300	500	800
Debt/equity (%)	33%	50%	100%

(ii) **Long-term loans to equity and long-term loans**

Long-term loans	200	200	600
Equity/LTL	500	700	1,400
Gearing (%)	40%	29%	43%

E8.4 Freshco plc

Liquidity ratios for Freshco plc for 2007 and the comparative ratios for 2006

Current ratio

$$\text{Current ratio } 2007 = \frac{\text{current assets}}{\text{current liabilities}} = \frac{£208}{£121} = 1.7 \text{ times}$$

$$\text{Current ratio } 2006 = \frac{£191}{£107} = 1.8 \text{ times}$$

Acid test (quick ratio)

$$\text{Quick ratio } 2007 = \frac{\text{current assets} - \text{stocks}}{\text{current liabilities}} = \frac{£208 - £124}{£121} = 0.7 \text{ times}$$

$$\text{Quick ratio } 2006 = \frac{£191 - £100}{£107} = 0.8 \text{ times}$$

Defensive interval

$$\text{Defensive interval } 2007 = \frac{\text{quick assets}}{\text{average daily cash from operations}} = \frac{£208 - £124}{(£80 + £894 - £70)/365}$$

$$= 34 \text{ days}$$

$$\text{Defensive interval } 2006 = \frac{£191 - £100}{(£60 + £747 - £80)/365} = 46 \text{ days}$$

Report on the liquidity of Freshco plc

The current ratio and the quick ratio have both dropped slightly to 1.7 times and 0.7 times respectively. However, the defensive interval has dropped significantly from 46 days to 34 days at which level the company could potentially survive if there were no further cash inflows.

Net cash flow from operations improved from £77m in 2006 to £84m in 2007. Investments in non-current assets were at lower levels in 2007 and matched by a reduction in long-term financing (debentures).

E8.7 Supermarket

	2007	2006	2005
Adjusted net assets	£5,000m	£4,769m	£4,377m
Market value	£17,808m	£11,531m	£11,995m
MVA	£12,808m	£6,762m	£7,618m

E8.9 Laurel and Hardy

(i) **Profitability ratios for Hardy plc for 2007 and the comparative ratios for 2006 and 2005**

Gross margin, GM

$$\text{Gross margin \% } 2007 = \frac{\text{gross margin}}{\text{sales}} = \frac{£161 \times 100\%}{£456} = 35.3\%$$

$$\text{Gross margin \% } 2006 = \frac{£168 \times 100\%}{£491} = 34.2\%$$

$$\text{Gross margin \% } 2005 = \frac{£143 \times 100\%}{£420} = 34.0\%$$

Profit before interest and tax, PBIT (or operating profit)

$$\text{PBIT \% 2007} = \frac{\text{operating profit}}{\text{sales}} = \frac{£52 \times 100\%}{£456} = 11.4\%$$

$$\text{PBIT \% 2006} = \frac{£61 \times 100\%}{£491} = 12.4\%$$

$$\text{PBIT \% 2005} = \frac{£50 \times 100\%}{£420} = 11.9\%$$

Net profit, PAT (return on sales, ROS)

$$\text{PAT\% 2007} = \frac{\text{net profit}}{\text{sales}} = \frac{£20 \times 100\%}{£456} = 4.4\%$$

$$\text{PAT\% 2006} = \frac{£28 \times 100\%}{£491} = 5.7\%$$

$$\text{PAT\% 2005} = \frac{£25 \times 100\%}{£420} = 6.0\%$$

Return on capital employed, ROCE (return on investment, ROI)

$$\text{ROCE\% 2007} = \frac{\text{operating profit}}{\substack{\text{total assets} - \text{current liabilities} \\ \text{(average capital employed)}}} = \frac{£52 \times 100\%}{(£284 + £292)/2} = \frac{£52 \times 100\%}{£288} = 18.1\%$$

$$\text{ROCE\% 2006} = \frac{£61 \times 100\%}{(£237 + £284)/2} = \frac{£61 \times 100\%}{£260.5} = 23.4\%$$

ROCE% 2005 is not available because we do not have the capital employed figure for 31 March 2004.

Return on equity, ROE

$$\text{ROE\% 2007} = \frac{\text{PAT}}{\text{equity}} = \frac{£20 \times 100\%}{£223} = 9.0\%$$

$$\text{ROE\% 2006} = \frac{£28 \times 100\%}{£215} = 13.0\%$$

$$\text{ROE\% 2005} = \frac{£25 \times 100\%}{£200} = 12.5\%$$

Capital turnover

$$\text{Capital turnover 2007} = \frac{\text{sales}}{\text{average capital employed in year}} = \frac{£456}{£288} = 1.6 \text{ times}$$

$$\text{Capital turnover 2006} = \frac{£491}{£260.5} = 1.9 \text{ times}$$

Capital turnover 2005 is not available because we do not have the capital employed figure for 31 March 2004.

Report on the profitability of Hardy plc

Sales for the year 2007 were 7.1% lower than sales in 2006, which were 16.9% above 2005. It is not clear whether these sales reductions were from lower volumes, fewer products, or changes in selling prices.

Gross margin improved from 34.0% in 2005 to 34.2% in 2006 to 35.3% in 2007, possibly from increased selling prices and/or from lower costs of production.

Operating profit to sales increased from 11.9% in 2005 to 12.4% in 2006 but then fell to 11.4% in 2007, despite the improvement in gross margin, because of higher levels of distribution costs and administrative expenses.

ROCE dropped from 23.4% to 18.1%, reflecting the lower level of operating profit. Return on equity increased from 12.5% in 1998 to 13.0% in 2006 but then fell sharply in 2007 to 9.0%. This was because of the large fall in profit after tax in 2007.

Capital turnover for 2007 was reduced from 1.9 times in 2006 to 1.6 in 2007, reflecting the fall in sales levels in 2007 over 2006.

Efficiency ratios for Hardy plc for 2007 and the comparative ratios for 2006 and 2005

Debtor days

$$\text{Debtor days } 2007 = \frac{\text{trade debtors} \times 365}{\text{sales}} = \frac{£80 \times 365}{£456} = 64 \text{ days}$$

$$\text{Debtor days } 2006 = \frac{£70 \times 365}{£491} = 52 \text{ days}$$

$$\text{Debtor days } 2005 = \frac{£53 \times 365}{£420} = 46 \text{ days}$$

Creditor days

$$\text{Creditor days } 2007 = \frac{\text{trade creditors} \times 365}{\text{cost of sales}} = \frac{£38 \times 365}{£295} = 47 \text{ days}$$

$$\text{Creditors days } 2006 = \frac{£38 \times 365}{£323} = 43 \text{ days}$$

$$\text{Creditors days } 2005 = \frac{£26 \times 365}{£277} = 34 \text{ days}$$

Stock days (stock turnover)

$$\text{Stock days } 2007 = \frac{\text{stock value}}{\text{average daily cost of sales in period}} = \frac{£147}{£295/365}$$
$$= 182 \text{ days (26.0 weeks)}$$

$$\text{Stock days } 2006 = \frac{£152}{£323/365} = 172 \text{ days (24.5 weeks)}$$

$$\text{Stocks days } 2005 = \frac{£118}{£277/365} = 155 \text{ days (22.2 weeks)}$$

Operating cycle days

Operating cycle 2007 = stock days + debtor days − creditor days = 182 + 64 − 47 = 199 days
Operating cycle 2006 = 172 + 52 − 43 = 181 days
Operating cycle 2005 = 155 + 46 − 34 = 167 days

Operating cycle %

$$\text{Operating cycle \% 2007} = \frac{\text{working capital requirement}}{\text{sales}} = \frac{(£147 + £80 - £38) \times 100\%}{£456}$$

$$= 41.4\%$$

$$\text{Operating cycle \% 2006} = \frac{(£152 + £70 - £38) \times 100\%}{£491} = 37.5\%$$

$$\text{Operating cycle \% 2005} = \frac{(£118 + £53 - £26) \times 100\%}{£420} = 34.5\%$$

Asset turnover

$$\text{Asset turnover 2007} = \frac{\text{sales}}{\text{total assets}} = \frac{£456}{£385} = 1.18 \text{ times}$$

$$\text{Asset turnover 2006} = \frac{£491}{£374} = 1.31 \text{ times}$$

$$\text{Asset turnover 2005} = \frac{£420}{£303} = 1.39 \text{ times}$$

Report on the working capital performance of Hardy plc

Average customer settlement days worsened successively over the years 2005, 2006, and 2007 from 46 to 52 to 64 days. This was partly mitigated by some improvement in the average creditors settlement period which increased from 34 to 43 to 47 days over the same period. The average stock turnover period worsened from 155 to 172 to 182 days over 2005, 2006, and 2007. Therefore, mainly because of the poor debt collection performance and increasingly high stock levels, the operating cycle worsened from 167 days in 2005 to 181 days in 2006 and to 199 days in 2007 (operating cycle 34.5% to 37.5% to 41.4%). Asset turnover reduced from 1.39 to 1.31 times from 2005 to 2006 and then to 1.18 in 2007, reflecting the degree to which sales had dropped despite increasing levels of total assets.

Liquidity ratios for Hardy plc for 2007 and the comparative ratios for 2006 and 2005

Current ratio

$$\text{Current ratio 2007} = \frac{\text{current assets}}{\text{current liabilities}} = \frac{£253}{£93} = 2.7 \text{ times}$$

$$\text{Current ratio 2006} = \frac{£251}{£90} = 2.8 \text{ times}$$

$$\text{Current ratio 2005} = \frac{£197}{£66} = 3.0 \text{ times}$$

Acid test (quick ratio)

$$\text{Quick ratio 2007} = \frac{\text{current assets} - \text{stocks}}{\text{current liabilities}} = \frac{£253 - £147}{£93} = 1.1 \text{ times}$$

$$\text{Quick ratio 2006} = \frac{£251 - £152}{£90} = 1.1 \text{ times}$$

$$\text{Quick ratio 2005} = \frac{£197 - £118}{£66} = 1.2 \text{ times}$$

Defensive interval

$$\text{Defensive interval 2007} = \frac{\text{quick assets}}{\text{average daily cash from operations}} = \frac{£253 - £147}{(£70 + £456 - £80)/365}$$

$$= 87 \text{ days}$$

$$\text{Defensive interval 2006} = \frac{£251 - £152}{(£53 + £491 - £70)/365} = 76 \text{ days}$$

Defensive interval 2005 is not available because we do not have the trade debtors figure for 31 March 2004.

Report on the liquidity of Hardy plc

The current ratio and the quick ratio have both dropped over the three years from 3.0 to 2.7 times, and 1.2 times to 1.1 times respectively. The defensive interval has increased from 76 days to 87 days at which level the company could potentially survive if there were no further cash inflows.

(ii) There are a number of areas that require further investigation. The following five ratios may be particularly useful to assist this investigation:

- Return on capital employed (ROCE)
- Debtor days
- Creditor days
- Stock days
- Current ratio.

(iii) The relevant information has not been provided to enable the following investment ratios to be calculated for Hardy plc, which would have improved the analysis of Hardy plc's performance:

Earnings per share, eps

Cannot be calculated because we do not have details of any preference share dividends and the number of ordinary shares in issue.

Dividend per share

Cannot be calculated because we do not have details of the number of ordinary shares in issue.

Dividend cover

Cannot be calculated because we have not been able to calculate earnings per share, eps, and dividend per share.

Dividend yield %

Cannot be calculated because we have not been able to calculate dividend per share, and we do not have the market prices of the company's shares.

Price/earnings ratio, P/E

Cannot be calculated because we have not been able to calculate earnings per share, and we do not have the market prices of the company's shares.

Capital expenditure to sales %

Cannot be calculated because we do not have details of capital expenditure.

Capital expenditure to gross fixed assets %

Cannot be calculated because we do not have details of capital expenditure.

E8.10 Dandy plc

As discussed in Chapter 8, there are many alternative ways in which ratios may be presented. This exercise illustrates some variations on the ratios shown in Chapter 8.

(i) Return on net assets (return on capital employed)

$$\frac{\text{net profit (before long-term interest and tax)}}{\text{total assets less current liabilities and long-term liabilities}} \times 100$$

2005	2006	2007
(£1,600/£3,400) × 100	(£2,400/£4,700) × 100	(£1,200/£5,350) × 100
47.1%	51.0%	22.4%

Return on equity (return on shareholders' funds)

$$\frac{\text{net profit (after long-term interest and tax)}}{\text{share capital and reserves}} \times 100$$

2005	2006	2007
(£1,000/£3,400) × 100	(£1,300/£4,700) × 100	(£650/£5,350) × 100
29.4%	27.6%	12.1%

Gross profit (gross margin)

$$\frac{\text{gross profit}}{\text{sales}} \times 100$$

2005	2006	2007
(£5,600/£11,200) × 100	(£5,000/£8,000) × 100	(£3,200/£6,000) × 100
50.0%	62.5%	53.3%

Net profit margin

$$\frac{\text{profit before long-term interest and tax}}{\text{sales}} \times 100$$

2005	2006	2007
$(£1,600/£11,200) \times 100$	$(£2,400/£8,000) \times 100$	$(£1,200/£6,000) \times 100$
14.3%	30.0%	20.0

Asset turnover

$$\frac{\text{sales}}{\text{total assets}} \times 100$$

2005	2006	2007
$(£11,200/£7,900) \times 100$	$(£8,000/£11,200) \times 100$	$(£6,000/£13,200) \times 100$
1.42 times	0.71 times	0.45 times

Stock turnover

$$\frac{\text{stock}}{\text{cost of sales}} \times 365$$

2005	2006	2007
$(£1,700/£5,600) \times 365$	$(£1,800/£3,000) \times 365$	$(£2,200/£2,800) \times 365$
111 days	219 days	287 days

Debtor days

$$\frac{\text{debtors}}{\text{sales}} \times 365$$

2005	2006	2007
$(£2,900/£11,200) \times 365$	$(£5,550/£8,000) \times 365$	$(£5,000/£6,000) \times 365$
95 days	253 days	304 days

Creditor days

$$\frac{\text{creditors}}{\text{cost of sales}} \times 365$$

2005	2006	2007
$(£1,300/£5,600) \times 365$	$(£1,200/£3,000) \times 365$	$(£1,000/£2,800) \times 365$
85 days	146 days	130 days

Operating cycle

stock days + debtors days − creditors days

2005	2006	2007
$111 + 95 − 85$	$219 + 253 − 146$	$287 + 304 − 130$
121 days	326 days	461 days

Current ratio

$$\frac{\text{current assets}}{\text{current liabilities}}$$

2005	**2006**	**2007**
(£5,300/£3,500)	(£9,200/£3,500)	(£8,100/£3,350)
1.51:1	2.63:1	2.42:1

Quick ratio (acid test)

$$\frac{\text{liquid assets}}{\text{current liabilities}}$$

2005	**2006**	**2007**
(£5,300 − £1,700)/£3,500	(£9,200 − £1,800)/£3,500	(£8,100 − £2,200)/£3,350
1.03:1	2.11:1	1.76:1

Debt to equity ratio

$$\frac{\text{total debt}}{\text{total equity}}$$

2005	**2006**	**2007**
(£1,000/£3,400) × 100	(£3,000/£4,700) × 100	(£4,500/£5,350) × 100
29.4%	63.8%	84.1%

Earnings per share

$$\frac{\text{profit after interest and tax}}{\text{number of ordinary shares}}$$

2005	**2006**	**2007**
£1,000/2,000	£1,300/2,200	£650/2,500
50p	59p	26p

Price/earnings ratio

$$\frac{\text{current market price per share}}{\text{earnings per share}}$$

2005	**2006**	**2007**
£0.80/£0.50	£0.90/£0.59	£0.45/£0.26
1.60	1.52	1.73

Dividend yield

$$\frac{\text{dividend per share}}{\text{current market price per share}}$$

2005	**2006**	**2007**
(£600/2,000)/£0.80	(£200/2,200)/£0.90	(£300/2,500)/£0.45
37.50%	10.10%	26.66%

Dividend cover

$$\frac{\text{profit after interest and tax}}{\text{total dividend}}$$

2005	2006	2007
£1,000/£600	£1,300/£200	£650/£300
1.66	6.50	2.17

Multivariate analysis – Altman Z score

$Z = 1.2R_1 + 1.4R_2 + 3.3R_3 + 0.6R_4 + 1.05R_5$ for a public company
(note that the private company formula is slightly different)

where

R_1 = working capital/total assets
R_2 = retained earnings/total assets
R_3 = earnings before interest and tax (PBIT)/total assets
R_4 = equity/total liabilities
R_5 = equity/total assets

For a public company

Z score above 2.99 indicated a company likely to be successful
Z score below 1.81 indicated a company likely to fail
Between 1.81 and 2.99 indicated a company's future was indeterminate.

	2005	2006	2007
Figures in £000			
working capital	1,800	5,700	4,750
total assets	7,900	11,200	13,200
retained earnings	1,400	2,500	2,850
PBIT	1,600	2,400	1,200
total liabilities	4,500	6,500	7,850
equity	3,400	4,700	5,350
R_1	0.228	0.509	0.360
R_2	0.177	0.223	0.216
R_3	0.203	0.214	0.091
R_4	0.756	0.723	0.682
R_5	0.430	0.420	0.405

2005

$Z = 1.2(0.228) + 1.4(0.177) + 3.3(0.203) + 0.6(0.756) + 1.05(0.430)$
$Z = 2.10$ (indeterminate)

2006

$Z = 1.2(0.509) + 1.4(0.223) + 3.3(0.214) + 0.6(0.723) + 1.05(0.420)$
$Z = 2.50$ (indeterminate)

2007

$$Z = 1.2(0.360) + 1.4(0.216) + 3.3(0.091) + 0.6(0.682) + 1.05(0.405)$$
$$Z = 1.87 \text{ (indeterminate)}$$

(ii) Please refer to the relevant sections in Chapter 8 to check your solution.

E9.1 Hearbuy plc

Hearbuy plc sales plan

Model assumptions	C	Sales	F Year 1	G Year 2	H Year 3	I Year 4	Total	Column I formulae
Growth	20.0%	Units 000	500.0	600.0	720.0	864.0	2,684.0	+H6+$C6*H6
Price/unit	£50	£m	25.0	30.0	36.0	43.2	134.2	+I6*C7

E9.2 Hearbuy plc

Hearbuy plc income statement for Year 1

Model assumptions	C	Income statement Figures in £m	F Year 1	Column F formulae
		Total sales	25.00	
% sales	70.0%	Cost of sales	(17.50)	+F6*C7
% sales	30.0%	PBIT	7.50	+F6+F7
% of debt	10.0%	Interest	(0.45)	+4.5*C9
		PBT	7.05	+F8+F9
% of PBT	35.0%	Tax	(2.47)	+F10*C11
		Net profit	4.58	+F10+F11
% of net profit	60.0%	Dividends	(2.75)	+F12*C13
% of net profit	40.0%	Retained earnings	1.83	+F12+F13

E9.3 Hearbuy plc

Hearbuy plc four-year plan

Model assumptions	C	Income statement Figures in £m	F Year 1	G Year 2	H Year 3	I Year 4	Column I formulae
Growth	20.0%	Total sales	25.00	30.00	36.00	43.20	+H6+$C6*H6
% sales	70.0%	Cost of sales	(17.50)	(21.00)	(25.20)	(30.24)	+I6*C7
% sales	30.0%	PBIT	7.50	9.00	10.80	12.96	+I6+I7
% of debt	10.0%	Interest	(0.45)	(0.45)	(0.80)	(1.22)	+H21*C9
		PBT	7.05	8.55	10.00	11.74	+I8+I9
% of PBT	35.0%	Tax	(2.47)	(2.99)	(3.50)	(4.11)	+I10*C11
		Net profit	4.58	5.56	6.50	7.63	+I10+I11
% of net profit	60.0%	Dividends	(2.75)	(3.34)	(3.90)	(4.58)	+I12*C13
% of net profit	40.0%	Retained earnings	1.83	2.22	2.60	3.05	+I12+I13

Model assumptions	C	Balance sheet Figures in £m	F Year 1	G Year 2	H Year 3	I Year 4	Column I formulae
Growth	20.0%	Non-current assets		13.50	16.20	19.44	23.33	+H18+$C6*H18
% of sales	60.0%	Working capital		15.00	18.00	21.60	25.92	+I6*C19
		Total assets	26.67	28.50	34.20	41.04	49.25	+I18+I19
		Debt	(4.50)	(4.50)	(7.98)	(12.22)	(17.38)	+H21-I24
			22.17	24.00	26.22	28.82	31.87	+I20+I21
		Equity	22.17	24.00	26.22	28.82	31.87	+H23+I14
		Additional funding required			3.48	4.24	5.16	+I20-H20-I14

E9.5 Hearbuy plc

No additional debt

Model assumptions	C	Income statement Figures in £m	F Year 1	G Year 2	H Year 3	I Year 4	Column I formulae
Growth	6.87%	Total sales	25.00	26.72	28.56	30.51	+H6+$C6*H6
% sales	70.00%	Cost of sales	(17.50)	(18.70)	(19.99)	(21.36)	+I6*C7
% sales	30.00%	PBIT	7.50	8.02	8.57	9.15	+I6+I7
% of debt	10.00%	Interest	(0.45)	(0.45)	(0.45)	(0.45)	+H21*C9
		PBT	7.05	7.57	8.12	8.70	+I8+I9
% of PBT	35.00%	Tax	(2.47)	(2.65)	(2.84)	(3.05)	+I10*C11
		Net profit	4.58	4.92	5.28	5.65	+I10+I11
% of net profit	60.00%	Dividends	(2.75)	(2.95)	(3.17)	(3.40)	+I12*C13
% of net profit	40.00%	Retained earnings	1.83	1.97	2.11	2.25	+I12+I13

Model assumptions	C	Balance sheet Figures in £m		F Year 1	G Year 2	H Year 3	I Year 4	Column I formulae
Growth	6.87%	Total assets		26.67	28.50	30.46	32.55	34.79	+H18+$C6*H18
		Debt		(4.50)	(4.50)	(4.49)	(4.47)	(4.46)	+H19-I22
				22.17	24.00	25.97	28.08	30.33	+I18+I19
		Equity		22.17	24.00	25.97	28.08	30.33	+H21+I14
		Additional funding effectively zero				−0.01	−0.02	−0.01	+I18-H18-I14
		Retention ratio	0.4	1.83/4.58				
		Return on capital employed	0.2066	4.58/22.17				
		Equity/assets ratio	0.8313					
		(0.4 × 0.2066 × 0.8313)	0.0687	= 6.87% **Growth rate**				

E9.6 Hearbuy plc

Constant gearing ratio

Model assumptions	C	Income statement Figures in £m	F Year 1	G Year 2	H Year 3	I Year 4	Column I formulae
Growth	8.26%	Total sales	25.00	27.07	29.30	31.72	+H6+$C6*H6
% sales	70.00%	Cost of sales	(17.50)	(18.95)	(20.51)	(22.20)	+I6*C7
% sales	30.00%	PBIT	7.50	8.12	8.79	9.52	+I6+I7
% of debt	10.00%	Interest	(0.45)	(0.45)	(0.49)	(0.52)	+H21*C9
		PBT	7.05	7.67	8.30	9.00	+I8+I9
% of PBT	35.00%	Tax	(2.47)	(2.68)	(2.90)	(3.15)	+I10*C11
		Net profit	4.58	4.99	5.40	5.85	+I10+I11
% of net profit	60.00%	Dividends	(2.75)	(3.00)	(3.24)	(3.51)	+I12*C13
% of net profit	40.00%	Retained earnings	1.83	1.99	2.16	2.34	+I12+I13

Model assumptions	C	Balance sheet Figures in £m		F Year 1	G Year 2	H Year 3	I Year 4	Column I formulae
Growth	8.26%	Total assets		26.67	28.50	30.85	33.40	36.16	+H18+$C6*H18
		Debt		(4.50)	(4.50)	(4.86)	(5.25)	(5.67)	+H19-I22
				22.17	24.00	25.99	28.15	30.49	+I18+I19
		Equity		22.17	24.00	25.99	28.15	30.49	+H21+I14
		Additional funding required				0.36	0.39	0.42	+I18-H18-I14
		Retention ratio	0.4	1.83/4.58				
		Return on capital employed	0.2066	4.58/22.17				
		(0.4 × 0.2066)	0.0826	= 8.26% **Growth rate**				

E9.7 Marx

(i)

	Chico	Groucho	Harpo
Average net operating assets	£7.5m	£17.5m	£12.5m
Operating profit	£1.5m	£1.4m	£2.0m
ROCE%	20%	8%	16%
Ranking of ROCE%	1	3	2

(ii)

	Chico	Groucho	Harpo
Average net operating assets	£7.5m	£17.5m	£12.5m
Divisional WACC	7%	5%	10%
Operating profit	£1.5m	£1.4m	£2.0m
Administrative expenses	£0.80m	£0.30m	£0.65m
Net income	£0.70m	£1.10m	£1.35m
Net assets × WACC	£0.525m	£0.875m	£1.250m
EVA = Net income × (NA × WACC)	£0.175m	£0.225m	£0.100m
Ranking of EVA	2	1	3

(iii) Please refer to the relevant section in Chapter 9 to check your solution.

(iv) (a) The ROCE% of each division is currently above its WACC with Chico being by far the best performer, followed by Harpo and then Groucho.

Chico and Harpo would be reluctant to pursue an investment opportunity that is expected to yield a return of 9% because they both currently earn 20% and 16% respectively.

In the case of Chico this represents a lost opportunity for Marx plc because taking on the investment would add value since Chico's WACC is 2% lower than the project's 9%.

Harpo's decision not to take on the investment is in the best interest of Marx plc since Harpo's WACC is 7% above the project's 9%.

Groucho would be keen to pursue an investment opportunity that is expected to yield a return of 9% because it currently earns only 8%.

Groucho's decision to take on the investment is also in the best interest of Marx plc since Groucho's WACC is 4% below the project's 9%.

(b) The current EVA of Groucho is the highest, followed by Chico and then Harpo.

If performance is measured using RI, then Chico and Groucho would take on an investment opportunity that yields 9% because even after capital charges on net operating assets at 7% and 5% respectively it would add to their residual incomes.

If performance is measured using EVA, Harpo would not take on an investment opportunity that yields 9% because after the capital charge on net operating assets at 10% there would be a reduction to residual income.

E9.8 Arby Ltd

(i)

Figures in £	Oct	Nov	Dec	Jan	Feb	Mar
Sales	200,000	205,000	180,000	200,000	205,000	200,000
Bad debts	7,000	7,175	6,300	7,000	7,175	7,000
Opening cash balance	25,000	−40,000	−15,500	−55,175	−62,975	−100,975
Cash sales 30%	60,000	61,500	54,000	60,000	61,500	60,000
Credit sales		133,000	136,325	119,700	133,000	136,325
Cash receipts	60,000	194,500	190,325	179,700	194,500	196,325
Wages	9,0000	105,000	90,000	85,000	90,000	100,000
Materials	0	30,000	65,000	67,500	67,500	62,500
Overheads	35,000	35,000	35,000	35,000	35,000	35,000
Non-current assets			40,000		40,000	
Cash payments	125,000	170,000	230,000	187,500	232,500	197,500
Closing cash balance	−40,000	−15,500	−55,175	−62,975	−100,975	−102,150
Materials	60,000	70,000	65,000	70,000	55,000	70,000
50%		30,000	30,000	35,000	32,500	35,000
50%			35,000	32,500	35,000	27,500
		0	30,000	65,000	67,500	67,500	62,500

(ii) Please refer to the relevant sections in Chapter 9 to check your solution.

E10.1 Oliver Ltd

Production costs

	£	
Raw materials	[40% × £5,300,000]	2,120,000	held in stock on average 4 days
Direct labour	[25% × £5,300,000]	1,325,000	finished goods
Overheads	[10% × £5,300,000]	530,000	held in stock on average 7 days
		3,975,000	

The production cycle is 14 days

Working capital requirement

			£	£
Raw materials	[£2,120,000 × 4/365]	=		23,233
Work in progress				
Raw materials	[£2,120,000 × 14/365]	=	1,315	
Direct labour	[£1,325,000 × 14/365 × 25%]	=	12,705	
Overheads	[£530,000 × 14/365 × 25%]	=	5,082	
				99,102
Finished goods	[£3,975,000 × 7/365]	=		76,233
Debtors	[£5,300,000 × 60/365]	=		871,223
Creditors	[£2,120,000 × 30/365]	=		(174,247)
Total working capital requirement				895,544

E10.5 Worrall plc

Cost of sales is 80% of sales		
Variable cost of sales	80% × 90%	= 72% of sales
Therefore		
Contribution		= 28% of sales
Proposed debtors		
Sales, increased by 20% are	120% × £8m = £9.6m	
Credit allowed increased to 90 days	£9.6m × 90/365	= £2,367,123
Current debtors	£8m × 60/365	= £1,315,068
Increase in debtors		£1,052,055
Gains		
Increase in contribution	(£9.6m − £8.0m) × 28%	= £448,000
Losses		
Increase in bad debts	(3% × £2,367,123) − (2% × £1,315,068) =	£44,713
Increase in financing costs	£1,052,055 × 10%	= £105,206
Total losses per annum		£149,919
Net gain	(£448,000 − £149,919)	£298,081

The net gain to Worrall Ltd is £298,081 per annum and so an increase to 90 days' credit may be recommended.

E11.5 Bank of Penderyn

This is about the minimisation of loss and the Bank of Penderyn has a responsibility not only to its shareholders but also to its account holders. However, it is also about how to deal with payment default arising from excessive country risk.

In terms of courses of action available to the Bank of Penderyn, there are perhaps three courses of action open:

(1) reject the offer

(2) seek to renegotiate the offer

(3) accept the offer.

If the Bank were to reject the offer, it would need to decide on what action to take. It could, for example, pursue international legal action against the central bank of Zorbia for immediate recovery of the outstanding loans. This course of action, whilst undoubtedly legitimate and ethically correct, is likely to be costly and ultimately fruitless given the problems associated with third world debt. In addition, even if the course of action were to be successful, it would be unlikely given the current political and economic instability in many Indulosian countries, that the Bank would ever be able to sequestrate sufficient Zorbian assets to cover the outstanding loans.

Alternatively, the Bank could seek to sell the outstanding debt on the open market. It would be likely that this course of action would not produce a sum sufficient to cover the outstanding debt. It would be likely that the market value of the debt would be substantially less than the current book value of the outstanding debt.

The Bank's second course of action would be to seek a renegotiation of the settlement terms. However, given that the Bank of Penderyn may not be the only Bank involved in the debt default and the offer has emerged after considerable discussion it seems unlikely that this would produce any improvement.

The Bank's final course of action, and perhaps the only feasible course of action, would be to accept the offer and seek to minimise overall losses.

Compared to the outstanding value of the loans this represents a potential loss of £0.2 billion at current exchange rates. However this loss may be exacerbated by the existence of Zorbian exchange control restrictions which may prevent the disposal of the shares and repatriation of the funds to the UK and the lack of any double taxation agreement between Zorbia and the UK, which may mean that any allowable repatriation of funds could be subject to excessively high withholding taxes. This could substantially increase the potential loss.

In addition, the excessive market disposal of shares in previously publicly owned Zorbian Utilities may result in a considerable downturn in the market value per share resulting in an even greater potential loss accruing.

There are a number of ways in which the Bank could seek to minimise this potential loss. First, the Bank of Penderyn may seek to undertake an equity swap to avoid exchange limits and restrictions imposed on programme trading in equities. Second, the Bank of Penderyn may consider the use of equity options to protect against a potential downturn in share prices. Third, the Bank may simply seek to hold on to the shares in the anticipation that the shares prices may rise.

E11.7 Benjamin plc

Calculate the company's weighted average cost of capital, based on:

- cost of ordinary share capital
- cost of preference share capital
- cost of debentures.

Using the dividend model (without growth) calculate the cost of ordinary share capital and cost of preference shares as follows:

Cost of ordinary shares = £0.10/£3.00 = 0.0333 or 3.33%

Cost of preference share capital = £0.05/£1.00 = 0.05 or 5.00%

Because the debentures are redeemable to calculate the cost of debentures we need to calculate the internal rate of return (IRR):

The debentures are 7% and the cum interest price is £104

Therefore the ex interest price is = £104 − £7 = £97

Calculate net present value (NPV) using a 7% and 5% discount rate:

Year £	Cost £	Interest £	Tax £	Net £
0	(97.00)			(97.00)
1		7.00	(2.45)	4.55
2		7.00	(2.45)	4.55
3	100.00	7.00	(2.45)	104.55

Discounting at 7%:

Year	Cash flow £	Discount factor	Present value £
0	(97.00)	1.00	(97.00)
1	4.55	0.93	4.23
2	4.55	0.87	3.96
3	104.55	0.82	85.69
		NPV	(3.12)

Discounting at 5%:

Year	Cash flow £	Discount factor	Present value £
0	(97.00)	1.00	(97.00)
1	4.55	0.95	4.32
2	4.55	0.91	4.14
3	104.55	0.86	89.91
		NPV	1.37

The IRR is:

$$5\% + \frac{£1.37 \times (7\% - 5\%)}{(£1.37 + £3.12)} = 5.61\%$$

Cost of debentures = 5.61%
    Using each of the above costs of capital we can calculate the weighted average cost of capital:

	Market Value £	Cost of capital	Weighting £
Ordinary shares	2,000,000	0.0333	66,600
Preference shares	1,000,000	0.0500	50,000
Debentures (£97 × 800,000)	776,000	0.0561	43,534
	3,776,000		160,134

$$\text{Weighted average cost of capital} = \frac{£160,134}{£3,776,000} = 0.0424 = 4.24\%$$

Convert all cash flows into £ sterling:

Year	Cash flows	Exchange rate	£ cash flows £m
0	£(20.0m)	1.00	(20.00)
1	€11.0m	1.70	6.47
2	€13.5m	1.75	7.71
3	€10.0m	1.80	5.56
4	€3.5m	1.85	1.89

Make adjustments for management fees and corporation tax:

Year	Cash flows £m	Management fee £m	Corporation tax 35% cash flows less management fee £m	Net cash flows £m
0	(20.00)	0.00	0.00	(20.00)
1	6.47	0.10	0.00	6.37
2	7.71	0.10	2.23	5.38
3	5.56	0.10	2.66	2.80
4	1.89	0.10	1.91	(0.12)
5	0.00	0.00	0.63	(0.63)

Evaluate the £ sterling net cash flows of the project using the company's weighted average cost of capital, a discount rate of 4.24%:

Year	Cash flows £m	Discount factor at 4.24%	Present value £m
0	(20.00)	1.000	(20.00)
1	6.37	0.959	6.11
2	5.38	0.920	4.95
3	2.80	0.883	2.47
4	(0.12)	0.847	(0.10)
5	(0.63)	0.813	(0.51)
		NPV	(7.08)

Using the company's weighted average cost of capital the project gives a negative NPV of £7.08m and so will reduce shareholder value. Therefore on a financial evaluation basis Benjamin plc should reject the project.

E11.9 Lee Ltd

(i) **All the project profits are remitted to the UK**

		Singapore $000
Profit		2,000,000
Singapore Corporation tax		
(18% × 2,000,000)		(360,000)
Dividend before tax		1,640,000
Withholding tax (10%)		(164,000)
Net dividend received		1,476,000
UK Corporation tax		
(30% × 2,000,000)	600,000	
Foreign tax credit	(524,000)	
		(76,000)
Net annual cash flow after tax		1,400,000

(ii)   **All the project profits are reinvested in Singapore**

	Singapore $000
Profit	2,000,000
Singapore Corporation tax (18% × 2,000,000)	(360,000)
Net annual cash flow after tax	1,640,000

(iii) **The investment is managed by a wholly owned German subsidiary with the dividends remitted to Germany for further investment outside the UK**

	Singapore $000
Profit	2,000,000
Singapore Corporation tax (18% × 2,000,000)	(360,000)
Dividend before tax	1,640,000
Withholding tax (10%)	(164,000)
Net annual cash flow after tax	1,476,000

In summary:

If all the project profits are reinvested in Singapore the net annual cash flow would be $1,640,000,000.

If the cash flows remain in Singapore, then the withholding tax of 10% is not imposed.

If all the project profits are remitted to the UK the net annual cash flow would be $1,400,000,000. However, if the investment in Singapore is held via a German holding company with the dividends remitted to Germany for further investment outside the UK, the net annual cash flow would be $1,476,000,000.

This difference of $76,000,000 is due to the differential tax rates between Singapore and the UK – that is, the effective overall tax in the UK is greater than the effective overall tax in Singapore.

The tax credit in the UK for overseas tax is limited to the tax imposed in the UK. However, if there is greater convergence between the tax rates between Singapore and the UK, the differential benefit becomes less.

Assume, for example, if the Singapore withholding tax was not 10%, but 14%.

If all the project profits were remitted to the UK, the net annual cash flow would be:

		Singapore $000
Profit		2,000,000
Singapore Corporation tax (18% × 2,000,000)		(360,000)
Dividend before tax		1,640,000
Withholding tax (14%)		(229,600)
Net dividend received		1,410,400
UK Corporation tax (30% × 2,000,000)	600,000	
Foreign tax credit	(589,600)	
		(10,400)
Net annual cash flow after tax		1,400,000

If the investment was managed by a wholly owned German subsidiary with the dividends remitted to Germany for further investment outside the UK, the net annual cash flows would be:

	Singapore $000
Profit	2,000,000
Singapore Corporation tax	
(18% × 2,000,000)	(360,000)
Dividend before tax	1,640,000
Withholding tax (14%)	(229,600)
Net annual cash flow after tax	1,410,400

E11.10 Drex plc

The overall expected after tax return of the UK company on existing projects (80% (800/800 + 200) of the total) + either of the new projects (20% (200/800 + 200) of the total).

With the Norwegian project the return would be:

$$(0.80 \times 0.10) + (0.20 \times 0.12) = 10.4\%$$

With the Malaysian project the returns would be:

$$(0.80 \times 0.10) + (0.20 \times 0.12) = 10.4\%$$

Both are the same. However, the risk (standard deviation) on each project and the expected correlation between the new project returns and the existing business are not the same.

We can calculate the variance of a two-investment portfolio as follows:

$$\sigma_p = \sqrt{(\alpha_x^2 \times \sigma_x^2) + (\alpha_y^2 \times \sigma_y^2) + (2 \times \alpha_x \times \alpha_y \times r \times \sigma_x \times \sigma_y)}$$

where σ^2 = variance
α = proportion of investment in portfolio
r = correlation coefficient of returns of the two investments

For the Norwegian option the portfolio variance would be:

$$(0.80)^2 \times (0.03)^2 + (0.20)^2 \times (0.04)^2 + 2(0.80) \times (0.20) \times (0.80) \times (0.03) \times (0.04) = 0.0009472$$

For the Norwegian project the standard deviation is $\sqrt{0.0009472} = 0.3078$ or 3.1%

For the Malaysian project the portfolio variance would be:

$$(0.80)^2 \times (0.03)^2 + (0.20)^2 \times (0.05)^2 + 2(0.80) \times (0.20) \times (0.30) \times (0.03) \times (0.05) = 0.00082$$

For the Malaysian project the standard deviation is $\sqrt{0.00082} = 0.02863$ or 2.9%

The Malaysian project should be chosen because it has the lower risk. By doing this, the company's overall variability of income would be reduced by approximately 13.4%. That is:

$$1 - (0.00082/0.0009472) = 1 - 0.866 = 13.4\%$$

E12.3 Ray & Co

(i) The foreign exchange operations may have occurred as follows:

On 30 September 2006, Ray & Co would have arranged four foreign exchange transactions:

(1) to obtain sufficient Cam$ to purchase 1,000 tonnes in October 2006, at the spot rate

(2) to obtain sufficient Cam$ to purchase 1,000 tonnes in November 2006, at the one-month forward rate, that is, at the beginning of November 2006

(3) to sell PF to be received from the customer (for the first 1,000 tonnes) in November 2006, at the end of November 2006 (two months forward)

(4) to sell PF to be received by the end of December 2006 on the final 1,000 tonnes at the end of December 2006 rate (three months forward).

The bank selling rate (customer buying rate) is the left-hand column of figures quoted, and the bank buying rate (customer selling rate) for foreign currency is the right-hand column of figures.

Purchases of melinium

		Cam$	£
(1) October 2006:	7,000 Cam$ × 1,000 tonnes @ 200 Cam$/£	7,000,000	35,000
(2) November 2006:	7,000 Cam$ × 1,000 tonnes @ 201 Cam$/£ (200 + 1 discount)	7,000,000	34,826
Total purchases			69,826

Sales of melinium

		PF	£
(3) October 2006:	300 PF × 1,000 tonnes @ 7.44 PF/£ (7.5 – 0.06 premium)	300,000	40,323
(4) November 2006:	300 Cam$ × 1,000 tonnes @ 7.39 PF/£ (7.5 – 0.11 premuim)	300,000	40,595
Total sales			80,918

The commission of 0.05% (maximum £20) is as follows:

(1) $0.05 \times £35,000/100 =$ £17.50
(2) $0.05 \times £34,826/100 =$ £17.41
(3) $0.05 \times £40,323/100 = £20.16$, therefore   £20.00
(4) $0.05 \times £40,595/100 = £20.30$, therefore   £20.00
Total commission   £74.91 or £75

	£
Sales	80,918
Less cost of sales	(69,826)
Gross profit	11,092
Less commission	(75)
Profit	11,017

(ii) If the November 2006 shipment had been cancelled after Ray & Co had entered into the forward exchange contracts, the contracts would still have to be honoured. They would still have to buy Cam$7,000,000 at a rate of 201, and would have to sell PF300,000 at a rate of 7.39. Without the November 2006 shipment, Ray & Co would be obliged to 'close out' the contracts. They would have to:

- sell the Cam$ they must buy, at the spot rate available at the time
- buy PF at the available spot rate (or at a suitable forward rate) on the foreign exchange market, for resale.

In both of the above transactions there would probably have been a loss because the resale of the foreign currencies would probably earn less in £ sterling than it would cost Ray & Co to buy them (depending on how exchange rates have moved since the original forward exchange contracts were entered into) and incur commission costs.

If the November 2006 shipment had been delayed for two months until January 2007, the contracts entered into at the end of September 2006 would still have to be honoured.

The Cam$7,000,000 would have been obtained too early and it is unlikely that Ray & Co would have had enough funds in the business to hold them for two months. Ray & Co may have sold the Cam$ they needed to buy in November 2006, and would have made a loss on this transaction, and then entered into another forward exchange contract to obtain Cam$7,000,000 in November 2006.

The merchant would have had to sell PF300,000 in December 2006, in which case he would have had to buy this amount at the spot rate in order to re-sell it. There would have been a loss on this transaction, just as if the November 2006 shipment had been cancelled.

The merchant would then probably have decided to enter into another forward exchange contract to sell PF300,000 two months later than originally expected, that is, in February 2007.

The effect of a delay in shipment would then have been similar to the effect of a cancellation, with the exception that Ray & Co would have arranged two further foreign exchange contracts, one to buy more Cam$ and the other to sell forward more PF. Ray & Co would really have been trying to extend each of their forward exchange contracts by a further two months. Ray & Co's bank may have offered them slightly better exchange rates to extend the contracts than they would have had to use to close out the contracts and make new contracts.

E12.4 Blud Ltd

(i) The finance director of Blud Ltd could take a chance on the future changes in the €/£ sterling exchange rate, and do nothing for three months. When the €40,000 are received, they can then be exchanged at the spot rate, whatever that happens to be.

However, this is not recommended. The company should have a policy of hedging against foreign exchange risk, in view of its regular export sales. There are two principal methods to consider:

- a forward exchange contract
- the currency market.

Forward exchange contract

The forward exchange rate for Blud Ltd to sell €40,000 in three months' time is as follows.

Spot rate	1.4652
Less premium	(0.0100)
Forward rate	1.4552

The sterling value of the receipts will be

$$\frac{€40,000}{1.4552} = £27,488$$

The currency market

The euros will be received in three months, so Blud Ltd should borrow euros now. At a borrowing rate of 2.1% per annum or 0.525% per three months, the amount to be borrowed so that €40,000 become payable in three months' time is:

$$\frac{€40,000}{1.00525} = €39,791$$

The borrowed euros will be converted into £ sterling at the spot rate of 1.4652 to yield

$$\frac{€39,791}{1.4652} = £27,157$$

Assuming that these funds could be invested to earn the deposit rate for £ sterling (4.5% per annum or 1.125% for three months) this would have a value in three months' time of:

$$£27,157 \times 1.01125 = £27,463$$

A forward exchange contract appears to be the more profitable, and is therefore recommended.

(ii) The payment of €20,000 could be partially matched with the receipt of €40,000, so that the foreign exchange risk exposure is eliminated by using euro receipts to make euro payments. A forward exchange contract should be taken out for the remaining €20,000, and the net receipts will be:

$$\frac{€20,000}{1.4552} = £13,744$$

E12.5 Cookies plc

Foreign exchange forward contract

Forward contract fixed at 1 August 2007

$$\frac{US\$730,000}{1.8109} = £403,114$$

Total cost of the payment of US\$730,000 = £403,114

Money market

Assuming it has sufficient £ sterling Cookies plc could buy US\$ and lend it in the money market
   Three-months US\$ lending rate = 2.85%/4 = 0.7125%

The amount today required to become US$730,000 in three months' time:

$$\frac{US\$730,000}{1.007125} = US\$724,836$$

Cost of buying US$724,836 at the current spot rate is:

$$\frac{US\$724,836}{1.8188} = £398,524$$

The three-month £ sterling lending rate = 4.5%/4 = 1.125%
Three months' interest lost on £398,524:

$$£398,524 \times 0.01125 = £4,483$$

Total cost of the payment of US$730,000 = £398,524 + £4,483 = £430,007

Currency option

Put options may be used and each contract would deliver 1.9 × £25,000 = US$47,500
The number of contracts required is:

$$\frac{US\$730,000}{US\$47,500} = 15.37, \text{ or } 15 \text{ contracts}$$

Cost of the put option contracts:

$$0.075 \times US\$47,500 \times 15 = US\$53,438$$

£ sterling cost of the options:

$$\frac{US\$53,438}{1.8188} = £29,381$$

£ sterling required to deliver 15 × US$47,500 or US$712,500 is:

$$15 \times £25,000 = £375,000$$

Shortfall = US$730,000 − US$712,500 = US$17,500
Cost of shortfall in £ sterling using the US$/£ three-month forward rate

$$\frac{US\$17,500}{1.8109} = £9,664$$

Total cost of using options = £29,381 + £375,000 + £9,664 = £414,045

The foreign exchange fixed forward contract is the cheapest method in this example for Cookies plc to use to hedge its US$730,000 transaction exposure, at a cost of £403,114.

E12.6 Gleeson plc

(i) One tick has a value of $0.0001 \times £500,000 \times 3/12 = £12.50$

$1\% = 100$ ticks

(a) Gleeson would sell £10m of interest rate futures contracts – 20 at 93.25, or 6.75% – to hedge against an interest rate rise on the three-month loan required on 1 August. If the futures rate increased by 1% then at 1 August Gleeson would close out its contracts by buying contracts at 92.25, or 7.75%

$$\text{giving a profit of } £10m \times 1\% \times 3/12 = £25,000$$
$$\text{or } 20 \times 100 \text{ ticks @ } £12.50 = \underline{£25,000}$$

If the interest rate increased by 1% then Gleeson would offset the futures contracts profit of £25,000 against the increased cost of borrowing £10m at 8% at 1 August

$$\text{cost of borrowing } £10m \times 8\% \times 3/12 = £200,000$$
$$\text{cost of borrowing } £10m \times 7\% \times 3/12 = \underline{£175,000}$$
$$\text{increased interest cost} = \underline{\ £25,000}$$

The hedge efficiency is

$$\frac{£25,000}{£25,000} = 100\%$$

which is a perfect hedge.

(b) Gleeson would sell £10m of interest rate futures contracts – 20 at 93.25, or 6.75% – to hedge against an interest rate fall on the three-month loan required on 1 August. If the futures rate fell by 1.5% then at 1 August Gleeson would close out its contracts by buying contracts at 94.75, or 5.25%

$$\text{giving a loss of } £10m \times 1.5\% \times 3/12 = £37,500$$
$$\text{or } 20 \times 150 \text{ ticks @ } £12.50 = \underline{£37,500}$$

Gleeson would offset the futures contracts loss of £37,500 against the lower cost of borrowing £10m at 5% at 1 August

$$\text{cost of borrowing } £10m \times 5\% \times 3/12 = £125,000$$
$$\text{cost of borrowing } £10m \times 7\% \times 3/12 = \underline{£175,000}$$
$$\text{reduced interest cost} = \underline{\ £50,000}$$

The hedge efficiency is $\dfrac{£50,000}{£37,500} = 133\%$.

(ii) Futures hedging costs

(a) Interest £10m × 8% × 3/12   = £200,000
     less gain from futures contracts £25,000 = £175,000

(b) Interest £10m × 5% × 3/12   = £125,000
     plus loss from futures contracts £37,500 = £162,500

The premium for the guarantee is £10m × 0.3% = £30,000.

If the interest rate increases then the cost of servicing the loan is:

$$£10m × 7% × 3/12 \quad = £175,000$$
$$\text{plus premium } £30,000 = £205,000$$

This costs more than the futures contracts hedge in (a) above and so would not be beneficial.

If the interest rate falls then the cost of servicing the loan is:

$$£10m × 5% × 3/12 \quad = £125,000$$
$$\text{plus premium } £30,000 = £155,000$$

This costs less than the futures hedge in (b) above and so would be beneficial.

E12.7 Houses plc

Houses plc has an absolute comparative advantage over Thinice plc with regard to its fixed interest rate:

6.5% compared with 7%

Houses plc's fixed interest rate loan is 0.5% cheaper than Thinice plc may obtain.
     Houses plc also has an absolute comparative advantage over Thinice plc with regard to its floating interest rate:

4.85% (4.75 + 0.1) compared with 4.95% (4.75 + 0.2)

Thinice plc floating interest rate loan is 0.1% more expensive than Houses plc may obtain.
     However, Thinice plc has a relative comparative advantage with regard to its lower cost of floating interest compared with its cost of fixed interest.
     Thinice plc's floating interest rate compared with its fixed interest rate is:

$$\frac{4.95\%}{7.0\%} = 70.7\%$$

Houses plc's floating interest rate compared with its fixed interest rate is:

$$\frac{4.85\%}{6.5\%} = 74.6\%$$

Therefore, since both companies have loans of the same value, they may both gain from a swap arrangement.

If the two companies arranged an interest rate swap, Thinice plc would effectively pay Houses plc's fixed rate of interest on its loan at 6%, while Houses plc would effectively pay Thinice plc's floating rate of interest on its loan at 4.95%.

Thinice plc is saving on the fixed rate, and is better off by 0.5% (7% − 6.5%).

Houses plc is worse off by 0.1% because of paying more on its floating rate (4.85% − 4.95%).

The net benefit is therefore 0.4% (0.5% − 0.1%).

If the gain of 0.4% is shared equally between the two companies, then both companies should be better off by 0.2%.

Therefore, Thinice plc should pay Houses plc 0.3%, and will then be better off by
0.2% (0.5% − 0.3%).

Houses plc will then be better off by 0.2% (−0.1% + 0.3%).

The result of the swap is that:

Houses plc will pay a floating interest rate of
LIBOR − 0.1% (4.65%) compared with LIBOR + 0.1% (4.85%)
instead of the fixed interest rate of 6.5%.

Thinice plc will pay a fixed interest rate of
6.8% compared with 7%
instead of the floating rate of 4.95% (4.75% + 0.2%)

E12.8 Privet plc

Forward rate agreements (FRAs) are agreements to fix the interest rate applying to a loan (borrowing or lending) for some period in advance. For example, a company can enter into an FRA with a bank that fixes the rate of interest for borrowing at a certain time in the future. If the actual interest rate proves to be higher than the rate agreed, the bank pays the company the difference. If the actual interest rate is lower than the rate agreed, the company pays the bank the difference. FRAs do not involve actual lending or borrowing of the principal sum. FRAs are usually for amounts of at least the currency equivalent of US$1,000,000.

In Privet's case, an FRA could be combined with taking out a loan for £5m, which would be separately arranged. This would enable Privet effectively to fix its borrowing costs in three months' time.

Interest rate futures are similar to FRAs, except that the terms, the amounts, and the periods involved are standardised. An interest rate future is a binding contract between a buyer and a seller to deliver or take delivery of (respectively) a specified interest rate commitment on an agreed specified date at an agreed price.

Futures contracts can be sold now in the expectation that, if interest rates increase, the contract value will fall: they can then be purchased at a lower price thus generating profits on the deal which can compensate for the increase in interest rate. If interest rates move in the opposite direction, there will be a loss on the contract, but this should be offset by the saving on the interest costs on the loan taken out as a result of the fall in rates. Interest rate futures can thus be used as a hedge against interest rate changes, and are available for a maximum period of one to two years.

The standard rates futures contracts are traded on futures exchanges. The London International Financial Futures provides a market for a limited number of interest rate contracts, including three-month sterling time deposits, three-month eurodollar, 20-year gilts, and 20-year US Treasury bonds. The cost of the contract being provided is reflected in a margin or initial deposit.

Interest rate futures provide Privet with another method of hedging against interest rate risk. Because of the standardised nature of the contracts, however, it will probably not be possible to hedge the risk perfectly.

Interest rate guarantees (IRGs) are more expensive for a company to obtain than FRAs. They are agreements with a bank on the maximum borrowing rate that will apply at a certain time in the future. For example, a company might obtain an IRG from its bank that the interest rate will not exceed 14%. If it does, the bank must pay the company the difference. If market interest rates turn out to be lower, the company is not bound to accept 14%. Instead, it can abandon the guarantee and borrow at the lower existing market rate. IRGs are sometimes referred to as interest rate options or interest rate caps, and have a maximum maturity of one year. Longer-term interest rates options (such as caps, floors, and collars) are also available.

Similar hedging against interest rate risk is possible with IRGs as with FRAs. The main difference is that, unlike with an FRA, with IRGs require the seller to be paid a premium, whether or not the option involved in the guarantee is exercised. Against this relative disadvantage of IRGs, they do offer the advantage that the option holder, while being protected against adverse interest rate movements, can take full advantage of favourable interest rate movements. If interest rates fall, the guarantee need not be used; the company can borrow the money at the lower interest rates, having paid the premium for the IRG. FRA and interest rate futures do not offer the same possibility of gaining from favourable interest rate movements.

Privet could make use of IRGs to avoid exposure to the risk of interest rate rises while benefiting from falls in rates. However, to pay for these advantages, a premium must be paid for an IRG, which makes them relatively expensive.

Please refer to the relevant sections of Chapter 12 for a full discussion on hedging.

E13.1 to E13.10

Please refer to the relevant sections in Chapter 13 to check your solutions.

E14.7 Gregor

The ungeared betas for each company can be calculated using:

$$\beta_u = \beta_e \times \frac{E}{E + D(1 - t)}$$

Tench plc

$$\beta_u = 1.25 \times \frac{80\%}{80\% + 20\% \times (1 - 30\%)}$$

$$\beta_u = 1.25 \times \frac{80\%}{80\% + (20\% \times 70\%)}$$

$$\beta_u = 1.25 \times 0.85$$

$$\beta_u = 1.06$$

Rudd plc

$$\beta_u = 1.15 \times \frac{75\%}{75\% + 25\% \times (1 - 30\%)}$$

$$\beta_u = 1.15 \times 0.81$$

$$\beta_u = 0.93$$

Pike plc

$$\beta_u = 1.10 \times \frac{70\%}{70\% + 30\% \times (1 - 30\%)}$$

$$\beta_u = 1.10 \times 0.77$$

$$\beta_u = 0.85$$

Because computer repairs represents 40% of Pike plc's business and is considered 50% more risky than the electrical components business then its ungeared beta must be adjusted accordingly to calculate its electrical components ungeared beta as follows:

$$\beta_u = 0.5 \times \text{computer repairs } \beta_u + 0.5 \times \text{electrical components } \beta_u$$

and

$$\text{computer repairs } \beta_u = 1.5 \times \text{electrical components } \beta_u$$

therefore

$$\beta_u = 0.5 \times 1.5 \times \text{electrical components } \beta_u + 0.5 \times \text{electrical components } \beta_u$$
$$0.85 = 1.25 \times \text{electrical components } \beta_u$$

therefore

Pike plc's electrical components $\beta_u = 0.68$

The average of Pike plc's adjusted ungeared beta and the other two ungeared betas is

$$\frac{1.06 + 0.93 + 0.68}{3} = 0.89$$

0.89 may be used as the surrogate ungeared beta for Gregor in order to calculate its surrogate equity beta by using the variation of the ungeared beta equation:

$$\beta_e = \beta_u \times \frac{E + D(1 - t)}{E}$$

$$\beta_e = 0.89 \times \frac{80\% + 20\% \times (1 - 30\%)}{80\%}$$

$$\beta_u = 1.18 \times 0.89$$

$$\beta_e = 1.05$$

We can now calculate Gregor's estimated return (R_s) by using the basic CAPM formula:

$R_s = R_f + \beta_e(R_m - R_f)$

$R_s = 4\% + 1.05 \times (10\% - 4\%)$

$R_s = 0.1030$

Gregor's expected return is therefore 10.3%.

E15.4 Wane plc

Option 1

6.5p/0.07 = 92.86p

Therefore the value of the company would be £0.93 × 785,000 = £730,050

Option 2

5.5p/(0.10 − 0.04) = 91.67p

Therefore the value of the company would be £0.92 × 785,000 = £722,200

Option 3

	Dividend		Discount factor at 10%		pence
	pence				
2007	5.00	×	0.909		4.55
2008	5.45	×	0.826		4.50
2009	5.94	×	0.751		4.46
2010	6.47	×	0.683		4.41
2011	7.05	+	0.621 × 148.05*		96.32
					114.24

*7.05 × 1.05/(0.10 − 0.05) = 148.05p

Therefore the value of the company would be £1.14 × 785,000 = £894,900

Option 4

	Dividend		Discount factor at 10%		pence
	pence				
2007	5.00	×	0.893		4.46
2008	5.50	×	0.797		4.38
2009	6.65	×	0.712		4.73
2010	7.32	×	0.636		4.66
2011	8.05	+	0.567 × 104.65*		63.90
					82.13

*8.05 × 1.04/(0.12 − 0.04) = 104.65

Therefore the value of the company would be £0.82 × 785,000 = £643,700

Option 3 gives the maximum valuation of the company.

E15.5 Wooden plc

(i) $(1+G)^4 = (9/7)$
$(1+G)^4 = 1.256$
$(1+G) = \sqrt[4]{1.286}$
$G = 6.5\%$

Using the dividend growth model

$$S = \frac{v(1+G)}{(K_e - G)}$$

$S = £0.09 \times 1.065/(0.12 - 0.065) = £1.74$

Therefore the value of the company would be £1.74 × 1,650,000 = £2,871,000

(ii)

	Dividend pence	Discount factor at 12%	PV pence
Year 1	6	0.893	5.35
Year 2	6	0.797	4.78
Year 3	6	0.712	4.27
Year 4	10	0.636	6.36
Year 4	270.00*	0.636	171.72
			192.48

$$\frac{*(10 \times 1.08)}{(0.12 - 0.08)} = 270.00$$

NPV = £1.92

Therefore the value of the company would be £1.92 × 1,650,000 = £3,168,000
It would therefore appear that the sacrifice of short-term dividends is worthwhile.

E15.6 Solva plc

	Current market value £		Current returns £
Equity	5,000,000	2m shares × 15p	300,000
Debt	2,500,000	£2.5m debt × 12%	300,000
	7,500,000		600,000

Cost of equity using the dividend growth model and assuming zero dividend growth:

$$K_e = \frac{v}{S} = \frac{15p}{£2.50} = 6\%$$

Current market value £7,500,000

Rights issue at £2 per share to redeem debt of £2.5m

£2,500,000/£2 = 1,250,000 shares

Total shares

Original shares	£5,000,000/£2.50 = 2,000,000
Rights issue	£2,500,000/£2.00 = 1,250,000
Total shares	3,250,000

Estimated new cost of equity after debt redemption = 6% − 1% = 5%

Share price using the dividend growth model and assuming zero dividend growth:

$$S = \frac{v}{K_e} = \frac{15p}{5\%} = £3$$

Total new market value 3,250,000 shares × £3 = £9,750,000	
Original market value	= £7,500,000
Increase in market value	= £2,250,000

E15.8 Angle plc

	Current market value £		Current returns £
Debt	4,000,000	£4m debt × 7%	280,000
Equity	9,000,000	3m shares × 30p	900,000
	13,000,000		1,180,000

Cost of equity using the dividend growth model and assuming zero dividend growth:

$$K_e = \frac{v}{S} = \frac{30p}{£3.00} = 10\%$$

$$WACC = \frac{£1,180,000 \times 100}{£13,000,000} = 9.076923\%$$

$$\text{New development evaluation NPV} = \frac{£500,000}{0.09076923} - £4,000,000 = +£1,508,474$$

Therefore the new development is worthwhile.

	£	
Current dividend	900,000	
Current interest	280,000	
	1,180,000	
New development earnings	500,000	
	1,680,000	
New total interest	(560,000)	(£4m + £4m) debt × 7%
	1,120,000	

New cost of equity 10% + 2% = 12%
Therefore, new value of equity = £1,120,000/0.12 = £9,333,333

Current value of equity	= £9,000,000
Increase in value of equity	= £333,333

New value of company at WACC = £1,680,000/0.09076923 = £18,508,474
Current value of company = £8,000,000 + £9,333,333   = £17,333,333
Increase in value   £1,175,141
NPV of project   £1,508,474
Increase in value of equity   £333,333

E15.9 Cresswell plc

(i) Cresswell's current eps are £30m/100m = 30p and its P/E ratio is £2.0/30p = 6.67 times

If Cresswell uses all its £20m cash it can buy 10m shares (£20m/£2).

Because it will not now be receiving interest on its cash balances its profits after tax will fall to £28m (£30 − £2m).

The number of shares remaining will be 90m (100m − 10m), therefore eps will increase to 31.1p (£28m/90m), and if its share price remained unchanged its P/E ratio would fall to £2.0/31.1p = 6.43 times.

(ii) If shareholders believe that the P/E ratio of 6.67 times is still appropriate, then they may be willing to pay £2.07 (31.1p × 6.67) for the shares. Therefore, in theory the share price should increase after the share buy-back. In practice, the share price will depend on how the market perceives a company's disposal of its cash, and its stage in its business life cycle.

If Cresswell plc had any growth prospects shareholders may be willing to pay more than £2.07, because Cresswell's potential profit growth would increase after returning the cash to shareholders, which was providing no more than average returns.

However, in practice, as a mature company, investors are unlikely to see Cresswell plc as having any growth prospects – it had not been able to invest its £20m surplus cash in new value-adding projects. Therefore, it is likely that investors may be not even willing to pay £2.07 per share.

E15.10 Cresswell plc

Using the information from E15.9 we can see what would happen if the original share price had been higher than £2 at £3.

Cresswell's current eps are £30m/100m = 30p
and its P/E ratio is £2.0/30p = 6.67 times

If the original share price had been higher than £2 at £3, then

£20m cash would have bought 6.67m shares (£20m/£3)
eps would have remained at the original 30p (£28m/93.34m)
P/E ratio would have been 10 times (£3/30p)

The share price of £3 is the 'equilibrium' price, which equals the original earnings level of 30p multiplied by the £20m cash divided by the annual interest of £2m. At any share price above £3 eps will fall, and the P/E ratio will increase. The company should therefore buy back its shares when its P/E ratio is at a relatively low level.

E16.1 Pitch plc

$$\text{number of Perfecto ordinary shares in issue} = \frac{\text{balance sheet value of ordinary shares}}{\text{nominal value of each ordinary share}}$$

$$= £600,000/£1$$

$$= 0.6\text{m shares}$$

stock market valuation of Perfecto plc = number of ordinary shares in issue $\times$ market price

$$= 0.6\text{m} \times £1.84$$

$$= \underline{£1,104,000}$$

	£000
Total assets less current liabilities	1,625
less	
Intangible non-current assets	(203)
	1,422
less	
Long-term debt	(85)
	1,337
Net asset value (NAV)	**£1,337,000**
Number of ordinary shares	0.6m
Value per ordinary share	= £1,337,000/600,000
	= £2.23 per share

It can be see from the above calculation that the valuation of the company based on the historical costs of its book assets is around 21% more than the market value.

E16.2 Pitch plc

The costs of acquiring the separate assets of a target company may be determined on an open market basis. These are the costs to replace the assets, rather than what they could be sold for. The advantage of this method is that replacement cost valuations are more relevant than historical cost book valuations, or current realisable valuations.

Disadvantages are that this method ignores goodwill, and it is usually difficult to identify separate assets, like separate individual factories, machinery, etc., and determine their replacement cost. Assets may also be complementary and therefore their separate valuation may not be totally realistic. There is no data available to value Perfecto plc in this way.

E16.3 Pitch plc

Using the data from E16.1 the directors of Pitch plc may calculate a capitalised earnings valuation of Perfecto plc.

capitalised earnings value $= \dfrac{\text{annual maintainable expected earnings}}{\text{required earnings yield}}$

required earnings yield $=$ eps/share price

Perfecto plc required earnings yield = the reciprocal of its P/E ratio

$$= 1 \times 100/7.36 = 13.587\%$$

Perfecto plc's capitalised earnings value = £150,000/0.13587 (assuming that current earnings are equal to its maintainable expected earnings)

$$= \underline{£1,104,000} \qquad \text{(rounded up)}$$

E16.4 Pitch plc

Using the data from E16.1 the directors of Pitch plc may calculate a price/earnings ratio valuation of Perfecto plc. Pitch plc must decide on a suitable P/E ratio and then multiply this by Perfecto plc's eps. Perfecto plc's eps may be its historical eps or its expected future eps.

Pitch may use one of a number of P/E ratios: Pitch plc's P/E ratio; Perfecto plc's P/E ratio; the weighted average of the P/E ratios of the two companies. We will consider valuations of Perfecto plc using its historical (2007) eps and the three different P/E ratios.

Pitch plc P/E ratio

Market value of Perfecto plc = Perfecto 2007 eps × Pitch P/E × number of Perfecto ord. shares

$$= £0.25 \times 9 \times 600,000$$
$$= \underline{\textbf{£1,350,000}}$$

Perfecto plc P/E ratio

Market value of Perfecto plc = Perfecto 2007 eps × Perfecto P/E × number of Perfecto ord. shares

$$= £0.25 \times 7.36 \times 600,000$$
$$= \underline{\textbf{£1,104,000}} \text{ (rounded up, and equal to the capitalised earnings valuation)}$$

Weighted average P/E ratio

The combined earnings (profit on ordinary activities after tax) = £150,000 + £800,000

$$= £950,000$$

Perfecto plc P/E ratio weighted by combined earnings $= \dfrac{7.36 \times £150,000}{£950,000} = 1.16$

Pitch plc P/E ratio weighted by combined earnings $= \dfrac{9 \times £800,000}{£950,000} = 7.58$

Weighted average P/E ratio = 1.16 + 7.58
$$= 8.74$$

Market value of Perfecto plc = £0.25 × 8.74 × 600,000
$$= \underline{\textbf{£1,311,000}}$$

E16.5 Pitch plc

Using the data from E16.1 the directors of Pitch plc may use the DCF method to compare the present value of the future cash flows of the combined entity with the present values of its future cash flows if the acquisition did not go ahead.

Using distributable earnings (profit on ordinary activities after tax) as an approximation of cash flows:

Present value of future cash flows – no acquisition

Pitch plc current distributable earnings = £800,000
    Discount factor = Pitch plc WACC = 6%

Present value of future expected cash flows $= \dfrac{£800,000}{0.06}$

$$= \underline{\textbf{£13,333,333}}$$

Present value of future cash flows – with acquisition

Pitch plc post-acquisition distributable earnings = £130,000 + £800,000.

The present values of future cash flows can then be calculated using Pitch plc's WACC, applied to distributable earnings, plus the estimated additional cash flows for 2008 to 2012.

Present value of post-acquisition cash flows

$$= \frac{£930,000}{0.06} + \frac{£130,000}{1.06} + \frac{£130,000}{1.06^2} + \frac{£150,000}{1.06^3} + \frac{£100,000}{1.06^4} + \frac{£130,000}{1.06^5}$$

$$= \underline{£16,040,638}$$

The difference between the present values of the future cash flows assuming acquisition and no acquisition are:

$$£16,040,638$$
$$\text{less } \underline{£13,333,333}$$

Maximum price that should be paid by Pitch plc for Perfecto plc = $\underline{\underline{£2,707,305}}$

E16.6 Pitch plc

Using the data from E16.1 the directors of Pitch plc may use the CAPM to value Perfecto plc. The risk-free rate of return R_f is 1% per annum and the market rate of return R_m is 6.5% per annum. Perfecto plc's beta factor $\beta = 1.20$.

Using
$$K_e = R_f + \beta \times (R_m - R_f)$$

Perfecto plc cost of equity $= 1\% + 1.20 \times (6.5\% - 1\%)$
$$= \underline{7.6\%}$$

Perfecto plc market value, assuming a 4% p.a. increase in future dividends

$$= \frac{£40,000 \times 1.04}{(0.076 - 0.04)}$$

$$= \underline{\underline{£1,155,555}}$$

It should be noted that this valuation is lower than Perfecto plc's book value of its net assets valuation of £1,337,000 at 30 September 2007, but higher than the valuation based on its share price 30 September 2007 of £1.84 × 600,000 = £1,104,000.

E16.7 Horse and Cart

(i) PV of gain = £2.5m/0.10 − £2m = **£23m**

(ii) If £70m offer is accepted the gain for Horse plc shareholders would be:

	£
Net acquisition cost (£70m − £50m)	20m
PV of gain	23m
Gain for Horse plc shareholders	**3m**

E16.10 Porgy plc

(i) Value created by merger

£158m − (£90m + £40m + £20m + £5m) = £3m
Present value £3.0m/0.10 = £30.0m

(ii) Cash Price

(£40m + £20m)/20m = £3.00 per share

(iii)

Value = (2/3 × £158m) − £90m = £15.3m

(iv)

Gain = (£158 − £90m − £60) = £8m

(v)

A target company may contest an offer on several grounds:

- offer is unacceptable because insufficient additional value will be created
- merger or acquisition has no obvious advantage
- employees may be strongly opposed.

(vi)

Defensive tactics:

- publicly refute profit forecasts
- lobby the OFT or DTI
- refer offer to Monopoly and Mergers Commission
- refer offer to the European Union
- find a 'white knight' company as an alternative buyer
- make a counter bid for the predator company
- arrange an MBO or MBI.

E16.11 Black Ltd

Alternative valuation models:

- Dividend model
- Dividend model (with growth)
- Assets based valuation
- Earnings based valuation – current
- Earnings based valuation – future
- Accounting rate of return (ARR)

Dividend model

$(£45,000/0.12)/300,000 = £1.25$ per share

Dividend model (with growth)

$(£45,000(1.04)/(0.12 - 0.04))/300,000 = £1.95$ per share

Assets based valuation

net assets £1,060,000 − non-current assets £1,305,000 + re-valued non-current assets $(£1,075,000 + £480,000 + £45,000) = £1,355,000/300,000 = £4.52$ per share

Earnings based valuation – current

$P/E = MV/earnings$

Average earnings over the last 5 years $= (£90,000 + £80,000 + £105,000 + £90,000 + £100,000)/5 = £93,000$

Average most recent market P/Es

$(8.5 + 9.0 + 10.0)/3 = 9.167$

Using an unadjusted P/E ratio

$(9.167 \times £93,000)/300,000 = £2.84$ per share

Adjusted P/E ratio (say reduced by 30% because Black is not a plc)

Say $9.167 \times 70\% = 6.41$
$(6.41 \times £93,000)/300,000 = £1.98$ per share

Earnings based valuation – future

Say over 5 years increase at 4% pa

Year 1	£100,000
Year 2	£104,000
Year 3	£108,160
Year 4	£112,486
Year 5	£116,985

Average $= £541,631/5 = £108,326$

Average most recent market P/Es

$(8.5 + 9.0 + 10.0)/3 = 9.167$

Using an unadjusted P/E ratio

$(9.167 \times £108,326)/300,000 = £3.31$ per share

Adjusted P/E ratio (say reduced by 30% because Black is not a plc)

Say $9.167 \times 70\% = 6.41$

$(6.41 \times £108,326)/300,000 = £2.31$ **per share**

Accounting rate of return

Assume ROCE $= 18\%$

$$\frac{\text{average profit over next five years/ROCE}}{\text{number of issued shares}} = \frac{£108,326/0.18}{300,000} = £2.00 \text{ per share}$$

E17.8 Blue Sky plc

(i) Reasons for mergers and acquisitions would include:

- operating economies of scale
- economies of vertical and horizontal integration
- combining complementary resource structures
- utilisation of surplus funds
- utilisation of tax shields
- strategic growth
- diversification
- asset backing
- increasing quality of earnings.

(ii) PV of gain

$(£2.75m/0.10) - £5m = £22.5m$

(iii) If £65m offer is accepted the gain for Blue Sky plc shareholders would be:

Net cost (£65m − £50m)	15.0m
PV of gain	22.5m
Gain for Blue Sky plc shareholders	7.5m

(iv) Value of 70% for Blue Sky plc of the merged company

$70\% \times (£80m + £50m + £22.5m) = £106.75m$

Value created for Blue Sky plc shareholders

$£106.75m - £80m = £26.75m$

(v) Defensive tactics would include:

- publicly refute profit forecasts
- lobby the OFT or DTI
- refer offer to Monopoly and Mergers Commission
- refer offer to the European Union
- find a 'white knight' company
- make a counter bid for the predator company
- arrange an MBO or MBI

E17.9 Arkwright plc

(i)

	£
Current profits	3,600,000
Increase	
(£2m – extra interest 8% × £10,000,000)	1,200,000
New profits after acquisition	4,800,000
New cost of equity	15%
New market value (£4.8m/0.15)	32,000,000
Old market value (£3.6m/0.12)	30,000,000
Increase in shareholders' wealth	2,000,000

(ii) NPV of the acquisition

(£2m/0.10) – £10m = £10m
Therefore impact of financing the acquisition = £10m – £2m = £8m

Change in the value of the company

	£
NPV of acquisition	10,000,000
Loss due to increase in cost of equity	(8,000,000)
Increase in shareholders' wealth	2,000,000

(iii) Reasons for an increase in cost of equity may include:

- greater perceived financial risk from an increase in debt and gearing
- reduced chance of dividend payments.

E18.7 Pomfrit Ltd

£m	Year 1	Year 2	Year 3	Year 4
Earnings	10.0000	11.8000	13.1275	14.6043
Dividends	(4.0000)	(2.9500)	(3.2819)	(7.3022)
Retained earnings	6.0000	8.8500	9.8456	7.3021
New equity	6.0000			
Funds invested	12.0000	8.8500	9.8456	
ROI (15%)	1.8000	1.3275	1.4768	
(add to next year's earnings)				

The growth rate G can be estimated assuming the expected long-term retention rate of 50%, and future return of 10%.

G = retention rate × expected future returns = 50% × 10% = 5%

The value in Year 3 would be £7.3022m/(0.10 – 0.05) = **£146.044m**
The value of the company today would therefore be:

£4m/1.10 + £2.95m/$(1.10)^2$ + £3.2819m/$(1.10)^3$ + £146.044m/$(1.10)^3$ = **£117.9921m** and the value of a share would be:

£117.9921m/1.5m = **£78.66 per share**

E18.8 Gillie plc

	Current market value £		Current returns £
Debt	2,000,000	£2m debt × 10%	200,000
Equity	6,000,000	3m shares × 40p	1,200,000
	8,000,000		1,400,000

Cost of equity using the dividend growth model and assuming zero dividend growth:

$$K_e = \frac{v}{S} = \frac{40p}{£2.00} = 20\%$$

$$WACC = \frac{£1,400,000 \times 100}{£8,000,000} = 17.5\%$$

Reorganisation evaluation NPV $= \dfrac{£525,000}{0.175} - £2,000,000 = +£1,000,000$

	£	
Current dividend	1,200,000	
Current interest	200,000	
	1,400,000	
Additional income	525,000	
	1,925,000	
New total interest	(400,000)	(£2m + £2m) debt × 10%
	1,525,000	

New cost of equity 20% + 5% = 25%
Therefore, new value of equity = £1,525,000/0.25 = £6,100,000
Current value of equity   = £6,000,000
Increase in value of equity   =   £100,000

New value of company at WACC = £1,925,000/0.175 = £11,000,000
Current value of company = £4,000,000 + £6,100,000 = £10,100,000
Increase in value   £900,000
NPV of project   £100,000
Increase in value of equity   £100,000

Although the reorganisation is viable, the method of financing has considerably reduced the net benefit.

Index

Definitions may be found in the Glossary for key terms that have page numbers highlighted in colour. The names of companies mentioned in the book are in **bold** type.